I0727817

OLIVIER FÖLLMI

My Himalaya

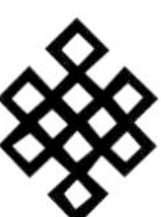

40 YEARS AMONG BUDDHISTS

teNeues

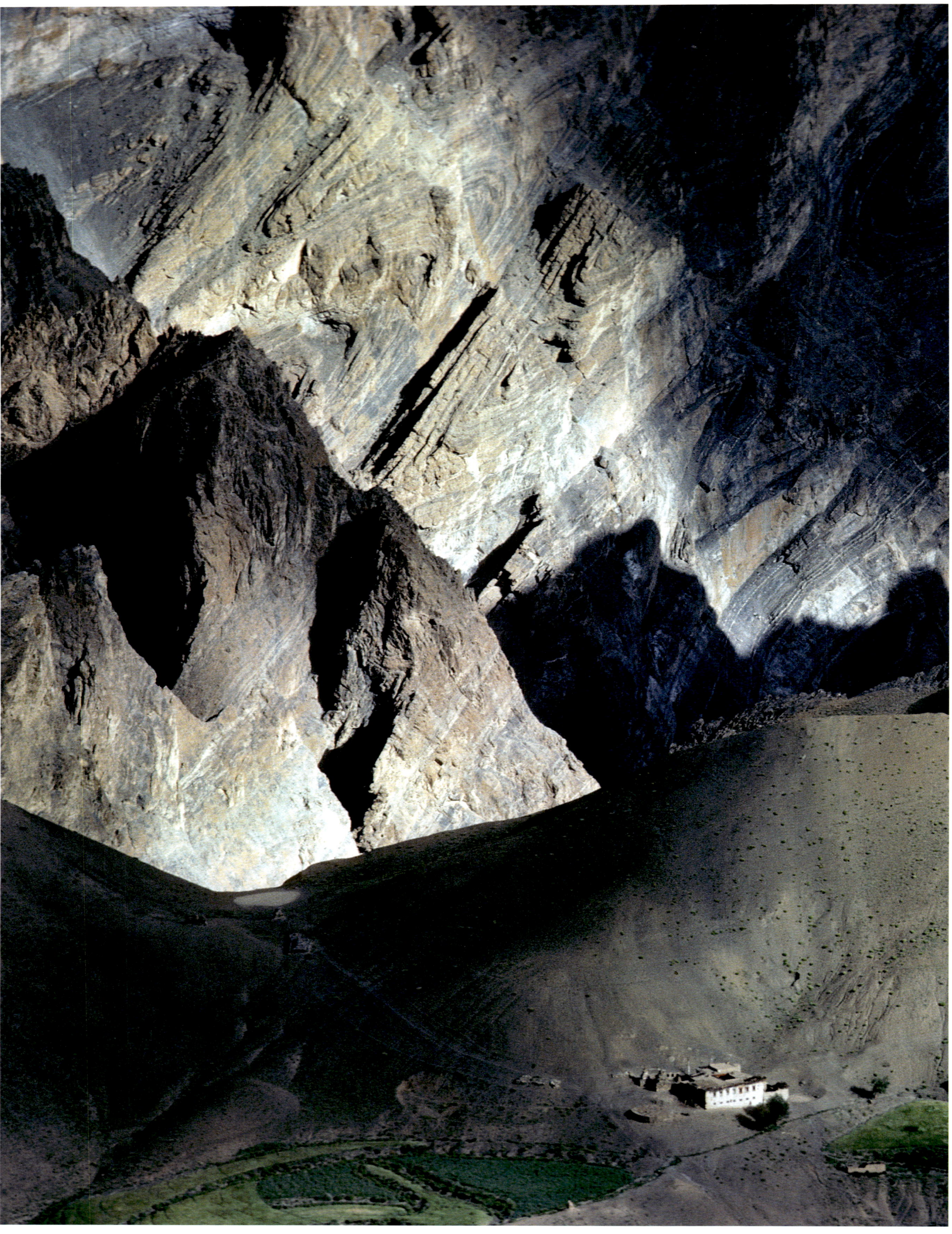

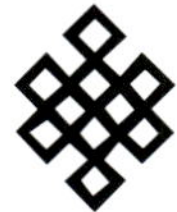

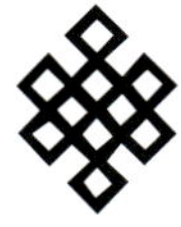

My Himalaya

40 YEARS AMONG BUDDHISTS

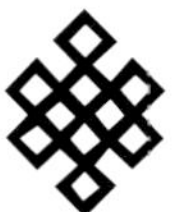

Spreading over some 1,500 miles from Afghanistan to Pakistan, India, Nepal, and Bhutan, and as far as Myanmar, the Himalayas are the longest and highest mountain range in the world. Covered with rice paddies and dense forestland, its southern side is irrigated by monsoon rains, grass grows in plenty, cows are sacred, and the villagers, mostly Hindus, drink sweet milky tea. To the west, in the Muslim Himalayas, minarets take pride of place in villages, green tea is the most popular beverage, and camels are a common sight. The barrier created by the hundreds of peaks rising up to 24,000 feet forms the natural boundary of the Himalayas. Beyond, the high plateaus and vast barren valleys of the northern side, sheltered from torrential rains, stretch into the distance 10,000 to 15,000 feet above sea level. This is the land where yaks live, where people drink salted butter tea, and where prayer flags flap in the wind. These are the Buddhist Himalayas of the Tibetan people where I grew up, learned and passed on knowledge, and loved. Our mutual adoption dates back forty years.

At the age of seventeen, my dream was to become a mountain guide. I was fearless, yearning for adventure, and wanting to live life fully. I set out by bus on the road to India, that road hippies took to use drugs in Kathmandu, Pokhara, Manali, and Goa. But rather than smoking ganja, I preferred to get high on walking and meeting people. With my pack on my back, I took my first steps in Nepal under a scorching sun in the rice terraces of the Himalayan foothills. In the distant horizon, although the far-off towering wall of glittering peaks galvanized me and spurred me to walk ever faster, I was forced to abide by the Himalayan laws of patience and perseverance. I ate lentils and white rice in small tea houses and slept in the barns of impoverished farmers who opened their doors to me for a few rupees. I loved this adventurous life and liked to think that the higher I climbed, the closer I got to the gods.

He who strives to attain Enlightenment
must expect to encounter dreadful obstacles:
anger, desire, mental confusion, pride and jealousy.
Dilgo Khyentse Rinpoche

In the rain and mist, I climbed up slippery paths at the bottom of deep and narrow valleys that were choked with forest and creepers. I passed by gushing mountain torrents that crashed noisily against the rocks. I didn't like those powerful torrents. I was frightened of their relentless violence, of my own insignificance, and of the truth of impermanence that sprang up from the frothy water. I felt horribly vulnerable in this green hell where leeches feasted on my blood. It took me days to reach the source of the torrents and finally savor the silence of quiet slopes. After pulling myself and panting through an interminable scree, I at last reached the windswept pass where my eyes once again were able to sweep the sky and the still far-off peaks. My spirit of exhilaration was revived. But, from the pass, I had to drop down again to the bottom of another valley, to return to hell, as in a bad rebirth, in order to draw step by step ever closer to my enlightenment, to my peaks.

During an expedition to climb the Minya Konka in Tibet, I succeeded in fulfilling my dream of getting closer to the gods, at more than 23,000 feet. But then, tortured by a raging storm and the lack of oxygen, I turned back before reaching the top. My spikes striking against the ice were but violence that I inflicted on myself. What could any god give me in that freezing hell? Breathless, exhausted, disappointed, I returned to base camp at 16,000 feet, where stones met snow. I was eager to embrace a gentler nature, reconnect with the world of men, and cease the combat of my ego, which was always looking for new victories. For two days, I climbed down through the scree slopes to reach a village nestling at the bottom of the sun-drenched valley.

The last bends of the path overlooked a handful of whitewashed houses scattered in the golden brown fields, through which a turquoise river flowed. Wreaths of smoke rose gracefully from the stone chimneys. I felt calm; my heart was at peace. Those gods whom I had sought on high had been here all along, in their mud houses. From village to village and journey to journey, they would teach me the path of inner triumph.

We continue to create suffering, waging war with what is good,
waging war with what is evil, waging war with what is too small,
waging war with what is too big, waging war with what is too short
or too long, or right or wrong, courageously carrying on the battle.
Ajahn Chah

At the age of twenty, on my return from a journey to the Himalayas, I nearly died in a car accident. To be frank, I should have died. But it wasn't written in my karma that I should die so young. When I reemerged on the surface of life, I sought to draw closer to the death I had brushed against in an attempt to rediscover the exaltation of the unfathomable peace I had felt. To try to relive the spiritual experience of my accident, I chose to spend a winter in Phuktal monastery in Zanskar, India, 13,000 feet above sea level, and to study Buddhism, which I thought would give me some of the answers I was looking for.

Before the first snowfall I set out from the Indus valley in Ladakh to reach the remote valleys of Zanskar by the Jumlam path. For one week, at temperatures near -4°F, I traveled through a maze of narrow, bleak valleys and crossed three passes nearly 16,000 feet high. At the end of this solitary journey, from the top of a headland and with the last gorges behind me, I contemplated at length the Zanskar valley and its small villages, set in another time, another world. I was overwhelmed. I had the cosmic feeling of having come home at last after a long journey in my past lives. The unutterable joy I felt was that of the disciple who has been finally reunited with his Master.

In the decades to come, I returned many times to Zanskar and even spent four winters there. In those valleys completely sealed off by snow from the outside world, winter lets you savor the beauty and fullness of life more keenly. There is nothing to do except share all this endless time with others. Sensitivity is heightened and emotions run wild. The gentle, noble nature of the villagers becomes even more apparent. Their words are whispered, their glances soft as velvet. Their gestures, like the graceful blessings of the monks, mirror the respect in their souls. It is with the villagers and monks of Zanskar that I was initiated into the Buddhism of the heart. Zanskar is thus my lotus flower, my benevolent Buddha who, for decades, spurred me on to meet other Tibetan peoples, those I speak of in this book, and to surround myself ever more with inner peace, kindness, tolerance, compassion, and nonviolence. So it is that, over the years, during the course of long fireside evenings watching the flickering flames, I have learned through simple words, thoughtful gestures, and soothing glances that while each person has a demon to fight, they also have a god in them that they can waken.

I wish you a long and lovely life, O my Himalaya,
and a very long life to His Holiness the 14th Dalai Lama.
Let peace and happiness shine out.
Olivier Föllmi

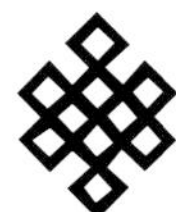

Der Himalaya erstreckt sich auf etwa 2400 Kilometern von Afghanistan und Pakistan über Indien, Nepal und Bhutan bis Myanmar. Er ist die längste und höchste Gebirgskette der Welt. Seine von Reisfeldern und dichten Wäldern bedeckte Südflanke wird vom Monsun bewässert. Hier wachsen viele Kräuter, die Kühe sind heilig und die Dorfbewohner – zumeist Hindus – trinken gezuckerten Milchtee. Im Westen beginnt der moslemische Himalaya dort, wo Minarette die Dörfer beherrschen, man grünen Tee trinkt und Kamele sieht. Ein Bollwerk aus Hunderten von Gipfeln zwischen 6000 und 8000 Meter Höhe bildet die natürliche Grenze des Himalaya. Dahinter erstreckt sich, geschützt vor sintflutartigen Regenfällen, die Nordflanke mit ihren Hochebenen und riesigen wüstenartigen Tälern in 3000 bis 5000 Meter Höhe. Hier leben Yaks, trinkt man gesalzenen Buttertee und klappern die Gebetsfahnen im Wind. In diesem buddhistischen Himalaya der Tibeter bin ich gereift, habe gelernt, gelehrt, geliebt. Mein Himalaya und ich sind uns vor 40 Jahren nahegekommen.

Mit 17 Jahren träumte ich davon, Bergführer zu werden. Ich war waghalsig, hungrig nach Abenteuern, nach dem Leben. Mit dem Reisebus bin ich nach Indien gefahren wie die Hippies, die in Kathmandu, Pokhara, Manali oder Goa Drogenerfahrungen suchten. Statt aber Ganja zu rauchen, berauschte ich mich lieber an langen Fußmärschen und Begegnungen. Mit dem Rucksack machte ich, unter einer erdrückenden Sonne, in den Reisterrassen der Ausläufer des Himalaya meine ersten Schritte in Nepal. Schon von Weitem begeisterte mich das ferne Spektakel aus gleißenden Bergspitzen und ließ mich meine Schritte beschleunigen, doch musste ich mich den himalayischen Gesetzen der Geduld und Beharrlichkeit beugen. Ich ernährte mich von Linsen und weißem Reis in schmutzigen Gaststätten und schlief in den ärmlichen Ställen der Bauern, die mir für wenige Rupien ihre Gastfreundschaft anboten. Ich liebte dieses abenteuerliche Leben und glaubte nur zu gern, dass ich mich den Göttern näherte, je höher ich kletterte.

Wer sich bemüht, Erleuchtung zu erlangen,
muss damit rechnen, auf schreckliche Hindernisse zu treffen:
Zorn, Begierde, geistige Verwirrung, Stolz und Neid.
Dilgo Khyentse Rinpoche

Bei Regen und Nebel bin ich eisglatte Wege in engen Tälern mit dichten Wäldern und Lianen gegangen. Ich bin sprudelnde Gebirgsbäche entlanggelaufen, die mit lautem Rauschen gegen Felsen schossen. Ich mochte diese starken Strömungen nicht, hatte Angst vor ihrer unaufhörlichen Gewalt, vor meiner Bedeutungslosigkeit und der Wahrheit der Vergänglichkeit, die aus dem schäumenden Wasser hervorsprudelte. Ich fühlte mich so verletzlich in dieser grünen Hölle, in der Blutegel mein Blut tranken. Es dauerte Tage, bis ich an der Quelle der Bäche angelangt war und endlich die Stille der friedvollen Hänge genießen konnte. Ich stapfte keuchend über schier endlose Geröllfelder und stieg hinauf bis zu windgepeitschten Satteln. Dort hatte ich wieder freien Blick auf den Himmel und die noch immer fernen Gipfel, dort fand ich meine Begeisterung wieder. Aber von oben musste ich in einen weiteren Talgrund hinabsteigen, zurückkehren in die Hölle, die mir wie eine schlechte Wiedergeburt erschien, um mich nach und nach meiner Erleuchtung, meinen Gipfeln zu nähern.

Auf einer Expedition zur Ersteigung des Minya Konka in Tibet gelang mir in 7000 Meter Höhe die Verwirklichung meines Traums, den Göttern näherzukommen. Aber gepeinigt von Wind, Sturm und Sauerstoffmangel verzichtete ich auf die Eroberung des Gipfels. Die Tritte meiner Steigeisen gegen das Eis waren nur Gewalt gegen mich selbst, und ich erwartete in dieser Eishölle nichts mehr von irgendeinem Gott. Keuchend, erschöpft und enttäuscht stieg ich zum Basislager in 5000 Meter Höhe an der Grenze zwischen Stein und Schnee hinab. Ich sehnte mich nach Wärme und Menschen und wollte dem Kampf meines siegeshungrigen Egos entsagen. Also ging ich zwei Tage lang über Geröllhalden zurück in ein Dorf am Ende eines sonnengebadeten Tals. Die letzten Serpentinen des Wegs wurden beherrscht von einer Handvoll weiß gekalkter Häuser, die sich über goldbraune Felder an einem türkisblauen Fluss verteilten. Rauchspiralen stiegen anmutig aus ihren steinernen Kaminen auf. Ich fühlte mich zur Ruhe gekommen, mit Frieden im Herzen. Die Götter, die ich so hoch droben gesucht hatte, sie waren hier, in diesen Lehmhäusern. Und sie waren es auch, die mir von Dorf zu Dorf und von Reise zu Reise den Weg zum inneren Triumph wiesen.

Wir schaffen weiterhin Leid.
Wir hadern mit dem Guten, mit dem Bösen,
mit dem, was zu klein ist, mit dem, was zu groß ist,
mit dem was zu kurz, zu lang oder falsch ist.
Verbissen führen wir unseren Kampf fort.
Ajahn Chah

Als ich mit 20 Jahren von einer Reise in den Himalaya zurückkehrte, hatte ich einen Autounfall, den ich eigentlich nicht hätte überleben dürfen. Aber es war nicht in meinem Karma, so jung zu sterben. Trotzdem versuchte ich, nachdem ich wieder an die Oberfläche des Lebens zurückgekehrt war, mich dem Tod zu nähern, den ich gestreift hatte, um das Hochgefühl der unergründlichen Ruhe wiederzufinden, welches ich durch ihn kennengelernt hatte. Weil ich die spirituelle Erfahrung meines Unfalls noch einmal erleben wollte, beschloss ich, einen Winter im 4000 Meter hoch gelegenen Kloster Phuktal in Zanskar zu verbringen und mich mit dem Buddhismus vertraut zu machen, der mir, wie es schien, Antworten geben konnte.

Vor den ersten Schneefällen brach ich also mit meinem Rucksack vom Tal des Indus in Ladakh auf, um über Jumlam zu den entlegenen Tälern von Zanskar zu gelangen. Eine Woche lang durchlief ich bei -25 °C ein Labyrinth aus engen, kargen Tälern und überquerte drei Pässe in fast 5000 Meter Höhe. Am Ende meiner einsamen Reise betrachtete ich nach der Überwindung der letzten Schluchten von einem Felsvorsprung aus lange das Tal von Zanskar und seine kleinen Dörfer, die aus einer anderen Zeit und Welt zu sein schienen. Ich war aufgewühlt, ergriff mich doch das kosmische Gefühl, nach einer langen Reise in meinen früheren Leben endlich bei mir selbst angekommen zu sein. Ich empfand die unsägliche Freude des Schülers, der endlich seinen Meister gefunden hat.

Im Lauf der letzten Jahrzehnte bin ich immer wieder nach Zanskar zurückgekehrt und habe dort sogar vier Winter verbracht. In den durch den Schnee völlig von der Außenwelt abgeschnittenen Tälern lässt einen der Winter die Schönheit und Tiefe des Lebens intensiver genießen. Es gibt nichts zu tun, und jeder hat viel Zeit, sie mit anderen zu teilen. Die Empfindsamkeit steigt, die Gefühle vervielfachen sich. Von den Dorfbewohnern empfängt man noch mehr Milde, noch mehr Edelmut. Ihre Worte werden gemurmelt, ihre Blicke sind wie Samt. Ihre Gesten erinnern an die anmutigen Segnungen der Mönche und offenbaren ihren respektvollen Geist. Bei den Dorfbewohnern und den Mönchen von Zanskar bin ich dem Buddhismus mit dem Herzen nähergekommen. Der Zanskar war daher meine Lotusblüte, mein gütiger Buddha, der mich veranlasst hat, jahrzehntelang die Begegnung mit anderen tibetischen Völkern – denen meines Himalaya – zu suchen, damit ich stets durchdrungen werde von innerem Frieden, Wohlwollen, Toleranz, Mitgefühl und Gewaltfreiheit. So habe ich im Lauf der Jahre und während langer Wachen an züngelnden Feuern durch einfache Worte, aufmerksame Gesten und zärtliche Blicke gelernt, dass, wenn in jedem Menschen ein Dämon steckt, den es zu bekämpfen gilt, auch in jedem ein Gott ist, der erweckt werden will.

Ein sehr langes und schönes Leben dir, o mein Himalaya,
und ein sehr langes Leben seiner Heiligkeit, dem 14. Dalai Lama.
Mögen Frieden und Glück erstrahlen.
Olivier Föllmi

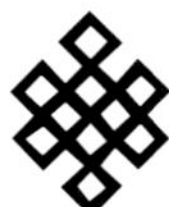

S'étalant sur près de 2 400 kilomètres, de l'Afghanistan au Pakistan, à l'Inde, au Népal, au Bhoutan, et jusqu'au Myanmar, l'Himalaya est la plus longue et la plus haute chaîne de montagnes du monde. Couvert de rizières et de forêts denses, son versant sud est irrigué par la mousson, l'herbe y est abondante, les vaches sont sacrées et les villageois, hindous pour la plupart, boivent du thé au lait sucré. À l'ouest, l'Himalaya musulmane commence dès lors que des minarets trônent dans les villages, qu'on boit du thé vert où qu'on aperçoit des chameaux. La barrière des centaines de sommets de 6 000 à 8 000 mètres d'altitude constitue la frontière naturelle de l'Himalaya. Au-delà, protégé des pluies torrentielles, le versant nord s'étale en hauts plateaux et en vastes vallées désertiques entre 3 000 et 5 000 mètres d'altitude. C'est là que vivent les yaks, que l'on boit du thé salé au beurre, que des drapeaux de prières claquent au vent, c'est là l'Himalaya bouddhiste des Tibétains où j'ai grandi, appris, transmis, aimé. Nous nous sommes adoptés il y a quarante ans.

À dix-sept ans, je rêvais de devenir guide de haute montagne. J'étais intrépide, j'avais soif d'aventure, soif de vivre. Je suis parti en autocar sur la route des Indes qu'empruntaient les hippies pour aller se droguer à Katmandou, Pokhara, Manali ou Goa. Plutôt que de fumer de la ganja, j'ai préféré m'enivrer de marche et de rencontres. Sac au dos, j'ai fait mes premiers pas au Népal sous un soleil écrasant, dans les rizières en terrasses des premiers contreforts de l'Himalaya. Au loin, la muraille lointaine hérissée de pics étincelants m'exaltait et m'incitait à forcer le pas, mais j'ai dû me plier aux lois himalayennes de la patience et de la persévérance. Je me nourrissais de lentilles et de riz blanc dans des gargotes et dormais dans les étables de paysans démunis qui m'offraient l'hospitalité contre quelques roupies. J'aimais cette vie aventureuse et j'aimais croire que plus je grimpais haut, plus je m'approchais des dieux.

Celui qui s'efforce d'atteindre l'Éveil
doit s'attendre à rencontrer d'épouvantables obstacles :
la colère, le désir, la confusion mentale, l'orgueil et la jalousie.
Dilgo Khyentsé Rinpotché

Sous la pluie, dans le brouillard, j'ai remonté des chemins glissants au fond de vallées encaissées, étouffées de forêts et de lianes. Je longeais des torrents bouillonnants qui se fracassaient bruyamment contre les rochers. Je n'aimais pas ces torrents trop puissants, j'avais peur de leur violence sans répit, de mon insignifiance et de la vérité de l'impermanence qui jaillissait de l'écume. Je me sentais si vulnérable dans cet enfer de verdure où des sangsues buvaient mon sang. Il m'a fallu des jours pour arriver jusqu'à la source des torrents et goûter enfin au silence des pentes apaisées. Haletant dans un interminable pierrier, je me suis hissé jusqu'au col battu par le vent. Là, j'ai retrouvé la vue sur le ciel et les sommets encore lointains, j'ai retrouvé l'exaltation. Mais du col, il m'a fallu redescendre tout au fond d'une autre vallée, retourner en enfer, comme lors d'une mauvaise renaissance, pour m'approcher peu à peu de mon éveil, de mes sommets.

Au cours d'une expédition pour gravir le Minya Konka au Tibet, j'ai réussi à réaliser mon rêve, celui de me rapprocher des dieux, à plus de 7 000 mètres d'altitude, mais torturé par le vent, la tempête et le manque d'oxygène, j'ai renoncé au sommet. Mes coups de crampons contre la glace n'étaient que violence contre moi-même et je n'attendais plus rien d'aucun dieu dans cet enfer du froid. Pantelant, épuisé, déçu, j'ai rejoint le camp de base à 5 000 mètres d'altitude, à la limite des pierres et de la neige. J'aspirais à retrouver de la douceur, à retrouver des hommes et cesser le combat de mon ego assoiffé de victoires. Je suis donc descendu dans les pierriers durant deux jours pour rejoindre un village tout en bas de la vallée baignée de soleil. Les derniers lacets du chemin dominaient une poignée de maisons blanchies à la chaux dispersées dans les champs mordorés, que traversait une rivière turquoise. Des volutes de fumée s'échappaient gracieusement des cheminées de pierre. Je me suis senti apaisé, le cœur en paix. Ces dieux que j'étais allé chercher si haut étaient là, dans leurs maisons de terre, et ce sont eux qui, de village en village, de voyage en voyage, m'enseigneraient le chemin de la victoire intérieure.

Nous continuons à créer la souffrance ; nous sommes en conflit
avec le bien, en conflit avec le mal, en conflit avec ce qui est trop petit,
avec ce qui est trop grand, avec ce qui est trop court, ou trop long, ou faux ;
vaillamment, nous poursuivons le combat.
Ajahn Chah

À vingt ans, au retour d'un voyage en Himalaya, j'ai eu un accident de voiture dont je n'aurais pas dû sortir vivant. Mais il n'était pas inscrit dans mon karma de mourir si jeune. Cependant, revenu à la surface de la vie, j'ai cherché à me rapprocher de la mort que j'avais effleurée pour retrouver l'exaltation de l'insondable quiétude qu'elle m'avait procurée. Pour tenter de renouer avec l'expérience spirituelle de mon accident, j'ai donc choisi de séjourner un hiver au monastère de Phuktal, à 4 000 mètres d'altitude, au Zanskar, et de me rapprocher du bouddhisme qui, me semblait-il, m'offrirait des réponses.

Avant les premières chutes de neige, je suis donc parti sac au dos de la vallée de l'Indus au Ladakh pour rejoindre les vallées isolées du Zanskar par le chemin du Jumlam. Pendant une semaine, par moins vingt degrés, j'ai parcouru un labyrinthe de vallées étroites et austères et franchi trois cols à près de 5 000 mètres d'altitude. Arrivé au bout de ce voyage solitaire, après avoir franchi les dernières gorges, j'ai longuement contemplé du haut d'un promontoire la vallée du Zanskar et ses petits villages hors du temps, hors du monde. J'étais bouleversé : j'avais le sentiment cosmique d'arriver enfin chez moi après un long voyage dans mes vies antérieures et j'éprouvais la joie indicible du disciple qui retrouve enfin son Maître.

Durant des décennies, je n'ai eu de cesse de retourner au Zanskar et j'y ai même séjourné quatre hivers. Dans ces vallées totalement isolées du monde par la neige, l'hiver permet de savourer plus intensément la beauté et la profondeur de la vie. Il n'y a rien à faire et chacun a tout son temps pour le partager avec les autres. La sensibilité y est exacerbée et les émotions sont décuplées. Il émane des villageois encore plus de douceur, de noblesse. Leurs paroles sont murmurées, leur regard est de velours. Leurs gestes, semblables aux bénédictions gracieuses des moines, reflètent leur âme respectueuse. C'est auprès des villageois et des moines du Zanskar que je me suis initié au bouddhisme du cœur. Le Zanskar a donc été ma fleur de lotus, mon bouddha bienveillant qui m'a incité à aller pendant des décennies à la rencontre des autres peuples tibétains, ceux de Mon Himalaya, pour m'imprégner toujours plus de paix intérieure, de bienveillance, de tolérance, de compassion et de non-violence. C'est ainsi qu'au cours des années, au cours de longues veillées autour des flammes vacillantes, j'ai appris par des mots simples, des gestes attentionnés, des regards caressants que si chaque homme a un démon à combattre, il a aussi un dieu à éveiller.

Très longue et belle vie à toi, Ô mon Himalaya,
et une très longue vie à sa Sainteté, le XIVe dalaï-lama.
Que la paix et le bonheur rayonnent.
Olivier Föllmi

Wisdom

Weisheit · Sagesse

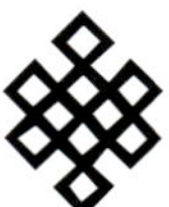

"You are responsible for your own confusion, and you are responsible for your own liberation. What saves us from confusion is our wisdom." Such are the words of the Buddha, who taught us how to free ourselves from suffering to attain enlightenment.

„Ihr seid verantwortlich für eure eigene Verwirrung, und ihr seid verantwortlich für eure eigene Befreiung. Vor der Verwirrung rettet uns unsere Weisheit." Dies waren die Worte Buddhas, der uns lehrte, wie wir uns vom Leid befreien, um Erleuchtung zu erlangen.

« Vous êtes responsable de votre propre confusion et vous êtes responsable de votre propre libération. Ce qui nous sauve de la confusion, c'est notre sagesse », déclara Bouddha, qui enseigna comment se libérer de la souffrance pour atteindre l'éveil.

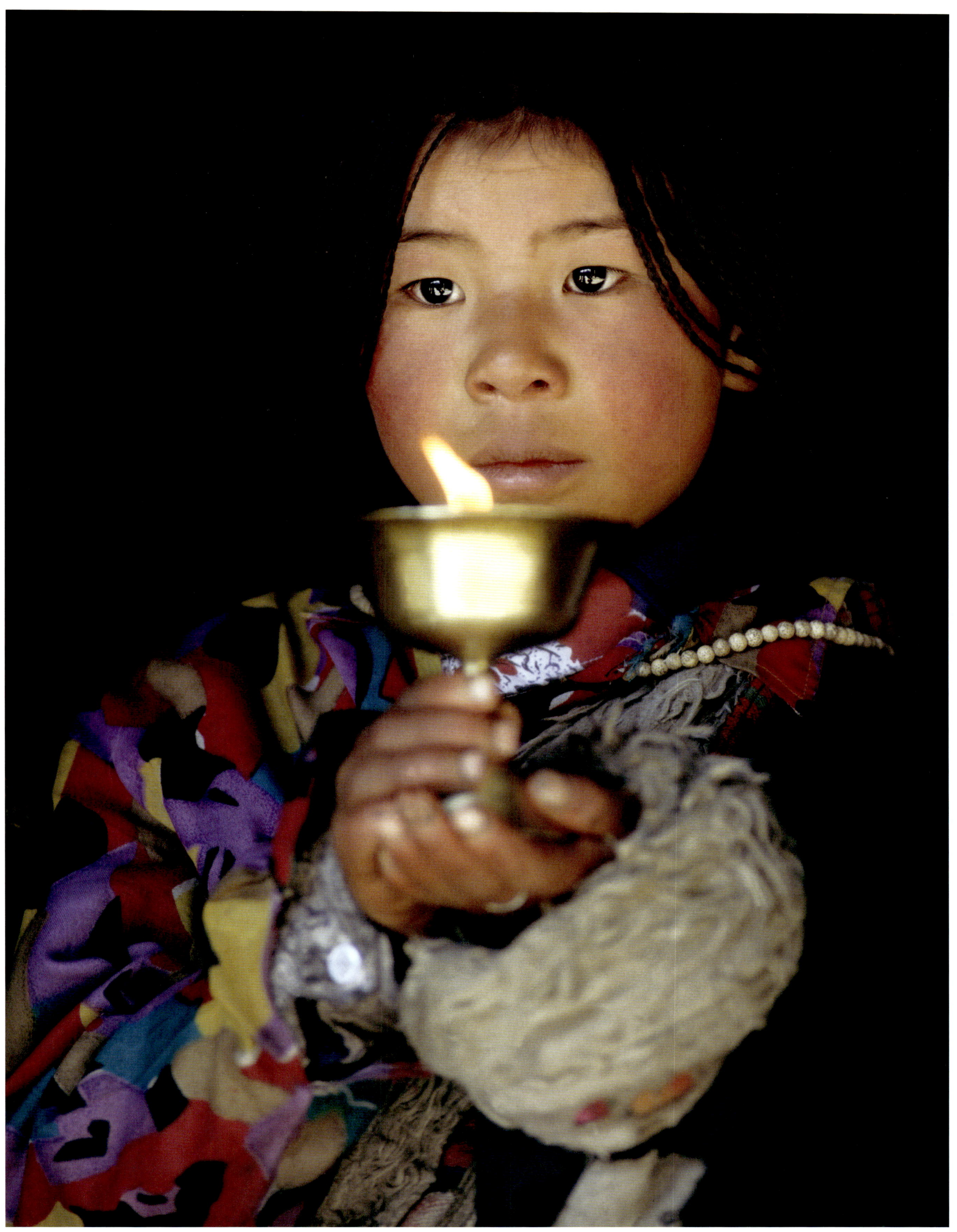

The 14th Dalai Lama, the Ocean of Wisdom Tenzin Gyatso, is acknowledged by Tibetans as the emanation of Chenrezik, the divinity of infinite love who teaches the path to enlightenment. My most moving experience with the Dalai Lama dates back to 1985, twenty-six years after he left Tibet to take refuge in India and escape the fanaticism of Mao's Red Guards. That year, the Dalai Lama gave one of his most precious teachings: the Kalachakra, the initiation of peace into the heart, at Bodhgaya, in the Indian plain where the Buddha attained enlightenment under a peepal tree at the foot of the Himalayas 2,500 years ago. For Buddhists, Bodhgaya is the most important pilgrimage of all. Announced the year before, this splendid news was spread throughout the Himalayas, from mouth to mouth and from valley to valley, reaching Tibetan refugees in all four corners of the world. Although Tibet had still not recovered from the horror of the Cultural Revolution, in which millions of people lost their lives, five thousand Tibetans from the high plateaus managed to cross 18,000-foot passes by walking, risking their lives to reach Bodhgaya. For the first time, they met their spiritual leader, the mention of whom or possession of whose image was punishable by imprisonment in Tibet.

In Gaya, the nearest station to Bodhgaya, trains from Delhi and Calcutta are all fully packed. Thousands of Tibetan refugees have come from southern India, their bags stuffed with green bananas. Thousands of villagers wrapped in multicolored shawls pour in from the far-off regions of Dolpo and Mustang. Others arrive from Ladakh and snow-sealed Zanskar dressed in madder wool coats, from Lahaul wearing small, flat, embroidered caps, from the kingdom of Bhutan, or from the depths of Mizoram and Arunachal Pradesh. Hundreds of Tibetans who found refuge in Switzerland, Germany, and the United States also converge toward Bodhgaya.

AT EIGHT O'CLOCK SHARP, HIS HOLINESS WILL APPEAR AND START THE KALACHAKRA, THE TEACHING OF WISDOM THAT LEADS TO DELIVERANCE.

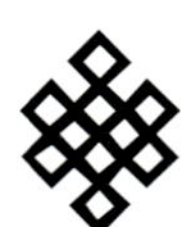

Three enormous tented camps encircle the tiny village of Bodhgaya. The first camp houses penniless pilgrims from Tibet, who are haggard and exhausted after weeks of walking. Their stay—accommodation and food—is entirely paid for by the Tibetan government in exile. Monks welcome them under a large white cotton tent. A weathered man enters the tent, a serious expression on his face. His hair, gray with dust, is tied back by a red woolen braid. He still carries his jute bag sandwiched between two wooden sticks, serving as his backpack. Overwhelmed by emotion, he slowly greets the monk, joining the palms of his hands in front of his forehead. Reaching into his large woolen coat that smells of smoke, he gently takes out a small roll protected by an old yellowed rag. He bends over its shabby gold-painted holy image that he saved from the ransacking of the Red Army and, with both hands, offers it to the monk: "I wish long life to our Master, the Precious Victorious One. I have walked three months to come to him with my four children. One of them died on the last pass."

Fingering their prayer beads, the thousands of pilgrims devoutly circumvent the holy tree and stupa, the quintessential symbol of Buddha and his all-knowing spirit, whose various parts evoke the series of steps on the path to illumination. That evening, Bodhgaya vibrates with an unusual tension, perceptible on each person's face. The stupa glows with thousands of candles, like stars in the sky, as though the entire universe was participating in the prayers. Tomorrow is the great day, the event of a lifetime for which they have given up their wealth and sapped their strength to get here. Tomorrow, at eight o'clock sharp, His Holiness will appear and start the Kalachakra, the teaching of wisdom that leads to deliverance. Tomorrow, after decades of suffering under the Maoist yoke, thousands of Tibetans from the high plateaus will finally see and hear their spiritual leader.

That evening, many of them have already settled under the huge 650-foot-long tent, at the end of which, seated on a throne, the Dalai Lama will offer up his teaching. At three in the morning, under the star-studded sky, all three hundred thousand pilgrims huddle together and murmur their prayer of peace and compassion while they gently finger their prayer beads. At four, the clear sound of a conch shell pierces the silence of the night. Seated in tight formation in front of the throne, eight thousand saffron-robed monks intone a low-pitched prayer, with one spirit, one voice. Although Buddhists have no god, that night I truly believed there was a god of Love. Another four hours and the Dalai Lama will appear there, on his throne, in front of the monks and the pilgrims. Everyone concentrates on their prayers, composes their mind, and focuses their attention. From time to time a baby cries, and its mother protects it with the fold of her cloak, offering her breast. The day dawns in the distance with a slowness that portends a great event. Like a heavenly offering, the sun rises above the horizon and hovers over the plain in a drop of red blood. Then, to the slow rhythm of the monks' prayers, it turns into a golden yellow flame. When its first rays caress my face under the great tent, I honor it with my thoughts, like the grace of heavenly gods also come to greet the man who will appear from one moment to the next. The monks' prayers intensify. Each fingers his prayer beads restlessly, all eyes are riveted on that door, down there. Under the heavy woolen cloaks, hearts are beating fast. The monks' prayers are humbler now, more confidential, and then slowly die down to a whisper. In a silence where no one is praying any more, he appears in the doorway. He remains standing in front of the throne, joining the palms of his hands in every direction, for each one of us. He makes our tears fall and we cry in silence, tears gushing from our heart. He is so far away, so small, and yet he is here, so very much present. I feel, we all feel, flooded with an indescribable compassion. His selflessness, the energy he gives off by his aura, and the path of Love that he preaches, shine within us. Around me, I no longer see people but gods, the palms of their hands joined in prayer.

O my Himalaya . . .

Der 14. Dalai Lama, Ozean der Weisheit Tenzin Gyatso, wird von den Tibetern als Wiedergeburt des Chenrezi (Avalokiteshvara) anerkannt, der Gottheit des unendlichen Mitgefühls, die den Weg zur Erleuchtung lehrt. Meine bewegendste Begegnung mit dem Dalai Lama hatte ich 1985 – 26 Jahre nachdem er gezwungen worden war, Tibet zu verlassen und sich ins indische Exil zu begeben, um den fanatischen Roten Garden Maos zu entkommen. In diesem Jahr gab der Dalai Lama in Bodhgaya eine seiner kostbarsten Kalachakra-Initiationen zur Erlangung des Herzensfriedens. Bodhgaya liegt in der indischen Ebene am Fuß des Himalaya, in der Buddha vor 2500 Jahren unter einer Pappelfeige Erleuchtung fand. Für Buddhisten ist Bodhgaya die wichtigste Pilgerstätte überhaupt. Die großartige Nachricht von der Initiation wurde ein Jahr im Voraus angekündigt und über Mundpropaganda von Tal zu Tal weitergegeben. So verbreitete sie sich im ganzen Himalaya, erreichte aber auch die über die Welt verstreuten Exiltibeter. Tibet hatte sich noch nicht von den Schrecken der Kulturrevolution erholt, die Millionen Tote forderte, dennoch gelang es 5000 Tibetern der Hochebenen, unter Lebensgefahr Pässe in 5600 Meter Höhe zu Fuß zu überqueren und nach Bodhgaya zu kommen. Zum ersten Mal begegneten sie dort ihrem geistlichen Oberhaupt. Von ihm ein Bild zu besitzen, ja, ihn auch nur zu erwähnen, wird in Tibet schon mit Gefängnis bestraft.

In Gaya, dem Bodhgaya nächstgelegenen Bahnhof, treffen die Züge aus Delhi und Kalkutta überfüllt ein. Tausende tibetischer Flüchtlinge kommen aus dem Süden Indiens, ihr Gepäck voll mit grünen Bananen. Man sieht unzählige Dorfbewohner in vielfarbigen Gewändern aus dem fernen Dolpo und Mustang. Andere in Mänteln aus roter Wolle stammen aus Ladakh, dem durch Schnee fast völlig von der Außenwelt abgeschnittenen Zanskar oder – wenn sie einen kleinen flachen, bestickten Hut auf dem Kopf tragen – aus Lahaul. Wieder andere finden sich aus dem Königreich Bhutan, dem hintersten Mizoram und aus Arunachal Pradesh ein. Hunderte Exiltibeter reisen ferner aus der Schweiz, aus Deutschland oder den Vereinigten Staaten nach Bodhgaya.

Drei riesige Zeltstädte werden um das winzige Dorf Bodhgaya aufgeschlagen. Im ersten übernachten völlig mittellose Pilger aus Tibet, scheu und erschöpft von wochenlangen Märschen. Ihr Aufenthalt mit Unterkunft und Verpflegung wird komplett von der tibetischen Exilregierung finanziert. Unter einem großen Zelt aus weißer Baumwolle heißen die Mönche sie willkommen. Ein zerfurchter Mann betritt das Zelt mit ernster Miene. Sein vor Staub graues Haar ist mit einem roten Wollband zusammengeflochten. Er trägt noch seinen Reisebeutel, den er zwischen zwei Holzstangen geklemmt zum Rucksack umfunktioniert hat. Zutiefst bewegt grüßt er einen Mönch langsam mit gefalteten Händen. Dann steckt er eine Hand in seinen großen, nach Rauch riechenden Wollmantel. Vorsichtig holt er eine kleine, in alten vergilbten Stoff eingeschlagene Rolle heraus, verneigt sich vor dem abgewetzten, in Gold gemalten Andachtsbild, das er vor den Plünderungen der Roten Armee gerettet hat, und reicht es mit beiden Händen dem Mönch: „Ich wünsche unserem Meister, dem kostbaren, siegreichen Dalai Lama, ein langes Leben. Ich bin drei Monate lang mit meinen vier Kindern hierher gegangen. Eines von ihnen ist am letzten Pass gestorben."

Tausende Pilger umrunden mit Gebetsschnüren gottesfürchtig den heiligen Baum und den Stupa, das Symbol der Erhabenheit des Buddha und seiner Allwissenheit. Die verschiedenen Elemente des Bauwerks stehen für die Stufen auf dem Weg zur Erleuchtung. An diesem Abend ist Bodhgaya von einer ungewöhnlichen Spannung erfüllt, die allenthalben deutlich wird. Der Stupa wird von Tausenden Kerzen erleuchtet. Sie sind so zahlreich wie die Sterne am Nachthimmel und gemahnen daran, das ganze Universum in die Gebete einzuschließen. Morgen ist der große Tag, das wichtigste Ereignis im Leben eines Buddhisten, für den er seinen ganzen Besitz hergibt und seine ganze Kraft auf dem Weg hierher verbraucht. Morgen um exakt acht Uhr erscheint seine Heiligkeit und leitet das Kalachakra ein, die zur Erlösung führende Lehre der Weisheit. Morgen werden nach jahrzehntelangem Leiden unter dem maoistischen Joch Tausende von Tibetern aus den Hochebenen endlich ihr spirituelles Oberhaupt sehen und hören.

Schon an diesem Abend begeben sich viele in das riesige, 200 Meter lange Zelt, an dessen Ende der Dalai Lama auf einem Thron seinen Rat erteilt. Um drei Uhr nachts haben sich unter dem sternenklaren Himmel bereits 300 000 Pilger in das Zelt gezwängt. Dicht gedrängt sitzen sie, murmeln ihre Gebete des Friedens und Mitgefühls und lassen dabei ihre Gebetsschnüre vorsichtig durch die Finger gleiten. Um vier Uhr durchbricht der klare Klang eines Muschelhorns die Stille der Nacht. Vor dem Thron beginnen

UM EXAKT ACHT UHR ERSCHEINT SEINE HEILIGKEIT UND LEITET DAS KALACHAKRA EIN, DIE ZUR ERLÖSUNG FÜHRENDE LEHRE DER WEISHEIT.

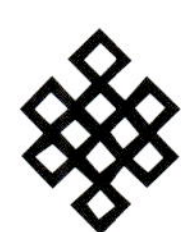

8000 Mönche in safranroten Roben wie mit einer Stimme und wie auf Kommando ein ernstes Gebet. Es gibt für Buddhisten keinen Gott, aber in dieser Nacht habe ich an den Gott der Liebe geglaubt. Nur noch vier Stunden, dann wird der Dalai Lama auf seinem Thron erscheinen und den Mönchen und Pilgern gegenübersitzen. Jeder konzentriert sich auf seine Gebete, bringt seinen Geist zur Ruhe und sammelt seine Aufmerksamkeit. Gelegentlich hört man ein Kleinkind schreien. Seine Mutter beruhigt es mit einem Zipfel ihres Kleides, stillt es. Der Tag bricht in der Ferne mit einer Langsamkeit an, die sich als Vorbote für ein großes Ereignis deuten lässt. Wie eine himmlische Opfergabe erhebt sich die Sonne als blutroter Tropfen über dem Horizont. Dann verwandelt sie sich im trägen Rhythmus der Mönchsgebete in eine goldgelbe Flamme. Als ihre ersten Strahlen mein Gesicht im großen Zelt streicheln, würdige ich sie in Gedanken wie eine Gnade himmlischer Mächte, gekommen, um auch diejenigen zu begrüßen, die unvermutet erscheinen. Das Gebet der Mönche wird eindringlicher. Jeder klammert sich fest an seine Gebetskette, die Augen starr auf die Tür weit hinten gerichtet. Unter den schweren Wollmänteln fangen die Herzen schneller zu schlagen an. Mit einem Mal beginnen die Mönche demütiger, langsamer und leiser zu sprechen, bis sie in ein Murmeln verfallen. In einer Stille, in der niemand mehr betet und jeder den Atem anhält, erscheint er in einer Türöffnung. Vor dem Thron bleibt er stehen. Er faltet die Hände in jede Richtung, für jeden von uns. Er lässt die Tränen fließen, lässt unsere Tränen still fließen, Tränen, die aus dem Herzen quellen. Er ist so weit weg, so klein und doch da, sehr präsent. Ich fühle mich, wir alle fühlen uns überwältigt von einem unbeschreiblichen Mitgefühl. Sein Altruismus, die Energie, die er uns durch seine Aura vermittelt, das Gesetz der Liebe, das er predigt, strahlt in uns. Um mich herum sehe ich keine Menschen mehr, ich sehe Götter mit gefalteten Händen.

O mein Himalaya …

Le XIVe dalaï-lama, l'Océan de Sagesse Tenzin Gyatso, est reconnu par les Tibétains comme l'émanation de Chènrezi, la divinité de l'amour infini qui enseigne le chemin de l'éveil. Mon expérience la plus émouvante avec le dalaï-lama remonte à 1985, vingt-six ans après qu'il fut contraint de quitter le Tibet pour se réfugier en Inde, afin d'échapper au fanatisme de l'armée des gardes rouges de Mao. Cette année-là, le dalaï-lama a donné l'un de ses plus précieux enseignements : le Kalachakra, l'initiation de la paix du cœur, à Bodh-Gaya, dans la plaine indienne où Bouddha atteignit l'éveil sous un arbre, un pipal, au pied de l'Himalaya, il y a 2 500 ans. Pour les bouddhistes, Bodh-Gaya est le plus important de tous les pèlerinages. Annoncée un an à l'avance, cette magnifique nouvelle circule dans tout l'Himalaya, de bouche à oreille, de vallée en vallée, jusqu'aux Tibétains réfugiés du monde entier. Le Tibet n'est pas encore remis de l'horreur de la révolution culturelle qui fit des millions de morts, mais 5 000 Tibétains des hauts plateaux réussissent à franchir à pied des cols à 5 600 mètres d'altitude au péril de leur vie pour se rendre à Bodh-Gaya. Pour la première fois, ils vont rencontrer leur chef spirituel, dont l'évocation verbale ou la possession de l'image sont punis d'emprisonnement au Tibet.

À HUIT HEURES PRÉCISES, SA SAINTETÉ APPARAÎTRA ET DÉBUTERA LE KALACHAKRA, L'ENSEIGNEMENT DE SAGESSE QUI MÈNE À LA DÉLIVRANCE.

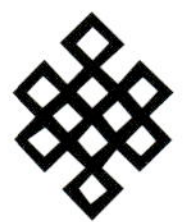

À Gaya, la gare la plus proche de Bodh-Gaya, les trains en provenance de Delhi ou Calcutta arrivent bondés. Des milliers de réfugiés tibétains viennent du sud de l'Inde, leurs sacs remplis de bananes vertes. Des milliers de villageois enveloppés dans des châles multicolores arrivent du lointain Dolpo et du Mustang, d'autres vêtus de manteaux de laine garance viennent du Ladakh, du Zanskar isolé dans la neige, d'autres encore du Lahaul, coiffés d'un petit chapeau plat et brodé, du royaume du Bhoutan, du fin fond du Misoram et de l'Arunachal Pradesh. Des centaines de Tibétains réfugiés en Suisse, en Allemagne ou aux États-Unis convergent aussi vers Bodh-Gaya.

Trois gigantesques camps de toile encerclent le minuscule village de Bodh-Gaya. Le premier camp héberge les pèlerins qui arrivent sans un sou du Tibet, hagards et épuisés après des semaines de marche. Leur séjour – logement et nourriture – est entièrement pris en charge par le gouvernement tibétain en exil. Sous une grande tente de coton blanc, des moines les accueillent. Un homme buriné entre sous la tente, le visage grave. Une tresse de laine rouge noue ses cheveux gris de poussière. Il porte encore son sac de jute enserré entre deux tiges de bois en guise de sac à dos. Profondément ému, il salue lentement le moine, les mains jointes à son front. Plongeant la main dans son grand manteau de laine à l'odeur de fumée, il retire doucement un petit rouleau protégé par un vieux tissu jauni. Il s'incline sur son image pieuse élimée et peinte d'or qu'il a sauvée du saccage par l'Armée rouge et l'offre des deux mains au moine : « Je souhaite une longue vie à notre Maître, le Précieux Victorieux. J'ai marché trois mois pour venir jusqu'à lui avec mes quatre enfants. L'un d'eux est mort au dernier col. »

Égrenant leur chapelet, les milliers de pèlerins contournent pieusement l'arbre sacré et tournent lentement autour du stupa, le symbole par excellence de Bouddha et de son esprit omniscient dont les différentes parties évoquent les étapes successives de la voie menant à l'illumination.

Ce soir, Bodh-Gaya vibre d'une tension inhabituelle, perceptible dans chaque regard. Le stupa luit de milliers de bougies comme autant d'étoiles dans le ciel, comme si l'univers entier s'impliquait dans les prières. Demain est le grand jour, l'événement d'une vie pour lequel on a sacrifié sa fortune, usé ses forces sur les chemins. Demain, à huit heures précises, Sa Sainteté apparaîtra et débutera le Kalachakra, l'enseignement de sagesse qui mène à la délivrance. Demain, après des décennies de souffrance sous le joug maoïste, des milliers de Tibétains des hauts plateaux vont enfin apercevoir et entendre leur chef spirituel.

Nombreux sont ceux qui s'installent dès le soir sous l'immense chapiteau long de 200 mètres au bout duquel, sur un trône, le dalaï-lama offrira son enseignement. À trois heures du matin, dans la nuit criblée d'étoiles, tous les pèlerins, 300 000 pèlerins, se serrent, assis les uns contre les autres, et murmurent leur prière de paix et de compassion en égrenant doucement leur rosaire. À quatre heures, une conque au son clair perce le silence de la nuit. Assis en rangs serrés devant le trône, 8 000 moines aux robes safran entonnent une prière grave, d'un seul élan, d'une seule voix. Il n'y a point de dieu pour les bouddhistes mais pourtant, cette nuit-là, j'ai cru au dieu Amour. Encore quatre heures et le dalaï-lama apparaîtra là, sur son trône, face aux moines, face aux pèlerins. Chacun se concentre sur ses prières, calme son esprit et rassemble son attention. Parfois, un bébé pleure et sa mère le protège du pan de son manteau, lui donne le sein. Le jour se lève au loin avec la lenteur qui présage un grand événement. Comme une offrande céleste, le soleil s'élève à l'horizon et se pose sur la plaine en une goutte rouge sang. Puis au rythme lent de la prière des moines, il se transforme en une flamme jaune d'or. Lorsque ses premiers rayons me caressent le visage sous le grand chapiteau, je l'honore de mes pensées comme la grâce de dieux célestes venus aussi accueillir celui qui va apparaître d'un instant à l'autre. La prière des moines s'intensifie. Chacun égrène son rosaire avec tension, tous les yeux sont rivés sur cette porte, là-bas. Sous les lourds manteaux de laine, les cœurs explosent. La prière des moines se fait plus humble, plus intime et, lentement, devient murmure. Dans un silence où plus personne ne prie, où plus personne ne respire, il apparaît alors dans l'embrasure de la porte. Il reste debout, devant le trône. Il joint les mains dans chaque direction, pour chacun d'entre nous. Il fait couler des larmes, il nous fait couler des larmes, en silence, des larmes qui jaillissent de notre cœur. Il est si loin, si petit et pourtant il est là, si présent. Je me sens, nous nous sentons inondés d'une indescriptible compassion. Son altruisme, l'énergie qu'il nous communique par son aura, la loi de l'Amour qu'il prône rayonne en nous. Autour de moi, je ne vois plus d'hommes, je vois des dieux, les mains jointes.

Ô mon Himalaya...

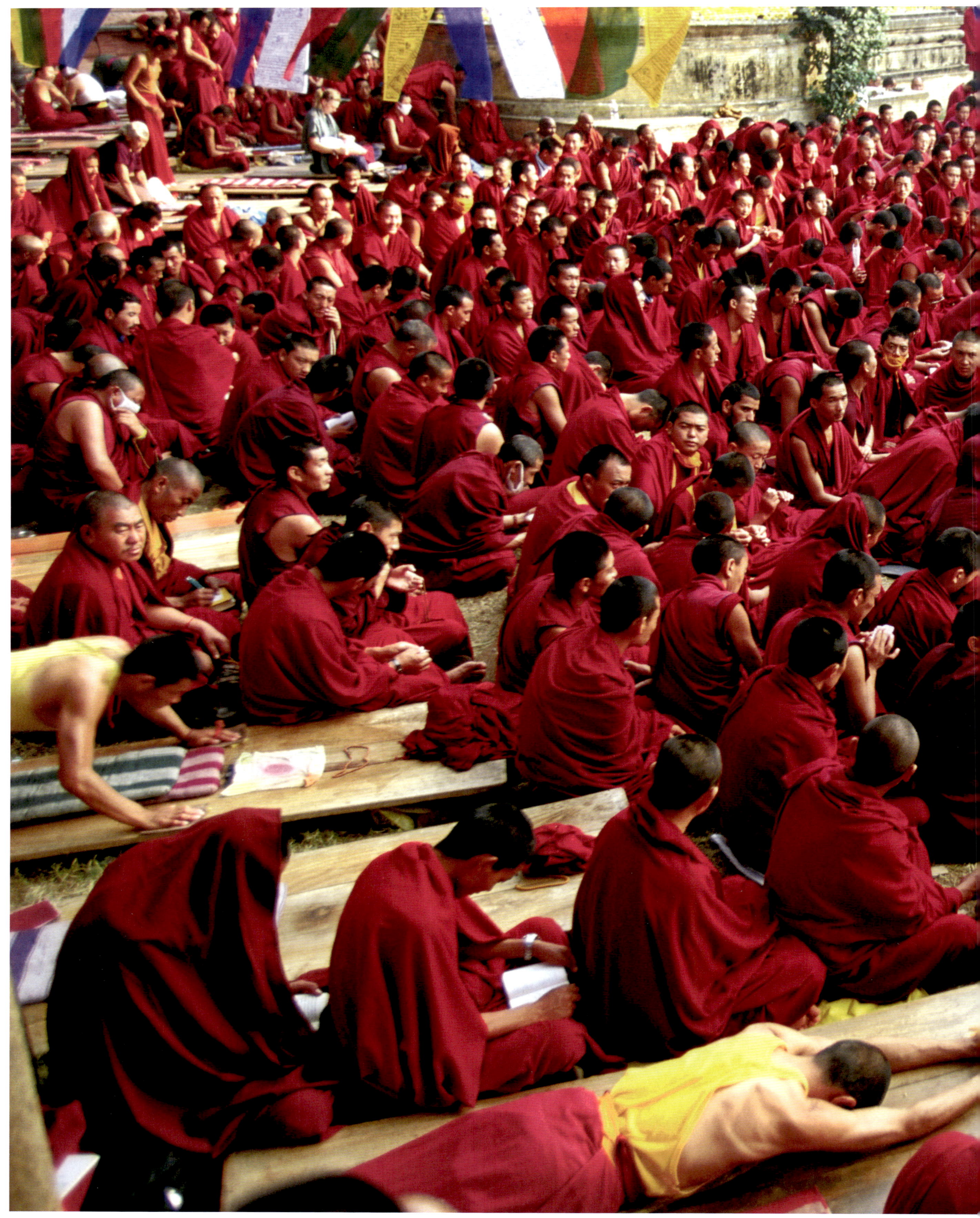

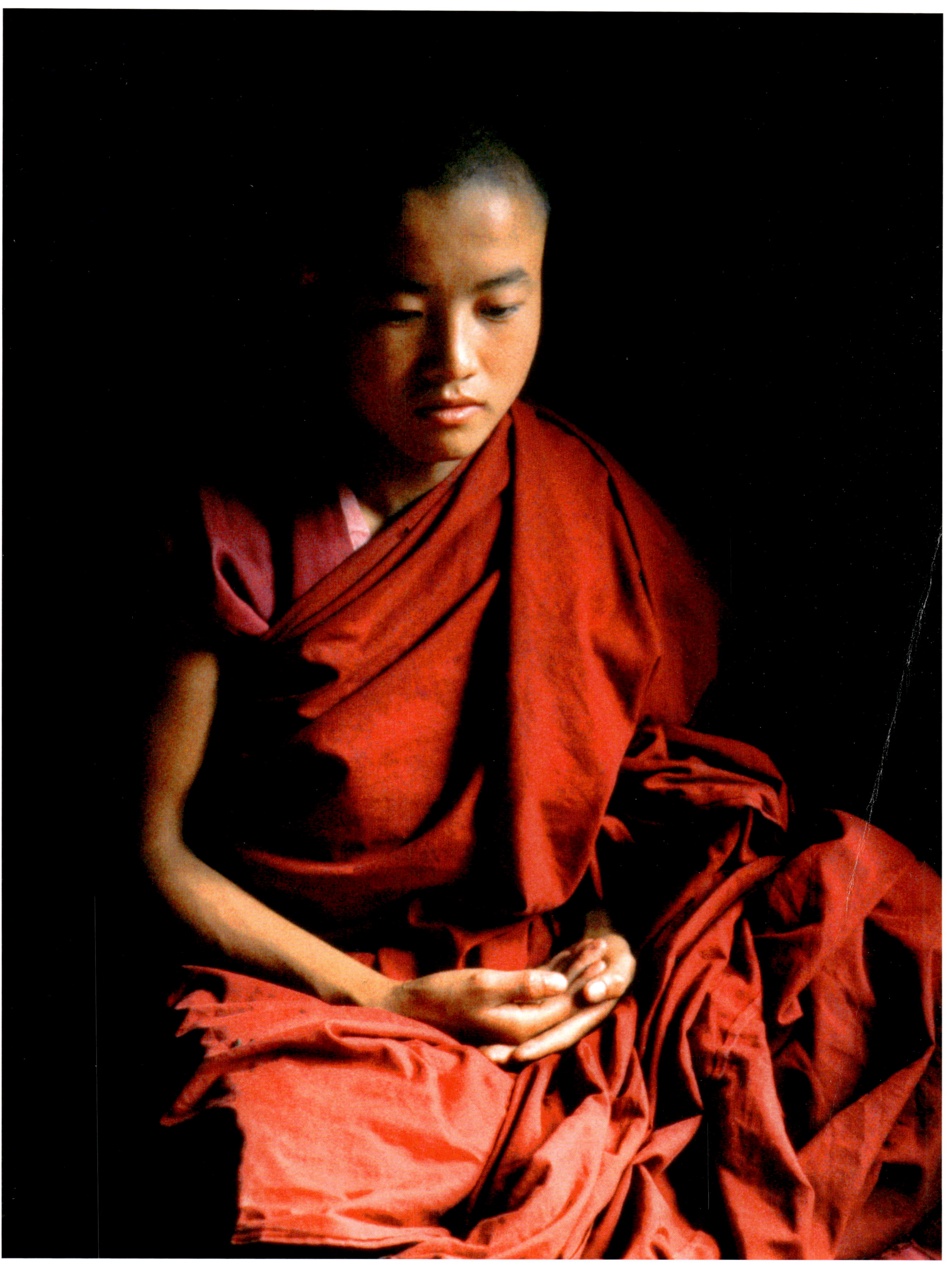

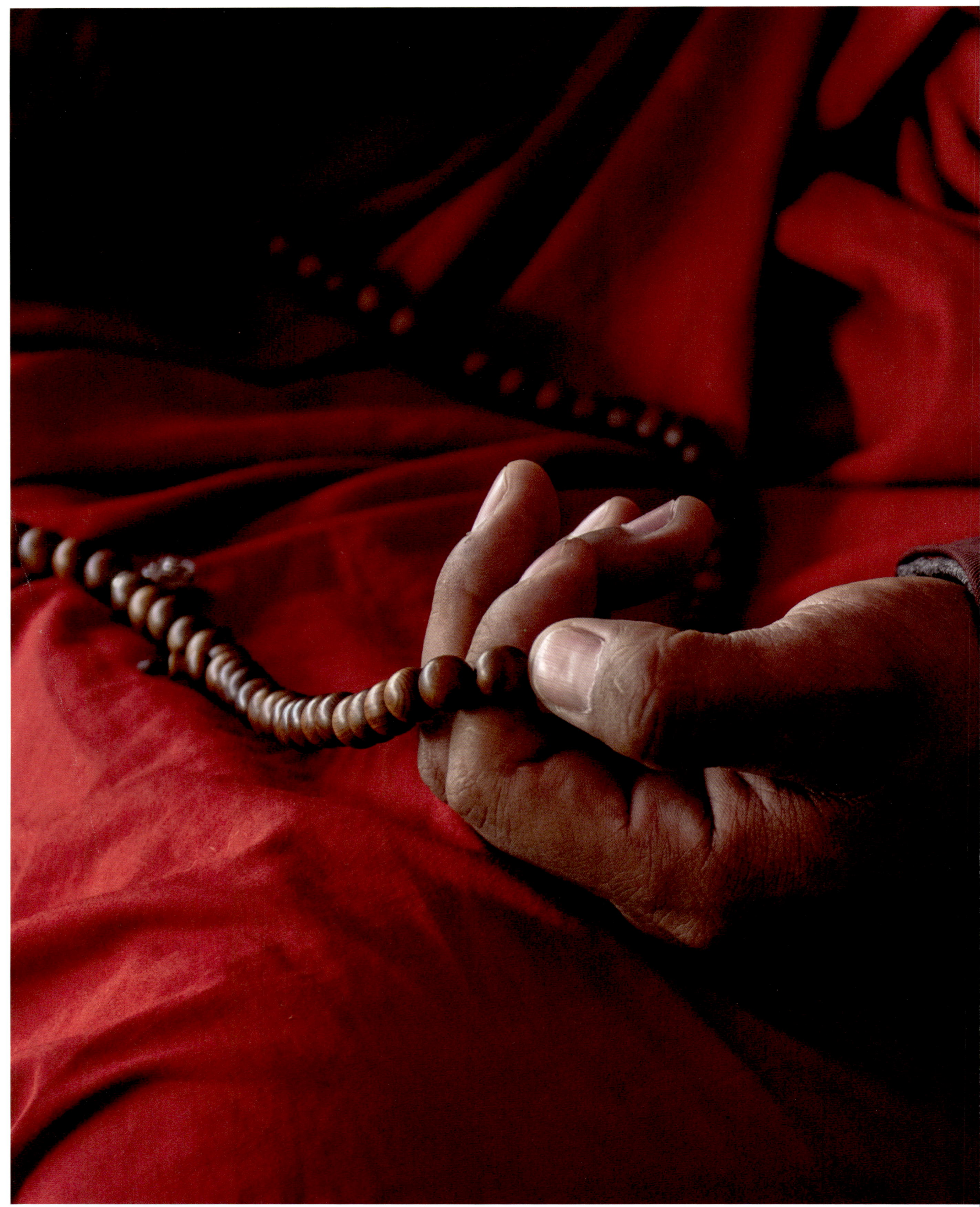

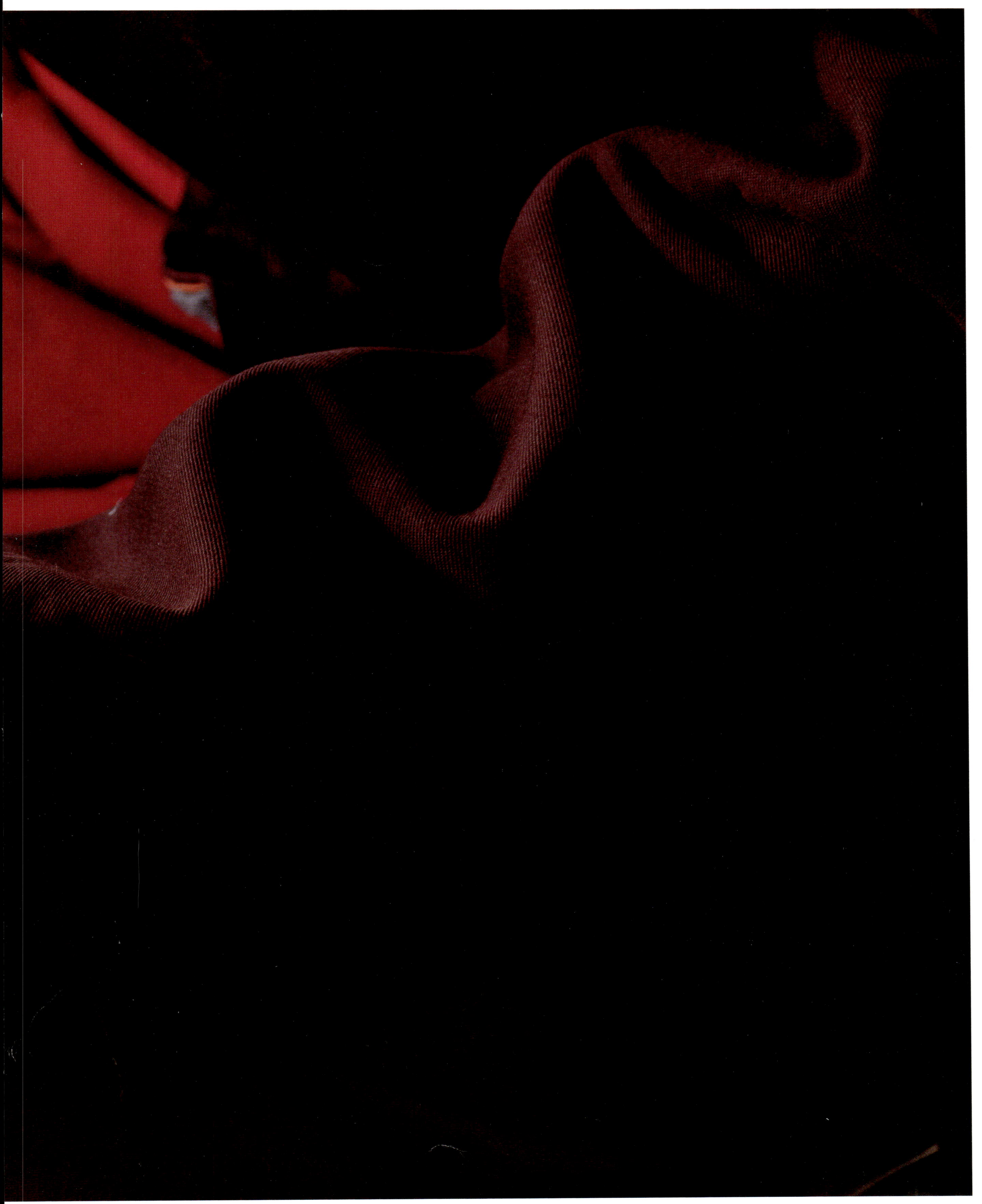

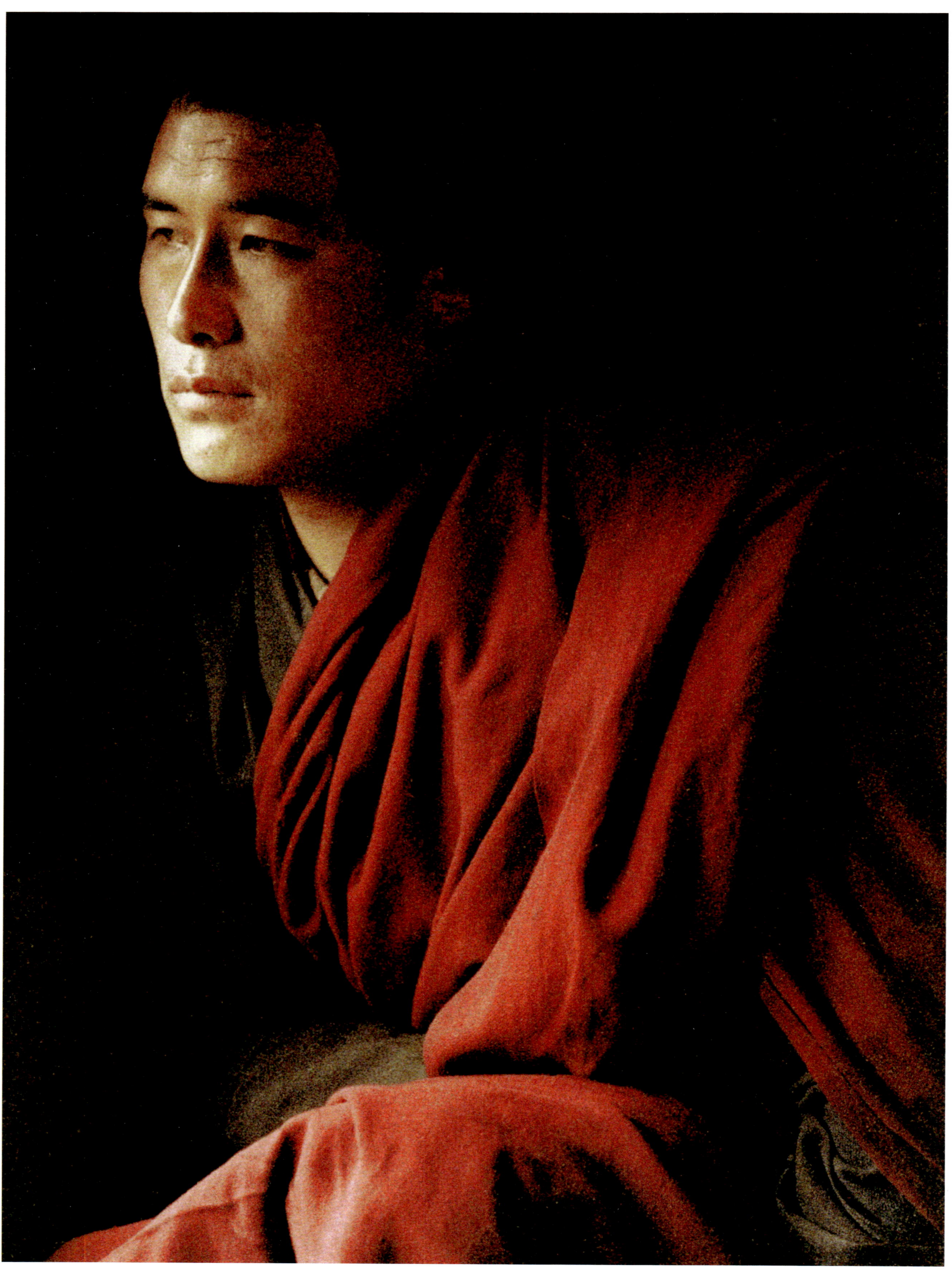

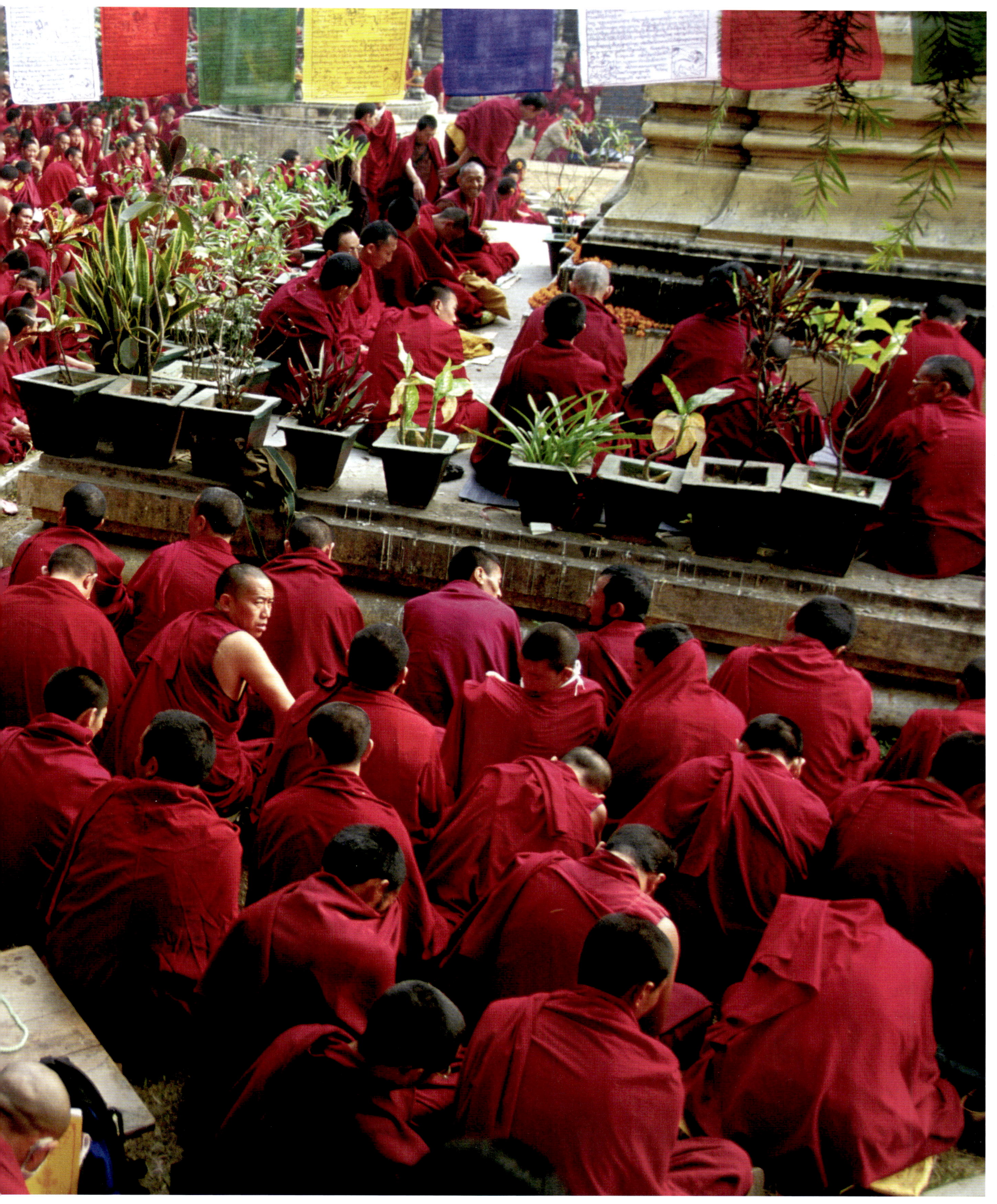

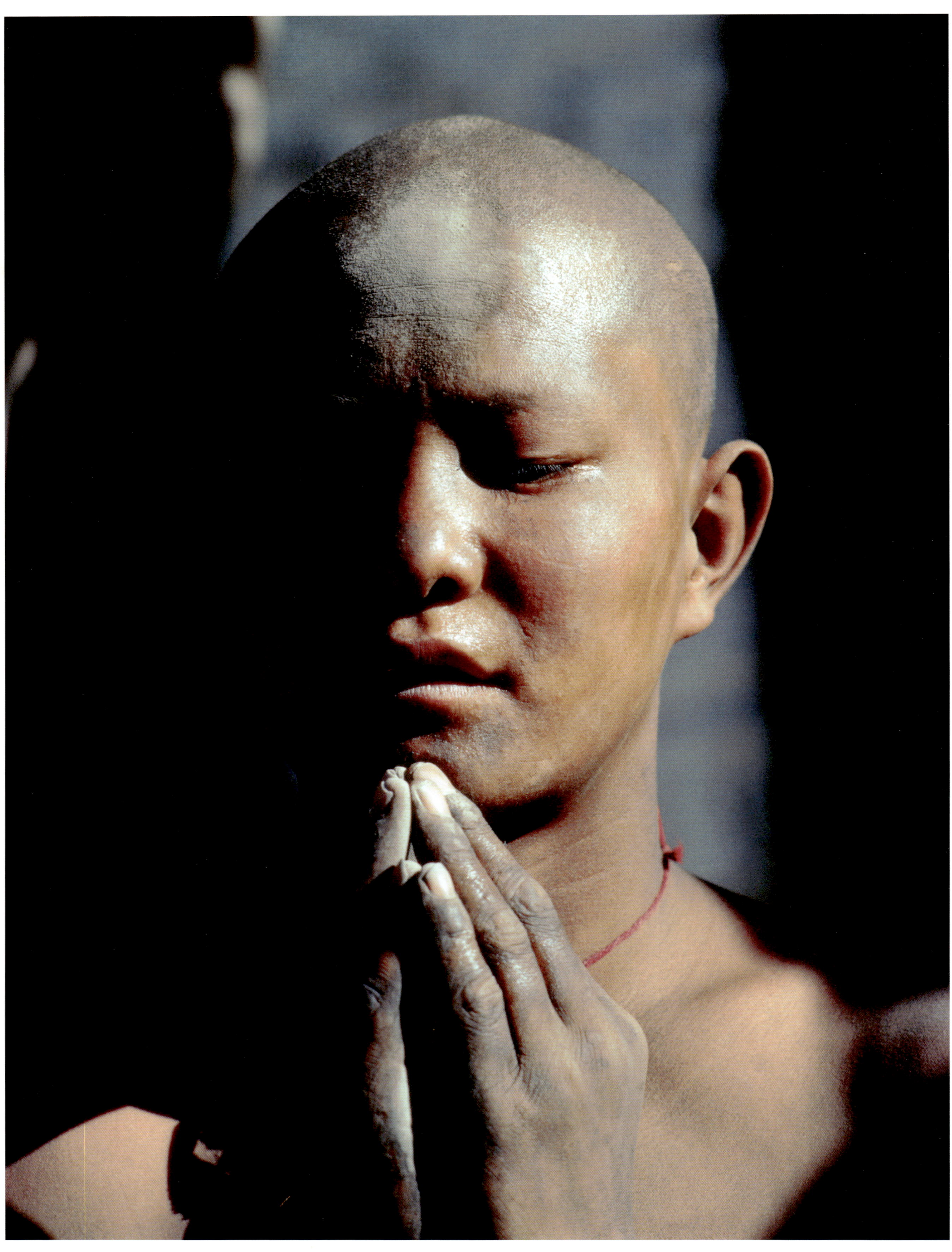

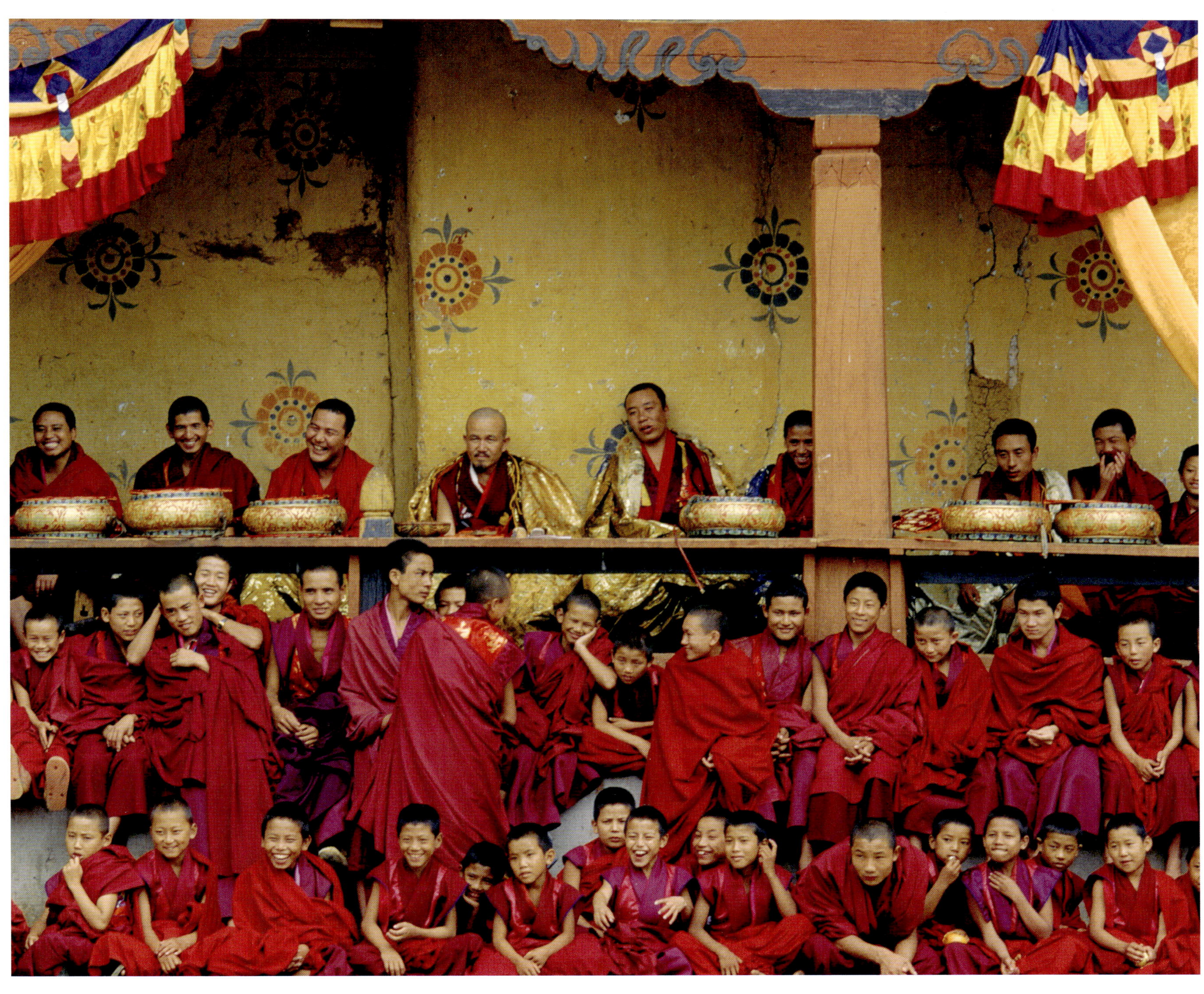

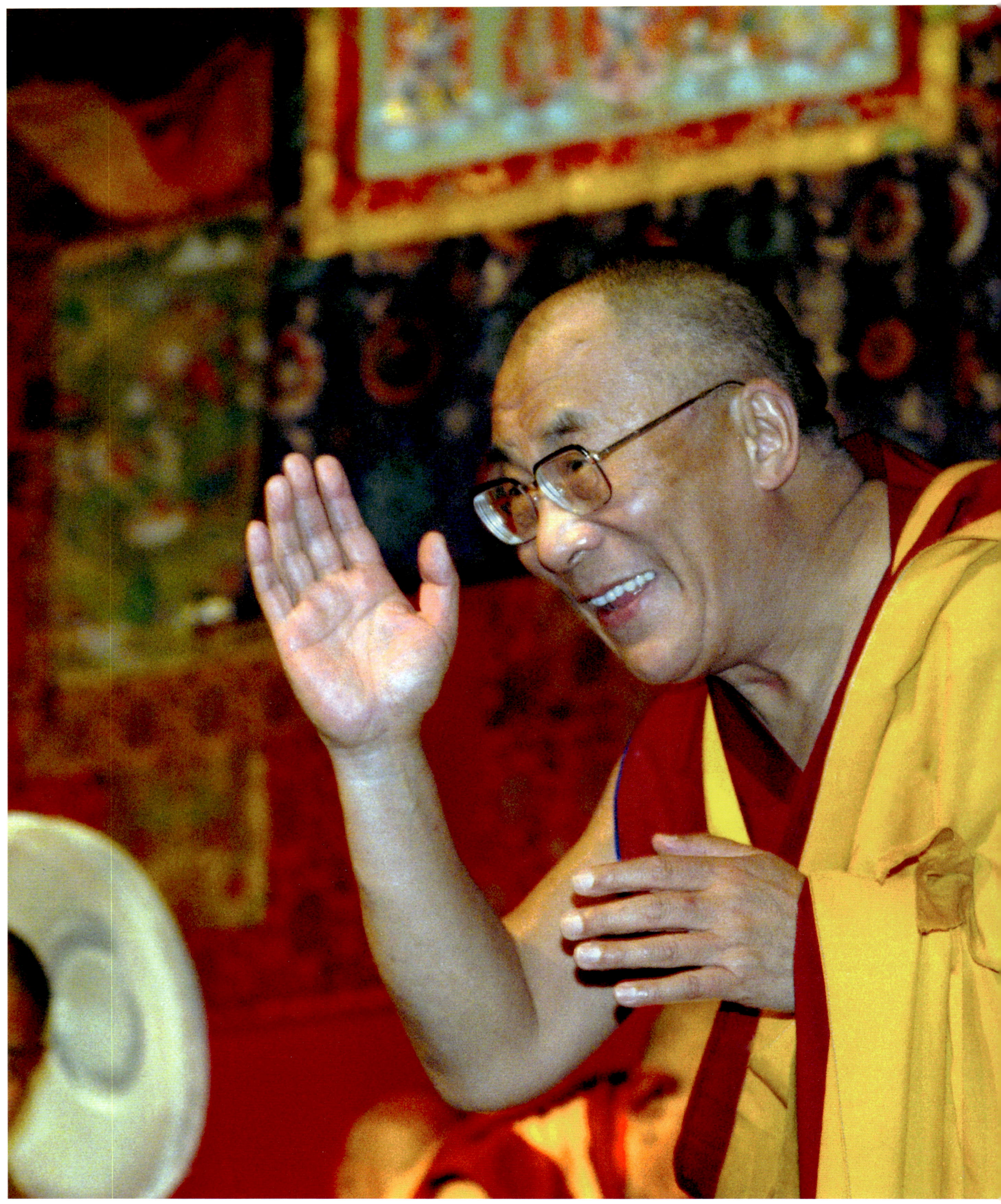

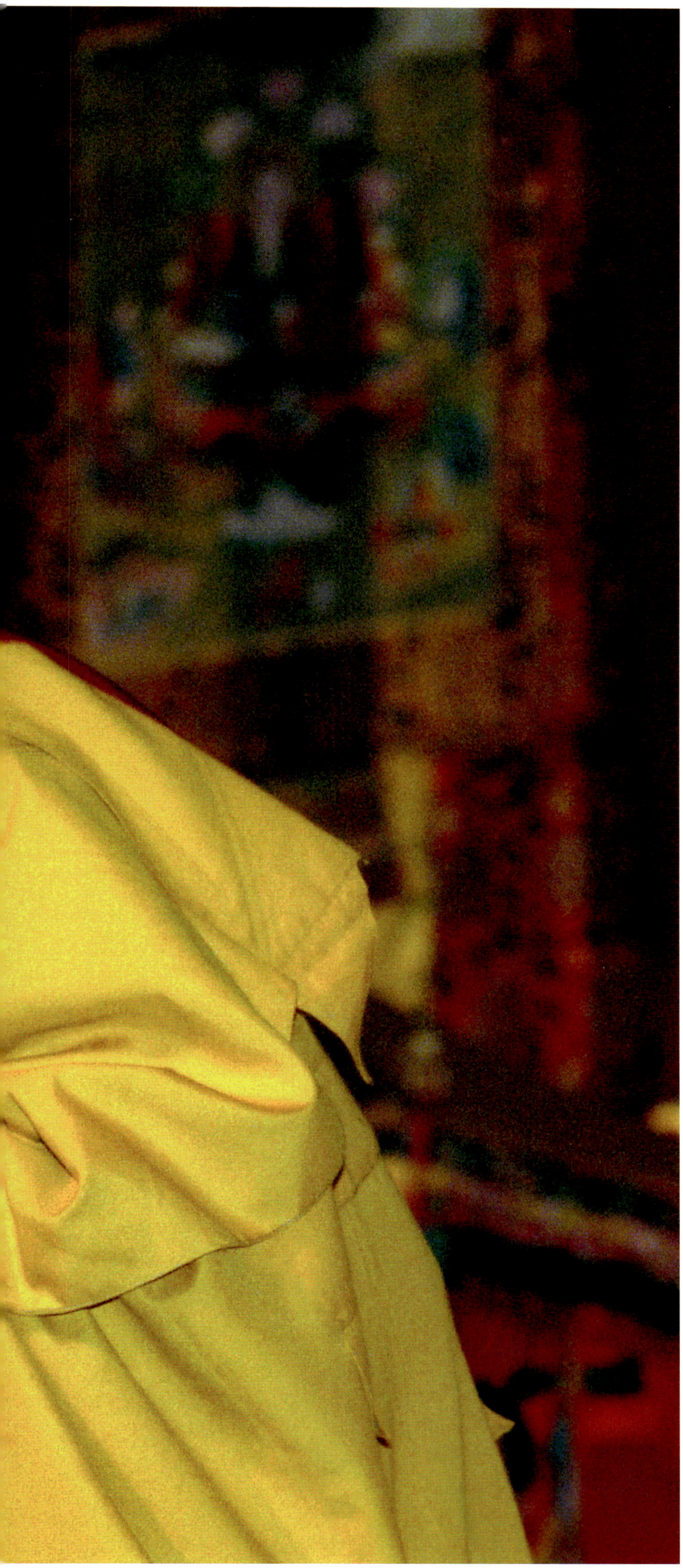

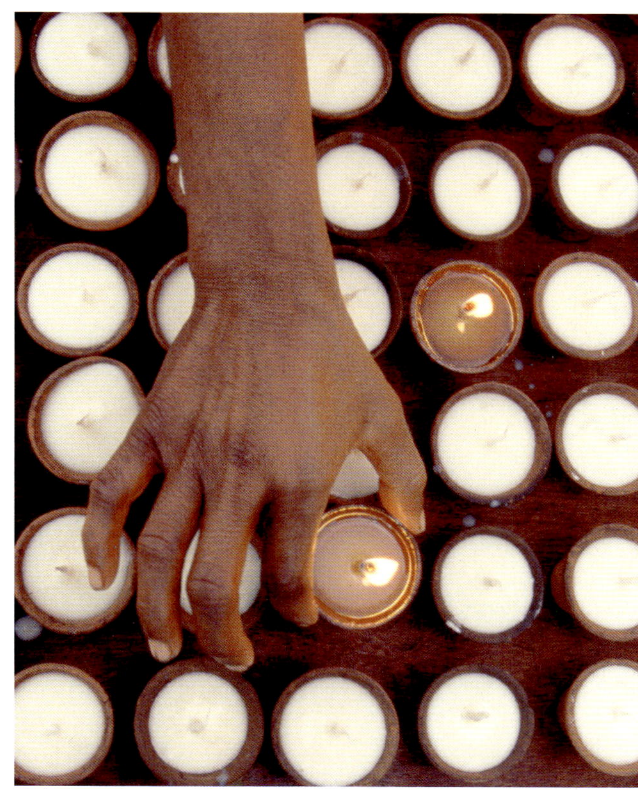

When he was awarded the Nobel Peace Prize, the Dalai
Lama humbly said, while joining the palms of his hands: "It is not the
monk you should reward, it is his motivation."

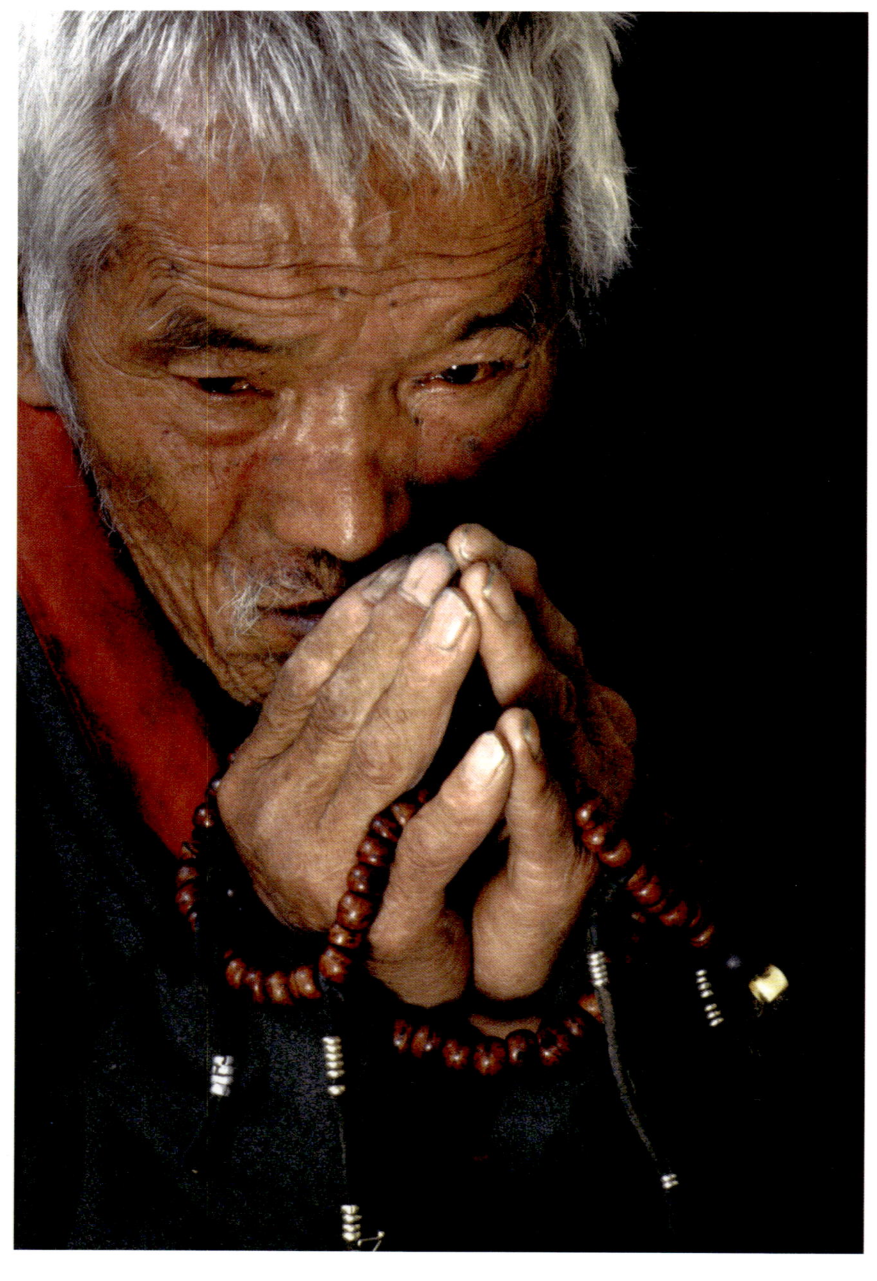

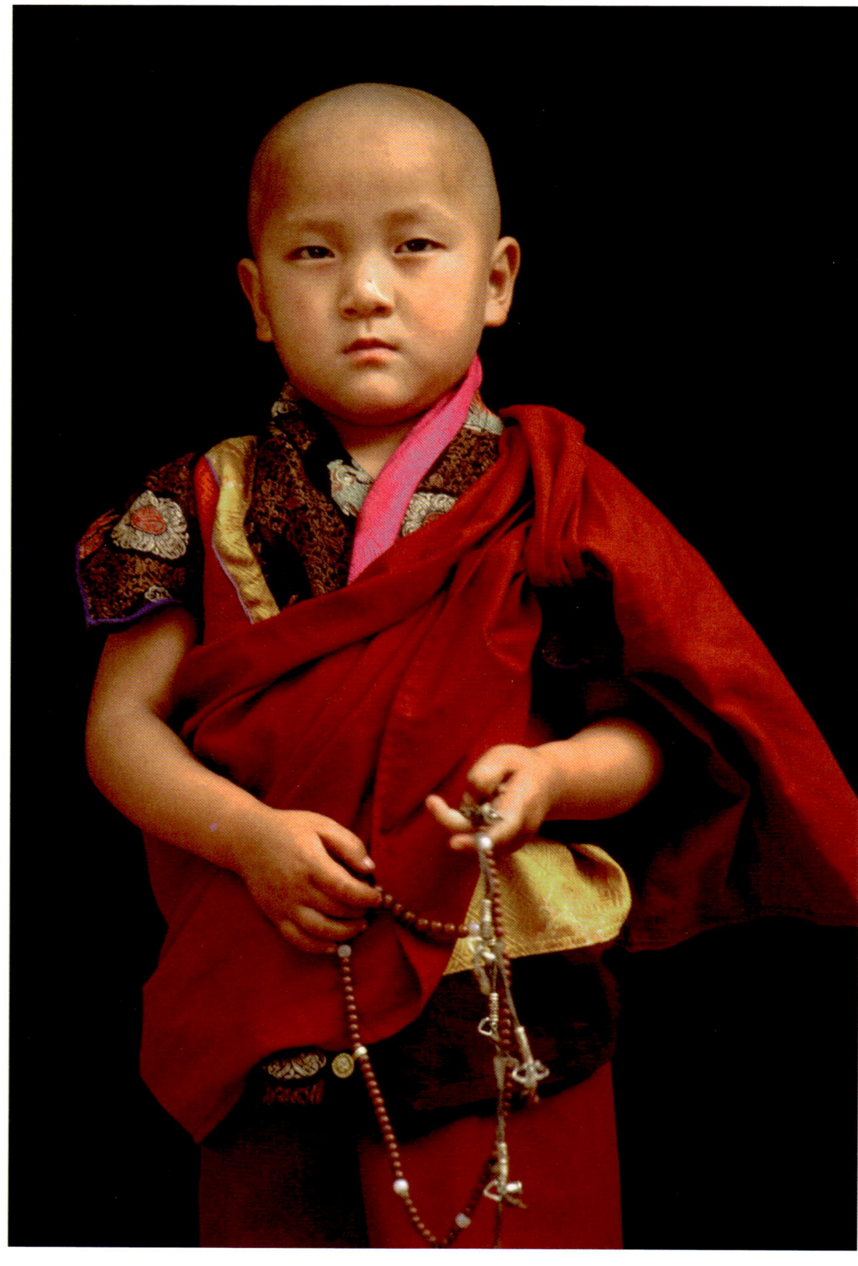

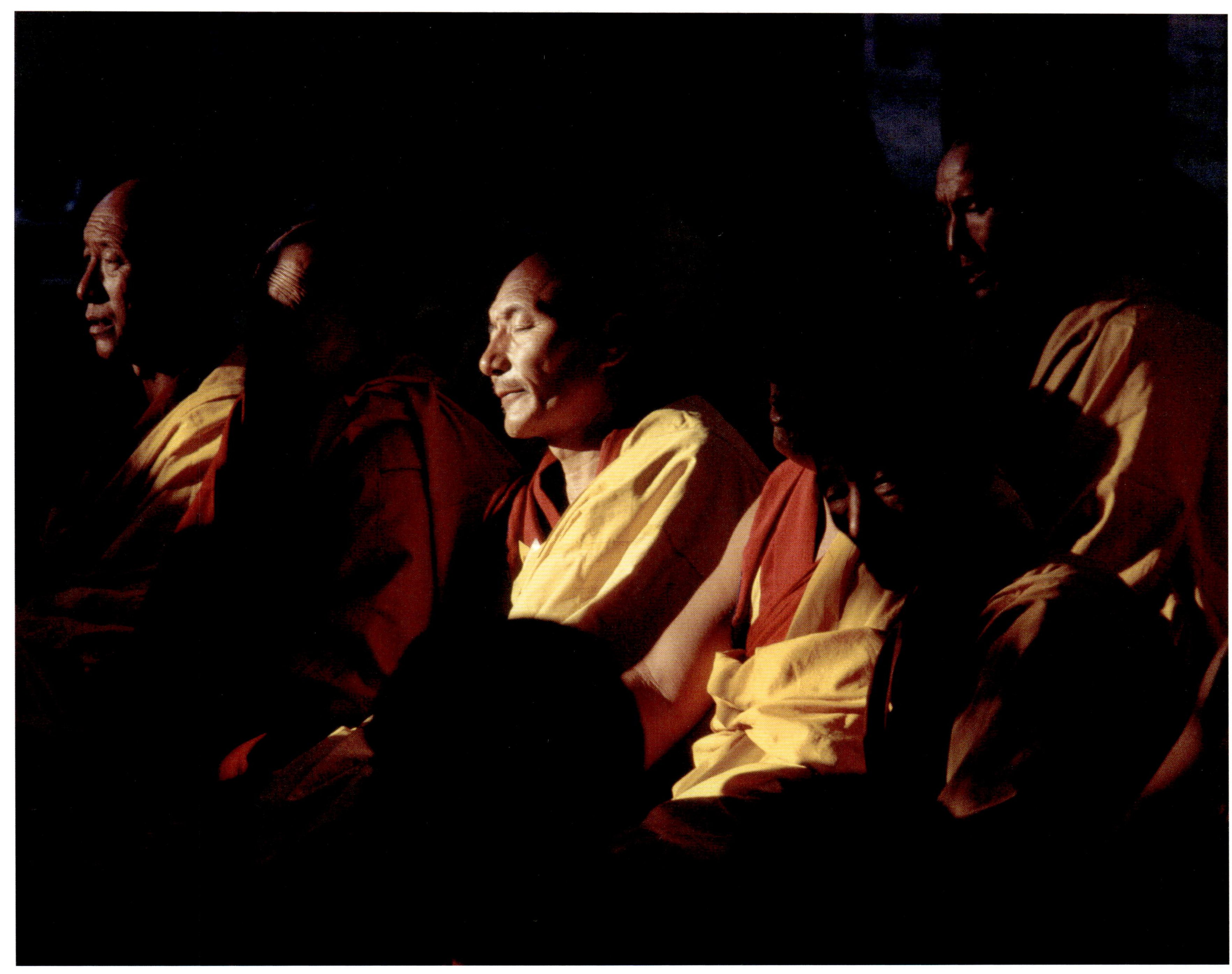

Als dem Dalai Lama der Friedensnobelpreis verliehen wurde, erklärte er mit gefalteten Händen: „Nicht den Mönch gilt es auszuzeichnen, sondern seine Motivation."

Lorsque le prix Nobel de la paix lui fut décerné, le dalaï-lama s'exprima humblement, les mains jointes : « Ce n'est pas le moine qu'il faut récompenser, c'est sa motivation. »

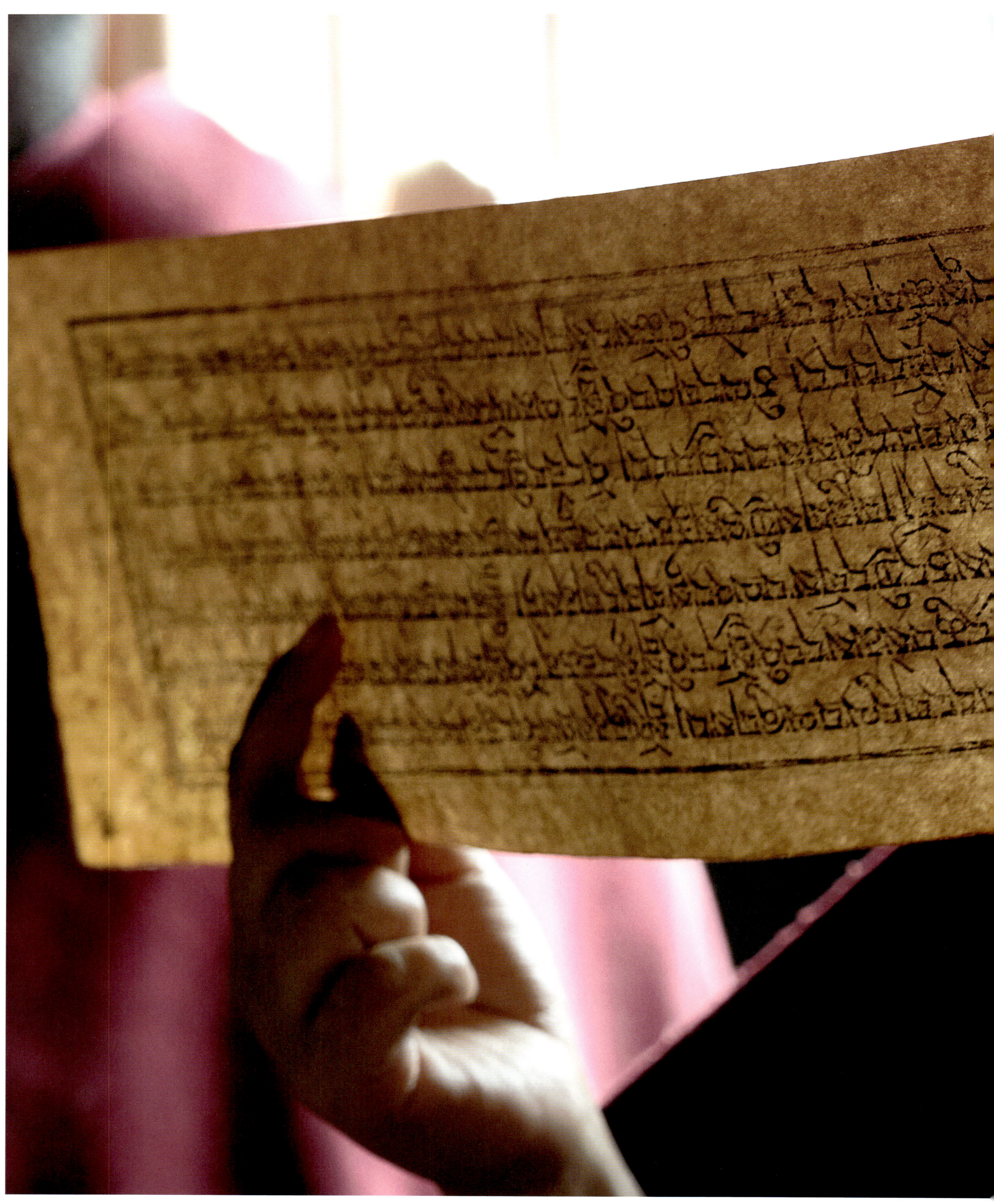

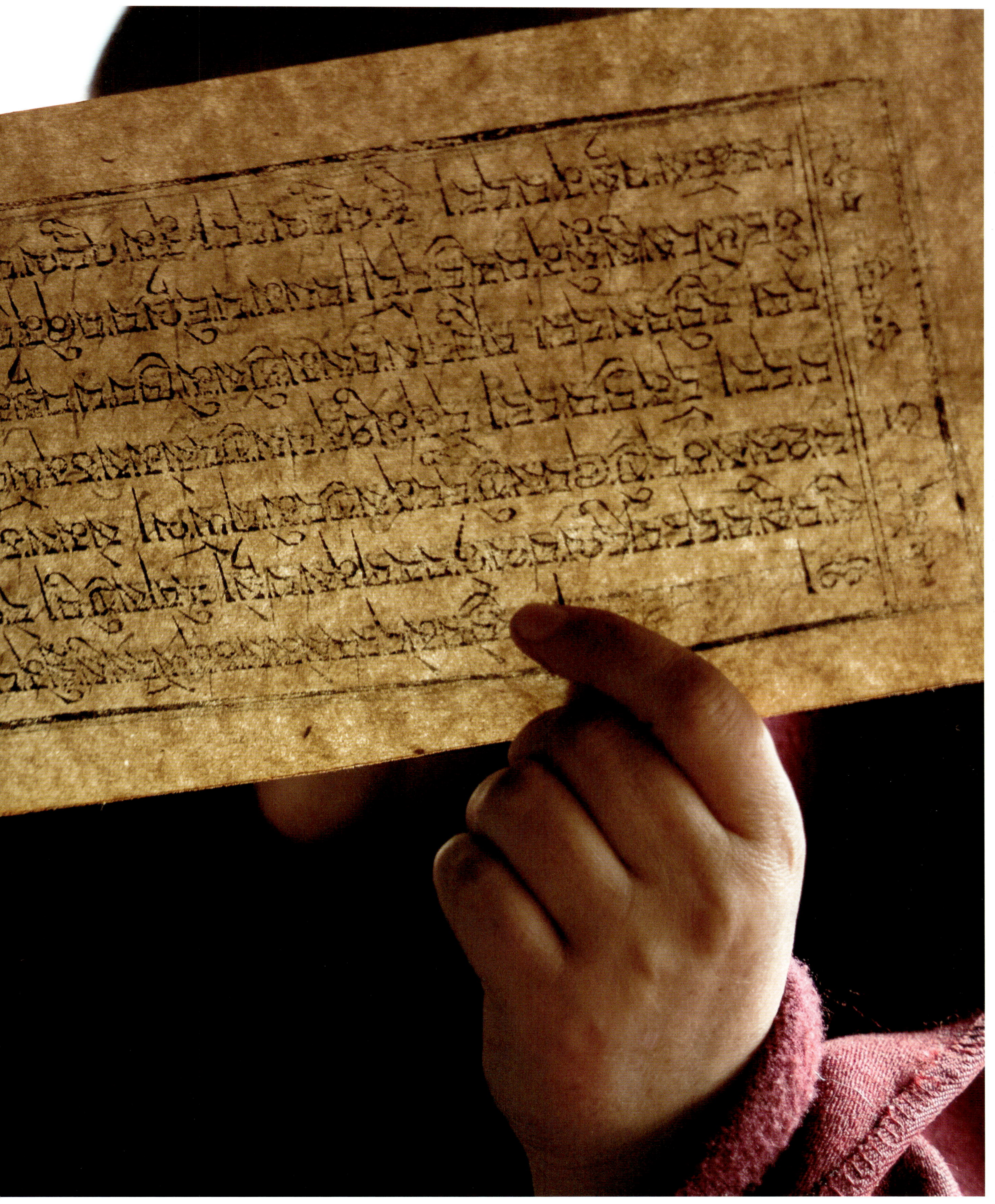

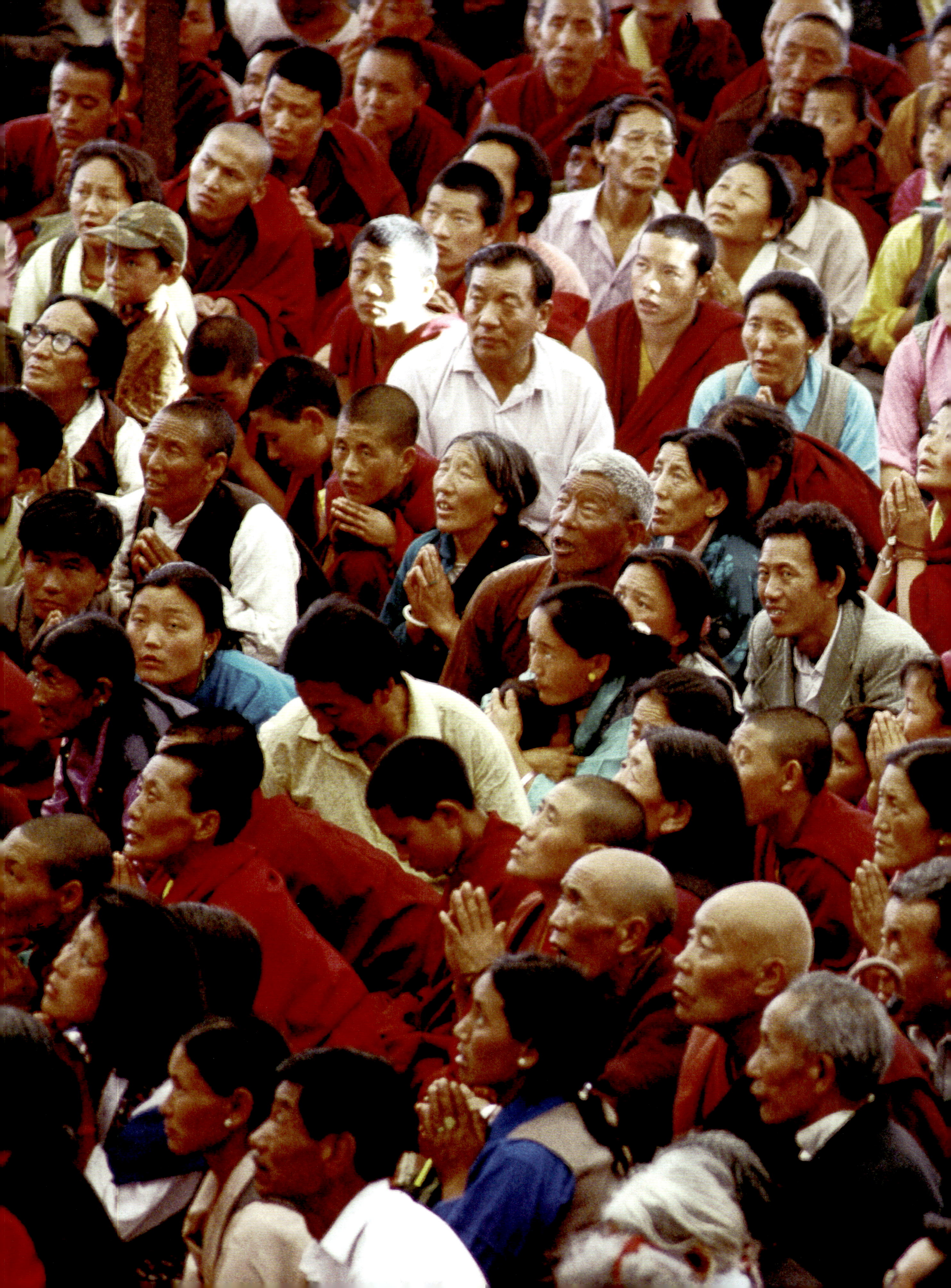

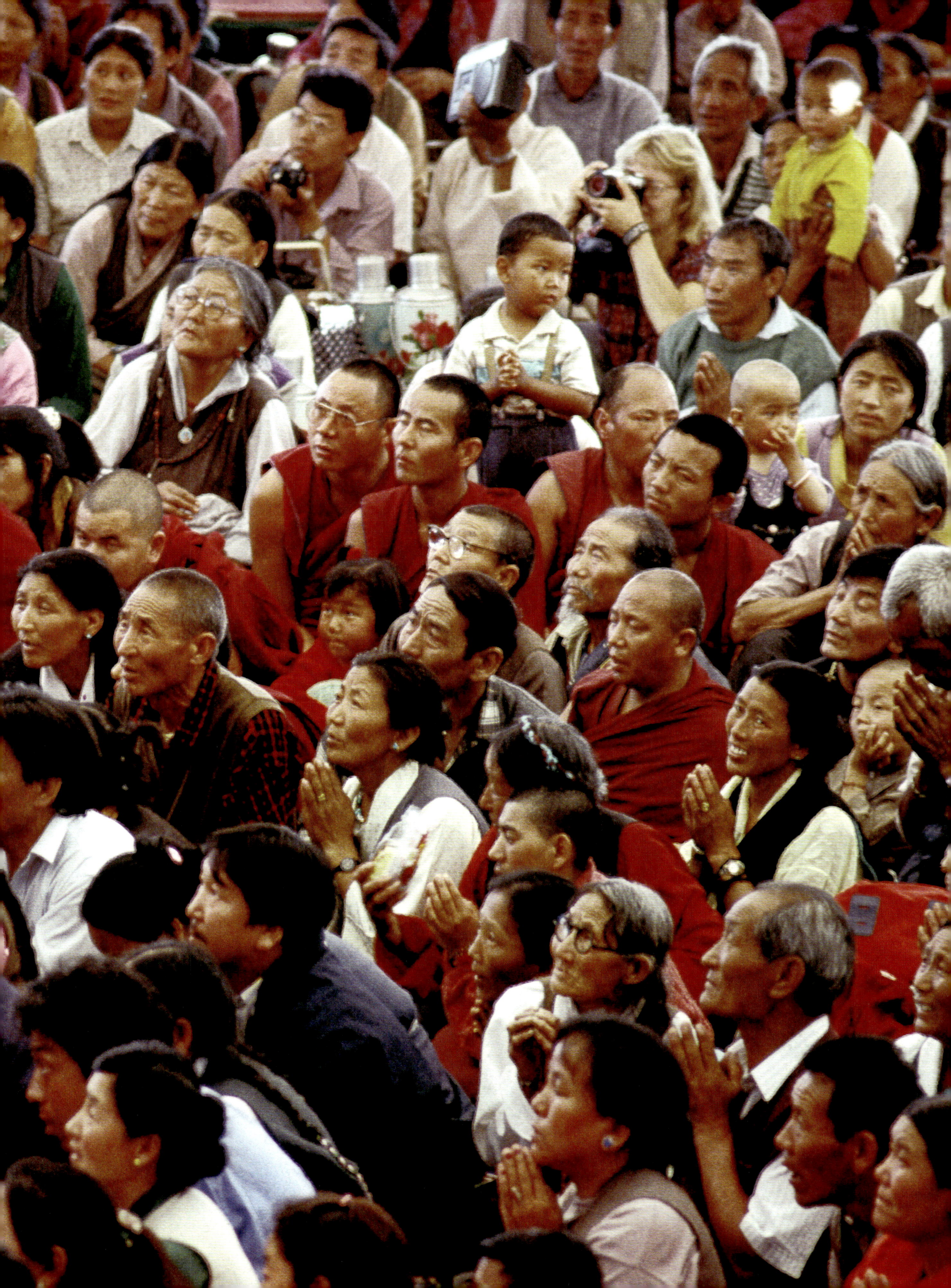

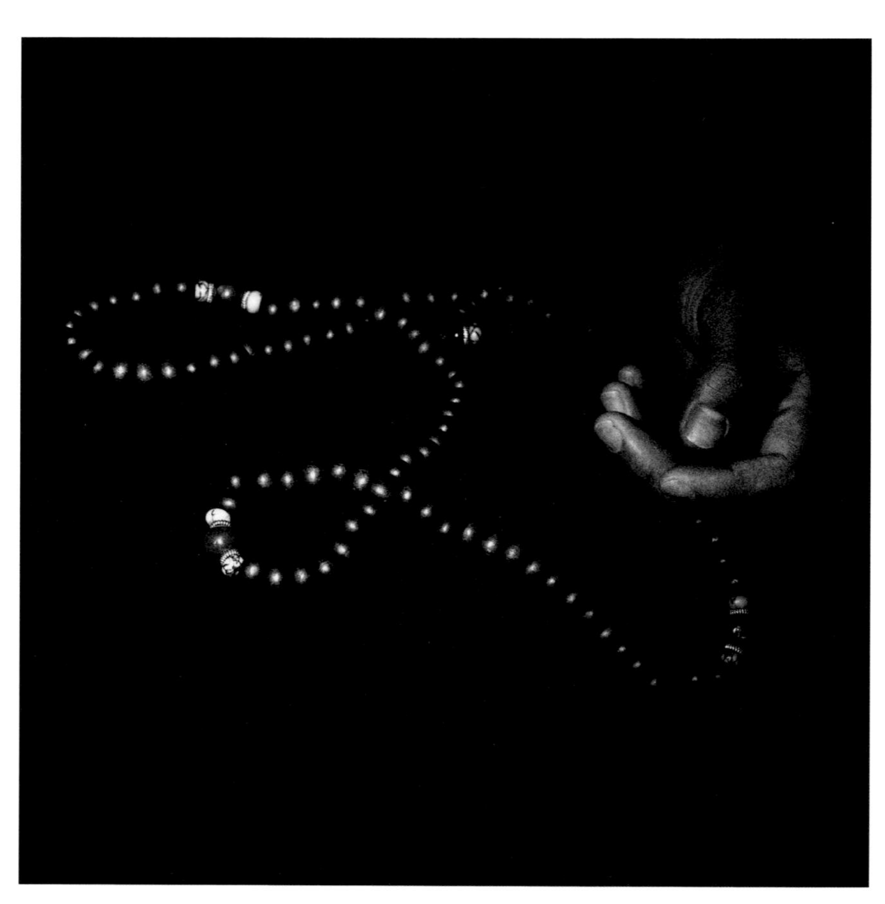

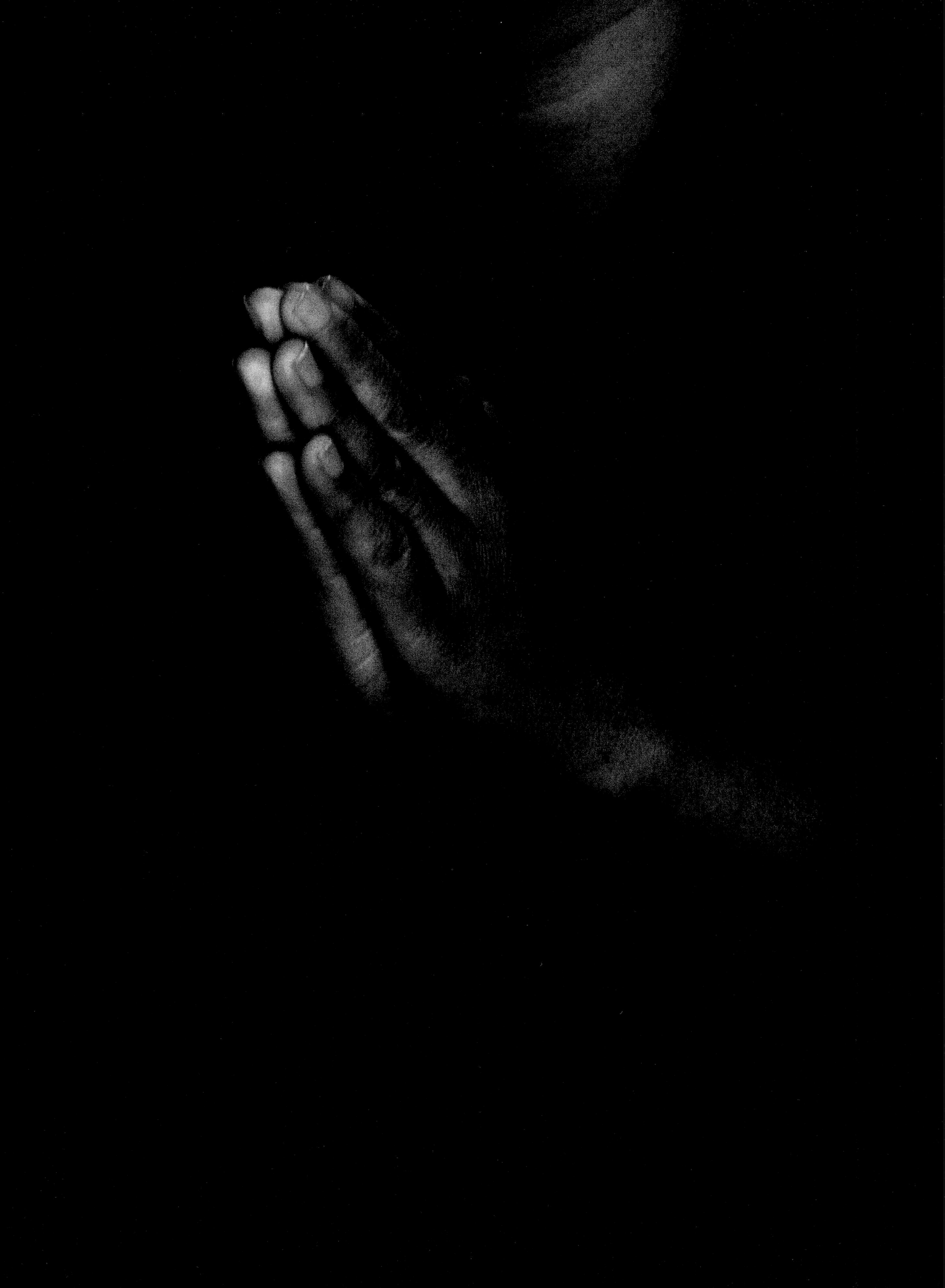

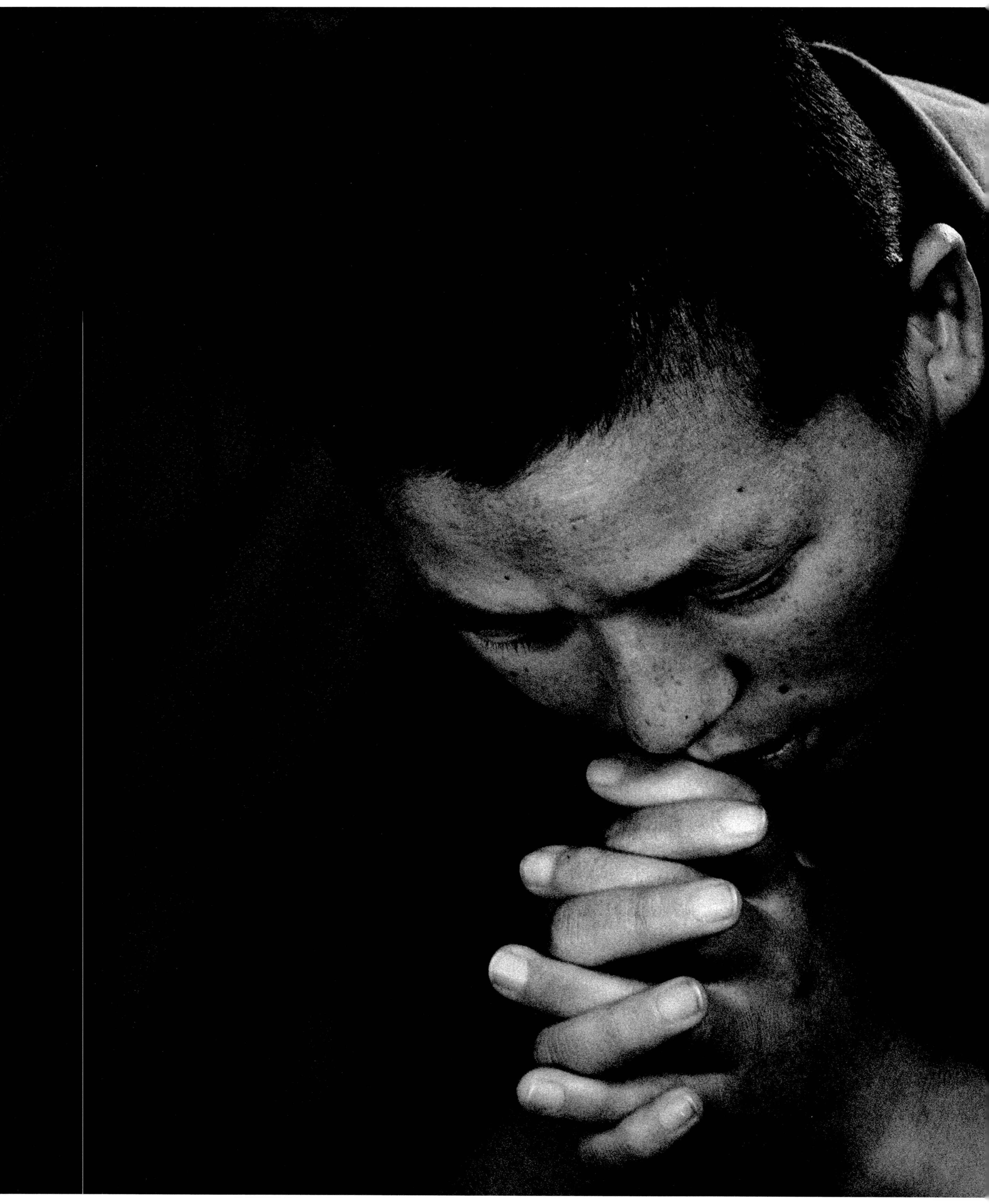

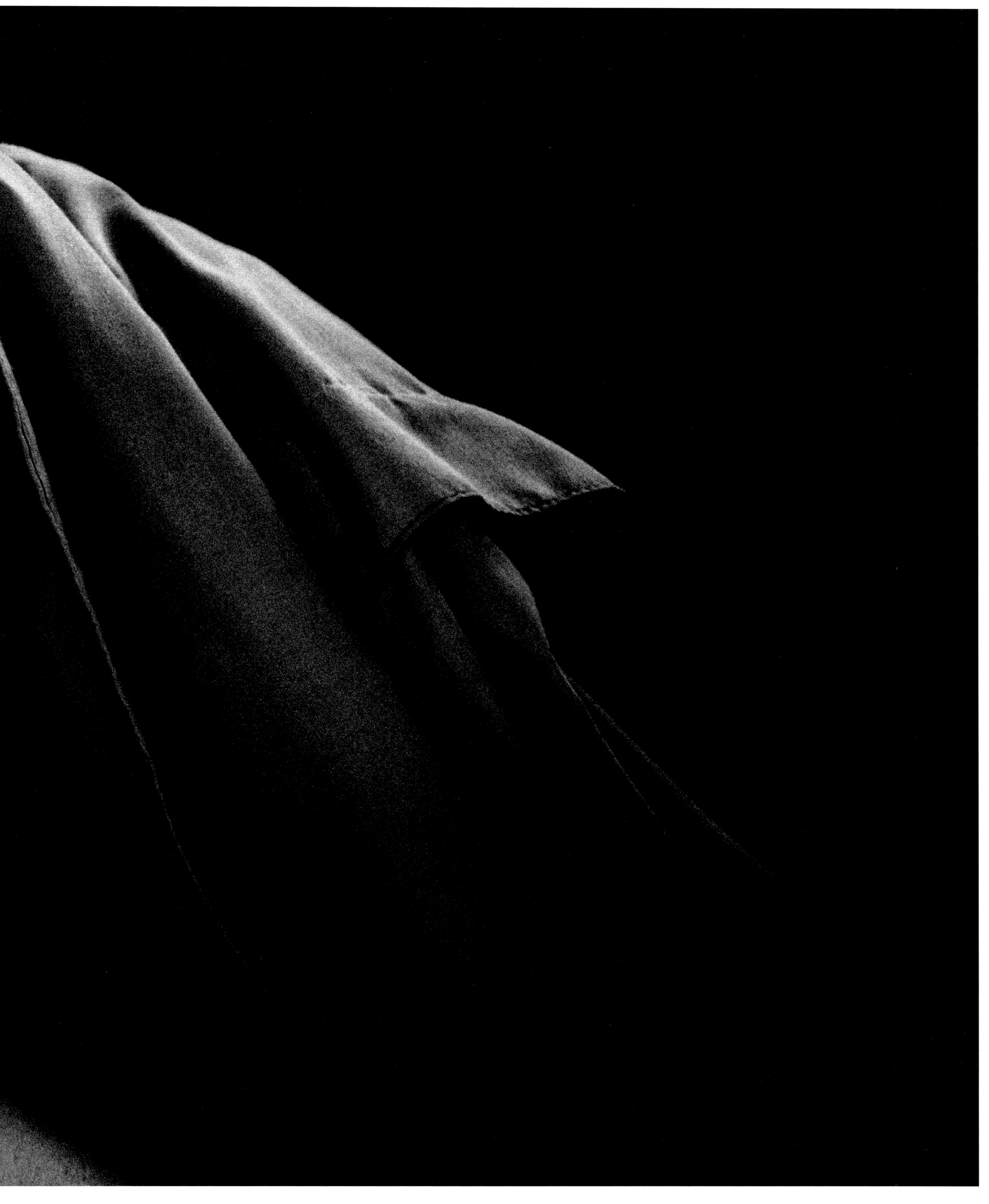

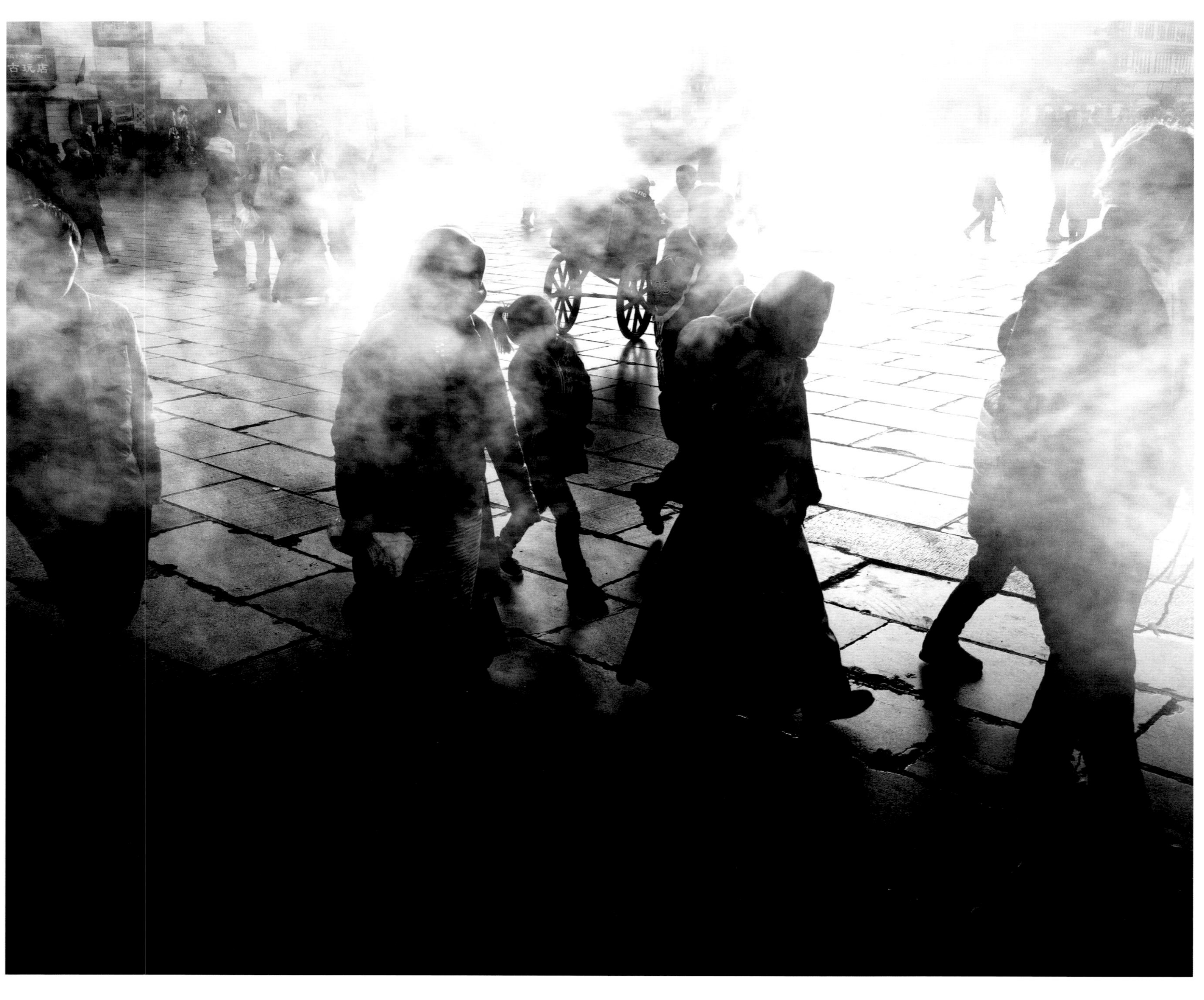

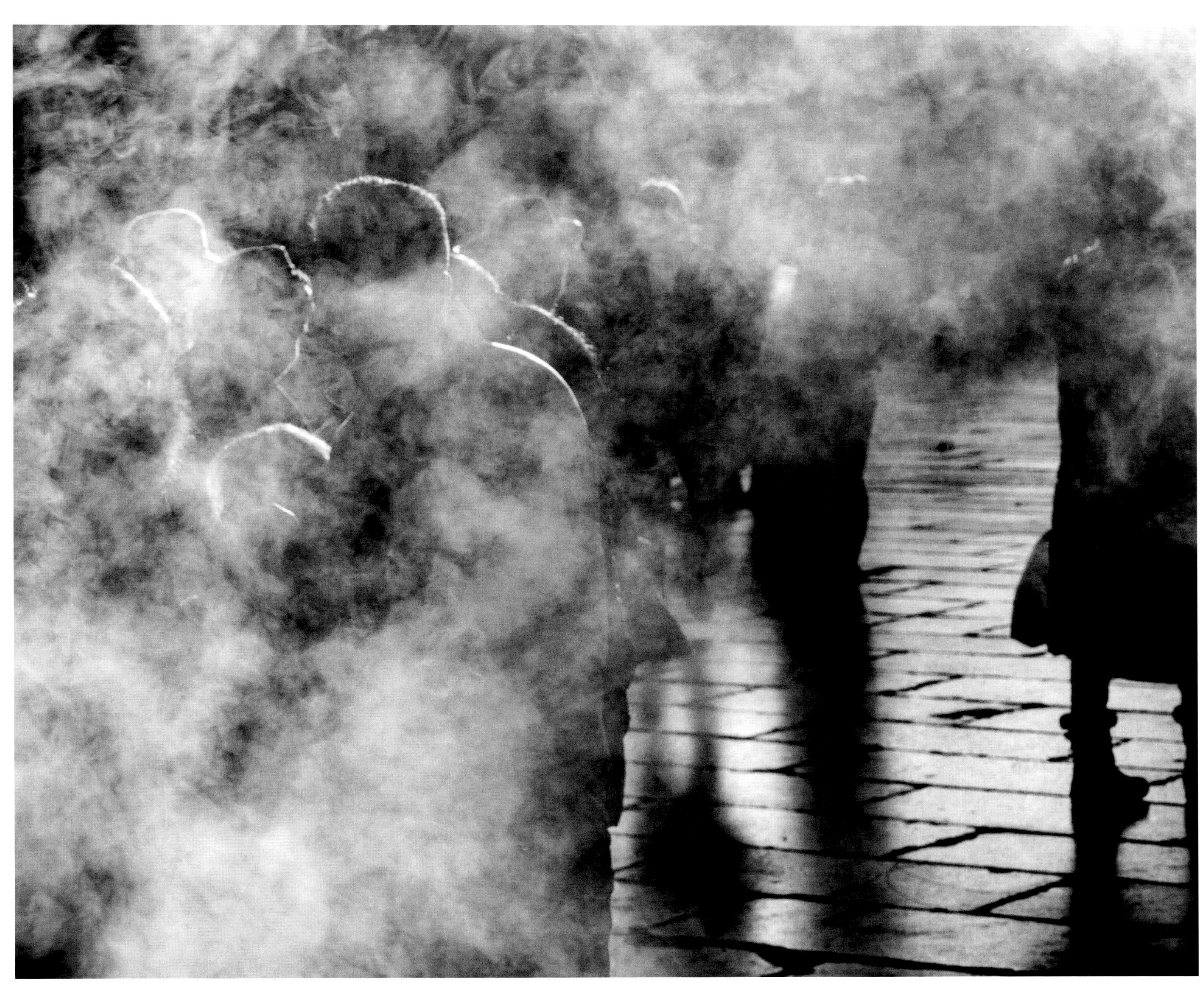

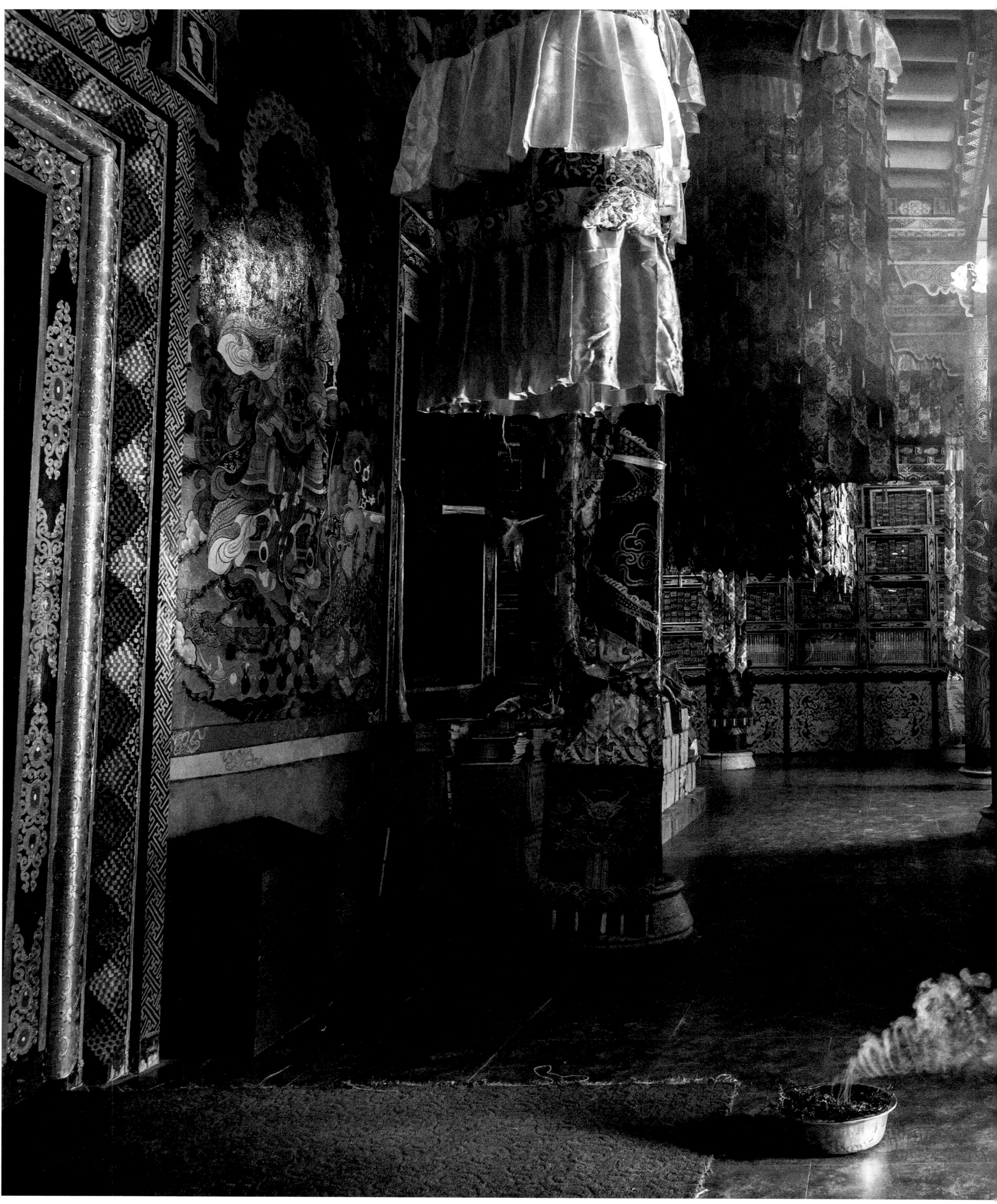

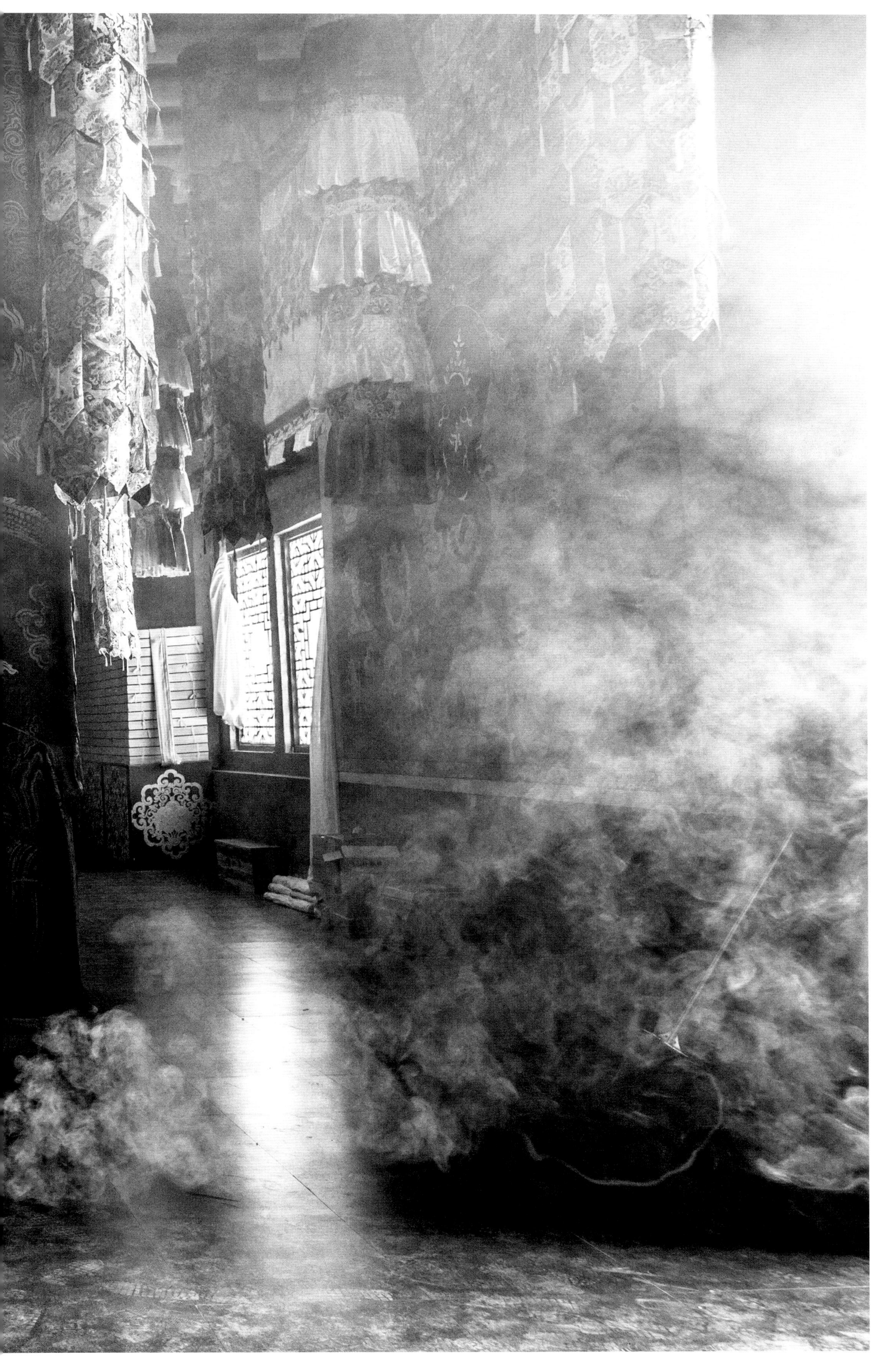

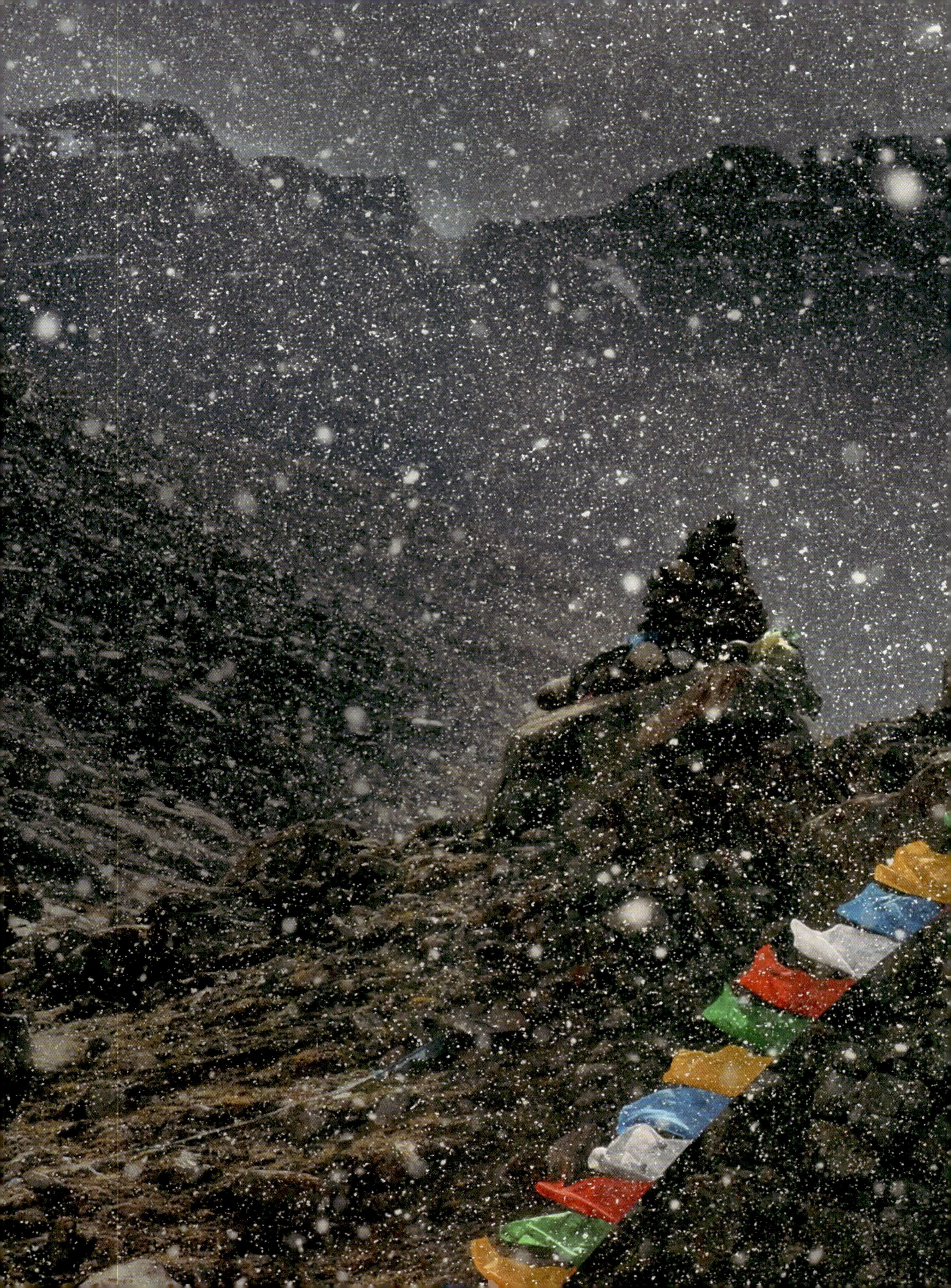

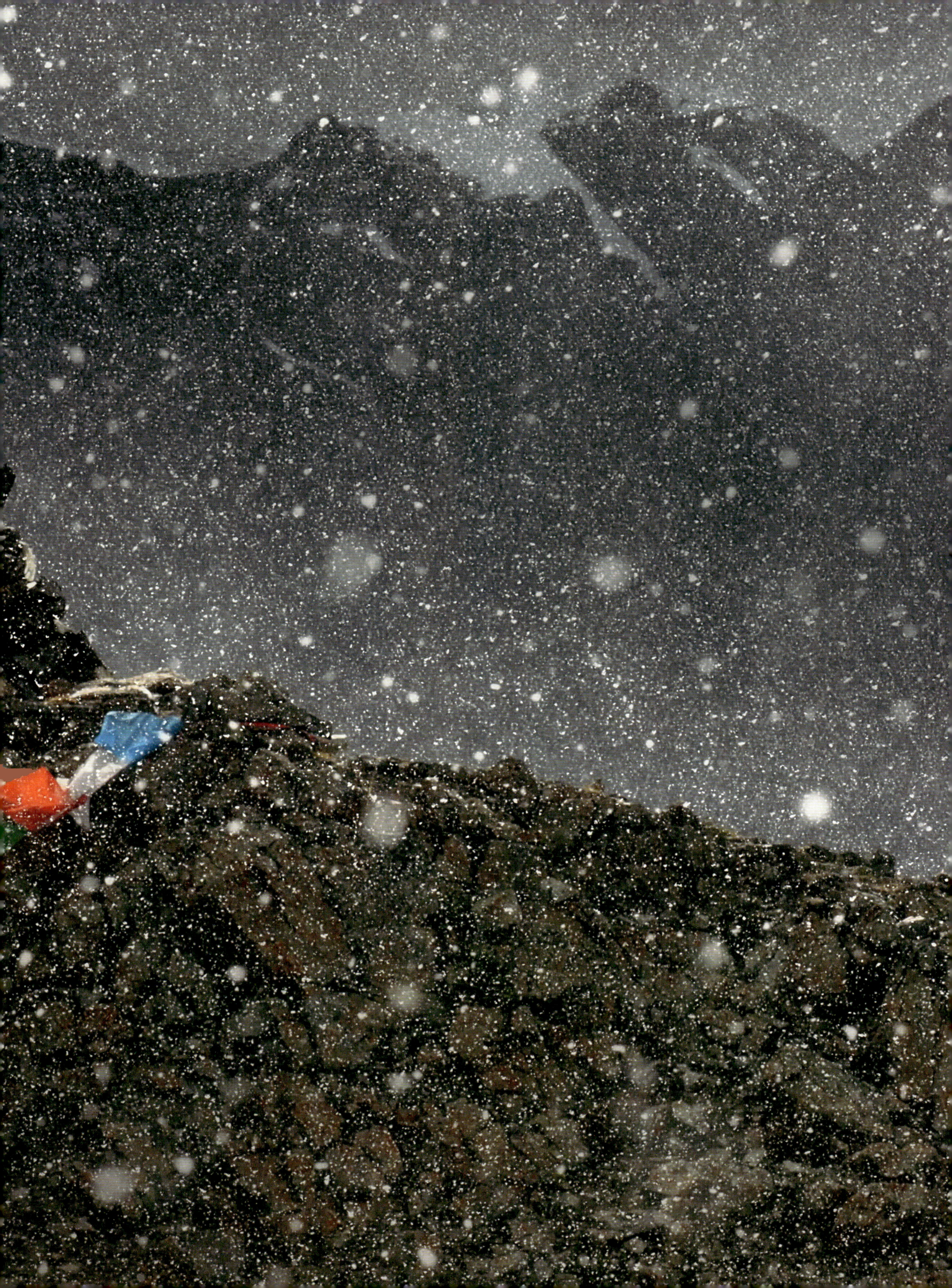

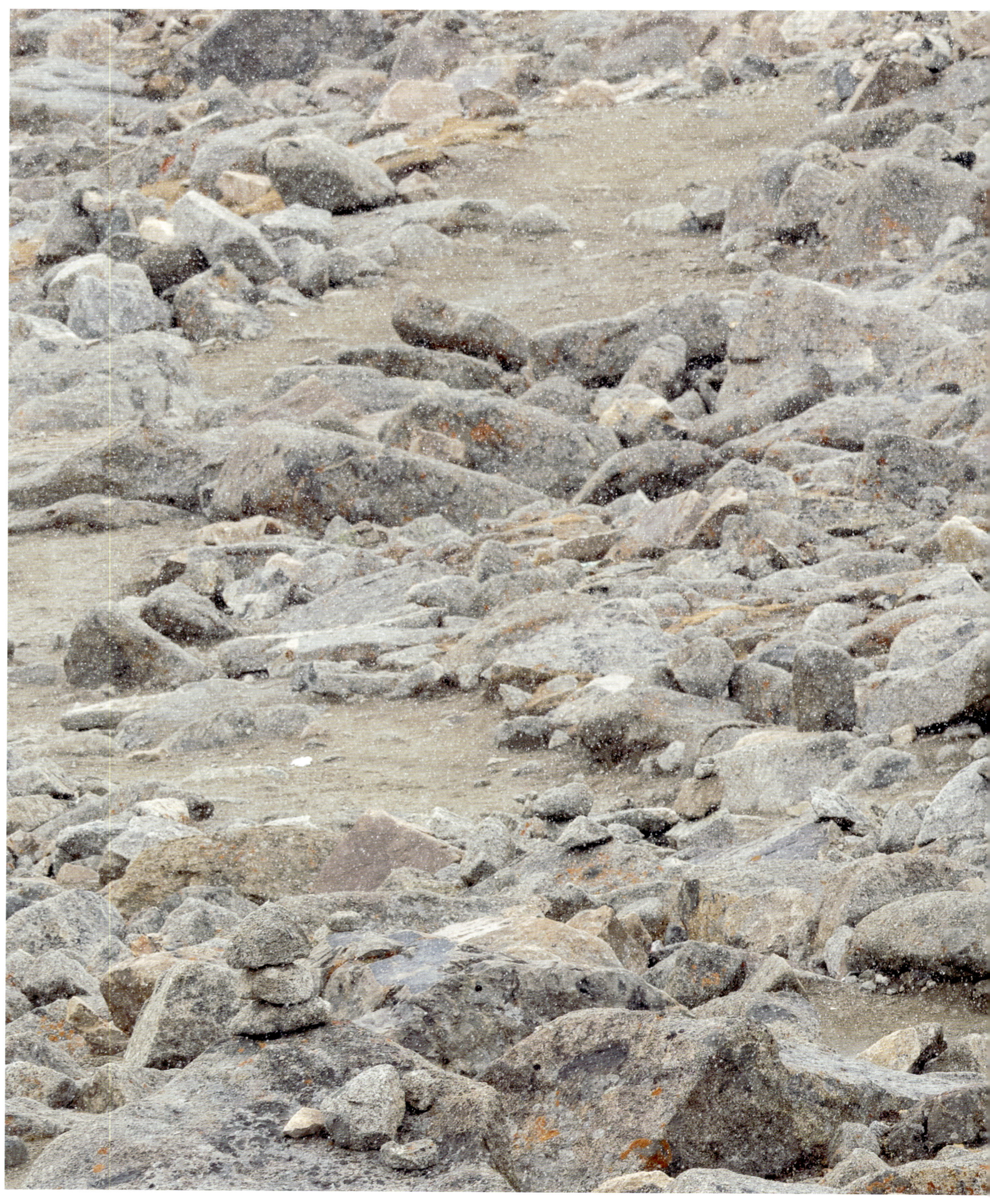

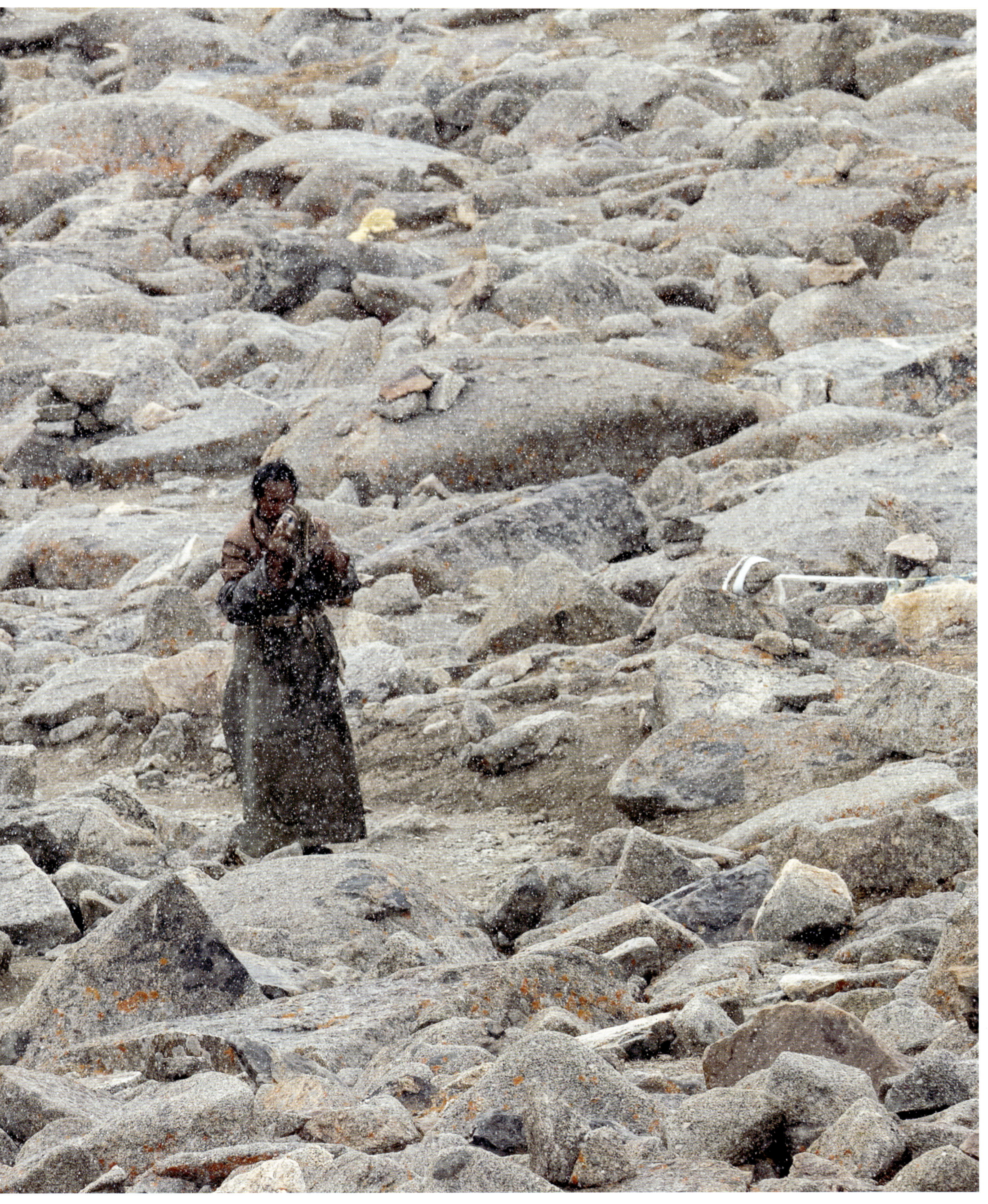

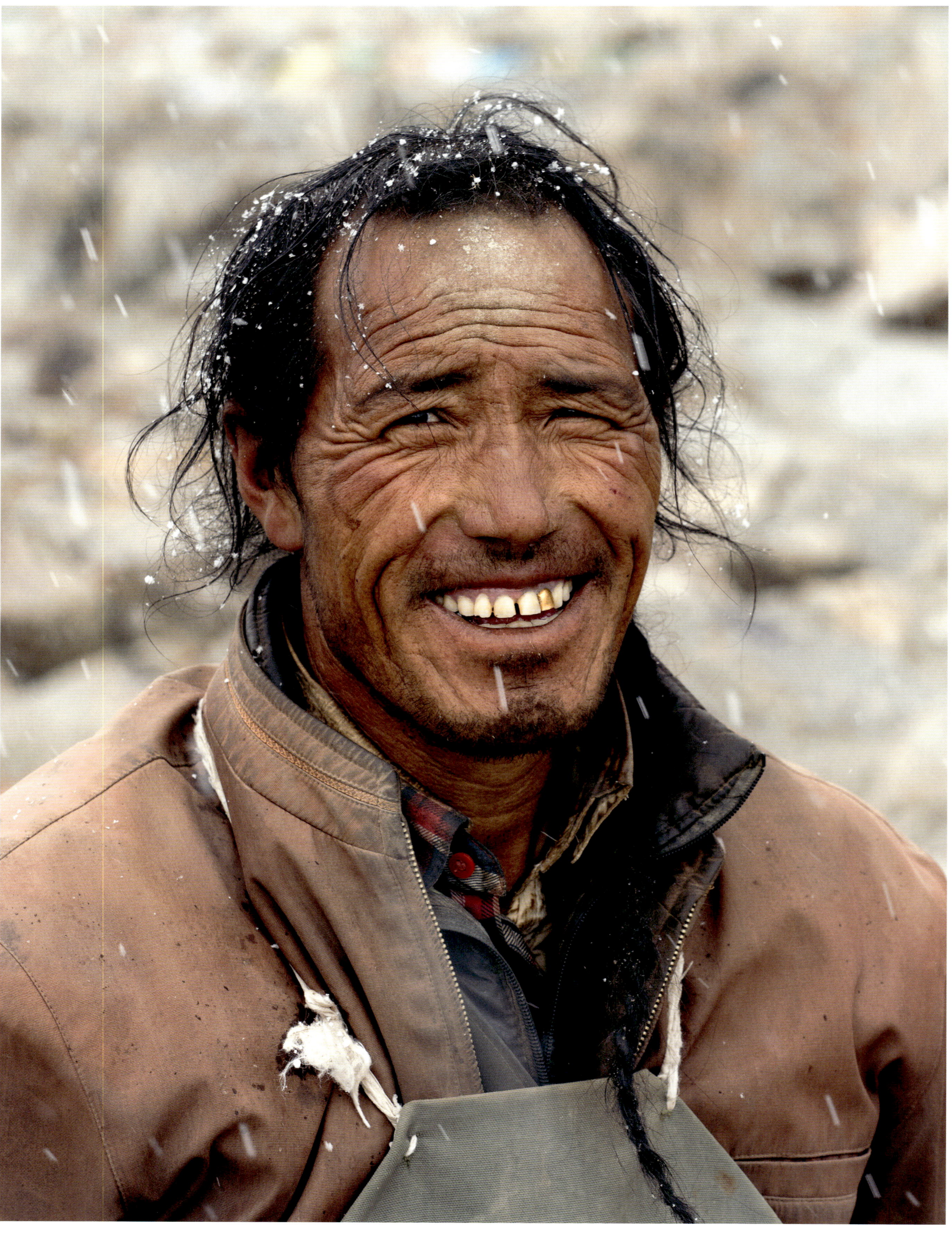

Prostrating myself with my forehead touching the ground, I whisper, "Buddha, Dharma, Sangha." I thus express my recognition, my joy, my respect, my trust in Buddha, in the pure path that he teaches and in the spiritual community who encourages me to discover my awakened nature.

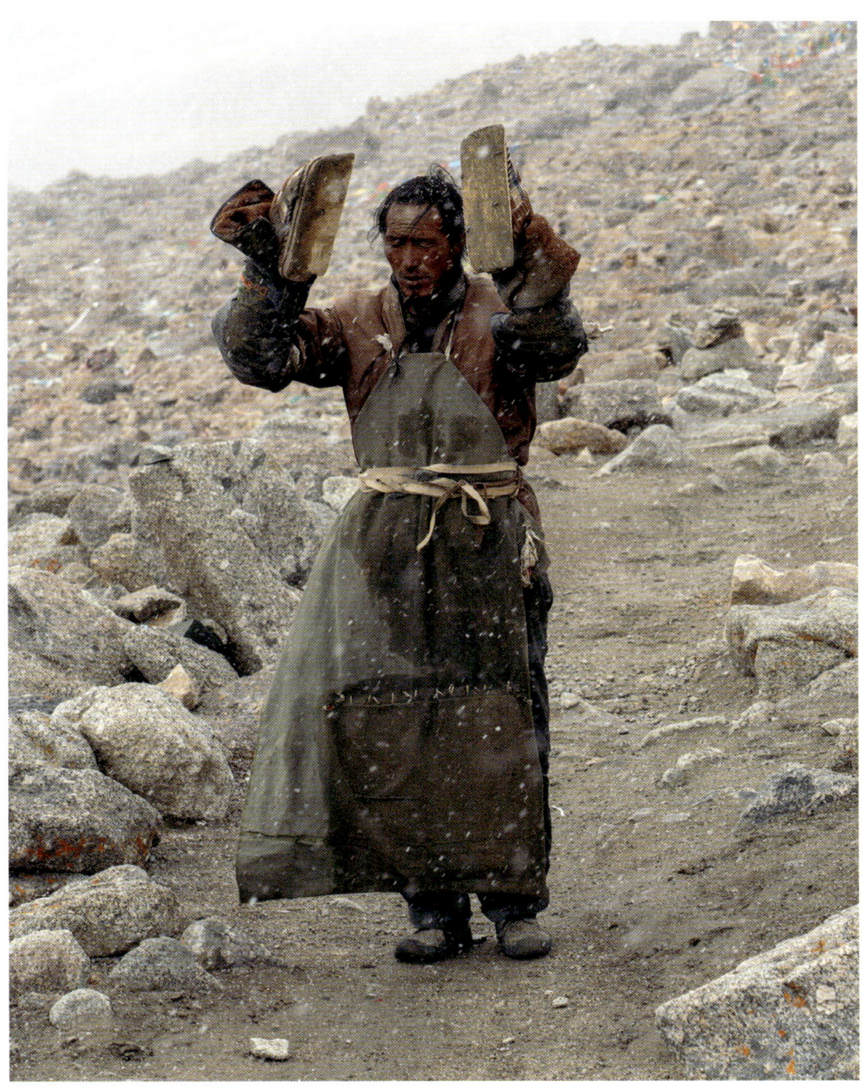
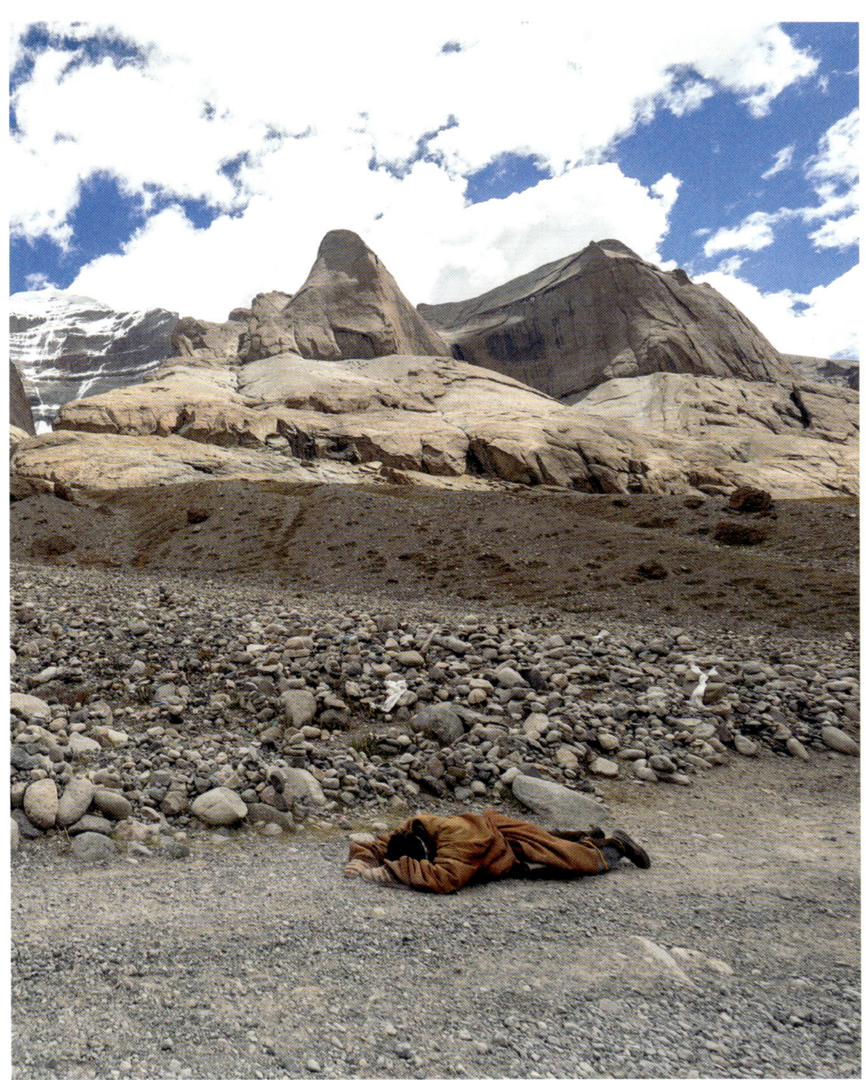

Indem ich mich demütig auf den Boden werfe, murmle ich: „Buddha, Dharma, Sangha". So bekunde ich meine Dankbarkeit, meine Freude, meinen Respekt und mein Vertrauen, das ich Buddha, dem reinen Weg, den er lehrt, und der spirituellen Gemeinschaft, die mich ermutigt, meinen erleuchteten Geist zu entdecken, entgegenbringe.

En me prosternant le front à terre, je murmure : « Bouddha, Dharma, Sangha ». Je manifeste ainsi ma reconnaissance, ma joie, mon respect, ma confiance envers Bouddha, le chemin pur qu'il enseigne et la communauté spirituelle qui m'encourage à découvrir ma nature éveillée.

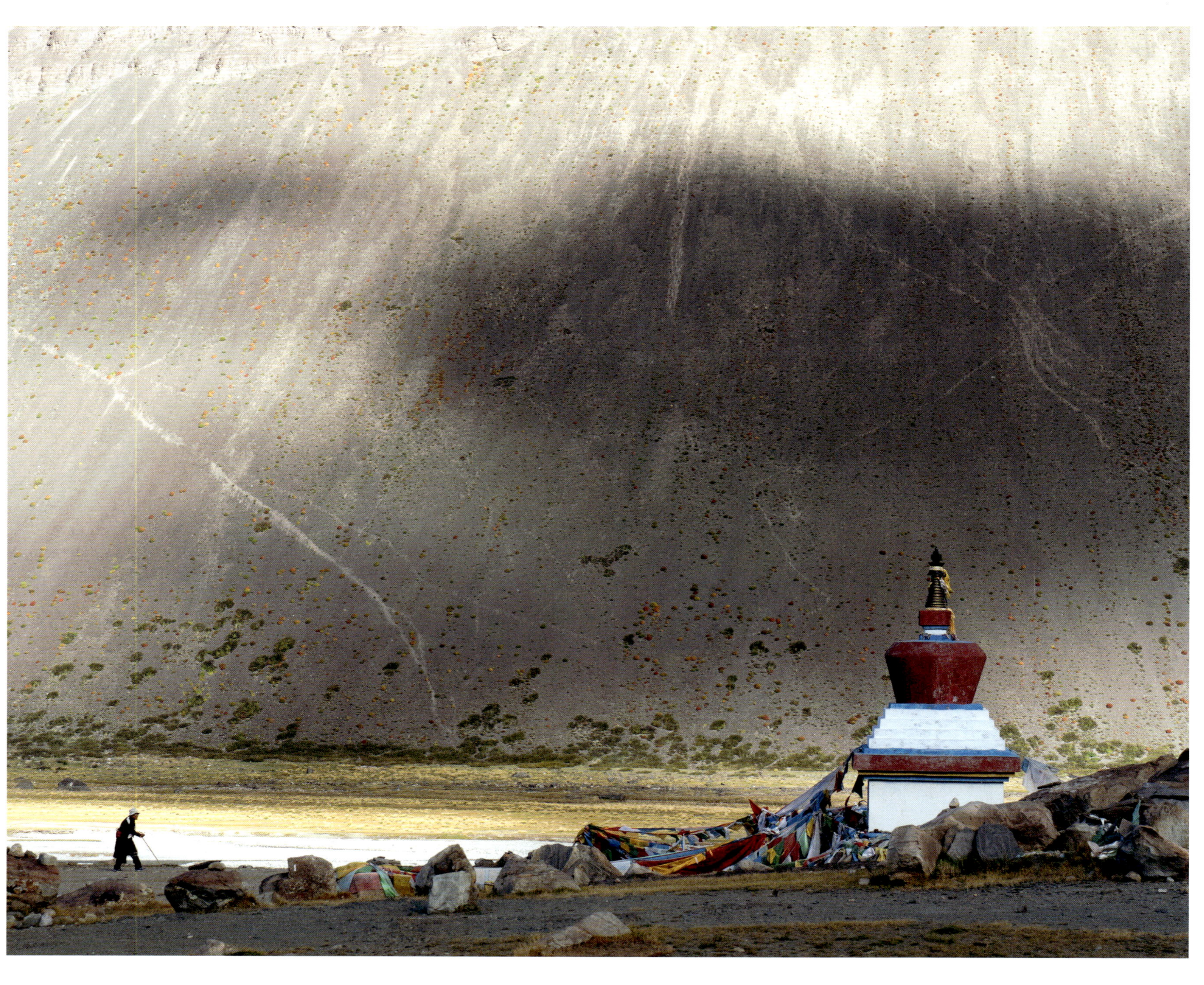

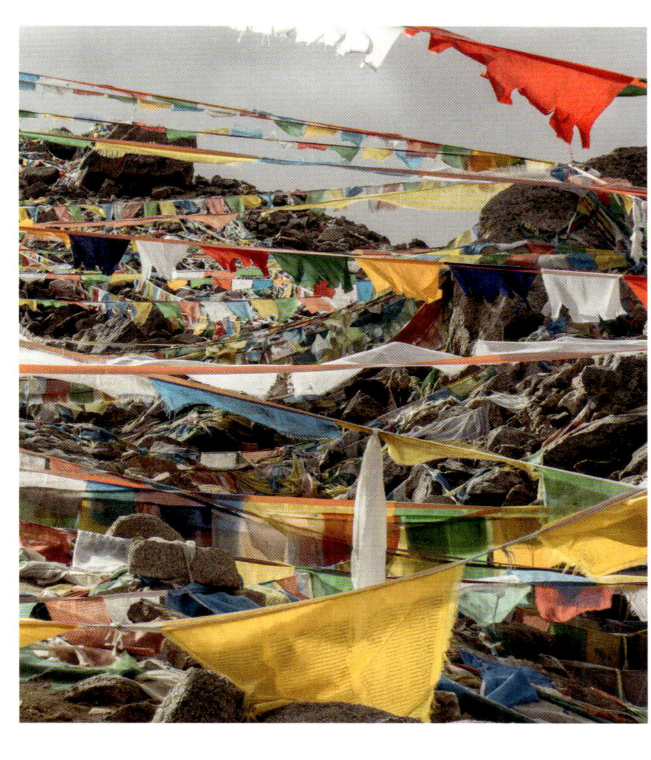

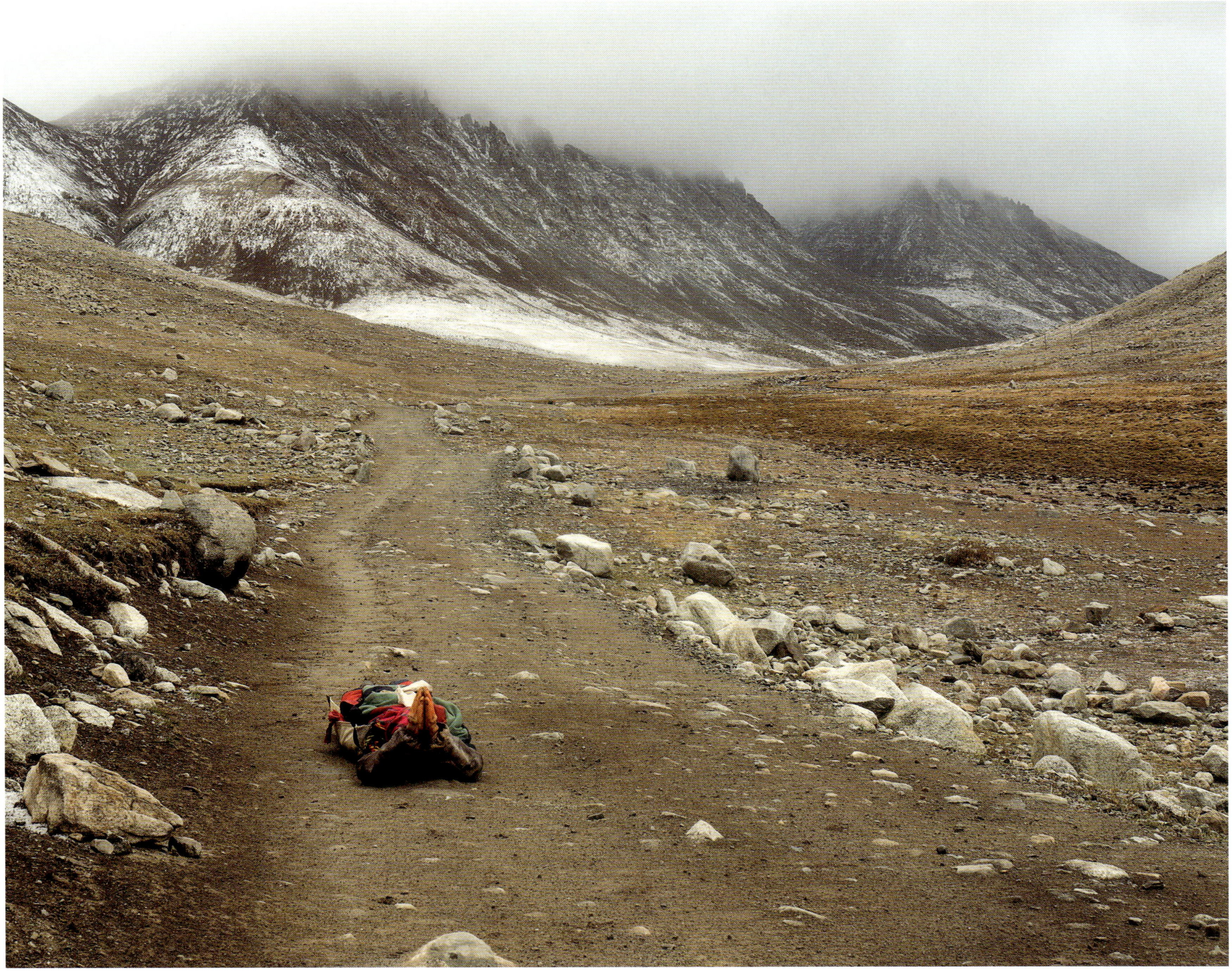

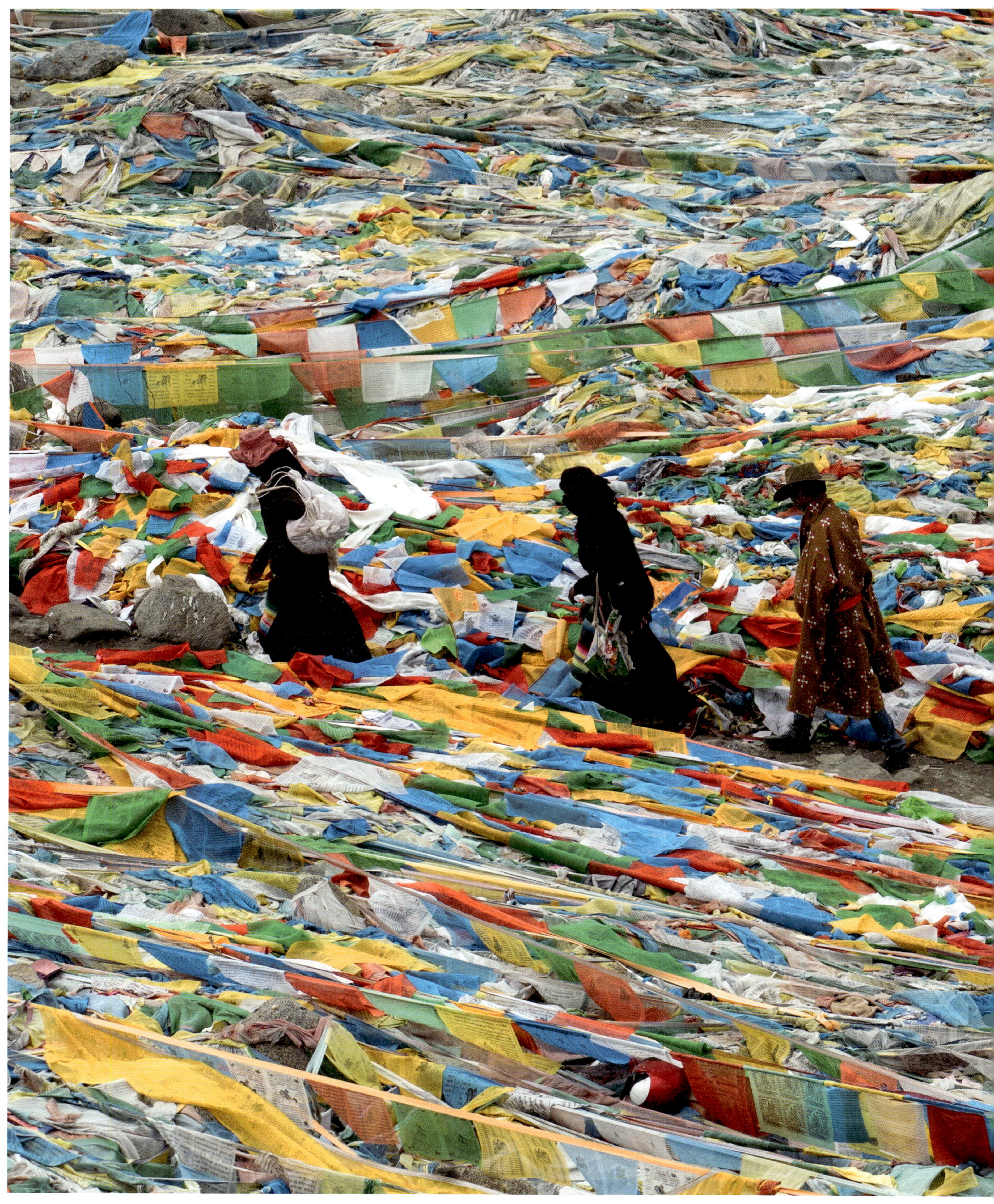

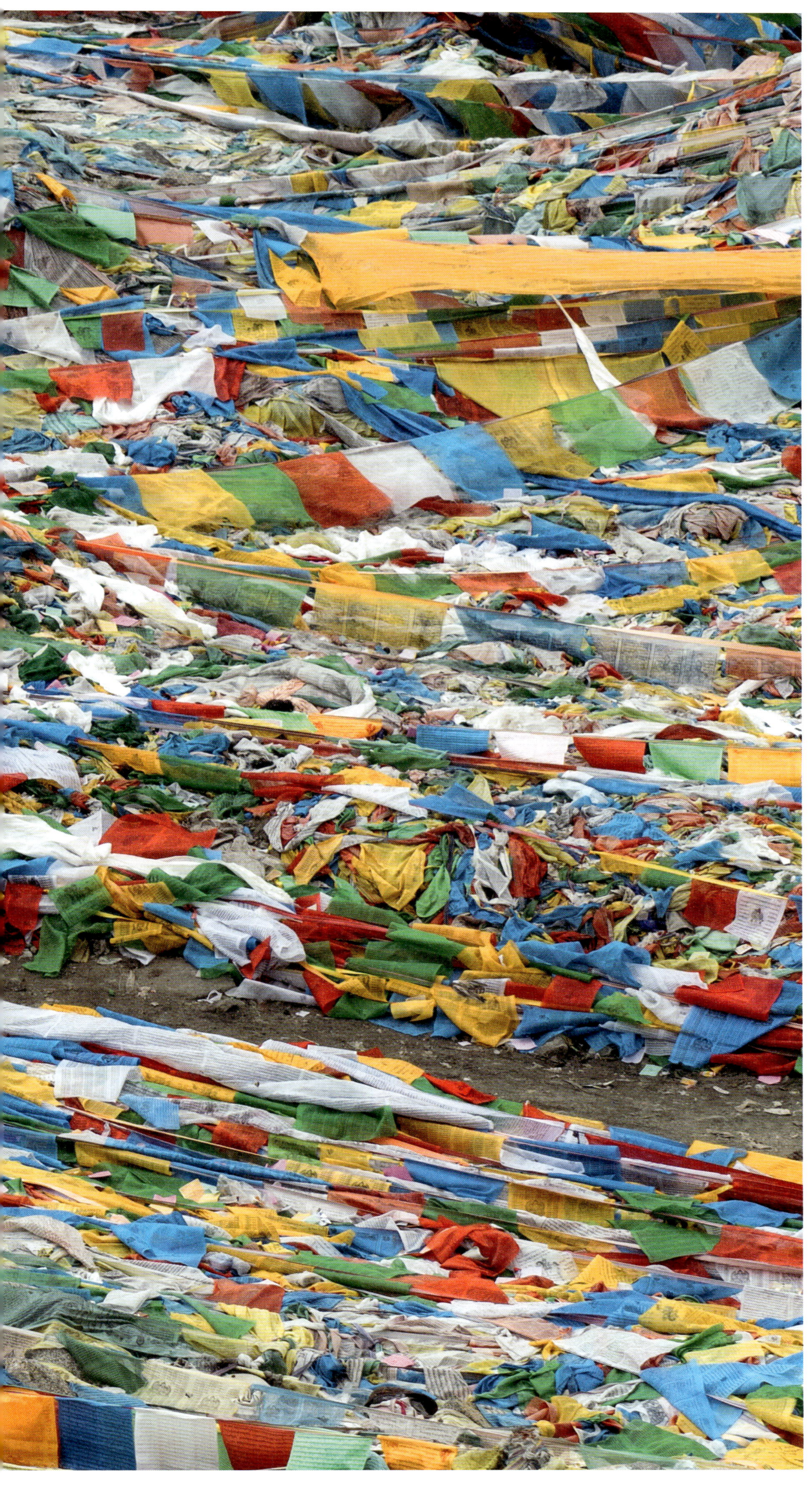

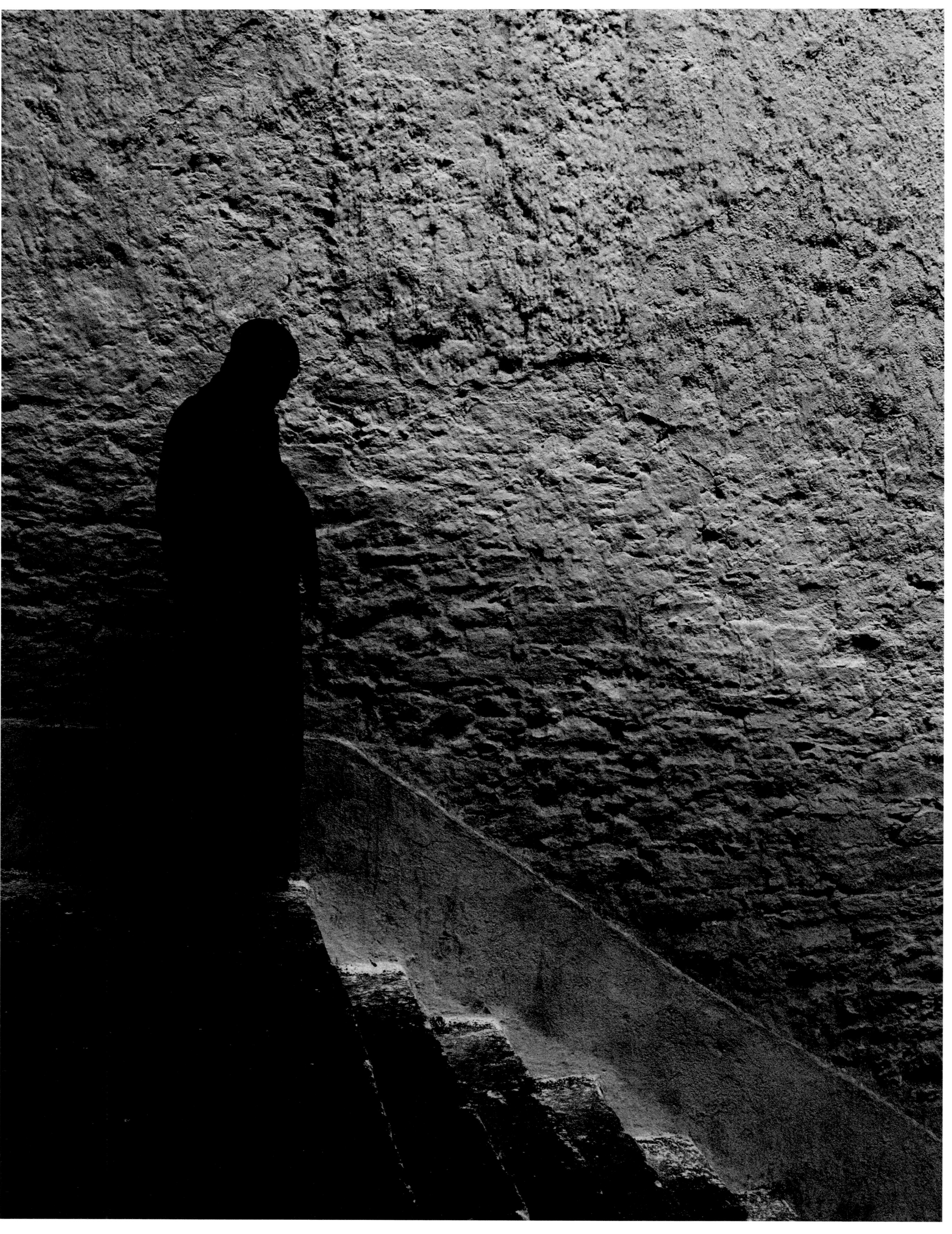

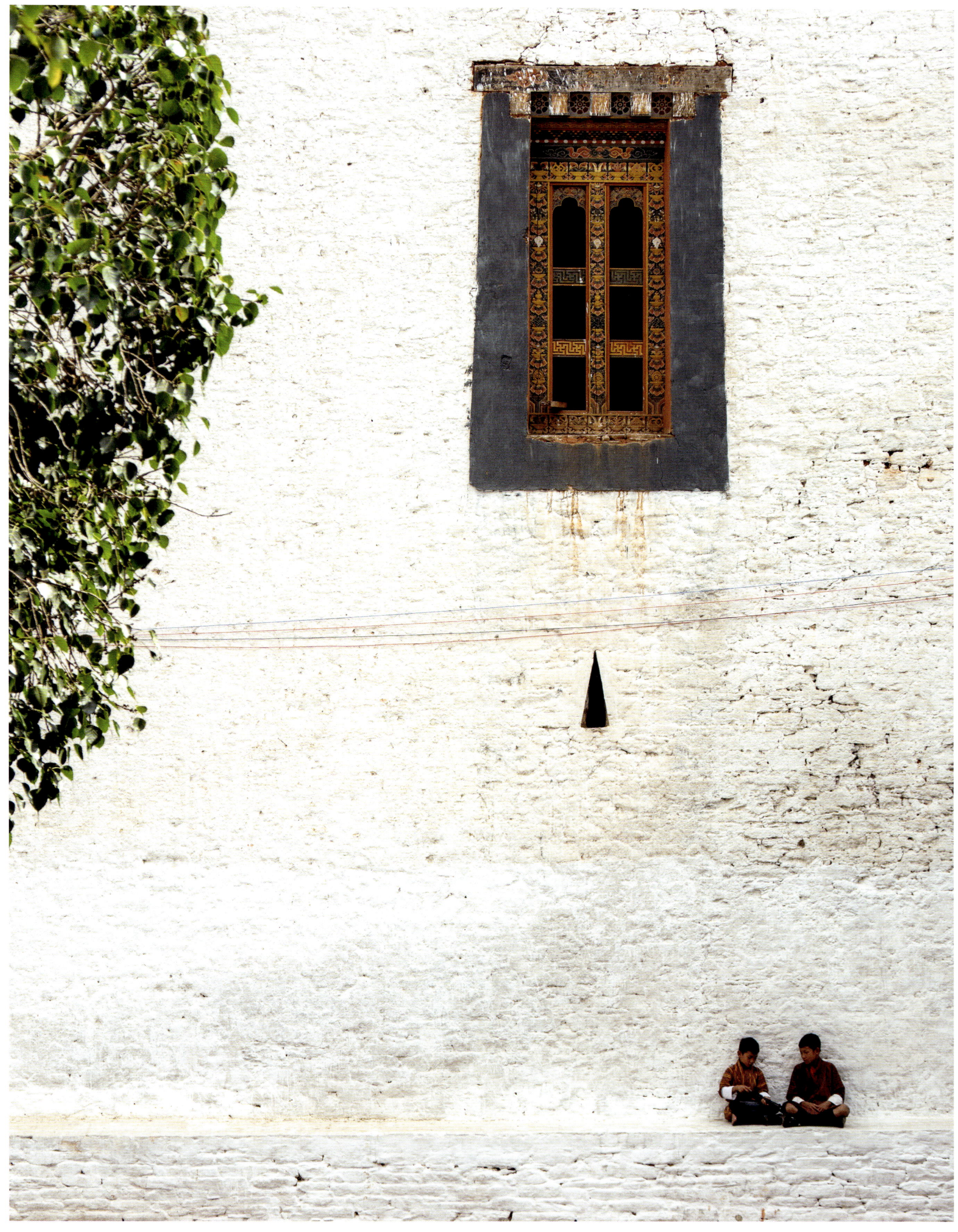

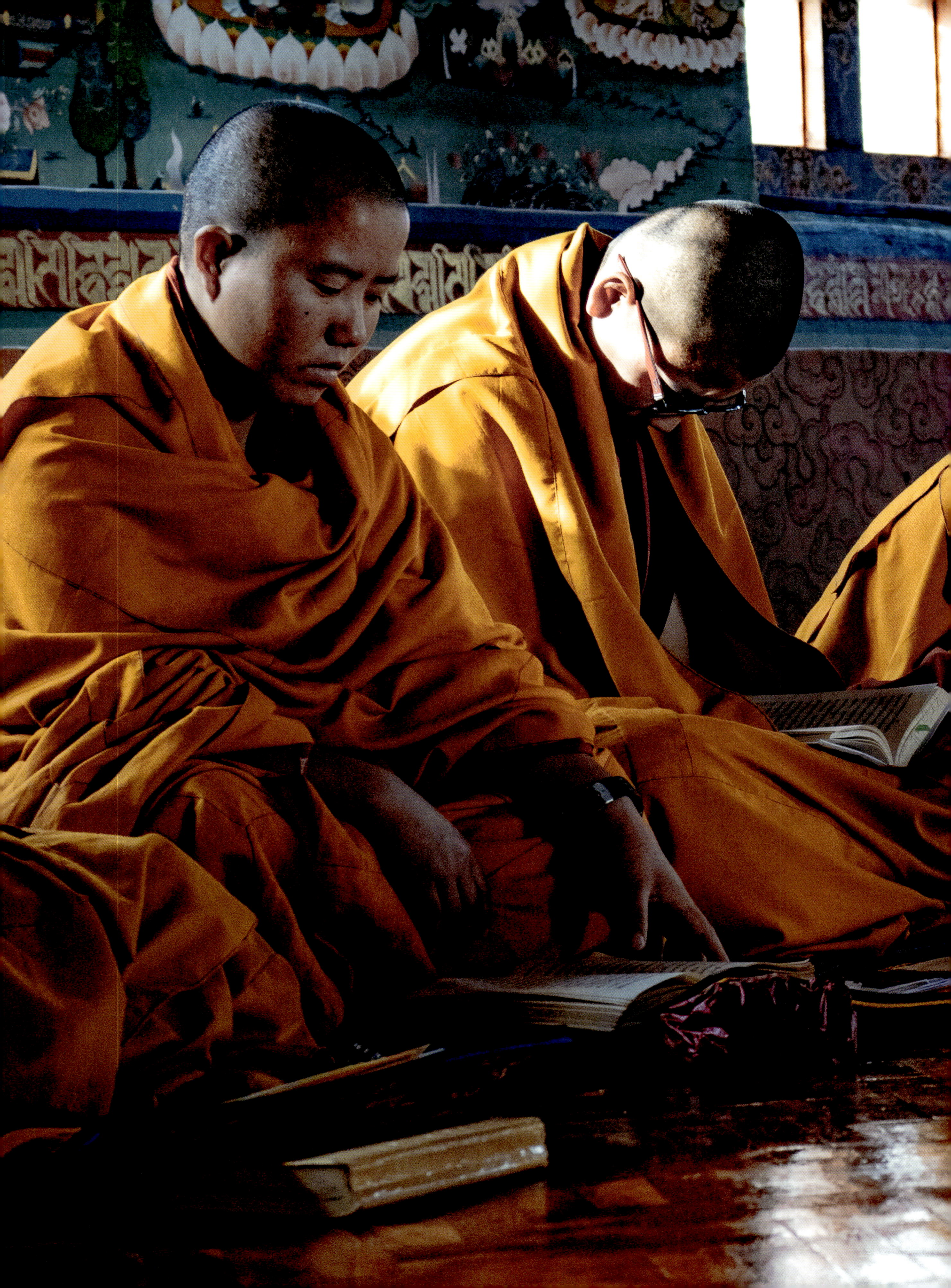

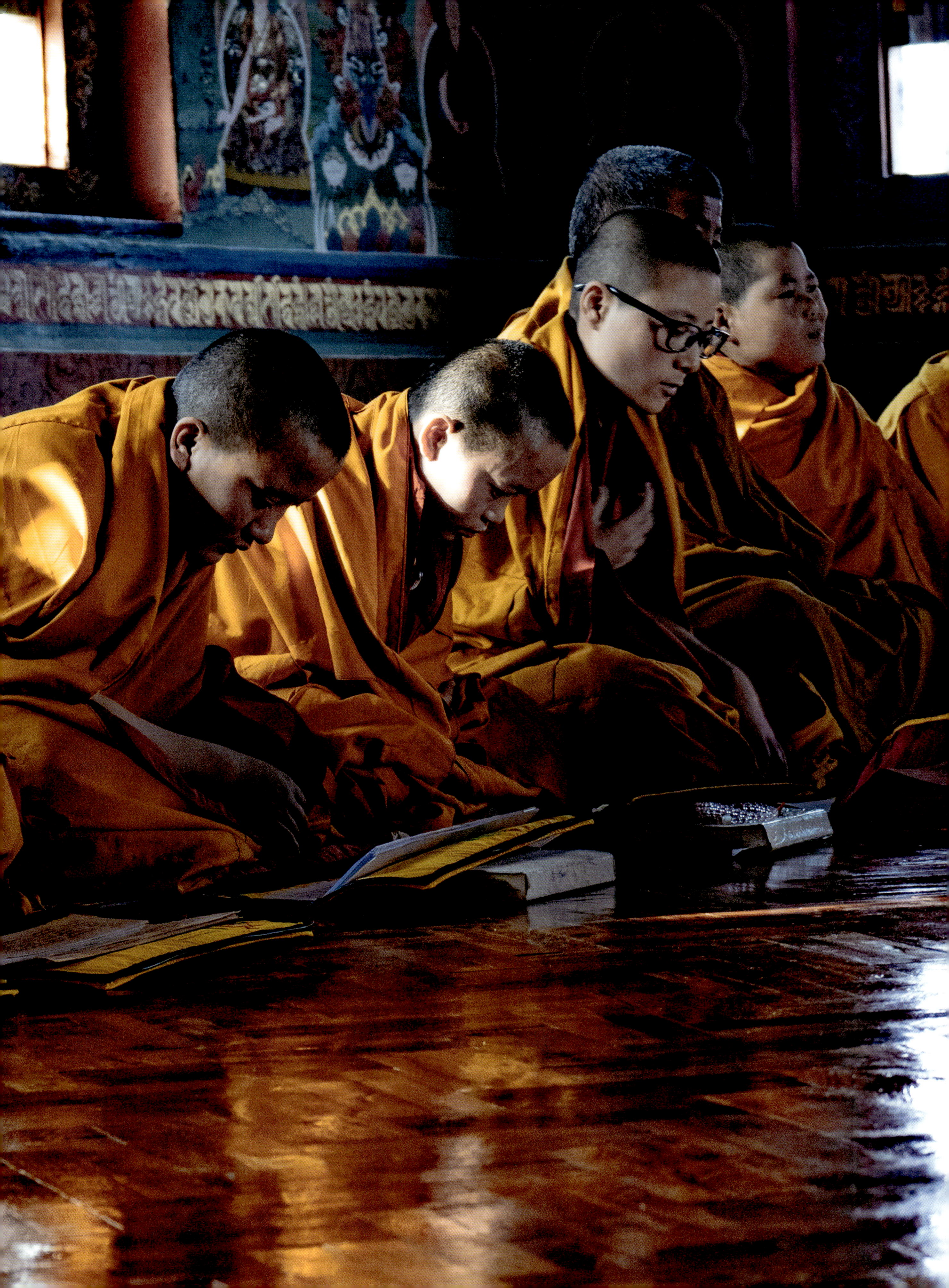

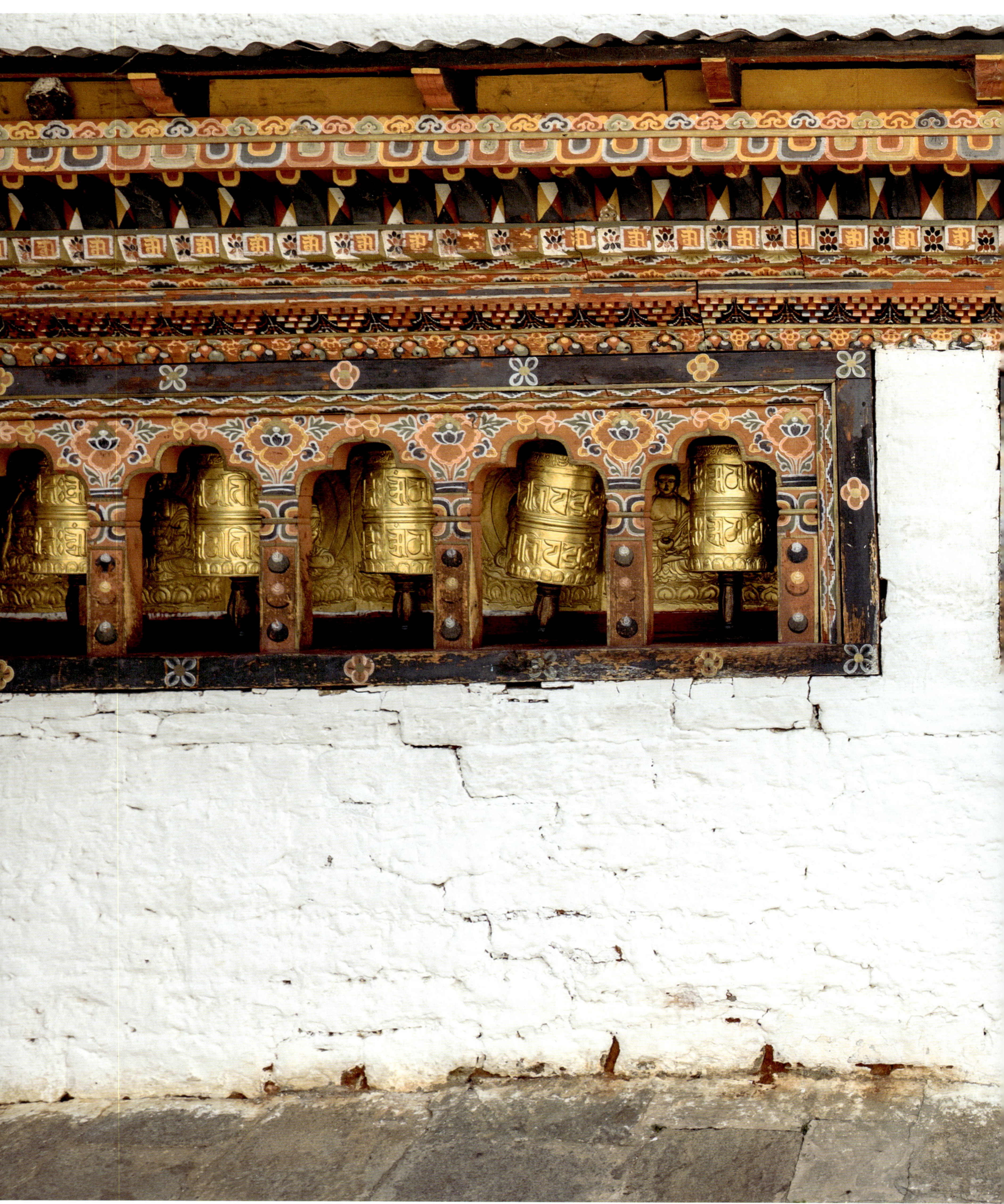

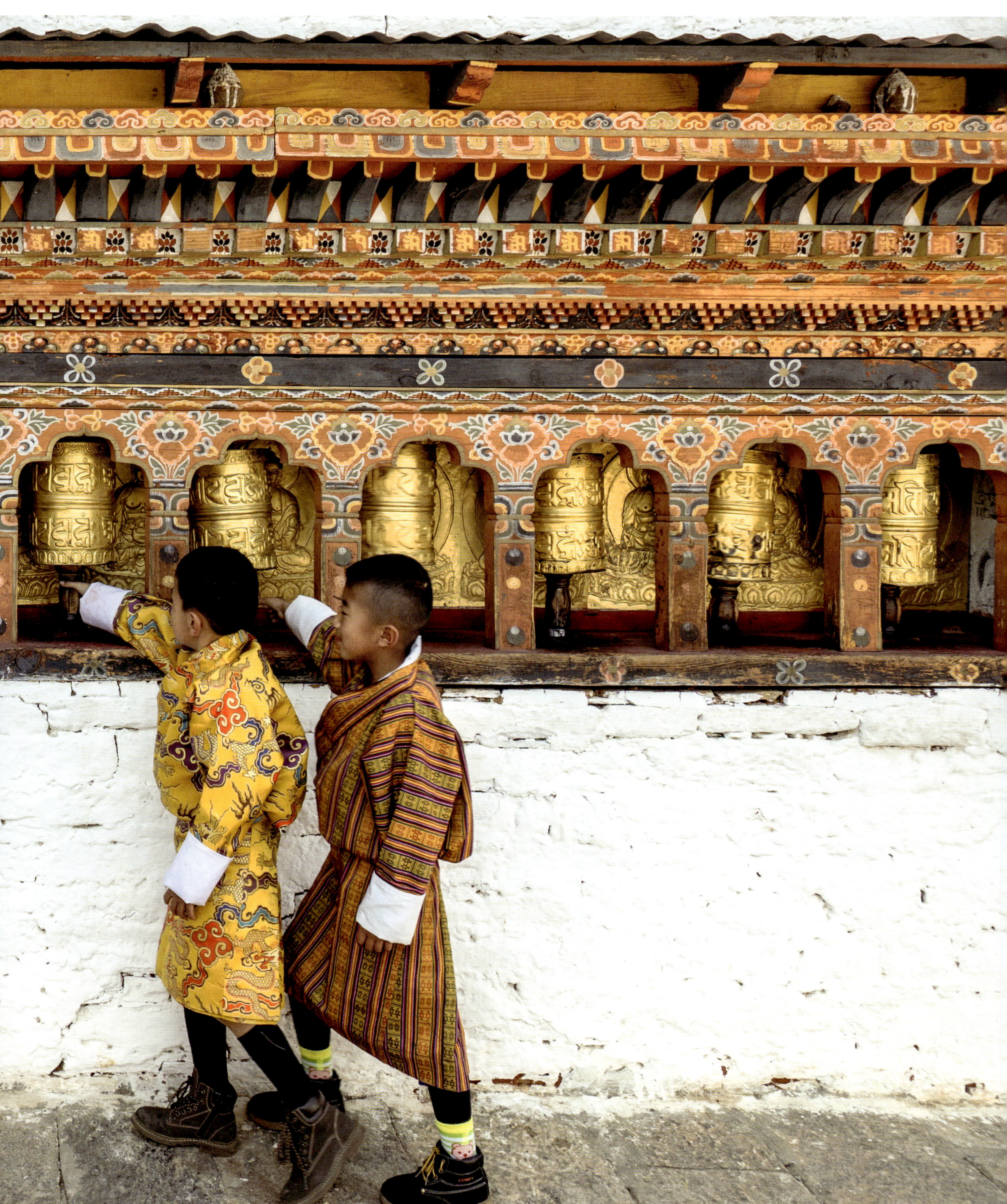

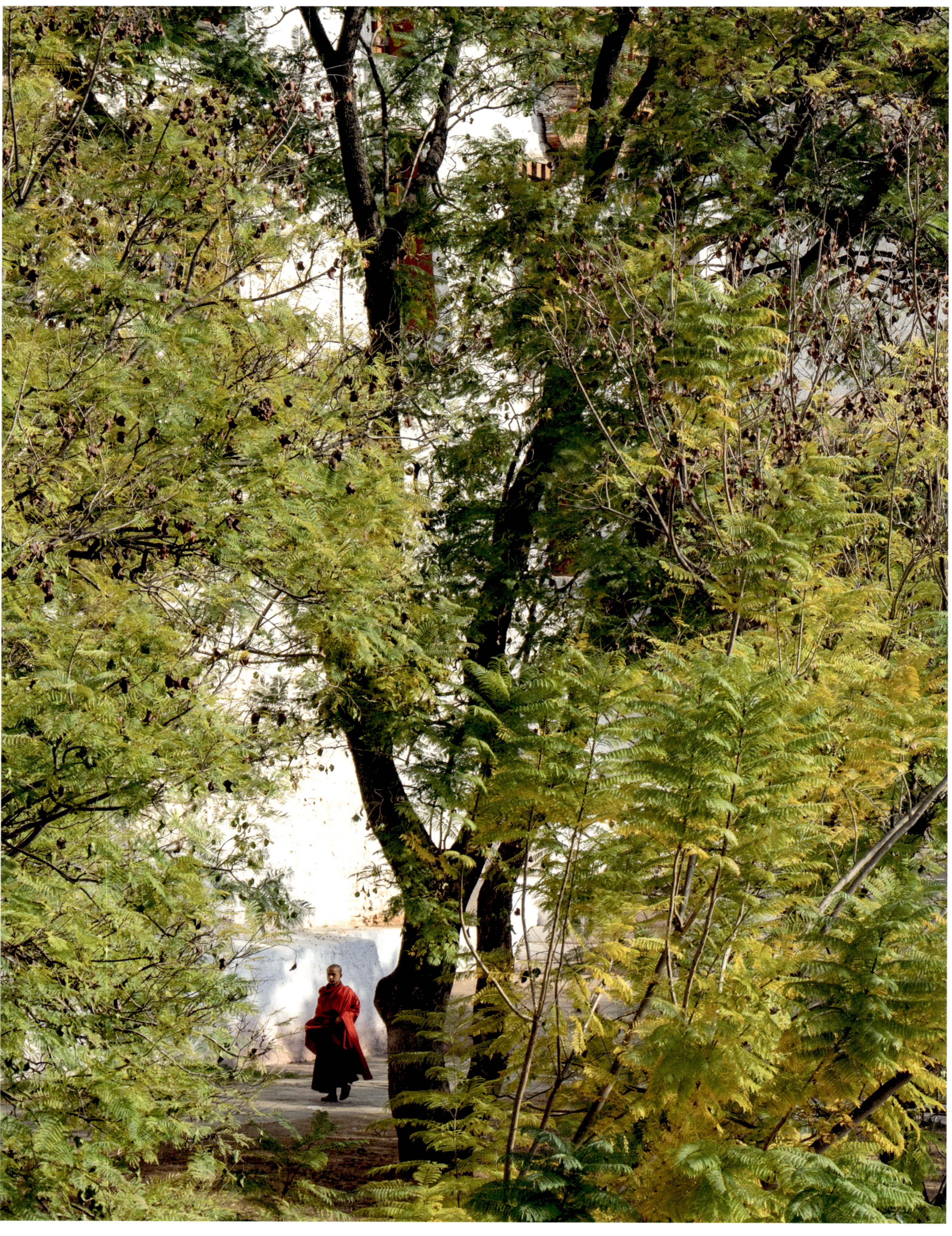

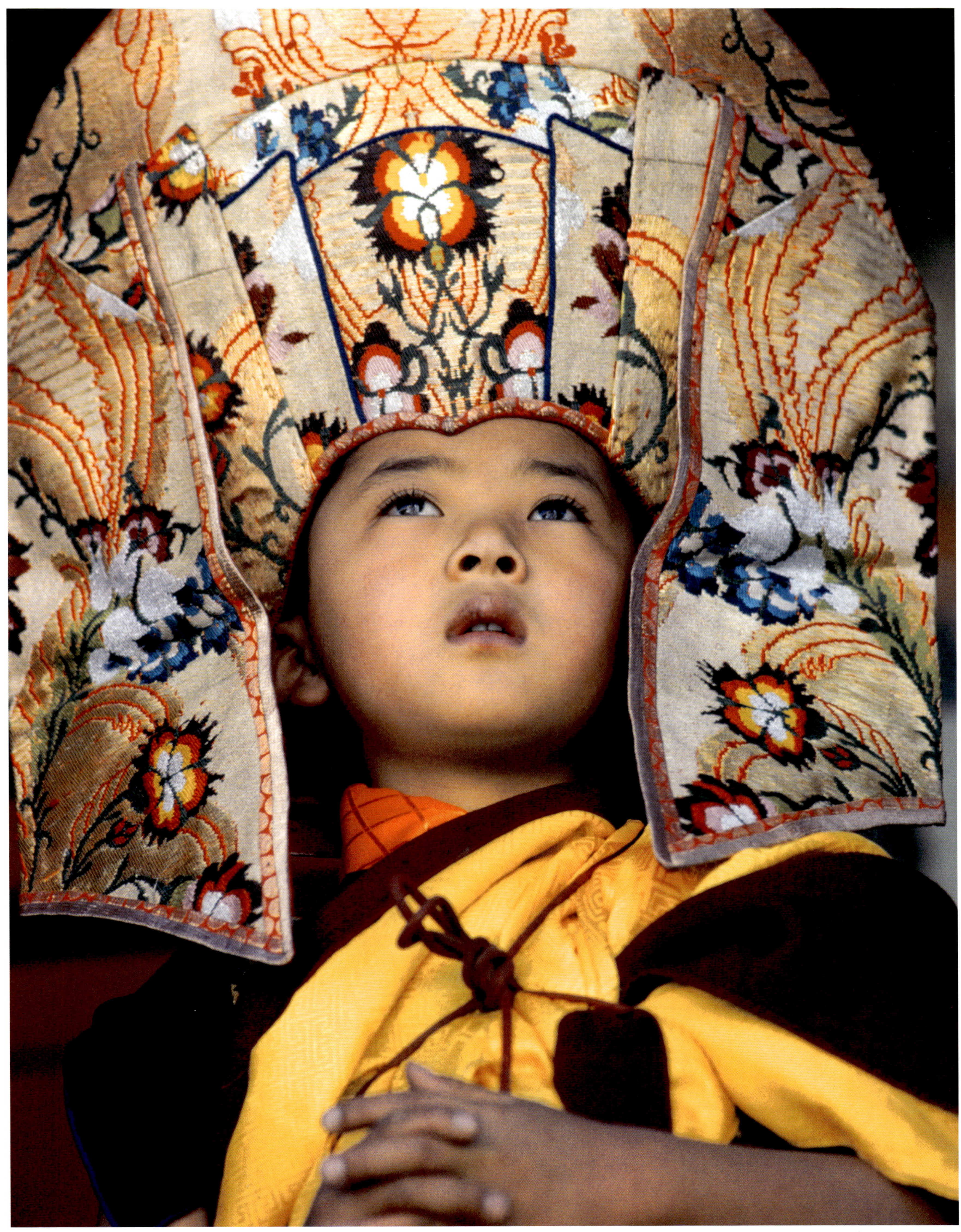

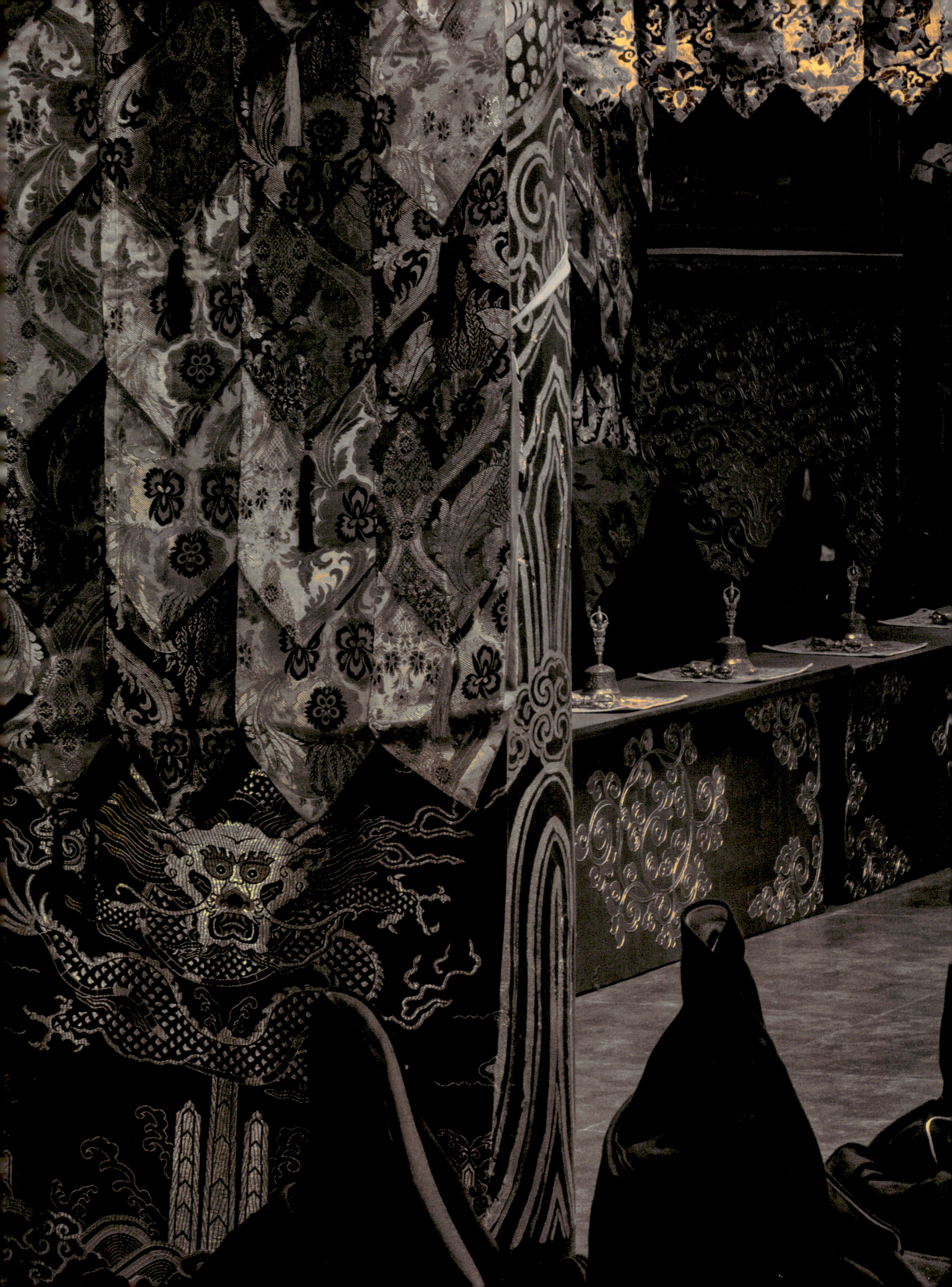

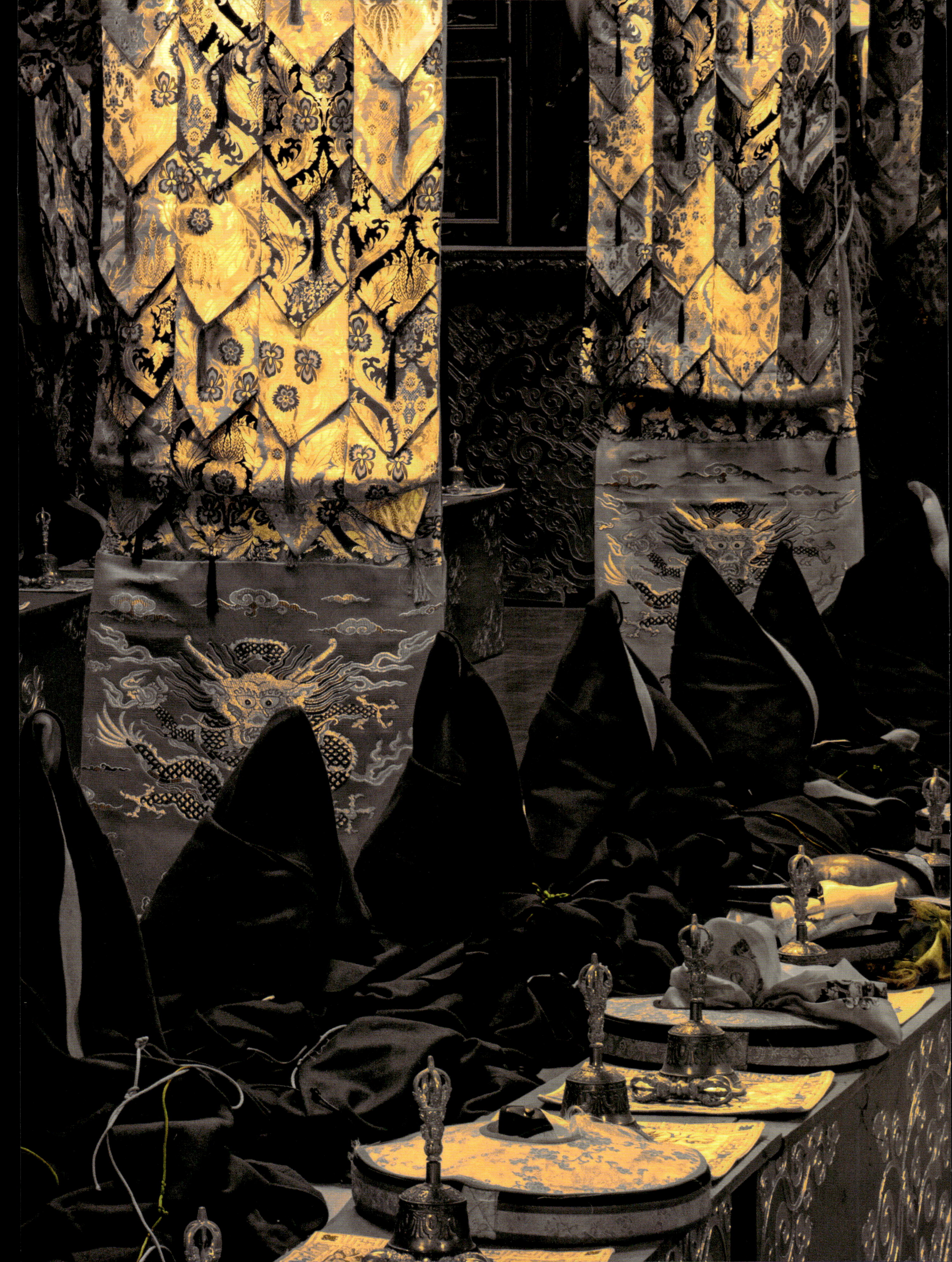

Happiness is no simple matter. It is very hard to find it in oneself and impossible to find it elsewhere.

Buddha Shakyamuni

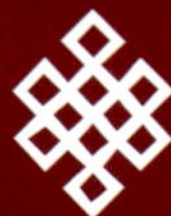

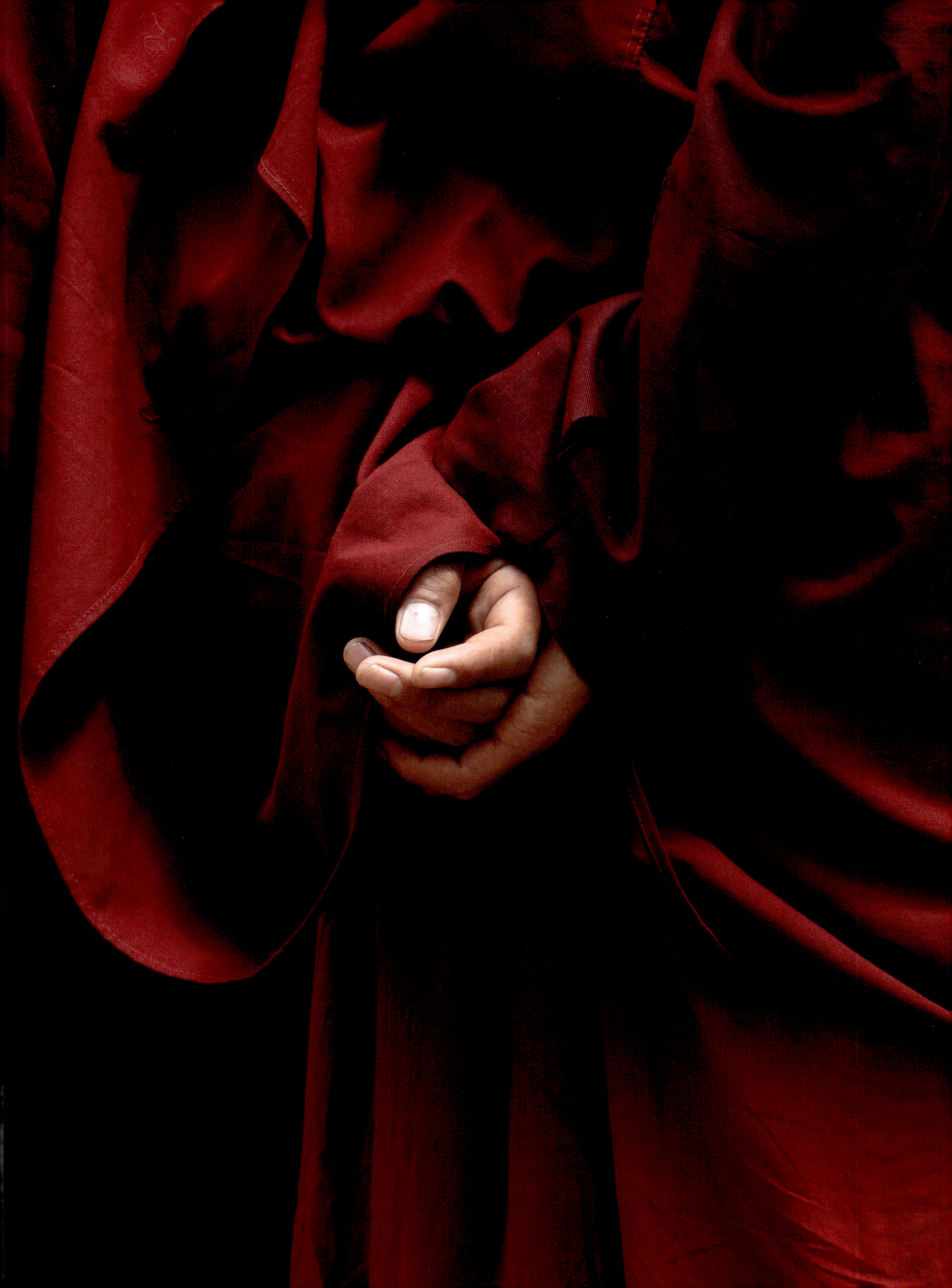

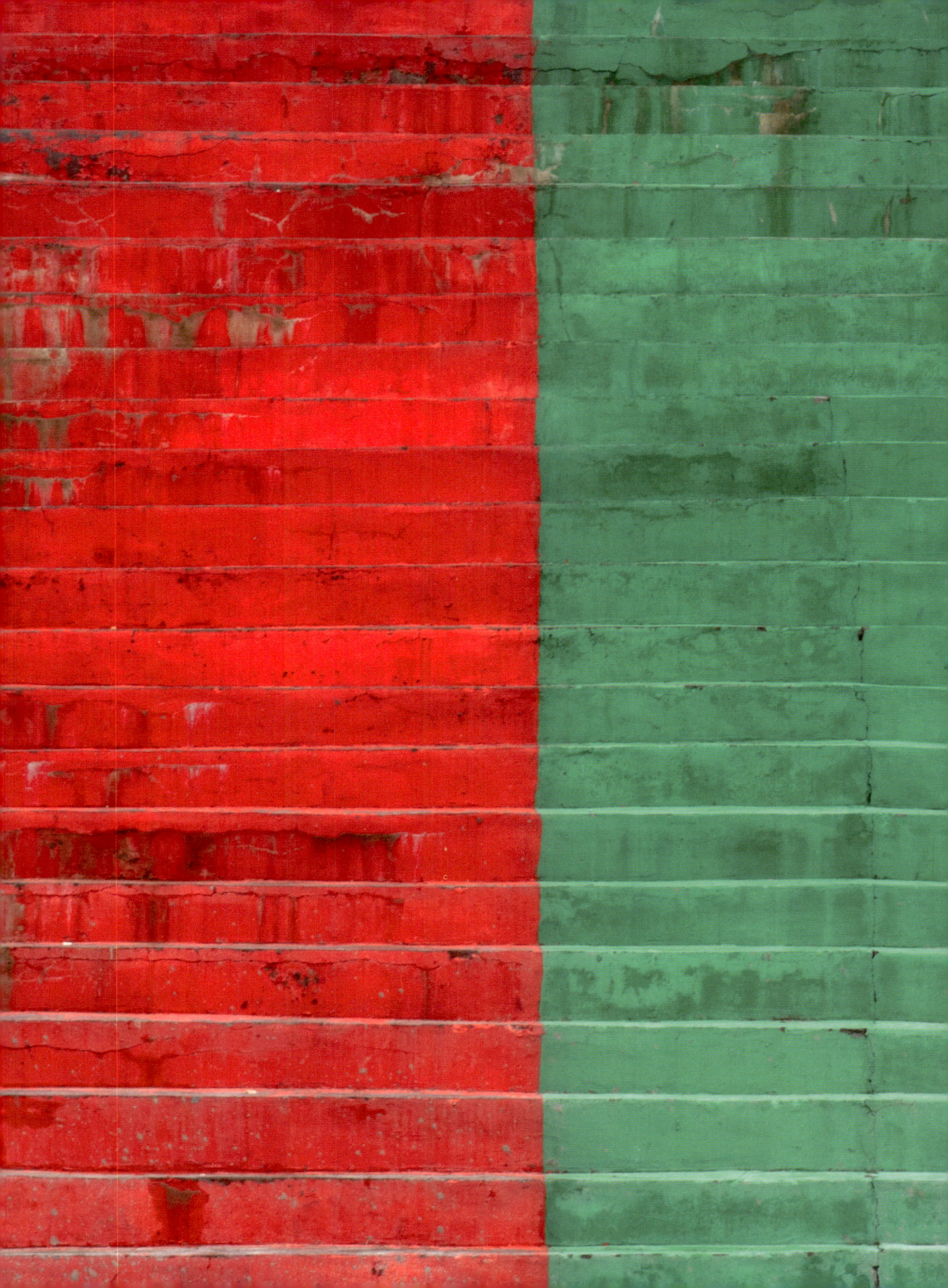

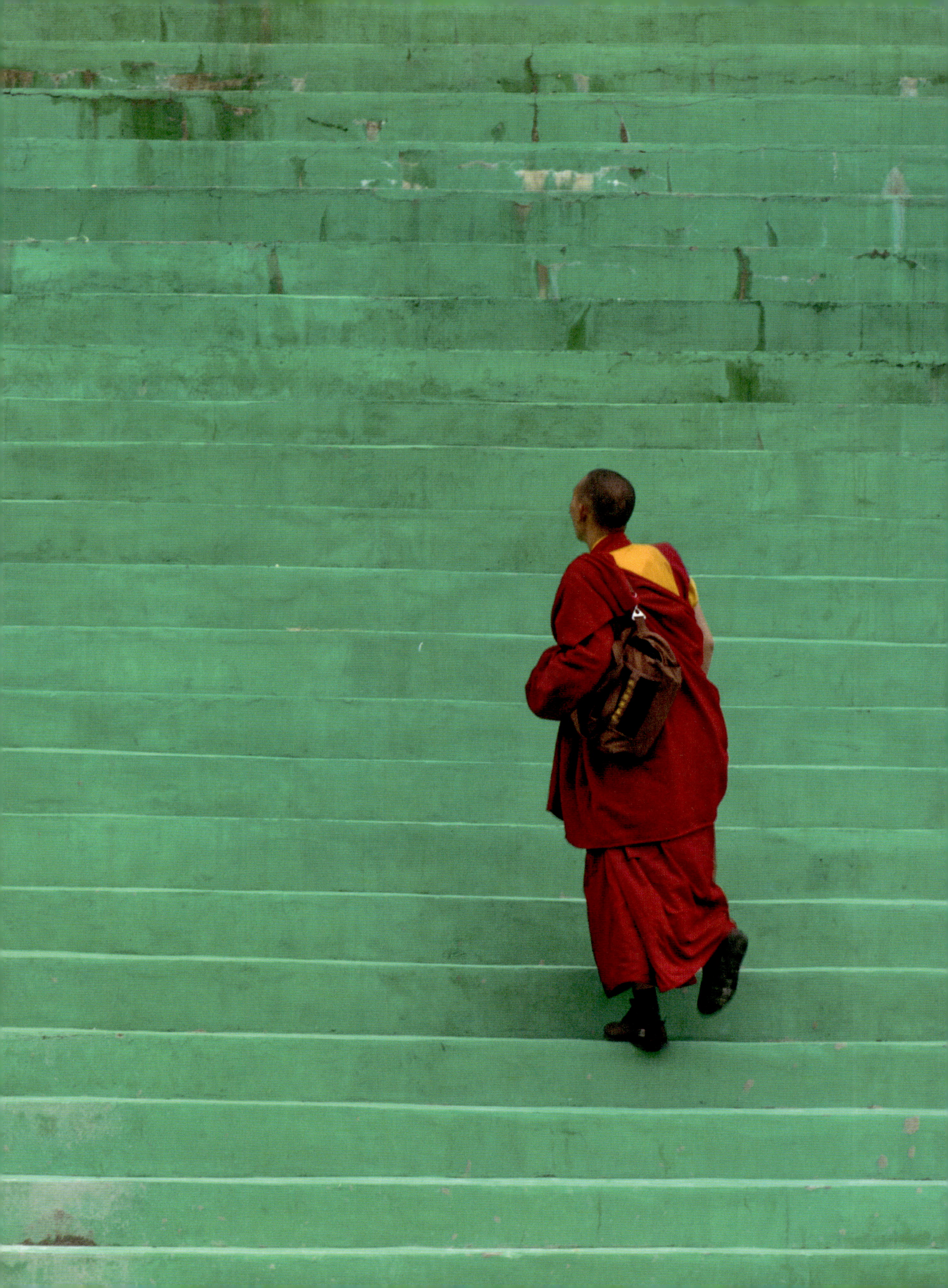

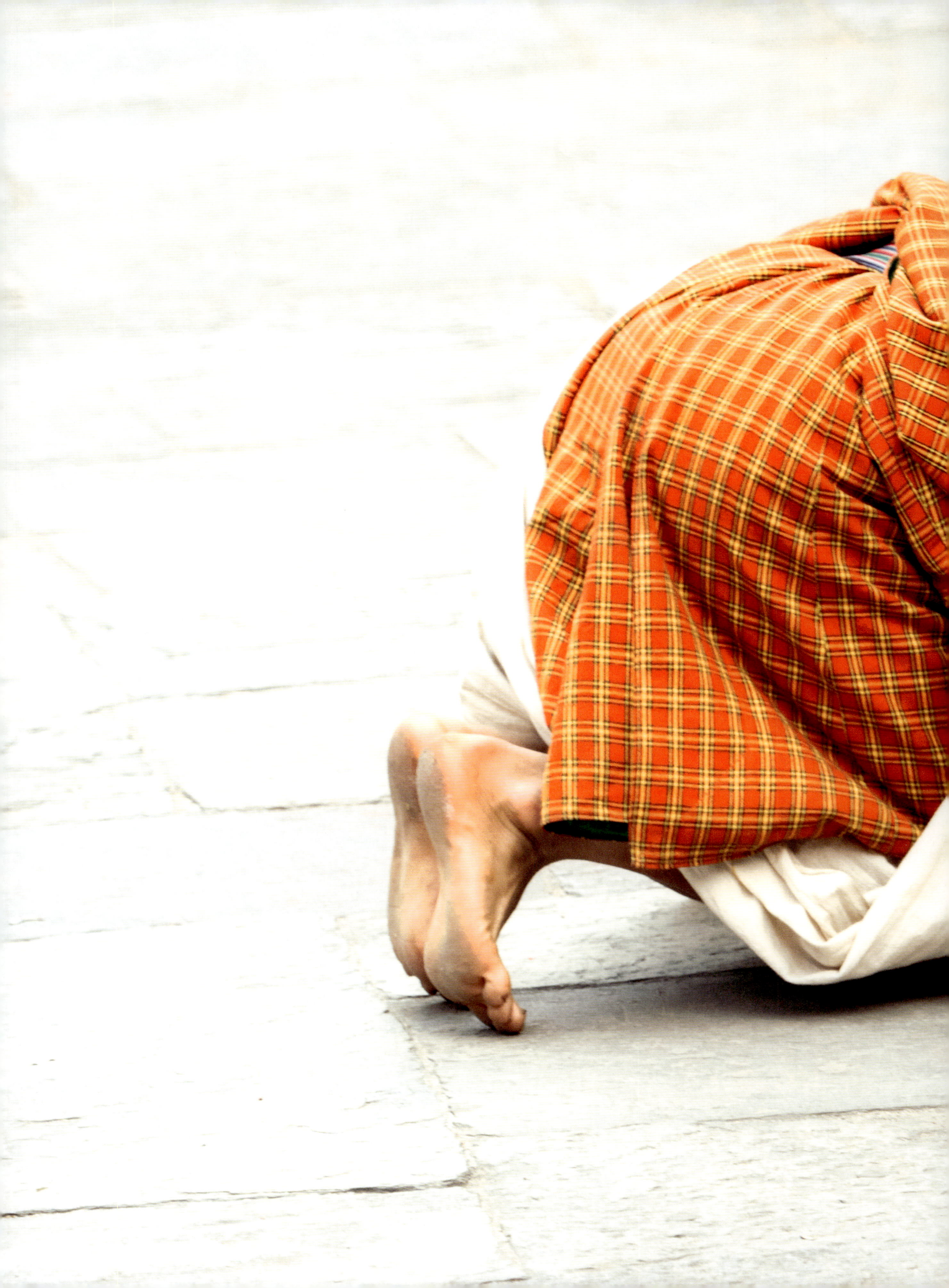

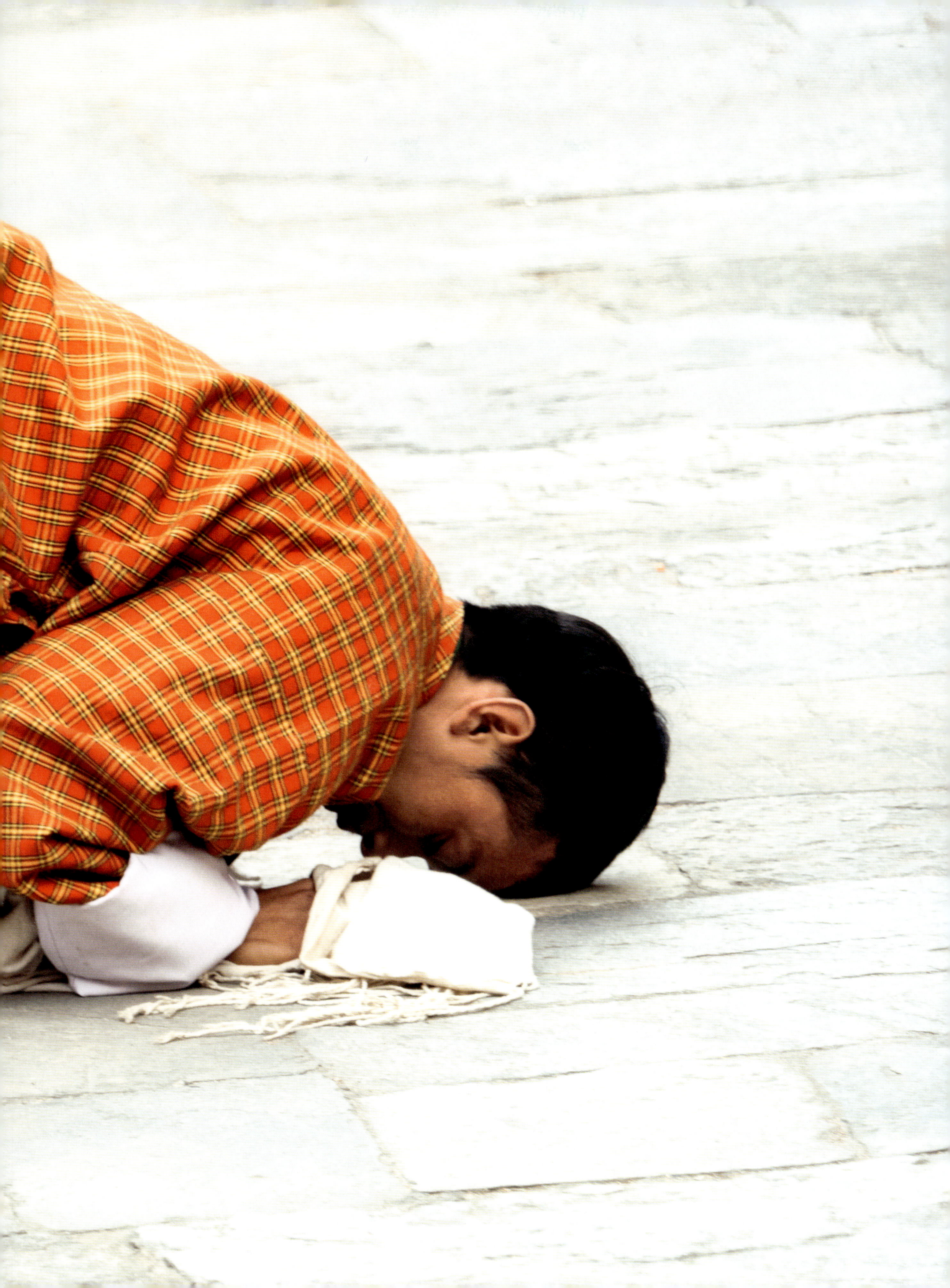

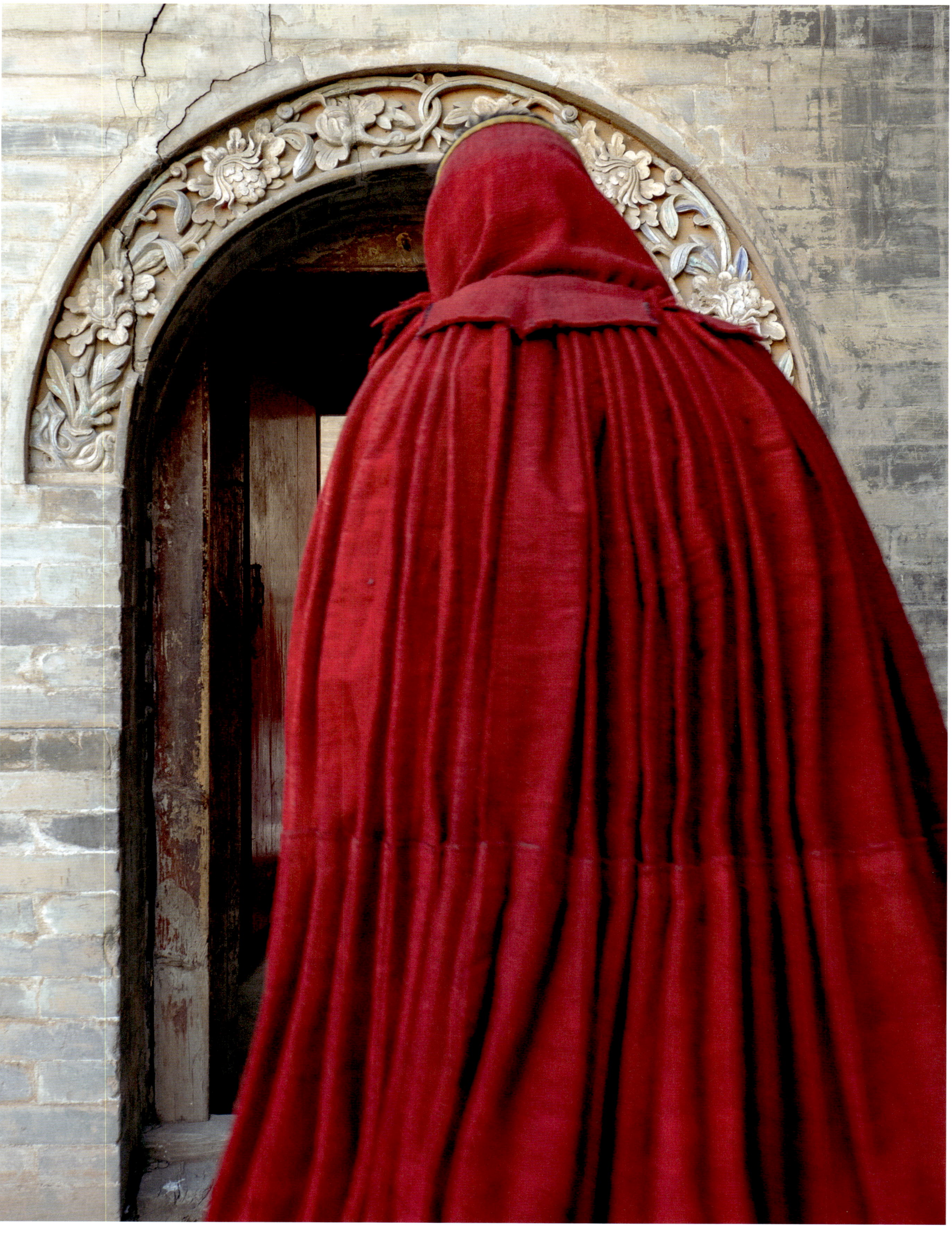

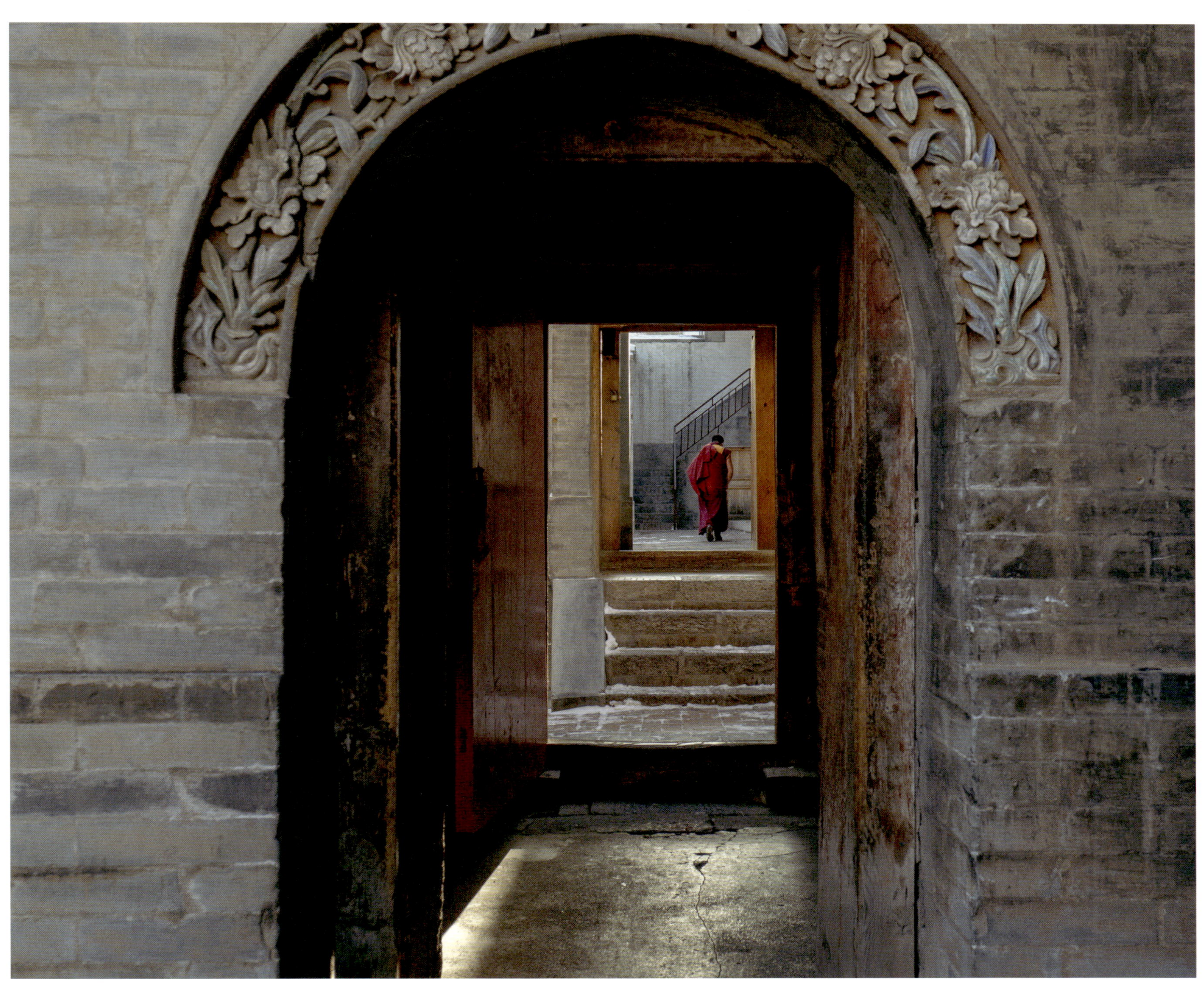

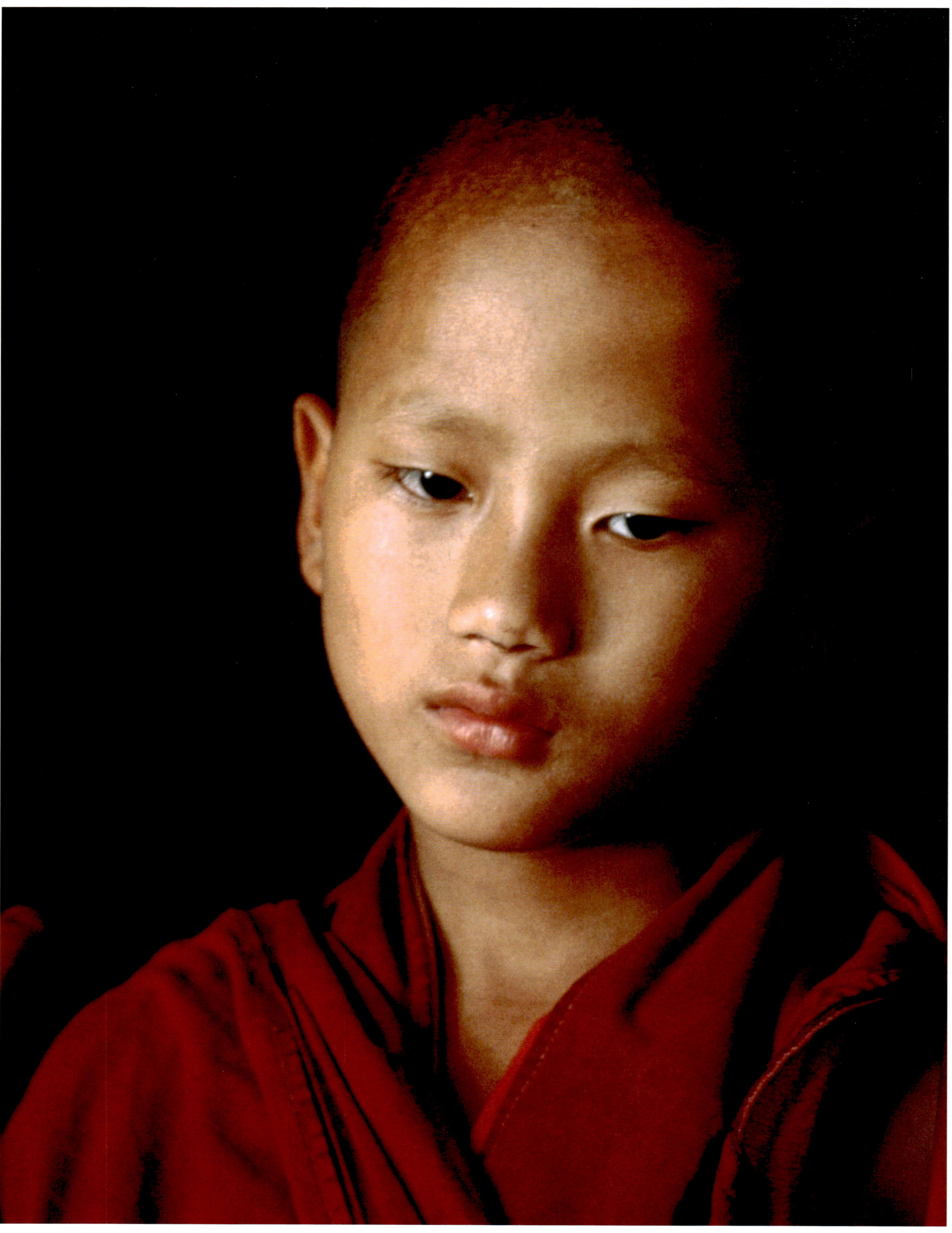

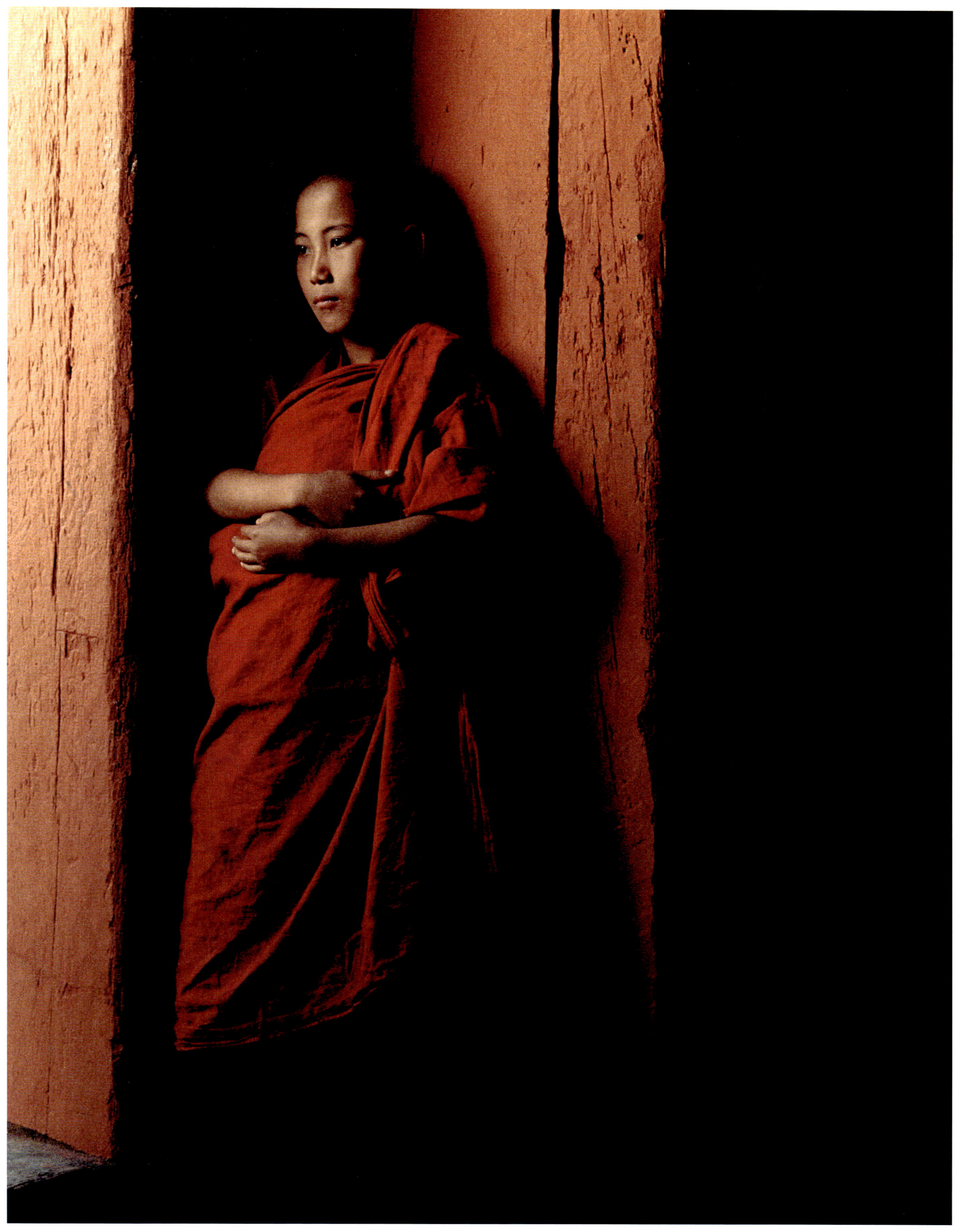

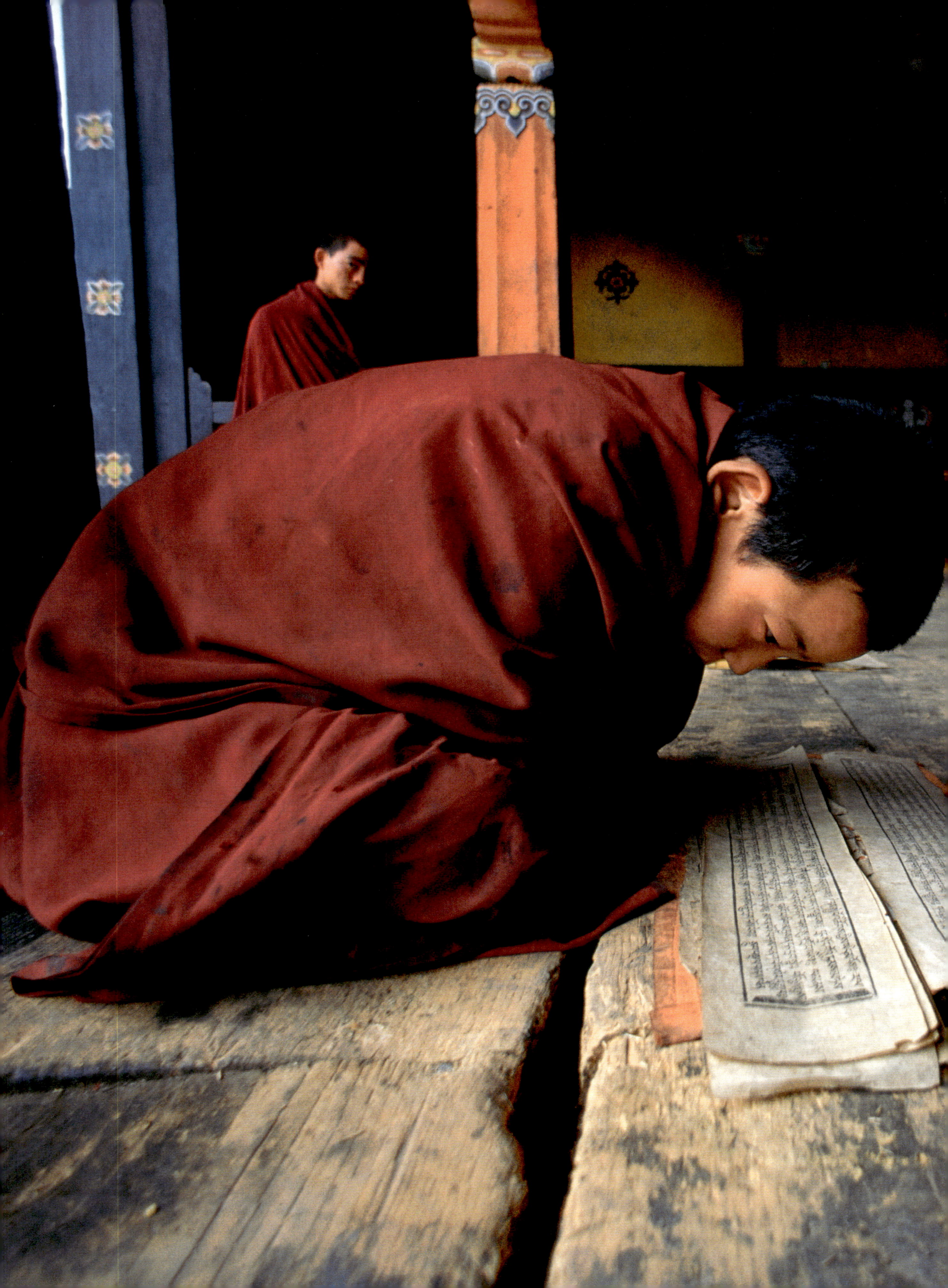

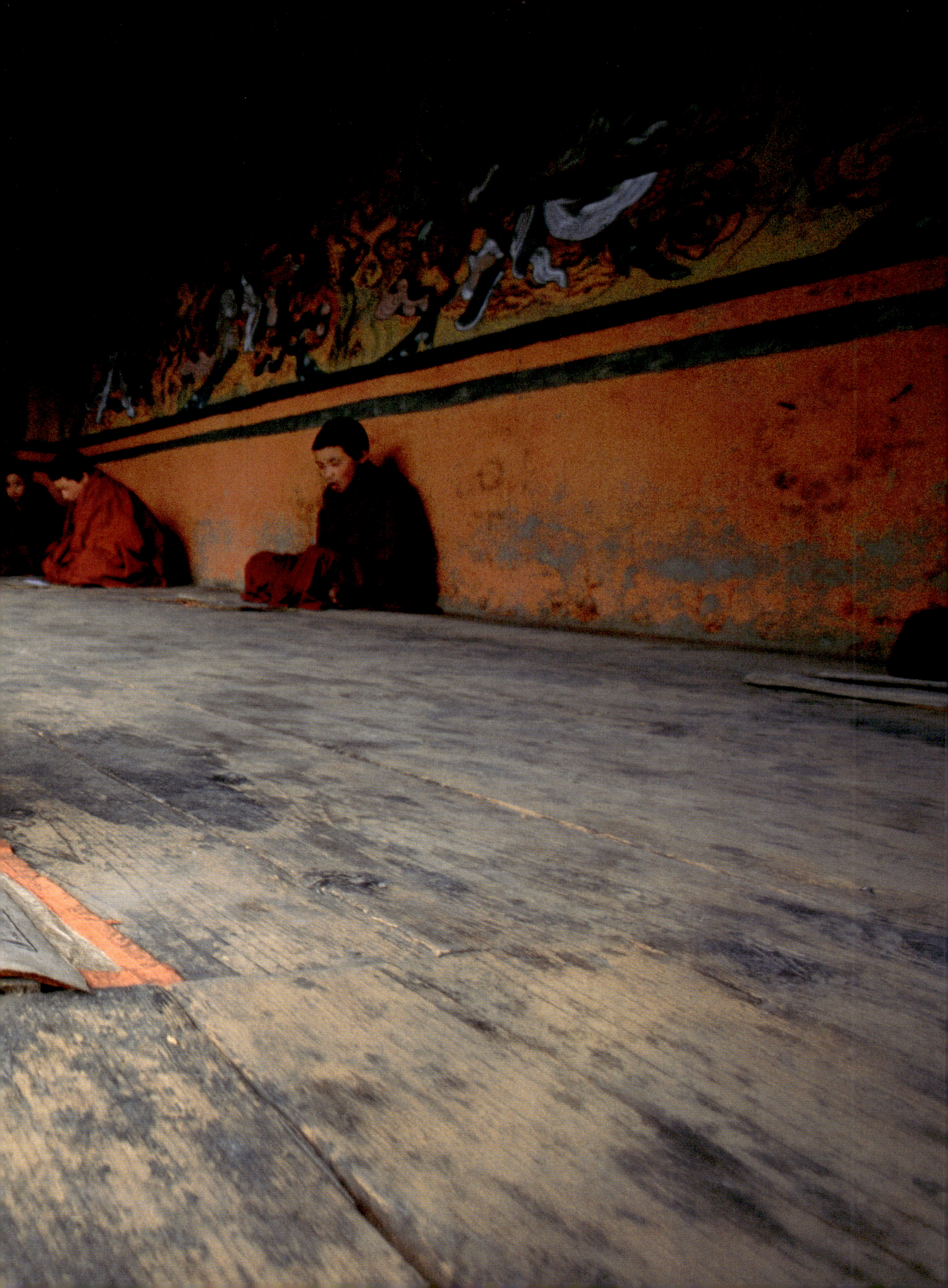

Karma

Karma · Karma

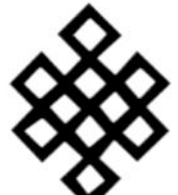

Each one of us is the master of his destiny and reaps what he has sown.
Nothing happens by chance or fate. Through the actions of our mind, we create our own
karma, positive and negative, in our life here and now and in our lives to come.

Jeder ist seines Schicksals Herr und erntet, was er sät. Nichts ist zufällig oder unabwendbar.
Durch unseren Geist schaffen wir unser eigenes Karma, ob gut oder schlecht, im jetzigen Leben
ebenso wie in allen kommenden Leben.

Chacun est le maître de son destin et récolte ce qu'il sème. Rien n'est dû au hasard
ni à la fatalité. Par les actions de notre esprit, nous créons notre propre karma, positif et négatif,
dans notre vie-ci ou dans nos vies à venir.

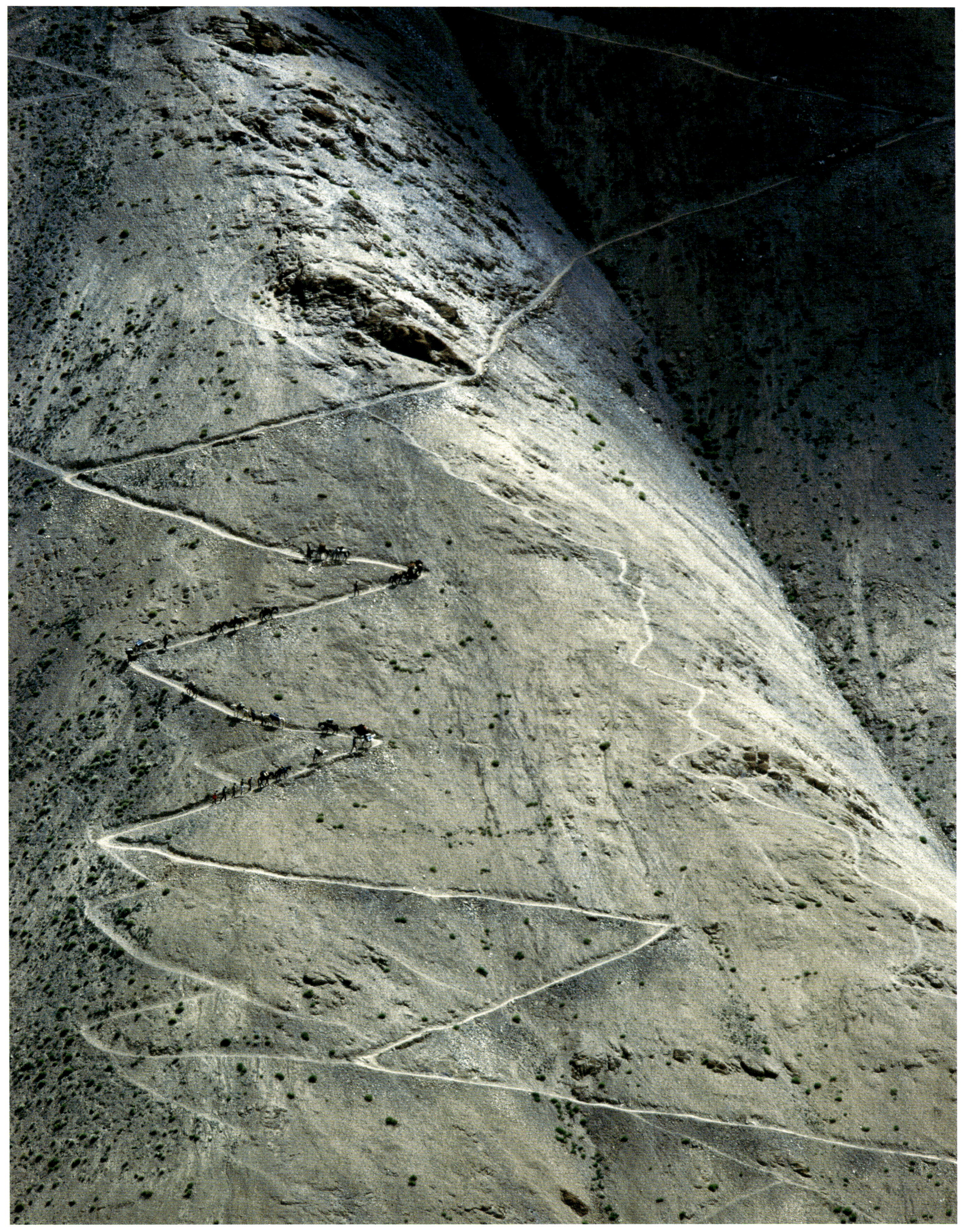

I cannot explain why, for twenty years, my karma has bound me so closely to the tiny Tibetan valleys of Zanskar, north of the Indian Himalayas. In these valleys, in which time has no hold and where I have spent many years, I made friends when first traveling there with Lobsang and Dolma, a couple of young farmers with three barley fields to cultivate and two yaks, ten goats, and one horse to their name. Their son, Motup, was then three years old, and Diskit, his little sister, was just one. Give or take a few years, Lobsang and I are the same age: in Zanskar you can guess people's age not only by their wrinkles but also by their smile. For several summers Lobsang and I traveled up and down the Zanskar valleys, at the pace of his horse's hooves. One evening, sitting by our campfire under the stars, I advised Lobsang, who can neither read nor write, to send Motup to school. "If our paths have crossed this way, Olivier, it is because we have shared the same family in a past life. Make the right decision for Motup, I trust you," he said.

So I took Motup, then age eight, through the mountains to enroll him in the nearest school, the Lamdon Model School in Ladakh, ninety miles from Zanskar. I was twenty-five years old and didn't have a penny to finance Motup's studies, but I placed my trust in my karma to find a solution. For three years, Motup remained a full-time boarder. He couldn't return home because the long school holidays are in winter when the passes connecting Zanskar to the outside world are blocked by snow. During the summer, I acted as a messenger between Motup at school in Ladakh and his parents in Zanskar. But one evening, in the glow of a butter lamp, we decided to bring Motup home for the holidays. The only passable route in winter is the river Zanskar, frozen on the surface, which rushes into a sixty-mile canyon that you have to walk up for six to fifteen days depending on the state of the ice. In January 1988, in the very heart of winter, my wife, Danielle, and I left Leh and our comfortable life, and with Lobsang, Motup, and ten porters drove by jeep on the bumpy track along the Indus River to the mouth of the river Zanskar, known as the Chadar, or frozen river, in winter. Our adventure was about to begin . . .

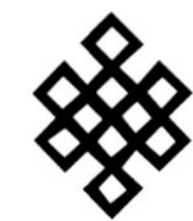

IF OUR PATHS HAVE CROSSED THIS WAY, OLIVIER, IT IS BECAUSE WE HAVE SHARED THE SAME FAMILY IN A PAST LIFE.

We advanced in single file on the Chadar, probing the ice with a long stick to test its solidity. The porters hummed a prayer while we walked beside frozen icefalls, which resembled giants' swords. The presence of death was all around us from our first steps on the river. At times, the stick broke through the ice and plunged into the dark water below. The river curled between the somber gorges and I had to raise my eyes up high to glimpse the sky. When I looked back down again at the icy river snaking before us, I saw the caravan of men, a pathetic sight, one behind the other, and I took fright at the evidence of our insignificance. Well before nightfall, we set up camp at the foot of the towering river wall and gathered the few dead branches we could find. Sitting in a circle around the flames to warm our hands, we made pawa, an insipid mixture of barley flour and melted butter that filled our stomachs. My friends began to murmur a gentle, distant prayer, which filled my soul and made me forget the cold. We then slipped fully clothed into our duvets, while Lobsang and the porters, huddled between us, rolled up in their coats under a blanket of sparkling stars. The silence was barely broken by the gentle crunching of the ice swept away by the river. The temperature was -13°F.

The dawn's cold burned our faces and woke us. Feverishly, we packed up our belongings and walked for three hours until our feet were warm. The sun was excruciatingly slow in reaching the bottom of the gorge, and we made a small fire on a bank to enjoy the supreme happiness of a cup of steaming hot salted butter tea. The sun then hugged us in its rays and I embraced its warmth as a divine gift. A school of life, a school of death: I love the Chadar, which teaches me the dharma, the truth of existence.

After walking for thirteen days, the canyon finally opened out to reveal the wide, pristine valley of Zanskar. We passed through a first village with its huddle of houses, tiny dots in the immensity of the glaring mountains. Following a long day when we made our trail in light snow, we finally reached the valley leading to the solitary house, and Motup picked up speed. At last he was going to be reunited with his mother, his sister, and his white long-haired goats.

For five days, we drank and danced to celebrate the family's reunion. The villagers joined in, swarming to admire the schoolboy, the only educated child in the valley. Diskit clung to her brother's side, asking him to tell her what he had done these last three years. "Atcho, big brother, can you see the moon from your school?" We then packed up our bags to take Motup back to school before the ice broke up. We had traveled one month so that Motup could spend just five days with his family.

On the eve of our departure, we shared a last festive meal of dumplings to which meat had been added, called mok moks. Lobsang and Dolma would never kill an animal, so we chewed on the meat of an old yak that had died from old age in autumn and been preserved for the winter. Dolma served us another bowl of chang, the barley beer she had fermented, before rising to her feet, overcome with emotion, and joining the palms of her hands in our direction: "Olivier, Danielle, we thank you for having allowed Motup to go to school. Please accept to give his sister, Diskit, the same opportunity. Take her with you too tomorrow." The next morning, as we were about to leave, Dolma, her voice shaky with tears, honored us by placing two white tulle scarves on our shoulders: "Olivier, Danielle, I entrust you with my children, they are also yours."

In Tibetan culture, a child is born into a family through the grace of its karma. The parents must do all they can to help him or her on the path to enlightenment, even if this means letting the child go. For twenty years we thus raised Motup and Diskit as our own, traveling each year to show them the world and returning with them to Zanskar to be reunited with their parents. On completion of their education in the best Indian schools, Motup and Diskit could speak four languages: English, French, Hindi, and Tibetan. Motup married Padma, a young Ladakhi woman he met at New Delhi University, and Diskit is now the wife of Angchuk, a young Ladakhi man who acts as an assistant to his uncle, a minister in Kashmir. In Zanskar, surrounded by all the villagers, in the grand tradition, we celebrated the marriages of the two children. Together we, the four parents, danced around the central wooden pole holding up the house and symbolizing the pillar of the Universe. We were in harmony with the stars and honored our mutual karma.

Today, Motup is the father of three children, and Diskit the mother of two. They both opened travel agencies in Ladakh, White Copper Travel and Föllmi Treks & Tours.

Ich kann nicht erklären, warum mein Karma mich 20 Jahre lang so eng mit den winzigen tibetischen Tälern von Zanskar im Norden des indischen Himalaya verbunden hat. In diesen weltfernen Tälern, in denen ich Jahre zubrachte, pflegte ich seit meiner ersten Reise eine enge freundschaftliche Beziehung zu Lobsang und Dolma, einem jungen Bauernpaar aus Zanskar, das drei Gerstenfelder bewirtschaftete und zwei Yaks, zehn Ziegen sowie ein Pferd hielt. Ihr Sohn Motup war damals drei Jahre, Diskit, die Jüngste, nicht einmal ein Jahr. Lobsang und ich haben bis auf wenige Jahre dasselbe Alter: In Zanskar bemisst man das Alter an den Falten der Zeit, aber auch denen des Lächelns. Mit Lobsang durchstreiften wir mehrere Sommer hintereinander die Täler von Zanskar im Rhythmus des Gangs seines Pferdes. Als wir eines Abends unser Nachtlager aufgeschlagen hatten und unter den Sternen am Lagerfeuer saßen, riet ich Lobsang, der weder lesen noch schreiben kann, Motup in die Schule zu schicken. „Wenn sich unser Leben so wie jetzt gekreuzt hat, Oliver", sagte er mir, „dann liegt es daran, dass wir in der Vergangenheit einer selben Familie angehört haben. Triff für Motup die richtige Entscheidung, ich vertraue dir."

Also führte ich Motup, damals acht Jahre alt, aus den Bergen und schrieb ihn in der nächsten Schule ein, der Lamdon Model School in Ladakh, etwa 150 Kilometer von Zanskar entfernt. Ich war damals 25 Jahre alt und hatte kein Geld, um ihm den Unterricht zu finanzieren. Aber ich hatte Vertrauen in mein Karma, das schon eine Lösung finden würde. Drei Jahre lang blieb Motup im Internat, ohne in dieser Zeit auch nur einmal nach Hause zurückkehren zu können, denn die großen Schulferien fielen auf den Winter – eine Zeit also, in der Zanskar durch den Schnee von der Außenwelt abgeschnitten war. Im Sommer fungierte ich als Kurier zwischen Motup in der Schule in Ladakh und seinen Eltern in Zanskar. Dort beschlossen wir eines Abends im Licht einer Butterlampe, Motup über die Ferien nach Hause zu bringen. Der einzige gangbare Weg im Winter war der Fluss Zanskar, der eine 100 Kilometer lange Schlucht durchfließt. Da seine Oberfläche in der kalten Jahreszeit gefroren ist, kann man je nach Zustand des Eises auf ihm nach Zanskar gehen, was ungefähr sechs bis 15 Tage dauert. Im Januar 1988 verließ ich mit Danielle, Lobsang, Motup und zehn Trägern im tiefsten Winter Leh und das schützende Dach über dem Kopf und rumpelte mit dem Jeep den Indus entlang bis zur Mündung des Flusses Zanskar, den man im Winter Chadar, den gefrorenen Fluss, nennt. Das Abenteuer nahm seinen Anfang ...

Wir kämpften uns im Gänsemarsch auf dem Chadar voran. Mit einem langen Stab prüften wir ständig die Festigkeit des Eises vor uns. Die Träger murmelten ein Gebet, während wir an gefrorenen Wasserkaskaden entlangliefen, die uns wie riesige Schwerter entgegenragten. Der Tod begleitete uns seit den ersten Schritten auf dem Fluss. Manchmal durchstieß der Stab das Eis und tauchte in das schwarze Wasser ein. Der Fluss zwängt sich zwischen dunklen Schluchten hindurch, und ich musste den Kopf weit heben, um den blauen Himmel zu sehen. Als mein Blick wieder auf die eisige Schlange des Flusses fiel, sah ich die Menschenkarawane, klein und unbedeutend, und bekam Angst angesichts unserer offensichtlichen Bedeutungslosigkeit. Lange vor Einbruch der Nacht schlugen wir unser Lager am Fuß einer Felswand auf und sammelten die wenigen dürren Zweige, die herumlagen. Später saßen wir um das Lagerfeuer, um unsere Hände zu wärmen und Pawa zuzubereiten, eine Mischung aus Gerstenmehl und zerlassener Butter, die zwar wenig Geschmack hat, aber sättigt. Meine Freunde stimmten ein leises Gebet an, das meine Gedanken abschweifen und mich die Kälte vergessen ließ. Dann schlüpften wir in voller Montur in unseren Daunenschlafsack, während Lobsang und die Träger sich unter einer Decke aus glitzernden Sternen in ihre Mäntel hüllten und zwischen uns legten. Die Stille wurde nur durchbrochen vom leicht knirschenden Eis des Flusses. Das Thermometer zeigte -25 °C.

Die morgendliche Kälte biss uns ins Gesicht und weckte uns. Hektisch packten wir unsere Sachen zusammen und marschierten drei Stunden lang, bis unsere Füße wieder warm waren. Die Sonne kroch viel zu langsam die Felswand herab. Wir machten an einem Steilufer ein kleines Feuer, um uns einen heißen Buttertee zu kochen. Welch ein Genuss! Dann umarmte uns die Sonne und ich genoss ihre Wärme wie ein göttliches Geschenk. Ich liebe diesen Chadar, der Schule des Lebens und des Todes zugleich ist und mich Dharma lehrt, die Wahrheit des Daseins.

Am 13. Tag unseres Marsches öffnete sich die Schlucht endlich zum weiten, makellosen Tal von Zanskar. Wir kamen an einem ersten Dorf aus geduckten Häusern vorbei, die vor der gewaltigen Größe der blendenden Berge noch kleiner wirkten. Nach einem langen Tag, an dem wir unsere Spuren im leichten Schnee hinterließen, gelangten wir endlich in die Talmulde, die zu einem alleinstehenden Haus führte. Motup beschleunigte seine Schritte. Endlich würde er seine Mutter, seine Schwester Diskit und seine Ziegen mit den langen weißen Haaren wiedersehen.

In den nächsten fünf Tagen feierten wir trinkend und tanzend die Wiedervereinigung mit der ganzen Familie und den Dorfbewohnern, die herbeieilten, um Motup zu bewundern, das einzige Kind des Tals, das eine Schule besuchte. Diskit bedrängte ihren Bruder, damit er ihr erzählte, was er die letzten drei Jahre gemacht hatte. „Atcho, großer Bruder, siehst du von deiner Schule aus den Mond?" Dann packten wir wieder unsere Rucksäcke, um Motup rechtzeitig vor dem Eisgang zur Schule zurückzubringen. Ein Monat Reise für fünf Tage bei der Familie …

Am Vorabend unserer Abreise setzten wir uns zu einem letzten Festmahl zusammen. Es gab eine Art Ravioli mit Fleisch, Mok Mok genannt. Weil Lobsang und Dolma niemals ein Tier töten würden, kauten wir auf einem alten Yak herum, das im Herbst an Altersschwäche gestorben und dessen Fleisch für den Winter haltbar gemacht worden war. Dolma drückte uns noch eine Schale Chang in die Hand, das Gerstenbier, das sie vergoren hatte. Dann erhob sie sich sehr bewegt und grüßte uns mit gefalteten Händen. „Olivier, Danielle, wir danken euch dafür, dass ihr Motup gestattet habt, in der Schule heranzuwachsen. Bitte gewährt auch seiner Schwester diese Gnade und nehmt Diskit morgen mit." Am nächsten Morgen war die Zeit des Abschieds gekommen. Mit tränenerstickter Stimme legte uns Dolma zwei Schals aus weißem Stoff um die Schultern: „Olivier, Danielle, ich vertraue euch meine Kinder an. Es sind auch die euren …"

> *„WENN SICH UNSER LEBEN SO WIE JETZT GEKREUZT HAT, OLIVER", SAGTE ER MIR, „DANN LIEGT ES DARAN, DASS WIR IN DER VERGANGENHEIT EINER SELBEN FAMILIE ANGEHÖRT HABEN."*

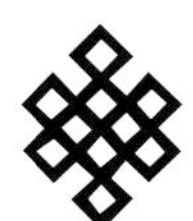

In der tibetischen Kultur wird ein Kind durch die Gnade seines Karmas in eine Familie hineingeboren. Die Eltern müssen alles tun, um es auf seinem Weg zur Erleuchtung zu unterstützen, selbst wenn das heißt, dass sie sich von ihm trennen müssen. 20 Jahre lang zogen wir Motup und Diskit daher wie unsere eigenen Kinder auf, reisten mit ihnen jedes Jahr, um ihnen die Welt zu öffnen, und kehrten mit ihnen nach Zanskar zu ihren Eltern zurück. Nach Abschluss ihrer Ausbildung in den großen indischen Schulen konnten die beiden sich in vier Sprachen – Englisch, Französisch, Hindi und Tibetisch – verständigen. Motup heiratete Padma, eine junge Frau aus Ladakh, die er an der Universität von Neu-Delhi kennengelernt hatte. Diskit wiederum ist mit Angchuk, einem jungen, ebenfalls aus Ladakh stammenden Mann, verheiratet, der für seinen Onkel, einen Minister in Kaschmir, arbeitet. Wir feierten in alter Tradition die Hochzeit der beiden Kinder mit allen Dorfbewohnern in Zanskar. Wir vier Eltern tanzten um den zentralen Holzpfeiler, der das Haus stützt und die Säule des Universums symbolisiert. So waren wir in Harmonie mit den Sternen und ehrten unser gemeinsames Karma.

Motup ist inzwischen Vater von drei, Diskit Mutter von zwei Kindern. Beide betreiben in Ladakh Reiseunternehmen: White Copper Travel und Föllmi Treks & Tours.

Je ne saurais expliquer pourquoi mon karma m'a tant lié durant vingt ans aux minuscules vallées tibétaines du Zanskar, au nord de l'Himalaya indien. Dans ces vallées hors du temps où j'ai passé des années, je me suis lié d'amitié dès mon premier voyage avec Lobsang et Dolma, un jeune couple de paysans du Zanskar qui cultivait trois champs d'orge et élevait deux yaks, dix chèvres et un cheval. Leur fils, Motup, avait trois ans, Diskit, la petite, avait un an à peine. À quelques années près, Lobsang et moi avons le même âge : au Zanskar, l'âge se devine aux rides du temps mais aussi du sourire. Avec Lobsang, nous avons sillonné plusieurs étés de suite les vallées du Zanskar, au rythme du pas de son cheval. Un soir, au bivouac, autour des flammes sous les étoiles, je conseille à Lobsang, qui ne sait ni lire ni écrire, d'envoyer Motup à l'école. « Si nos vies se sont ainsi mêlées, Olivier, c'est que nous avons partagé une même famille dans une vie passée. Prends la bonne décision pour Motup, je te fais confiance », me dit-il.

J'emmène donc Motup, alors âgé de huit ans, par les montagnes pour l'inscrire dans l'école la plus proche, la Lamdon Model School au Ladakh, à 150 kilomètres du Zanskar. J'ai vingt-cinq ans, je n'ai pas un sou pour financer les études de Motup, mais je fais confiance à mon karma pour m'en sortir. Durant trois ans, Motup reste en pensionnat sans pouvoir retourner chez lui : les grandes vacances scolaires ont lieu en hiver alors que les cols pour rejoindre le Zanskar sont bloqués par la neige. Pendant l'été, je sers de messager entre Motup, à l'école, au Ladakh, et ses parents au Zanskar où, un soir, à la lueur d'une lampe à beurre, nous décidons de ramener Motup au pays pour les vacances. Le seul chemin praticable l'hiver est le fleuve Zanskar, gelé en surface, qui s'engouffre dans un canyon de 100 kilomètres que l'on remonte à pied durant six à quinze jours selon l'état de la glace. En janvier 1988, au plus cruel de l'hiver, nous quittons Leh et notre confort avec Danielle, Lobsang, Motup et dix porteurs, et cahotons en jeep le long de l'Indus jusqu'à l'embouchure du fleuve Zanskar, que l'on appelle en hiver le Tchadar, le fleuve gelé. L'aventure commence...

Nous progressons en file indienne sur le Tchadar en sondant la glace avec un long bâton pour en éprouver la solidité. Les porteurs fredonnent une prière, tandis que nous longeons des cascades figées, telles des épées géantes. La présence de la mort ne nous quitte plus dès les premiers pas sur le fleuve. Parfois, le bâton passe au travers de la glace et plonge dans l'eau noire. Le fleuve s'incurve entre les gorges sombres et je dois lever haut les yeux pour apercevoir le ciel. Lorsque je les pose à nouveau sur le serpent de glace, j'aperçois la caravane des hommes, les uns derrière les autres, dérisoires, et je prends peur devant l'évidence de notre insignifiance. Bien avant la nuit, nous établissons notre bivouac au pied de la paroi et dénichons de rares branchages morts. En cercle autour des flammes pour réchauffer nos mains, nous cuisinons de la pawa, une mixture insipide de farine d'orge et de beurre fondu qui nous cale. Mes amis amorcent une prière douce, lointaine, qui me transporte et me fait oublier le froid. Puis nous nous glissons tout habillés dans nos duvets, tandis que Lobsang et les porteurs se serrent entre nous, roulés dans leurs manteaux sous une couverture d'étoiles scintillantes. Le silence est à peine troublé par la glace que le fleuve charrie en un léger crissement. Il fait moins vingt-cinq degrés.

> *SI NOS VIES SE SONT AINSI MÊLÉES, OLIVIER, C'EST QUE NOUS AVONS PARTAGÉ UNE MÊME FAMILLE DANS UNE VIE PASSÉE.*

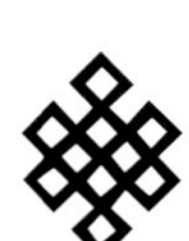

Le froid de l'aube nous brûle le visage et nous réveille. Fébrilement, nous paquetons nos affaires et marchons trois heures jusqu'à réchauffer nos pieds. Le soleil descend trop lentement le long de la paroi et nous faisons un maigre feu sur une berge pour goûter au bonheur suprême d'un thé salé au beurre brûlant. Puis le soleil nous étreint et j'embrasse sa chaleur comme un cadeau divin. École de la vie, école de la mort, j'aime ce Tchadar qui m'enseigne le dharma, la vérité de l'existence.

Au treizième jour de marche, le canyon s'ouvre enfin sur la vallée évasée du Zanskar, immaculée. Nous passons un premier village de quelques maisons blotties, minuscules dans l'immensité des montagnes aveuglantes. Après une longue journée à faire la trace dans la neige légère, nous parvenons enfin dans le vallon qui mène à la maison solitaire, et Motup force le pas. Enfin, il va retrouver sa mère, sa sœur, Diskit, et ses chèvres aux longs poils blancs.

Cinq jours durant, nous buvons, dansons pour fêter nos retrouvailles avec toute la famille et les villageois qui accourent pour admirer l'écolier, le seul enfant instruit de la vallée. Diskit talonne son frère pour qu'il lui raconte ce qu'il a fait pendant trois ans. « Atcho, grand frère, est-ce que tu vois la lune de ton école ? » Puis nous paquetons nos sacs pour ramener Motup à l'école avant la débâcle des glaces. Un mois de voyage pour cinq jours en famille…

La veille de notre départ, nous partageons un dernier repas de fête, des raviolis enrichis de viande : les mok mok. Lobsang et Dolma ne tueraient jamais un animal ; nous mastiquons un vieux yak mort de vieillesse à l'automne et conservé pour l'hiver. Dolma nous serre encore un bol de tchang, la bière d'orge qu'elle a fermentée, puis elle se lève très émue et joint les mains vers nous : « Olivier, Danielle, nous vous remercions d'avoir permis à Motup de grandir à l'école. S'il vous plaît, acceptez de donner la même chance à sa sœur, Diskit, repartez avec elle aussi, demain… » Le lendemain matin, au moment du départ, des larmes dans la voix, Dolma nous honore de deux foulards de tulle blanc sur les épaules : « Olivier, Danielle, je vous confie mes enfants, ce sont aussi les vôtres… »

Dans la culture tibétaine, un enfant naît au sein de la famille par la grâce de son karma. Les parents doivent tout faire pour l'aider sur son chemin d'éveil, quitte à s'en séparer. Pendant vingt ans, nous avons donc élevé Motup et Diskit comme nos propres enfants, voyageant chaque année pour les ouvrir au monde, retournant avec eux au Zanskar auprès de leurs parents. À la fin de leurs études dans des grandes écoles indiennes, Motup et Diskit s'expriment en quatre langues : l'anglais, le français, l'hindi et le tibétain. Motup a épousé Padma, une jeune Ladakhie rencontrée à l'université de New Delhi. Diskit est mariée avec Angchuk, un jeune Ladakhi qui seconde son oncle, ministre au Cachemire. Entourés de tous les villageois, dans la grande tradition, nous avons célébré au Zanskar le mariage des deux enfants et nous, les quatre parents, avons dansé autour du poteau de bois central qui soutient la maison et symbolise le pilier de l'univers. Nous étions ainsi en harmonie avec les astres et honorions notre karma commun.

Motup est aujourd'hui père de trois enfants, Diskit est mère de deux enfants. Tous deux ont ouvert une agence de voyage au Ladakh : White Copper Travel et Föllmi Treks & Tours.

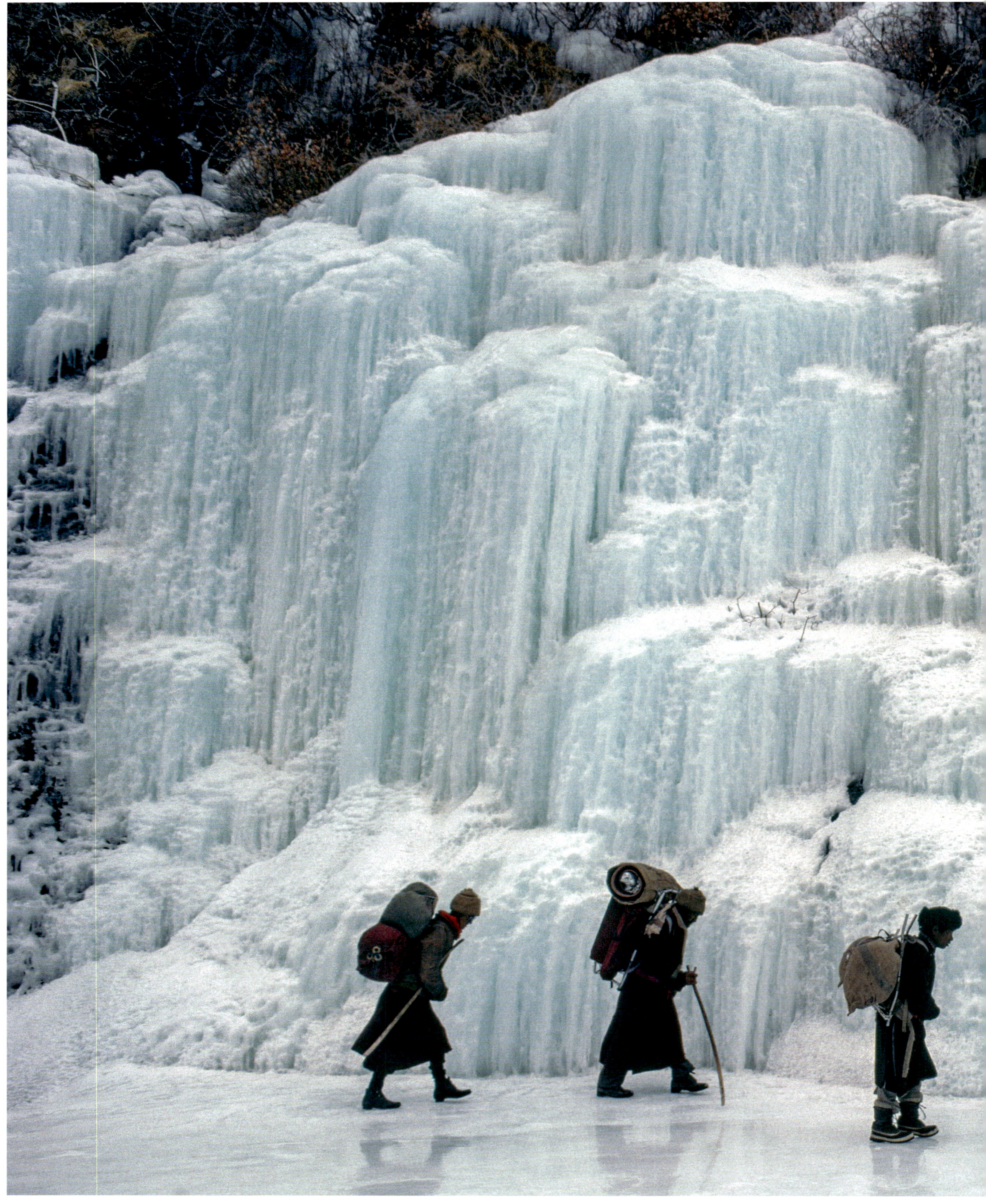

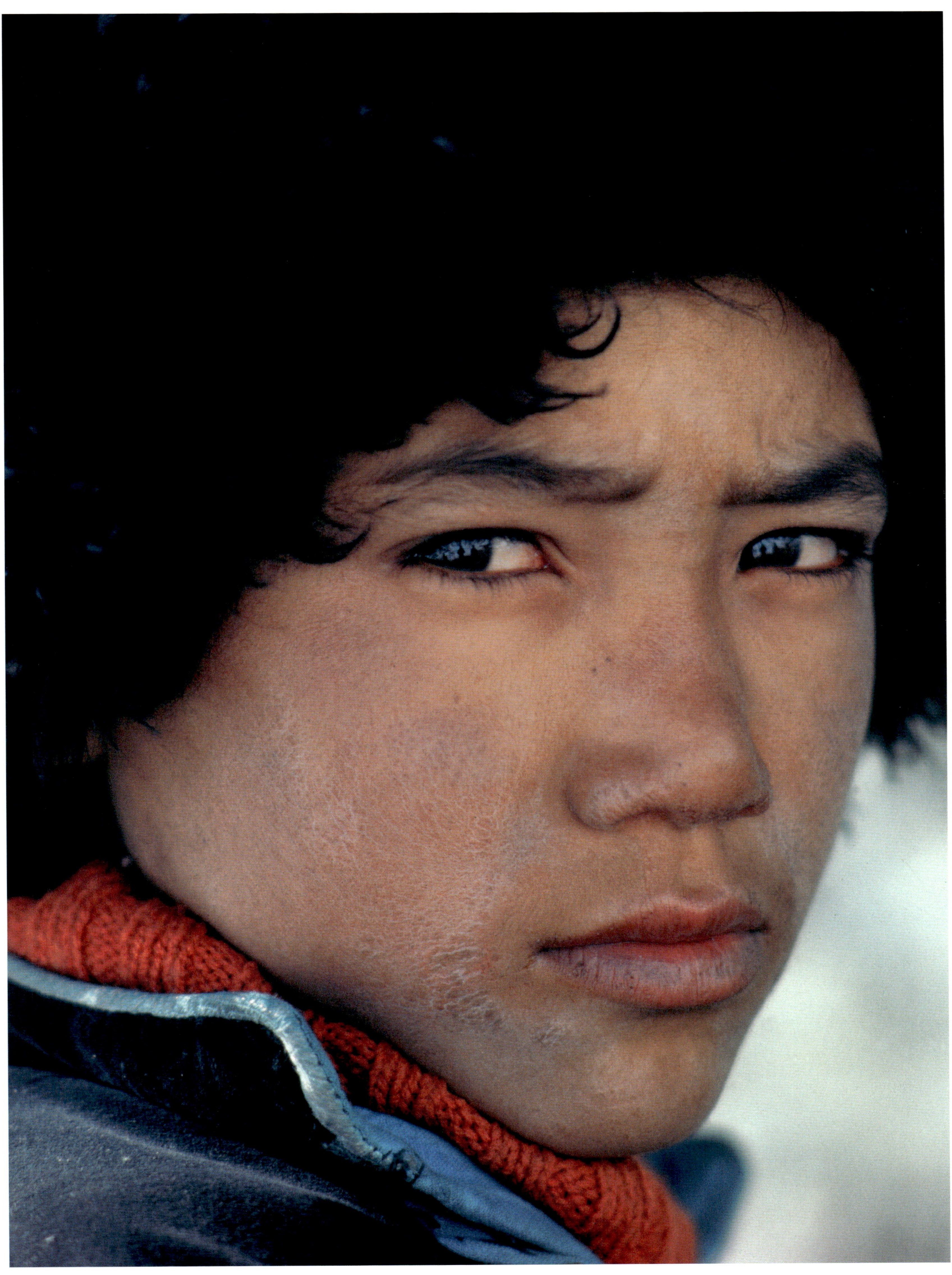

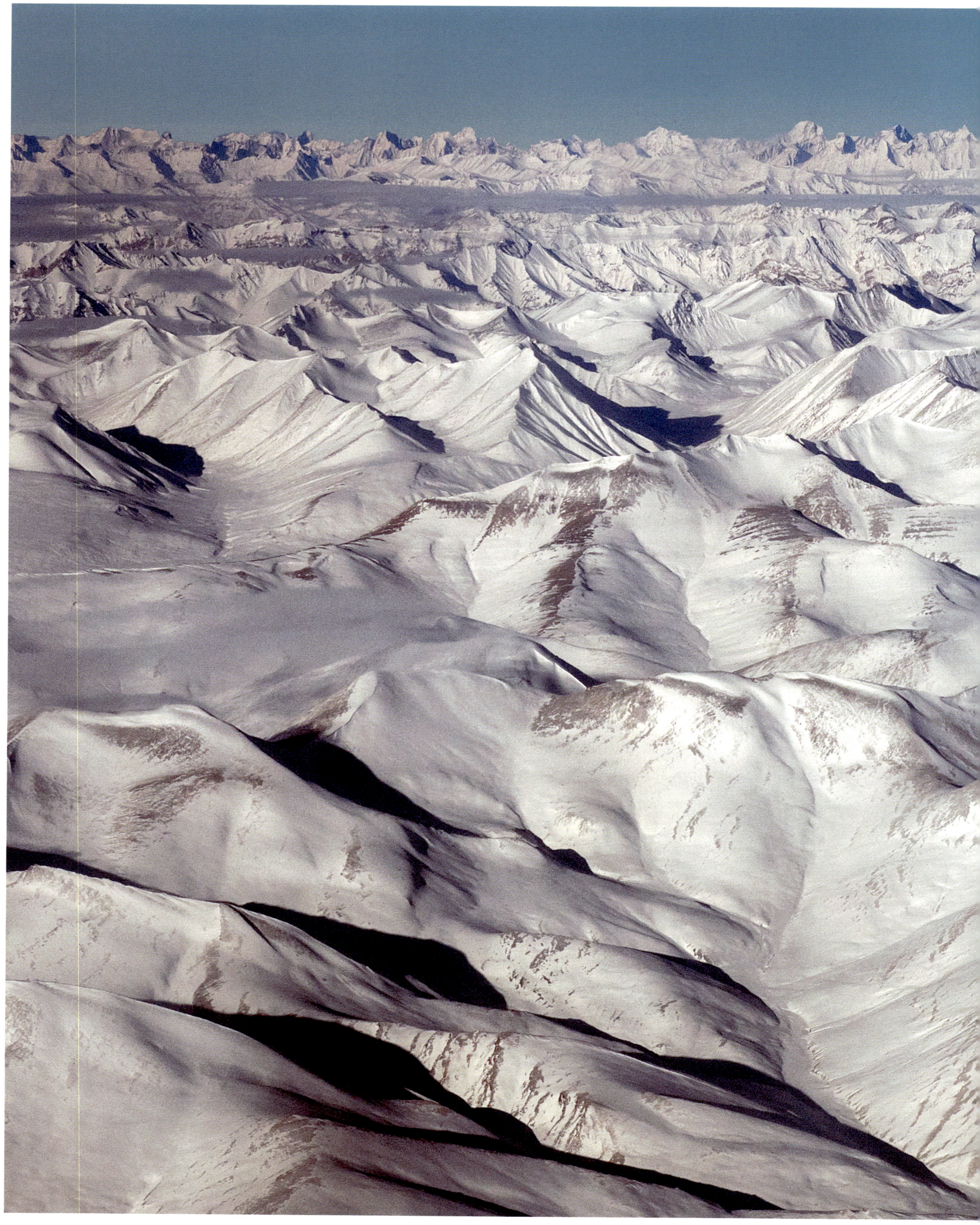

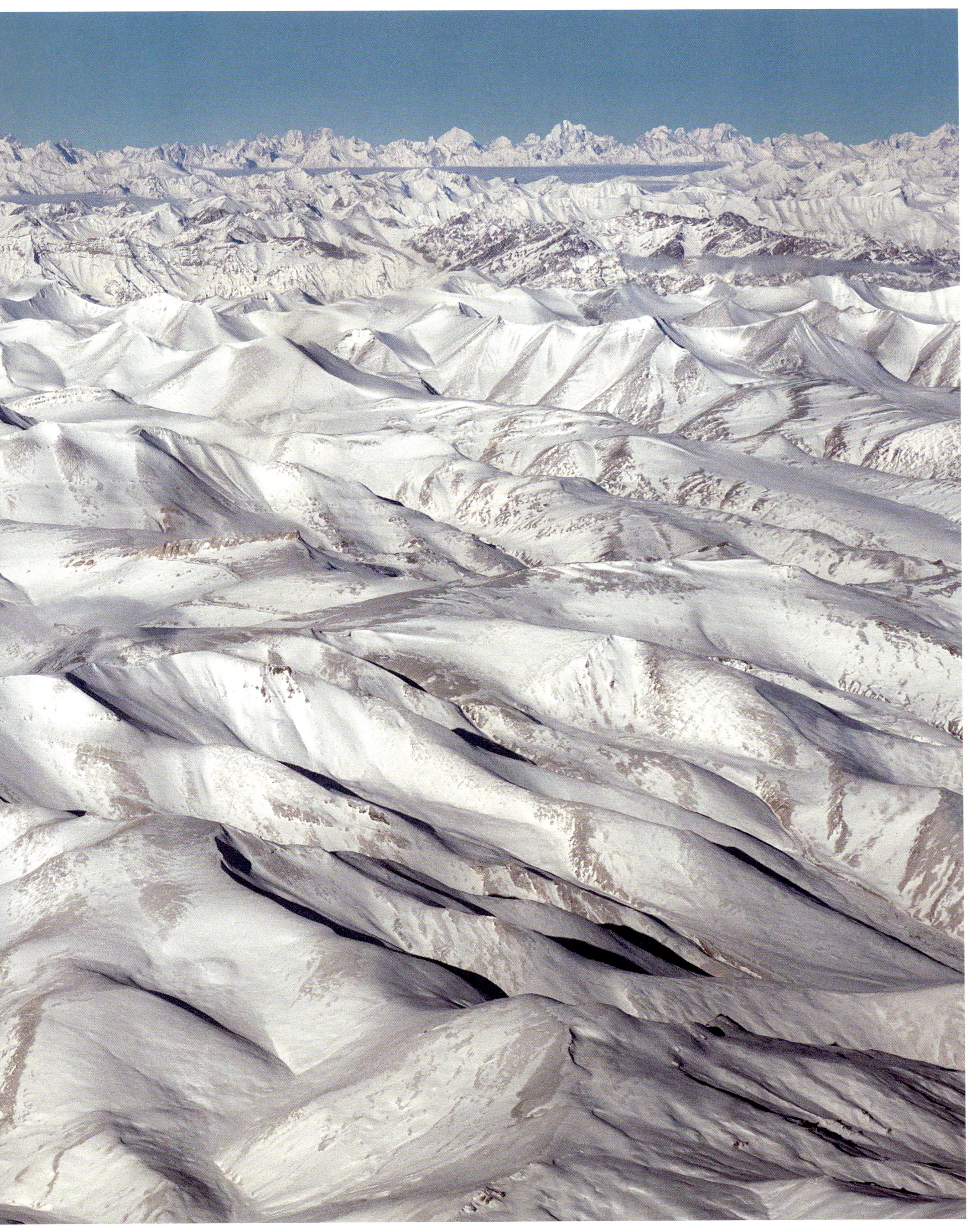

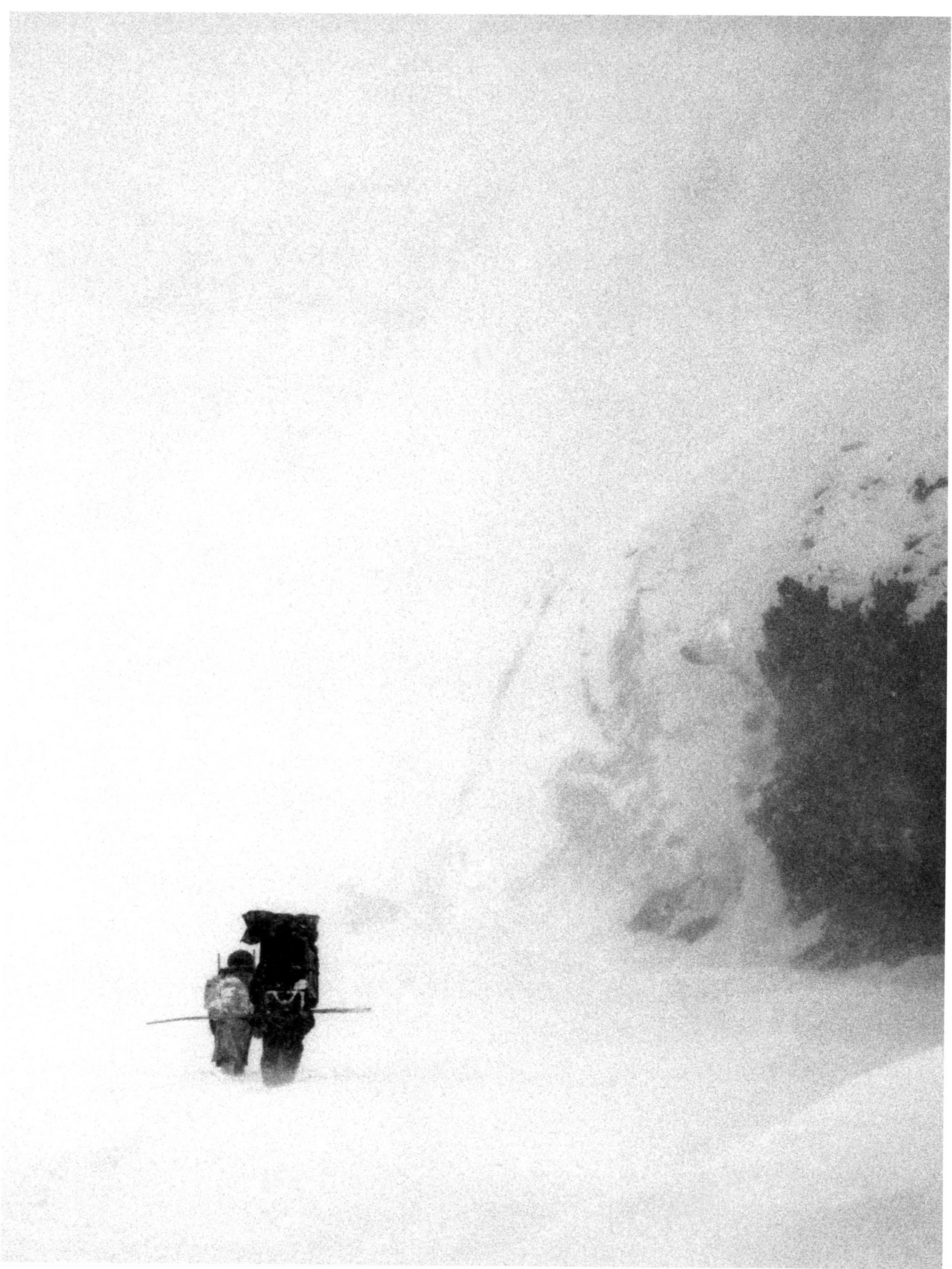

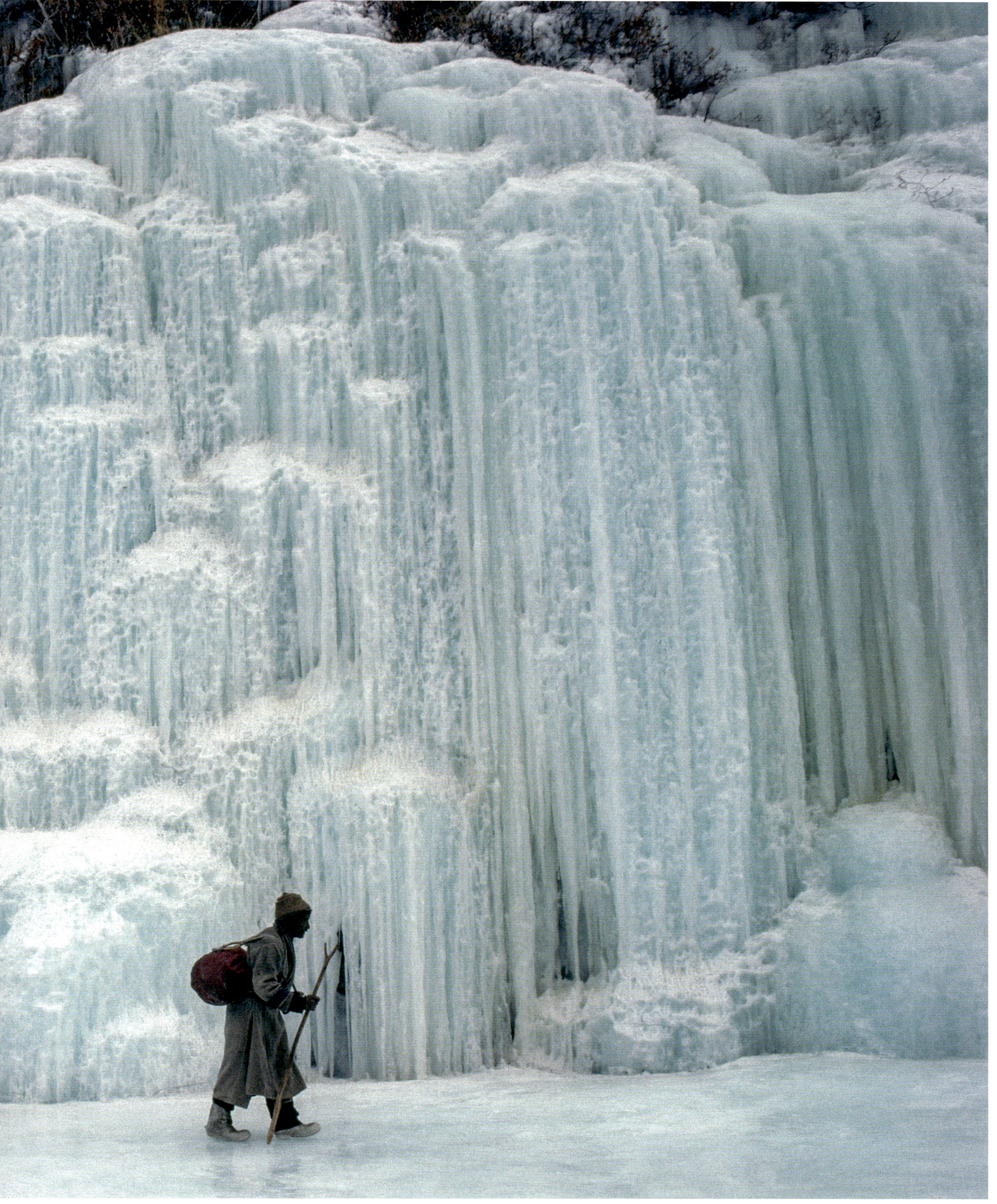

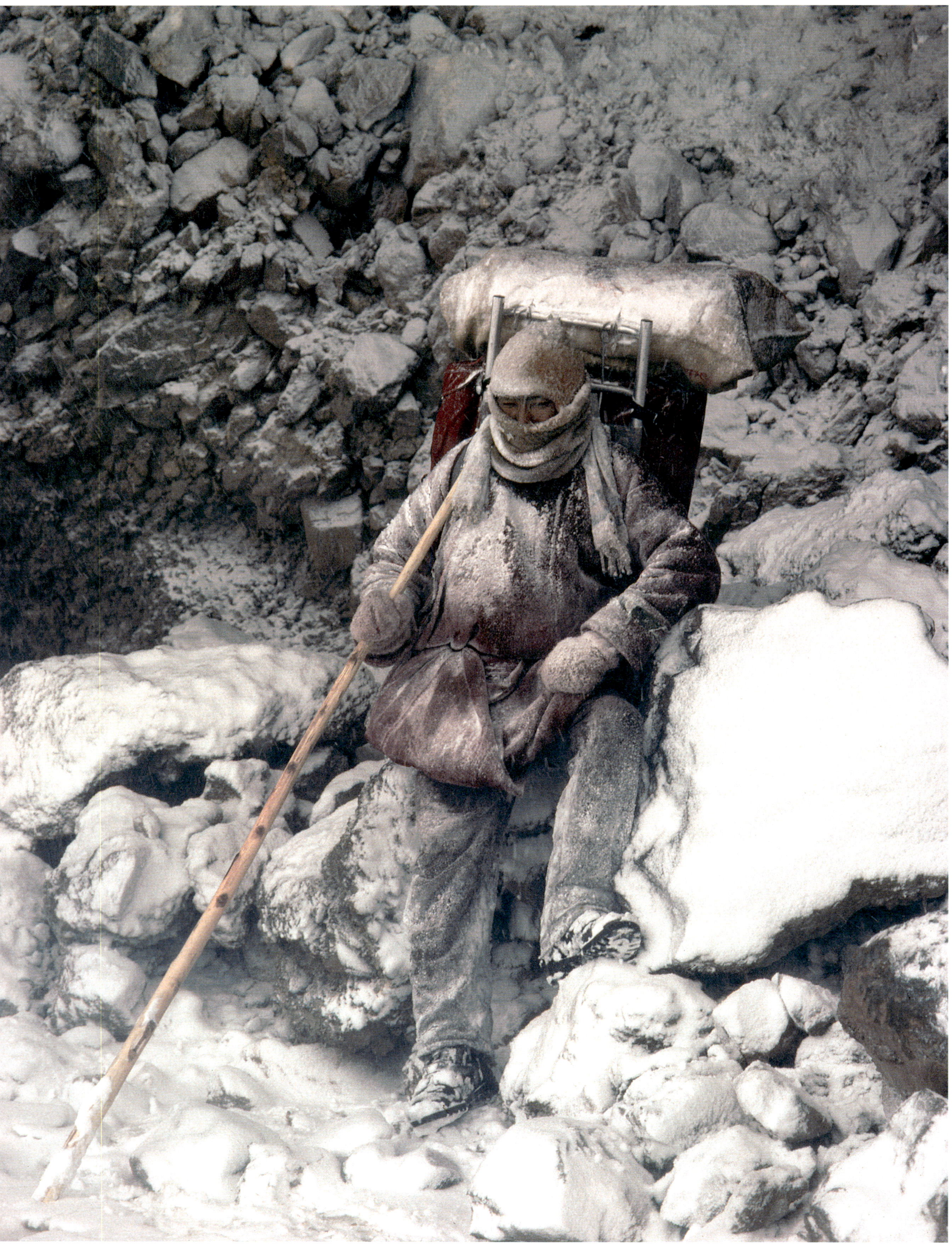

Depending on the state of the ice, we need to walk between six and fifteen days to cover the full length of the Zanskar River, the only route in winter to reach the Ladakh valleys and the nearest school, where Motup and Diskit are going to study.

Je nach Zustand des Eises dauert der Marsch auf dem Zanskar sechs bis 15 Tage. Er ist im Winter der einzig gangbare Weg zwischen den Tälern von Ladakh und der nächstgelegenen Schule – jener, die auch Motup und Diskit besuchten.

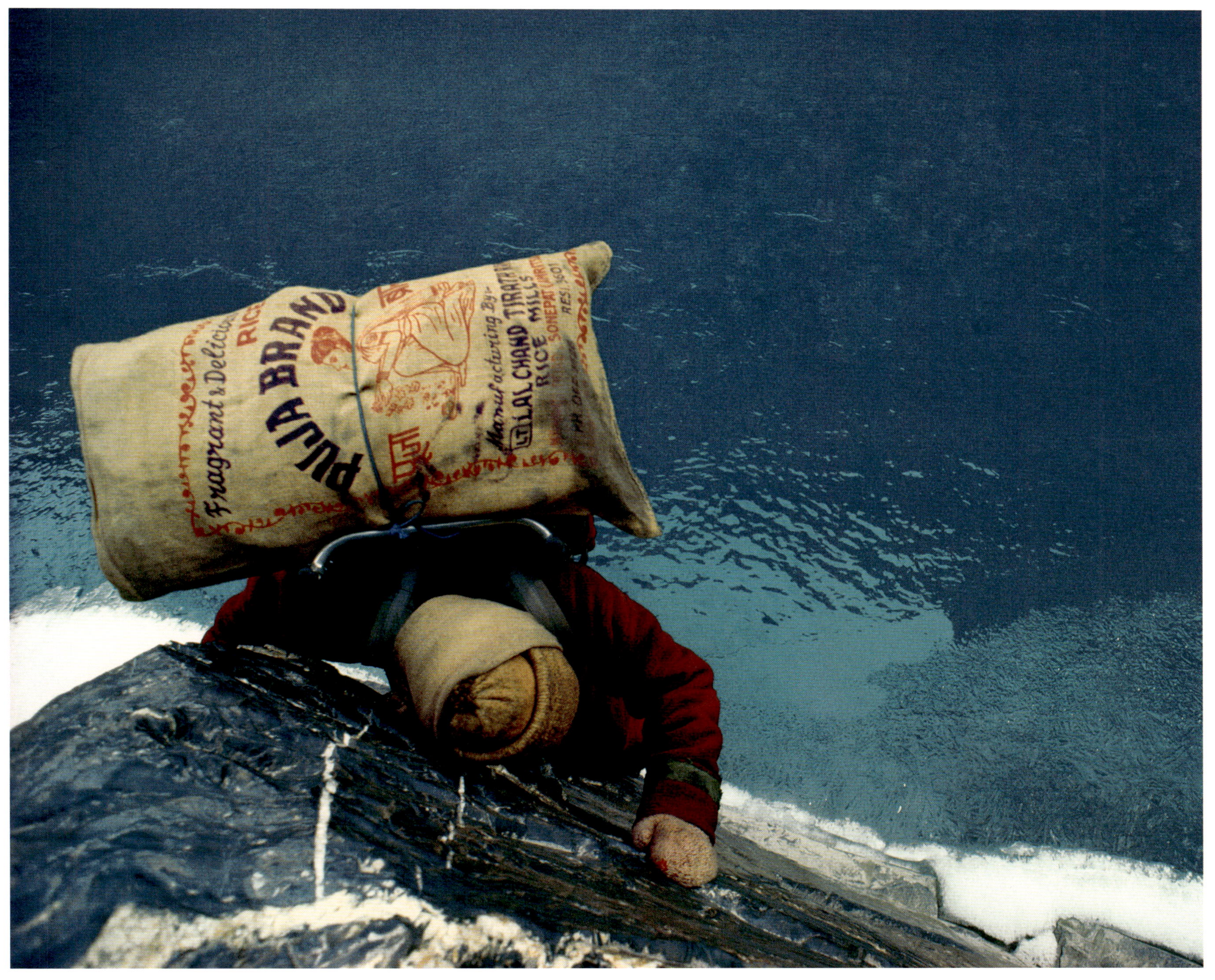

Selon l'état de la glace, six à quinze jours de marche sont nécessaires pour parcourir le fleuve Zanskar, le seul chemin en hiver pour rejoindre les vallées du Ladakh et l'école la plus proche où partent étudier Motup et Diskit.

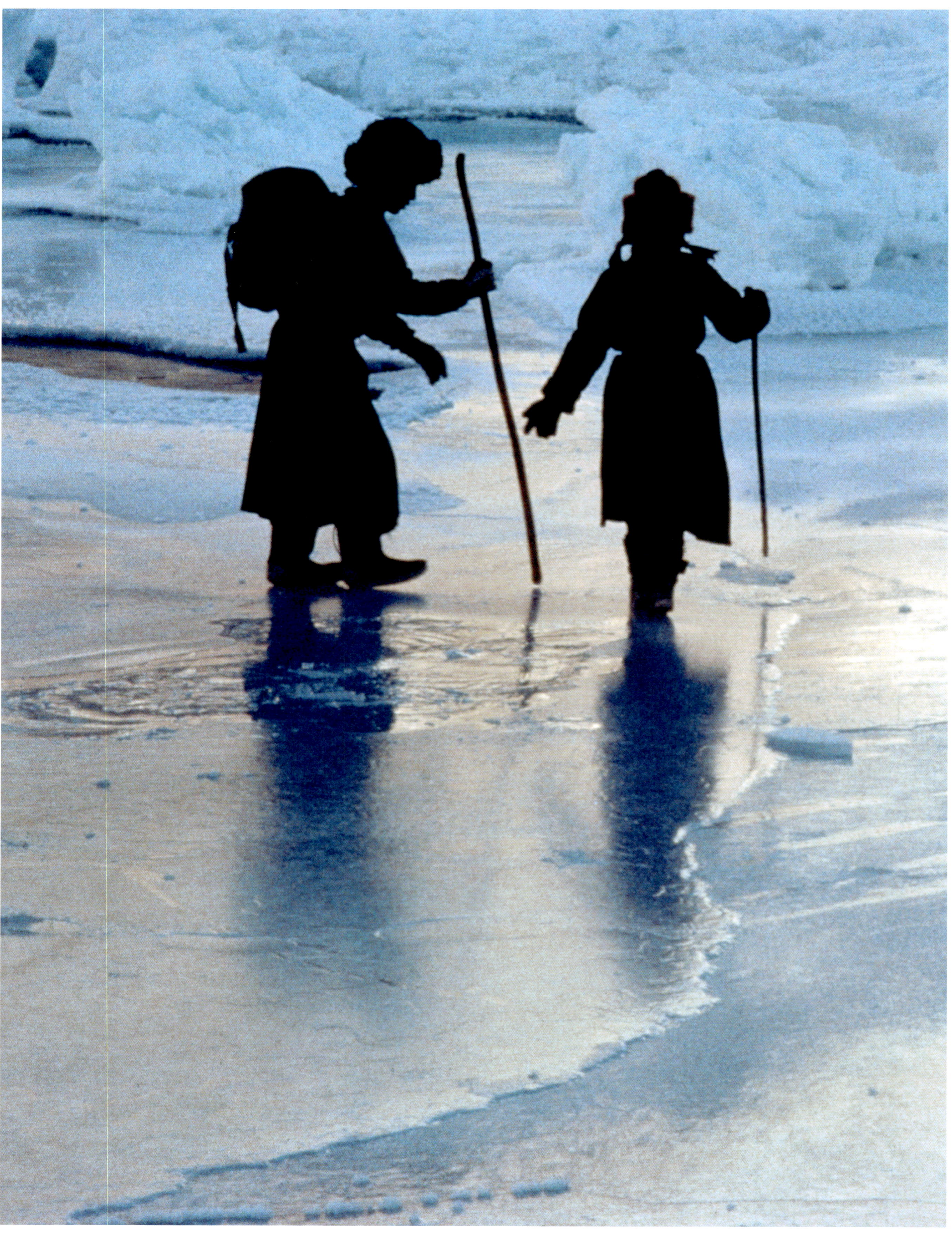

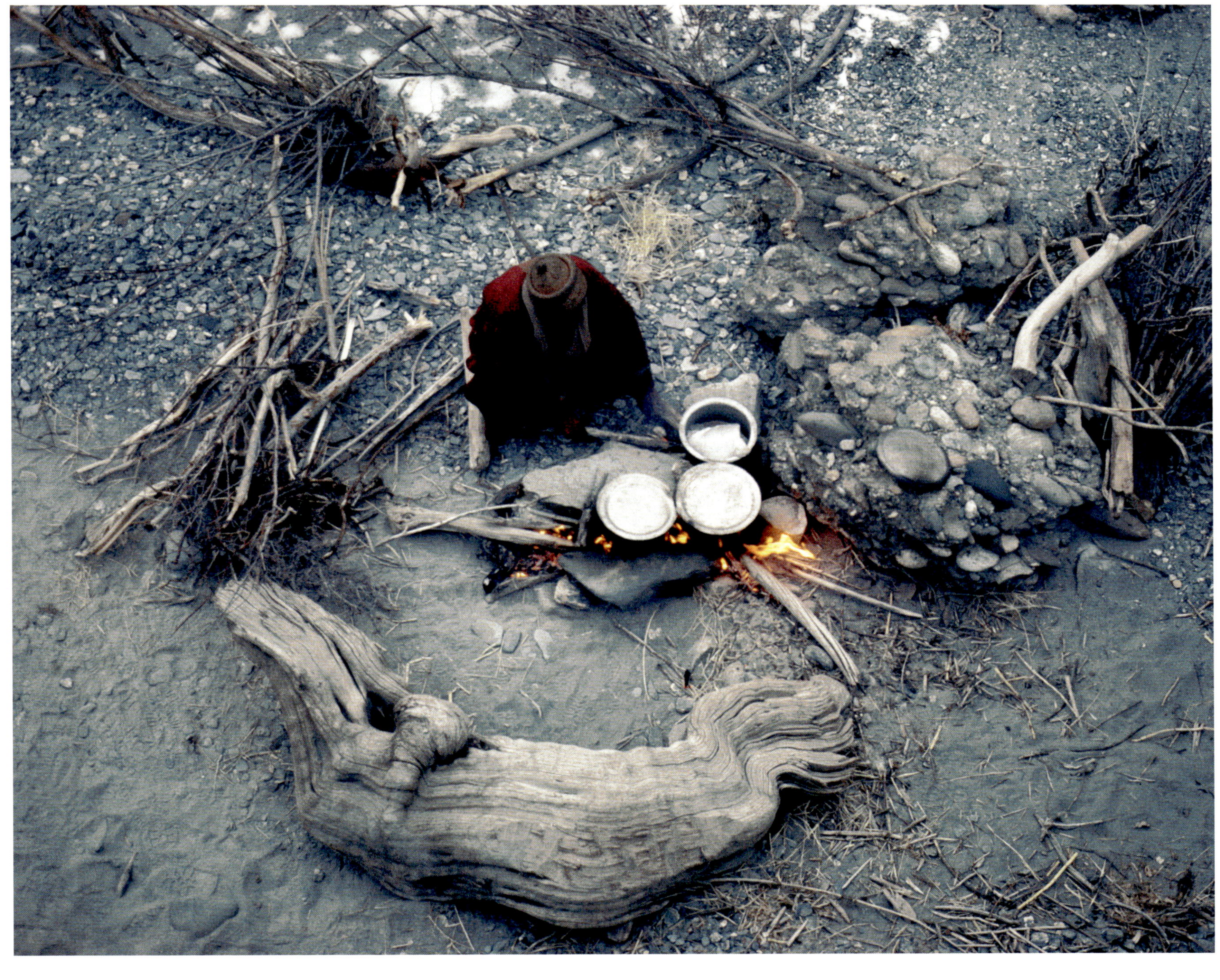

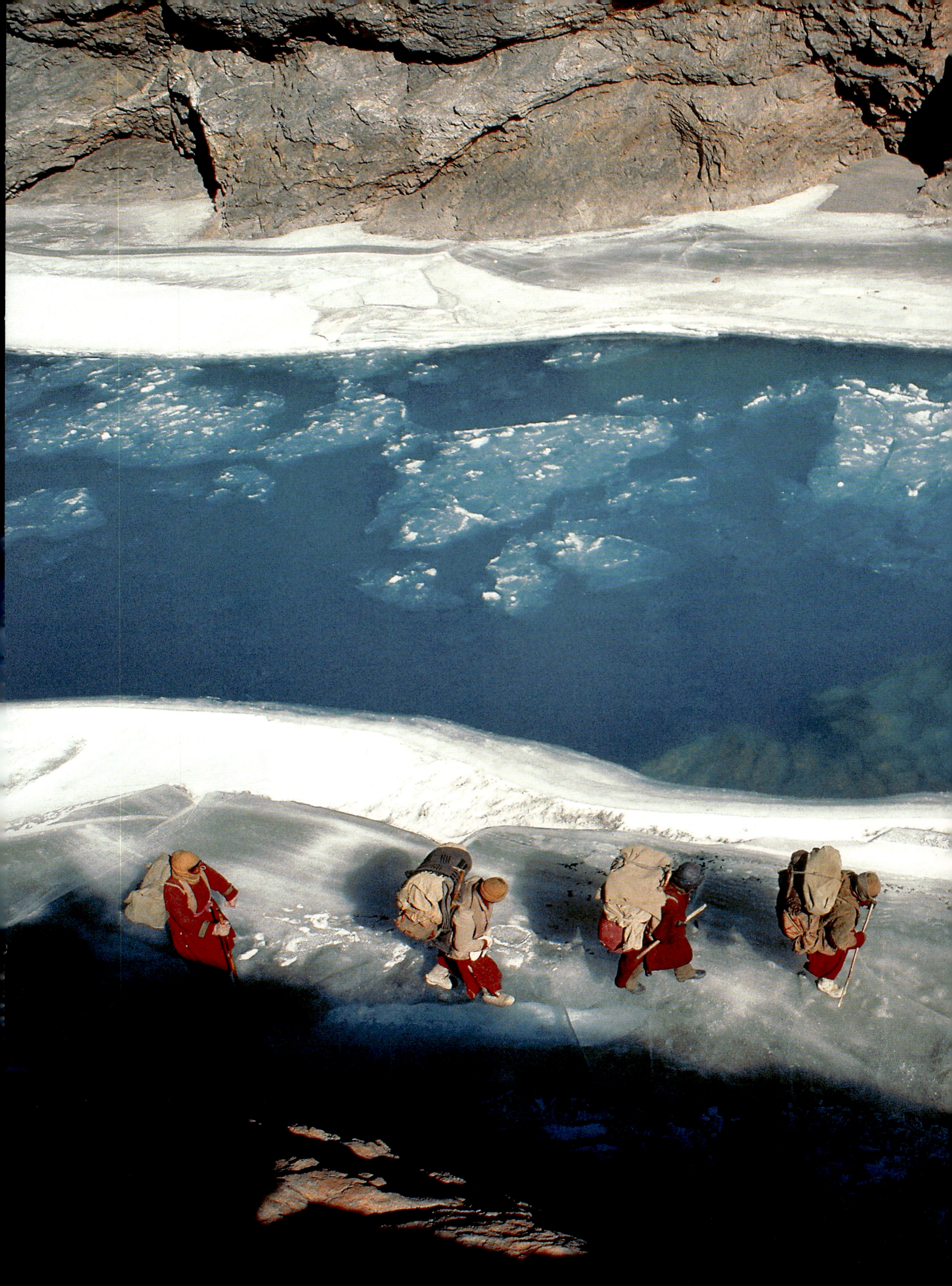

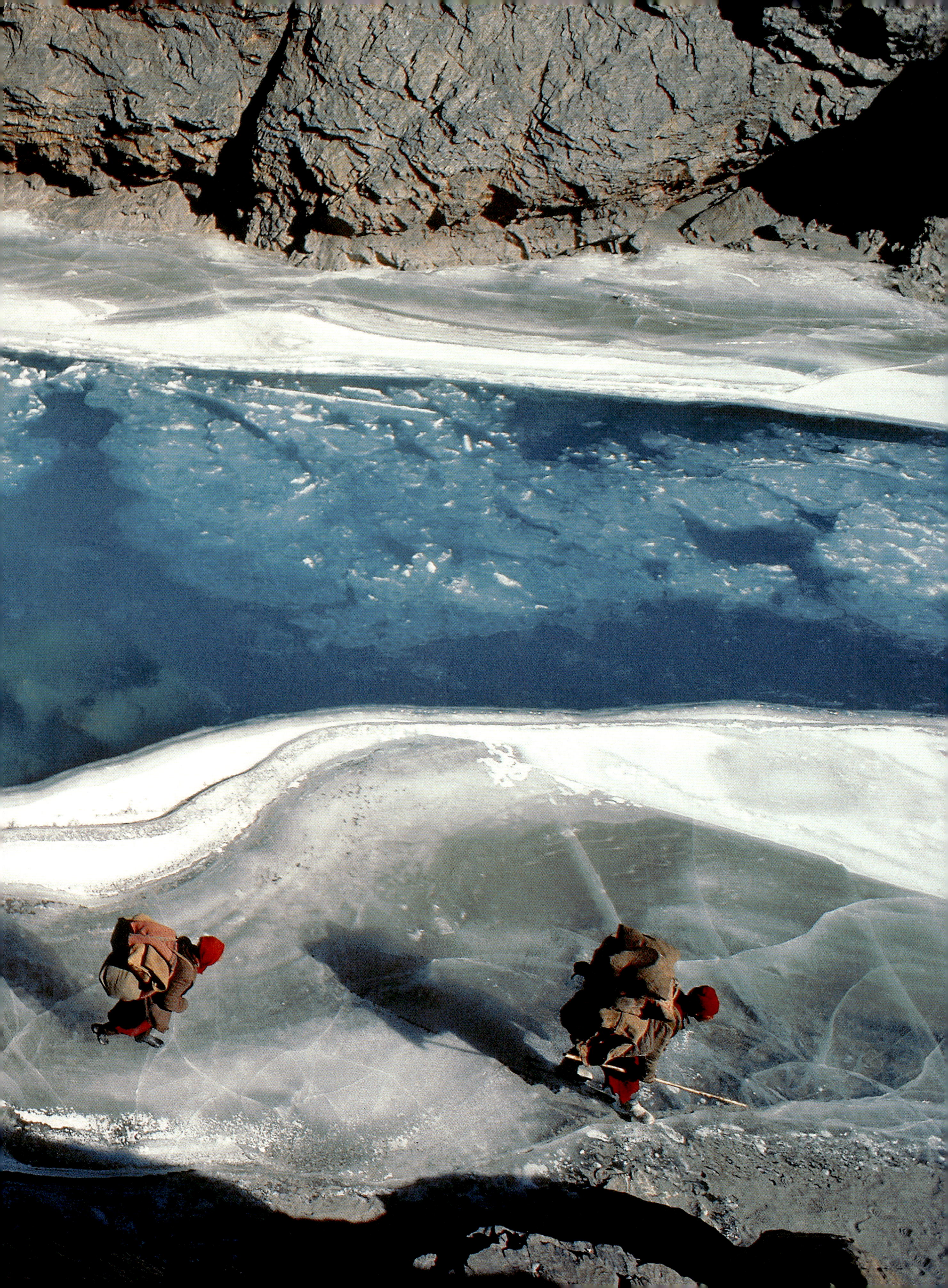

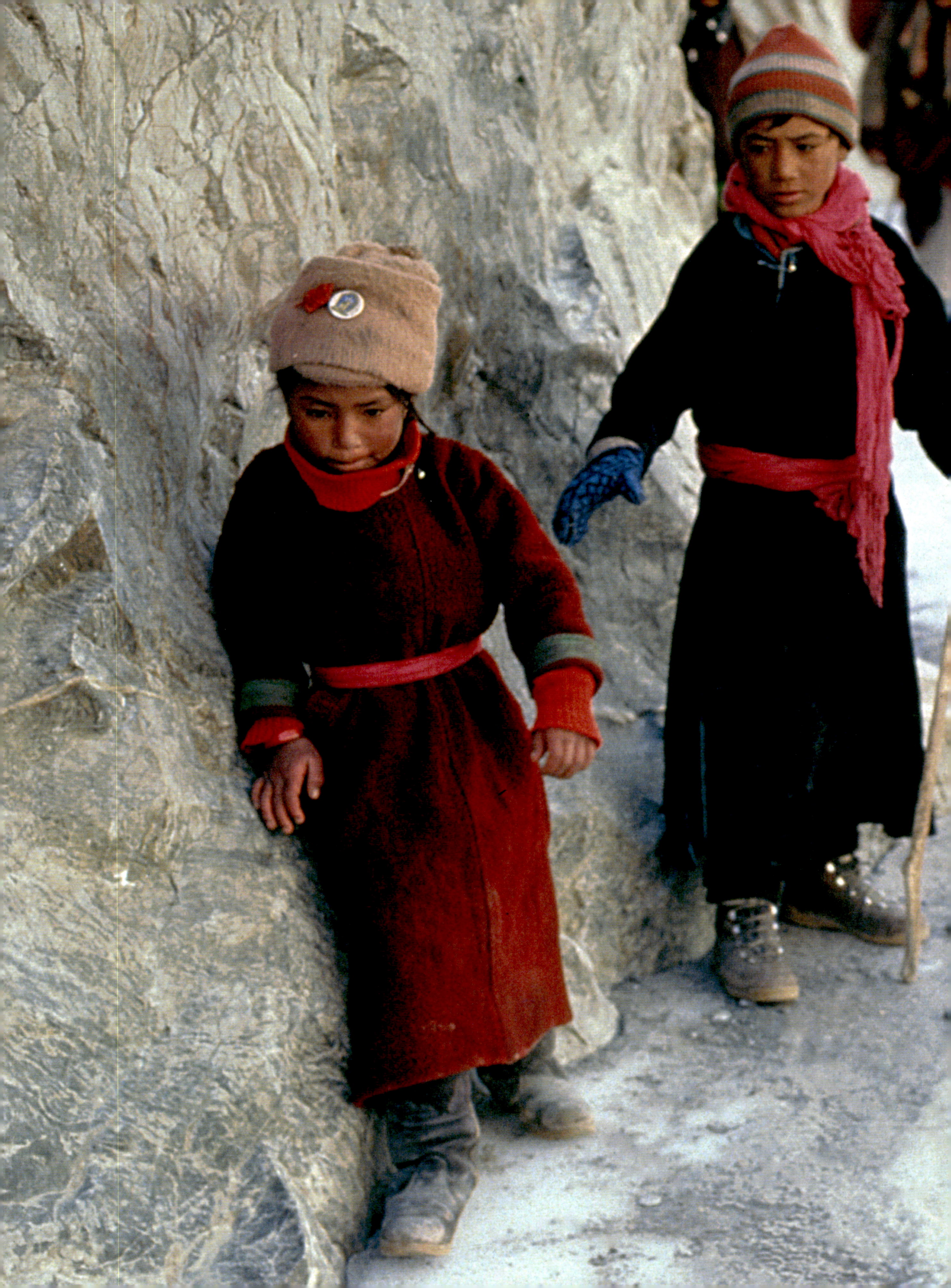

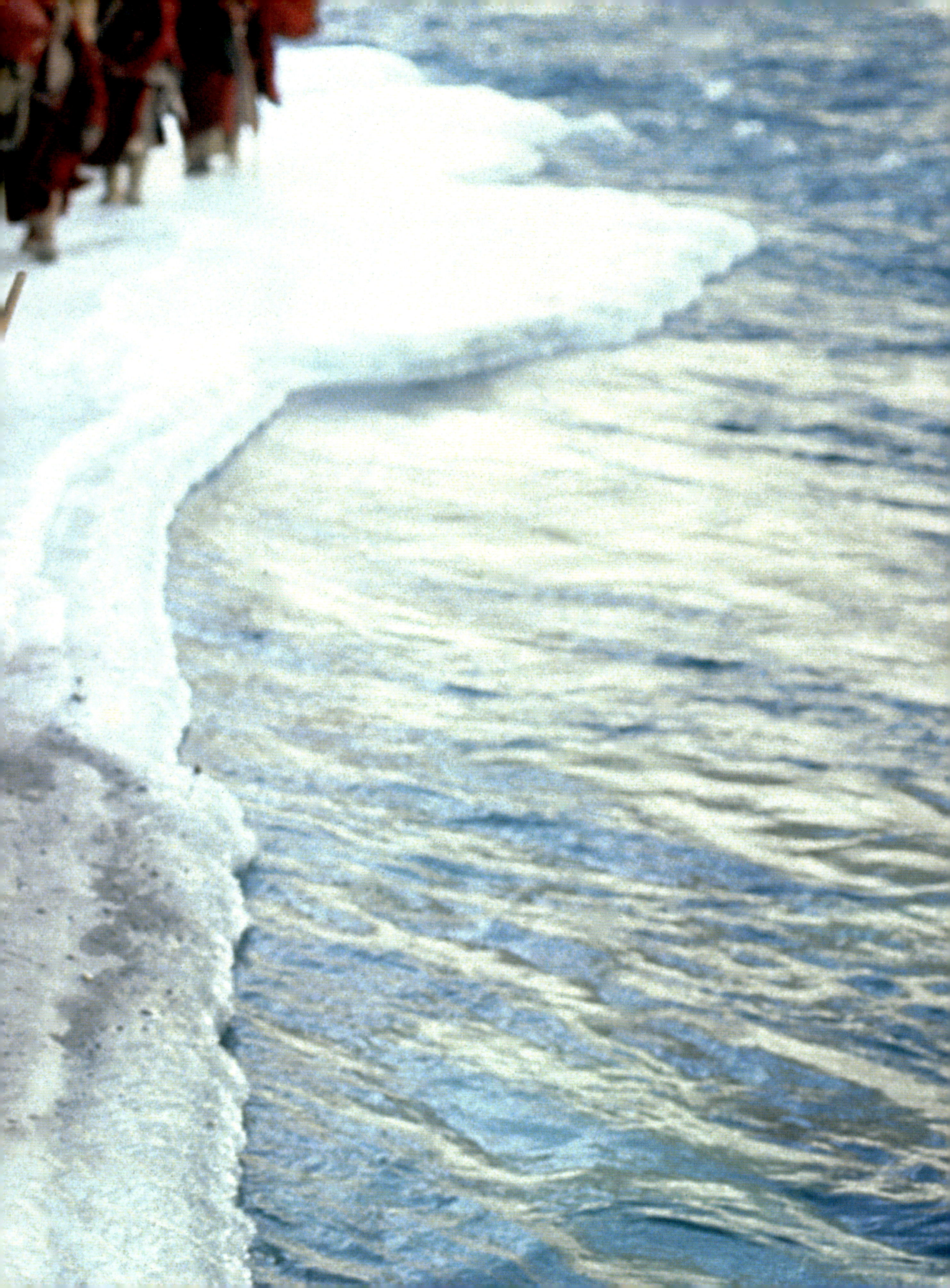

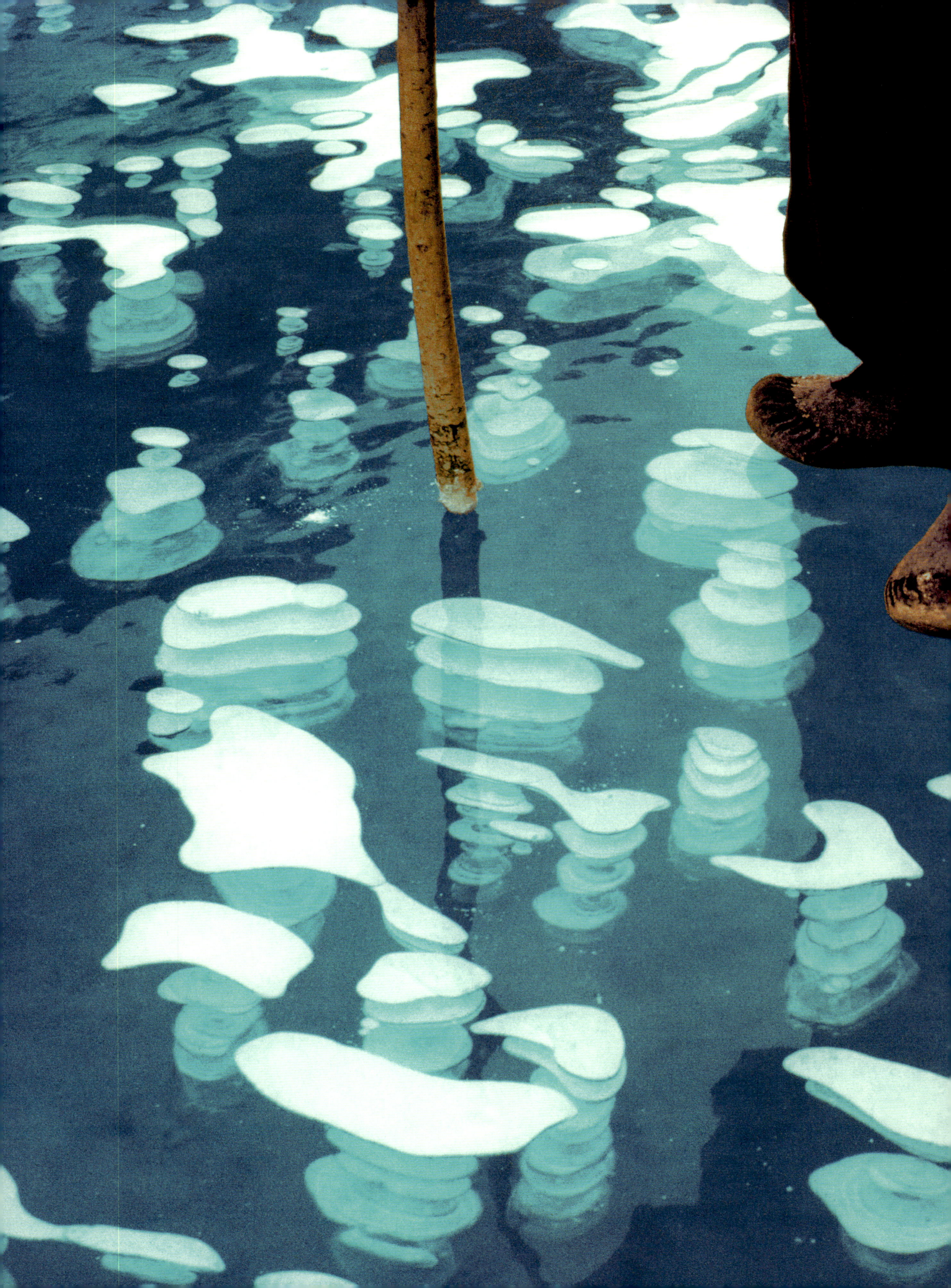

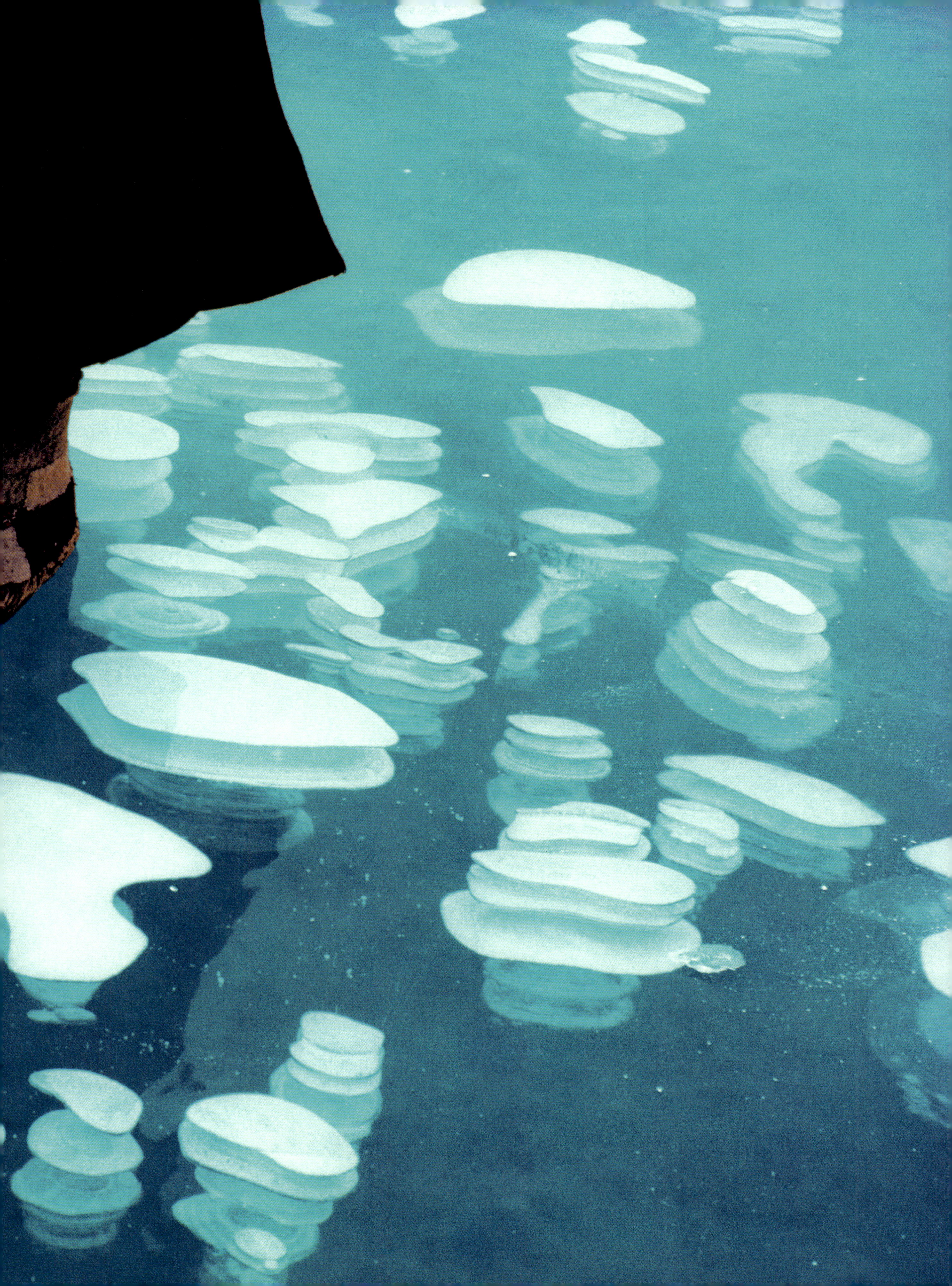

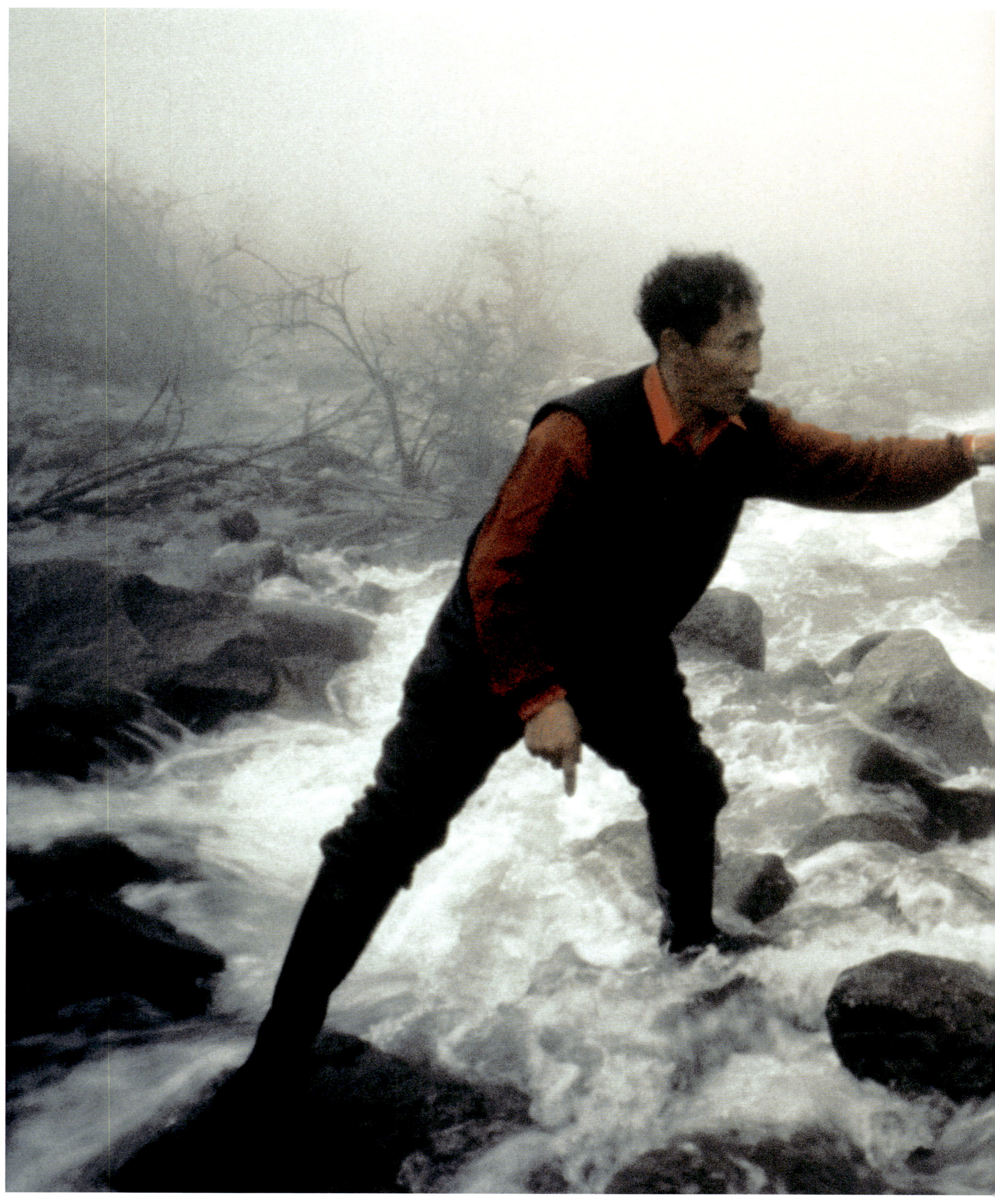

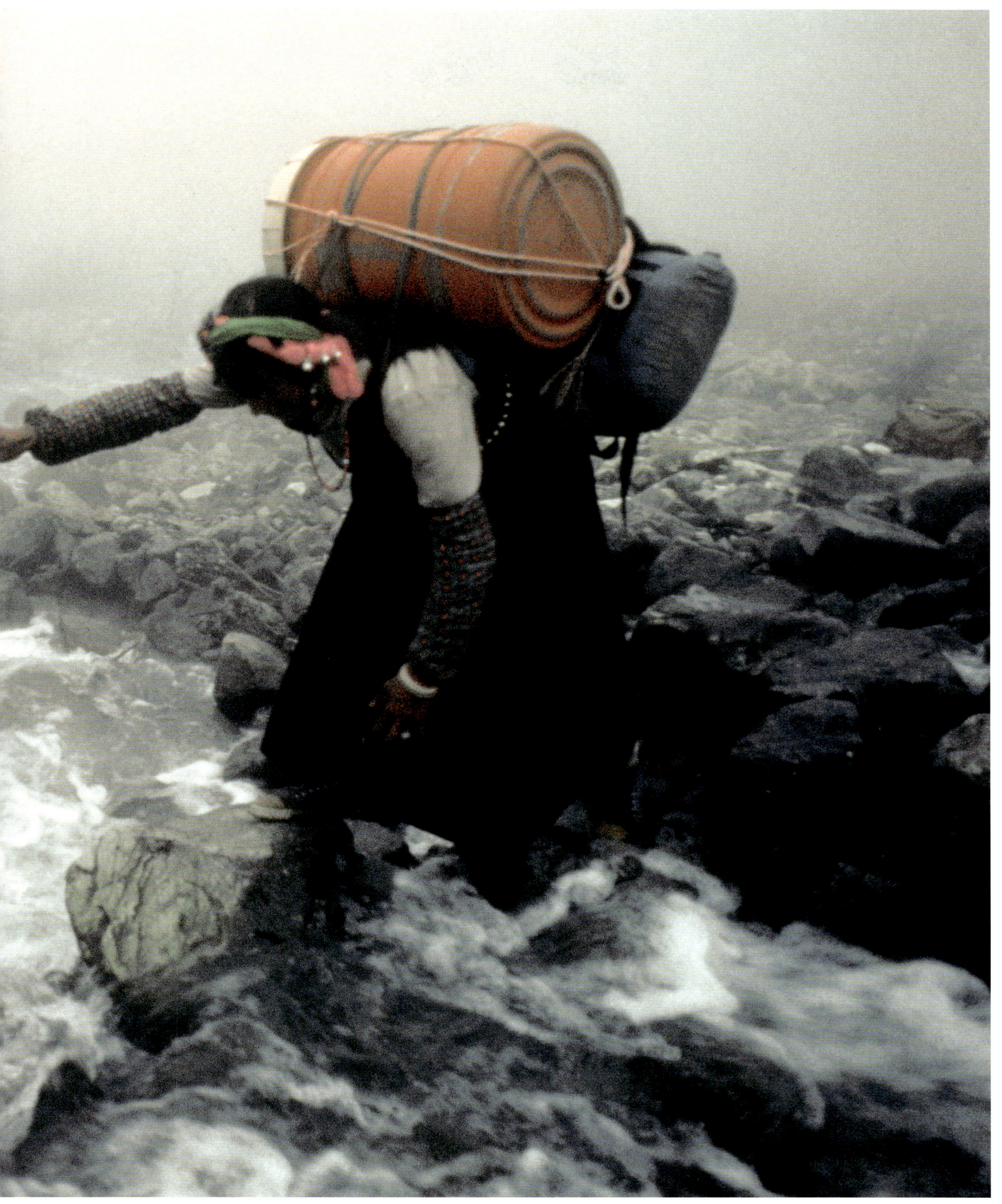

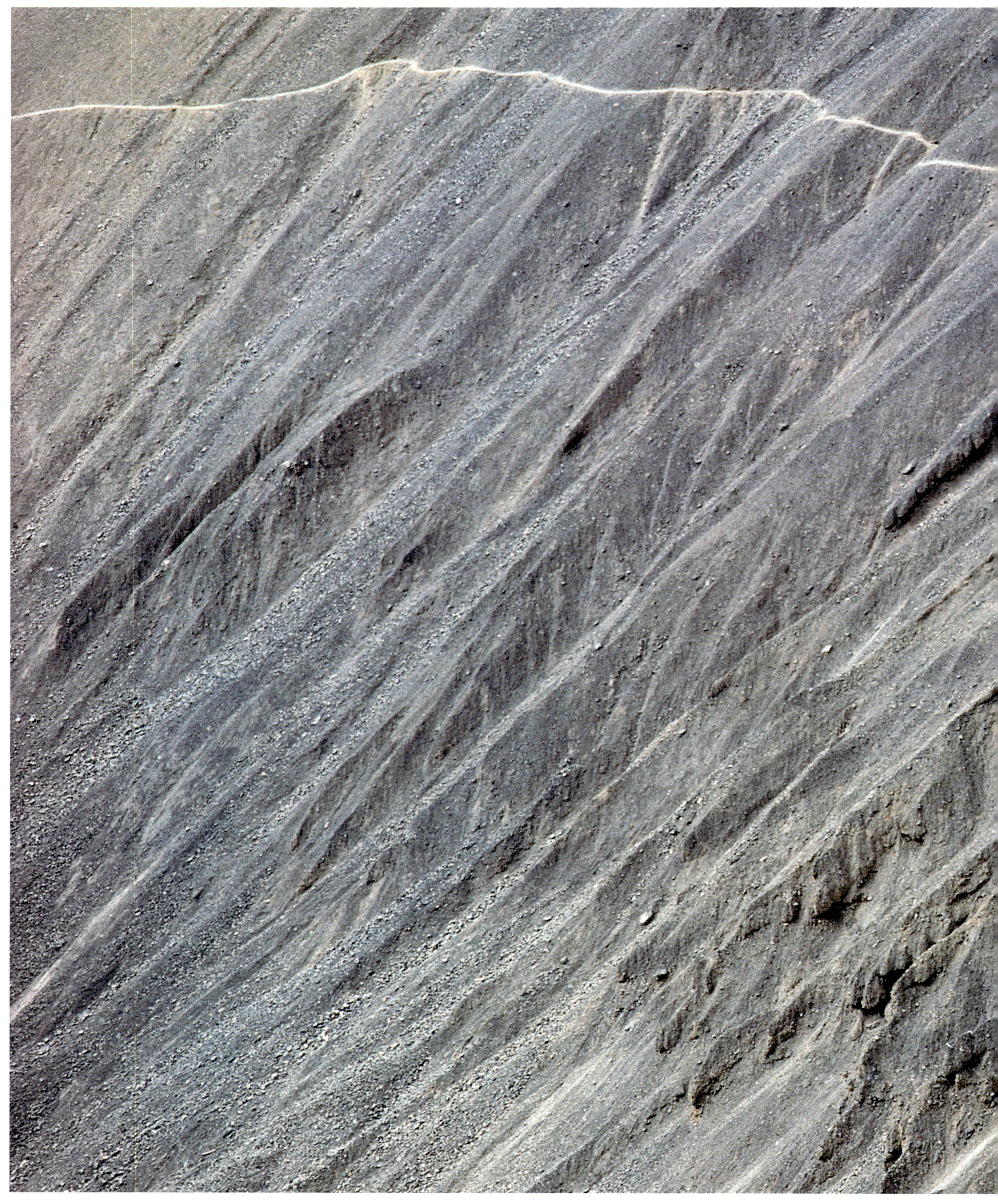

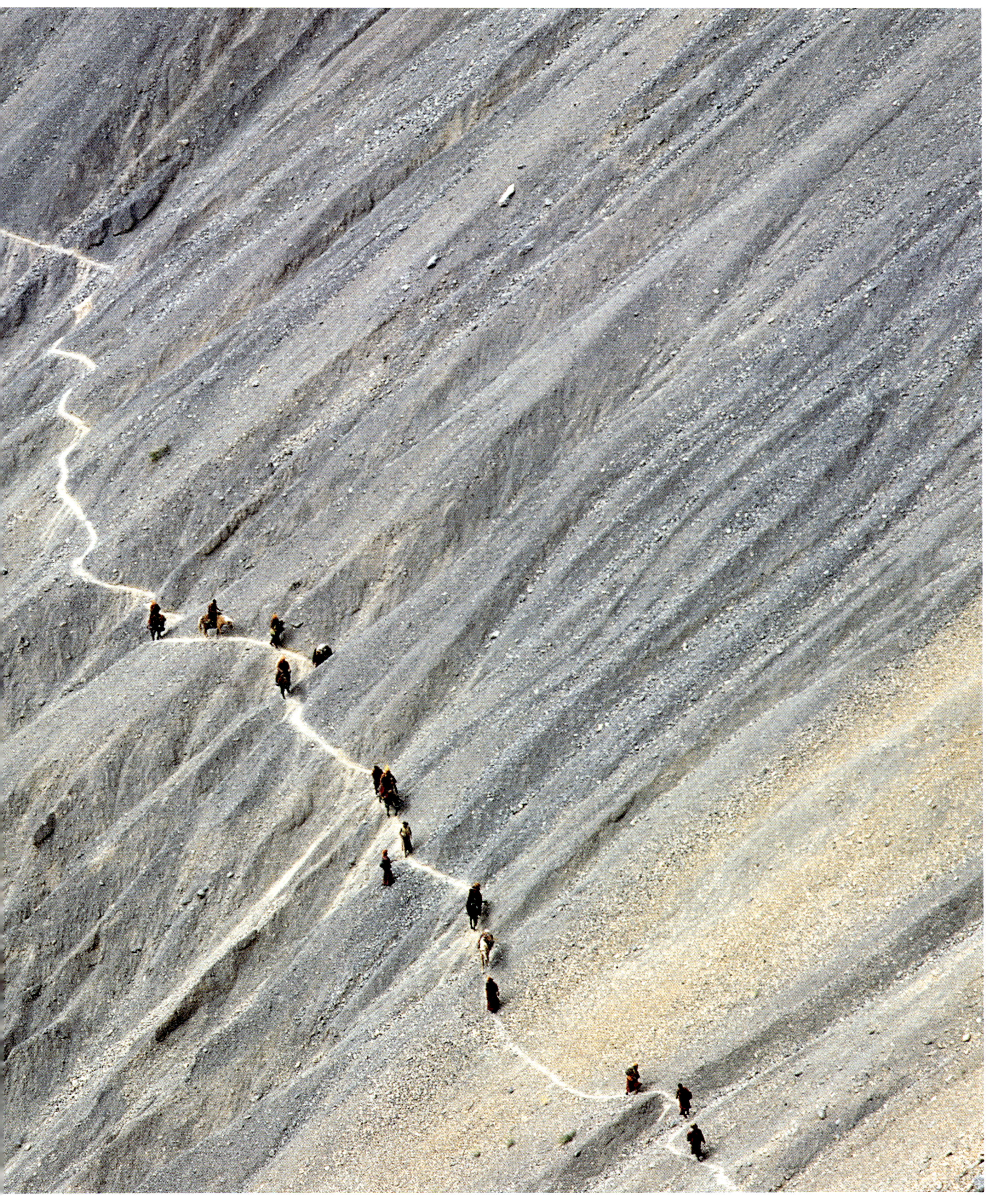

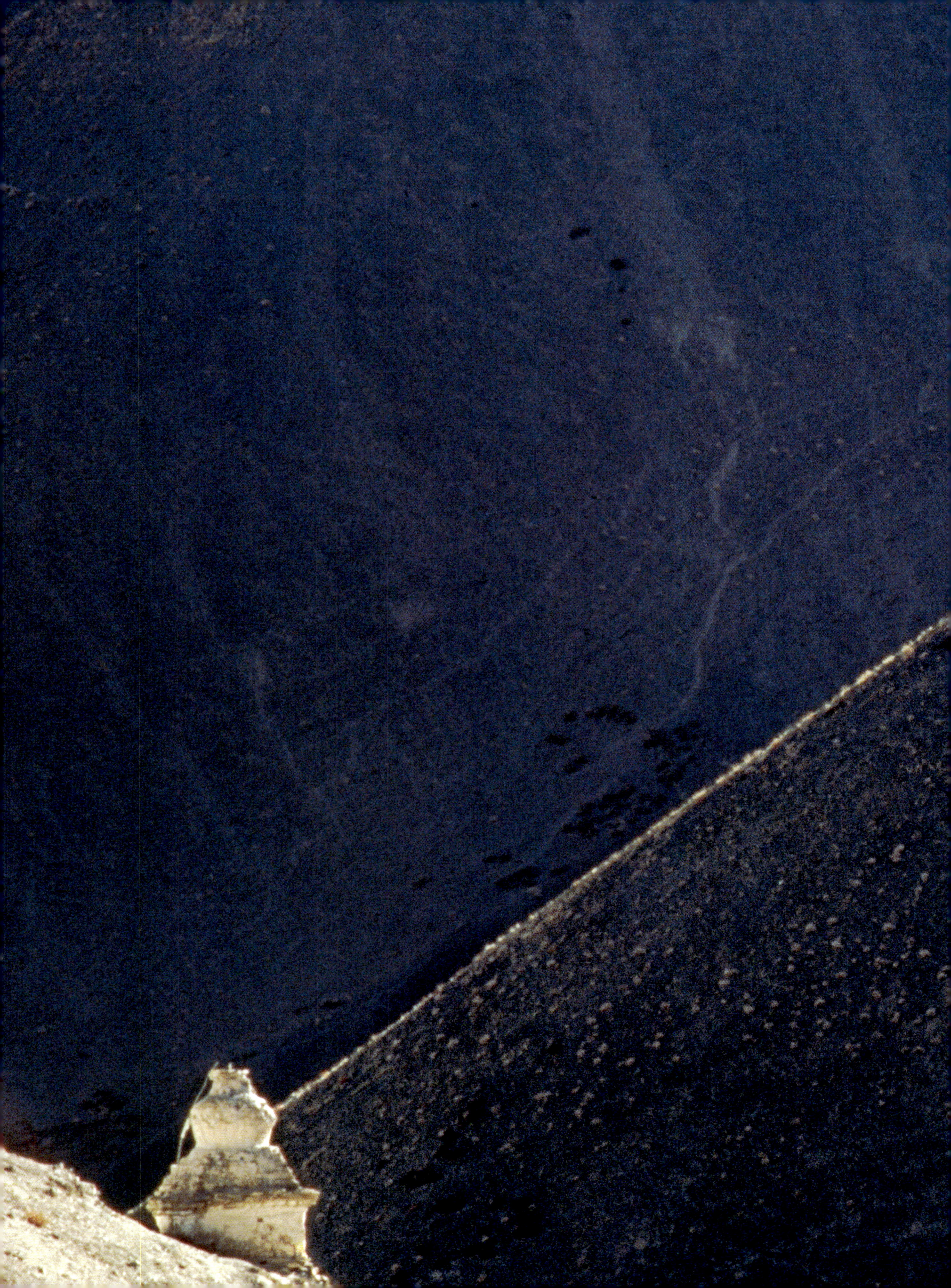

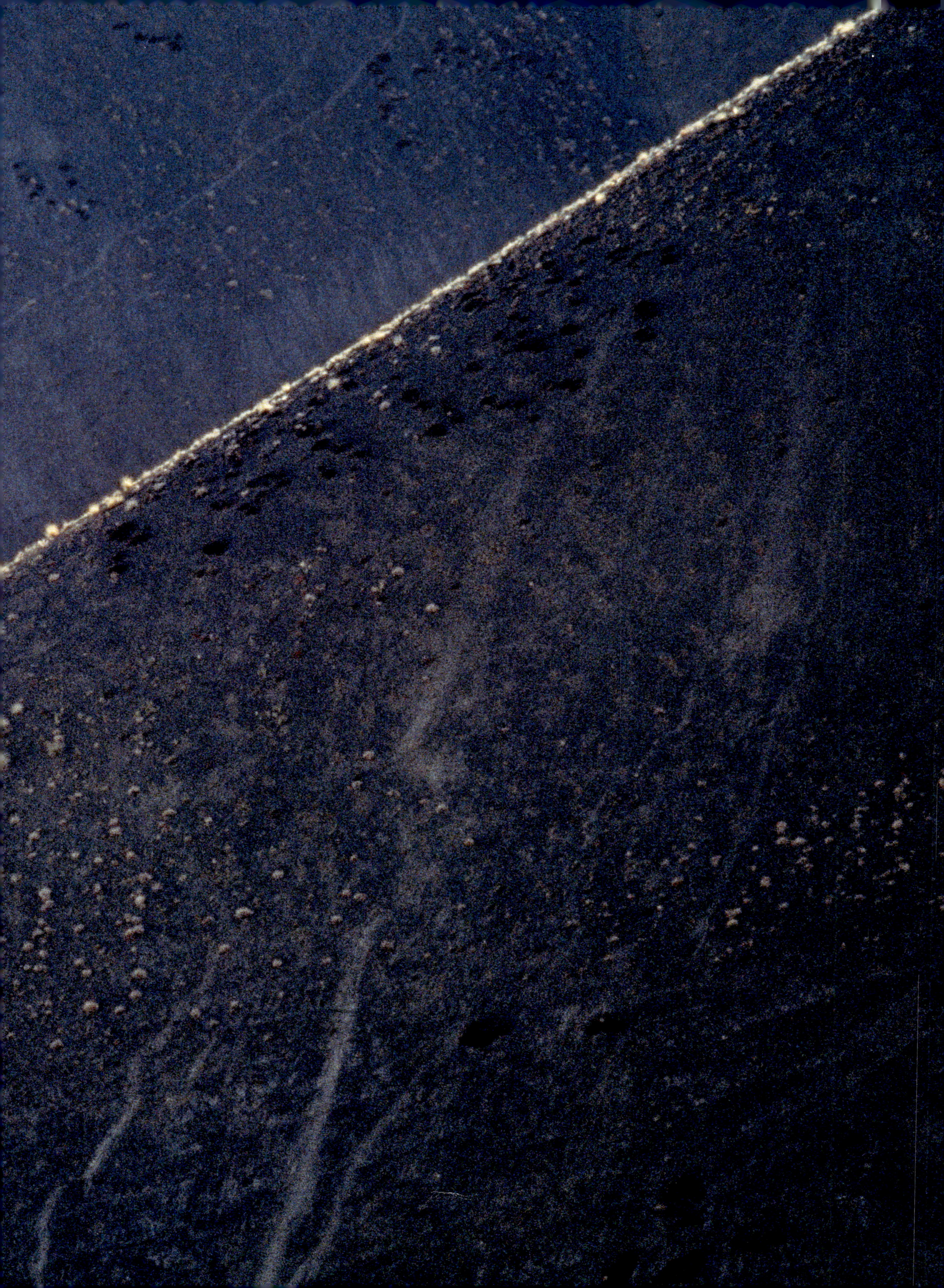

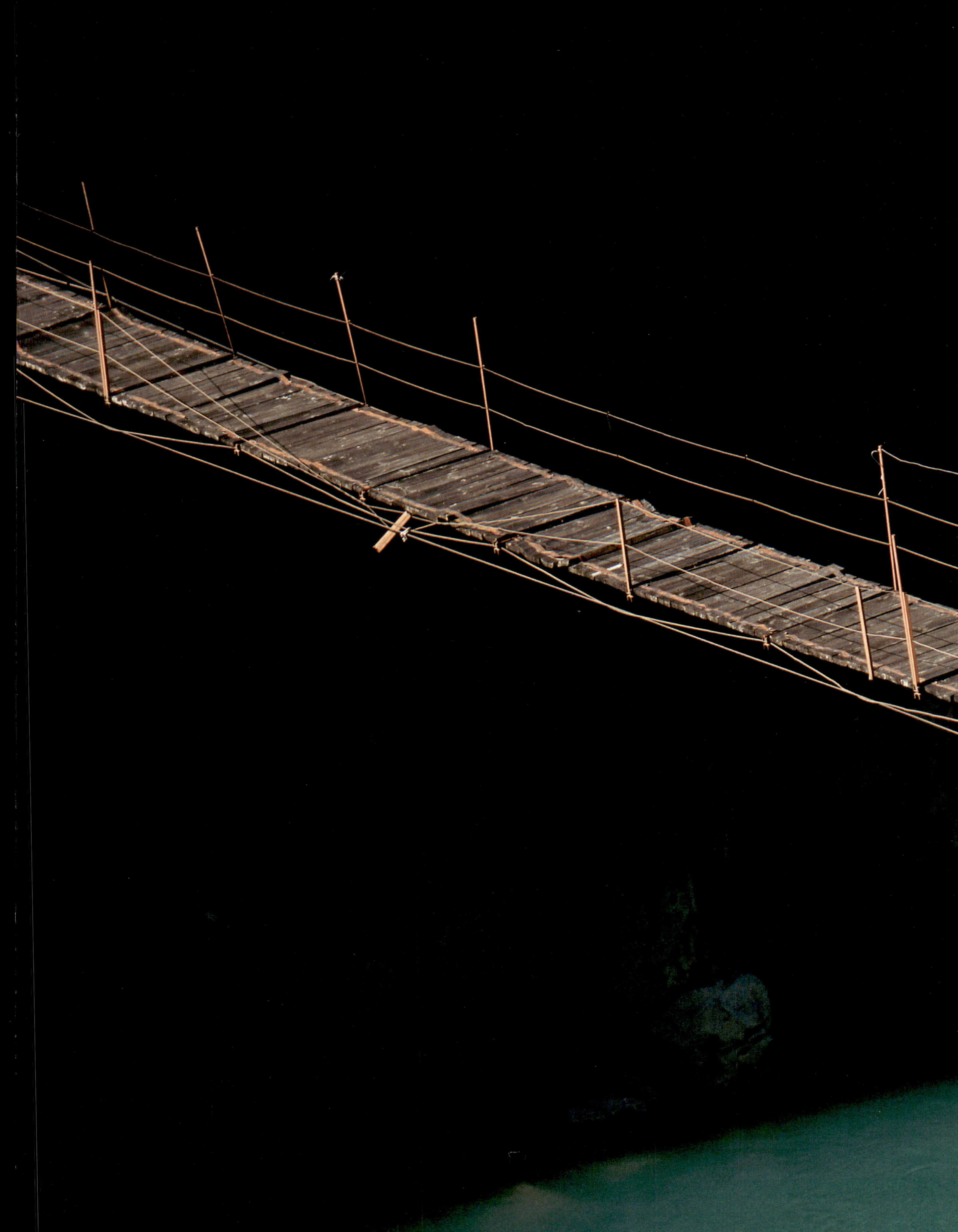

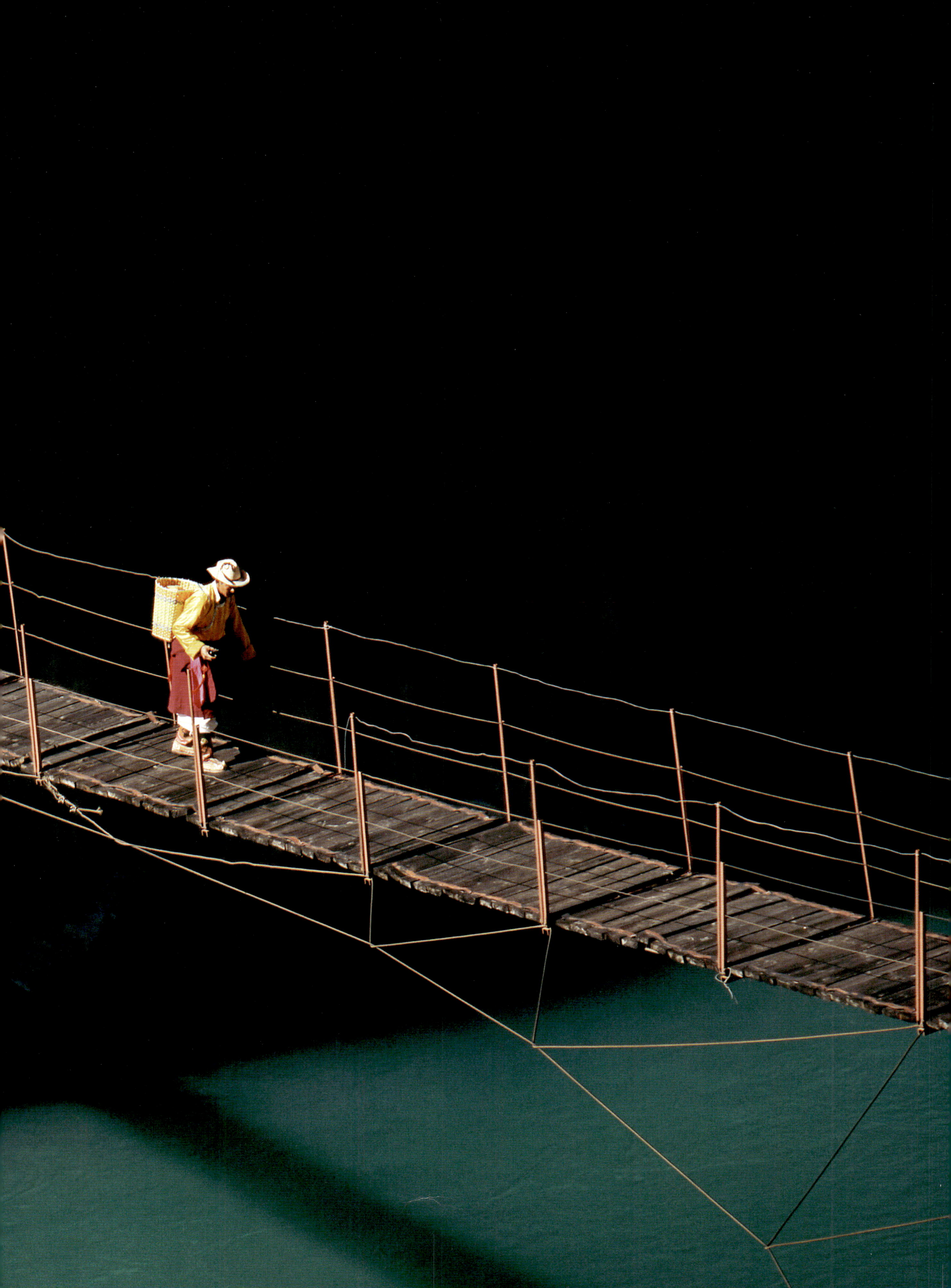

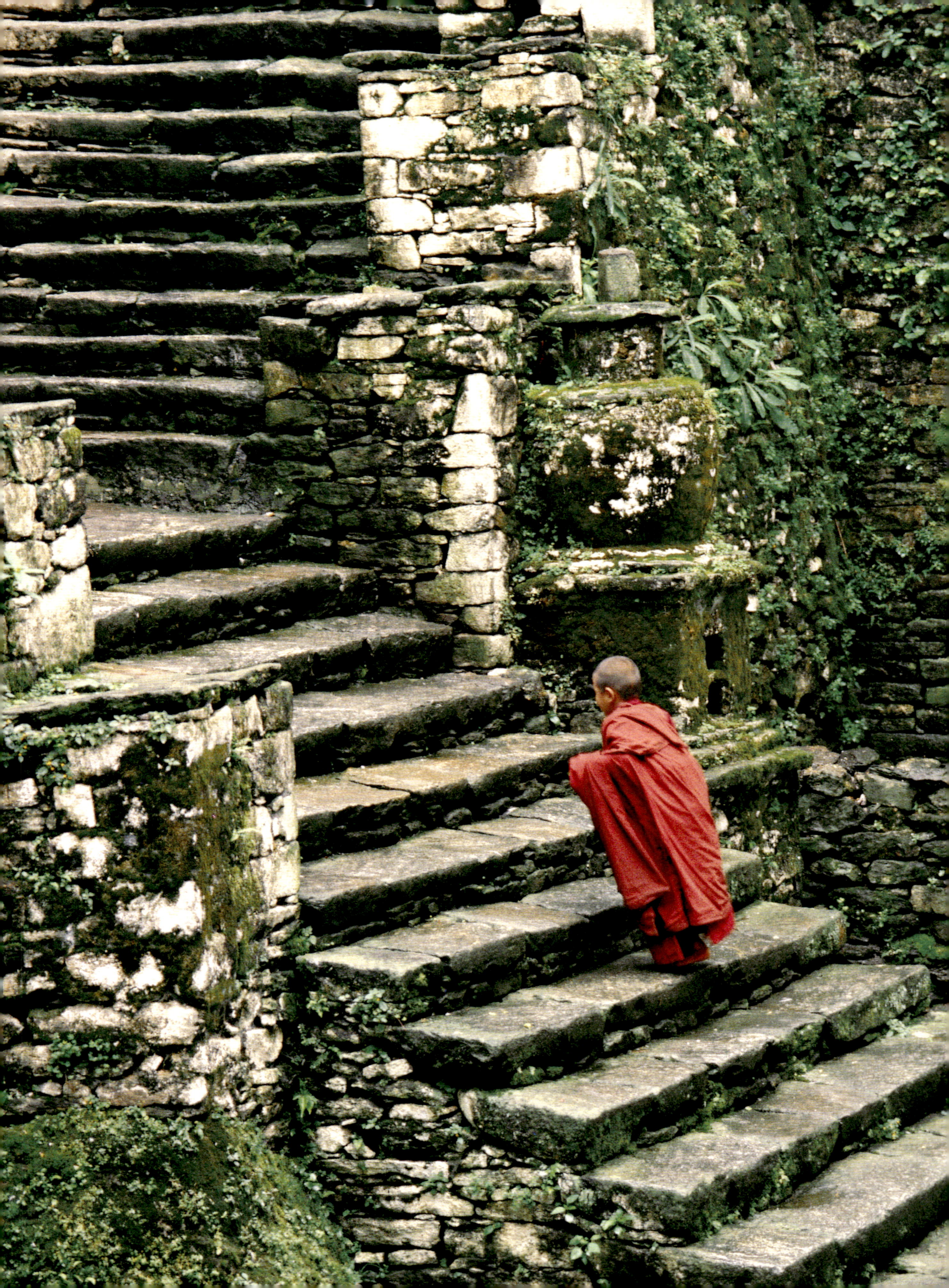

*Our acts, words and thoughts
determine our karma,
in other words, the happiness
and suffering that will
be our lot.*

Dilgo Khyentse Rinpoche

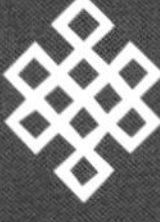

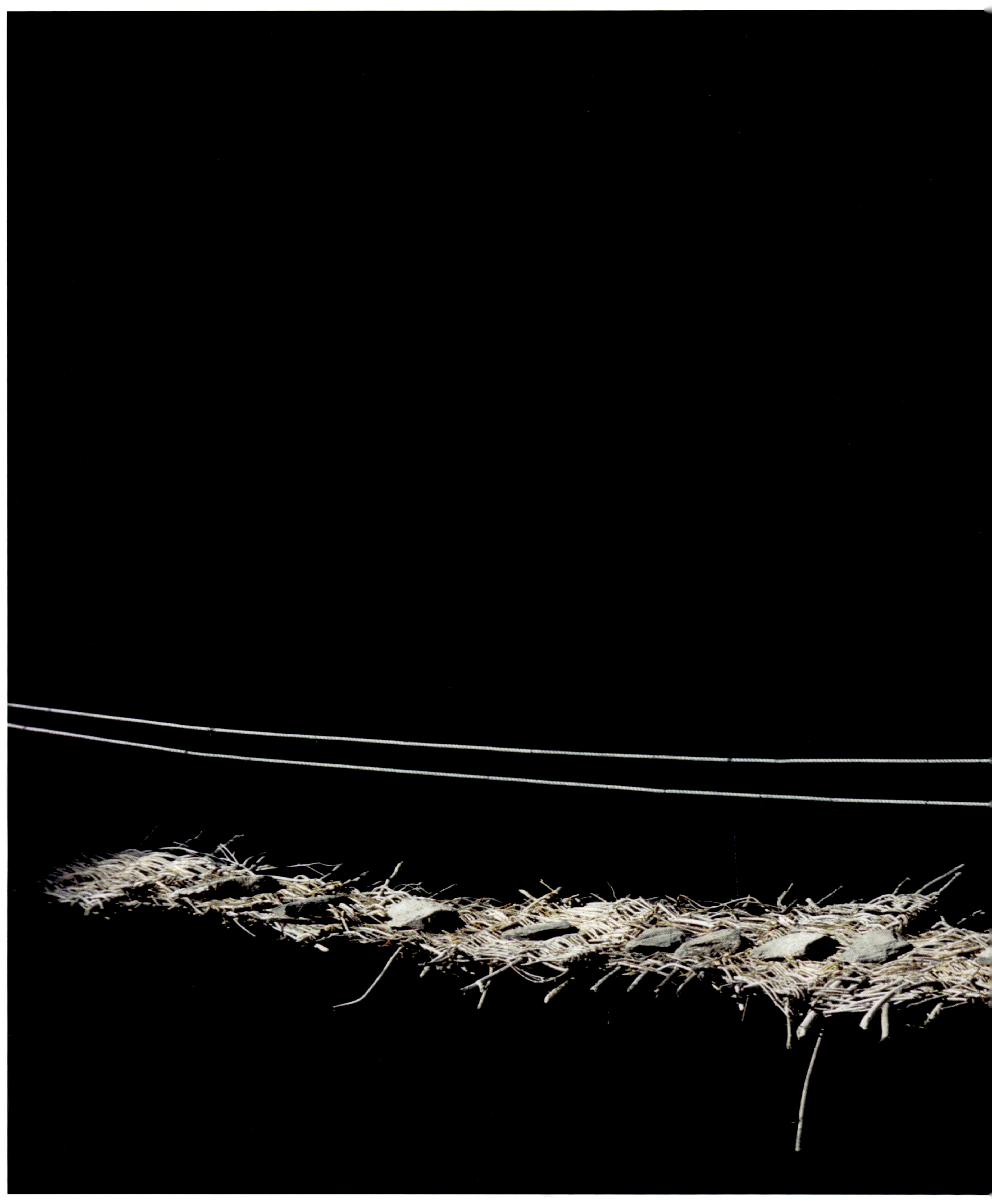

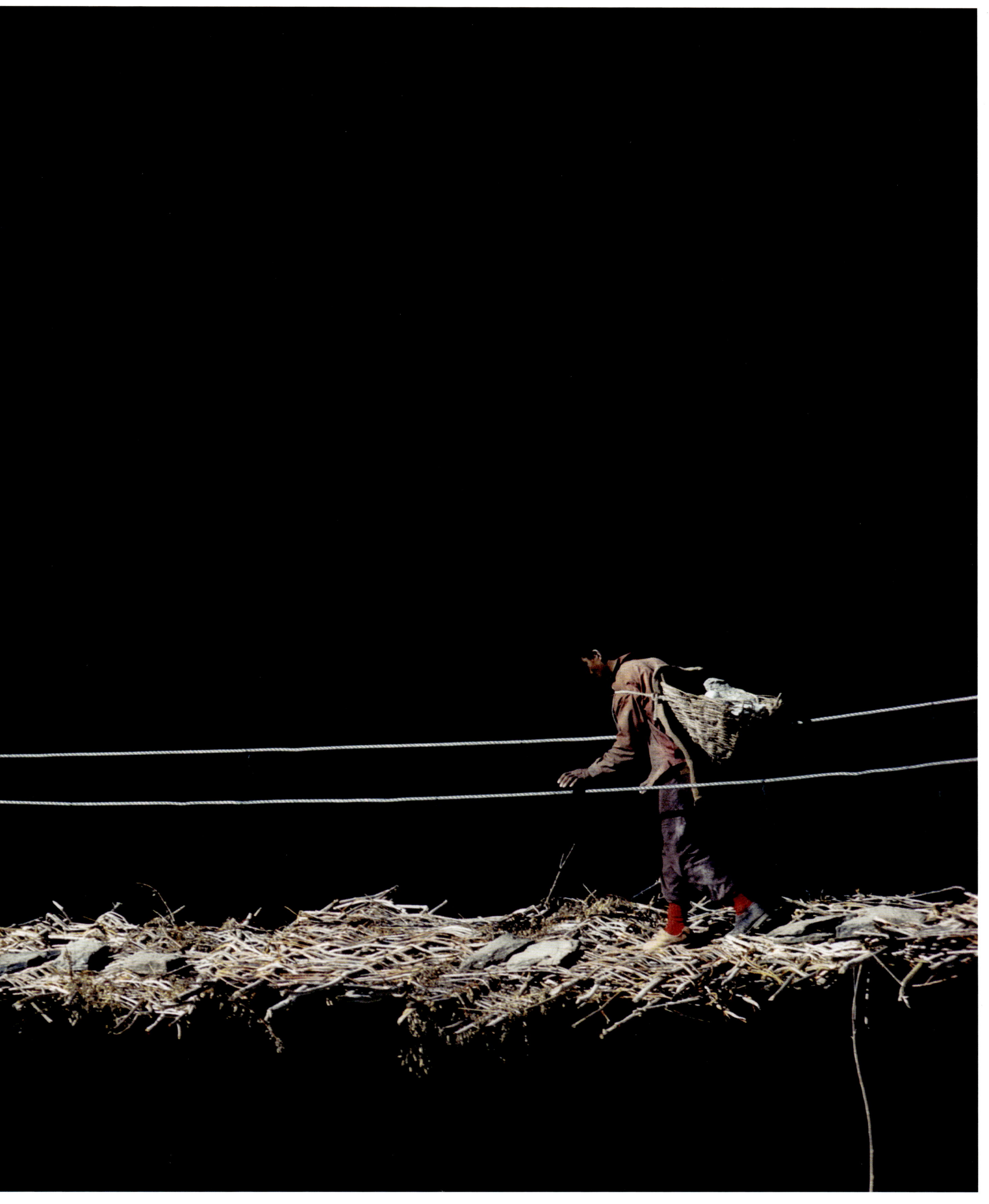

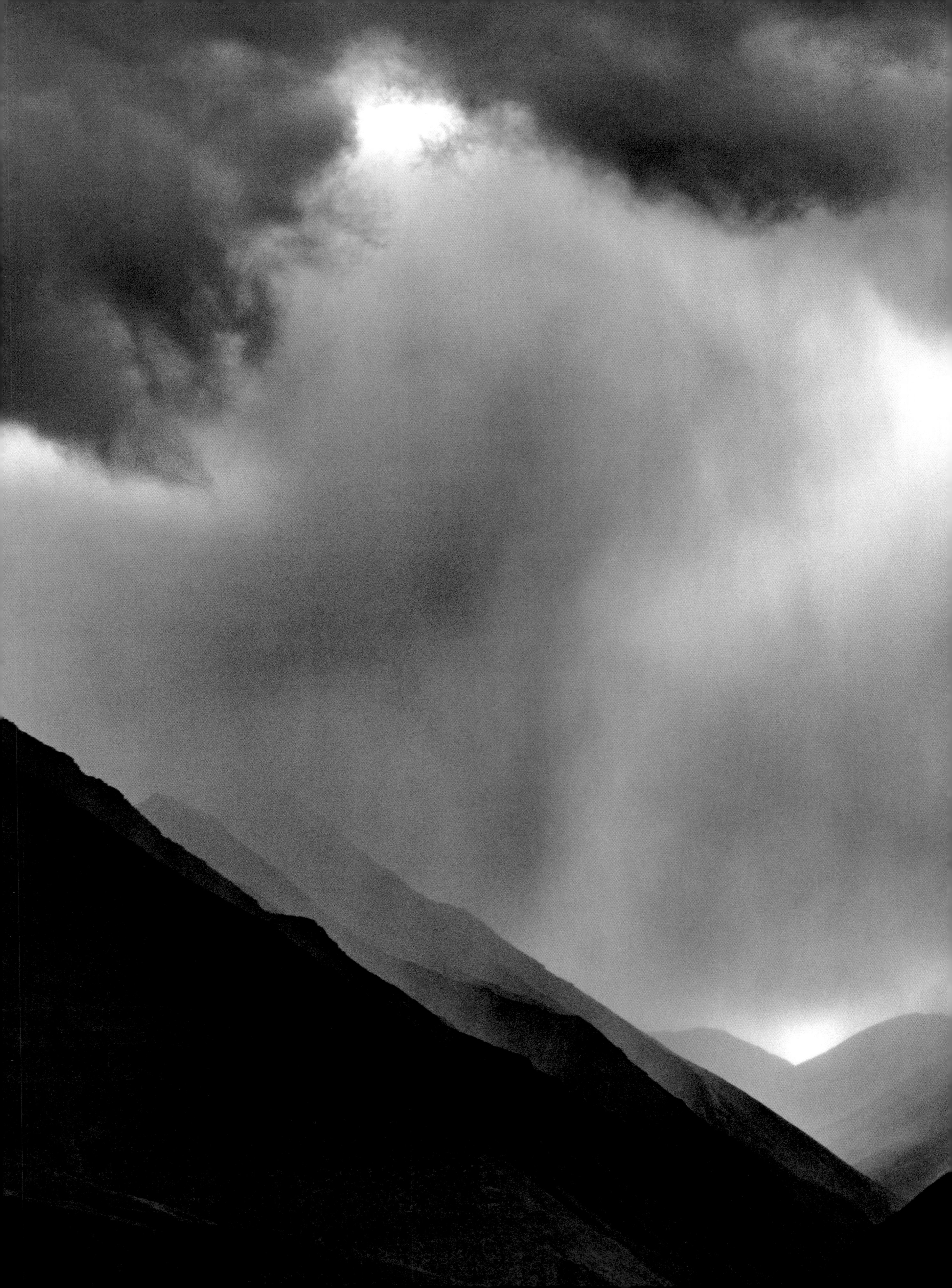

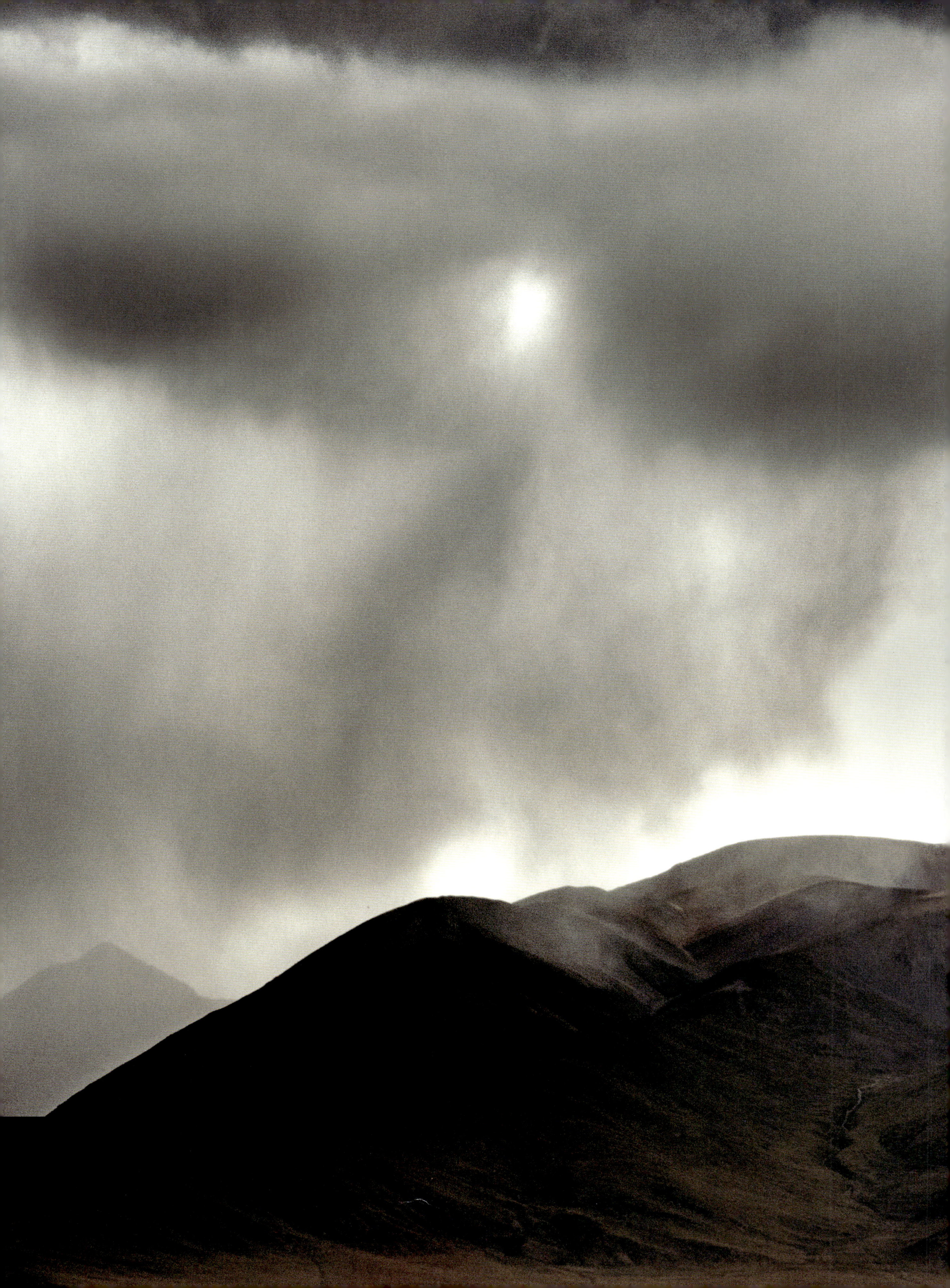

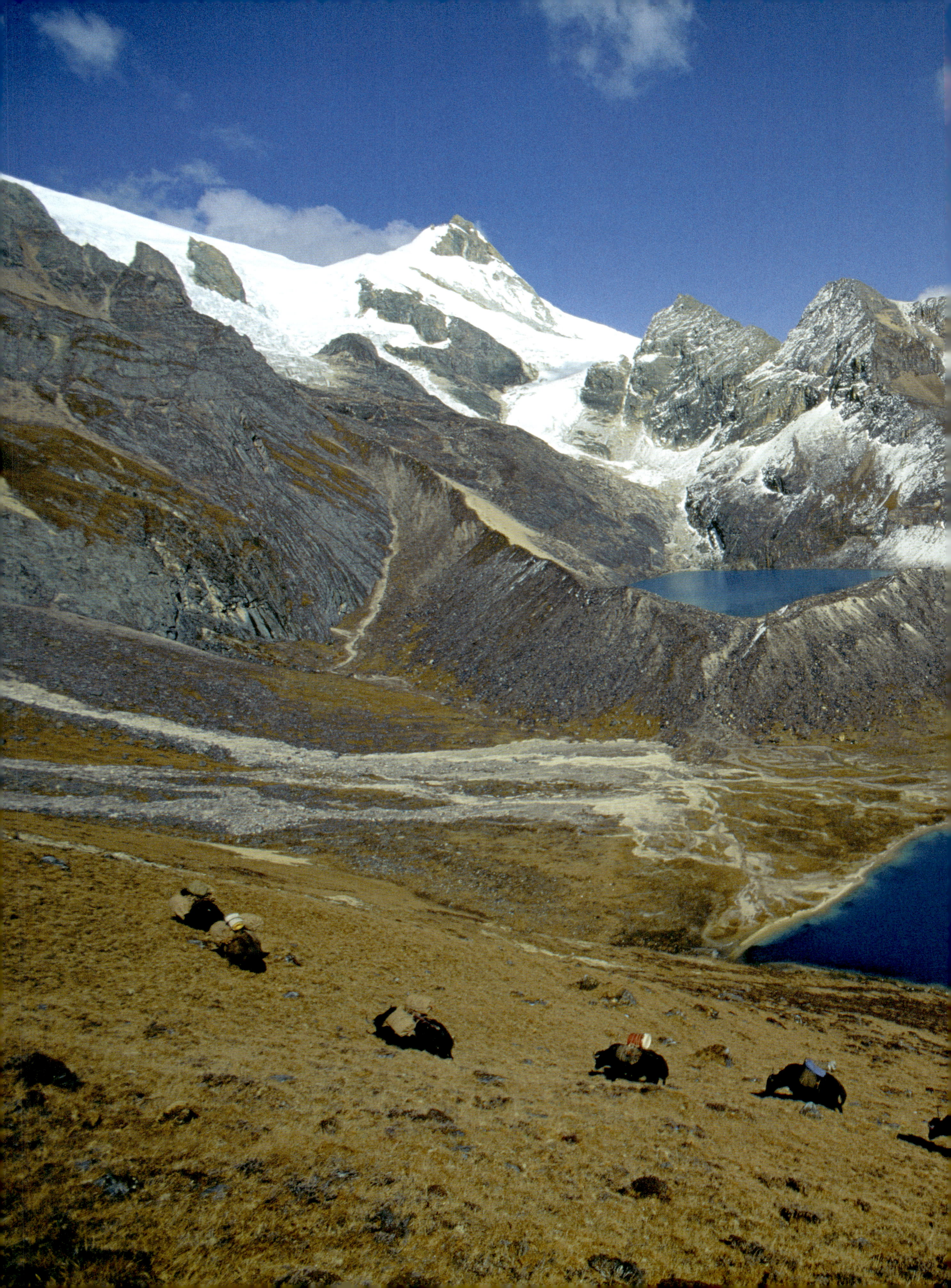

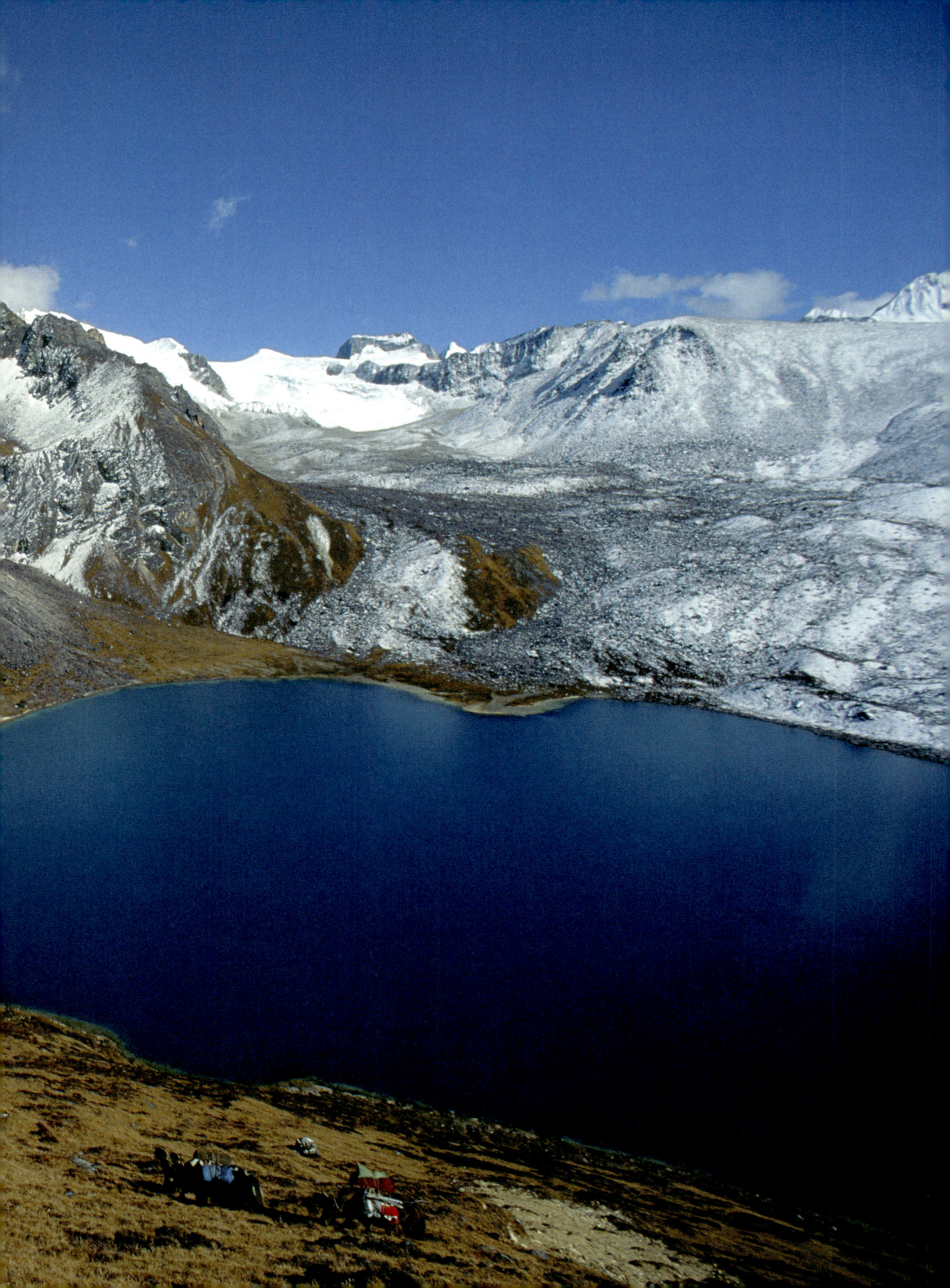

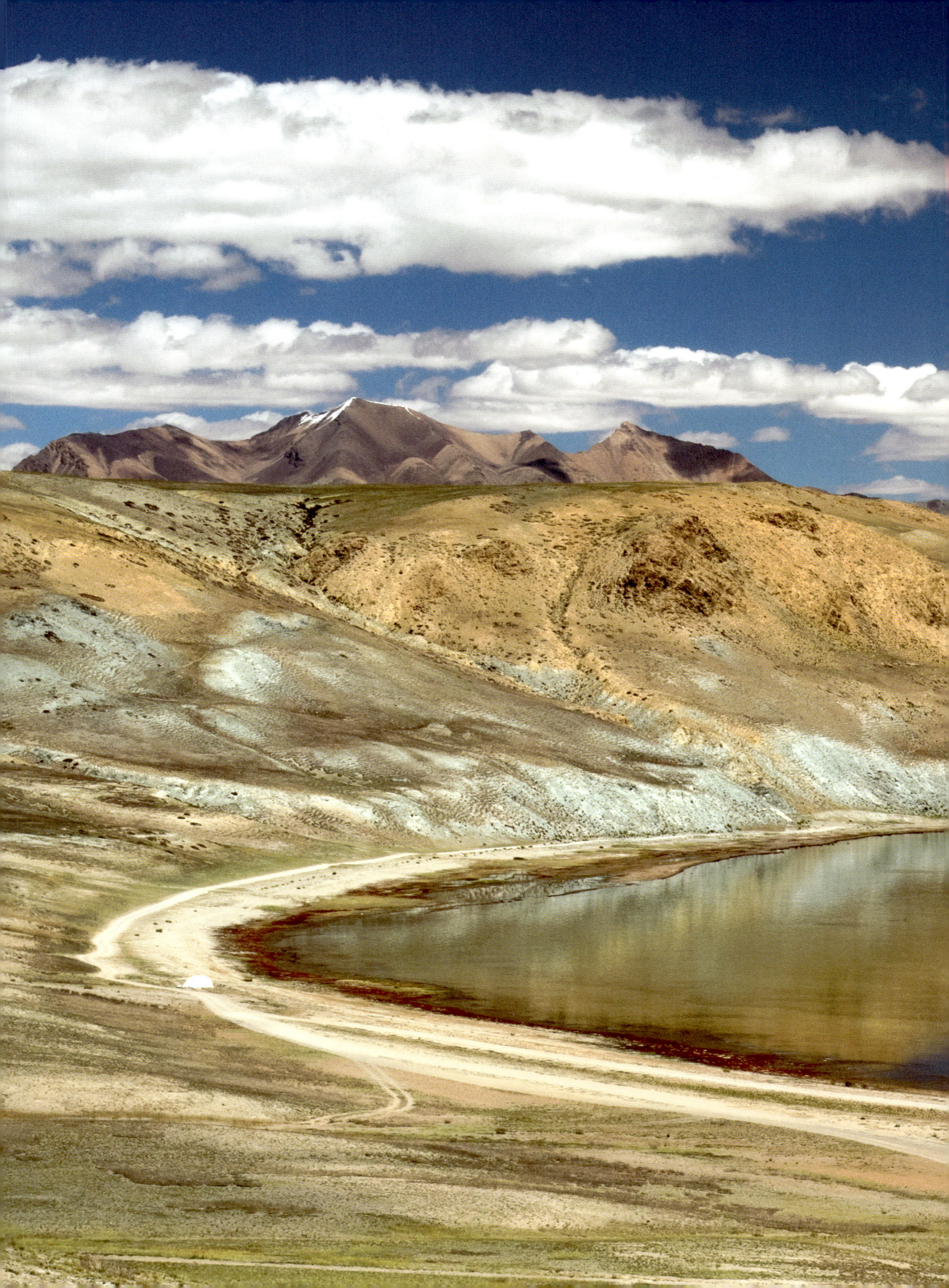

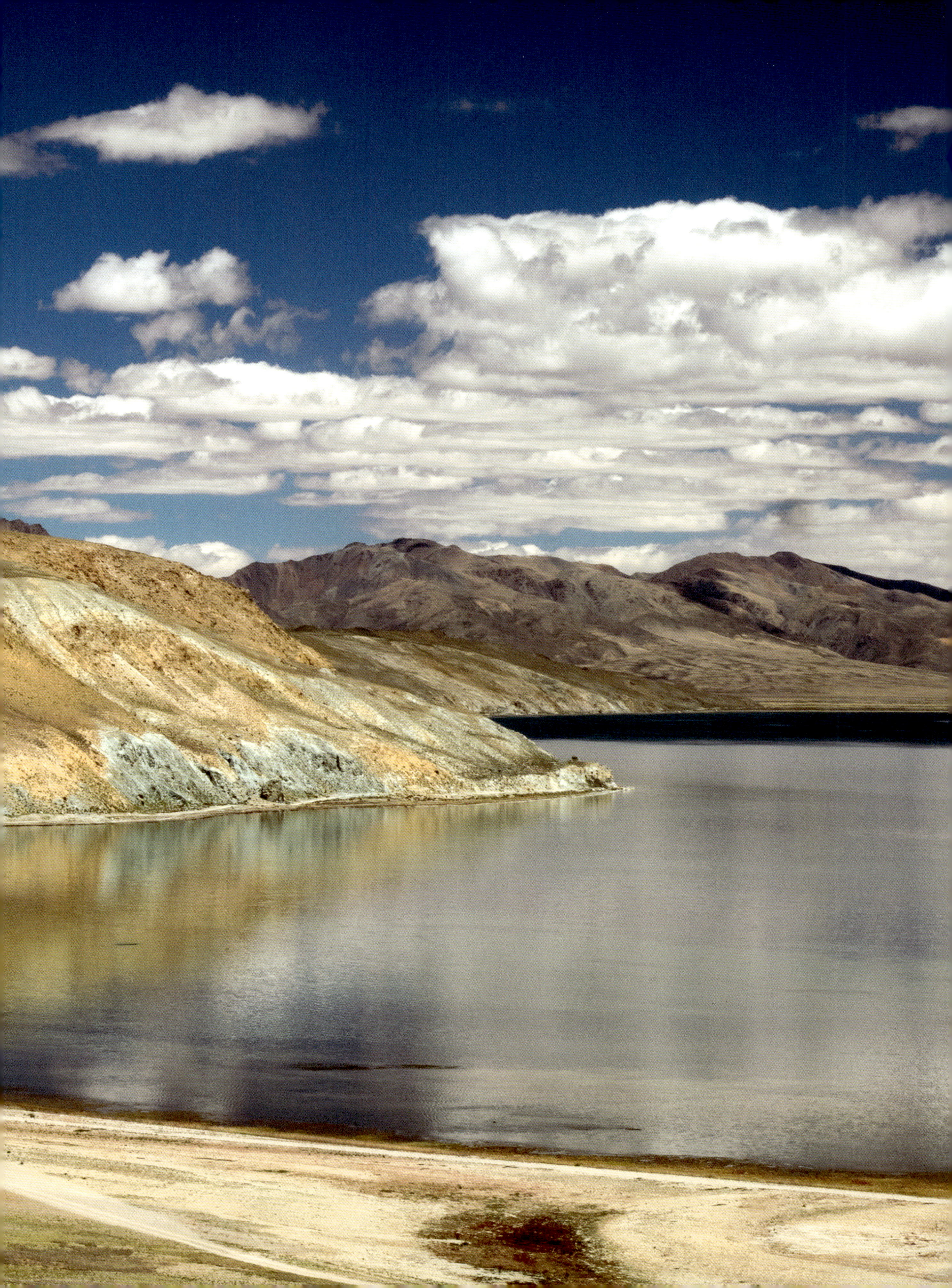

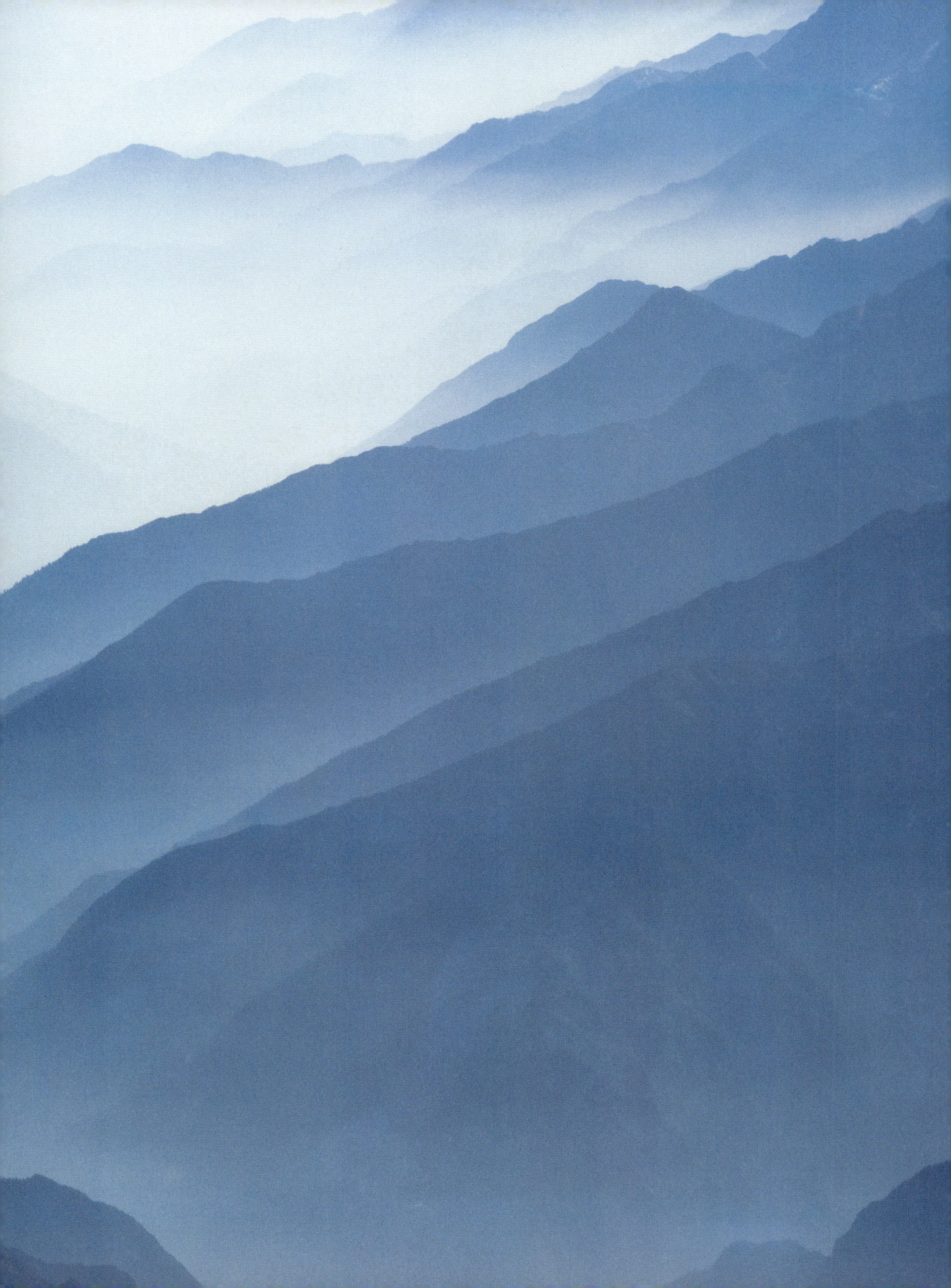

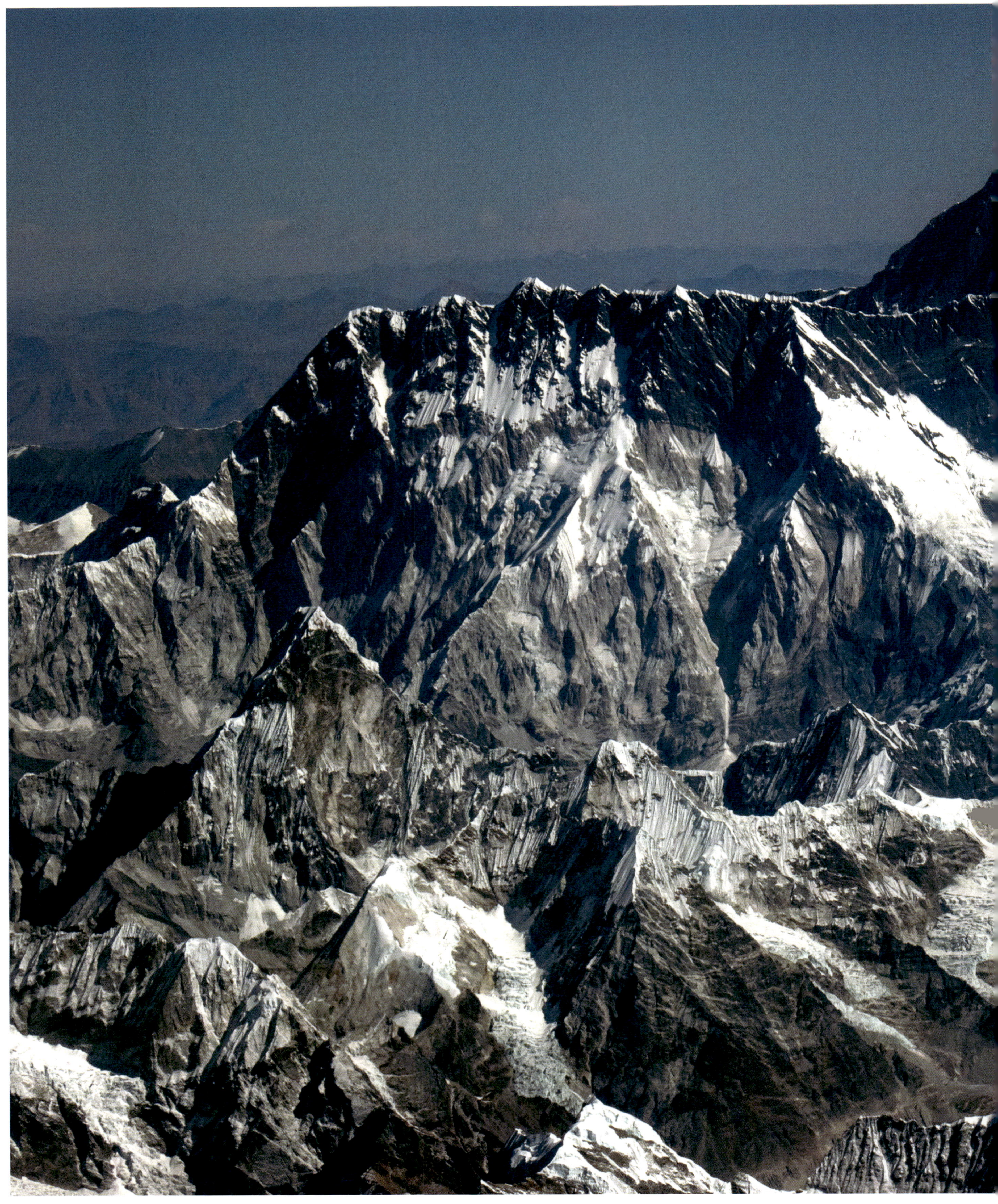

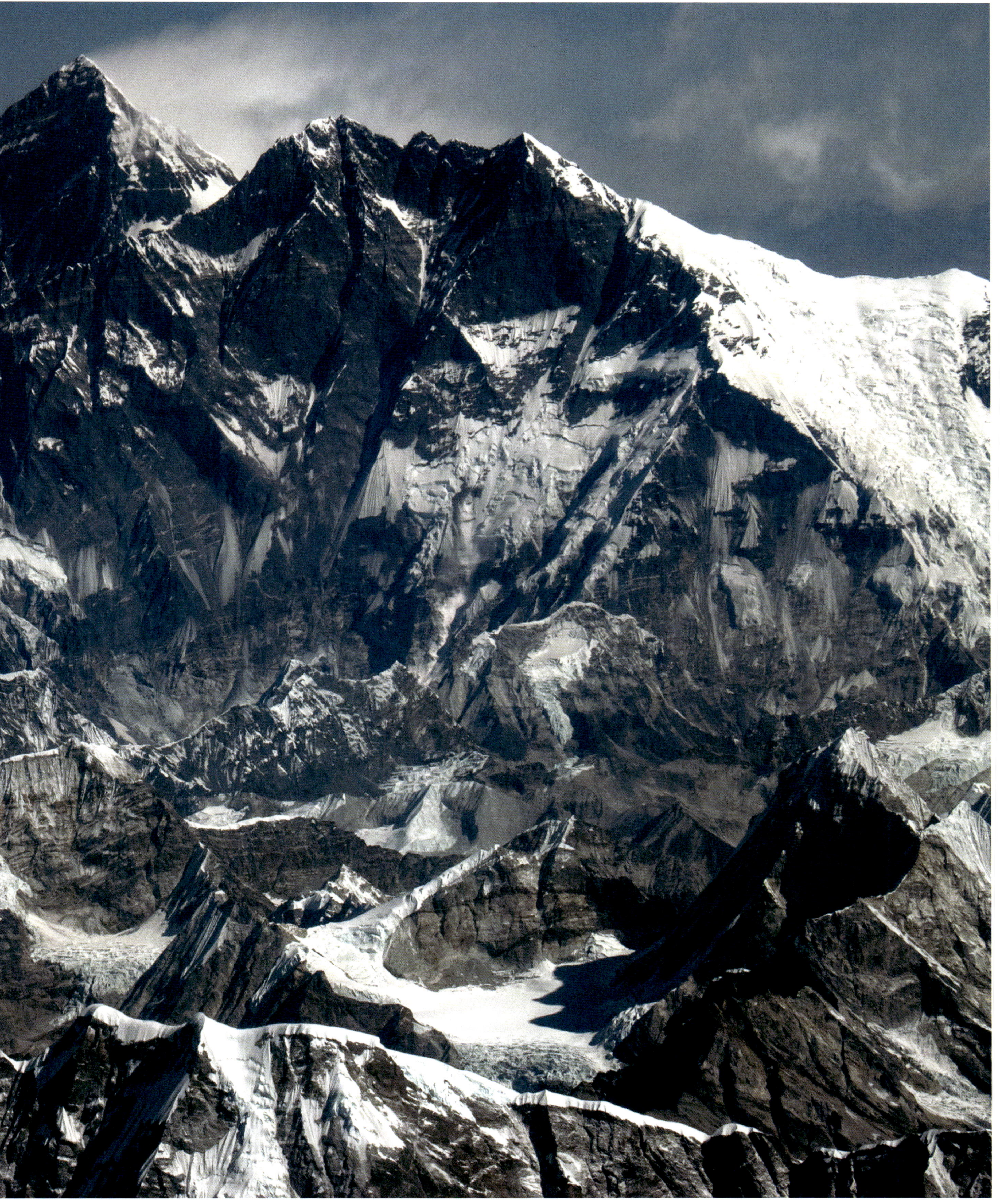

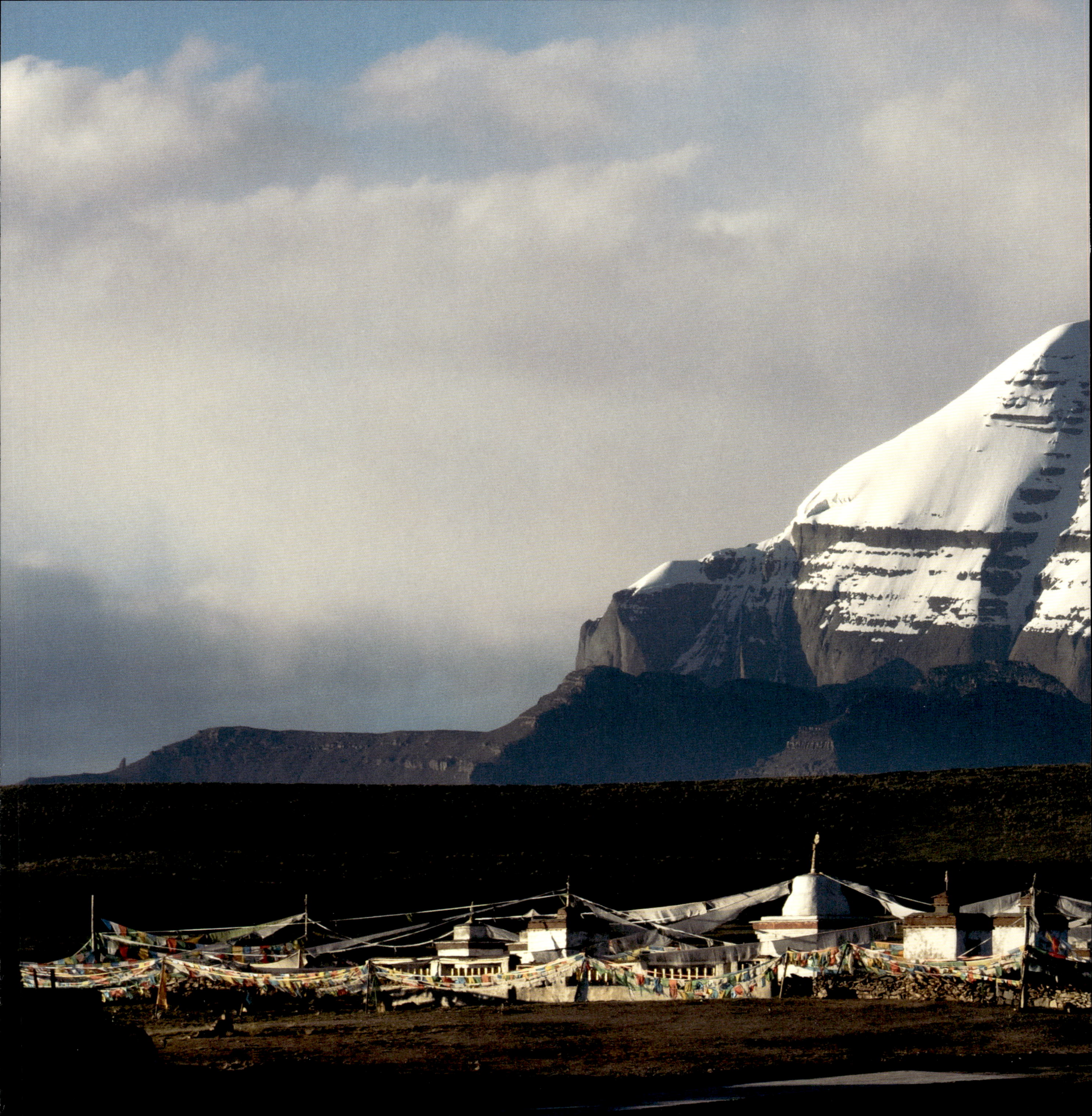

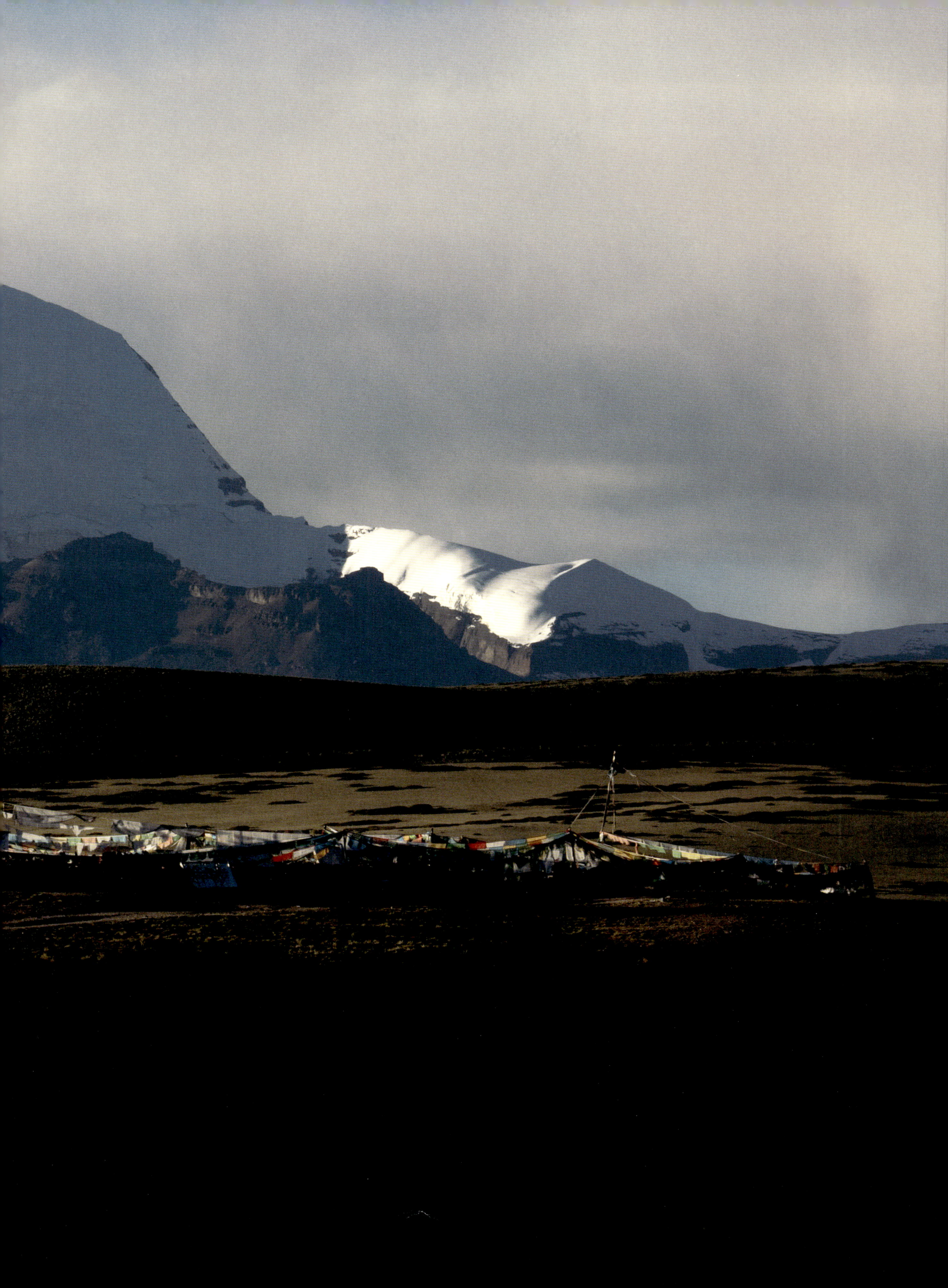

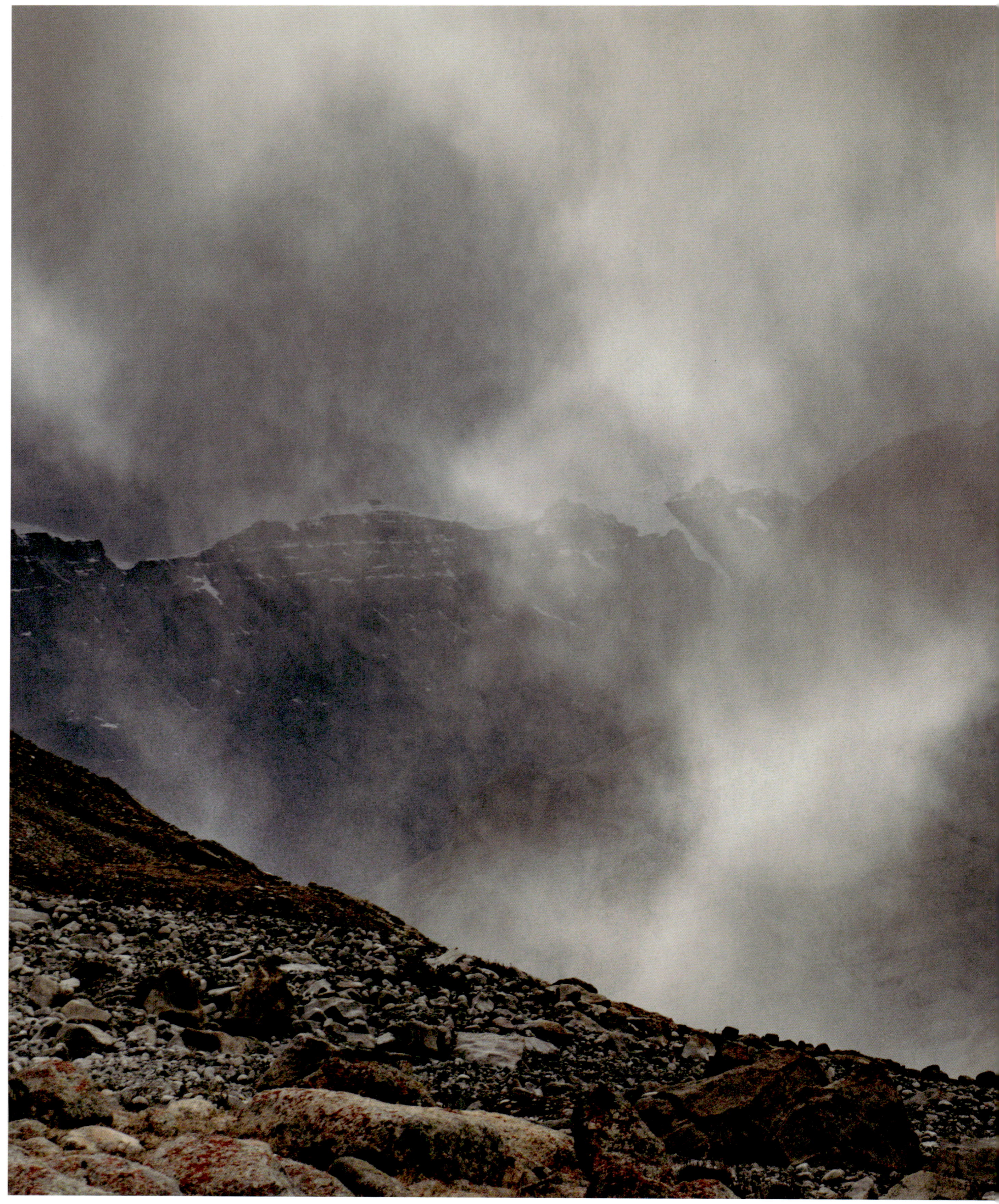

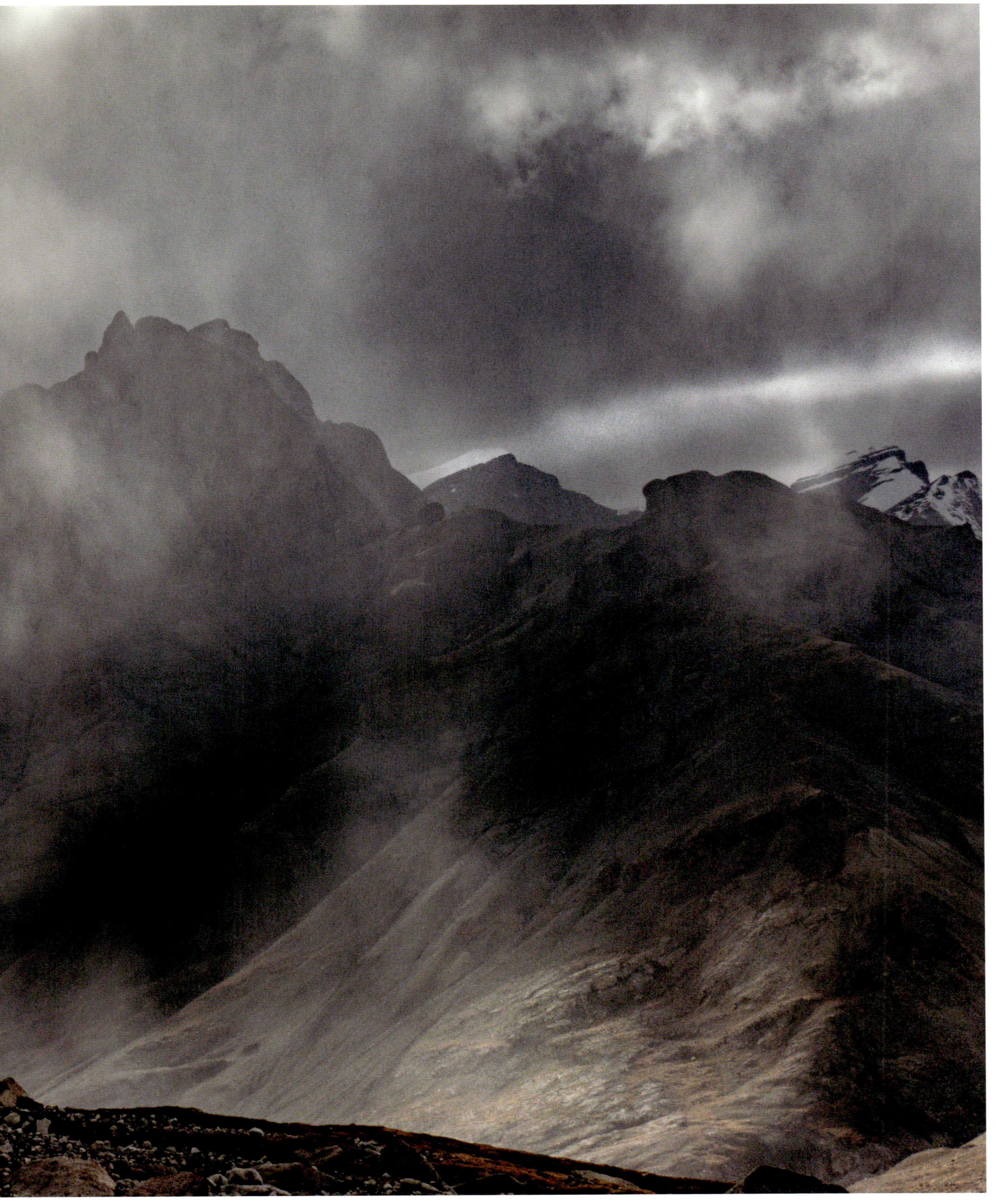

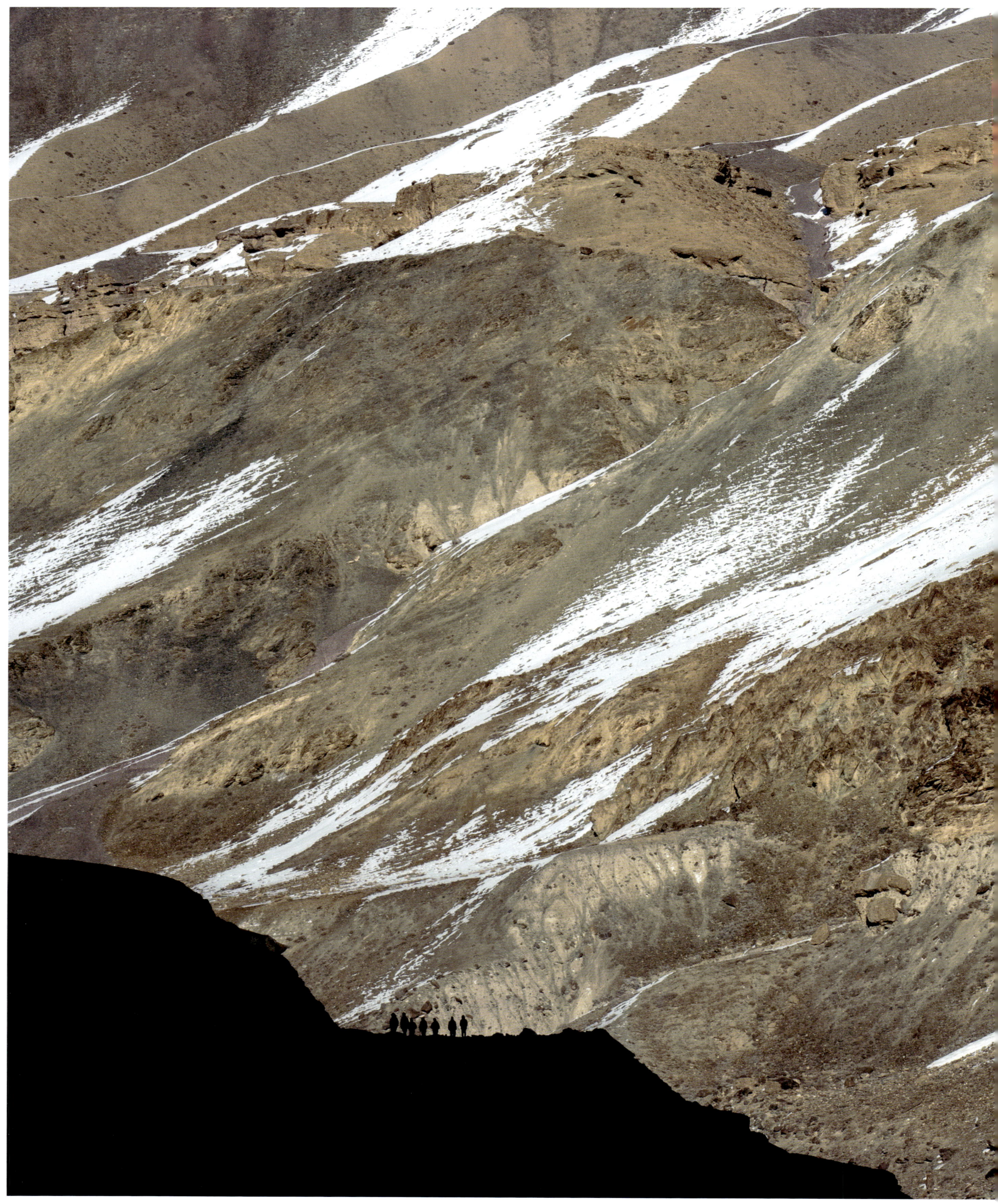

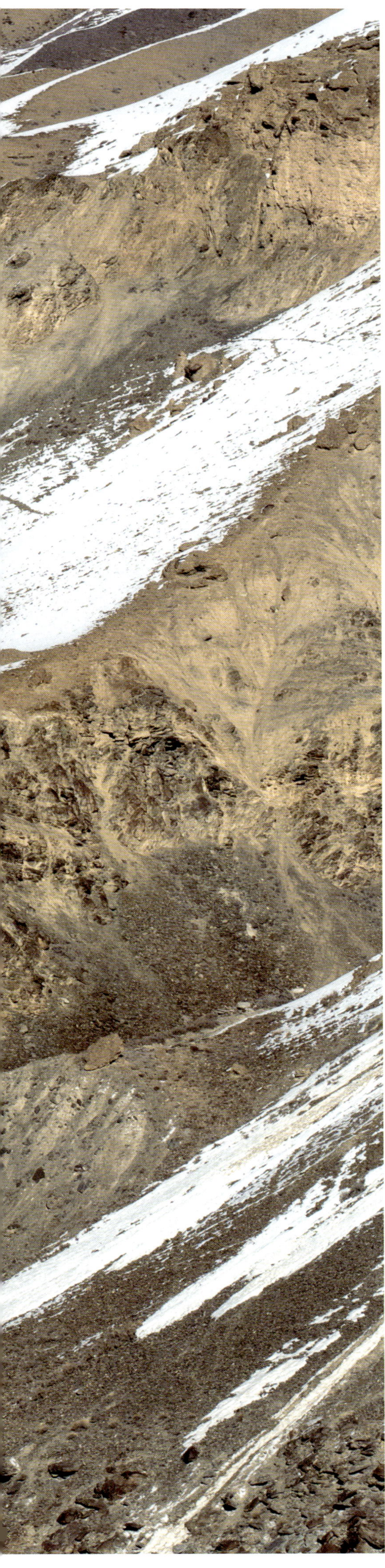

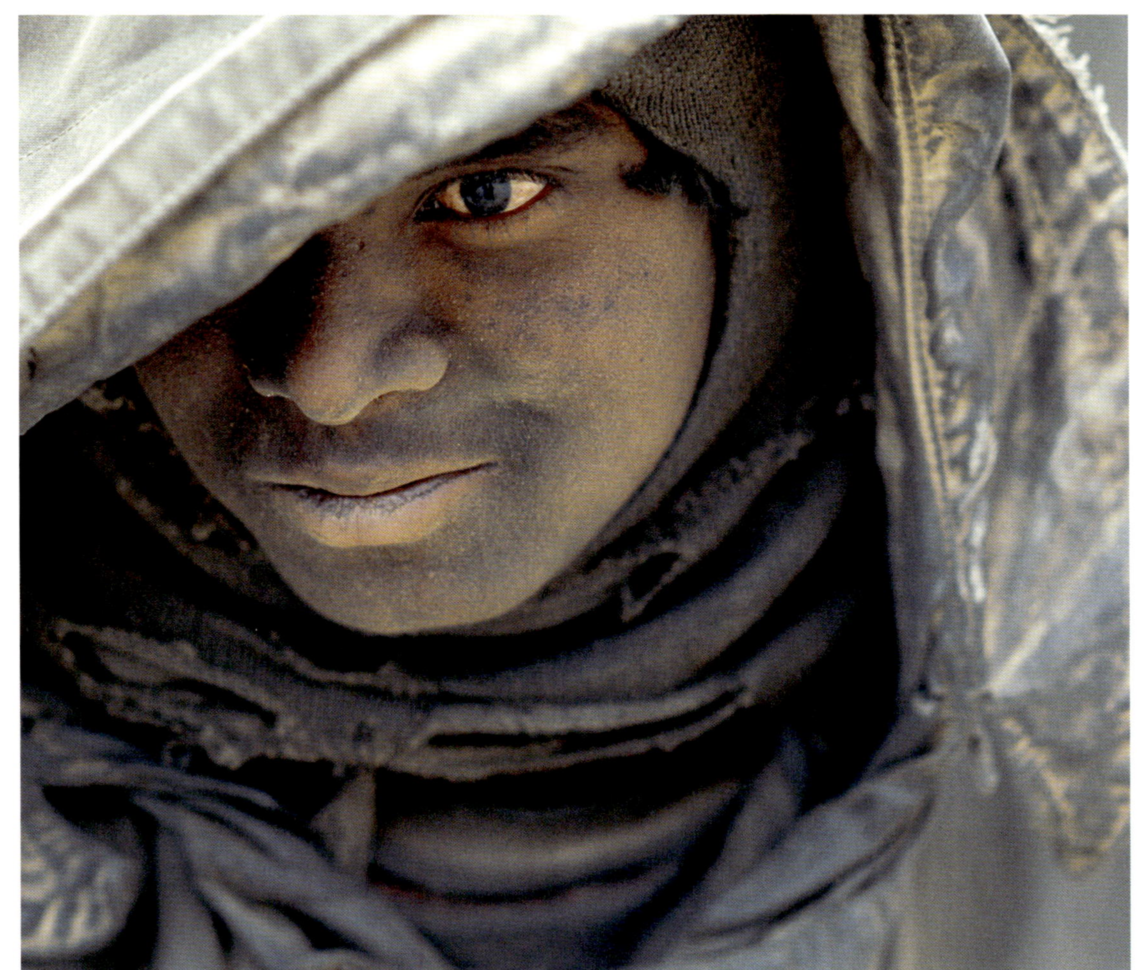

Coming from the sweltering plains that are the poorest in India, the men from Dumka construct the world's highest roads at 16,000 feet above sea level for the Indian army. They dig and pave with stones and tar by hand. Thanks to these men from Dumka, these channels of communication will ensure the prosperity of the Himalayas in the twenty-first century. We pay tribute to them, these phantoms of tar, for their courage and resignation.

Die Menschen von Dumka stammen aus heißen Ebenen, in denen die Ärmsten Indiens leben. Von Hand hacken, schottern und teeren sie für die indische Armee die höchsten Straßen der Welt in 5000 Metern über dem Meer. Diese Kommunikationswege begründeten im 21. Jahrhundert den Reichtum des Himalaya. Wir verbeugen uns vor ihnen, den Menschen von Dumka, jenen so mutigen wie illusionslosen Geistern des Asphalts.

Venus des plaines torrides les plus pauvres de l'Inde, les hommes de Dumka piochent, empierrent, goudronnent à la main les routes les plus hautes du monde à 5 000 mètres d'altitude, pour l'armée indienne. Ces voies de communication feront la prospérité de l'Himalaya du XXIe siècle grâce aux hommes de Dumka. Hommage à eux, fantômes de goudron, si courageux, si résignés.

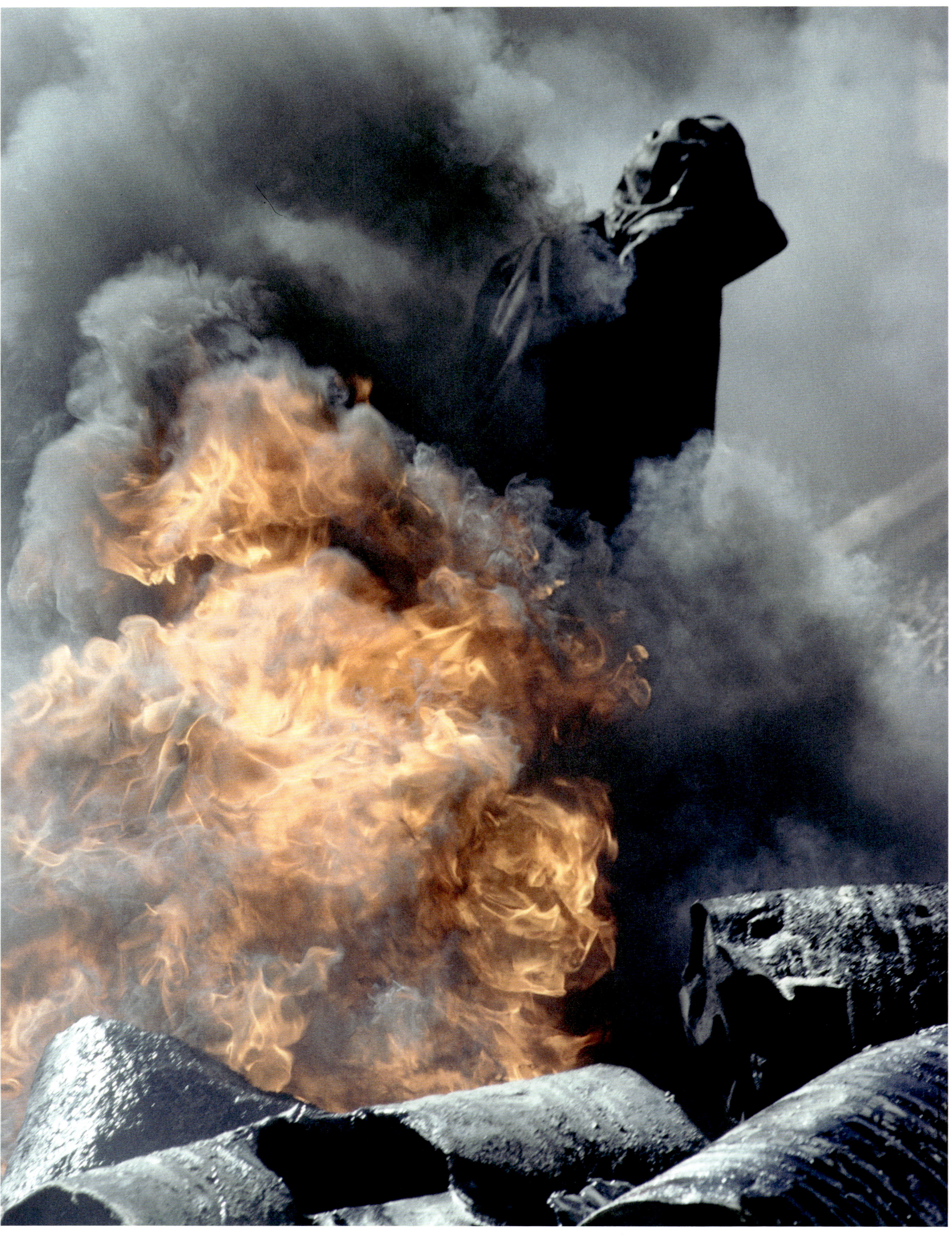

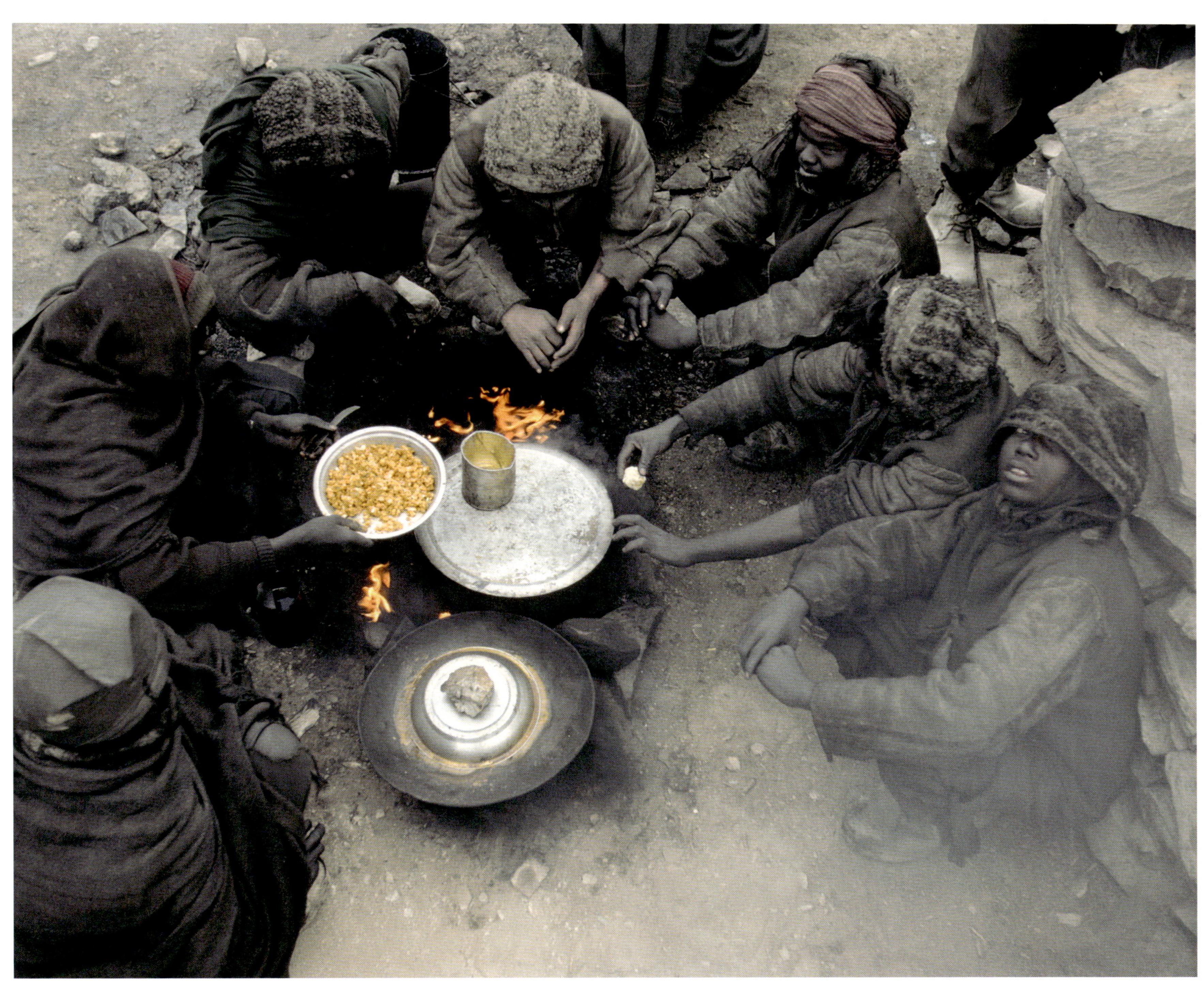

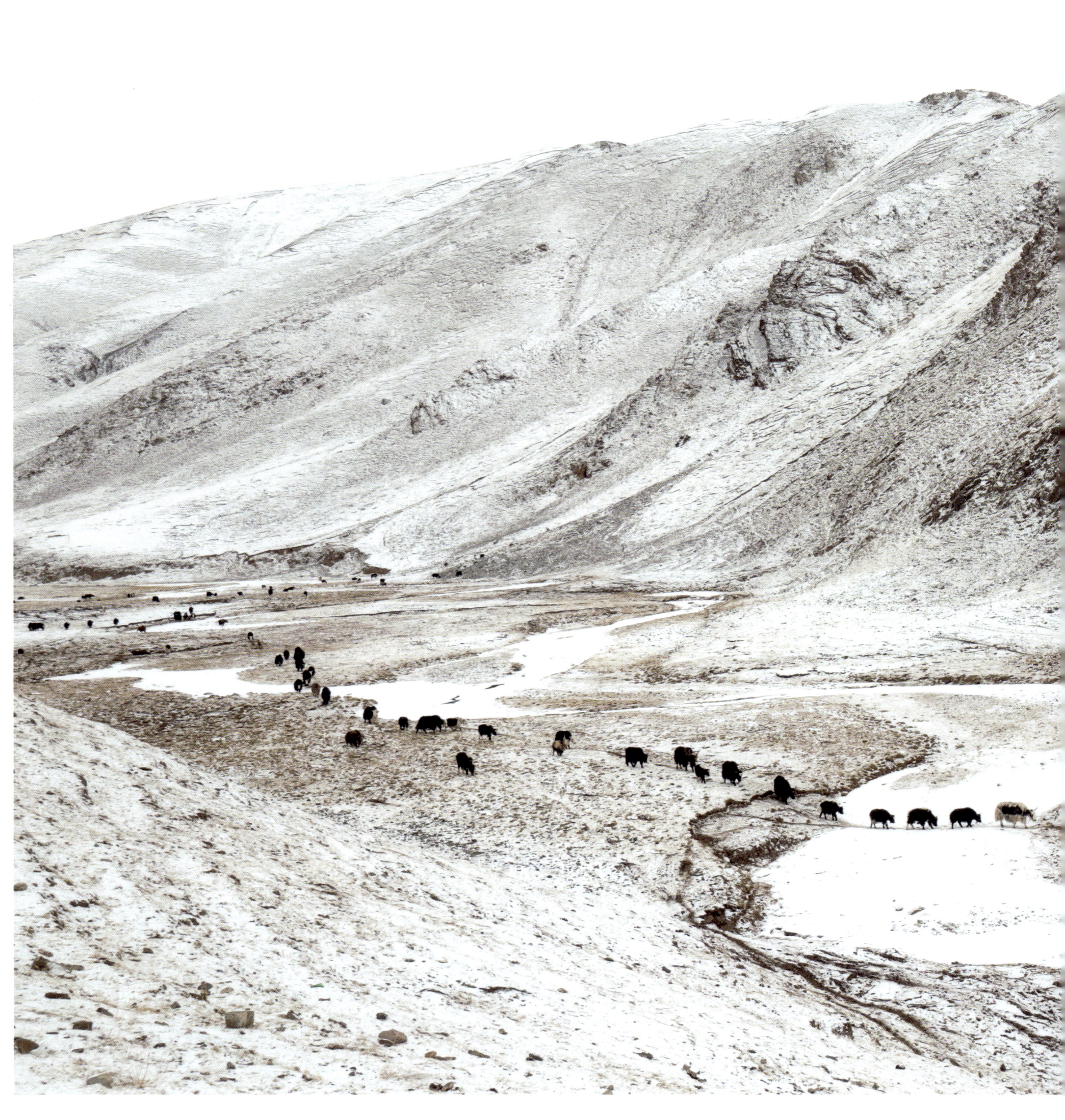

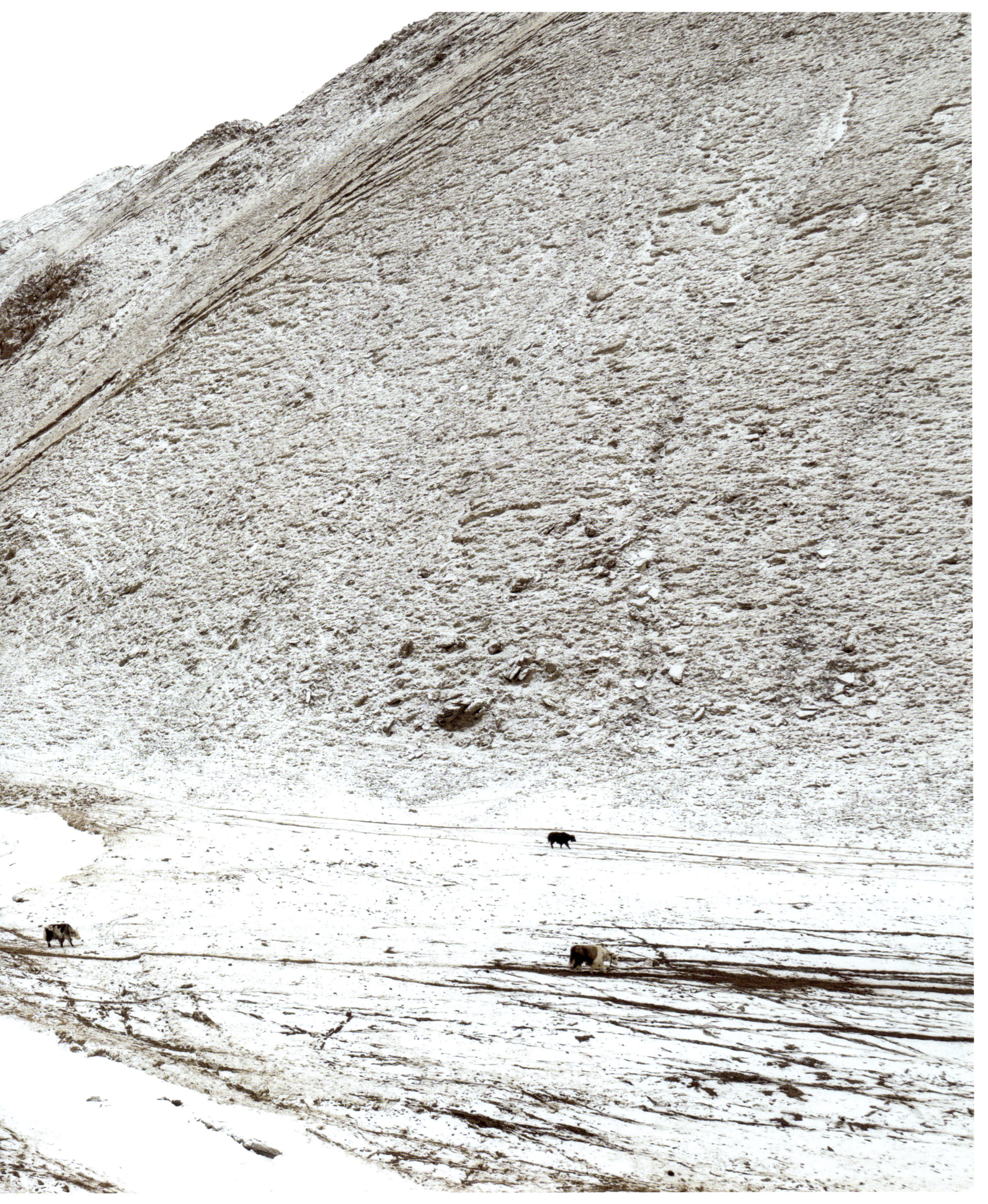

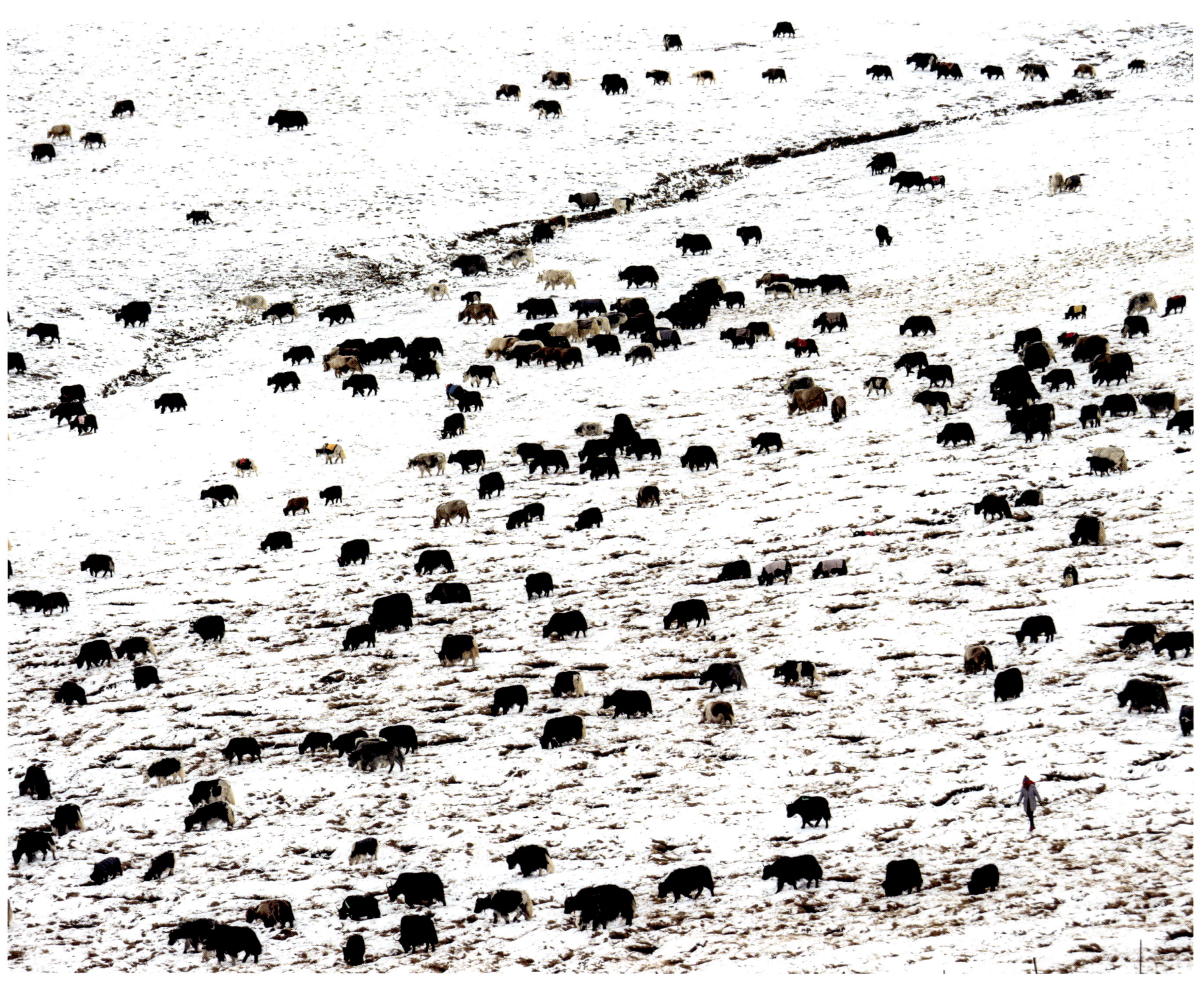

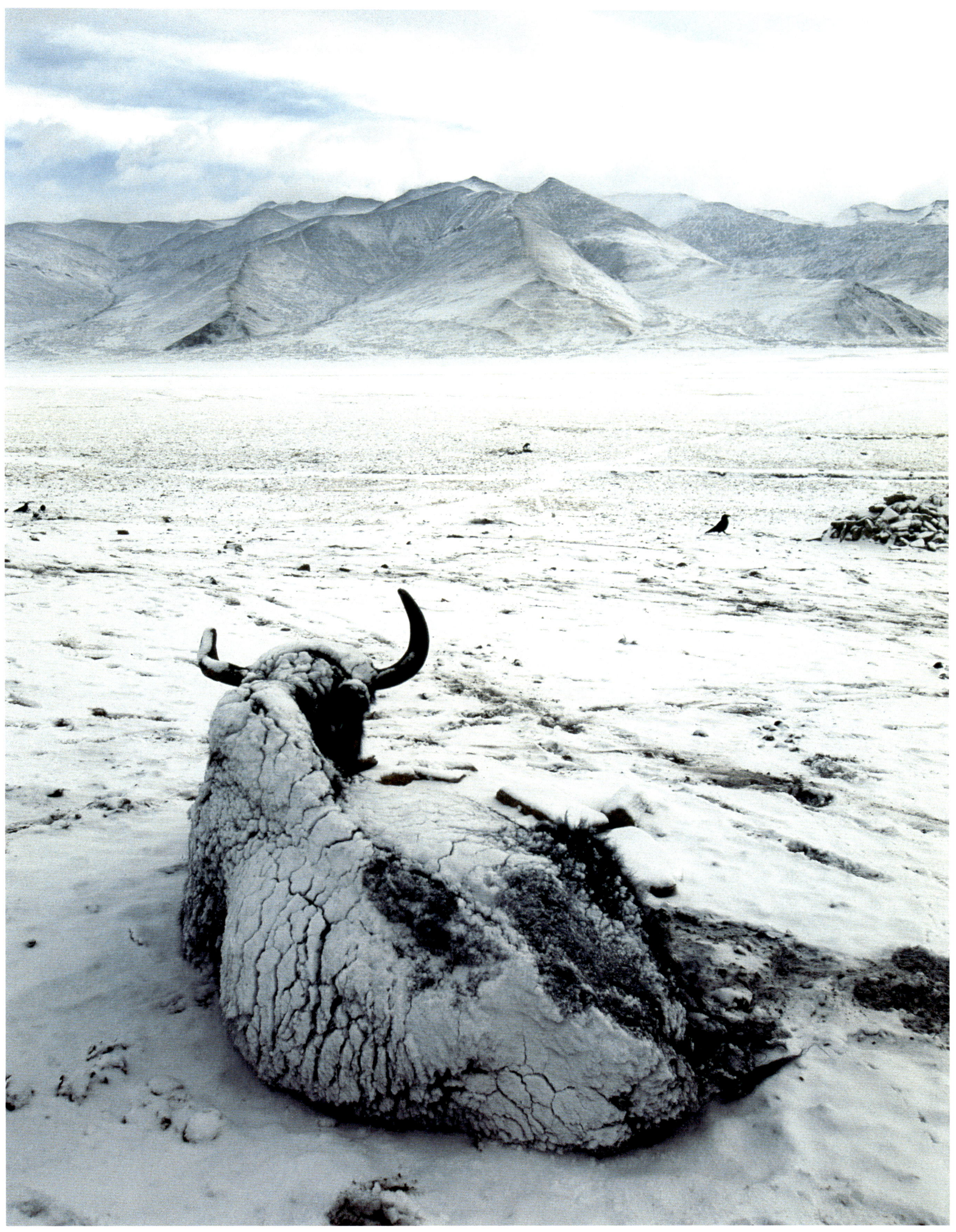

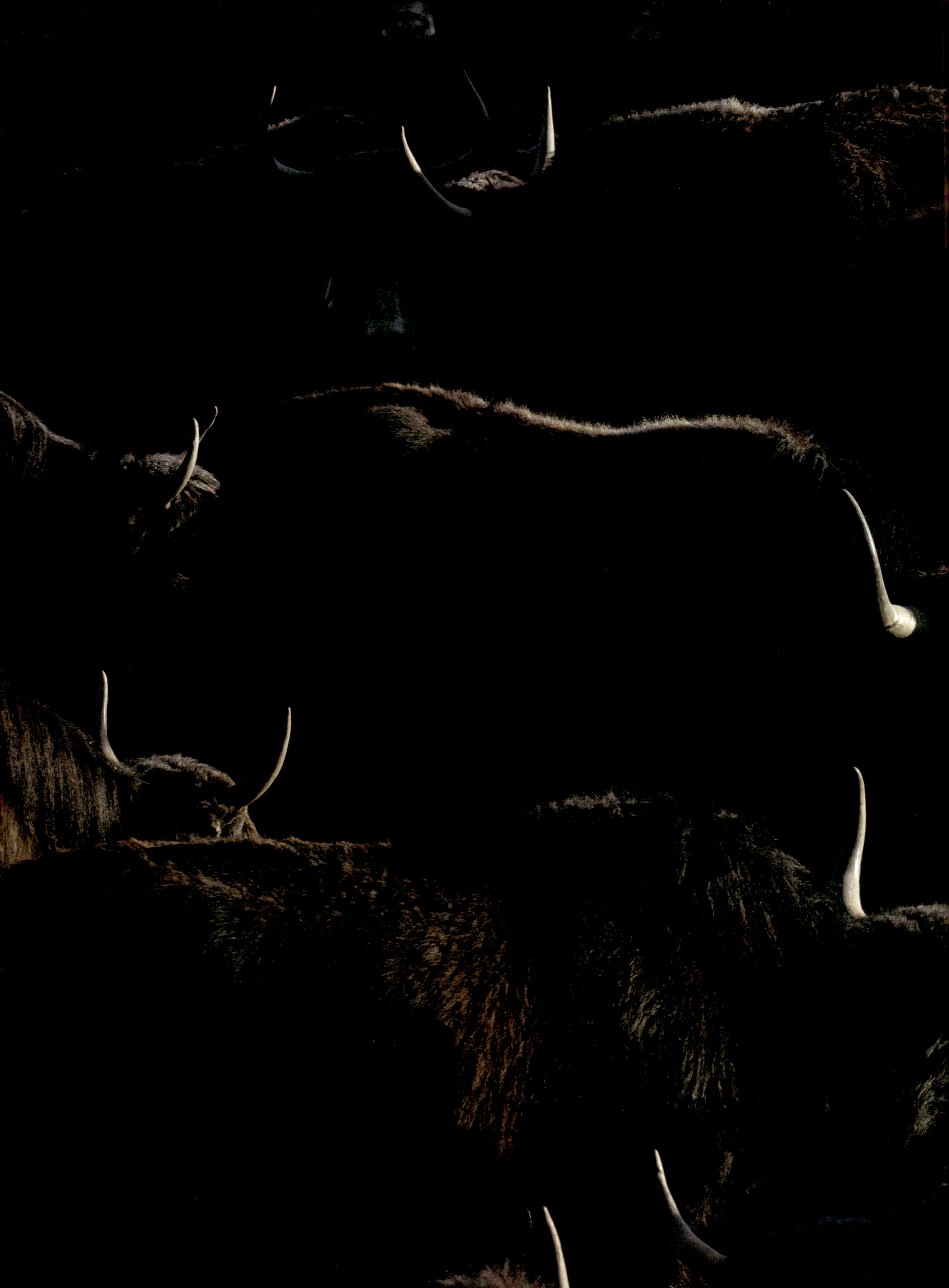

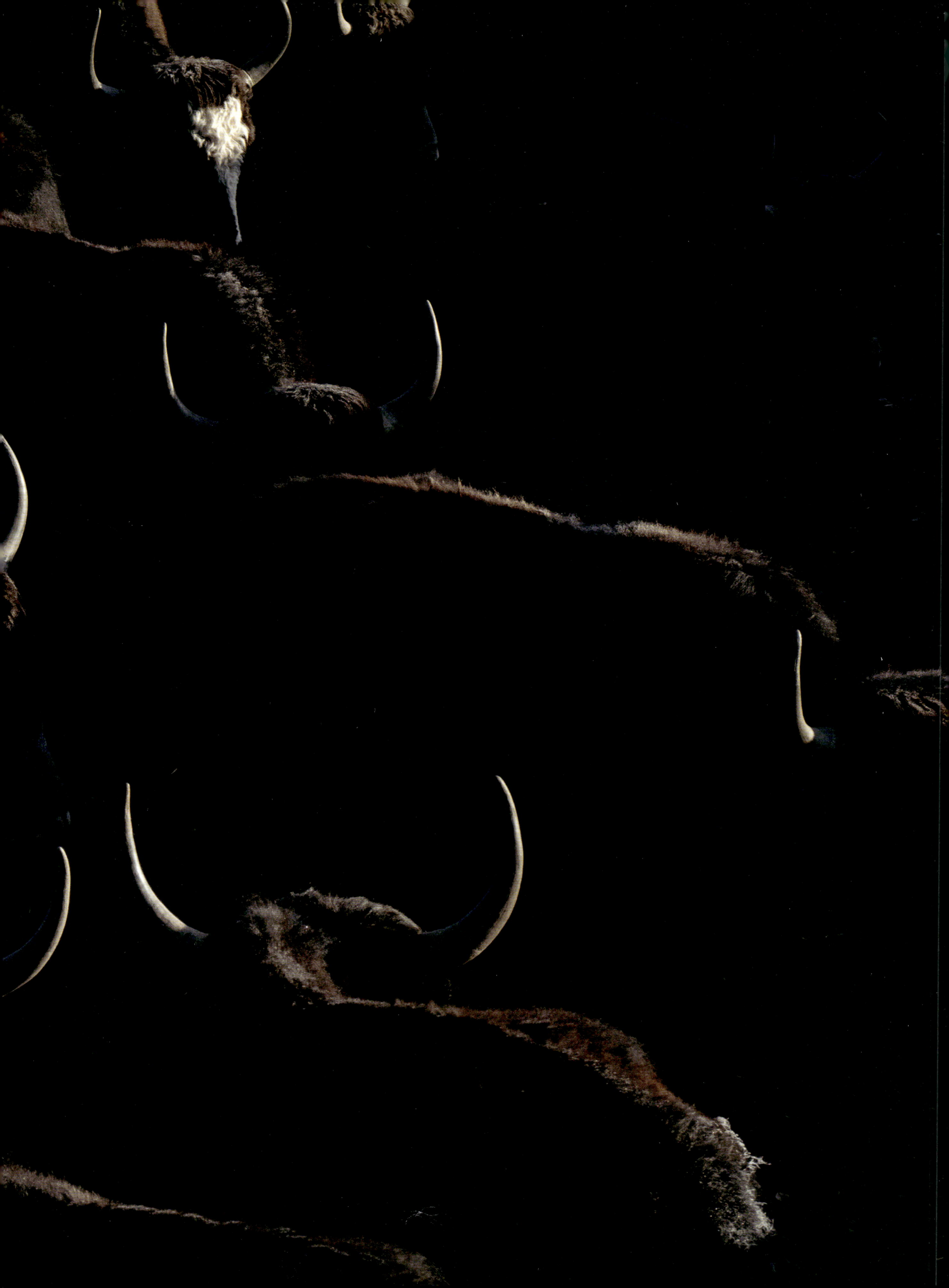

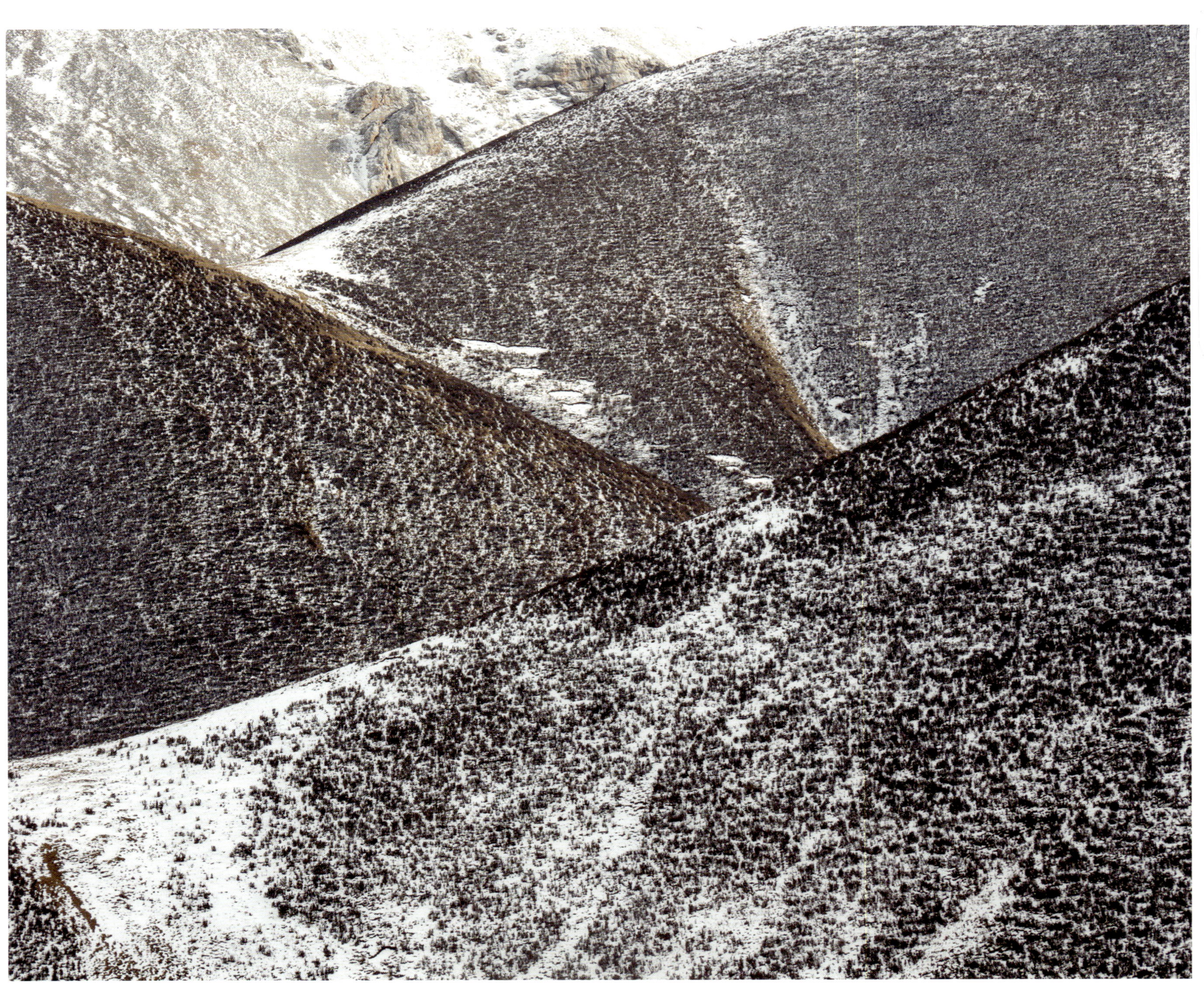

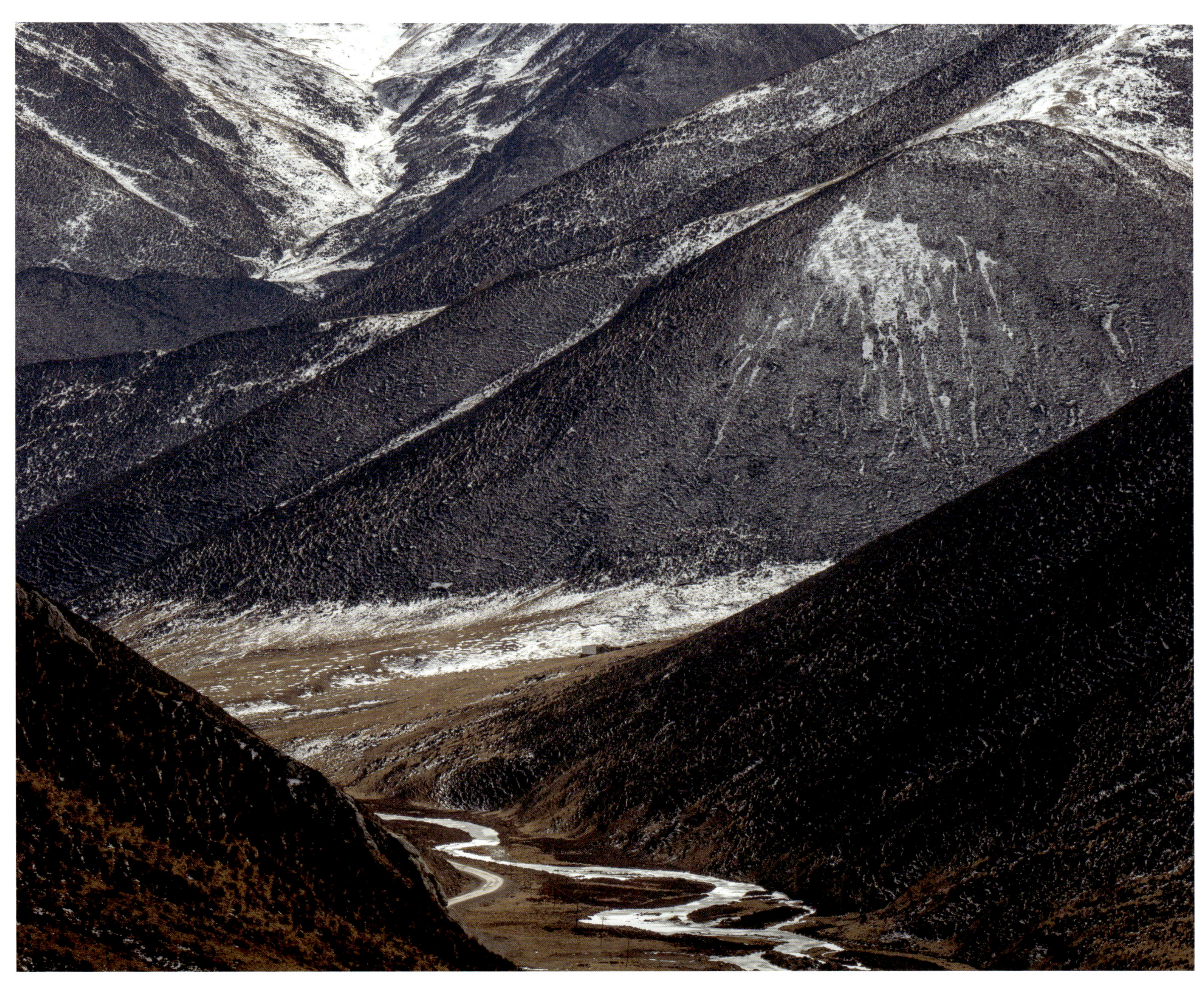

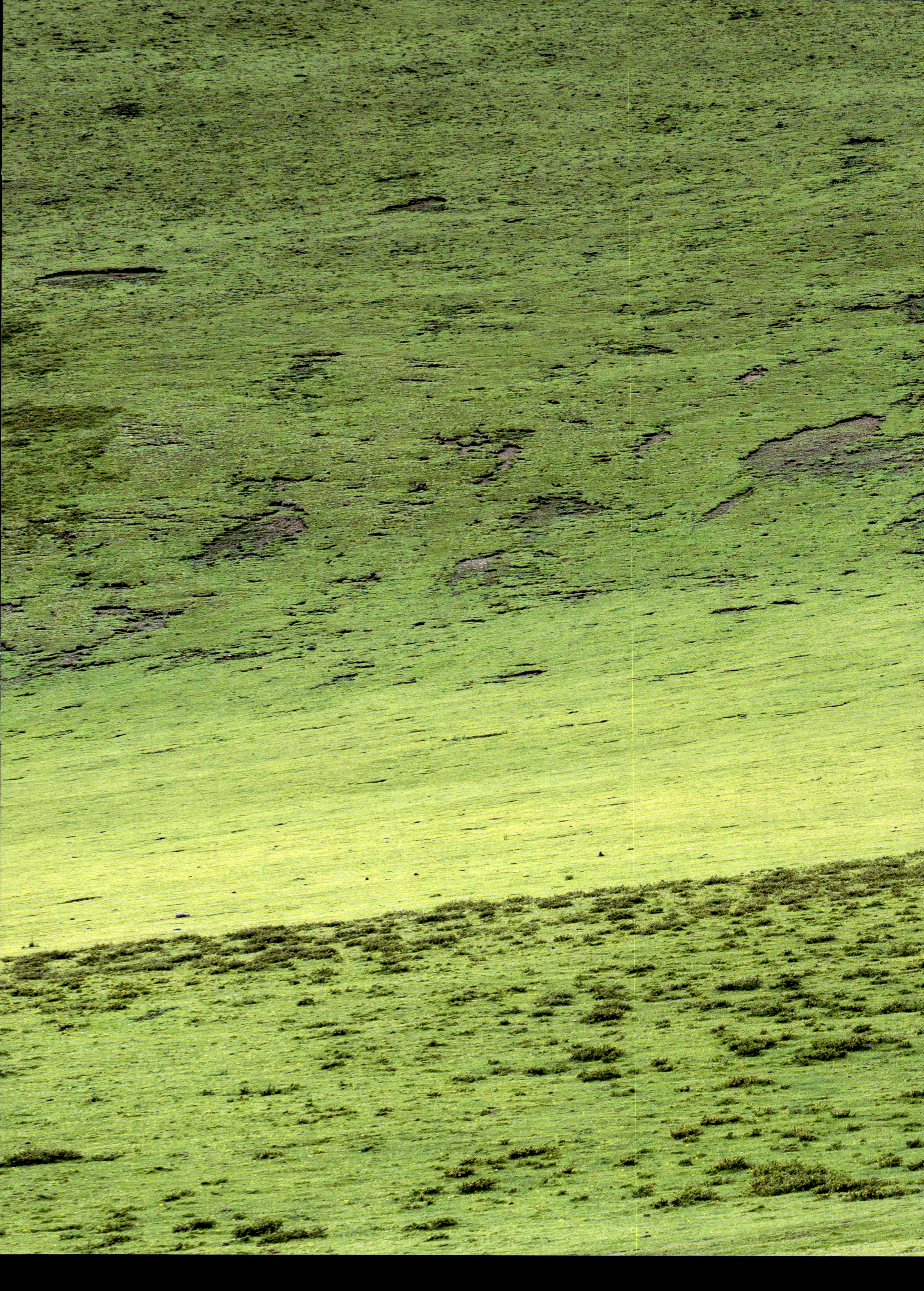

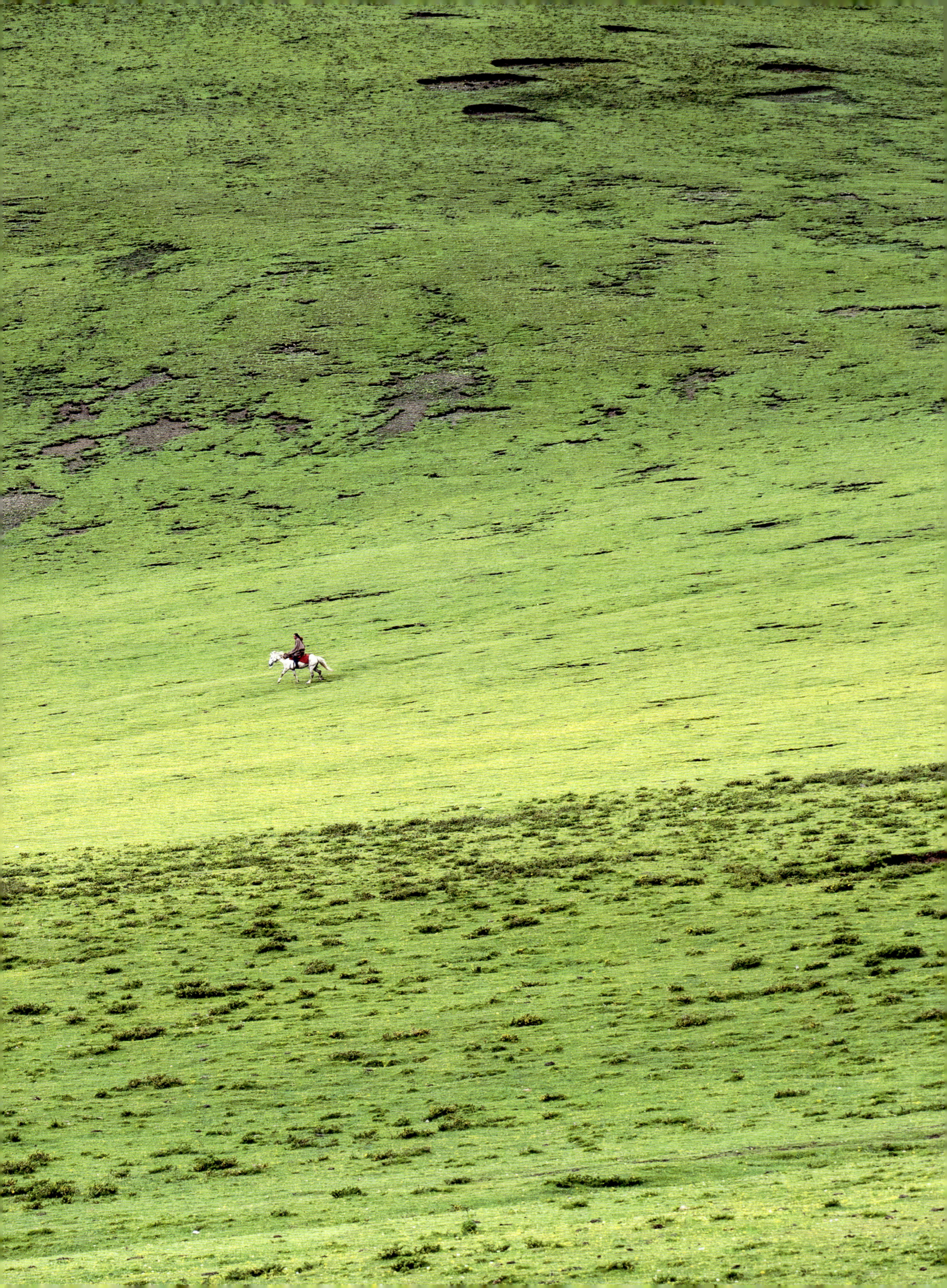

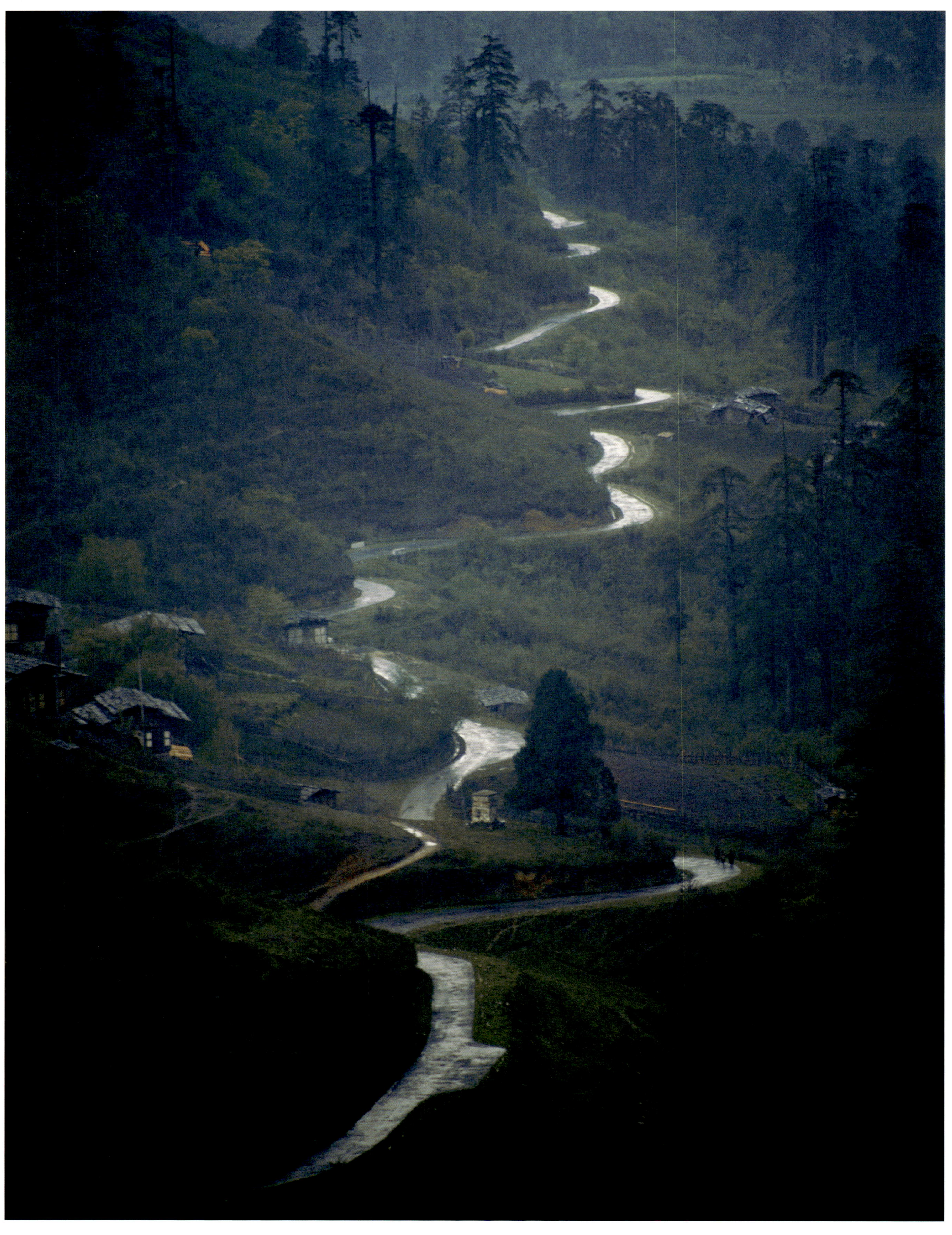

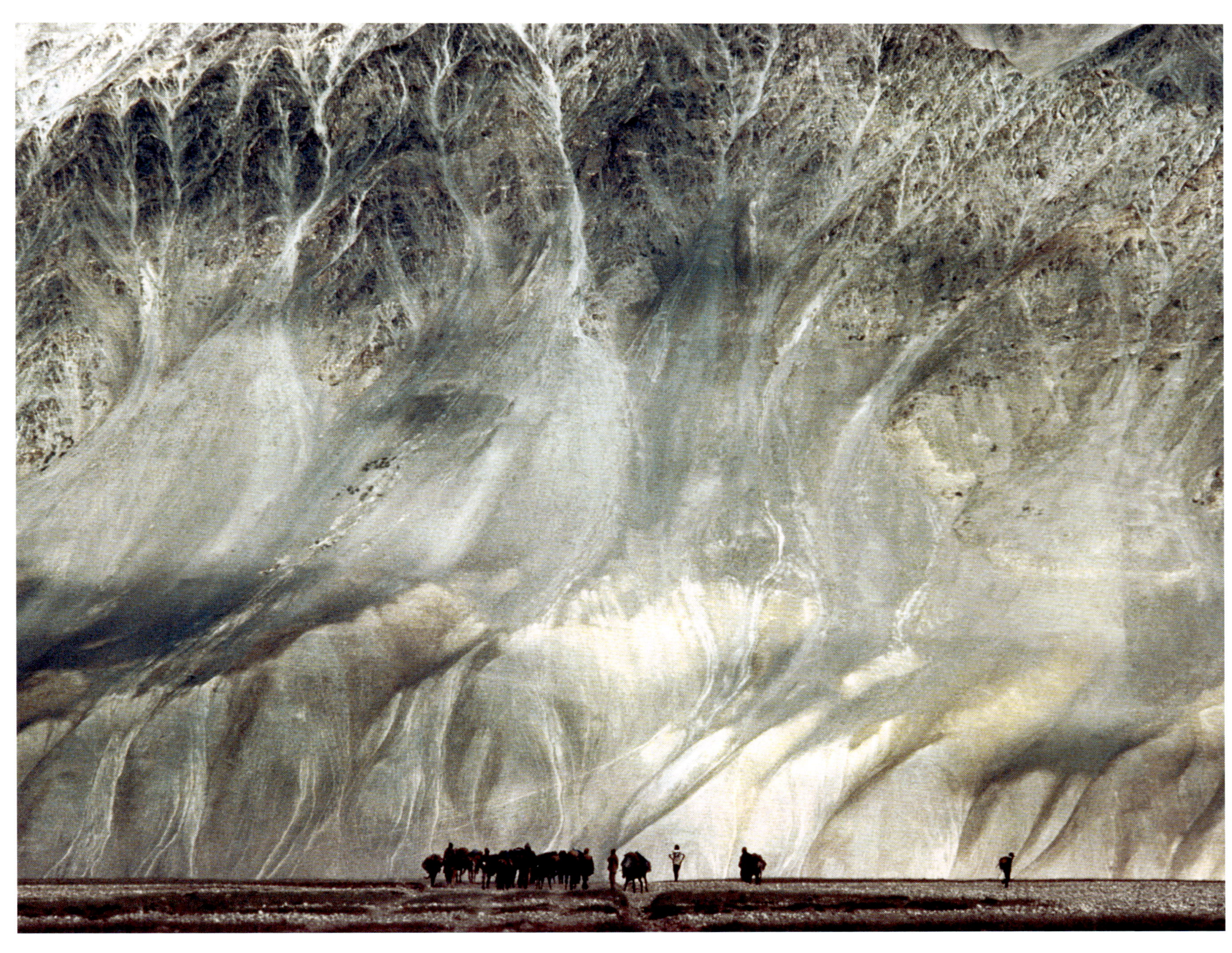

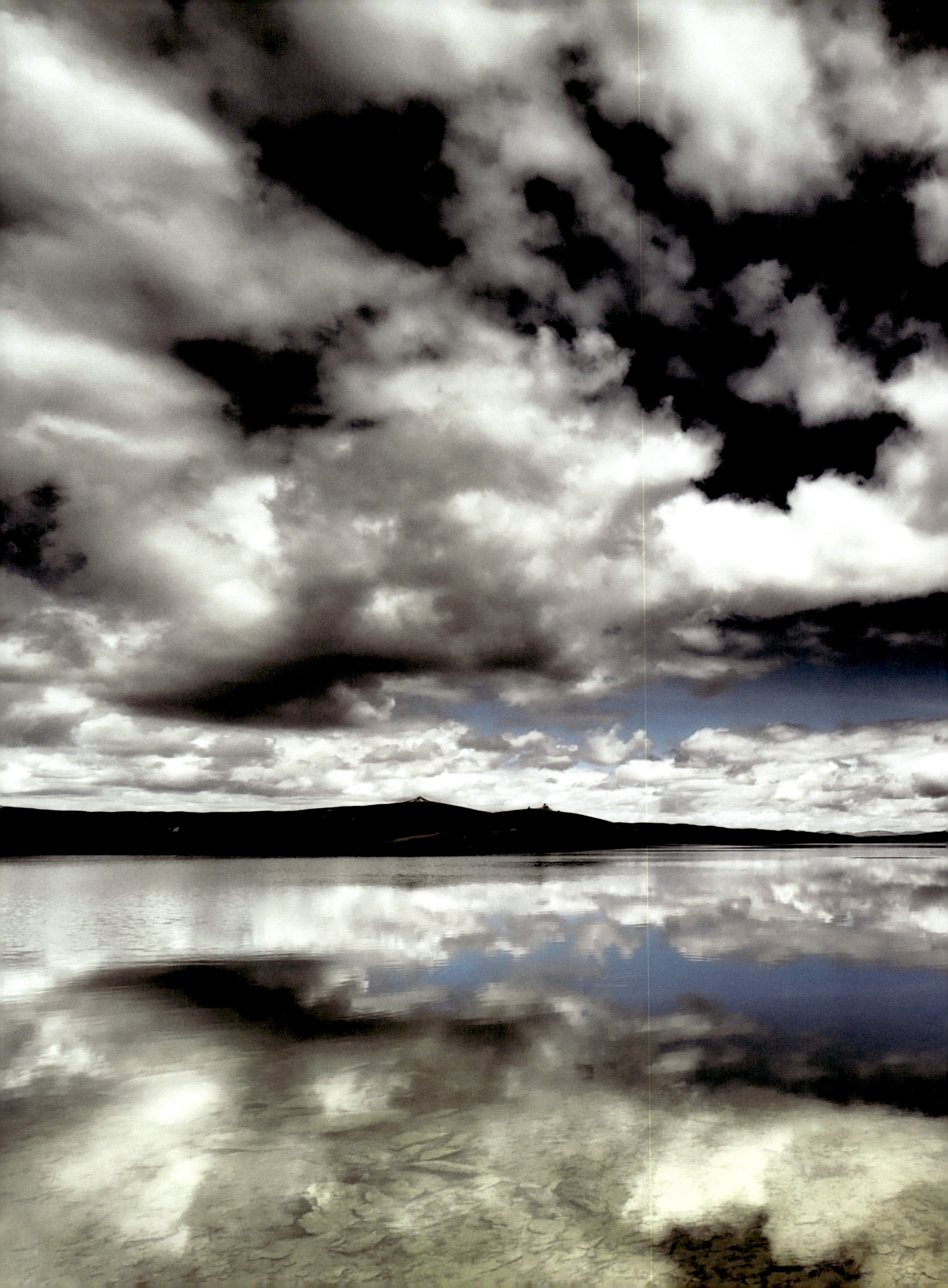

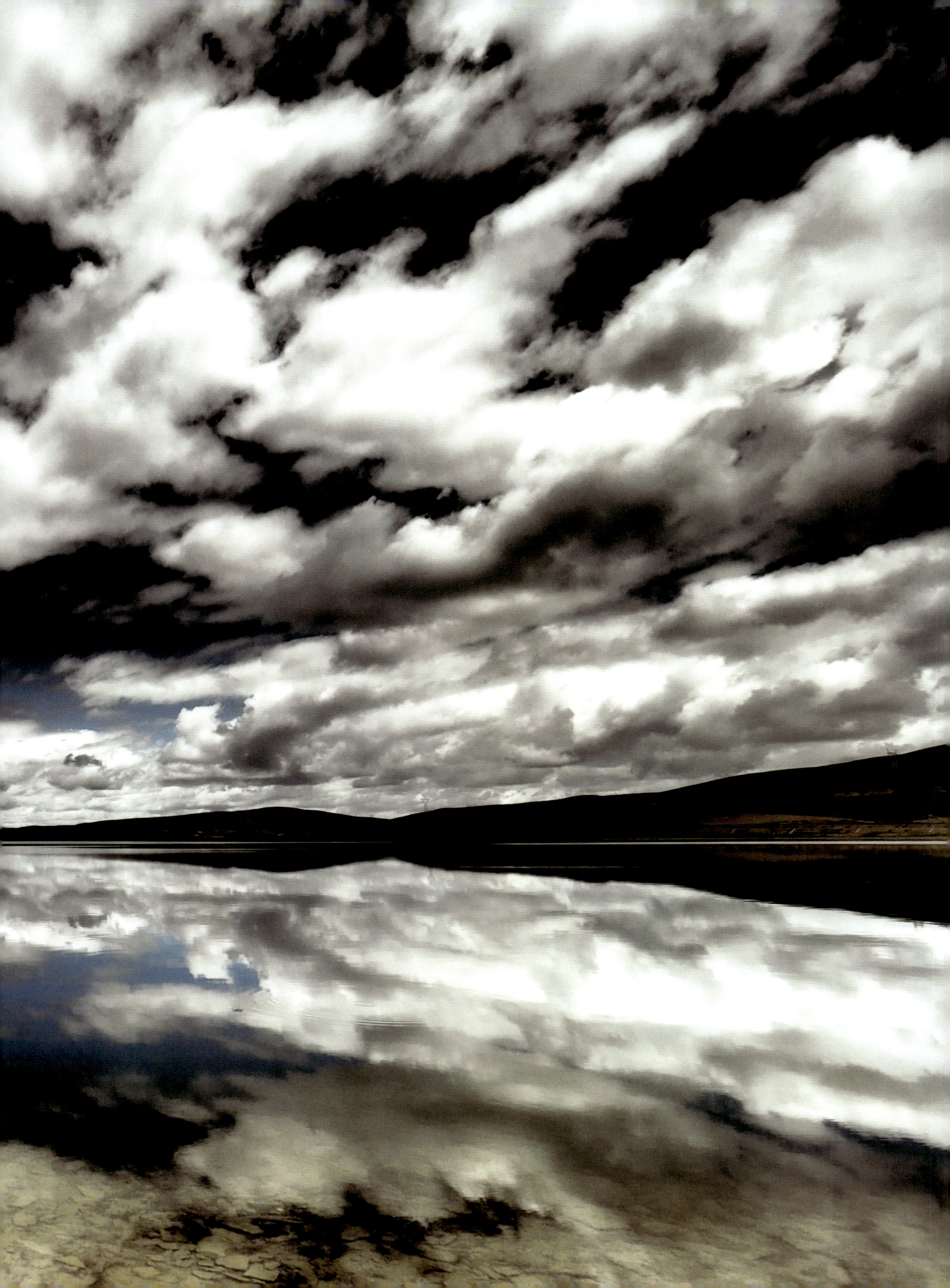

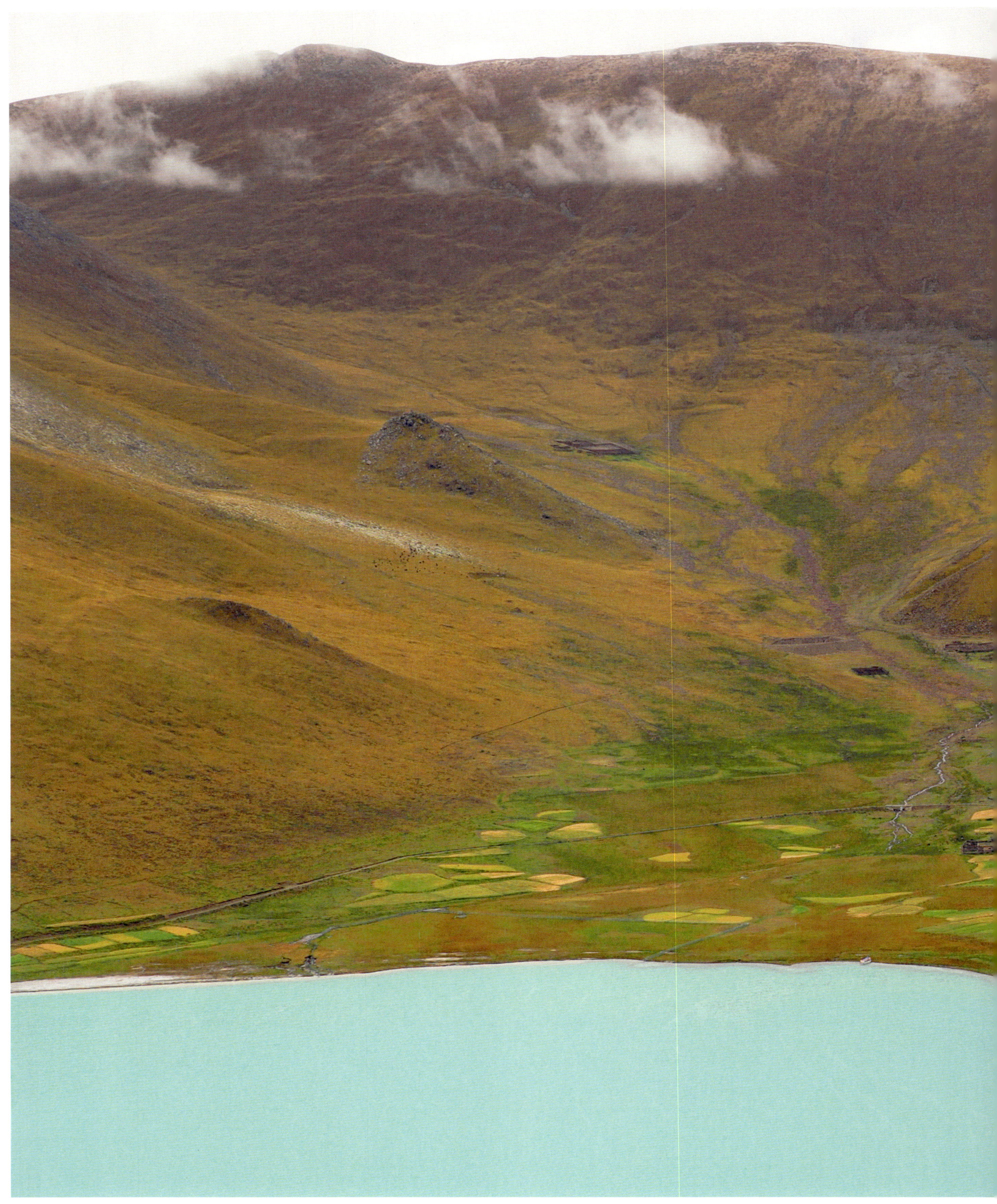

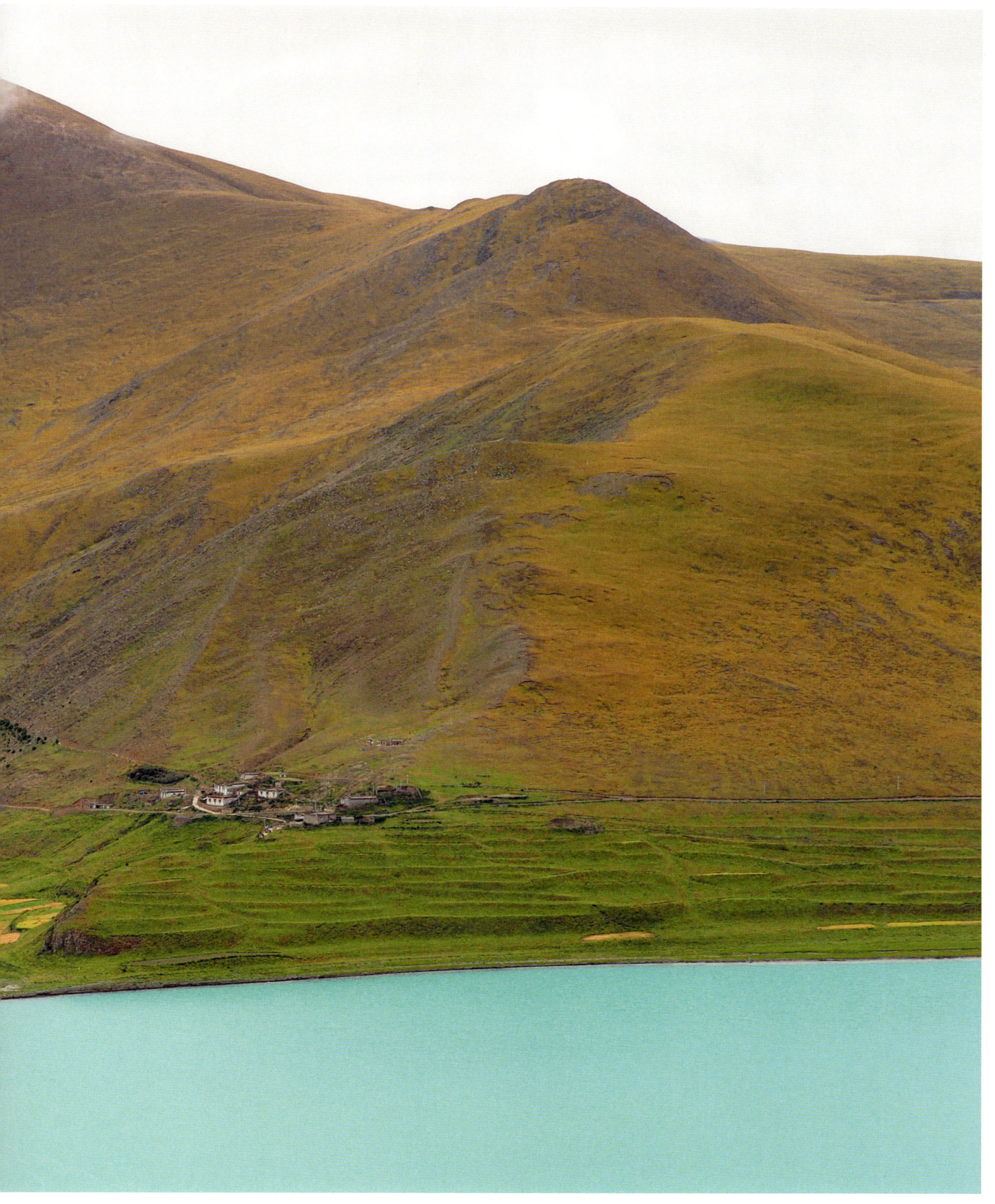

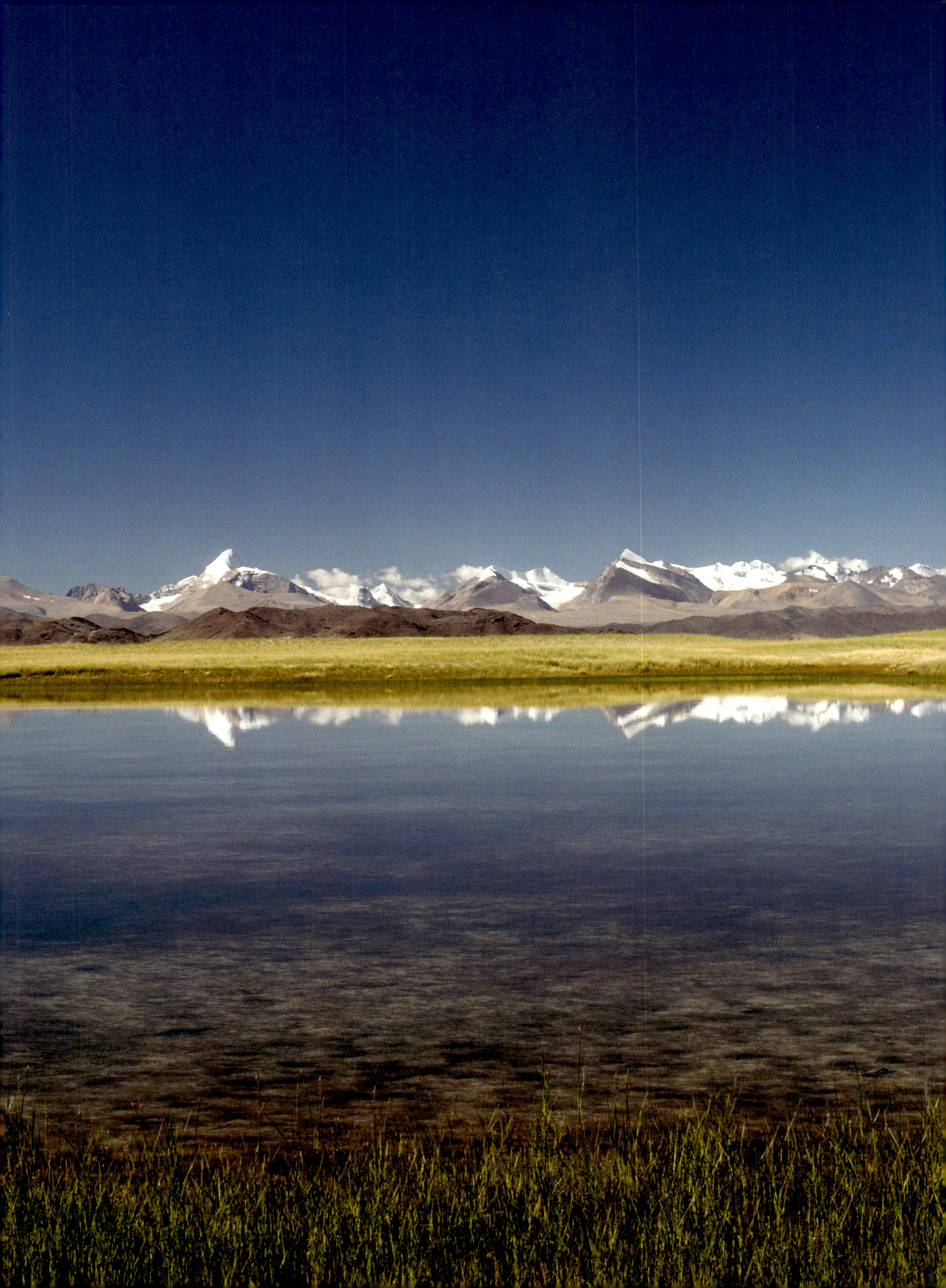

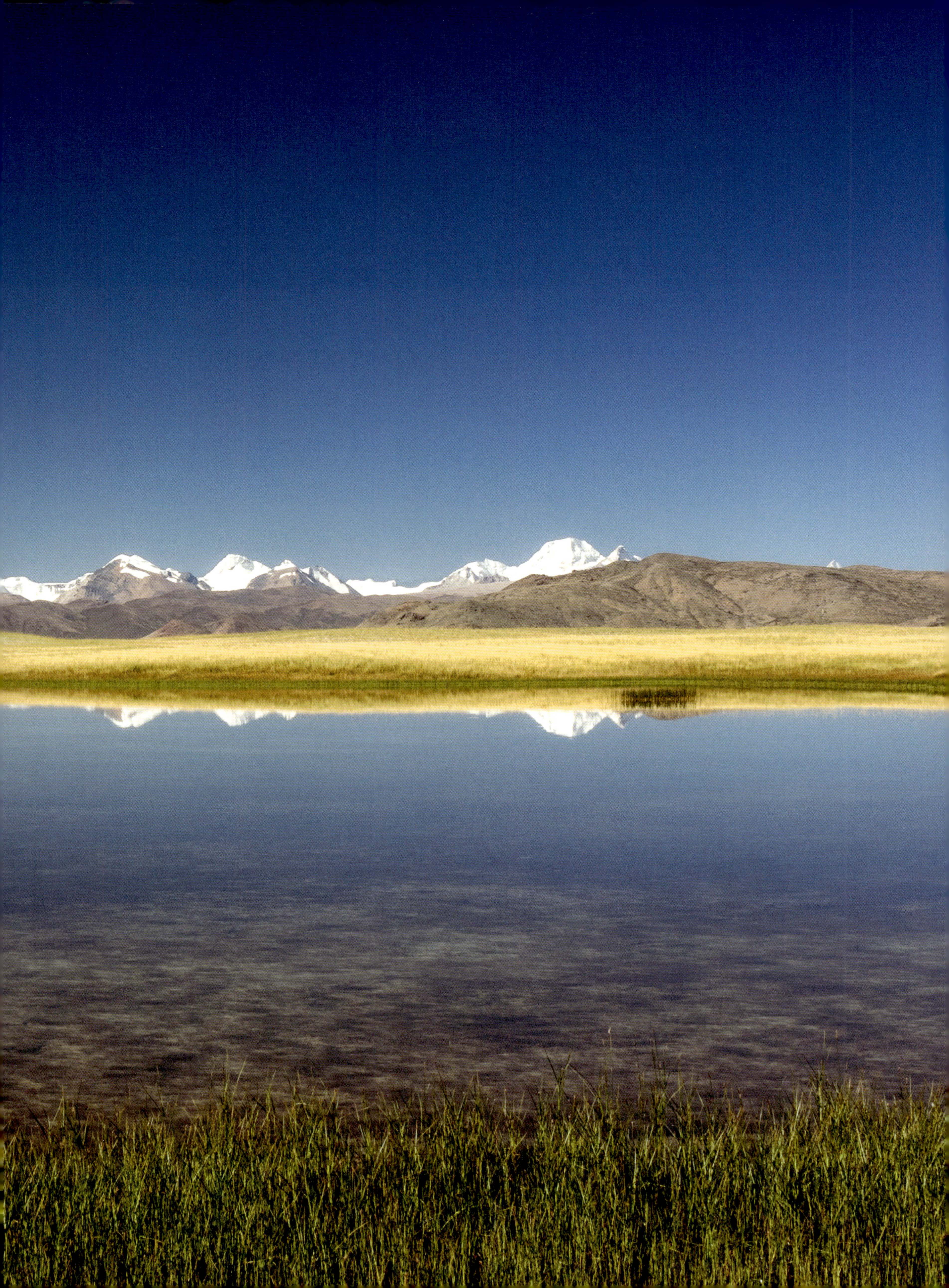

Impermanence

Vergänglichkeit · Impermanence

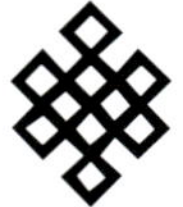

Our life is like an hourglass that never stops. From moment to moment, life trickles away like sand: we are first children, then adults, and finally old and dead. Our mind is responsible for our suffering as it places too much importance on the permanence of things.

Unser Leben ist wie eine Sanduhr, die nie aufhört zu rieseln ... mit jedem Augenblick versiegt das Leben ein Stück mehr. Wir sind Kinder, dann Erwachsene, schließlich alt und tot. Unser Geist ist die Ursache unseres Leids, denn er misst der Dauerhaftigkeit der Dinge zu viel Bedeutung bei.

Notre vie est comme un sablier qui ne s'arrête jamais... D'instant en instant, la vie s'épuise : nous sommes enfants, puis adultes, puis vieux et morts. Notre mental cause notre souffrance, car il attache trop d'importance à la permanence des choses.

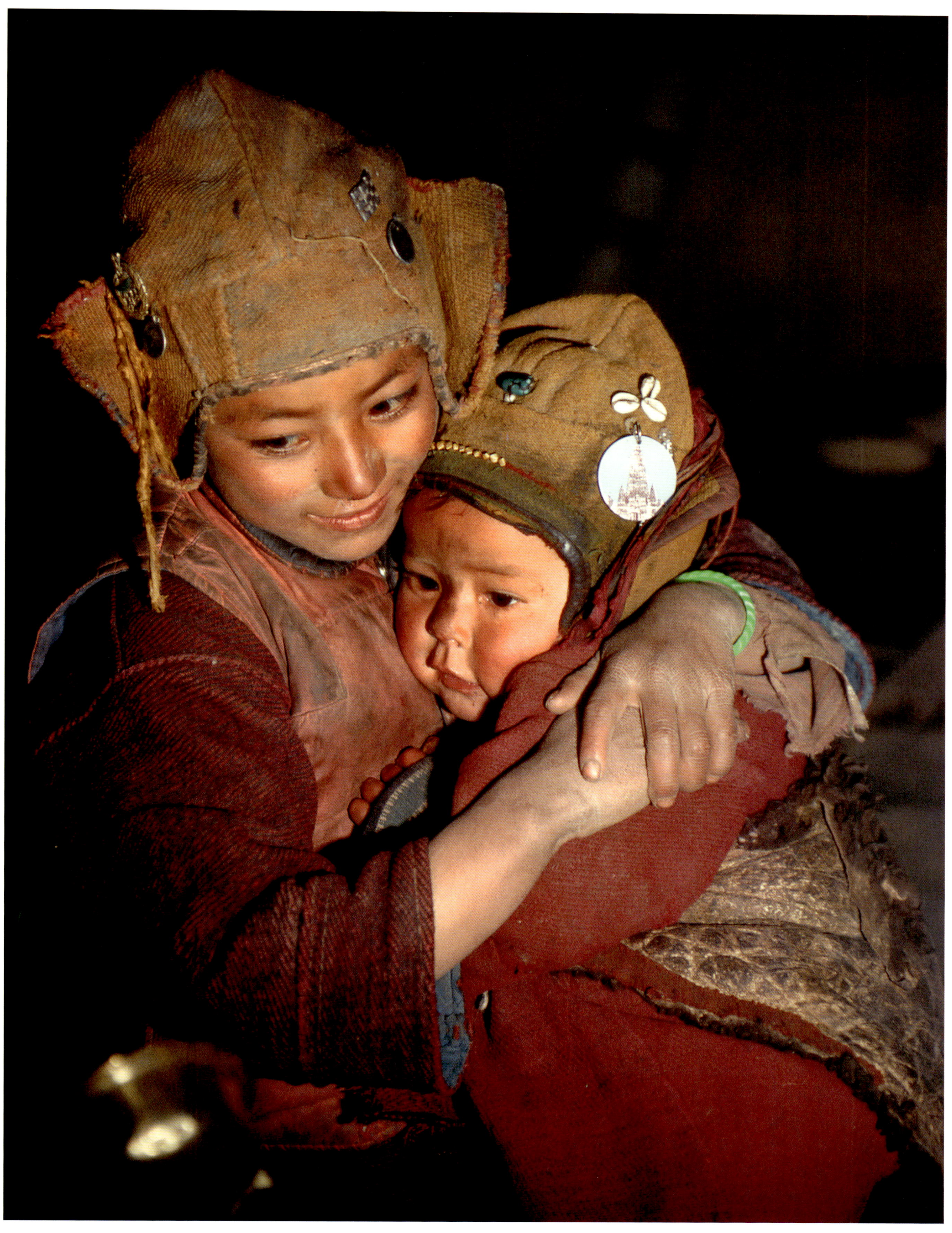

At more than 13,000 feet above sea level, the high and wide-mouthed valley of Lungnak in Zanskar is cut off by snow for eight months a year, and the high passes cannot be crossed. However, it is possible to walk from village to village by making a trail in the snow. But the few villages in the bleak and narrow lower valley are far more isolated on the steep slopes, and many a bold caravan has perished in avalanches while trying to reach them. Families thus spend the winter there, confined to their village and their stone houses. Life in the hamlet of Surle is particularly lonely, as there are only four houses perched above the frozen river. This is where my friend Dorjee lives with his wife, Diskit Lhamo, and their two children. Calm and composed, Dorjee always has his prayer beads in his hand and a prayer on his lips, and is respected by all the villagers as far as the high valley since he is the schoolteacher. In summer, he travels from village to village to teach children who have not migrated to the mountain pastures. In winter, Dorjee remains with his family in Surle. Prisoner of the snow for more than a month now in the high valley, I take the risk of going to find Dorjee in Surle and, anxiously probing the ice on the frozen Tsarap River, I pray that my karma will protect me from avalanches.

The blue shadows are creeping over the ice when, with a sigh of relief, I reach the foot of the hamlet and climb up the icy path. The hamlet is deserted, the animals have returned to their barns, and the cold air tears at my face. It is not even three o'clock. Joyfully, I push open the wooden door of Dorjee's house and, groping around in the narrow maze of the dark corridor, I pass through the barns, stumble against a yak, hit my head on a beam, and cross six tiny doors to reach the winter room, caulked beneath the house. The doors not only protect from the cold but also alert the family of my arrival as they squeak and squeal.

"Ya Djulley, Dorjee Lé!"
"Oh Olivier Lé, Djulley, skiot lé!"

In the half-light of the room where it's barely possible to stand, the family is sitting cross-legged on the dirt floor, in a circle around a small metal stove. In his large madder wool coat, his forehead against the floor, Dorjee is trying to revive the dried dung embers. "You didn't tell me you were coming!" he said, apologizing for not meeting me at the bottom of the path. "How did you expect me to tell you?!"

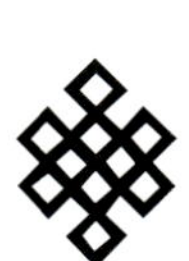

A glowing red flame escapes from the hearth, and the greasy smoke filling the room slowly disperses. Two small windows on the roof let in a little daylight. It is below freezing, and everyone is wearing their woolen coat and hat. These clothes are worn all winter long, even inside the house. Diskit Lhamo welcomes me with a large cheerful grin and, using her straw whisk, dissolves barley flour and mountain butter into quivering water. She then throws a handful of hard cheese in and leaves the soup to simmer in its stone pan. Tukpa, which warms all the body, is the gift of winter evenings. The two silent children and Meme Angchuk, the grandfather, who is busy praying, patiently wait for it to be served. Diskit Lhamo, whose name means happy goddess in Tibetan, has the gentle and reassuring gestures of a satisfied mother. On her head is a heavy turquoise and coral headdress, known as a peyrac, that her mother gave her when she married Dorjee, and on her back is a white long-haired goat's pelt. A necklace of turquoises embellishes her heavy burgundy-colored woolen coat, her only attire, which smells of smoke. Her sewn goat-skin shoes are enhanced by woolen gaiters. Like all women in Tibetan culture, she is the boss in her family. The men are always more reserved. On the go from dawn to dusk, she milks the goats, fetches water from the stream, cooks, cleans the barns, and purifies the house every morning with a melodious prayer and a sprig of juniper incense. While the soup simmers, she spins goat's wool with a caressing gesture. Every time she bends her arm toward her and then slowly straightens it again, she watches her hand that, skillfully, twists the wool. Her peaceful face, which she gently turns toward the heat of the flame, lights up little by little. "Tukpa tong," she says, gracefully handing me a bowl of steaming hot soup.

I love taking part in these scenes of daily life, reminiscent of the Bible, so harmonious that I want them to last forever. But the impermanence of life is one of the first evidences taught by Buddha.

A year later, in autumn, I go back to see my friends, but Dorjee, normally so cheerful, is taciturn. We drink chang on the flat roof of his house, and after a few bowls have loosened his tongue, he explains that he hasn't spoken with Tsering, his neighbor, in six months. Dorjee suspects Tsering of pilfering one of his hoes, while Tsering accuses Dorjee of stealing wood from him. This is a serious accusation for Dorjee, who strictly follows the Buddha's precepts of never killing, lying, or stealing. While the problem may seem futile, the situation has become very uncomfortable for everyone in the hamlet, given that two out of the four families living there are not on speaking terms.

In Zanskar, a dispute is never solved directly between protagonists. A third party who is not involved in the problem always acts as a mediator. This avoids lack of self-control and prevents anger, which for Buddhists is one of the worst evils there is to combat. "Dorjee, Tsering is my friend too, I'll talk to him." "Dju Olivier, thank you," whispers my friend, with downcast eyes.

Therefore, the next day I go to find Tsering at his house. We drink chang on his flat roof all afternoon without bringing up the problem. I really don't know how to broach the matter. "Tsering, tomorrow I'm leaving for the monastery. Please come to Dorjee's house in the morning so we can say goodbye." "Dju Olivier," my friend answers, who cannot refuse my proposal. The categorical "no" does not exist here, as it is too violently direct. Lying in the hay on the roof of Dorjee's house, I try to draw inspiration from the stars to resolve the conflict before falling asleep.

The next morning, in the dirt-floored kitchen, Dorjee is sitting cross-legged next to Tsering. I am seated opposite, and a jar of chang separates us. None of us speak. "Tchang done," I say to my two friends, pouring them a drink. We drink at least ten bowls, and their tense faces begin to relax. A few more bowls and we start to crack jokes. The jar is almost empty and I get up, taking from the flap of my coat two honorific khatas that I place on my friends' shoulders. I then join the palms of my hands: "Dorjee, Tsering, your quarrel is now over!" I say with emotion. "Dju Olivier, Dju," they stutter in a quavering voice, also joining the palms of their hands. Dorjee gets up and brings back a jar of chang. The two friends insist on serving each other. We burn an incense stick to drive out the demons of confusion and thank the spirits of clear-sightedness.

The mental poisons that cause our sufferings and those that we inflict on others are hate, greed, arrogance, jealousy, lack of discernment, and ignorance, which consists of wrongly perceiving the way in which things truly exist.

Das 4000 Meter hoch gelegene, weite obere Lungnak-Tal in Zanskar ist acht Monate im Jahr durch den Schnee von der Außenwelt abgeschnitten. Die Pässe sind in dieser Zeit nicht begehbar, doch kann man von einem Dorf zum anderen marschieren und dabei seine Spuren im Schnee hinterlassen. Noch viel stärker isoliert sind allerdings die wenigen Dörfer im tiefer gelegenen, abgeschiedenen und schluchtartigen unteren Tal mit seinen Steilhängen. Viele wagemutige Expeditionen sind bei dem Versuch, dorthin zu gelangen, unter Lawinen begraben worden. Die Familien im unteren Tal verbringen deshalb den Winter eingeschlossen in ihrem Dorf und ihren Steinhäusern. Besonders einsam ist das Leben im Weiler Surle, denn er besteht aus lediglich vier Häusern, die oberhalb des zugefrorenen Flusses am Hang kauern. Hier lebt mein Freund Dorjee mit seiner Frau Diskit Lhamo und ihren beiden Kindern. Dorjee, ein ruhiger, bedächtiger Mann, hat immer eine Gebetskette in der Hand und ein Gebet auf den Lippen. Er wird von allen Dorfbewohnern bis hinauf ins Hochtal respektiert, denn er ist Lehrer. Im Sommer geht er von Dorf zu Dorf und unterrichtet die Kinder, die nicht auf den Bergweiden arbeiten. Den Winter dagegen verbringt er bei seiner Familie in Surle. Ich bin nun schon seit einem Monat im Hochtal Gefangener des Schnees und will es wagen, Dorjee in Surle zu besuchen. Ängstlich untersuche ich das Eis auf dem zugefrorenen Fluss Tsarap und bete, dass mich mein Karma vor Lawinen bewahren möge.

Die blauen Schatten kriechen über das Eis, als ich erleichtert am unteren Rand des Weilers ankomme und den vereisten Weg hinaufsteige. Der Weiler ist verlassen, die Tiere sind in ihre Ställe zurückgekehrt und die Kälte beißt mir ins Gesicht. Es ist nicht einmal drei Uhr. Freudig drücke ich die Holztür des Hauses von Dorjee auf, taste mich im dunklen Flur voran wie in einem engen Labyrinth, vorbei an den Ställen. Dabei stoße ich an ein Yak, schlage mir den Kopf an einem Balken an und muss durch sechs kleine Türen, um zum Winterzimmer im unteren Teil des Hauses zu gelangen. Die vielen Türen schützen vor der Kälte, kündigen der Familie aber auch meine Ankunft an, denn sie knarren, als wollten sie klagen.

„Ya Djulley, Dorjee Le!"
„Oh Olivier Le, Djulley, skiotle!"

Im Halbdunkel des Raums, in dem man kaum aufrecht stehen kann, sitzt die Familie im Schneidersitz um einen kleinen Blechherd auf dem Erdboden. Dorjee versucht ganz außer Atem in seinem großen roten Wollmantel, die Stirn knapp über dem Boden, die Glut in den getrockneten Kuhfladen zu entfachen. „Du hast mir gar nicht gesagt, dass du kommst!", sagt er, als wollte er sich entschuldigen, dass er mich nicht am Ende des Wegs empfangen hat. „Wie hätte ich das denn machen sollen?", antworte ich.

Eine rötliche Flamme flackert aus der Feuerstelle. Der dichte Rauch, der das Zimmer erfüllt, verzieht sich nur langsam. Zwei Luken schicken einen Teil der Schwaden in den ärmlichen Tag hinaus. Es ist null Grad kalt, und jeder trägt seinen Mantel und seine Wollmütze. Man nimmt sie im Winter nie ab, nicht einmal im Haus. Freudig schenkt mir Diskit Lhamo ein breites, einladendes Lächeln und rührt mit ihrem Strohbesen Gerstenmehl und Bergbutter in das siedende Wasser. Dann wirft sie eine Handvoll Hartkäse hinein und lässt die Suppe im Steintopf köcheln. Die Tukpa wärmt den ganzen Körper; im Winter dient sie als Abendessen. Die beiden stillen Kinder und der im Gebet versunkene Großvater Mémé Angchuk warten geduldig. Diskit Lhamo bedeutet „glückliche Göttin". Sie hat die sanften, beruhigenden Gesten einer unbeschwerten Mutter. Auf dem Kopf trägt sie eine schwere Haube aus Türkisen und Korallen, die sie von ihrer Mutter zur Hochzeit bekommen hat. Über ihren Rücken hat sie ein Ziegenfell mit langen weißen Haaren gelegt. Eine Türkiskette ziert ihren schweren, bordeauxroten, nach Rauch riechenden Wollmantel, ihre einzige Kleidung. Die Schuhe aus genähtem Ziegenleder sind mit Wollgamaschen bedeckt. Wie alle Frauen des tibetischen Kulturkreises führt sie die Familie. Die Männer sind stets zurückhaltender. Sie arbeitet von morgens bis in die Nacht hinein, melkt die Ziegen, holt Wasser aus dem Gebirgsbach, kocht, mistet die Ställe aus und reinigt jeden Morgen das Haus mit einem melodiösen Gebet und einem Räucherstäbchen aus Wacholder. Während die Suppe köchelt, spinnt sie die Ziegenwolle mit zärtlicher Geste. Jedesmal wenn sie den Arm zu sich zieht, um ihn gleich wieder langsam zu entspannen, folgt ihr Blick ihrer Hand, die den Wollfaden geschickt flicht. Ihr ruhiges Gesicht, das sie sanft zur Hitze der Flamme wendet, beginnt nach und nach immer mehr zu strahlen. „Tukpa tong", sagt sie und reicht mir anmutig eine Schale kochend heißer Suppe.

Ich bin gern bei solchen biblischen Alltagsszenen dabei; sie wirken so harmonisch, dass es mir am liebsten wäre, sie würden ewig dauern. Die Vergänglichkeit des Lebens ist allerdings eine der ersten Grundwahrheiten, die Buddha gelehrt hat.

Ein Jahr später kehrte ich im Herbst wieder zu meinen Freunden zurück, doch Dorjee, sonst immer fröhlich, war schweigsam. Wir tranken auf der Terrasse des Hauses Chang und als er nach einigen Schalen gelöster wurde, erzählte er mir, dass er und Tsering, sein Nachbar, seit sechs Monaten nicht mehr miteinander geredet hätten. Dorjee verdächtigte Tsering, ihm eine Hacke gestohlen zu haben, während Tsering wiederum Dorjee Holzdiebstahl vorwarf. Das war eine schwere Anschuldigung für Dorjee, der nach den Lehren Buddhas lebt, in denen es heißt, dass man weder töten noch lügen noch stehlen darf. Eigentlich eine Belanglosigkeit, aber die Situation belastete jeden im Dorf, denn zwei von vier Familien waren verfeindet.

In Zanskar wird eine Meinungsverschiedenheit nie direkt zwischen den Beteiligten gelöst. Stets dient eine dritte Person von außen als Schlichter, um zu vermeiden, dass sie nicht die Kontrolle über sich und ihren Zorn verlieren, was eine der schlimmsten Sünden unter Buddhisten wäre. „Dorjee, Tsering ist auch mein Freund. Ich spreche mit ihm." „Dju Olivier, danke", murmelte mein Freund mit gesenktem Blick.

Am nächsten Tag suchte ich also Tsering bei sich zu Hause auf und wir tranken den ganzen Nachmittag auf seiner Terrasse Chang, ohne das Problem anzusprechen. Was sollte ich auch zu ihm sagen? „Tsering, morgen reise ich ab, um zum Kloster zu gehen. Bitte komm morgen früh zu Dorjee, damit wir uns verabschieden können." „Dju Olivier", antwortete mein Freund, der meinen Vorschlag nicht ablehnen konnte.

IN ZANSKAR WIRD EINE MEINUNGSVERSCHIEDENHEIT NIE DIREKT ZWISCHEN DEN BETEILIGTEN GELÖST.

Das kategorische Nein existiert hier nicht, es ist zu unverblümt direkt. Als ich bei Dorjee auf dem Dach im Heu lag, versuchte ich mich auf der Suche nach einer Lösung des Konflikts von den Sternen inspirieren zu lassen, bevor ich einschlief.

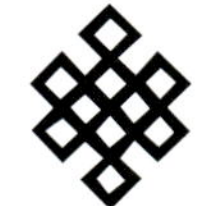

Am nächsten Morgen saß Dorjee in seiner Erdküche im Schneidersitz neben Tsering. Ich saß den beiden gegenüber, einen Krug Chang zwischen uns. Keiner sprach. „Chang done", sagte ich zu meinen beiden Freunden und goss ihnen zu trinken ein. Wir tranken wenigstens zehn Schalen, und allmählich begannen sich die Gesichter zu entspannen. Noch einige Schalen, und wir fingen an zu scherzen. Als der Krug fast leer war, stand ich auf und holte aus meinem Mantel zwei Ehren-Khata. Ich legte die Schals meinen Freunden über die Schulter und faltete die Hände. „Dorjee, Tsering, von nun an ist euer Streit beendet", erklärte ich bewegt. „Dju Olivier, dju", stammelten sie mit zittriger Stimme und falteten ebenfalls die Hände. Dorjee erhob sich und holte einen neuen Krug mit Chang. Die beiden Freunde bestanden darauf, sich gegenseitig einzugießen. Wir verbrannten einen Weihrauchstab, um die Dämonen der Verwirrung zu vertreiben und den Geistern für ihre Klarsicht zu danken.

Die geistigen Gifte, die unser Leid und das, was wir anderen zufügen, hervorbringen, sind Hass, Gier, Hochmut, Eifersucht, mangelnde Urteilsfähigkeit und eine Ignoranz, die darin besteht, die Art und Weise, wie die Dinge in Wirklichkeit sind, nicht zu sehen.

À plus de 4 000 mètres d'altitude, la haute vallée évasée de la Lungnak au Zanskar est isolée par la neige huit mois par an, les hauts cols sont impraticables, mais on peut marcher d'un village à l'autre en faisant sa trace dans la neige. En revanche, les quelques villages de la basse vallée, austère et encaissée, sont beaucoup plus isolés dans les pentes raides, et bien des caravanes téméraires ont péri à cause des avalanches en essayant de les rejoindre. Les familles y passent donc l'hiver, recluses dans leur village et leurs maisons de pierre. La vie au hameau de Surlé est particulièrement solitaire, car il n'y a que quatre maisons perchées au-dessus

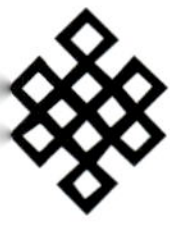

de la rivière gelée. C'est là que vit mon ami Dorjee avec sa femme, Diskit Lhamo, et leurs deux enfants. Calme et mesuré, Dorjee a toujours un rosaire à la main, une prière aux lèvres et il est respecté par tous les villageois jusque dans la haute vallée car il est instituteur. L'été, il passe de village en village pour instuire les enfants qui ne sont pas à l'alpage. L'hiver, Dorjee reste en famille, à Surlé. Prisonnier de la neige depuis plus d'un mois dans la haute vallée, je prends le risque d'aller retrouver Dorjee à Surlé et, sondant anxieusement la glace sur la Tsarap gelée, je prie pour que mon karma me préserve des avalanches.

Les ombres bleues rampent sur la glace lorsque, soulagé, j'arrrive au pied du hameau et grimpe le chemin verglacé. Le hameau est désert, les bêtes sont rentrées dans leurs étables et le froid me lacère le visage. Il est à peine trois heures. Joyeusement, je pousse la porte de bois de la maison de Dorjee et, en tatônnant dans le couloir obscur en labyrinthe étroit, je traverse les étables, bute contre un yak, me tape la tête contre une poutre et franchit six portes minuscules pour rejoindre la pièce d'hiver, calfeutrée sous la maison. Les portes ont l'avantage de protéger du froid, mais aussi d'avertir la famille de mon arrivée car elles grincent comme une plainte.

« Ya Djulley, Dorjee Lé! »
« Oh Olivier Lé, Djulley, skiot lé! »

Dans la pénombre de la pièce où l'on tient à peine debout, la famille est assise en tailleur sur le sol de terre, en cercle autour d'une petite cuisinière de tôle. Dans son grand manteau de laine garance, le front contre le sol, Dorjee s'essouffle sur la braise de bouse séchée. « Tu ne m'as pas prévenu de ton arrivée ! » me dit-il pour s'excuser de ne pas m'avoir accueilli au bas du sentier. « Comment veux-tu que je te prévienne ! »

Une flamme rougeoyante s'échappe de l'âtre et la fumée grasse qui envahissait la pièce se dissipe lentement. Deux lucarnes diffusent un peu du jour chétif. Il fait zéro degrés et chacun porte son manteau et son bonnet de laine. On ne les quitte jamais de tout l'hiver, même dans la maison. Enjouée, Diskit Lhamo me lance un large sourire accueillant et délaie avec son fouet de paille de la farine d'orge et du beurre d'alpage dans de l'eau frémissante. Puis elle jette une poignée de fromage dur et laisse mijoter la soupe dans sa casserole de pierre. La tukpa, qui réchauffe tout le corps, est le cadeau des soirs d'hiver. Ses deux enfants silencieux et Mémé Angchuk, le grand-père occupé à prier, l'attendent patiemment. Diskit Lhamo signifie déesse heureuse. Elle a les gestes doux et rassurants d'une mère épanouie. Elle est coiffée d'un lourd peyrac de turquoises et de coraux hérité de sa mère lors de son mariage avec Dorjee. Dans le dos, elle porte une peau de chèvre aux longs poils blancs. Un collier de turquoises embellit son lourd manteau de laine bordeaux à l'odeur de fumée, son seul habit. Ses chaussures en peau de chèvre cousue sont réhaussées de guêtres de laine. Comme toutes les femmes dans la culture tibétaine, c'est elle qui mène la famille. Les hommes sont toujours plus réservés. Active de l'aube à la nuit, elle trait les chèvres, cherche l'eau au torrent, cuisine, nettoie les étables, purifie la maison chaque matin d'une prière mélodieuse et d'un brin d'encens de genévrier. Tandis que la soupe mijote, elle file la laine de chèvre d'un geste caressant. Chaque fois qu'elle ramène son bras vers elle pour ensuite le détendre lentement, elle suit des yeux sa main qui, habilement, fait vriller la laine. Son visage tranquille, qu'elle tourne doucement vers la chaleur de la flamme, s'illumine peu à peu. « Tukpa tong », dit-elle en me tendant gracieusement un bol de soupe brûlante.

J'aime participer à ces scènes quotidiennes bibliques, si harmonieuses que j'aimerais les voir durer toujours. Mais l'impermanence de la vie est l'une des premières évidences enseignées par Bouddha.

Un an plus tard, à l'automne, je retourne auprès de mes amis, mais Dorjee, d'habitude jovial, est taciturne. Nous buvons du tchang sur la terrasse de sa maison et, plus détendu au bout de quelques bols, il m'explique que Tsering, son voisin, et lui ne se parlent plus depuis six mois. Dorjee soupçonne Tsering de lui avoir chapardé une pioche, et Tsering a accusé Dorjee de lui avoir volé du bois. C'est une accusion grave pour Dorjee, qui suit à la lettre les préceptes de Bouddha consistant à ne jamais ni tuer, ni mentir, ni voler. Le problème paraît futile, mais la situation accable tout le monde dans le hameau car, sur quatre familles, la moitié est en froid.

Au Zanskar, un différend ne se règle jamais directement entre protagonistes. C'est toujours une tierce personne extérieure à la cause qui sert de médiateur pour éviter le non contrôle de soi et la colère, l'un des pires maux à combattre chez les bouddhistes. « Dorjee, Tsering est aussi mon ami, je vais lui parler. » « Dju Olivier, merci », murmure mon ami, les yeux baissés.

Le lendemain, je vais donc trouver Tsering chez lui et nous buvons du tchang sur sa terrasse tout l'après-midi sans évoquer le problème. Que puis-je bien en dire ? « Tsering, demain, je pars au monastère, s'il te plaît, viens chez Dorjee demain matin pour qu'on se dise au revoir. » « Dju Olivier », répond mon ami, qui ne peut refuser ma proposition. Le non catégorique n'existe pas ici, il est trop violemment direct. Couché dans le foin sur le toit, chez Dorjee, je tâche de m'inspirer des étoiles pour dénouer le conflit avant de m'endormir.

Le lendemain matin, dans la cuisine de terre, Dorjee est assis en tailleur à côté de Tsering. Je suis assis en face et une jarre de tchang nous sépare. Aucun de nous ne parle. « Tchang done », dis-je à mes deux amis en leur versant à boire. Nous buvons au moins dix bols et les visages tendus commencent à s'adoucir. Quelques bols encore et nous commençons à plaisanter. La jarre est presque vide et je me lève, sors du pan de mon manteau deux khatas honorifiques que je dépose sur les épaules de mes amis puis joins les mains : « Dorjee, Tsering, à partir de maintenant, votre brouille est terminée ! » dis-je, ému. « Dju Olivier, Dju », bredouillent-ils d'une voix chevrotante, joignant aussi leurs mains. Dorjee se lève et ramène une jarre de tchang. Les deux amis insistent pour se servir l'un l'autre. Nous brûlons un bâtonnet d'encens pour chasser les démons de la confusion et remercier les esprits de la clairvoyance.

Les poisons mentaux qui causent nos souffrances et celles que nous infligeons à autrui sont la haine, l'avidité, l'arrogance, la jalousie, le manque de discernement et l'ignorance, qui consiste à mal percevoir la façon dont les choses existent réellement.

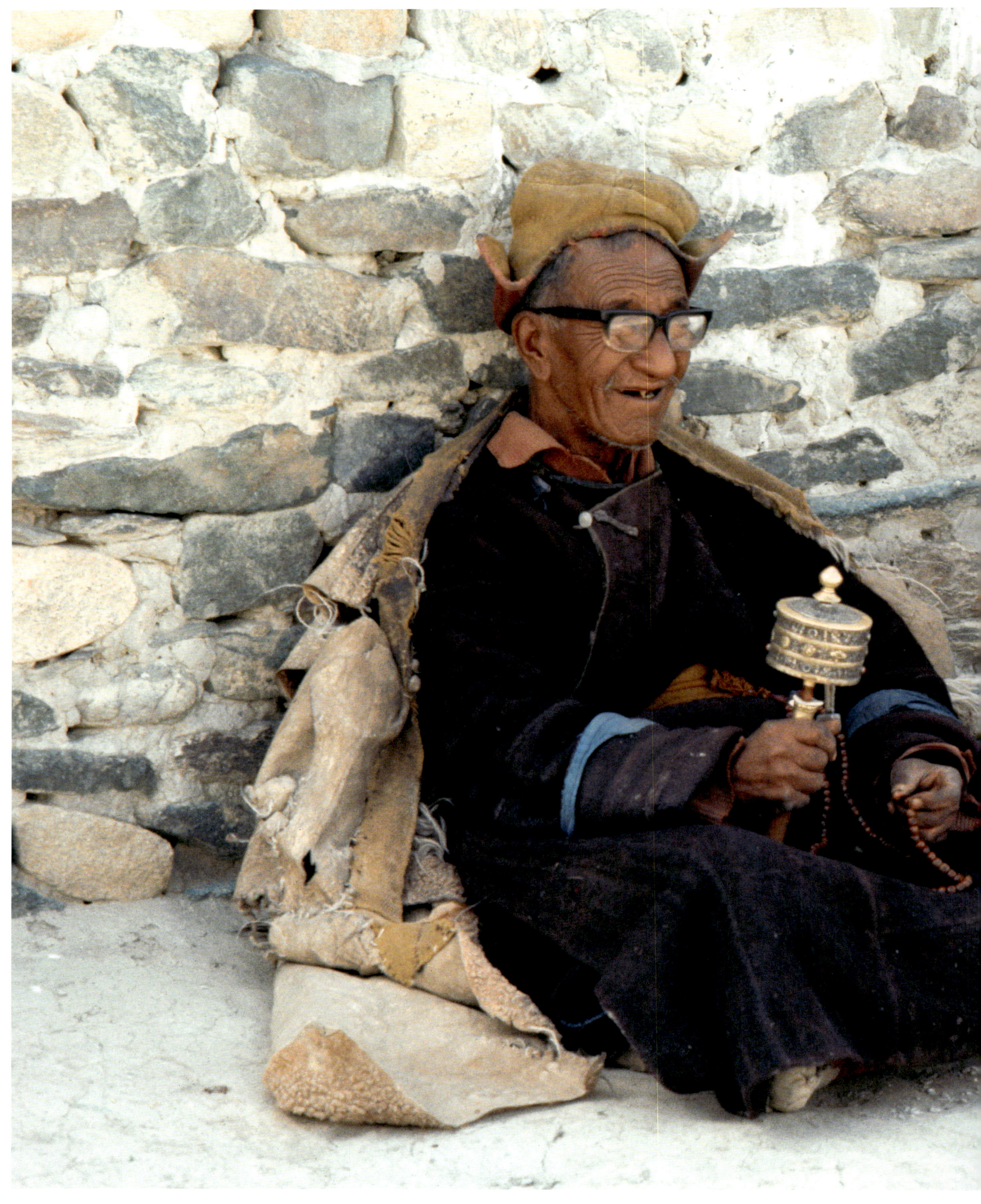

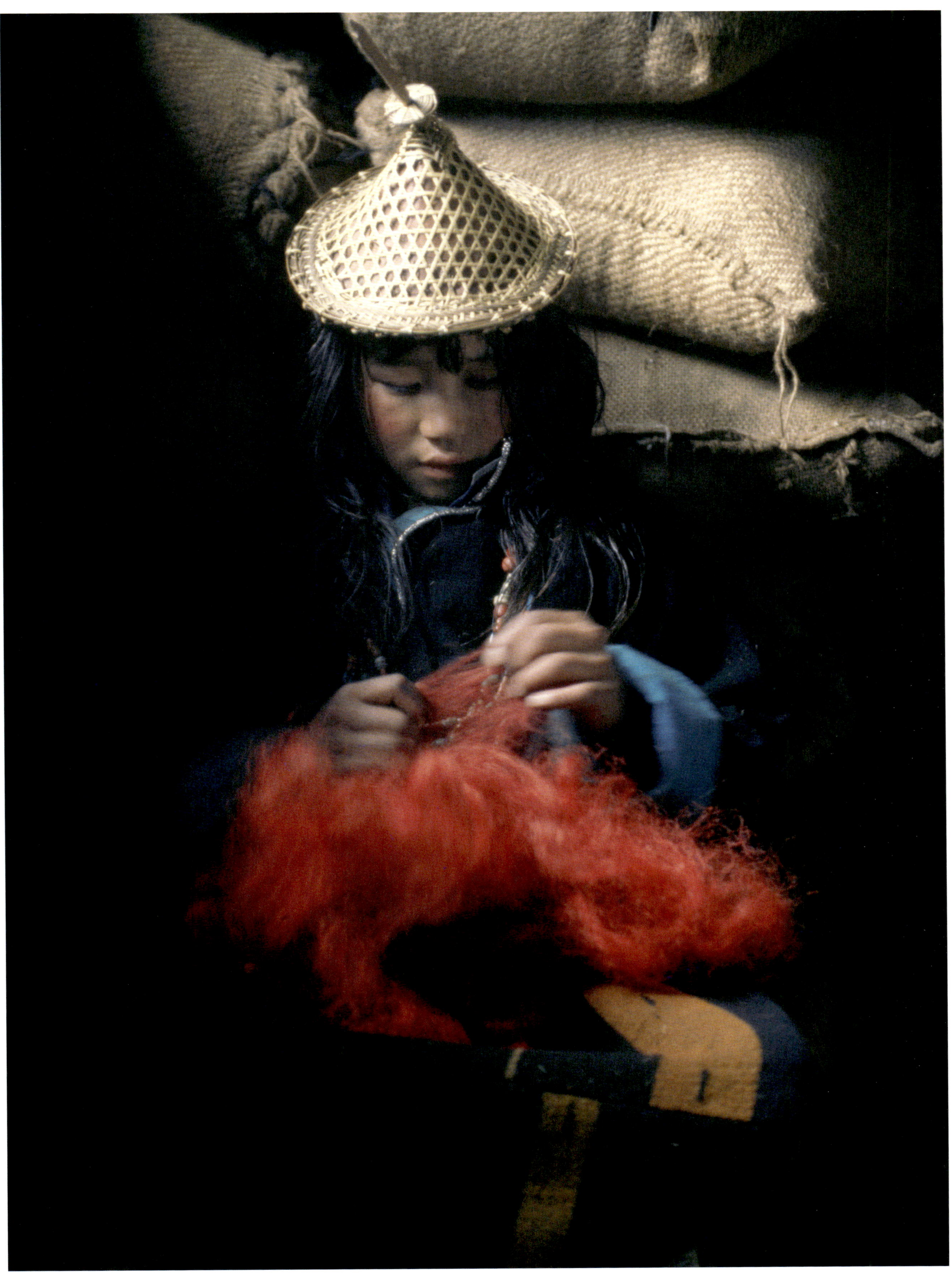

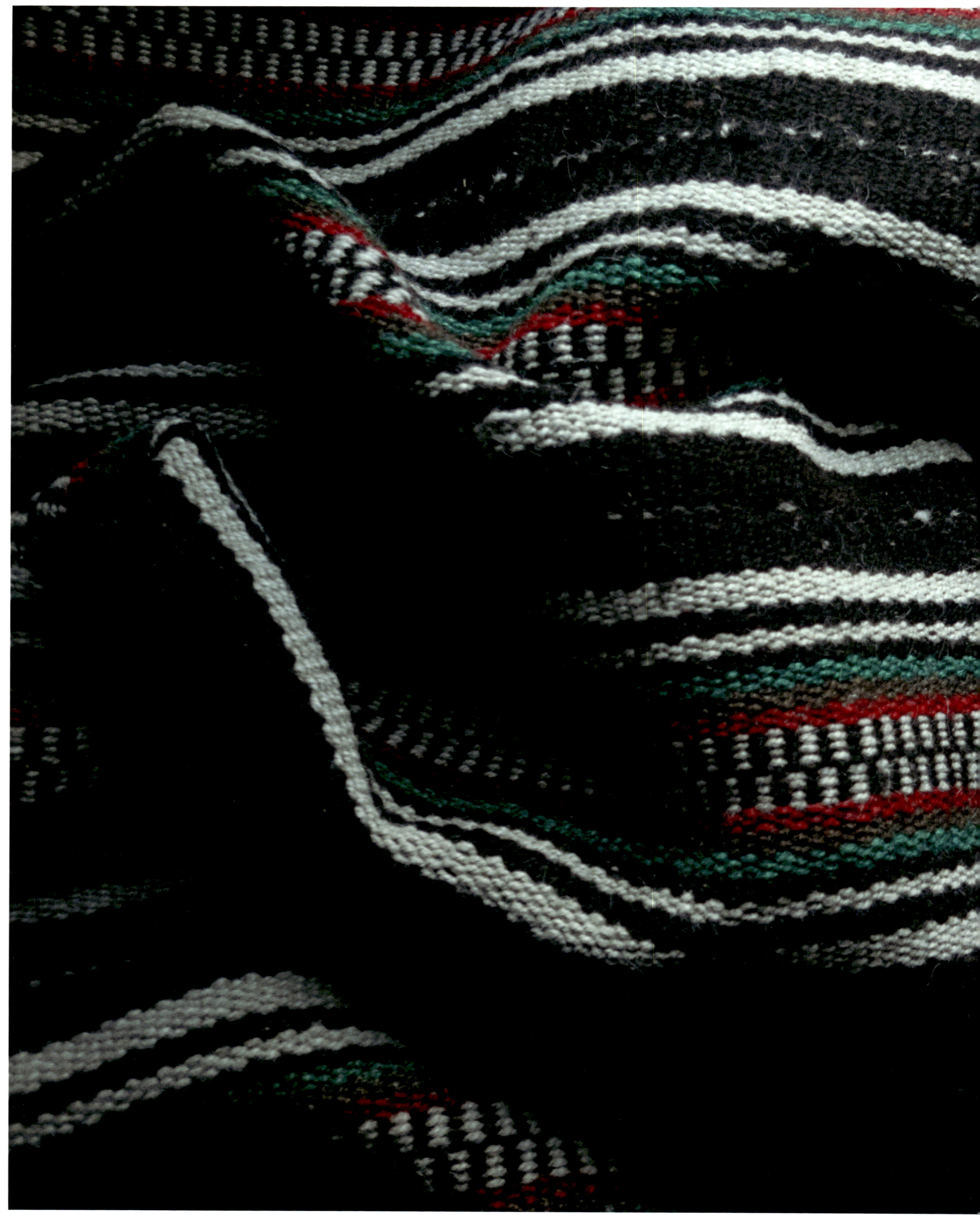

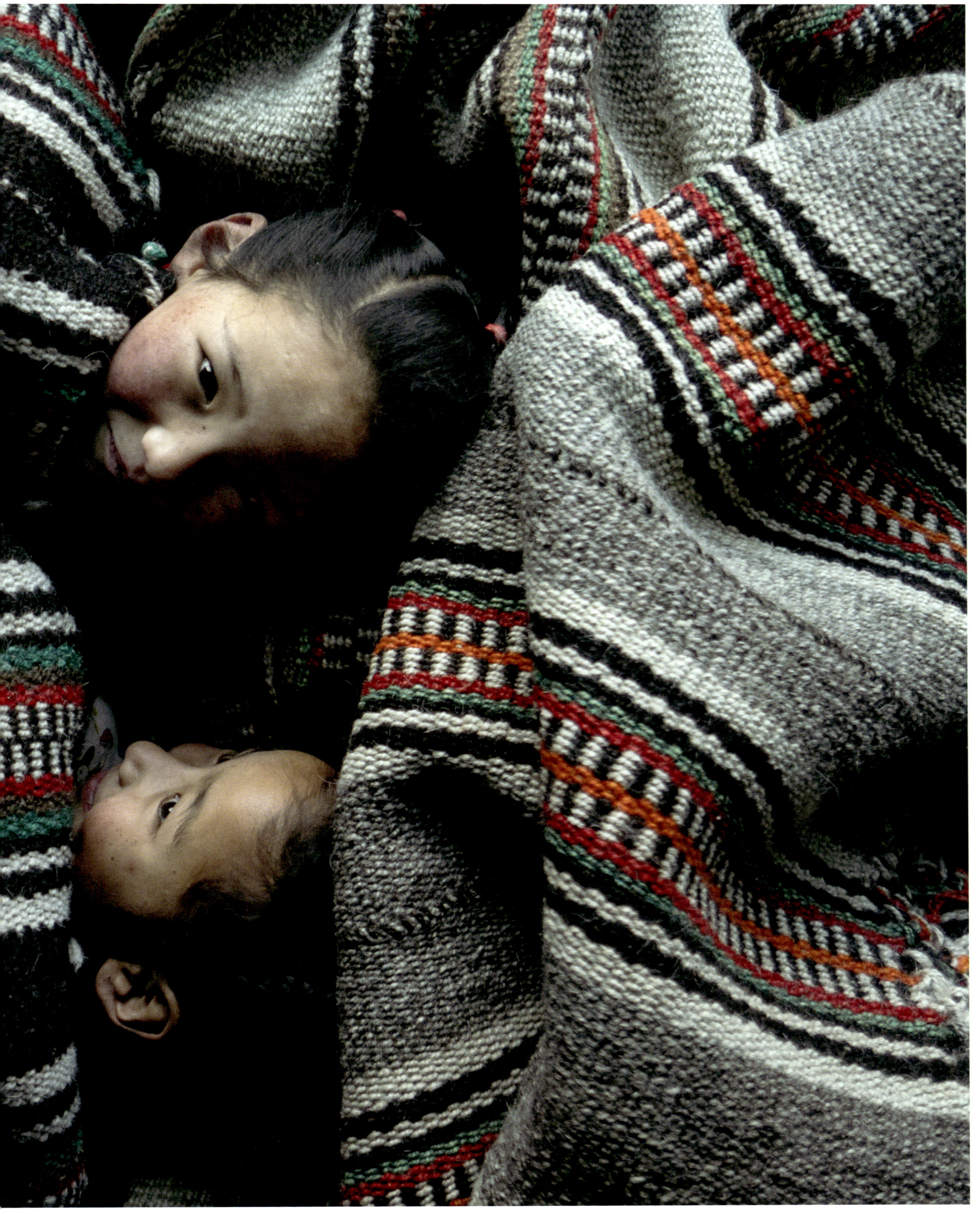

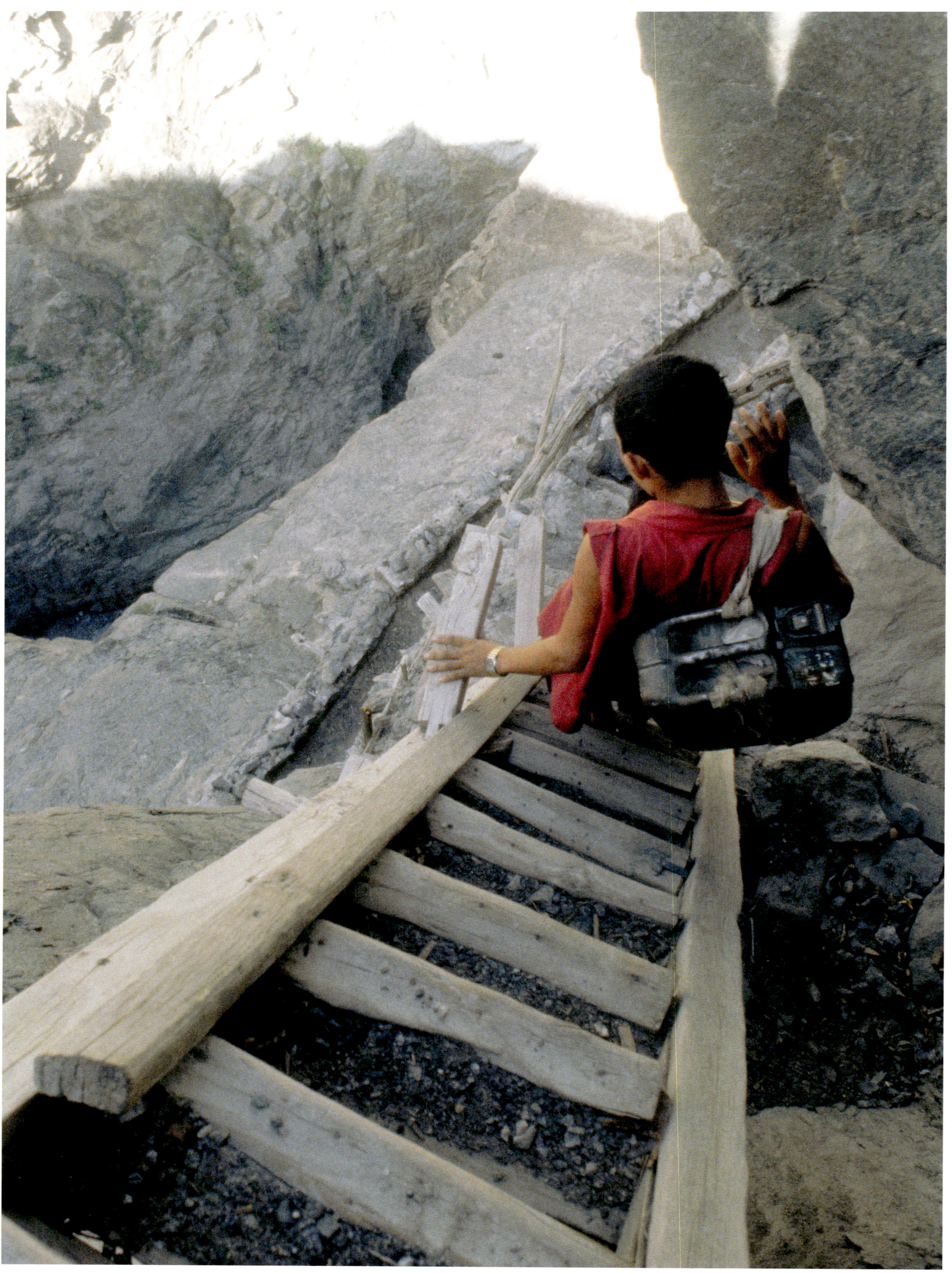

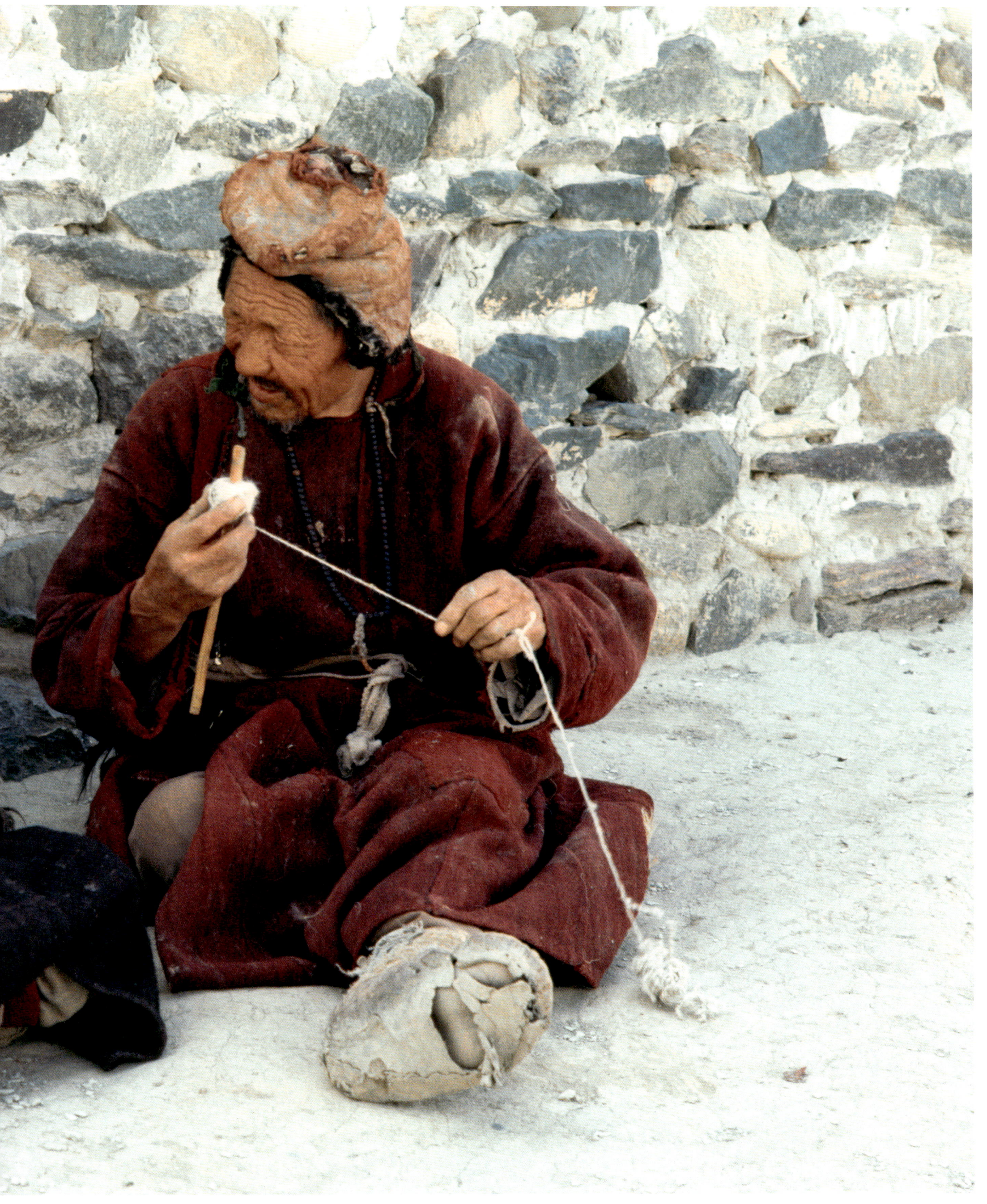

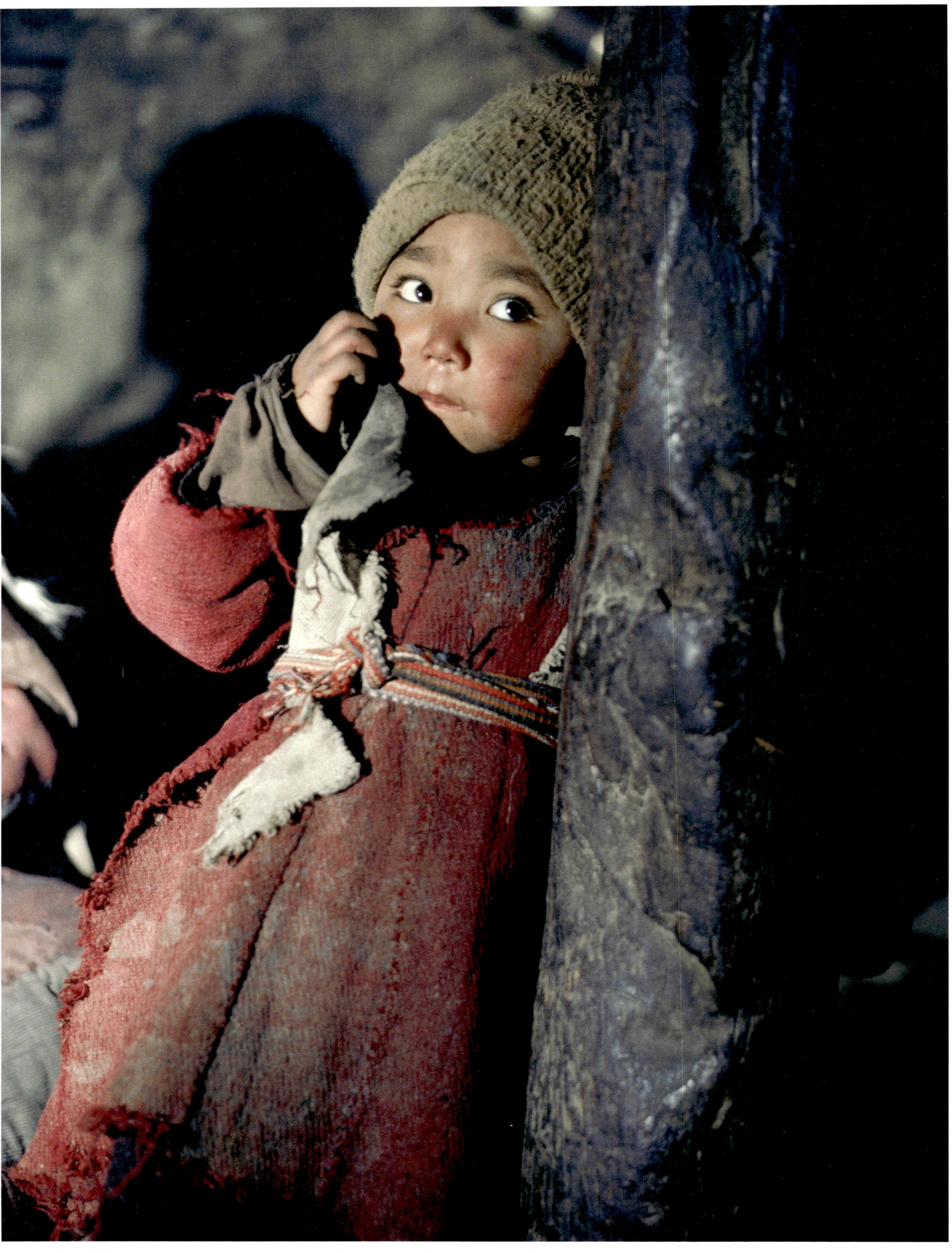

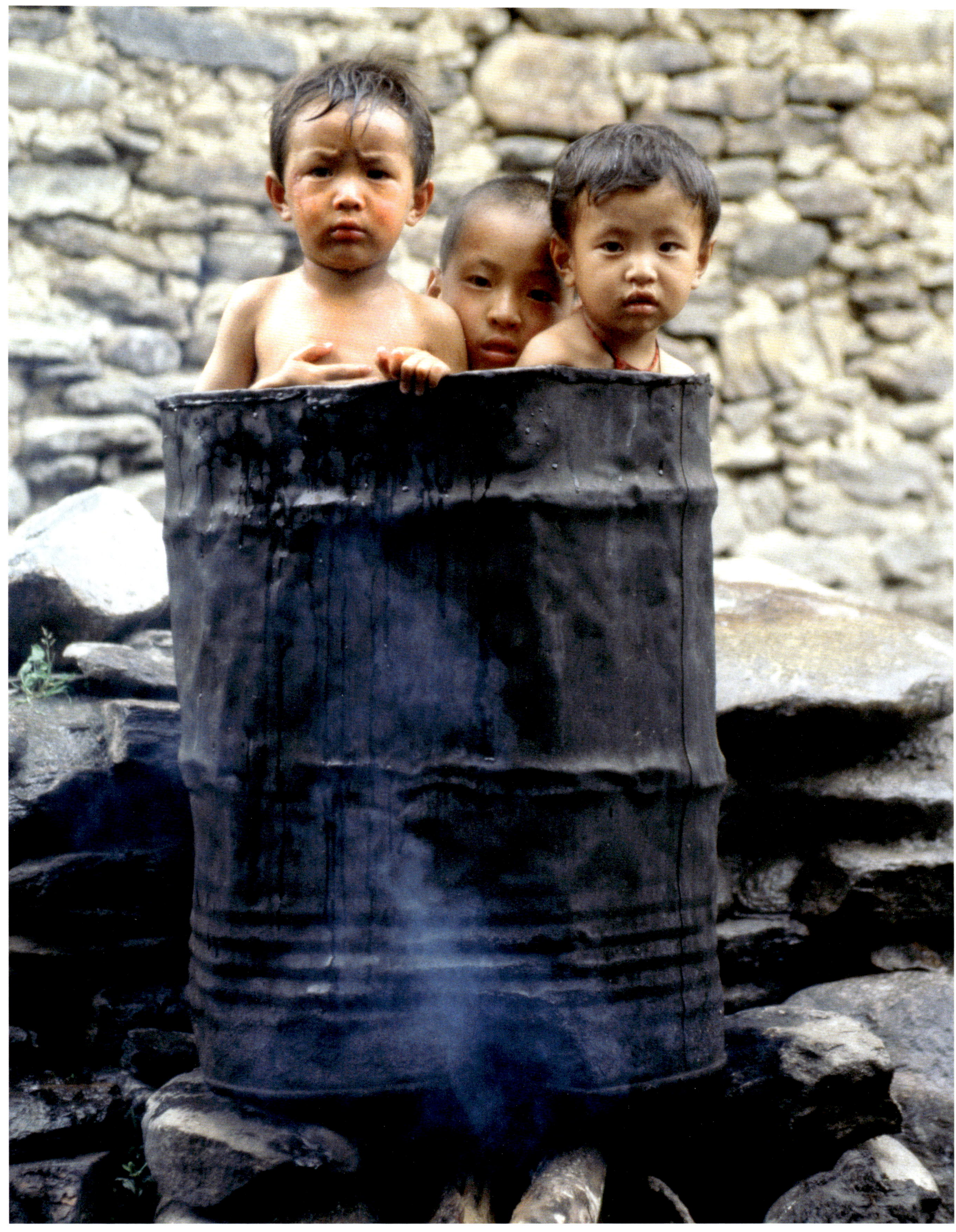

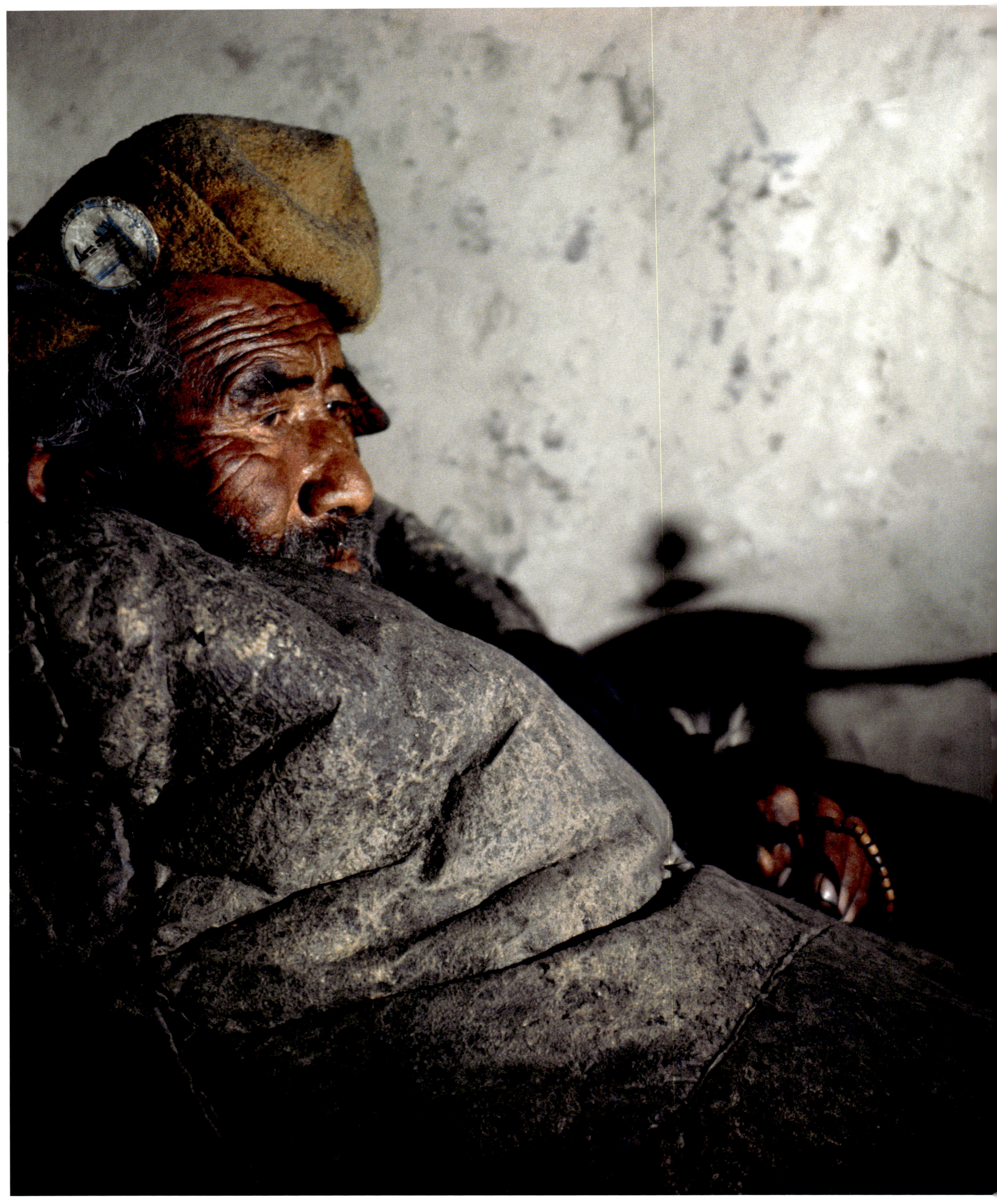

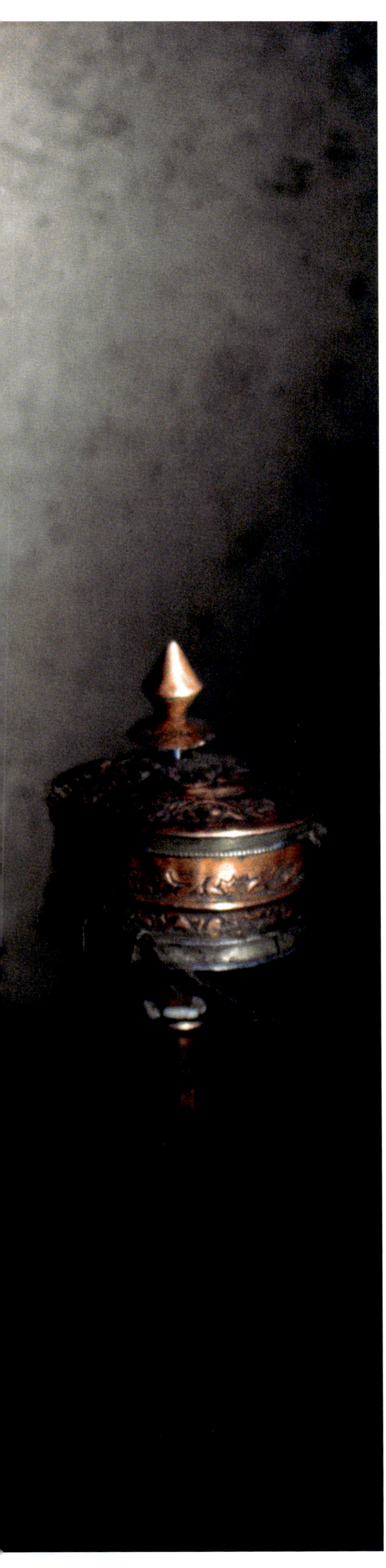

One month before his death, the old King of Zanskar took my hand as I was about to leave him. "Olivier, I won't survive this new winter. Please don't leave with a heavy heart. I have accomplished this life as best I could and I rejoice in the next one."

Einen Monat vor seinem Tod nahm der alte König von Zanskar meine Hand, als ich gerade im Begriff war, ihn zu verlassen. „Olivier, ich werde den kommenden Winter nicht überleben. Geh nicht mit traurigem Herzen. Ich habe mein Leben so gut wie möglich gelebt und freue mich auf das nächste."

Un mois avant sa mort, le vieux roi du Zanskar m'a pris la main alors que j'allais le quitter. « Olivier, je ne survivrai pas à ce nouvel hiver. Ne t'en va pas le cœur triste, j'ai accompli au mieux cette vie, je me réjouis de la suivante. »

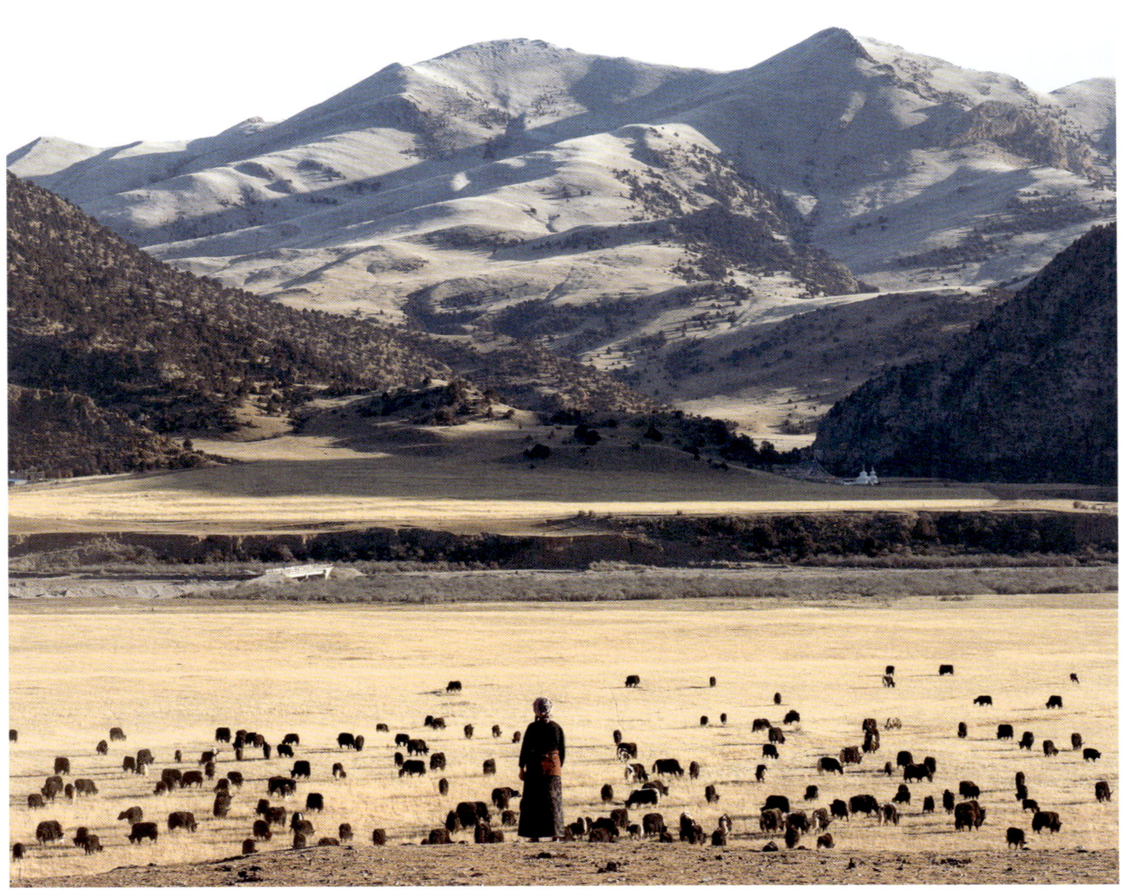

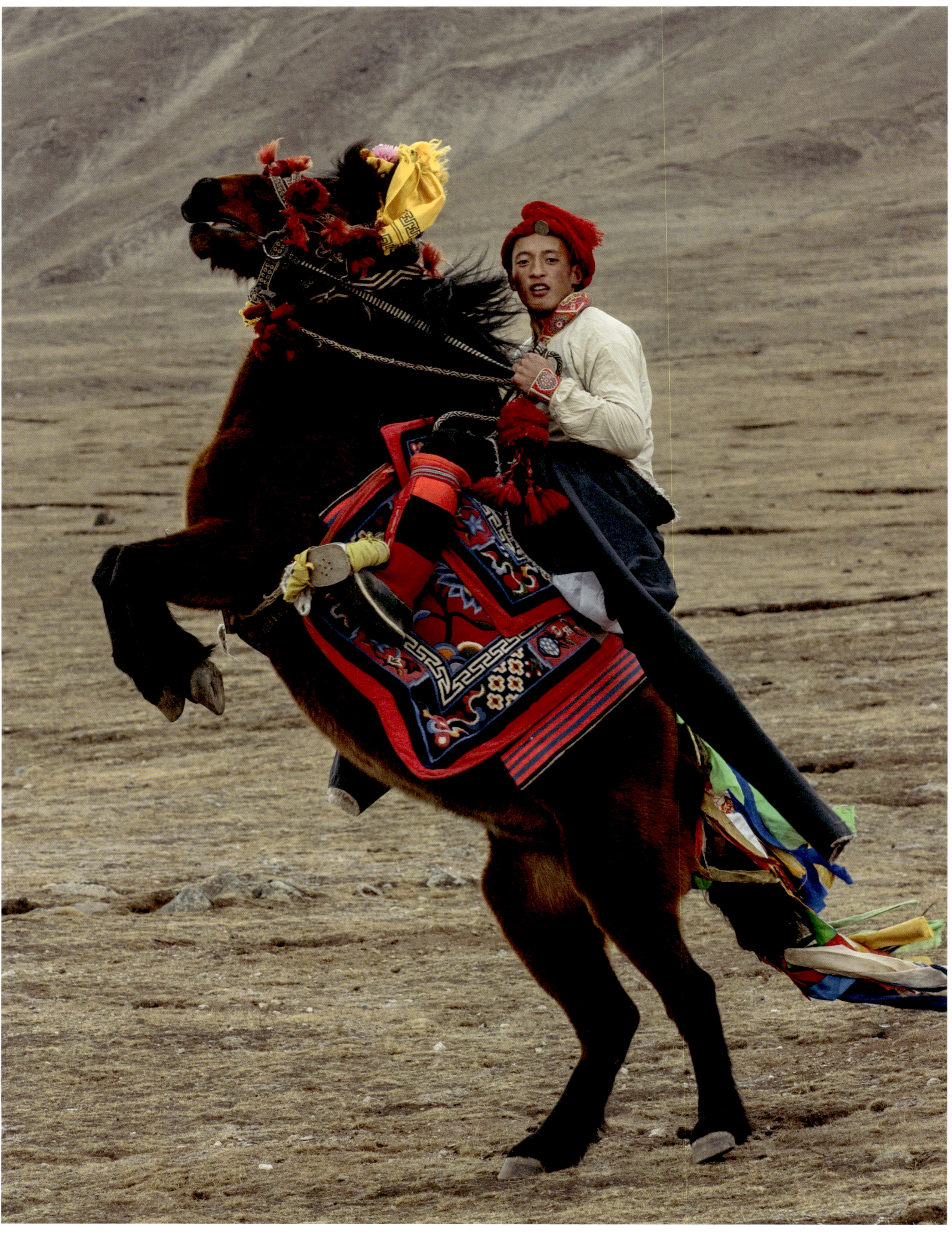

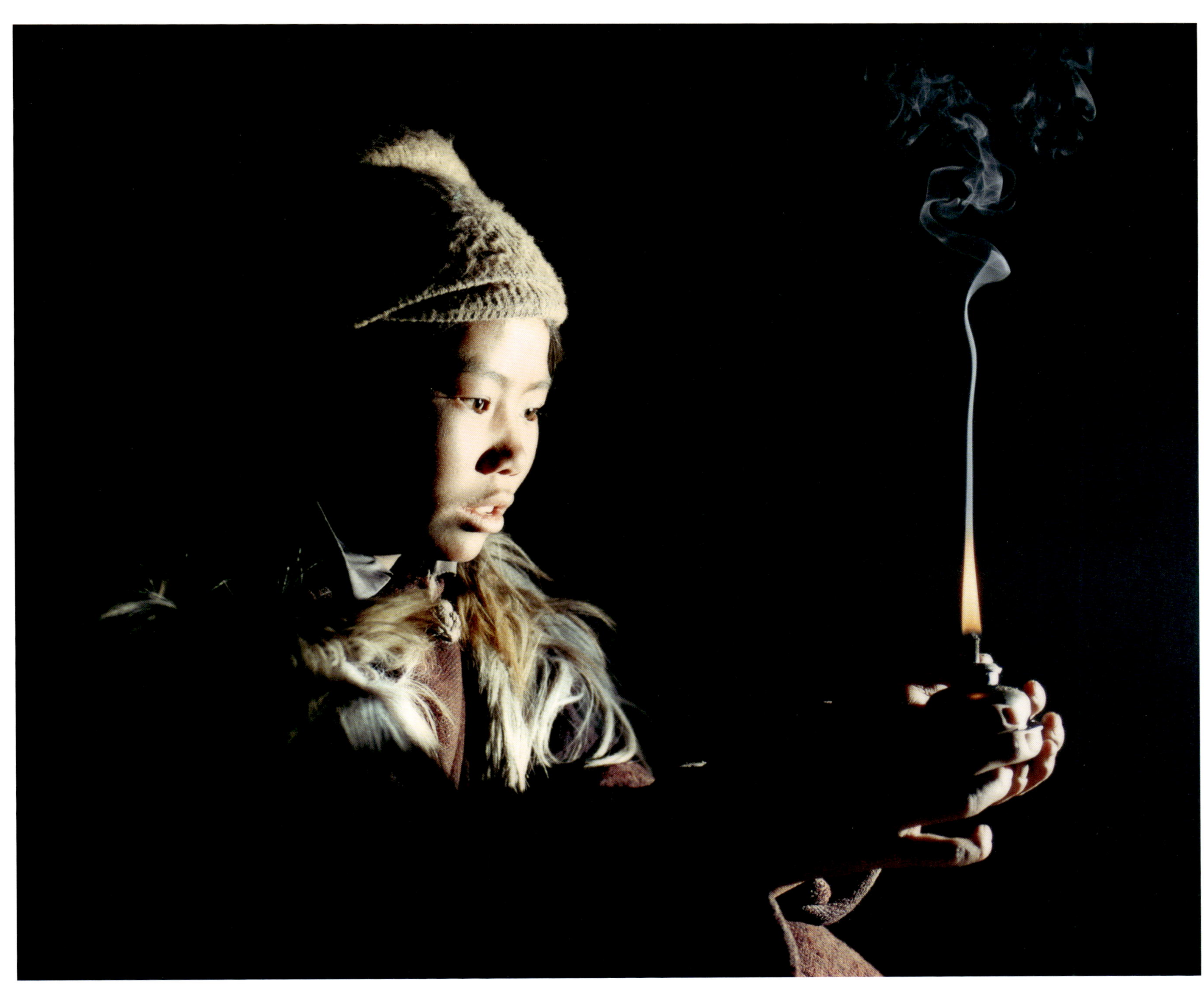

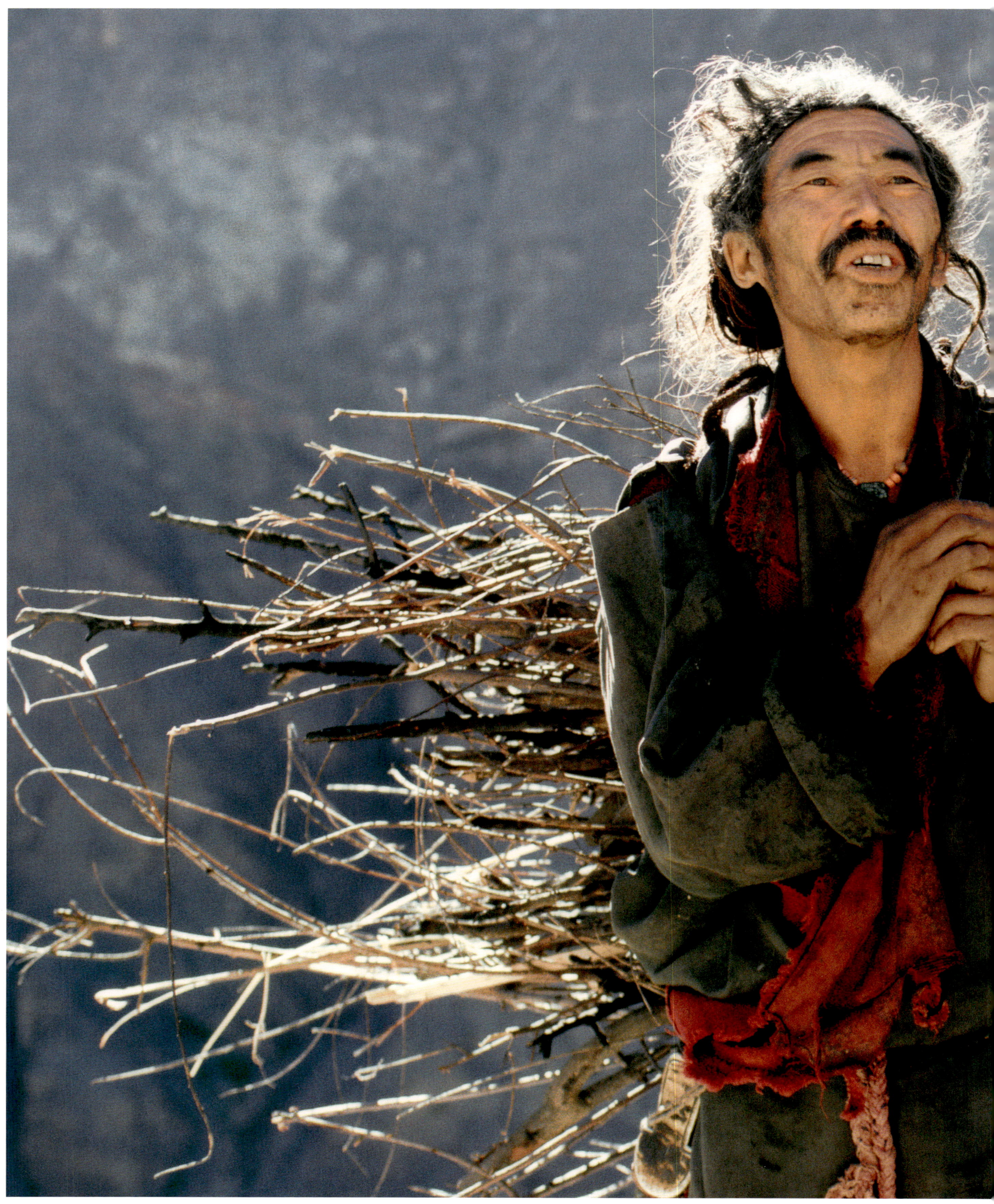

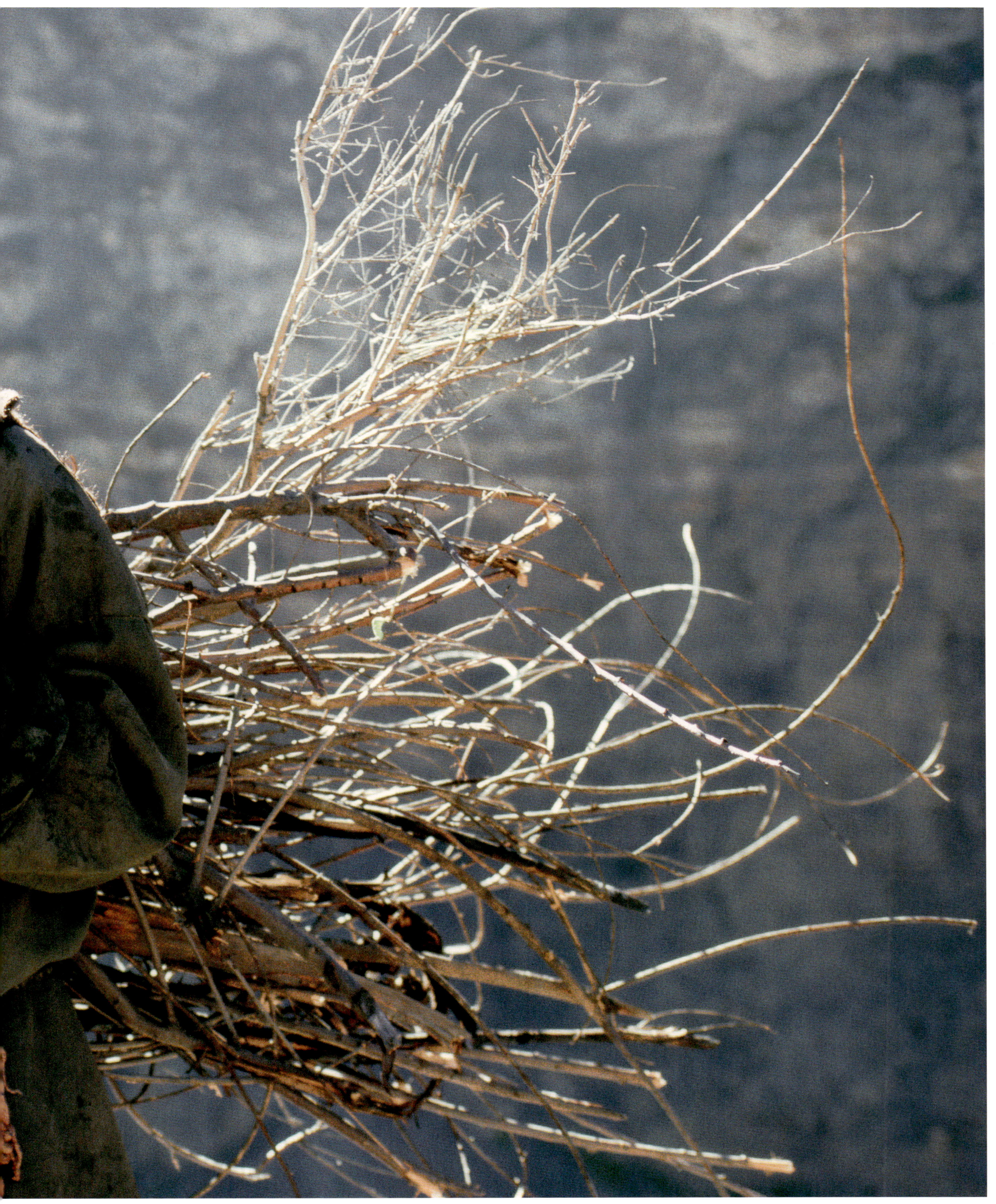

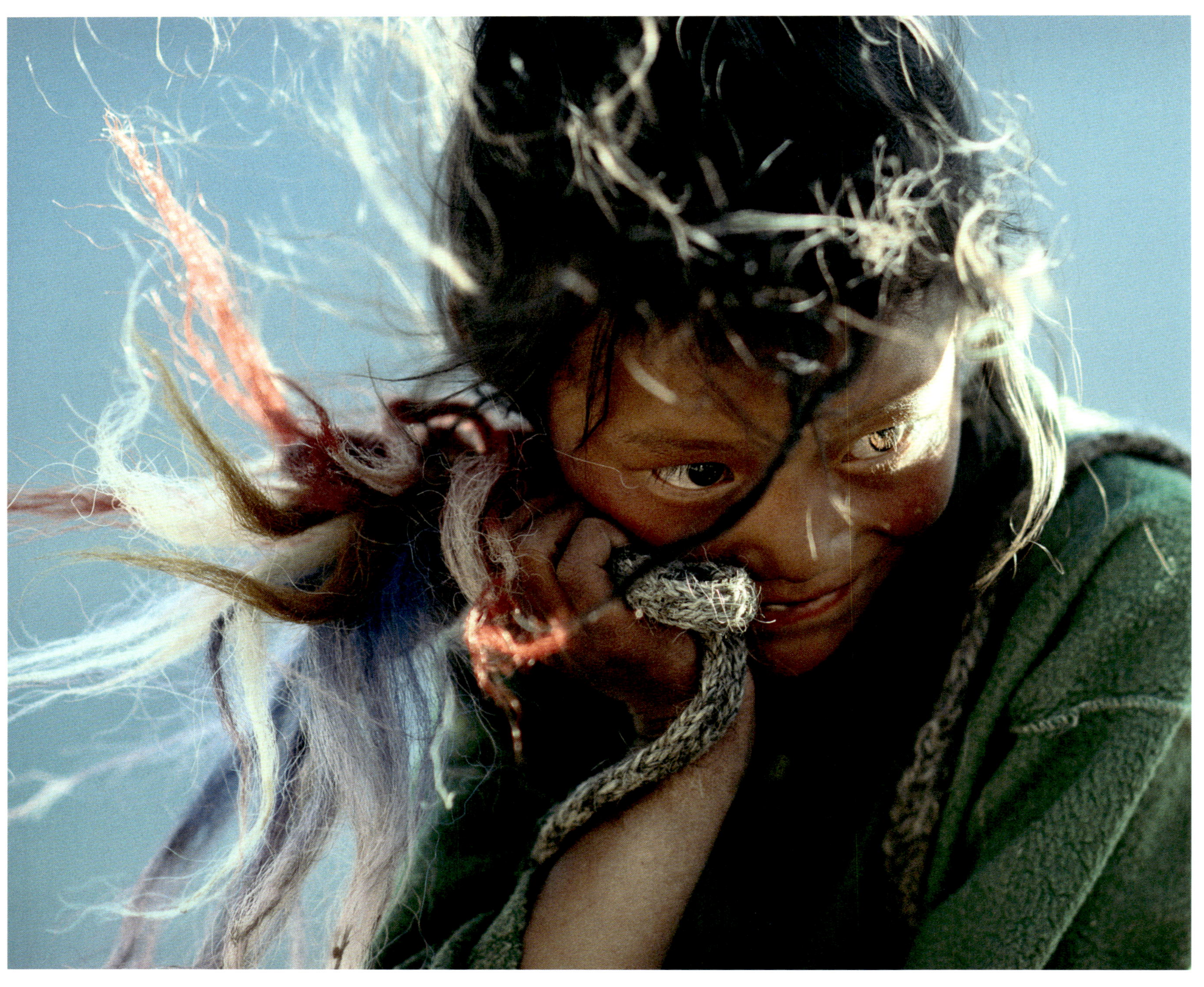

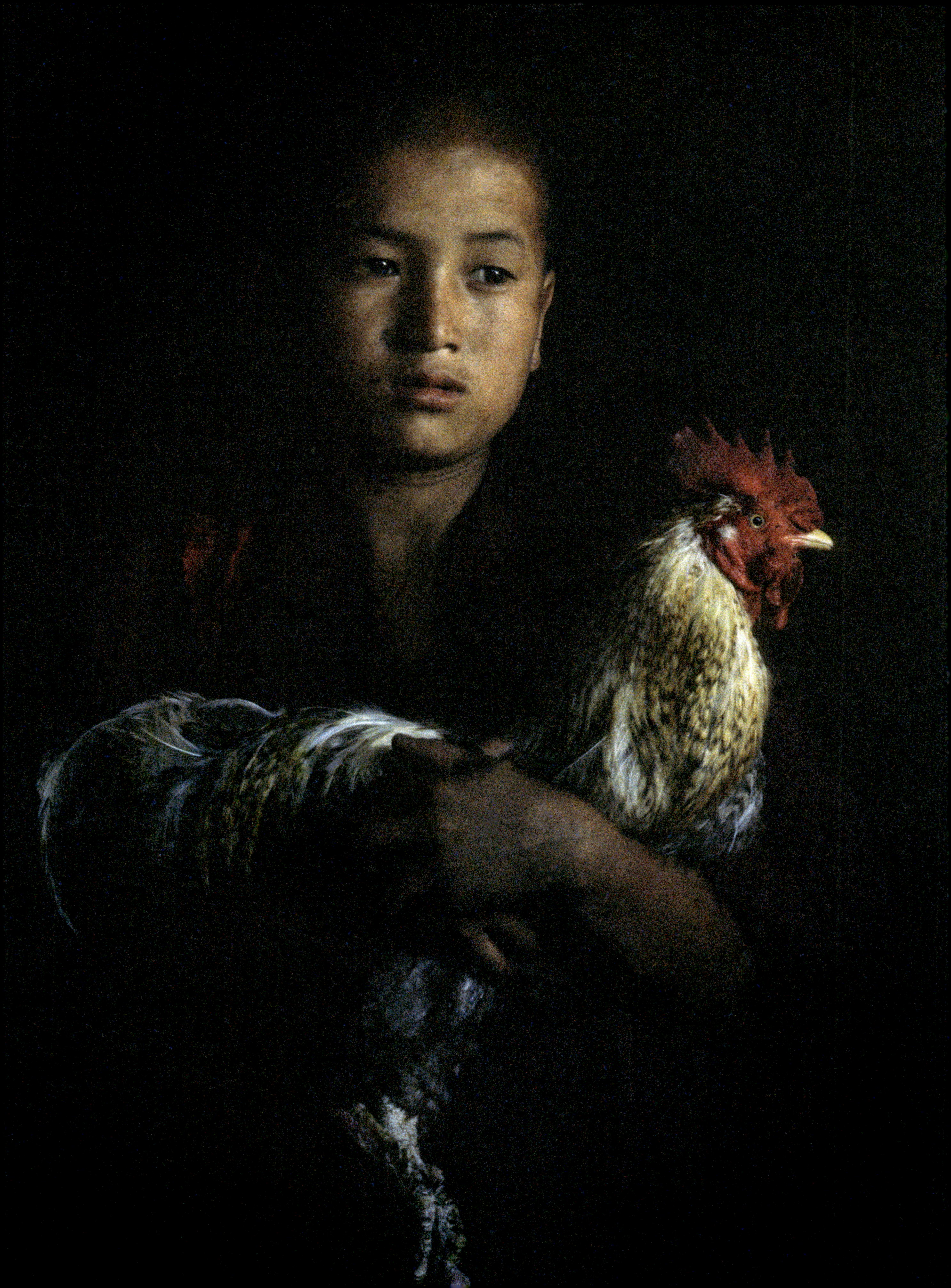

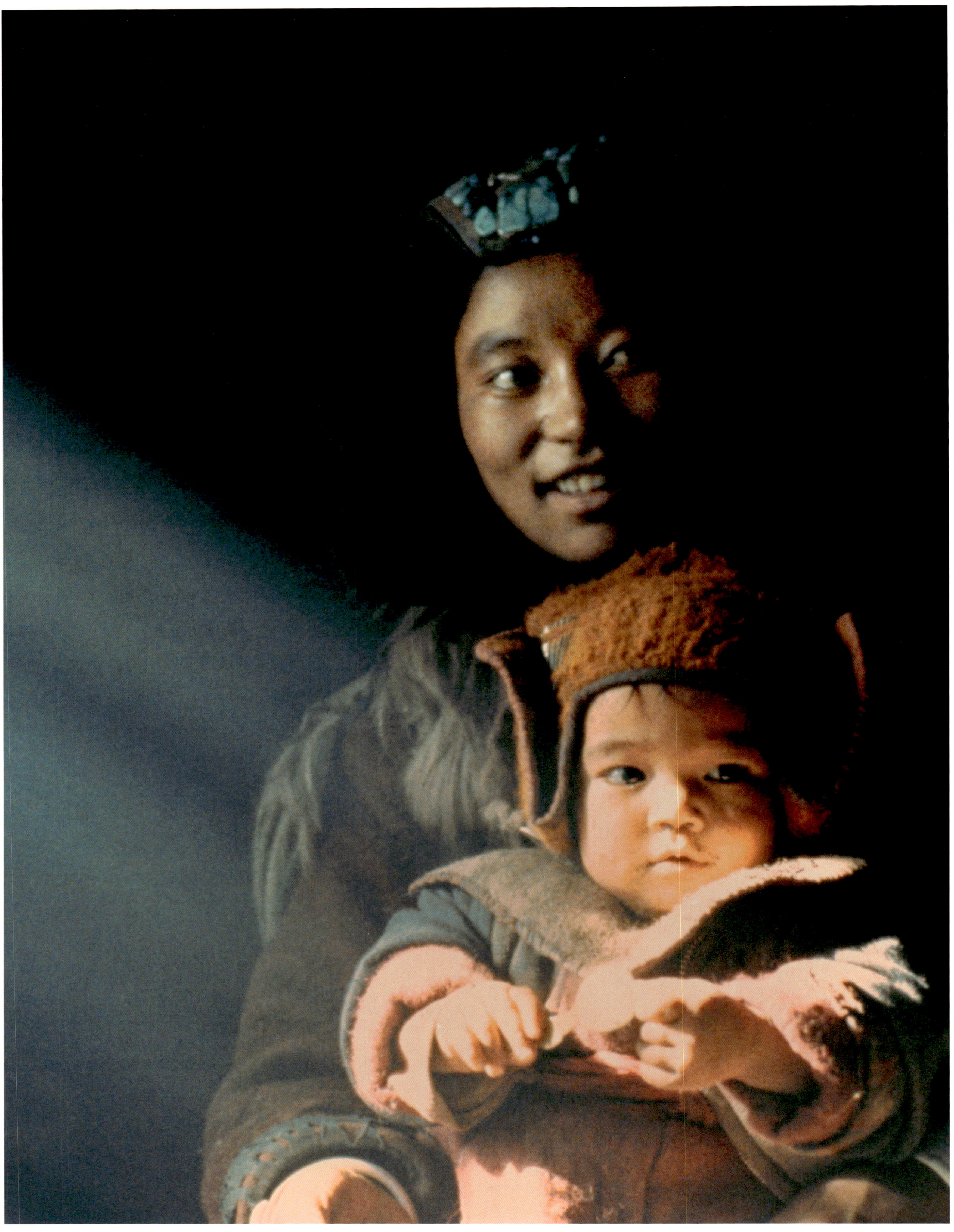

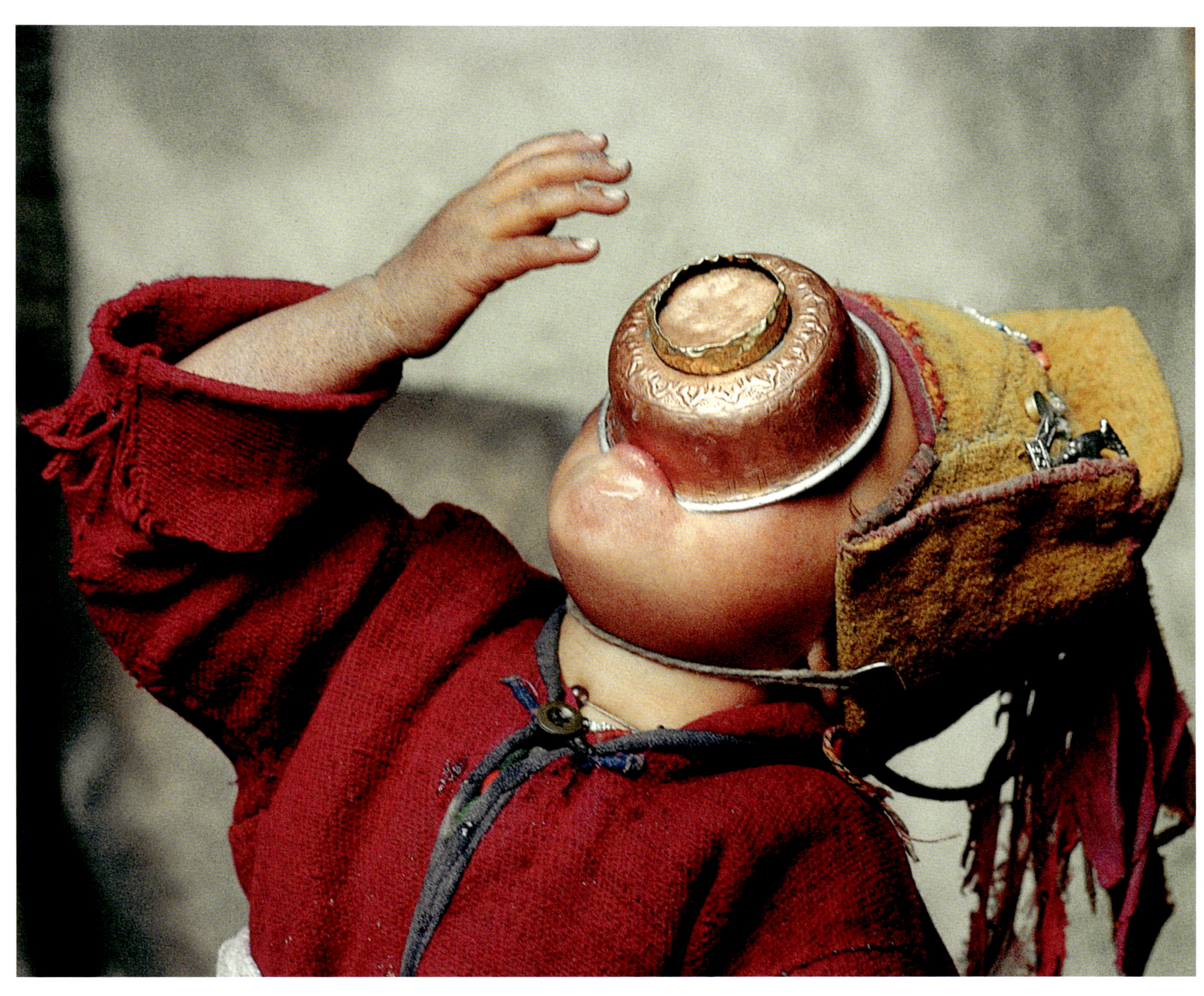

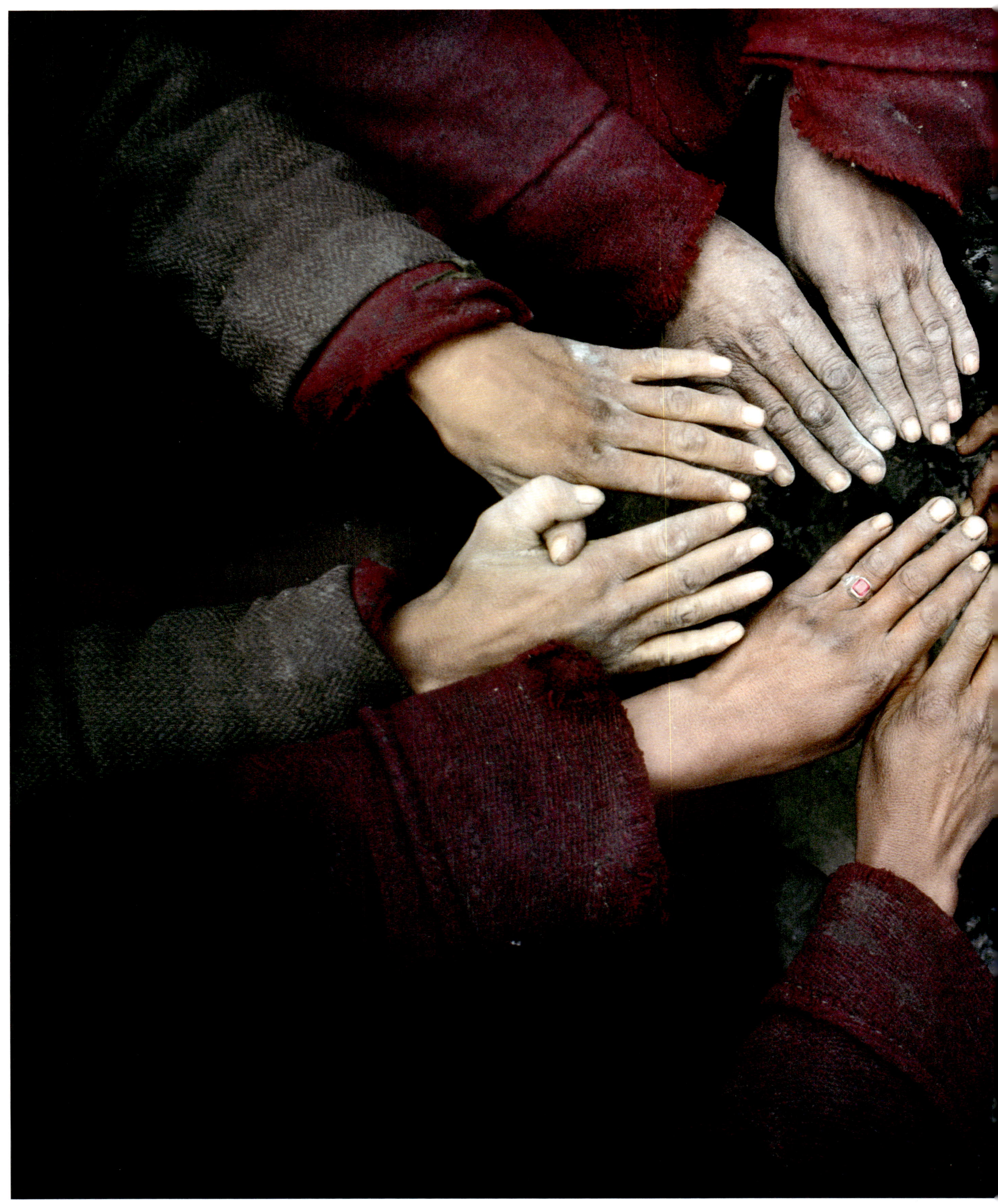

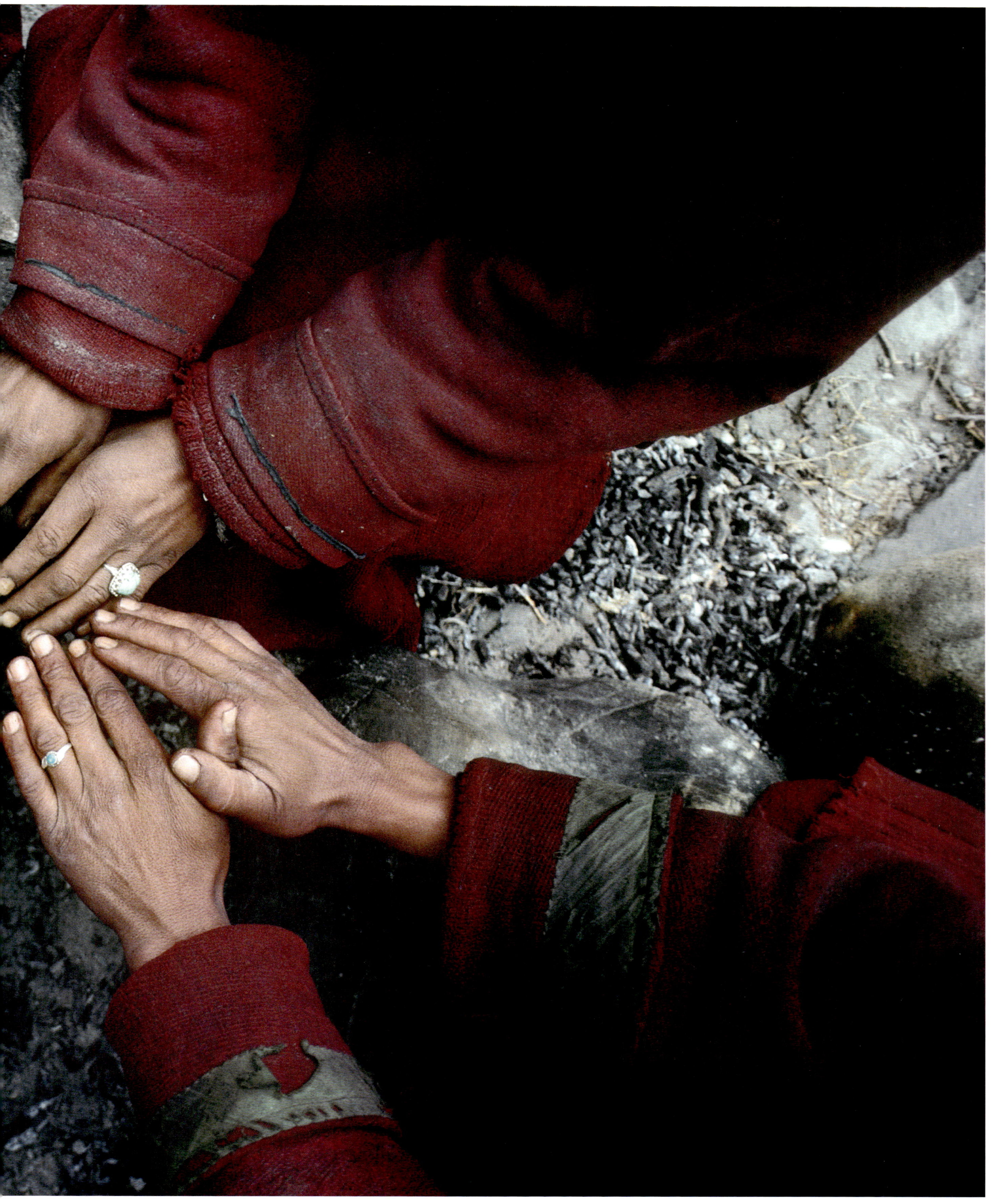

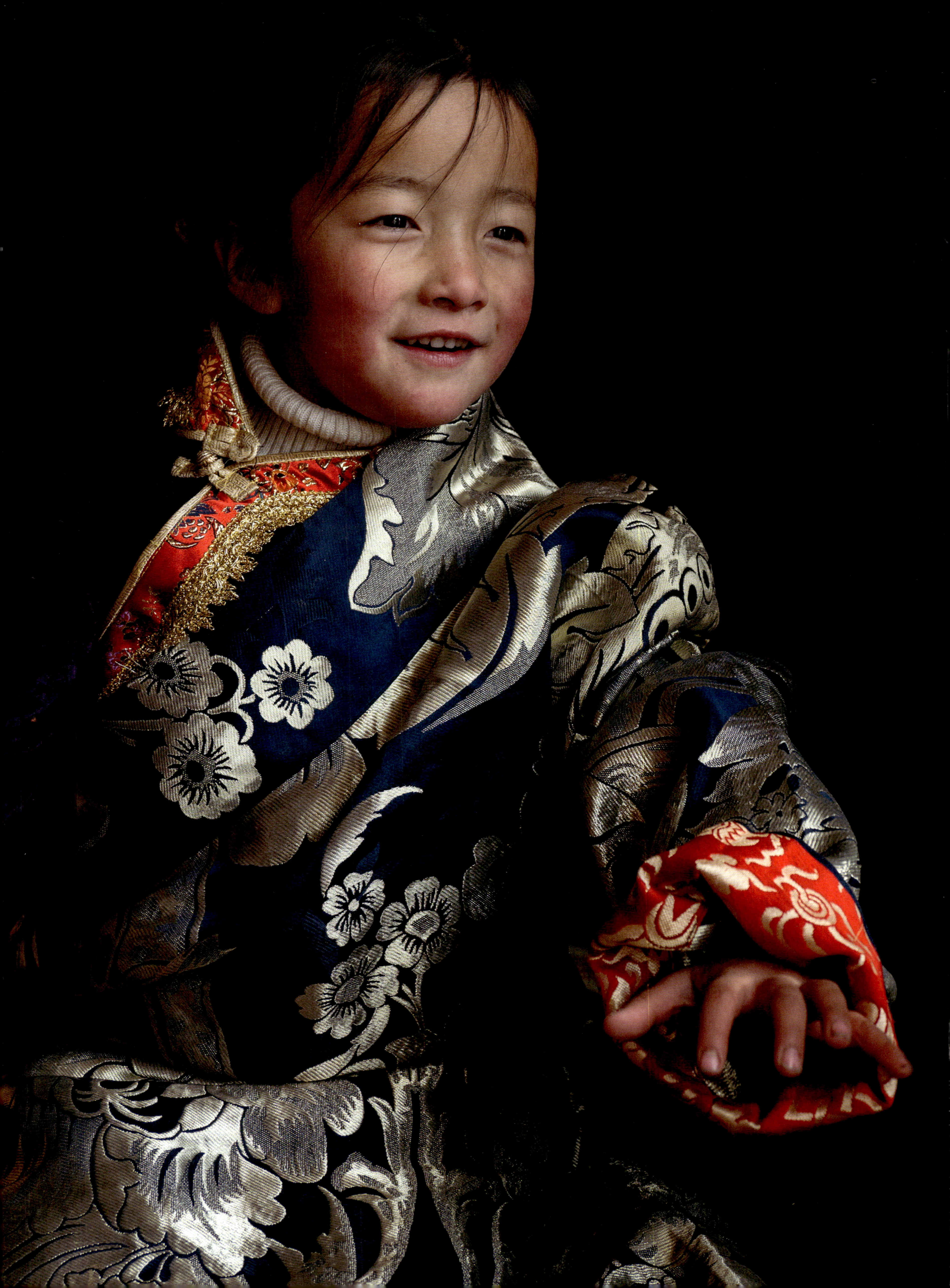

Impermanence is a principle of harmony. When we do not fight against it, we are in harmony with reality.

Pema Chödrön

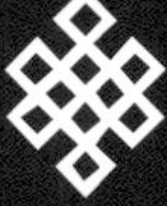

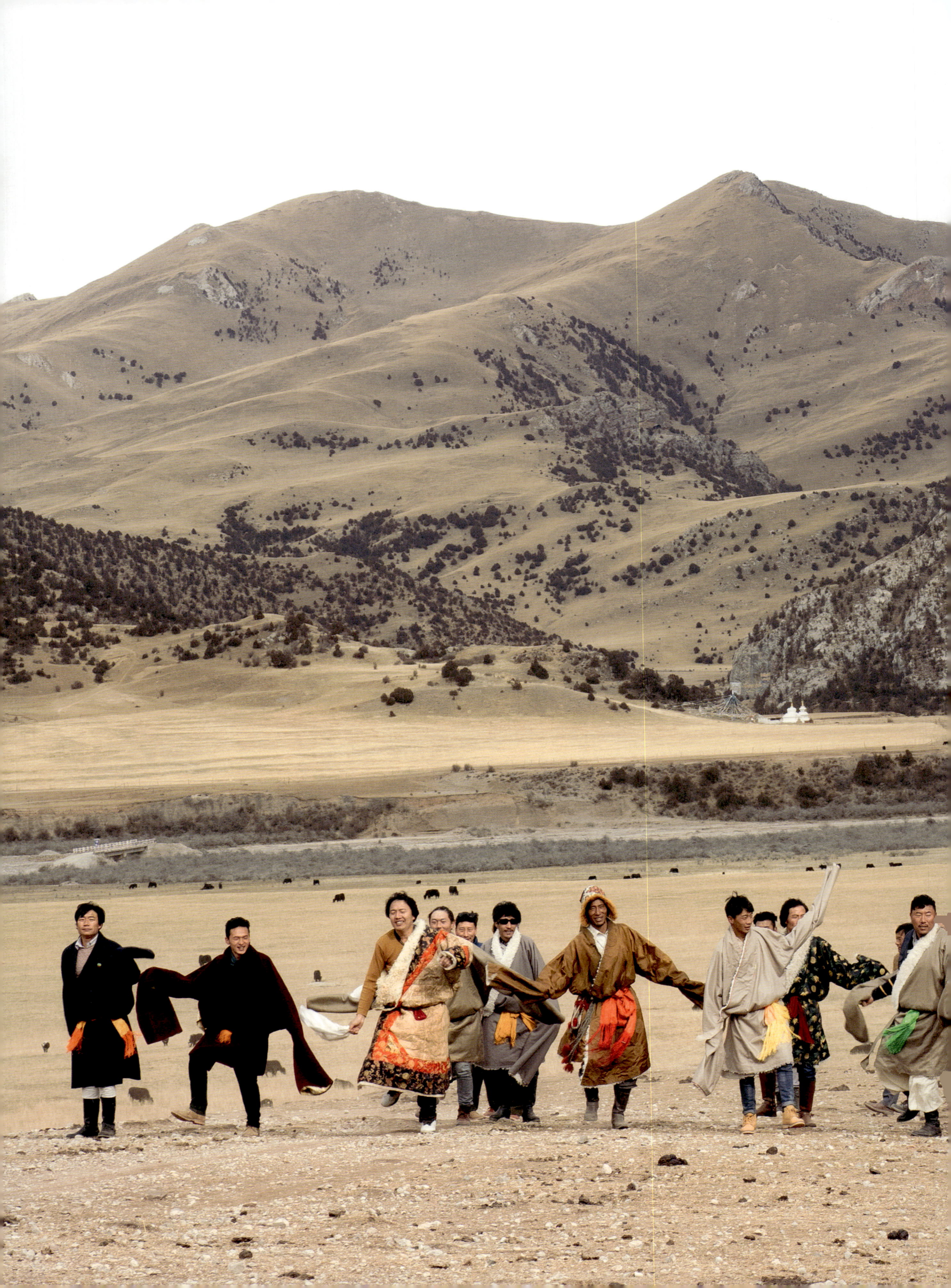

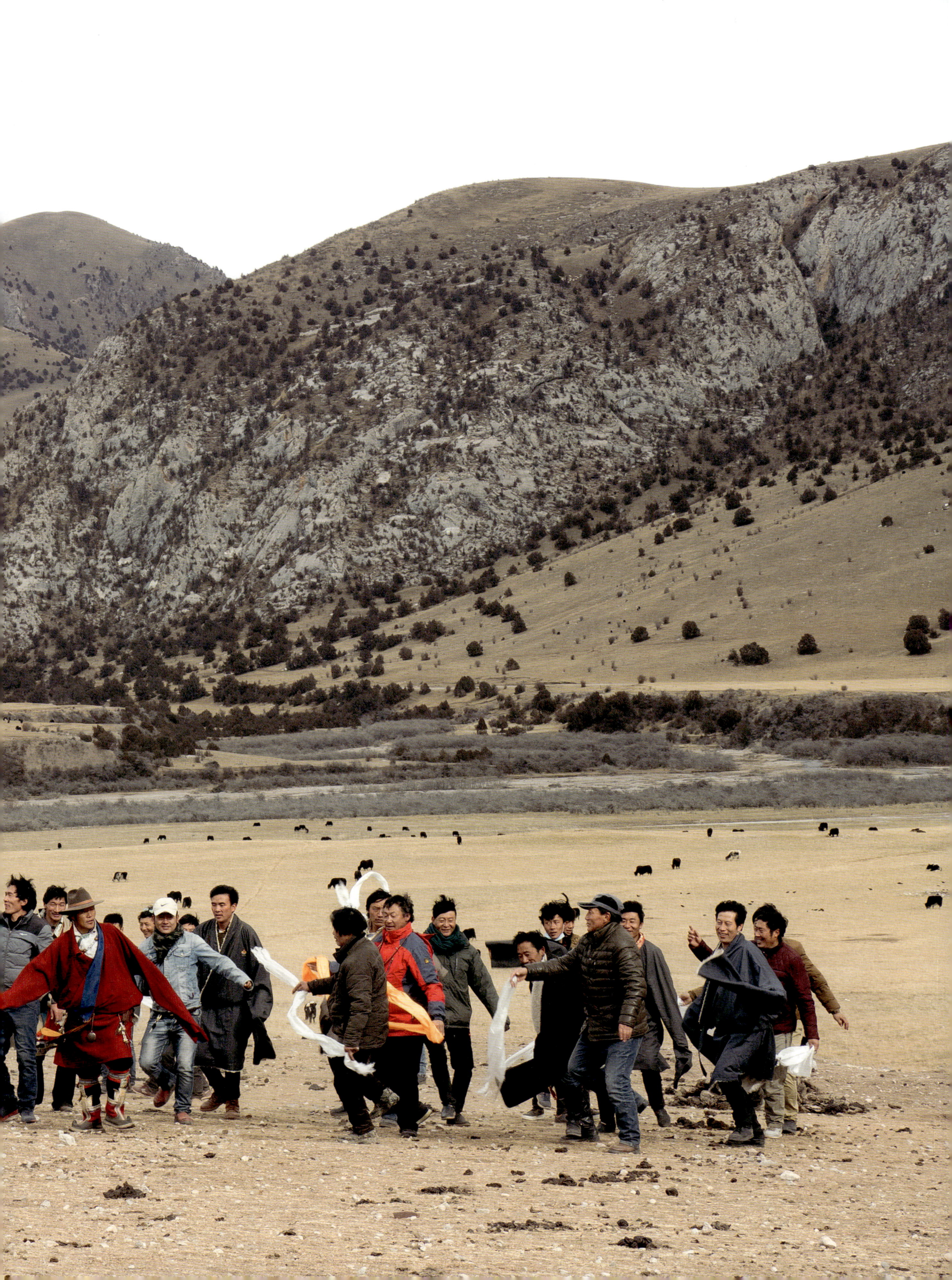

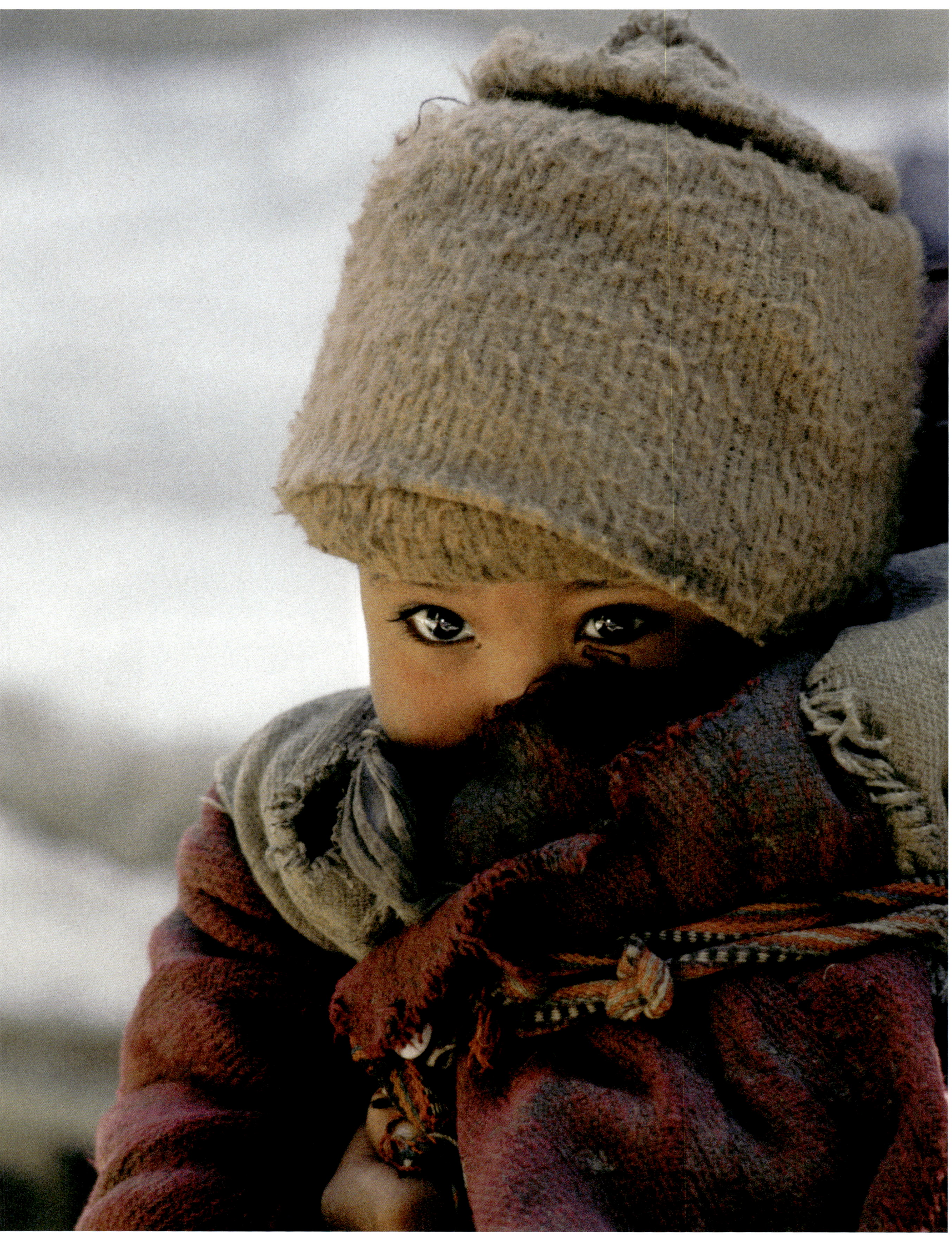

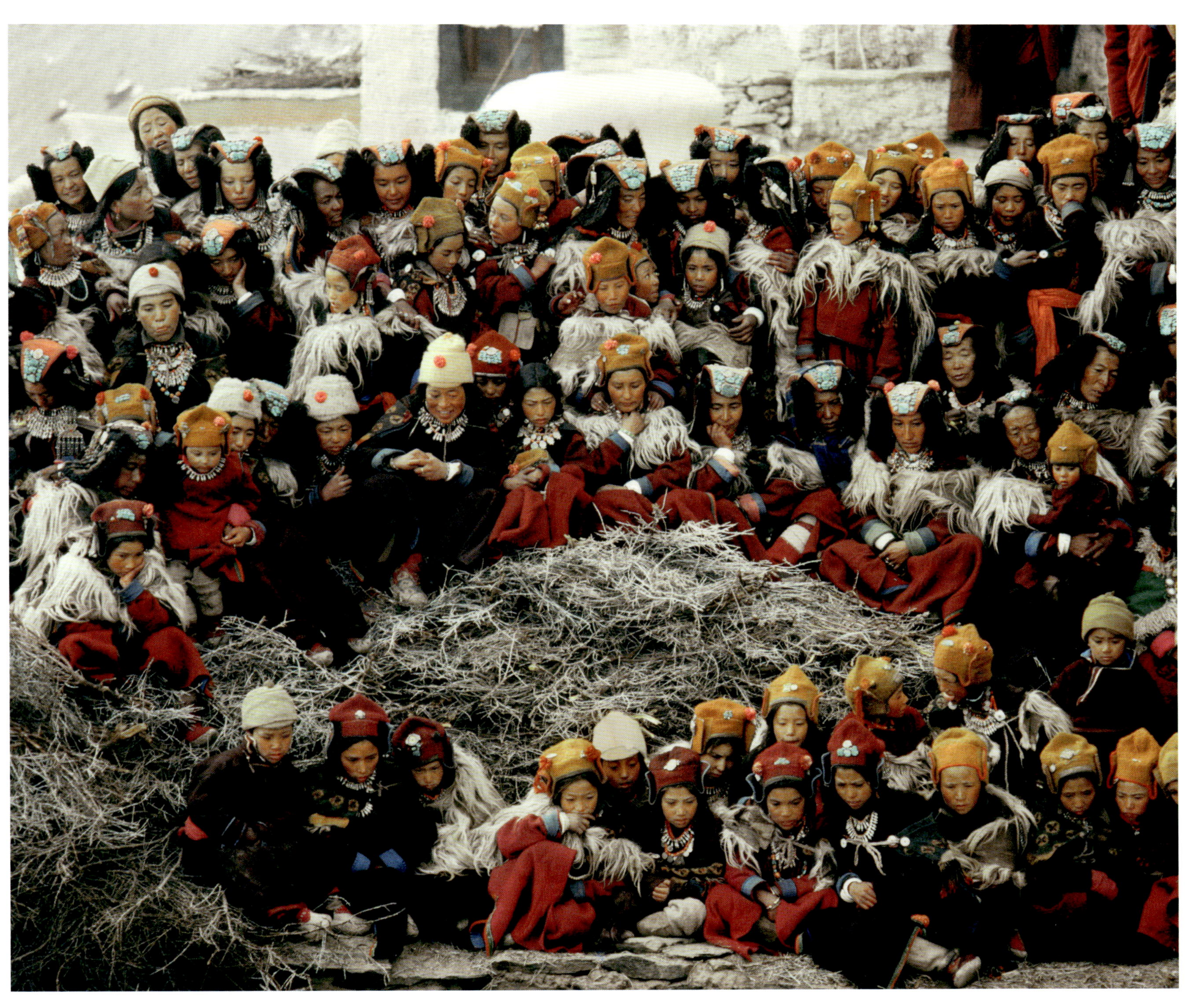

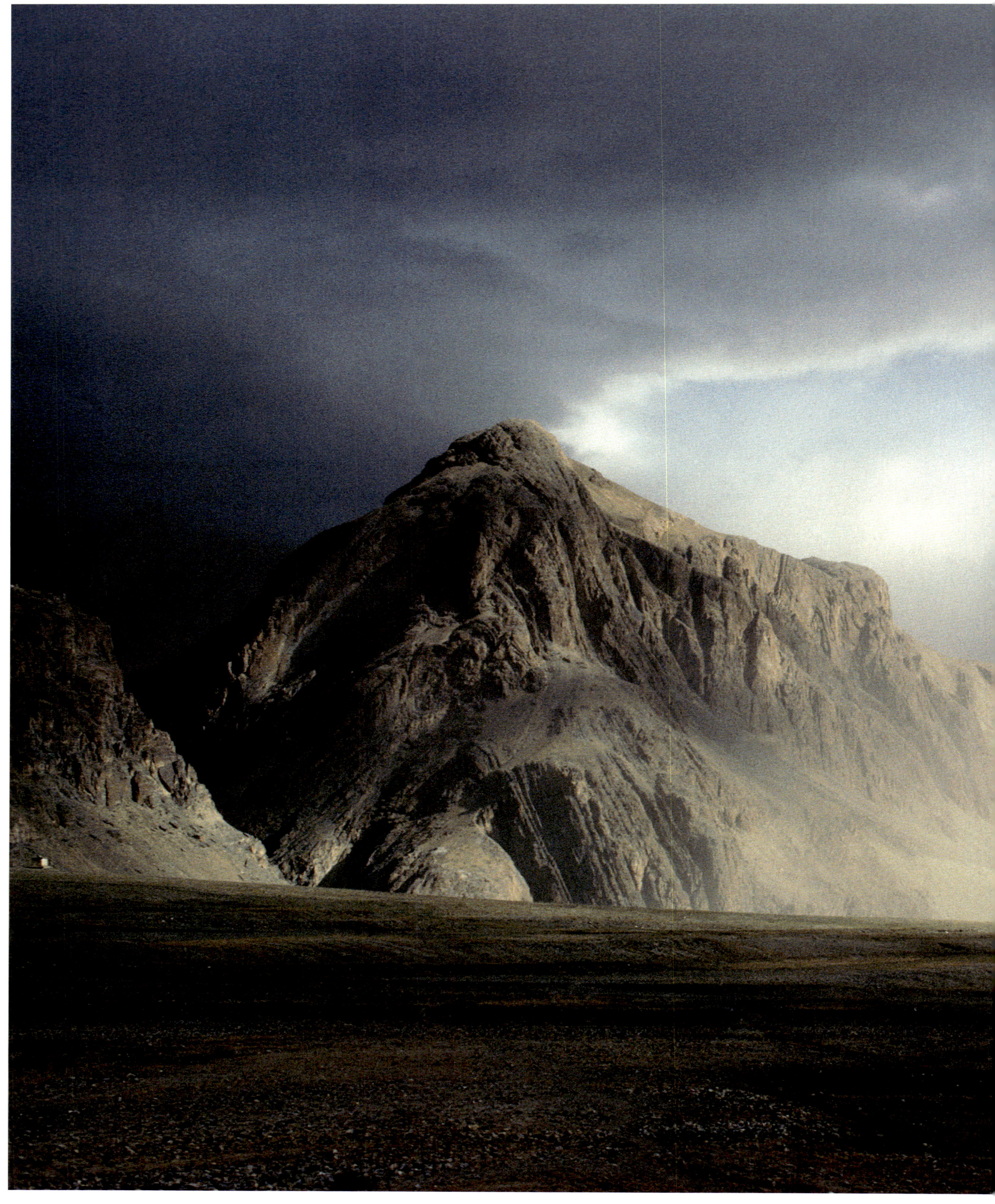

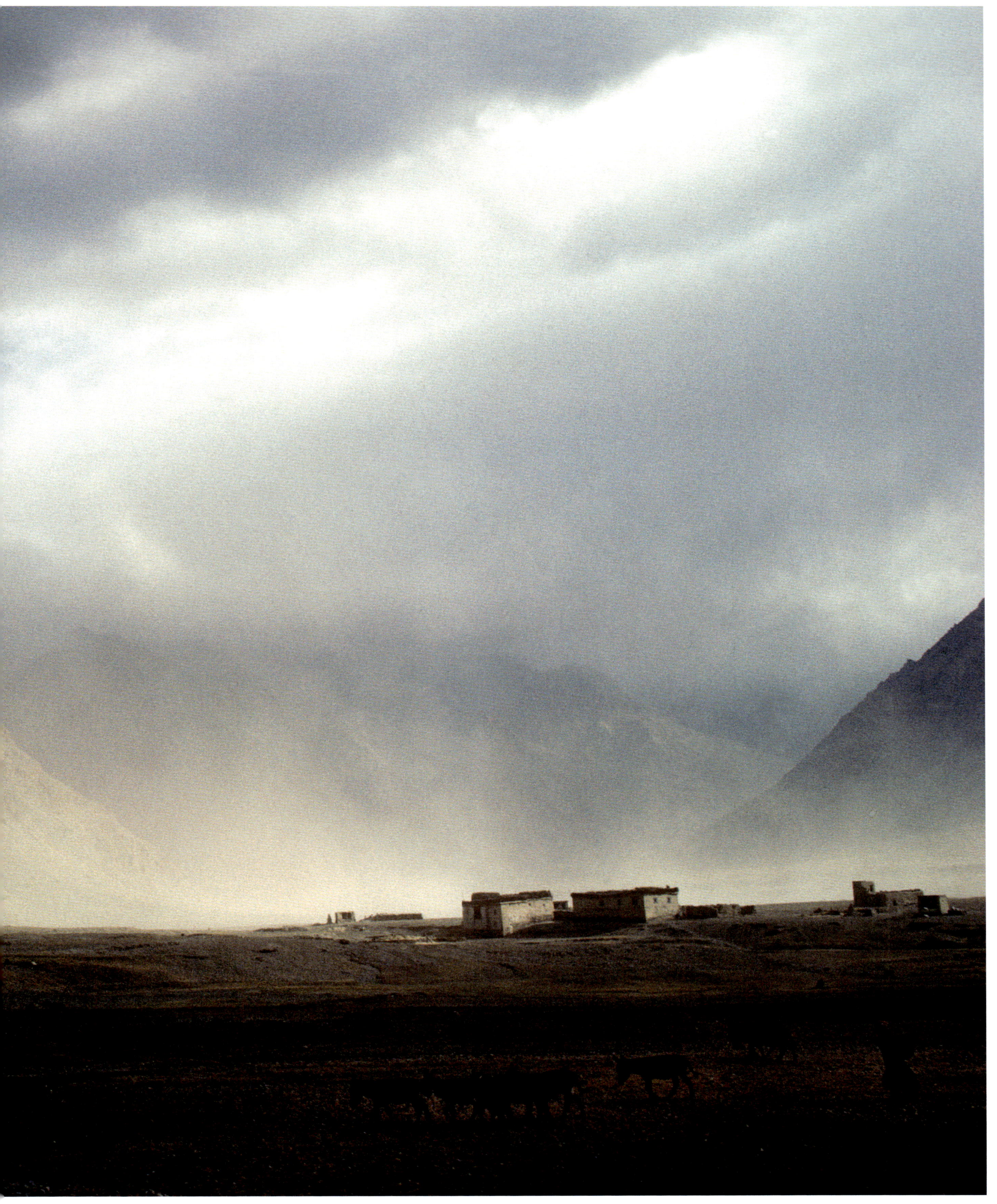

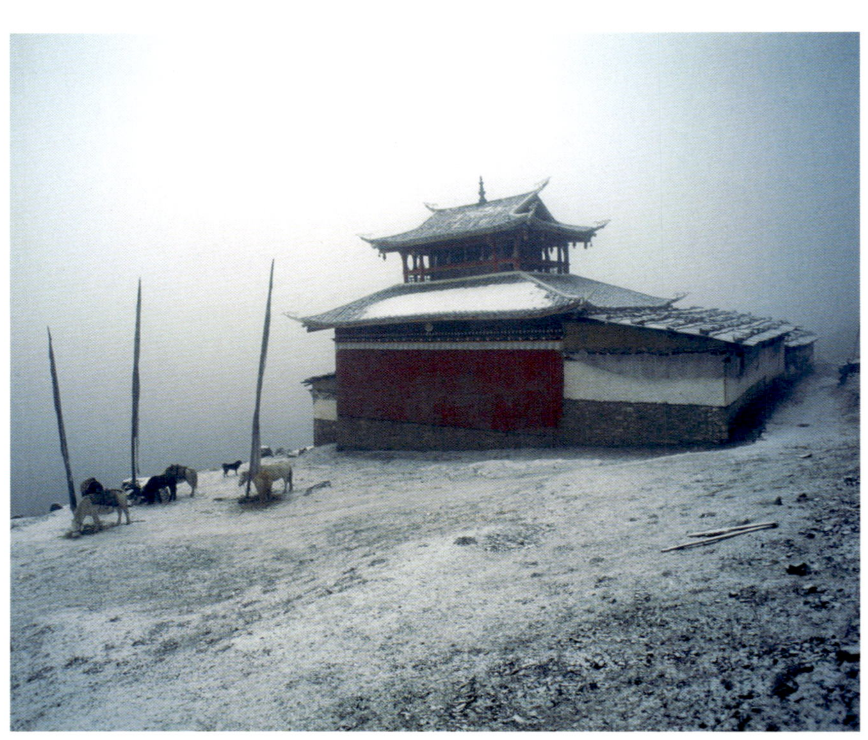

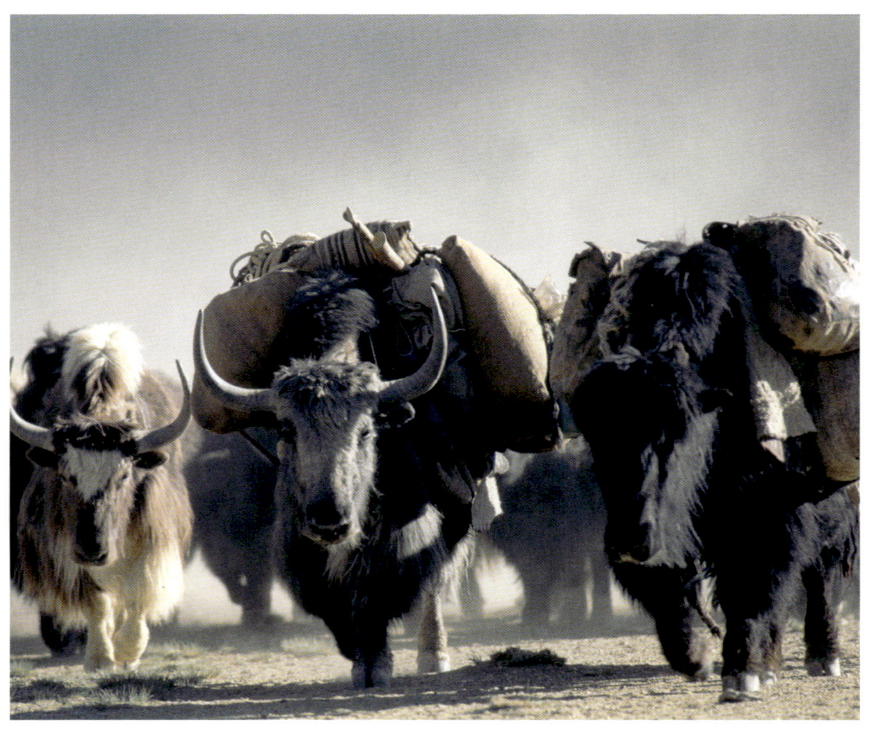

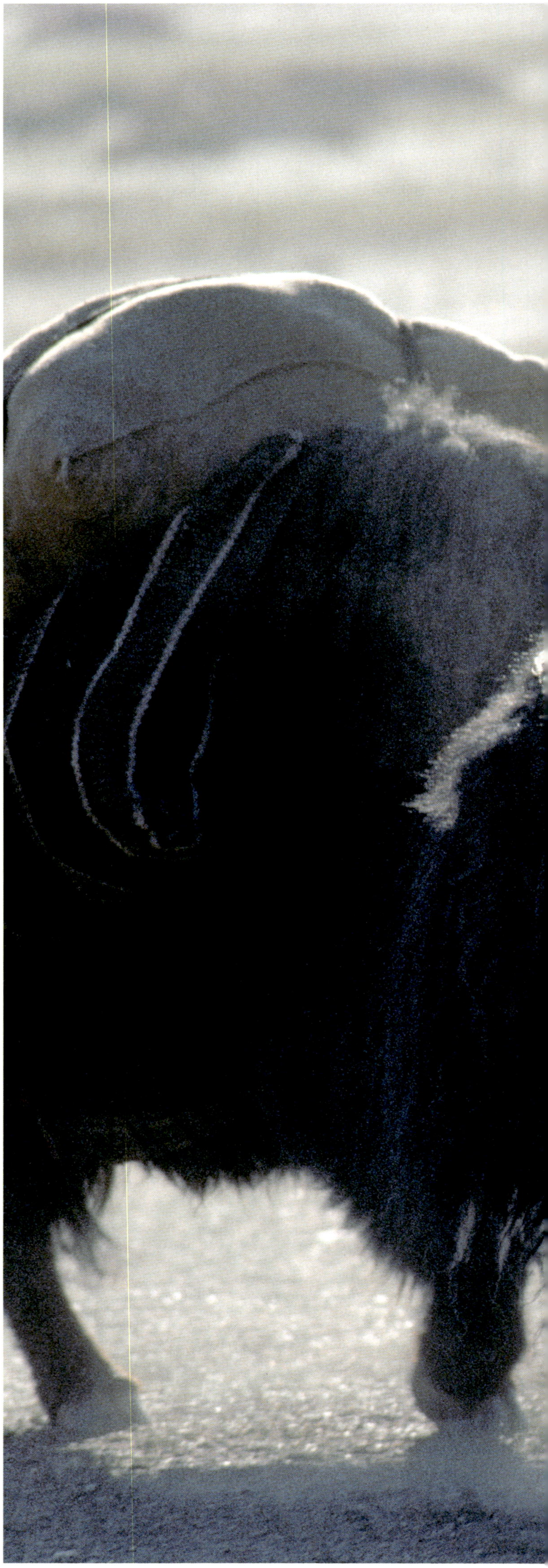

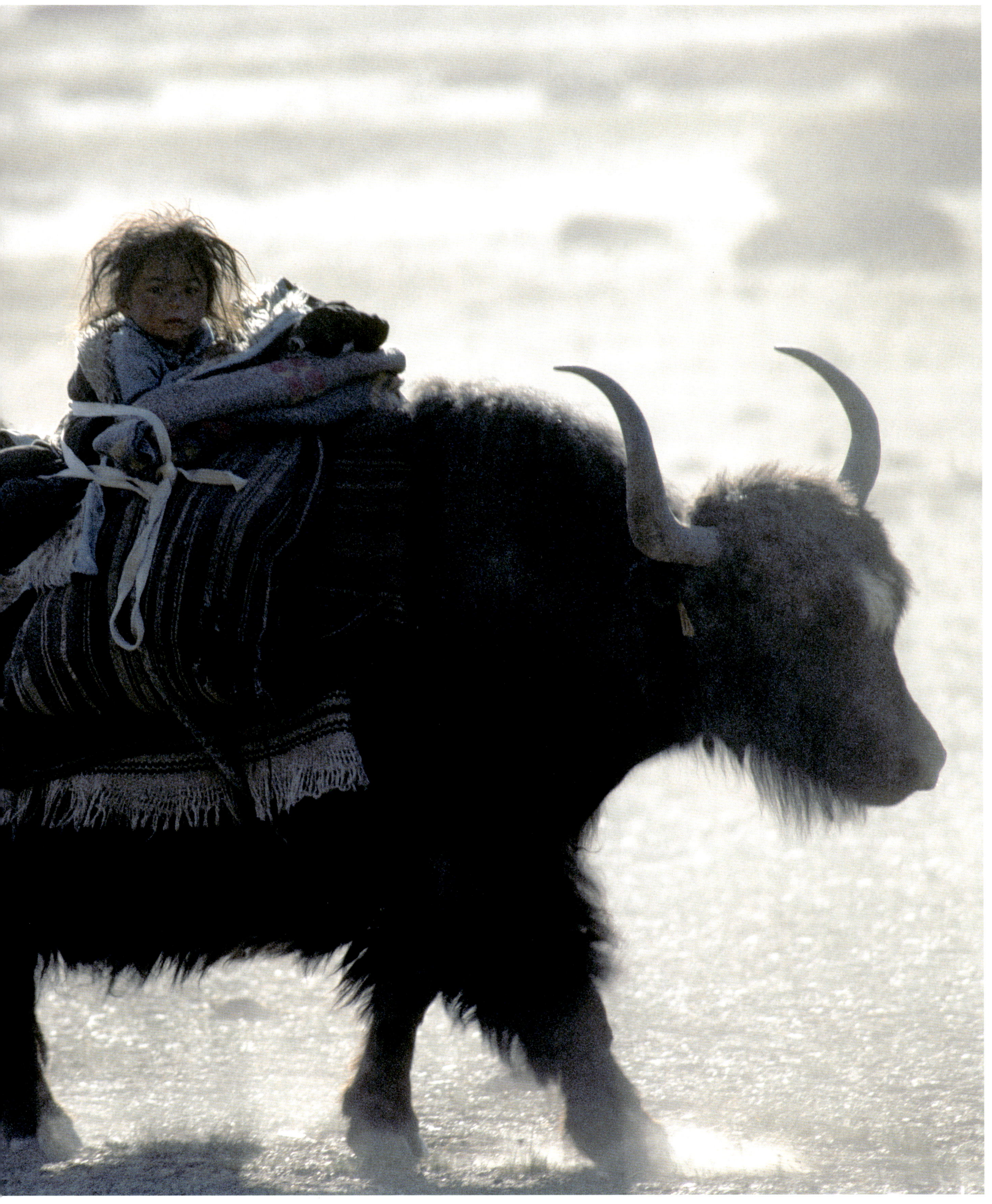

Dependent on the vagaries of weather at 15,000 feet above sea level, the lives of the Rupshu herders in Ladakh are some of the most precarious in the Himalayas. Sheltering under rough yak wool tents, they migrate with their herds four times a year, moving from one mountain pasture to another, taking with them only what their animals can carry. Each winter, facing the threat of snow for five months, they do their best to survive.

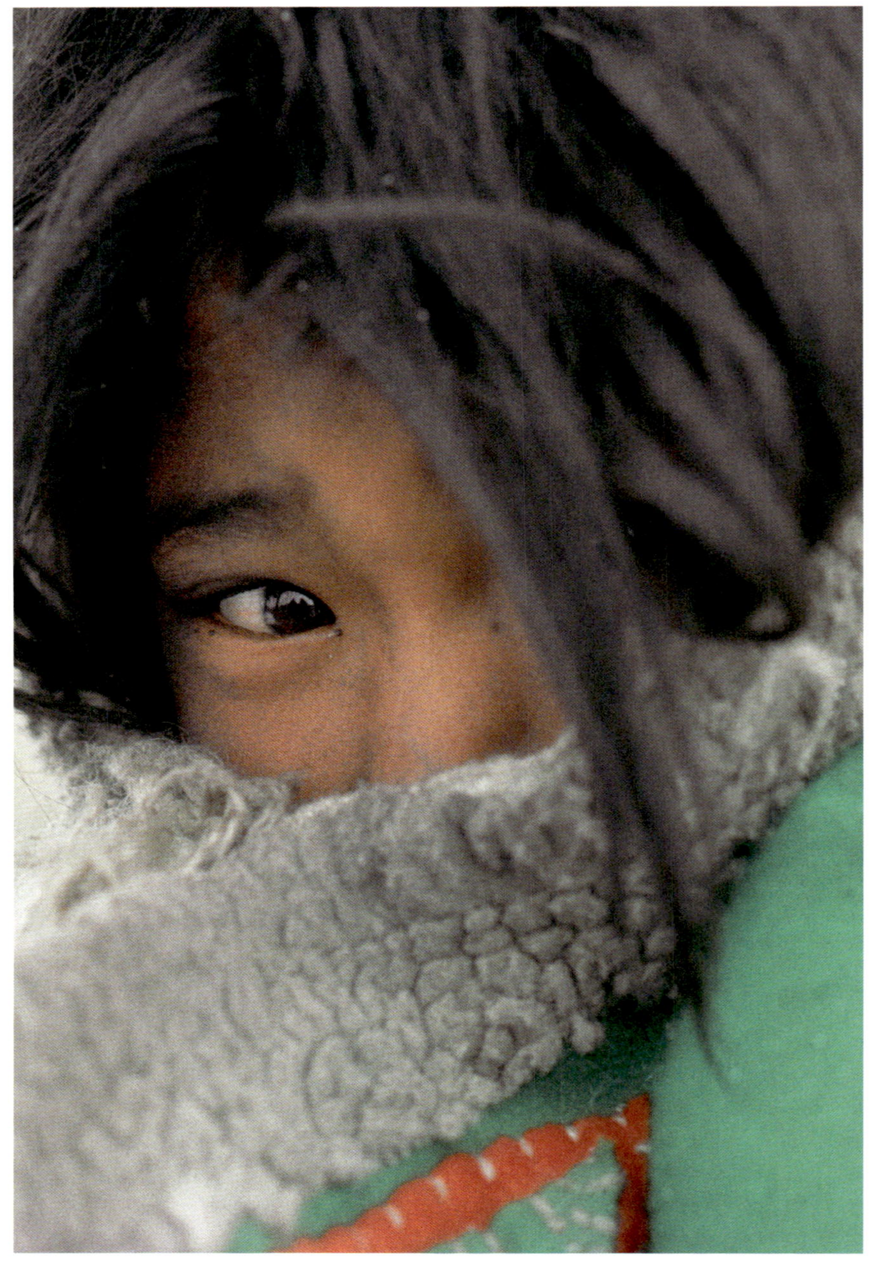

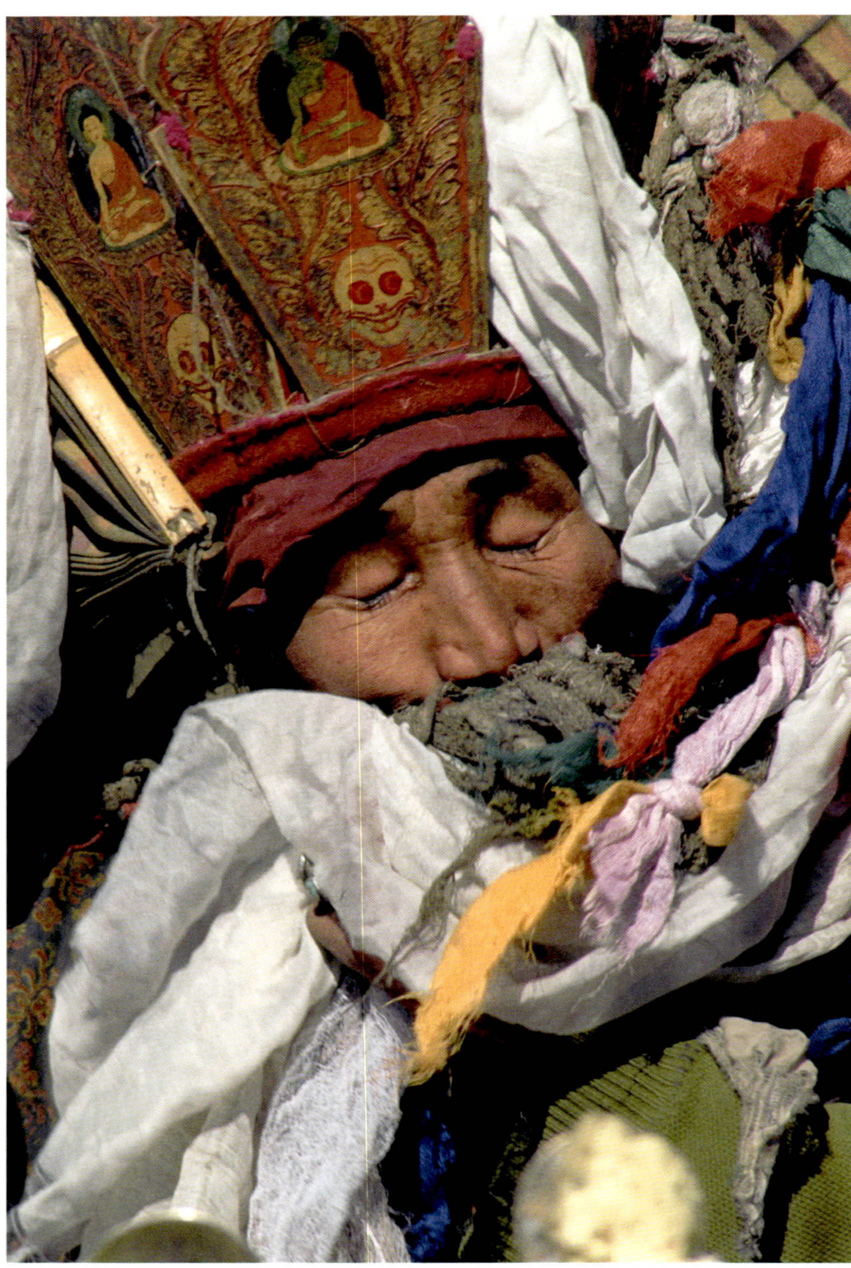

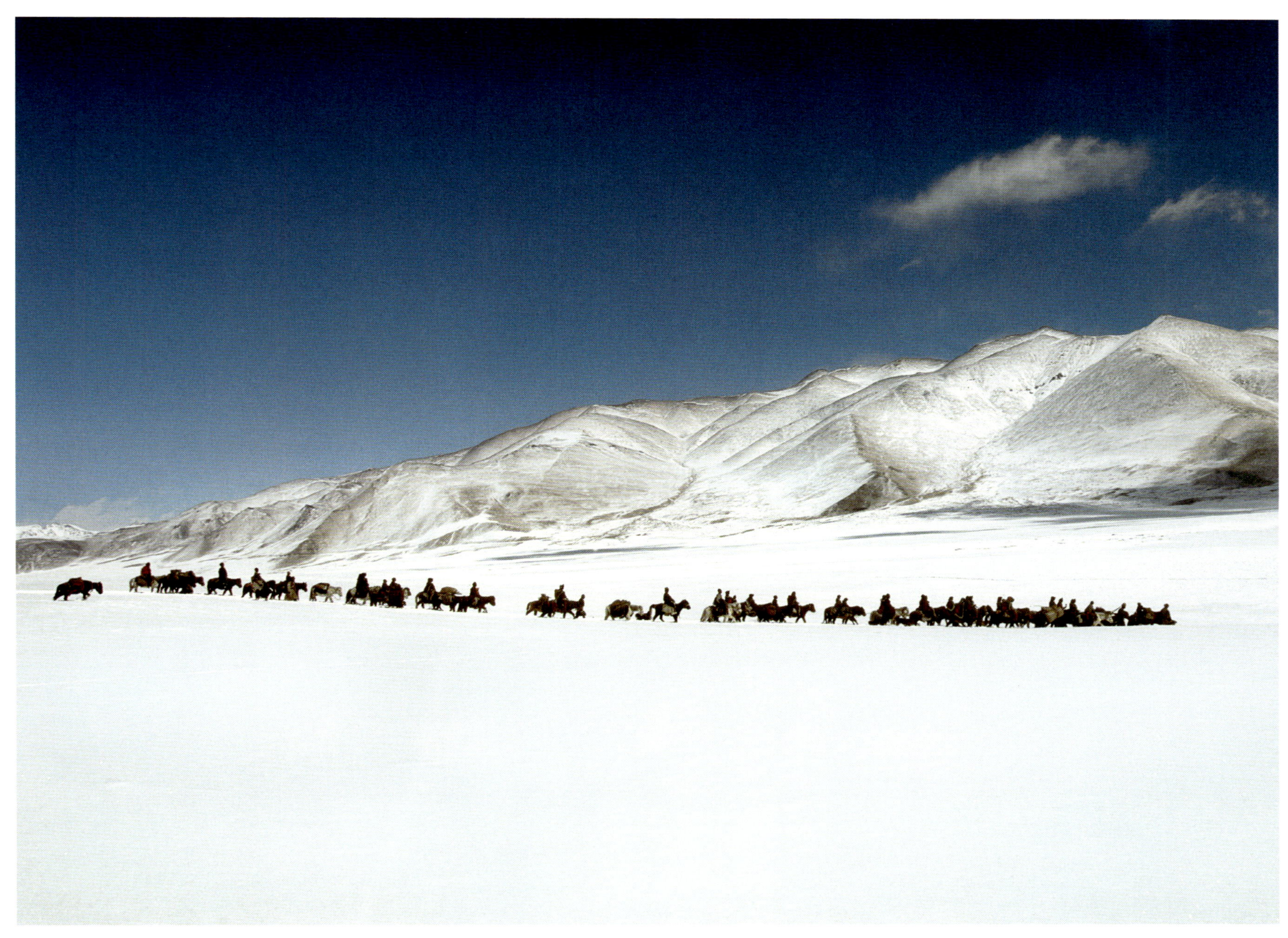

Das Leben der Schäfer von Rupshu in Ladakh ist eines der unsichersten und gefährlichsten im Himalaya. In 4500 Meter Höhe sind sie ganz den Unbilden des Wetters ausgeliefert. Ihr einziger Schutz sind Zelte aus rauer Yak-Wolle. Mit ihren Herden ziehen sie viermal im Jahr von einer Bergweide zur anderen. Sie führen nur so viel Habe mit, wie ihre Tiere tragen können. Jeden Winter kämpfen sie fünf Monate lang gegen den bedrohlichen Schnee ums Überleben.

Dépendante des caprices du temps à 4 500 mètres d'altitude, la vie des bergers du Rupshu au Ladakh est l'une des plus précaires de l'Himalaya. S'abritant sous des tentes en laine rêche de yak, ils migrent avec leurs troupeaux quatre fois par an d'un alpage à l'autre, transportant leurs affaires, réduites au chargement que les bêtes peuvent porter. En survie chaque hiver, ils doivent faire face à la neige menaçante pendant cinq mois.

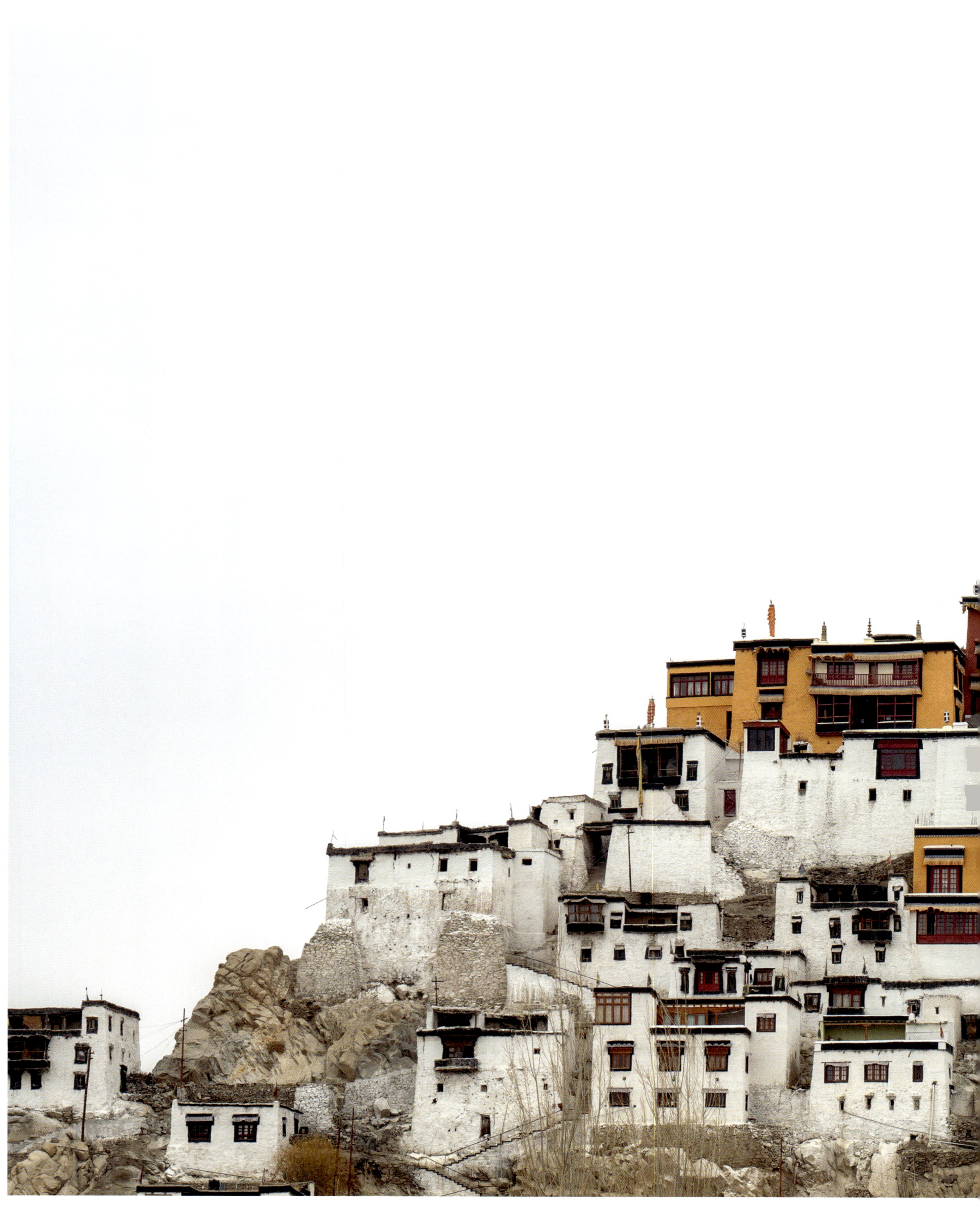

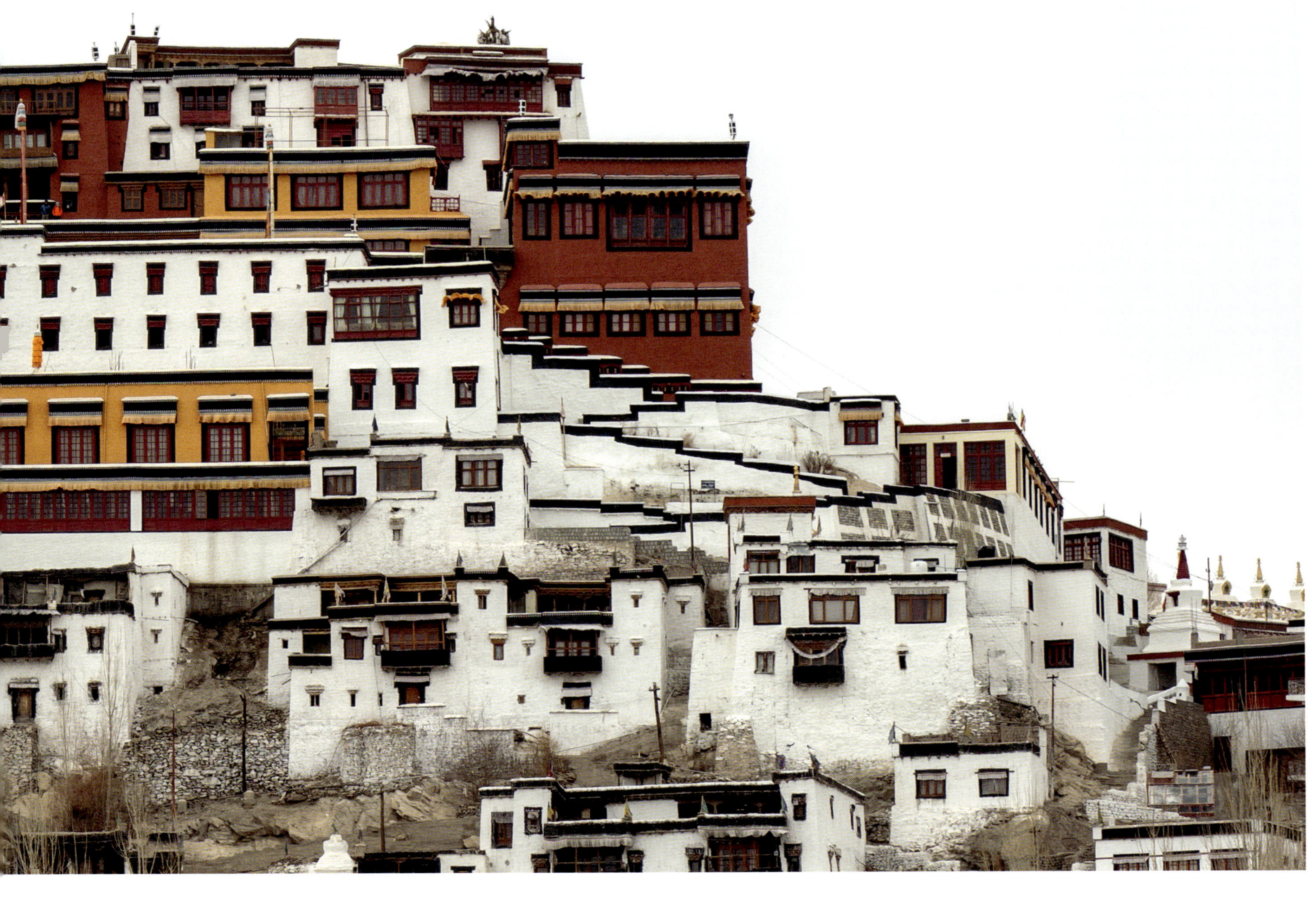

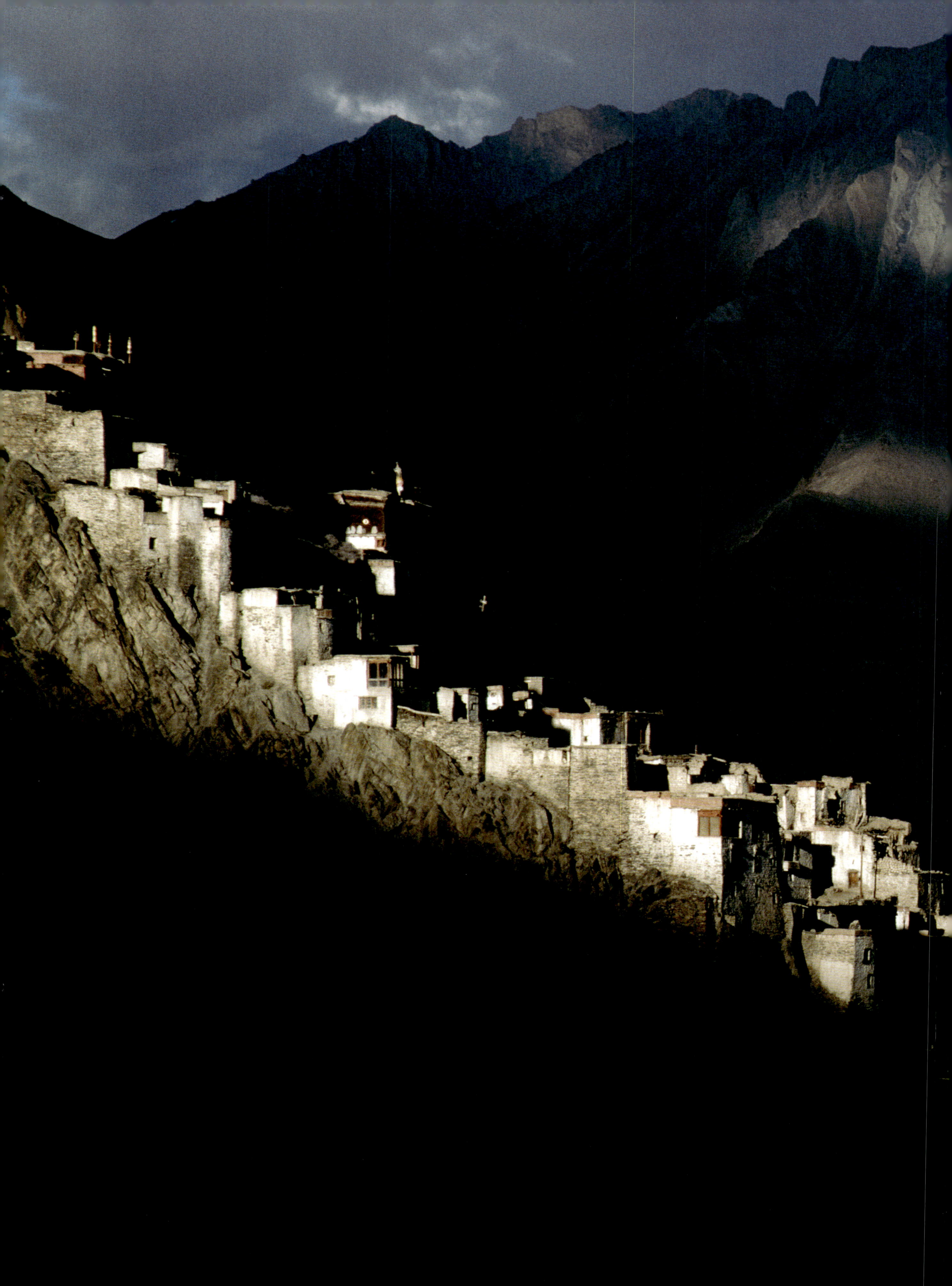

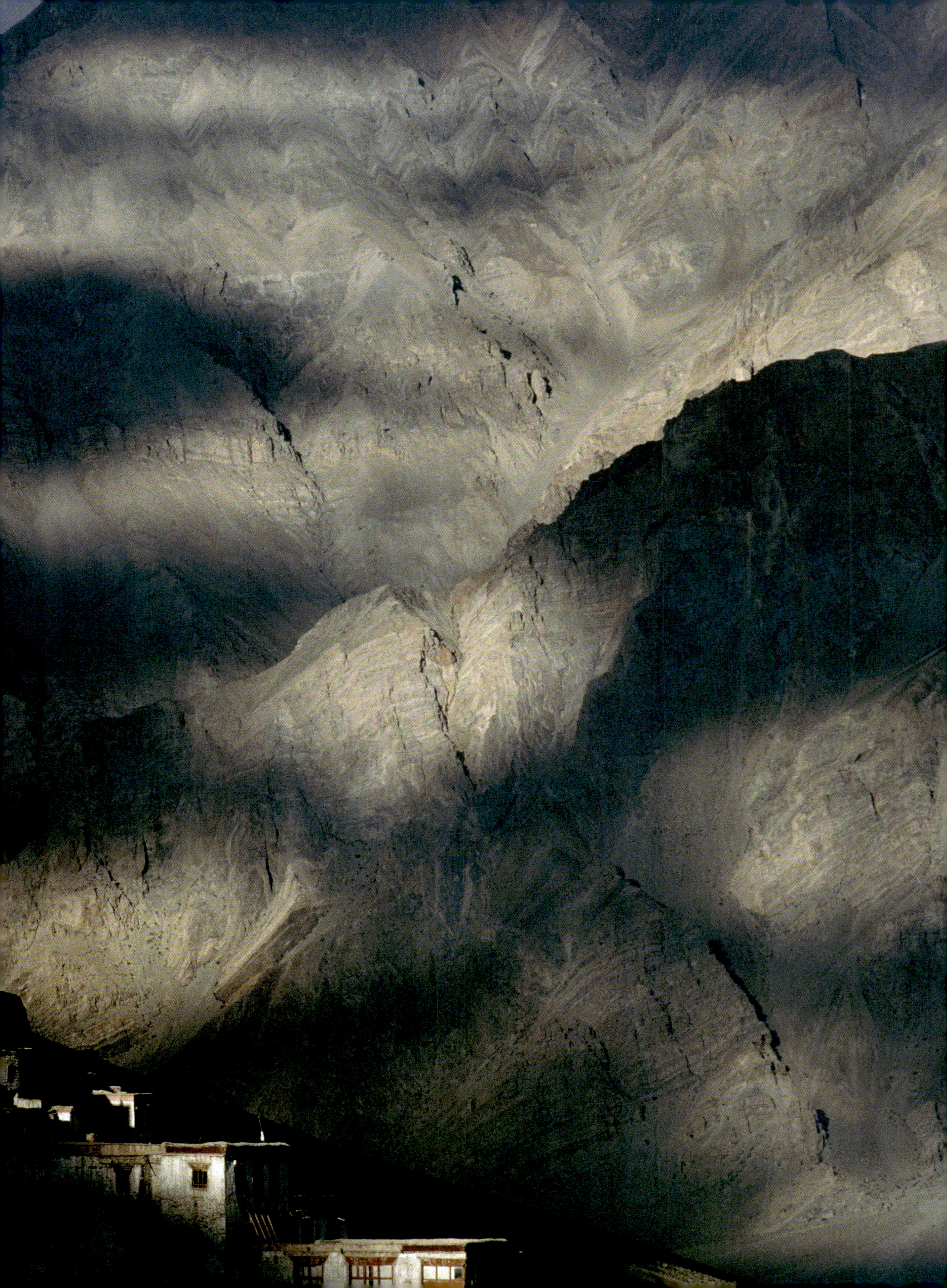

Interdependence

Interdependenz · Interdépendance

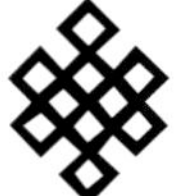

No individual happiness can be completely independent
from other people. We share the same family relationship with
all the beings of the Universe.

Es gibt kein Glück des Einzelnen in völliger Unabhängigkeit von anderen.
Wir teilen dieselben Familienbande mit allen Wesen des Universums.

Il n'existe pas de bonheur individuel totalement indépendant d'autrui.
Nous partageons une même relation de famille
avec tous les êtres de l'univers.

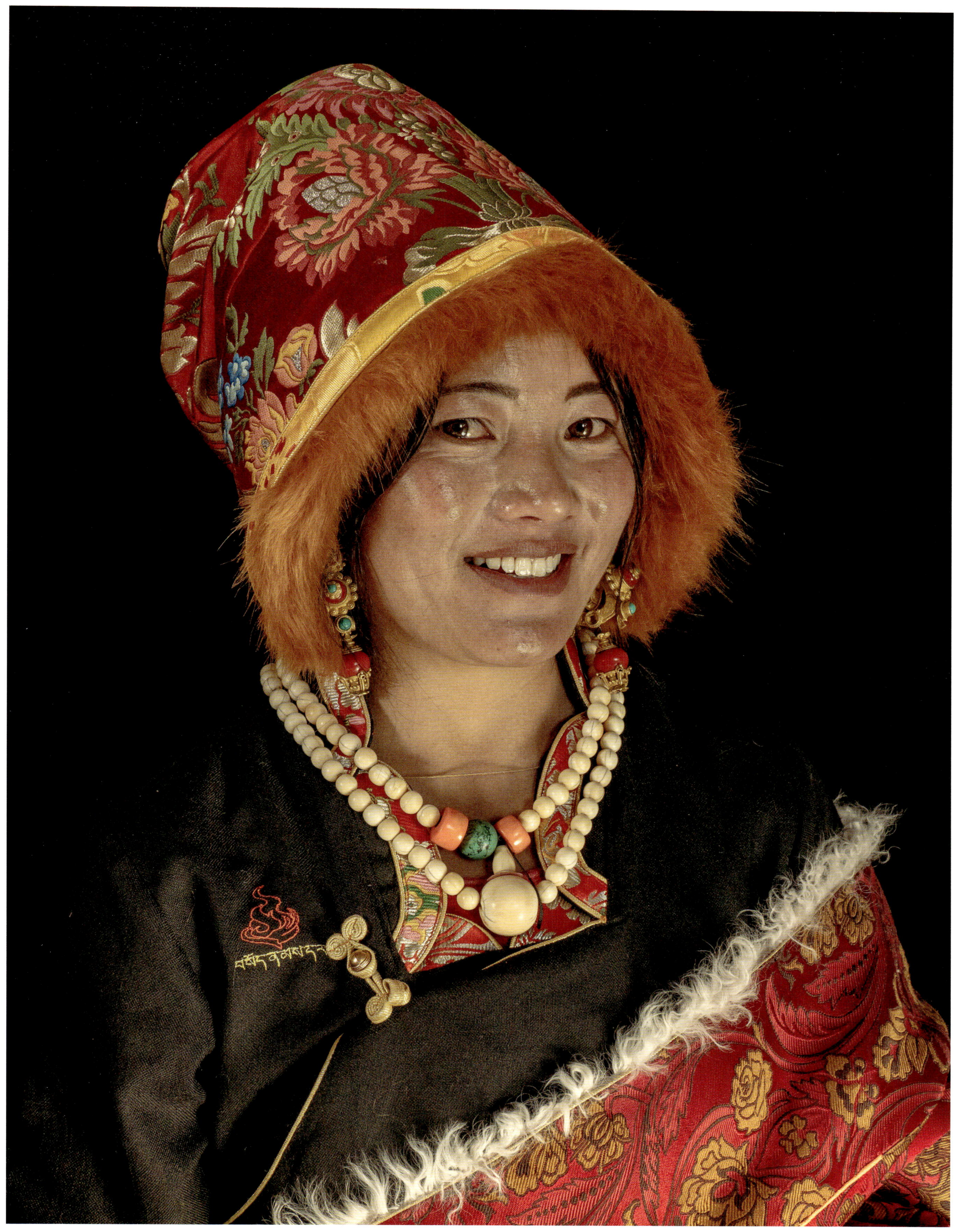

During my first winter in Zanskar, I stayed in Phuktal monastery, which clung to the mountain face like an eagle's nest at an altitude of 13,000 feet, facing the frozen river. I was contemplating becoming a Buddhist monk and wanted to experience life in a monastery. To reach the monastery from the main Zanskar valley 11,500 feet above sea level, you have to walk for four days at a good pace on the frozen river passing through the Lungnak valley, or walk for one week if you go via Shade, the most remote village in Zanskar, and the Stongde pass at an altitude of 18,000 feet. I wanted to discover Shade in winter, so, to reach Phuktal, I decided to cross the Stongde pass. No one had tried to cross it this winter but there didn't seem to be much snow. Also, I was accompanied by Tsering Norboo, one of my faithful friends from Zanskar who, strong as a yak, would help me make the trail.

Step by step, we climbed up to the pass, which took us all day. The air was pure and icy, and I felt free and happy. I love exploring, as my whims take me, in the maze of rugged valleys to reach a village. After days of solitude, I always feel an exhilarating joy in finding people again. We reached the pass at sunset, the slopes flooded with a soft, iridescent light. A bitter wind had arrived, chilling us to the bone and burning the insides of our throats. We were now at an altitude of 18,000 feet and night was falling. Luckily, the moon bathed the valley in a milky light and we climbed down for three hours before finding a cave and some wood. Sitting cross-legged around three stones, we listened to the fire crackling. A man of few words, my companion much preferred the calm of the mountains. In Tibetan regions, talking for the sake of talking is considered impolite.

For three days we walked without meeting a single human being. Our only encounter was with a snow leopard, this morning, on the river. We were walking silently on sheer ice when, going round a rock, we found ourselves face-to-face with the majestic animal. I don't know who was more surprised. The size of a gray-and-white mottled guard dog, the leopard stopped in its tracks, arched on its large furry paws. We looked at each other for a split second before the leopard vanished among the rocks with the suppleness and rapidity of all felines. "We were lucky," whispered Tsering, "it could have attacked us."

> A MAN OF FEW WORDS, MY COMPANION MUCH PREFERRED THE CALM OF THE MOUNTAINS. IN TIBETAN REGIONS, TALKING FOR THE SAKE OF TALKING IS CONSIDERED IMPOLITE.

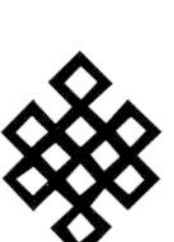

We reached Shade valley as the sun was setting and slowly climbed the path along the frozen stream. When I saw the tiny village with its fifteen houses, I had the impression I was entering another planet. However, the astonishment on the villagers' faces was just as great as they watched from their flat roofs while we climbed up, ensconced in our heavy woolen coats with our large packs strapped to our back. The village of Shade benefits from a microclimate as it gets plenty of sunshine, and families live upstairs, even in winter. Life here is thus easier than in the other villages. The astrologer, a jovial man whose age it was impossible to guess, offered us his hospitality. From his beaten earth roof, he sang the praises of his small valley: "You see, in Shade, stream water is close, the pastures are not far, there is wood nearby; the grass is lush, yaks are plentiful, there's no shortage of wool, and the butter is excellent! No village has a better location than Shade!" I agreed, to avoid upsetting our host, but thought of the long route we had taken to get here. Shade's astrologer is renowned throughout the region. People consult him to determine the best day to set off on a journey, to choose a good date for a wedding, or to know the value of a child's karma on its birth. He is paid in seeds, wool, or butter. Money does not yet have any value here. After all, how many rupees should you pay for a woolen coat that has taken weeks to spin? No one would be able to say.

Some thirty villagers turned up joyfully at the astrologer's home. Seated cross-legged the length of the four walls in a large dirt-floored room, we huddled against one another to protect ourselves from the icy air coming from the windows with no glass. The astrologer invited me to sit down next to him, and I gladly squeezed up to make the most of the warmth coming from his large turned-back goat-skin coat, fully aware that his fleas would soon be joining mine.

Crouched in the middle of the room, a pretty young woman, the astrologer's daughter-in-law, served us chang using a large copper ladle with a handle set with a small turquoise. The young woman didn't stop staring at me and, once she had served me a few ladles of chang, asked me spiritedly: "What village do you come from?" Her husband, Phuntsok, burst out laughing: "He doesn't live in Zanskar, he's a stranger!" The woman then waved her hand vaguely at me to ask whether I lived behind those mountains, and I replied with the same gesture. Then, sticking her tongue between her teeth and nodding her head, she made me understand, in Zanskari manner, that I really did live a long way away. But Phuntsok wanted to know more. "Do you live far from Zanskar?" As Europe meant nothing to him, nor did Delhi, I began to explain using the village as my starting point: "From Shade, if you walk for four days you reach Padum." Phuntsok was familiar with Padum, the largest town in Zanskar, as he had been there twice. "From Padum, in summer, if you drive by truck for two days, you reach Kargil." But Phuntsok had never seen a truck and preferred to talk in "days on horseback." He knew Kargil by name and raised his eyebrows, aware of how far away it was. I mentioned the city of Srinagar, but then stopped: Why explain exactly where I lived? What use was it to flaunt my knowledge? What was it worth here? Phuntsok had no notion of country, race, religion, or political affiliation. He was free of all prejudices and judgments and thus more serene.

However, the astrologer was curious and asked me some questions about my country. I had brought a few photos with me and showed him my house with its sloping roof, bordered by a field and three apple trees. "Aren't you cold in your house with all those windows?" he asked me, surprised. "And how can you store forage on your roof?" The field intrigued his son: "Your grass is lush, do you have many yaks?" When I told him that, in my country, some people eat horses and donkeys, all those present burst out laughing and asked me to repeat what I had said. The family and neighbors found it hilarious—they had never heard anything like it before! I explained the photo of a church and a cemetery, and the young woman brought the photo respectfully to her forehead, murmuring a prayer. The photo of a display of apples was a source of amazement, and that of a herd of cows in a pasture provoked endless discussions. The photo of a yacht on the ocean was simply incomprehensible, and that of a condominium produced consternation after a few explanations.

"You are very intelligent, as you know all that," the astrologer said to me admiringly. I lowered my eyes humbly, without replying. In this culture, pride is one of the worst forms of ignorance. But more than that, what merit could I truly claim? I was born into a good place in my society, I benefit from so-phisticated health care, knowledgeable teaching, and a comfortable lifestyle, but what is my merit? Past generations have worked toward my well-being; I am a link in interdependence. Also, I remain humble, as I have come here in search of answers that I have not found elsewhere.

Während meines ersten Winters in Zanskar war ich im Kloster Phuktal zu Gast, das über dem zugefrorenen Fluss wie ein Adlernest in 4000 Meter Höhe an einer Felswand kauert. Ich zögerte zwar zunächst, in den buddhistischen Orden einzudringen, wollte aber die Erfahrung eines Aufenthalts dort wagen. Um vom Zanskar-Haupttal in das 3500 Meter hoch gelegene Kloster zu gelangen, muss man vier Tage lang zügig auf dem gefrorenen Fluss durch das Tal des Lungnak gehen oder sich eine Woche lang über Shade, das entlegenste Dorf von Zanskar, sowie den Stongde-Pass in 5600 Meter Höhe zu den Mönchen vorarbeiten. Ich wollte Shade im Winter kennenlernen und beschloss, über den Stongde-Pass nach Phuktal zu gelangen. Niemand hatte in diesem Winter versucht, ihn zu überqueren, aber es schien mir nicht besonders viel Schnee zu liegen. Außerdem war ich in Begleitung von Tsering Norboo, einem meiner treuesten Freunde aus Zanskar, der nicht nur stark wie ein Yak war, sondern mir auch helfen würde, den Weg zu finden.

Schritt für Schritt näherten wir uns dem Pass. Der Aufstieg dauerte den ganzen Tag. Die Luft war klar und eisig, und ich fühlte mich frei und glücklich. Ich mag es, aufs Geratewohl das Labyrinth der wilden Täler zu durchlaufen, um zu einem Dorf zu gelangen. Nach tagelanger Einsamkeit empfinde ich jedes Mal große Begeisterung und freue mich sehr, wieder auf Menschen zu treffen. Als die Sonne unterging und die Hänge in ein mildes Licht tauchte, erreichten wir die Passhöhe. Es kam ein eisiger Wind auf, der uns das Blut in den Adern gefrieren ließ. Wir befanden uns auf 5600 Meter Höhe, und die Nacht brach herein. Zum Glück tauchte der Mond das Tal in ein milchiges Licht. Wir stiegen drei Stunden lang ab, bis wir eine Höhle und etwas Holz fanden. Im Schneidersitz saßen wir um drei Steine und hörten dem knisternden Feuer zu. Mein schweigsamer Freund fügte sich gern in die Stille der Berge. In Tibet gilt es als unhöflich zu reden, wenn man nichts zu sagen hat.

Drei Tage waren wir unterwegs, ohne auf eine Menschenseele zu stoßen. Unsere einzige Begegnung hatten wir an einem Morgen mit einem Schneeleoparden auf dem Fluss. Wir marschierten schweigend auf dem glänzenden Eis dahin, als wir an einer Biegung hinter einem Felsen unvermutet dem majestätischen Raubtier, das genauso überrascht war wie wir, Auge in Auge gegenüberstanden. Es war groß wie ein Hofhund, weiß und grau gefleckt. Abrupt blieb der Leopard mit seinen dicken, behaarten Pfoten stehen und machte einen Buckel. Wir blickten uns für den Bruchteil einer Sekunde an, dann verschwand das Tier mit der für Katzen typischen Gewandtheit und Schnelligkeit zwischen den Felsen. „Wir haben Glück gehabt", flüsterte mir Tsering zu, „er hätte uns auch angreifen können."

Mit den letzten Sonnenstrahlen kamen wir in der Talmulde von Shade an und kletterten langsamen Schrittes den Trampelpfad neben dem gefrorenen Bach hoch. Als ich das Dorf aus 15 Häusern sah, hatte ich das Gefühl, auf einem anderen Planeten zu landen. Doch auch den Dorfbewohnern stand die Überraschung ins Gesicht geschrieben. Von ihren flachen Dächern aus sahen sie uns mit großen Rucksäcken beladen in unseren schweren Wollmänteln heraufsteigen. Shade profitiert dank guter Sonnenexposition von einem günstigen Mikroklima. Die Familien können sogar im Winter im Obergeschoss bleiben. Das Leben ist hier also leichter als in anderen Dörfern. Der Astrologe des Dorfes bot uns seine Gastfreundschaft an. Er war ein jovialer Mann, dessen Alter sich unmöglich schätzen ließ. Von seinem Lehmdach aus lobte er unablässig sein kleines Tal: „Seht, in Shade fließt der Bach gleich nebenan, die Weiden sind nicht weit entfernt, man findet Holz, es gibt viele Kräuter und Yaks, es fehlt uns nicht an Wolle und die Butter ist ausgezeichnet! Shade liegt einfach ideal!" Ich wollte unserem Gastgeber nicht widersprechen und pflichtete ihm deshalb bei, dachte aber an den Weg, den wir nehmen mussten, um überhaupt hierher zu gelangen. Der Astrologe von Shade steht im ganzen Land in hohem Ansehen. Man wendet sich an ihn, um von ihm zu hören, wann der günstigste Tag für den Antritt einer Reise oder eine Hochzeit ist, aber auch, um den Wert des Karmas eines Kindes bei seiner Geburt zu erfahren. Entlohnt wird er mit Getreide, Wolle oder Butter. Geld hat hier keinen Wert. Wie viele Rupien ist ein Wollmantel wert, den man wochenlang webt? Niemand weiß es.

Etwa 30 Dorfbewohner hatten sich beim Astrologen eingefunden. Wir reihten uns im Schneidersitz entlang der vier Wände eines großen Lehmzimmers auf und drückten uns aneinander, um uns vor dem eisigen Luftzug zu schützen, der durch die scheibenlosen Fenster strich. Der Astrologe lud mich ein, neben ihm zu sitzen. Ich klebte förmlich an ihm, um von der Wärme seines dicken Mantels aus nach innen gewendetem Ziegenfell zu profitieren – der Tatsache wohlbewusst, dass sich seine Flöhe nun zu meinen gesellen würden.

In der Mitte des Zimmers saß eine hübsche junge Frau, die Schwiegertochter des Sternendeuters. Sie goss mir mit einer Schöpfkelle, deren Griff mit einem kleinen Türkis besetzt war, Chang ein. Ohne Unterlass starrte sie mich an und fragte lebhaft, nachdem sie mir einige Schöpfkellen Chang serviert hatte: „Du, aus welchem Dorf kommst du?" Ihr Mann Phuntsok lachte laut auf: „Er lebt nicht in Zanskar. Er ist ein Fremder." Die Frau fragte mich mit einer unmerklichen Geste ihrer Hand, ob ich hinter den Bergen leben würde, und ich antwortete ihr mit derselben Geste. Sie klemmte daraufhin ihre Zunge zwischen die Zähne und schüttelte den Kopf, um mir auf typisch zanskarische Art zu bedeuten, dass ich wirklich sehr weit weg wohnen würde. Aber Phuntsok wollte mehr wissen. „Wohnst du weit weg von Zanskar?" Europa sagte ihm nichts, Delhi auch nicht. Also versuchte ich es ihm mit seinem Dorf als Bezugspunkt zu erklären. „Von Shade gelangt ihr nach einem viertägigen Fußmarsch nach Padum." Phuntsok kannte Padum, das größte Städtchen von Zanskar, gut, er war schon zweimal dort gewesen. „Von Padum wiederum gelangt man im Sommer mit einem Lastauto nach Kargil." Phuntsok hatte jedoch noch nie einen Lastwagen gesehen, er rechnete lieber in Tagesetappen mit dem Pferd. Ich erwähnte die Stadt Srinagar, brach meine Erklärungen aber ab. Was hatte es für einen Sinn, darzulegen, wo ich wohne? Was würde es bringen, mein Wissen hier auszubreiten? Welchen Wert hatte es hier? Phuntsok hatte keine Vorstellung von Ländern, Ethnien, Religion oder politischer Zugehörigkeit. Er war frei von allem Vorurteil, ja, von allem Urteil. Das gab ihm Gelassenheit.

> *MEIN SCHWEIGSAMER FREUND FÜGTE SICH GERN IN DIE STILLE DER BERGE. IN TIBET GILT ES ALS UNHÖFLICH ZU REDEN, WENN MAN NICHTS ZU SAGEN HAT.*

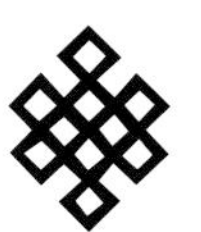

Der Astrologe indes war neugierig und fragte mich über mein Land aus. Ich hatte einige Fotos dabei und zeigte ihm mein Haus mit spitzem Dach, daneben ein Feld und drei Apfelbäume. „Frierst du in deinem Haus mit so vielen Fenstern nicht?", fragte er mich erstaunt. „Und wie schaffst du es, auf dem Dach das Futter für die Tiere zu lagern?" Sein Sohn kam auf das Feld zu sprechen. „Du hast üppiges Gras, hast du viele Yaks?" Als ich ihnen erzählte, dass in meinem Land manche Menschen Pferde und Esel essen, gab es unter den Anwesenden ein großes Gelächter. Man bat mich, das zu wiederholen. Die Familie, die Nachbarn, sie amüsierten sich köstlich – so etwas hatten sie noch nie gehört! Ich erklärte ihnen das Foto mit der Kirche und dem Friedhof. Die junge Frau hielt es sich respektvoll an die Stirn und murmelte ein Gebet. Eine Aufnahme von einer Auslage mit Äpfeln brachte sie zum Staunen, eine andere mit einer Herce Kühe auf der Weide zog nicht enden wollende Diskussionen nach sich. Das Bild von einem Segelschiff auf dem Meer erzeugte Verständnislosigkeit. Als sie ein Hochhaus sahen, waren sie selbst nach einigen Erklärungen noch immer konsterniert.

„Du bist sehr intelligent, weil du das alles weißt", meinte der Astrologe bewundernd. Ich senkte bescheiden die Augen, ohne zu antworten. Stolz ist eine der schlimmsten Formen der Ignoranz. Vor allem: Welche Verdienste hätte ich schon anführen können? Ich bin in meine Gesellschaft hineingeboren, ich komme in den Genuss ihrer hoch entwickelten Fürsorge, einer guten Bildung, eines leichten Lebens, aber was ist mein Verdienst? Generationen vor mir haben die Voraussetzungen für mein Wohlergehen geschaffen, ich bin nur ein Glied in einem Geflecht. Ich bleibe hier auch demütig, denn ich bin auf cer Suche nach Antworten hergekommen, die ich anderswo nicht finde.

Lors de mon premier hiver au Zanskar, j'ai séjourné au monastère de Phuktal accroché à la paroi comme un nid d'aigle, à 4 000 mètres d'altitude, face à la rivière gelée. J'hésitais à entrer dans les ordres bouddhistes et je voulais en tenter l'expérience monastique. Pour rejoindre le monastère depuis la vallée principale du Zanskar à 3 500 mètres d'altitude, il faut marcher quatre jours d'un bon pas sur la rivière gelée en passant par la vallée de la Lungnak, ou une semaine si l'on passe par Shadé, le village le plus isolé du Zanskar, et le col de Stongdé, à 5 600 mètres d'altitude. Souhaitant découvrir Shadé, je décide de passer par le col de Stongdé pour me rendre à Phuktal. Personne n'a tenté encore de le franchir cet hiver, mais il ne paraît pas très enneigé et je suis accompagné de Tsering Norboo, l'un de mes fidèles amis du Zanskar qui, aussi fort qu'un yak, m'aidera à faire la trace.

Pas à pas, l'ascension du col nous prend toute la journée. L'air est pur et glacé et je me sens libre et heureux. J'aime parcourir à l'aventure le labyrinthe de vallées sauvages pour rejoindre un village. Après des jours de solitude, j'éprouve toujours une joie exaltante à retrouver les hommes.

Au coucher du soleil qui irise les pentes d'une lumière douce, nous arrivons au col. Un vent polaire se lève, nous glace les veines et nous brûle les bronches. Nous sommes à 5 600 mètres d'altitude et la nuit tombe. Heureusement, la lune baigne la vallée dans une lumière laiteuse et nous descendons trois heures avant de trouver une grotte et un peu de bois. Assis en tailleur autour de trois pierres, nous écoutons crépiter le feu. Peu bavard, mon compagnon s'unit volontiers au calme des montagnes. En pays tibétain, parler pour ne rien dire est une impolitesse.

PEU BAVARD, MON COMPAGNON S'UNIT VOLONTIERS AU CALME DES MONTAGNES. EN PAYS TIBÉTAIN, PARLER POUR NE RIEN DIRE EST UNE IMPOLITESSE.

Pendant trois jours, nous marchons sans croiser une seule vie humaine. Notre unique rencontre est un léopard des neiges, ce matin, sur la rivière. Nous marchions silencieusement sur la glace vive lorsqu'au détour d'un rocher, nous nous sommes trouvés face à face avec cette bête majestueuse, aussi surprise que nous. De la taille d'un molosse tacheté blanc et gris, le léopard a stoppé net, arqué sur ses grosses pattes velues. Nous nous sommes regardés une fraction de seconde, puis le léopard a disparu

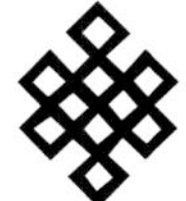

dans les rochers avec la souplesse et la rapidité des félins. « Nous avons eu de la chance, a soufflé Tsering, il aurait pu nous attaquer. »

Nous arrivons dans le vallon de Shadé aux derniers rayons de soleil et grimpons d'un pas lent le sentier le long du torrent gelé. En apercevant le village de quinze maisons, j'ai le sentiment d'arriver sur une autre planète, mais la stupéfaction se lit aussi sur les visages des villageois qui, de leur toit en terrasse, nous regardent monter, harnachés de gros sacs et engoncés dans nos lourds manteaux de laine.

Shadé bénéficie d'un microclimat grâce à un très bon ensoleillement, et les familles vivent à l'étage, même en hiver. La vie y est donc plus facile que dans les autres villages. L'astrologue nous offre l'hospitalité. C'est un homme jovial à qui il est impossible de donner un âge. De son toit de terre battue, il ne tarit pas d'éloges sur sa petite vallée : « Voyez-vous, à Shadé, l'eau du torrent est à côté, les pâturages ne sont pas loin, il y a du bois à proximité ; l'herbe est riche, les yaks sont nombreux, la laine ne manque pas, le beurre est excellent ! Il n'y a pas mieux situé que Shadé ! » J'acquiesce pour ne pas contrarier notre hôte, mais je pense au chemin qu'il nous a fallu parcourir pour arriver ici.

L'astrologue de Shadé est réputé dans tout le pays. On fait appel à lui pour déterminer le jour propice au départ d'un voyage, pour le choix d'une date bénéfique à un mariage, pour connaître la valeur du karma d'un enfant à sa naissance. On rémunère l'astrologue en grains, en laine ou en beurre. L'argent ici n'a pas encore de valeur. Combien de roupies vaut un manteau de laine que l'on tisse durant des semaines ? Personne ne saurait le dire.

Une trentaine de villageois s'invitent joyeusement chez l'astrologue. Assis en tailleur le long des quatre murs dans une grande pièce de terre, nous nous serrons les uns contre les autres pour nous protéger des courants d'air glacés qui vont et viennent par les fenêtres sans vitre. L'astrologue m'invite à m'asseoir à ses côtés et je me colle à lui pour profiter de la chaleur de son gros manteau de peau de chèvre retourné, conscient que ses puces s'ajouteront aux miennes.

Accroupie au centre de la pièce, une jolie jeune femme, la belle-fille de l'astrologue, nous sert à boire du tchang avec une grosse louche en cuivre au manche serti d'une petite turquoise. La jeune femme me dévisage sans arrêt et, après m'avoir servi quelques louches de tchang, elle m'interroge vivement : « Toi, tu viens de quel village ? » Son mari, Phuntsok, éclate de rire : « Il n'habite pas au Zanskar, c'est un étranger ! » La femme m'adresse alors un vague signe de la main pour me demander si j'habite derrière ces montagnes, et je réponds par le même geste. Se coinçant alors la langue entre les dents et hochant la tête, elle me fait comprendre, à la manière zanskarie, que j'habite vraiment très loin. Mais Phuntsok aimerait en savoir davantage. « Tu habites loin du Zanskar ? » L'Europe n'évoquant rien pour lui, Delhi non plus, j'entreprends mes explications à partir du village : « Depuis Shadé, en quatre jours de marche, vous allez jusqu'à Padum. » Phuntsok connaît bien Padum, le plus gros bourg du Zanskar, il y est allé deux fois. « De Padum, l'été, en deux jours de camion, vous arrivez à Kargil. » Mais Phuntsok n'a jamais vu de camion et préfère parler en jours de cheval. Il connaît Kargil de nom et hausse les sourcils, sachant combien c'est loin. J'évoque la ville de Srinagar, mais j'arrête là mes explications. Quelle importance d'expliquer exactement où j'habite ? À quoi sert d'étaler mes connaissances ? Que valent-elles ici ? Phuntsok n'a pas la notion de pays, de race, de religion ou d'appartenance politique. Il est libre de tout préjugé, de tout jugement. Il est donc plus serein.

Cependant, l'astrologue est curieux et me questionne sur mon pays. J'ai apporté quelques photos de chez moi et je montre ma maison au toit pointu, bordée par un champ et trois pommiers. « Tu n'as pas froid dans ta maison avec autant de fenêtres ? me demande-t-il, étonné. Et sur ton toit, comment fais-tu pour mettre le fourrage ? » Le champ interpelle son fils : « Ton herbe est riche, tu as beaucoup de yaks ? » Lorsque je raconte que, dans mon pays, certains mangent du cheval et de l'âne, l'assemblée part d'un énorme éclat de rire. On me demande de répéter ; la famille, les voisins sont hilares, ils n'ont jamais rien entendu de pareil ! J'explique la photo d'une église et d'un cimetière ; la jeune femme la porte respectueusement à son front et murmure une prière. Le cliché d'un étalage de pommes provoque la stupéfaction, celui d'un troupeau de vaches dans un pâturage, des discussions interminables, la photo d'un voilier sur l'océan, l'incompréhension, et celle d'un immeuble, la consternation après quelques explications.

« Tu es très intelligent pour connaître tout ça », me dit l'astrologue, admiratif. Je baisse humblement les yeux, sans répondre. L'orgueil ici est l'une des pires formes de l'ignorance. Surtout, de quel mérite pourrais-je me prévaloir ? Je suis bien né dans ma société, je jouis de soins sophistiqués, d'une instruction savante, d'une vie aisée, mais quel est mon mérite ? Les générations passées ont œuvré à mon bien-être, je suis un maillon de l'interdépendance. Je reste humble aussi, car je suis venu jusqu'ici en quête de réponses que je ne trouve pas ailleurs.

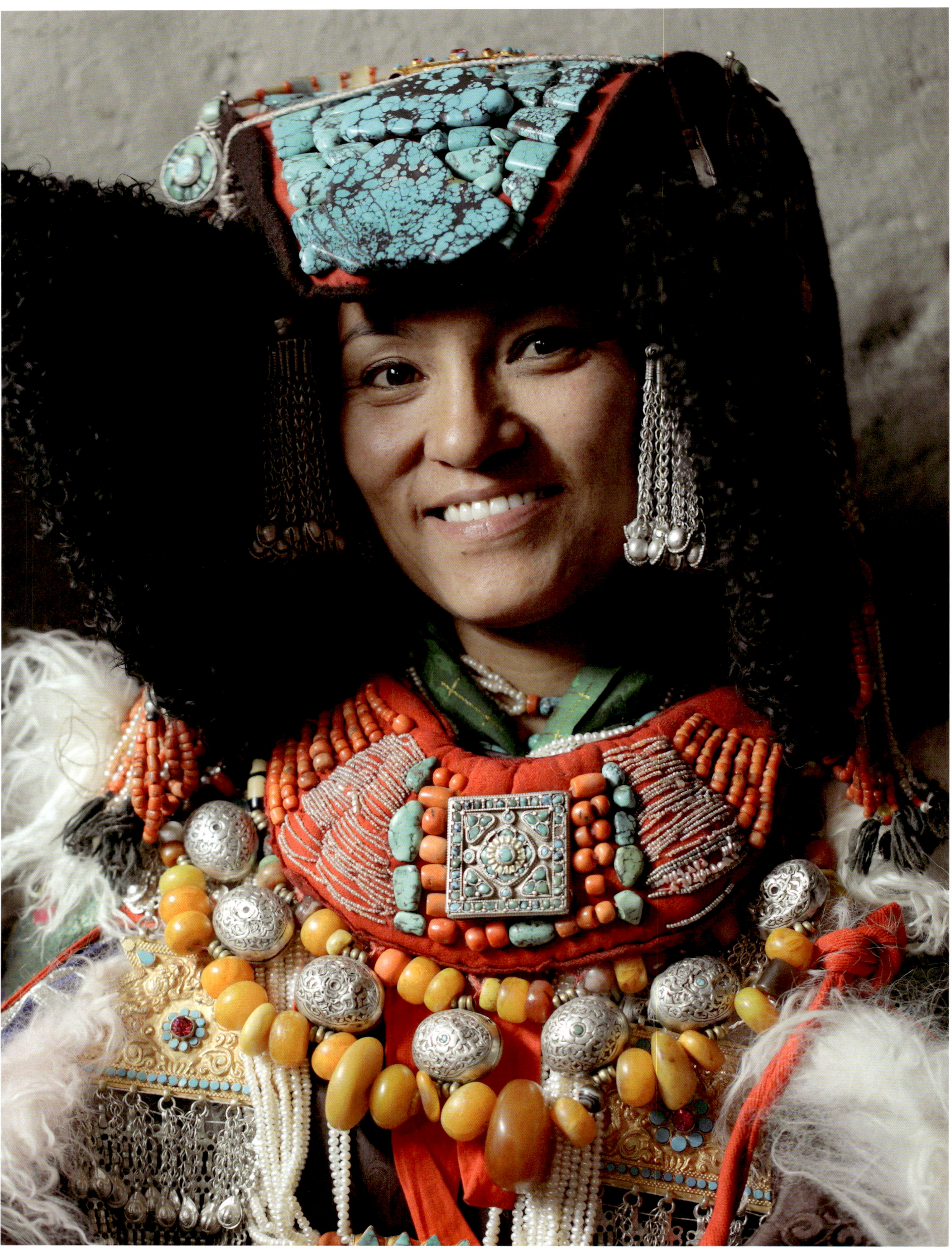

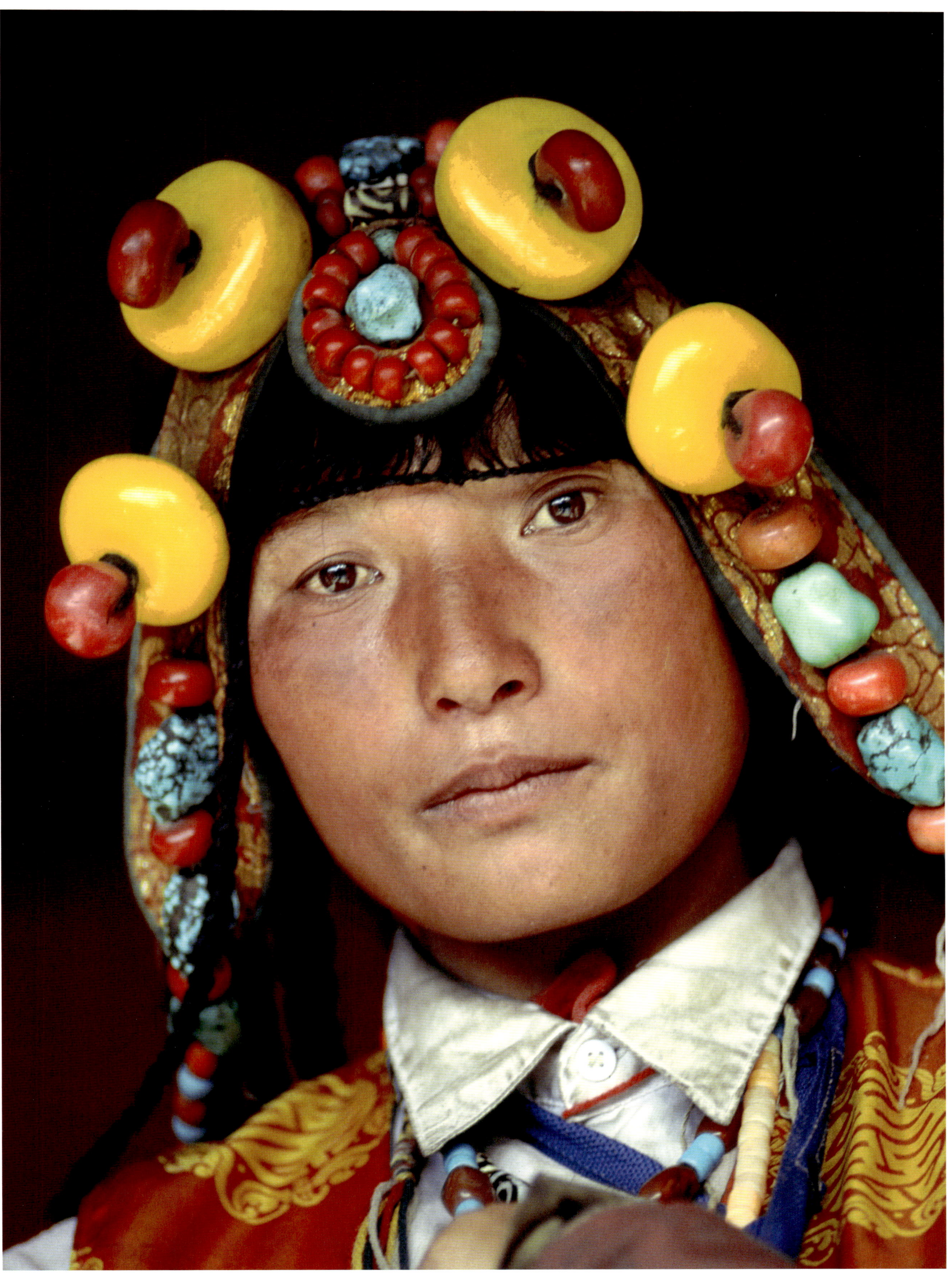

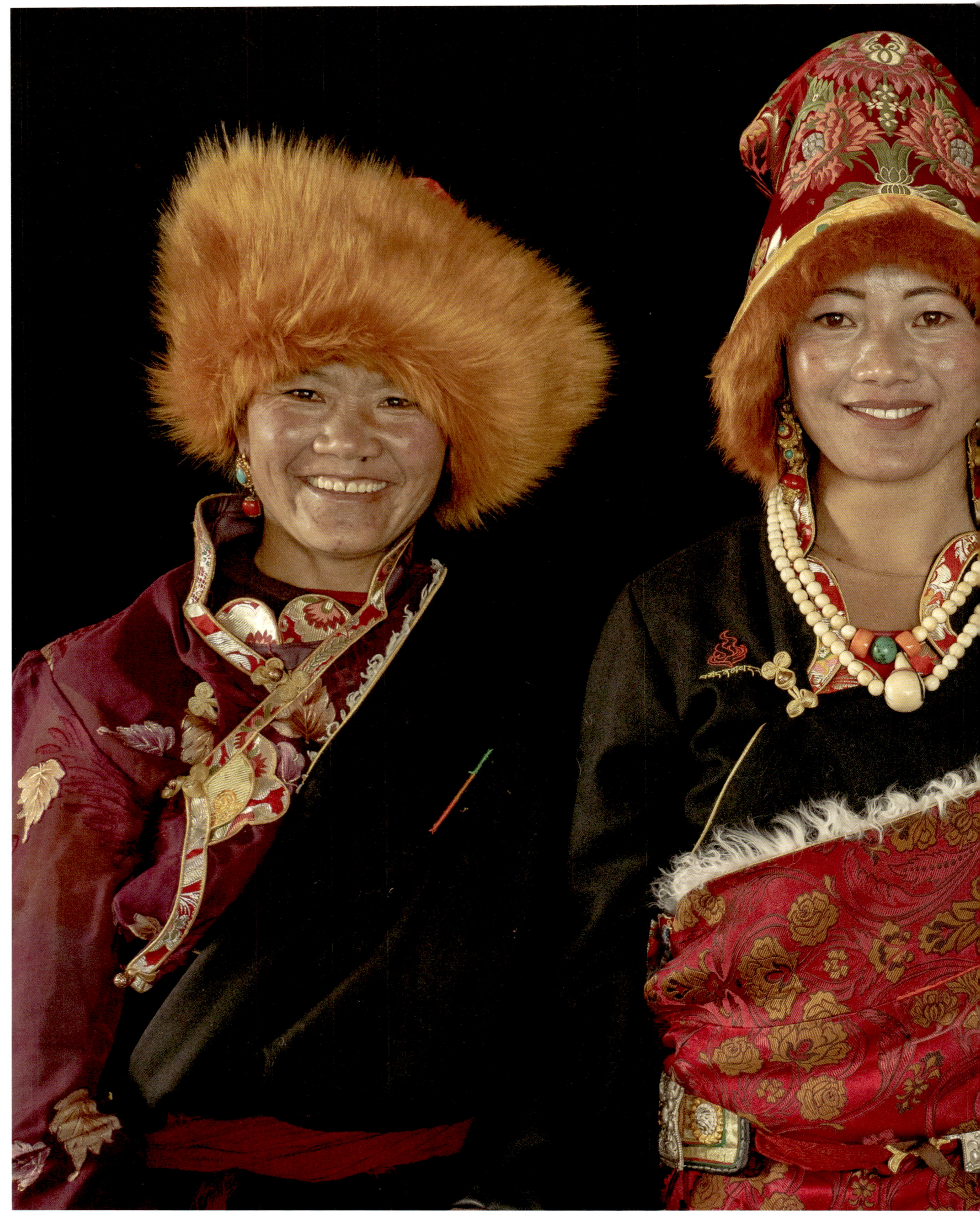

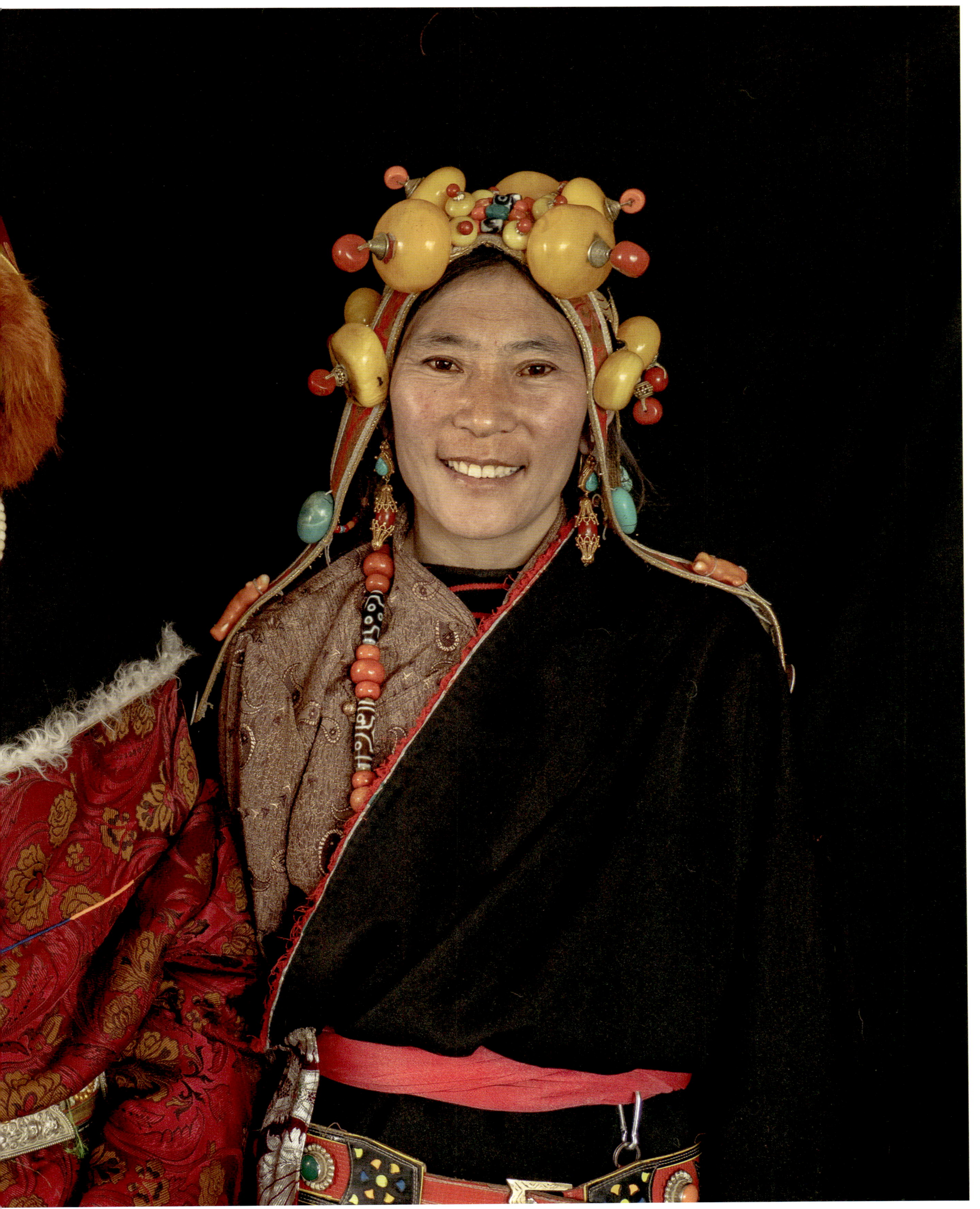

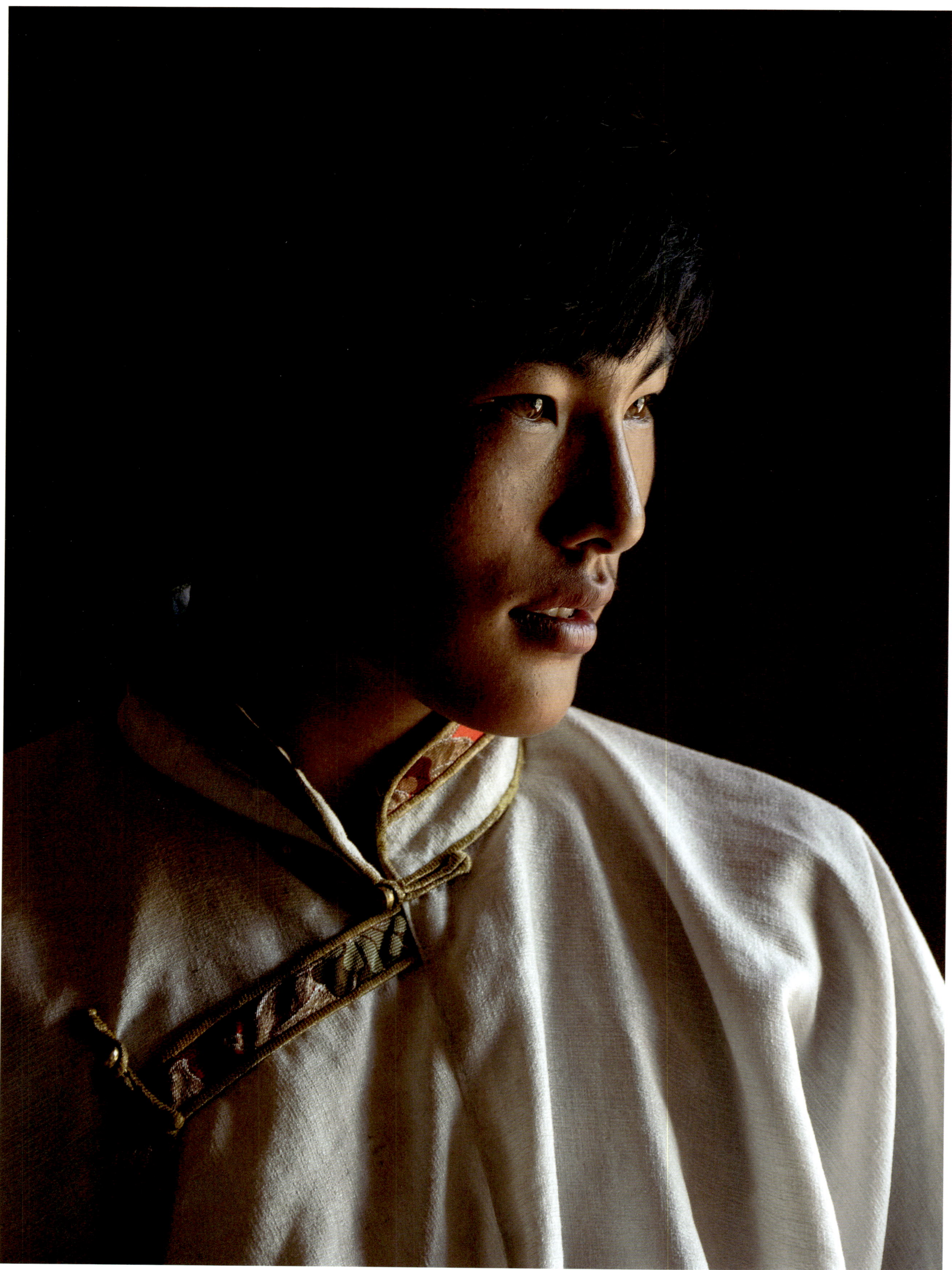

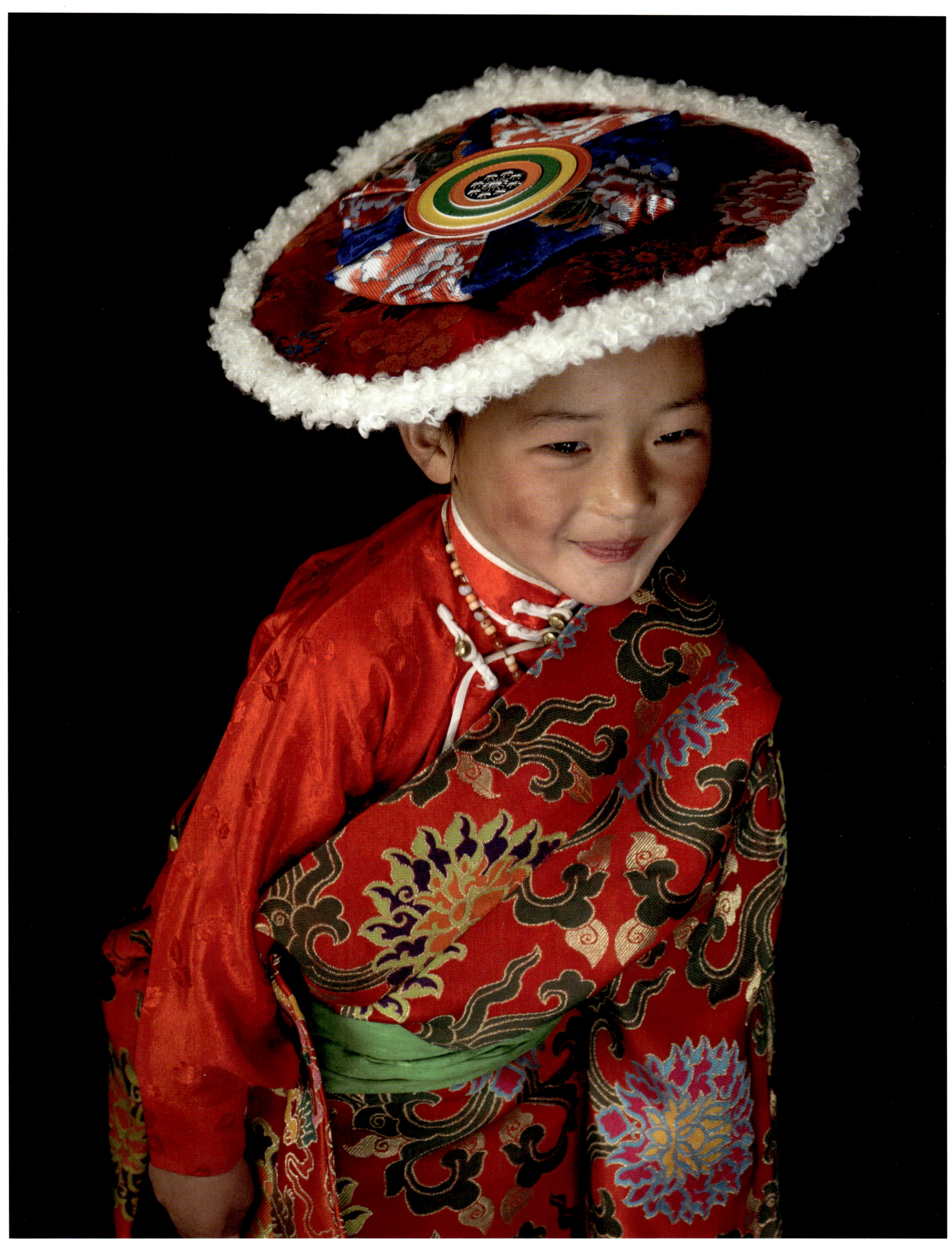

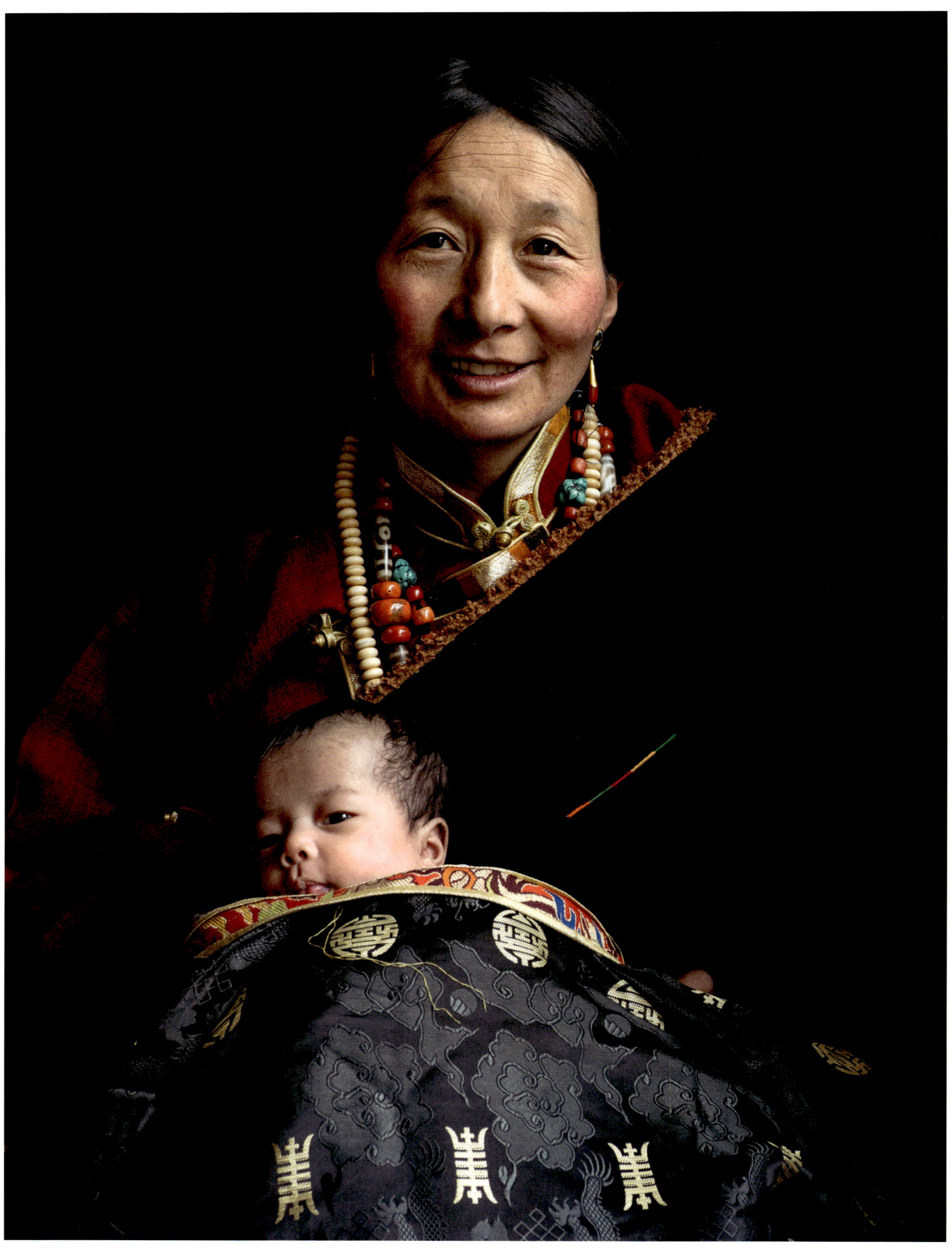

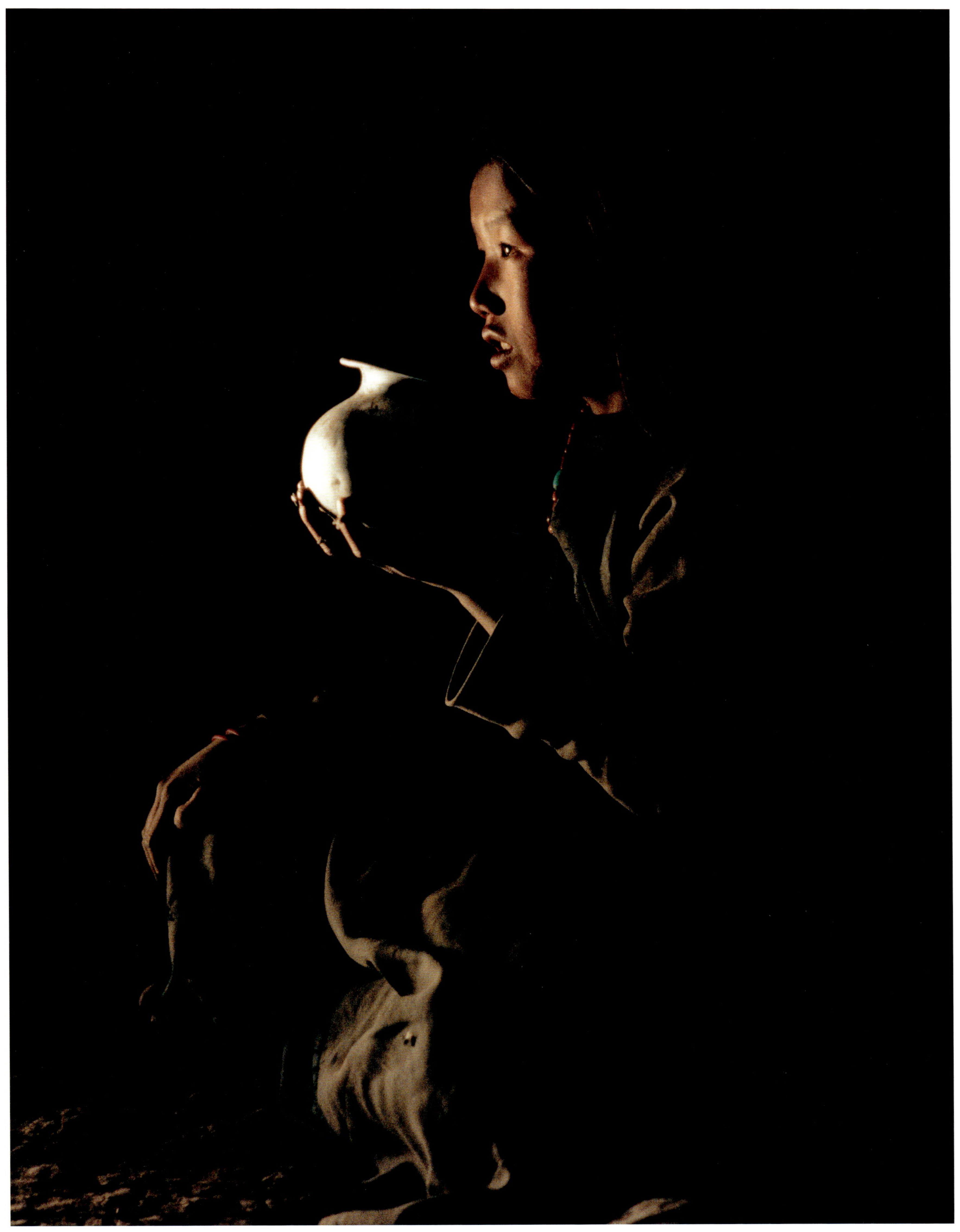

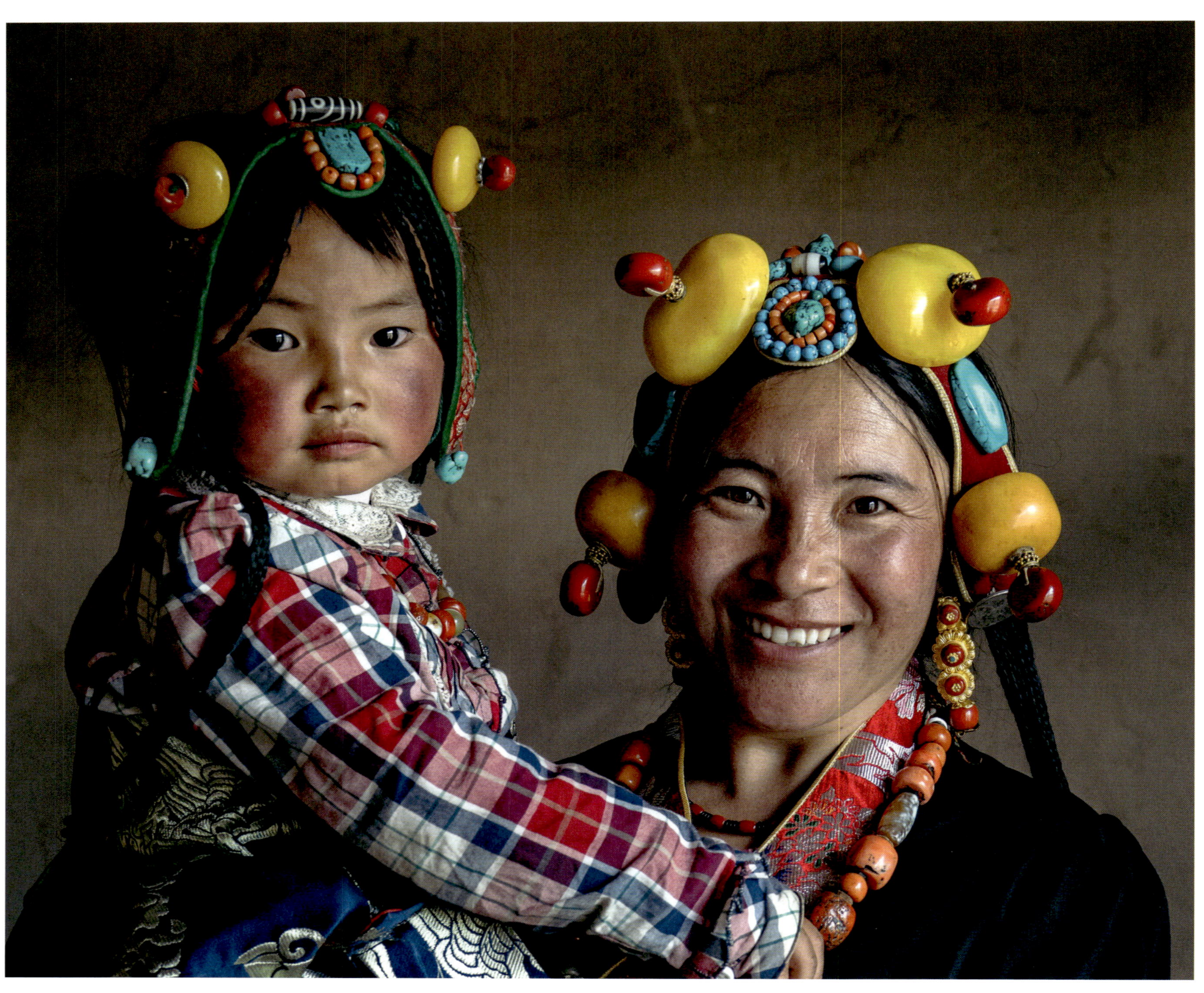

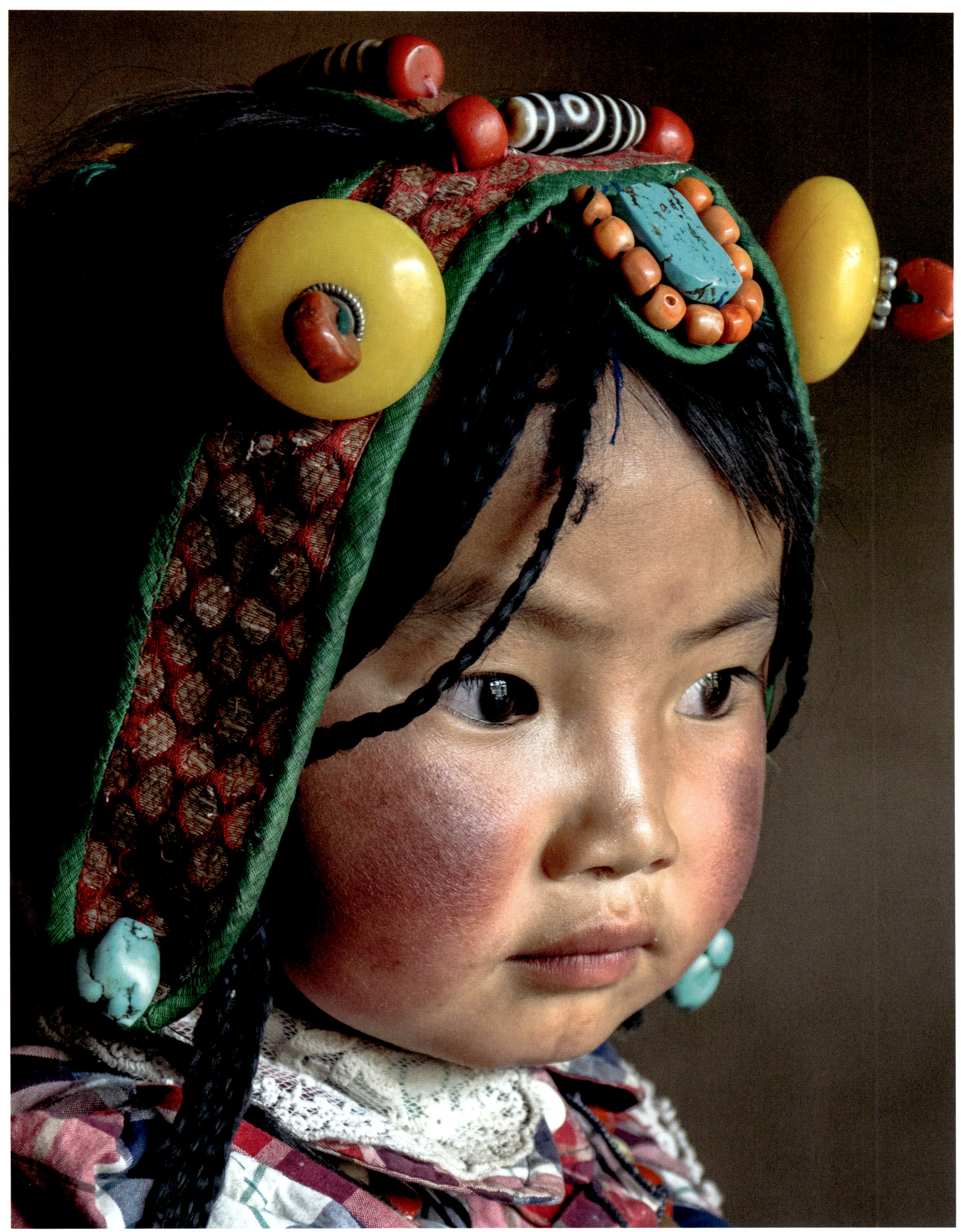

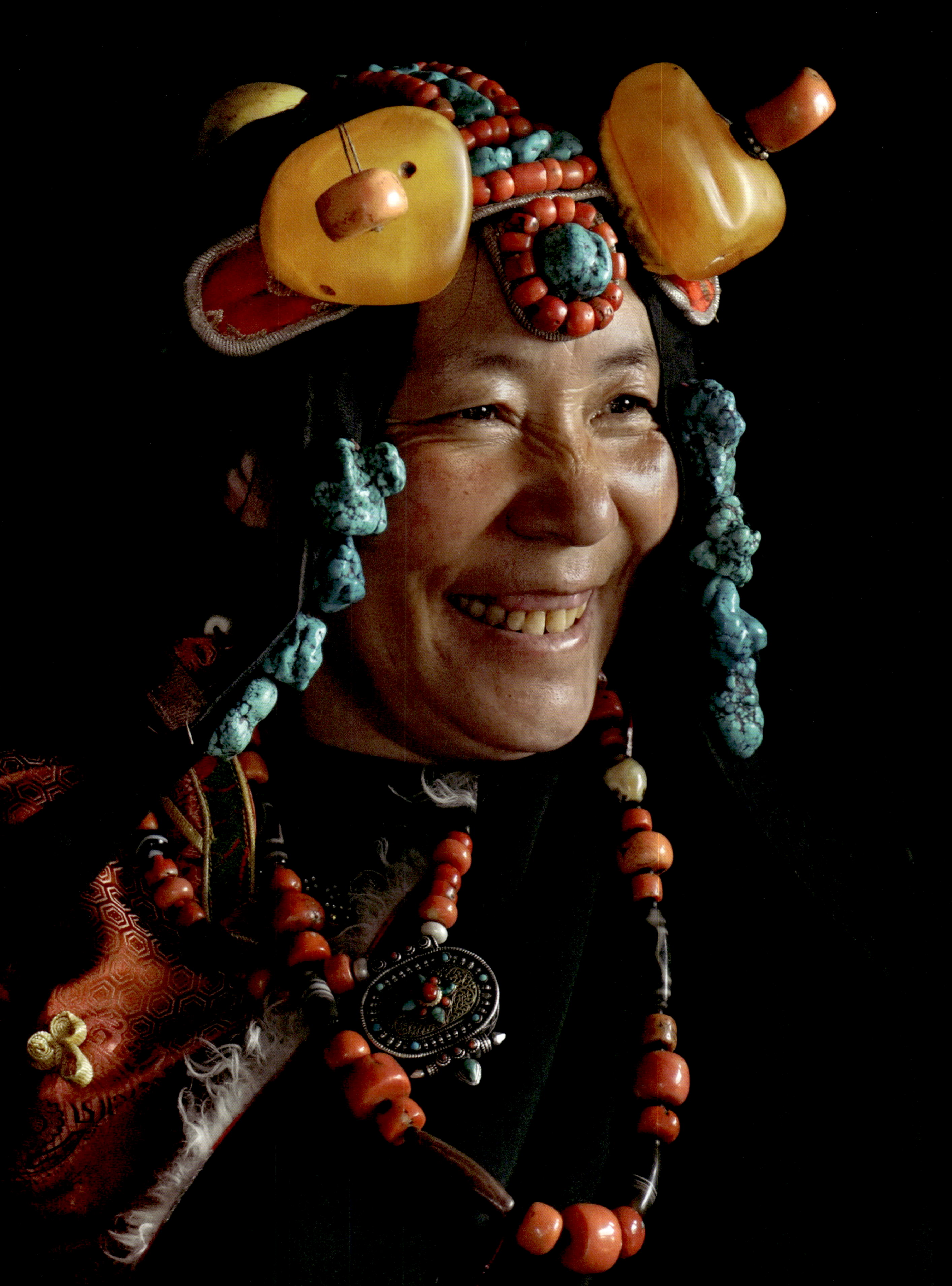

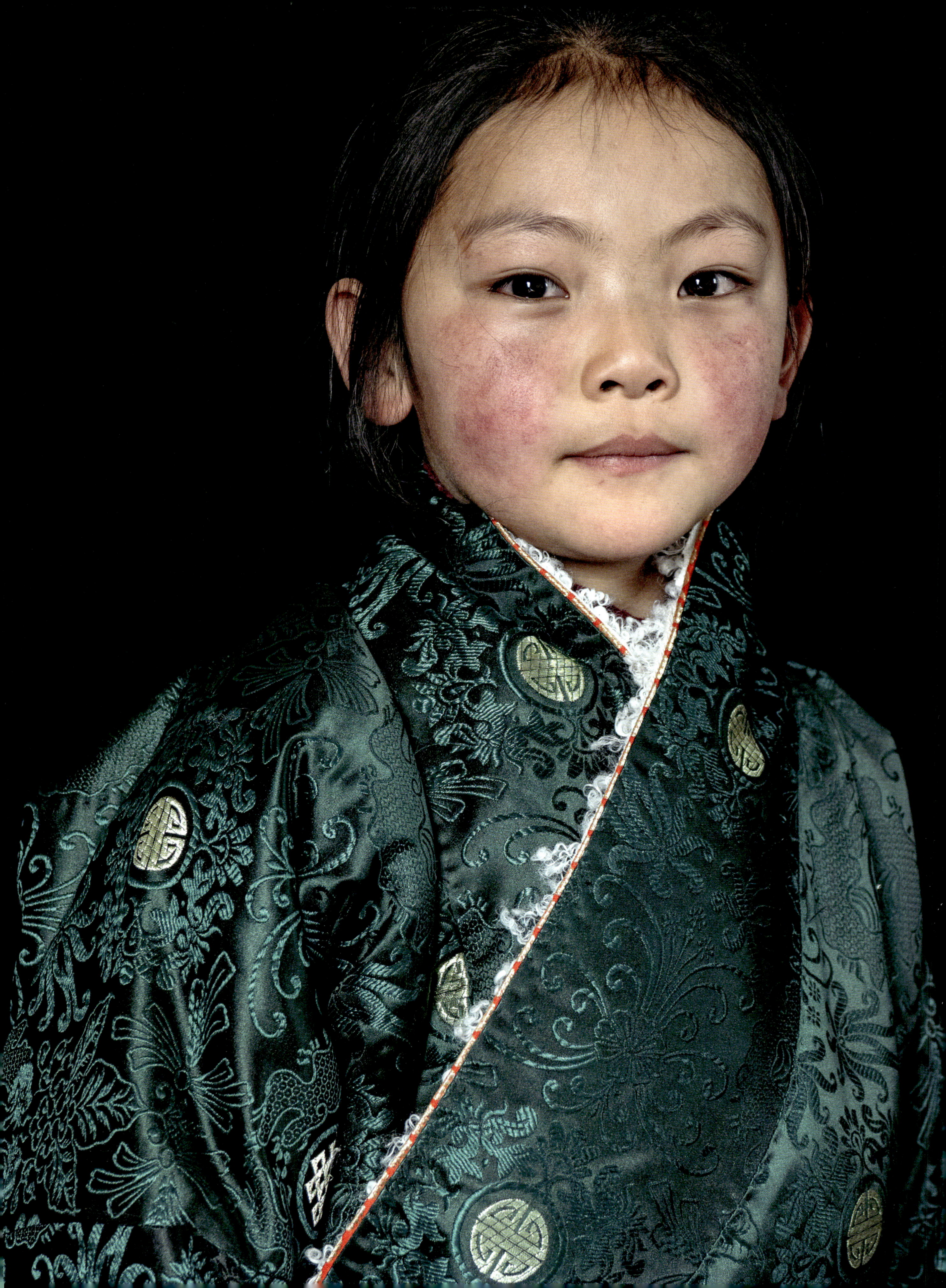

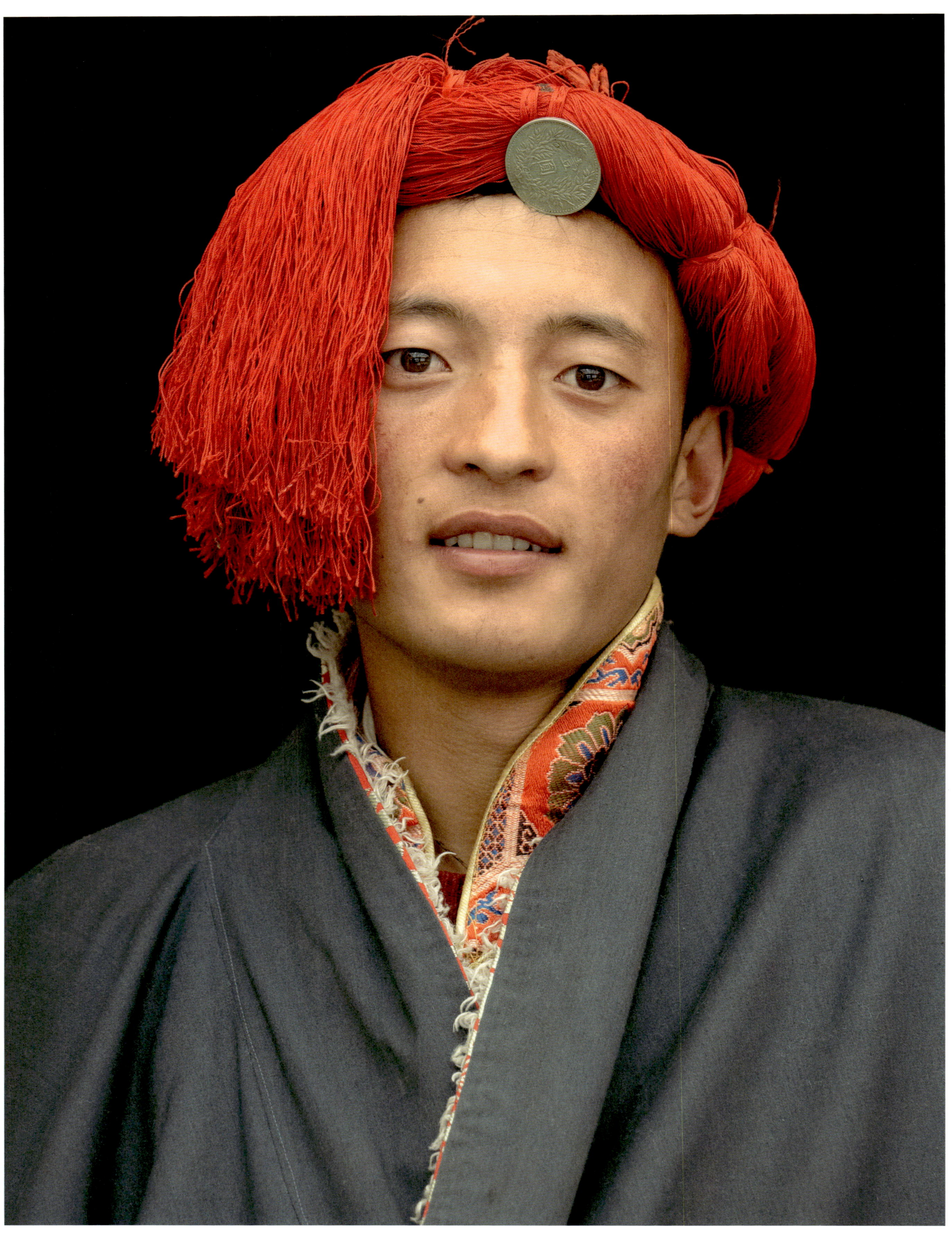

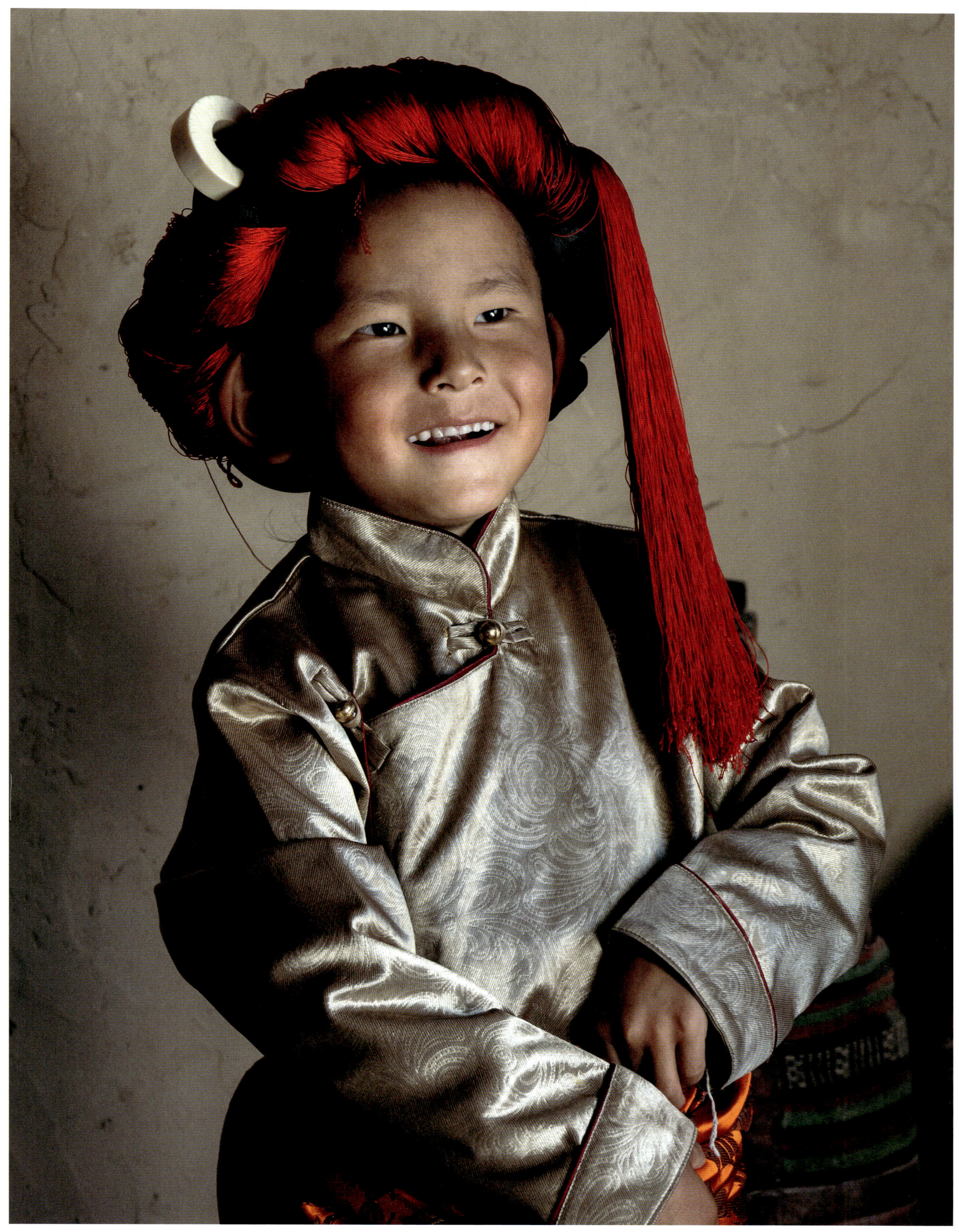

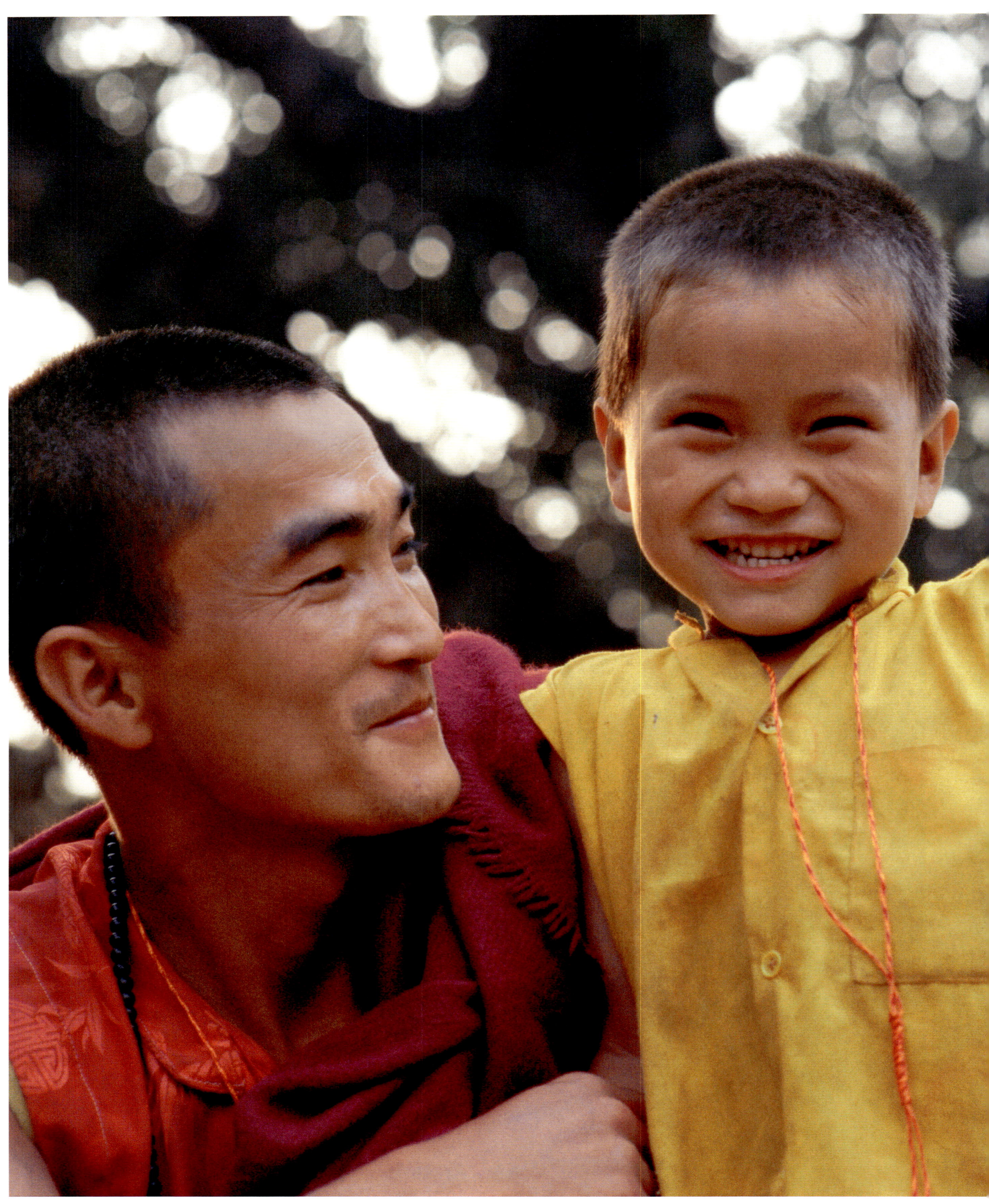

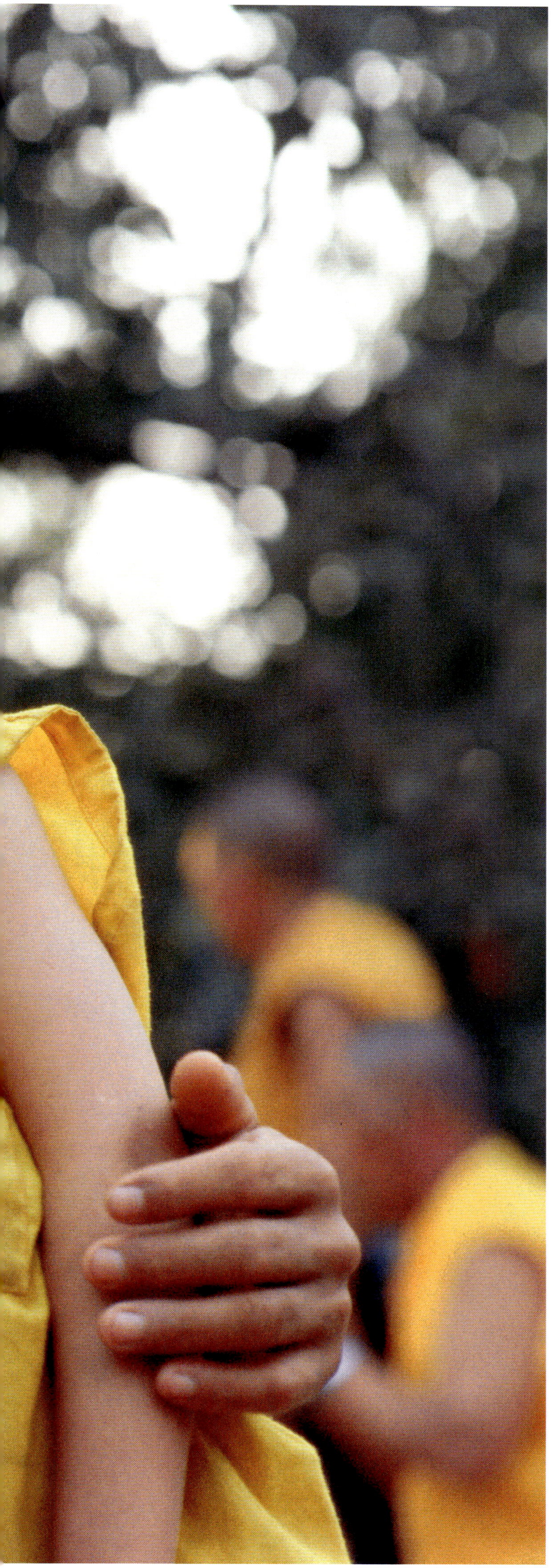

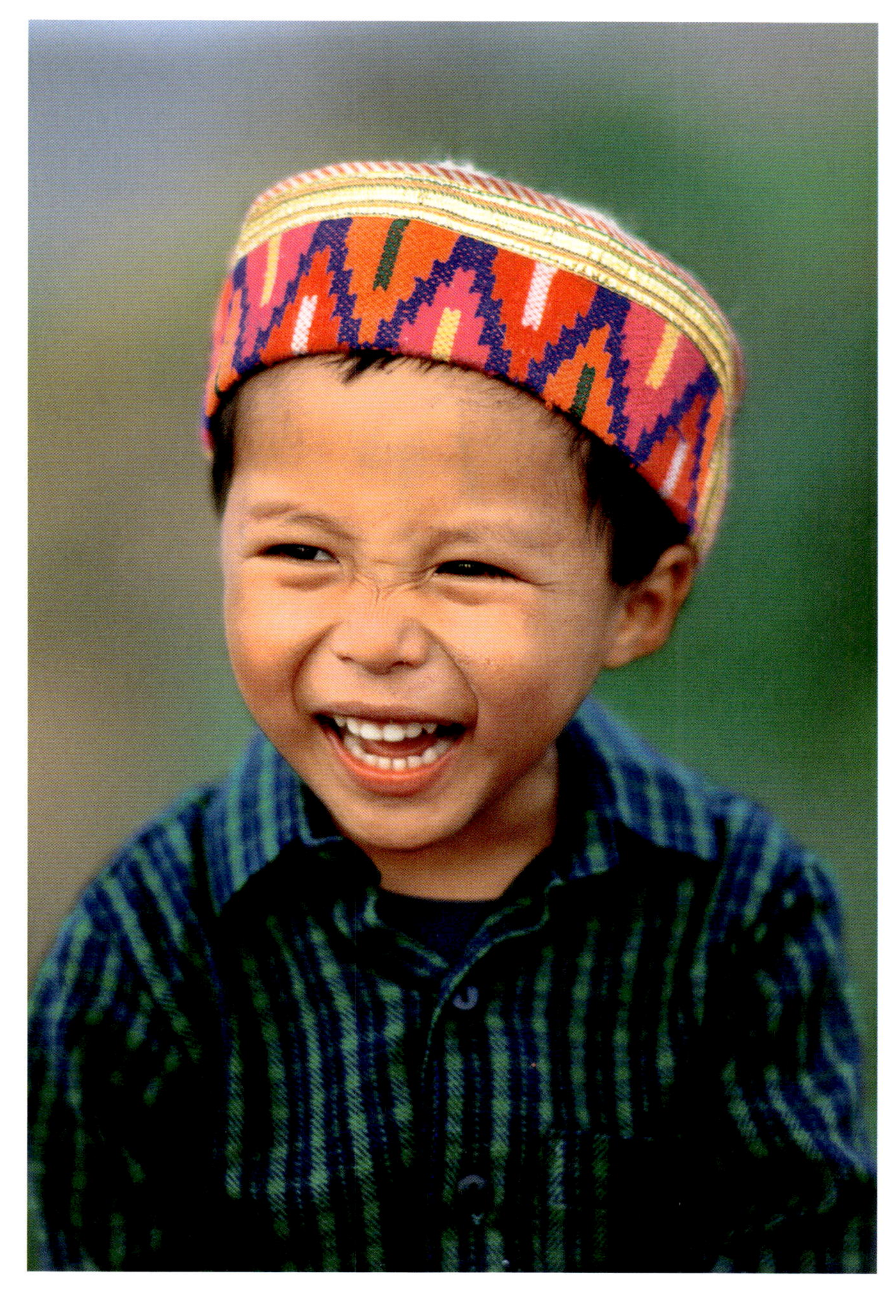

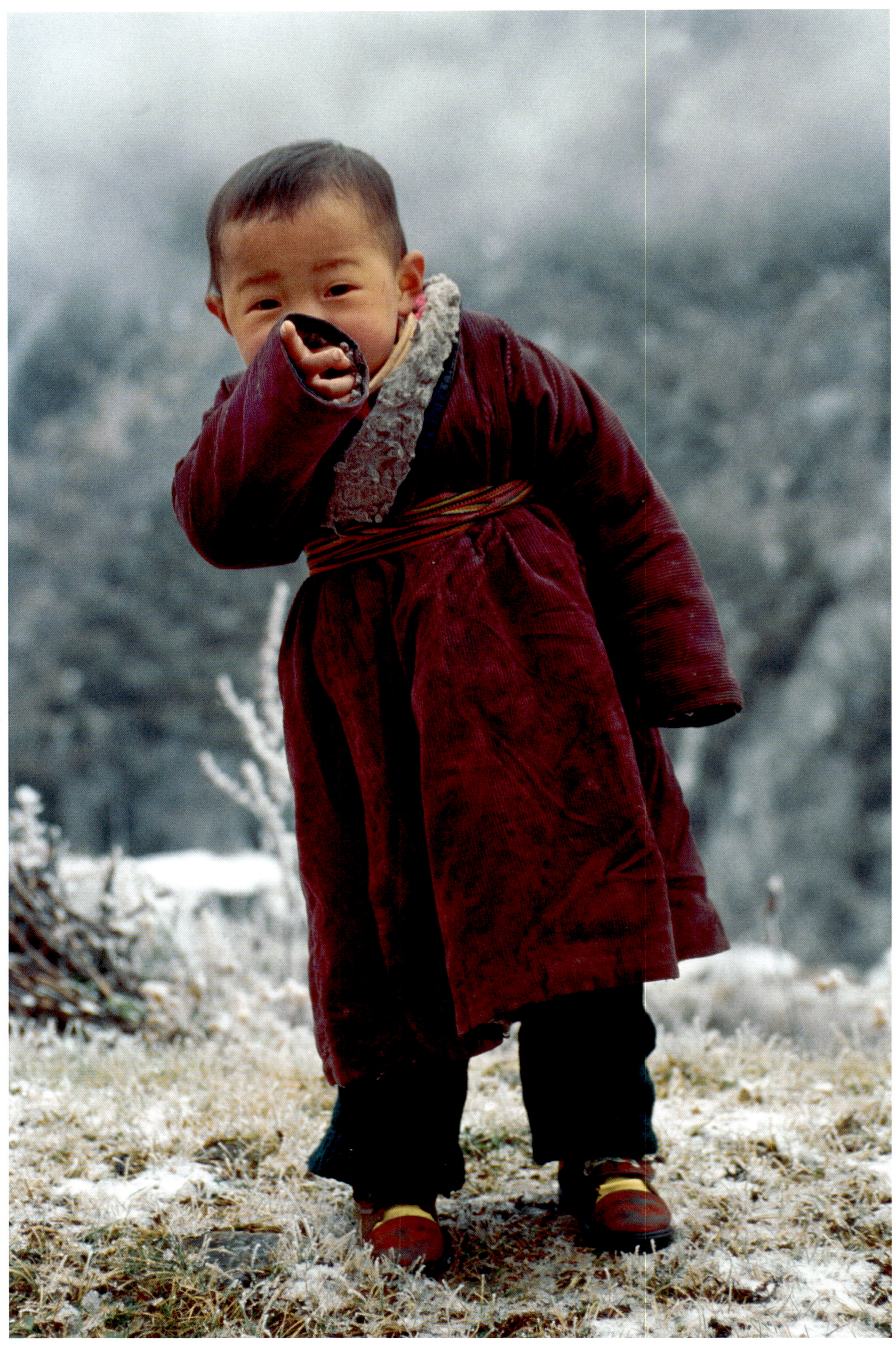

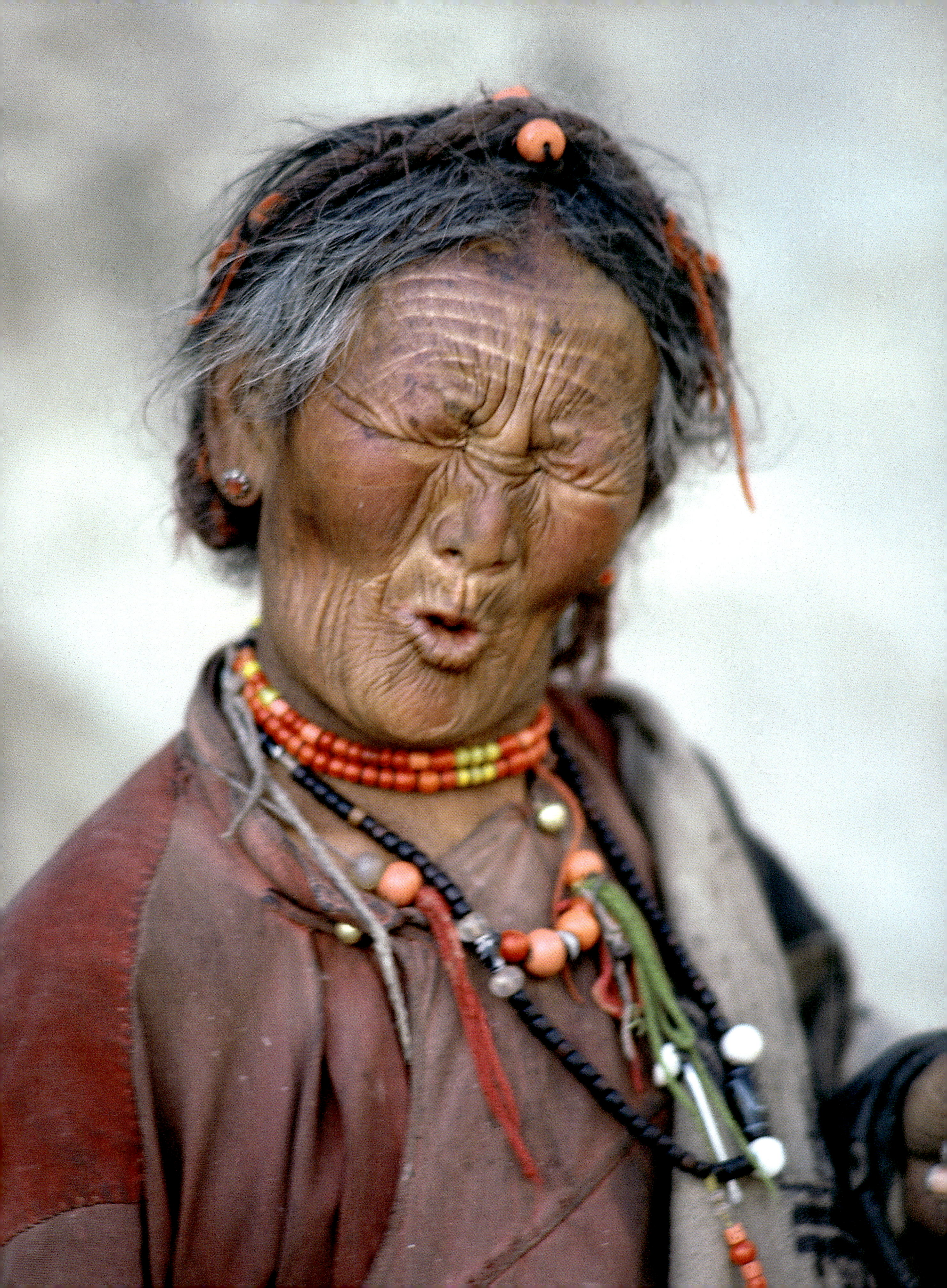

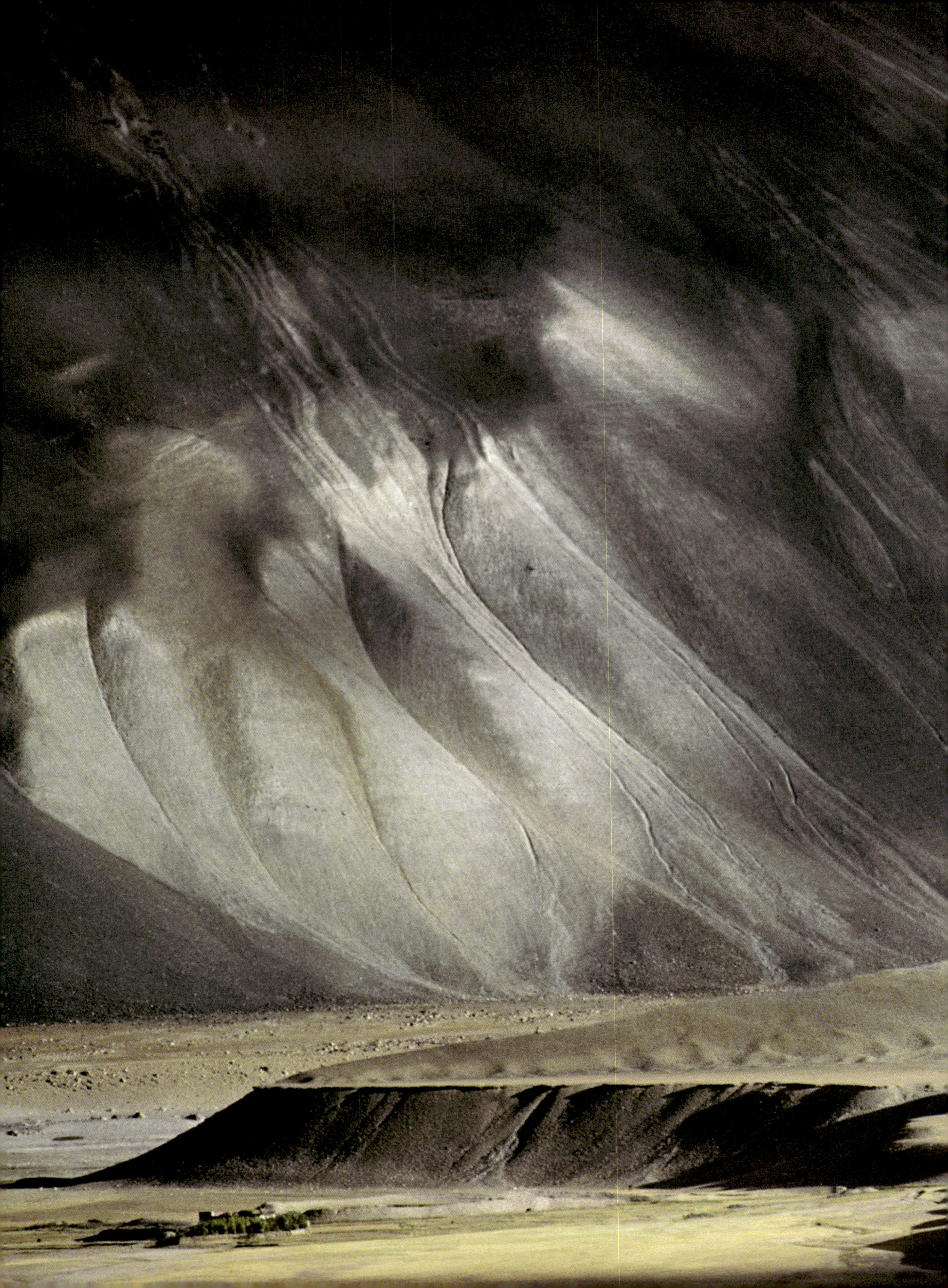

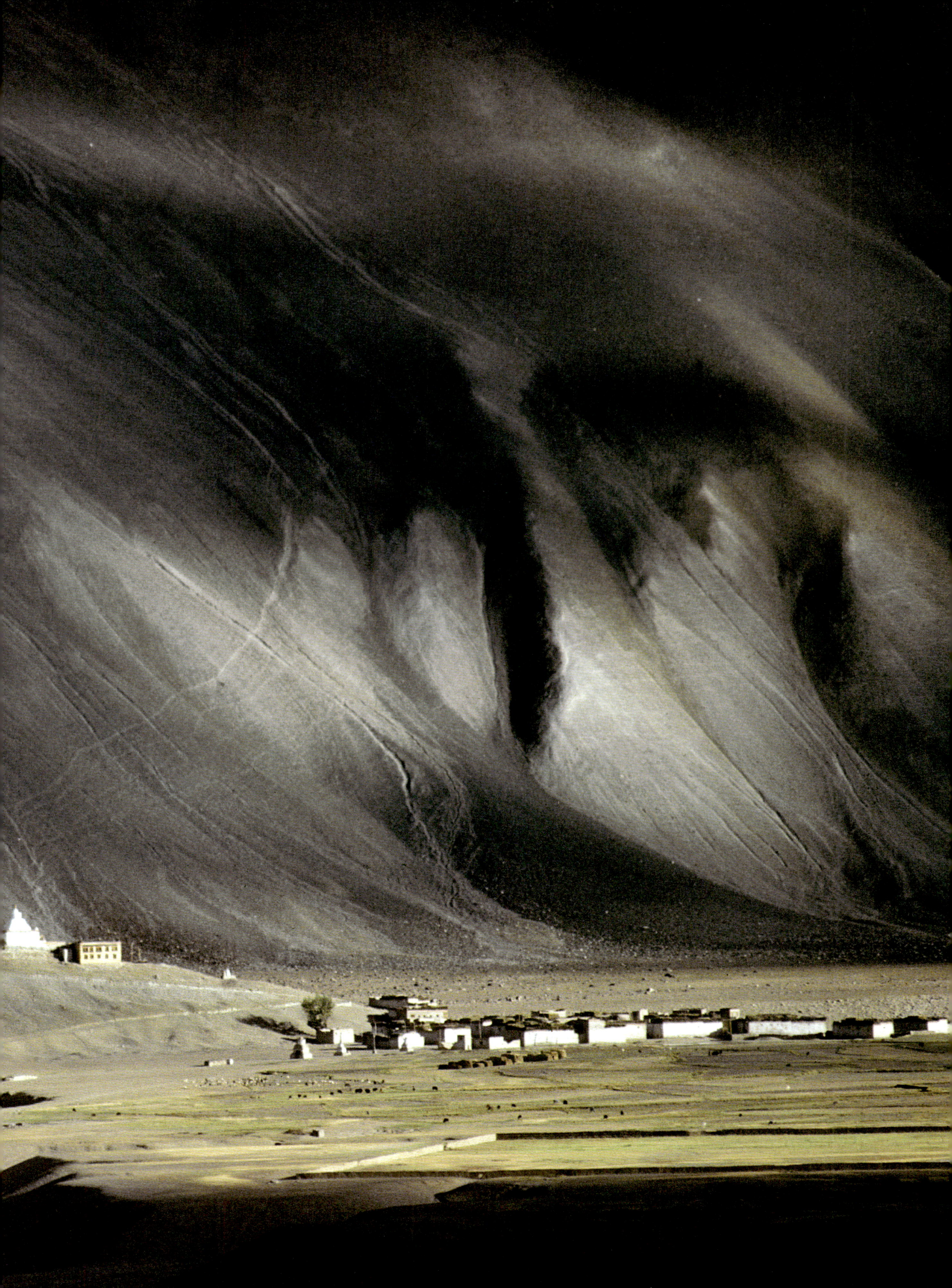

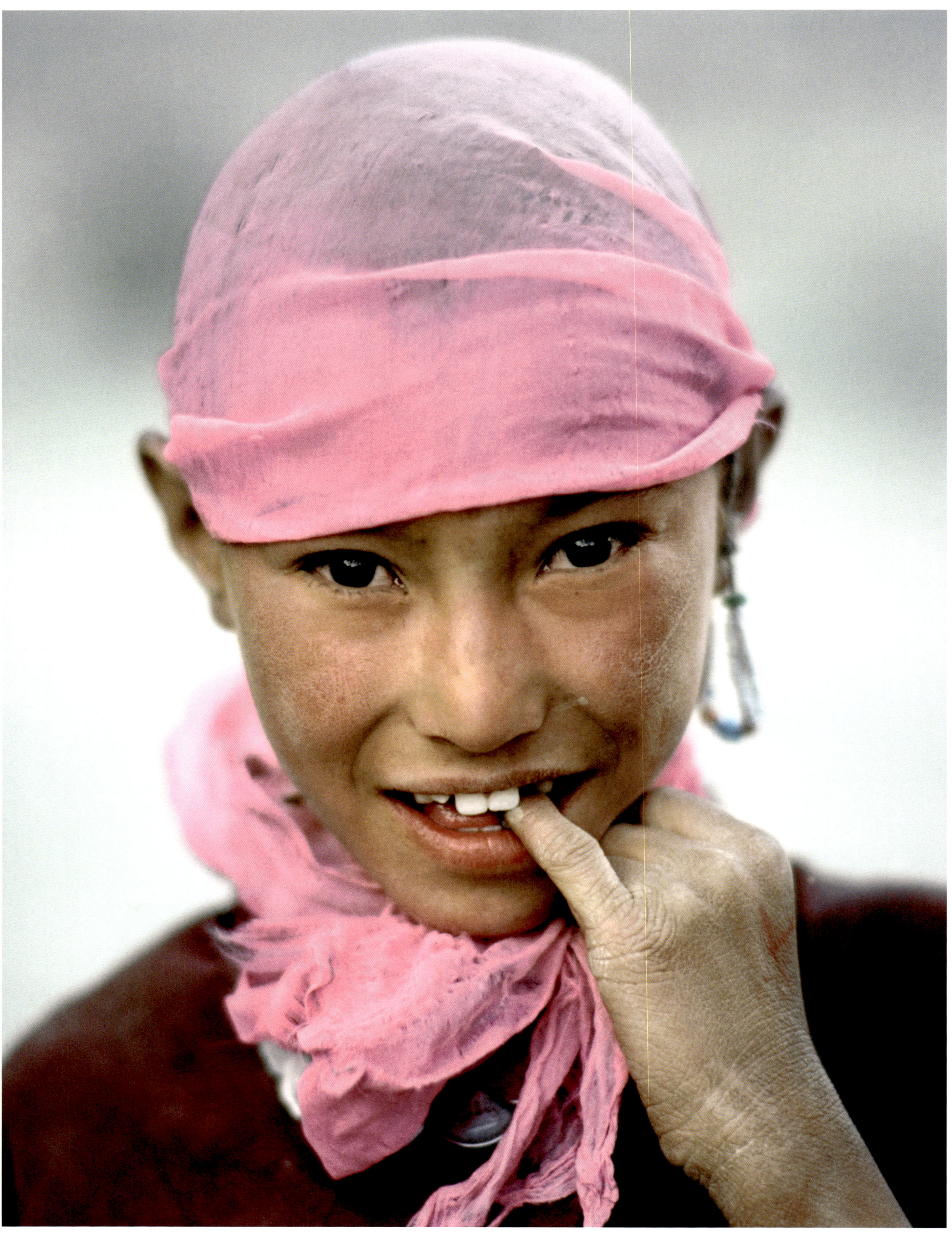

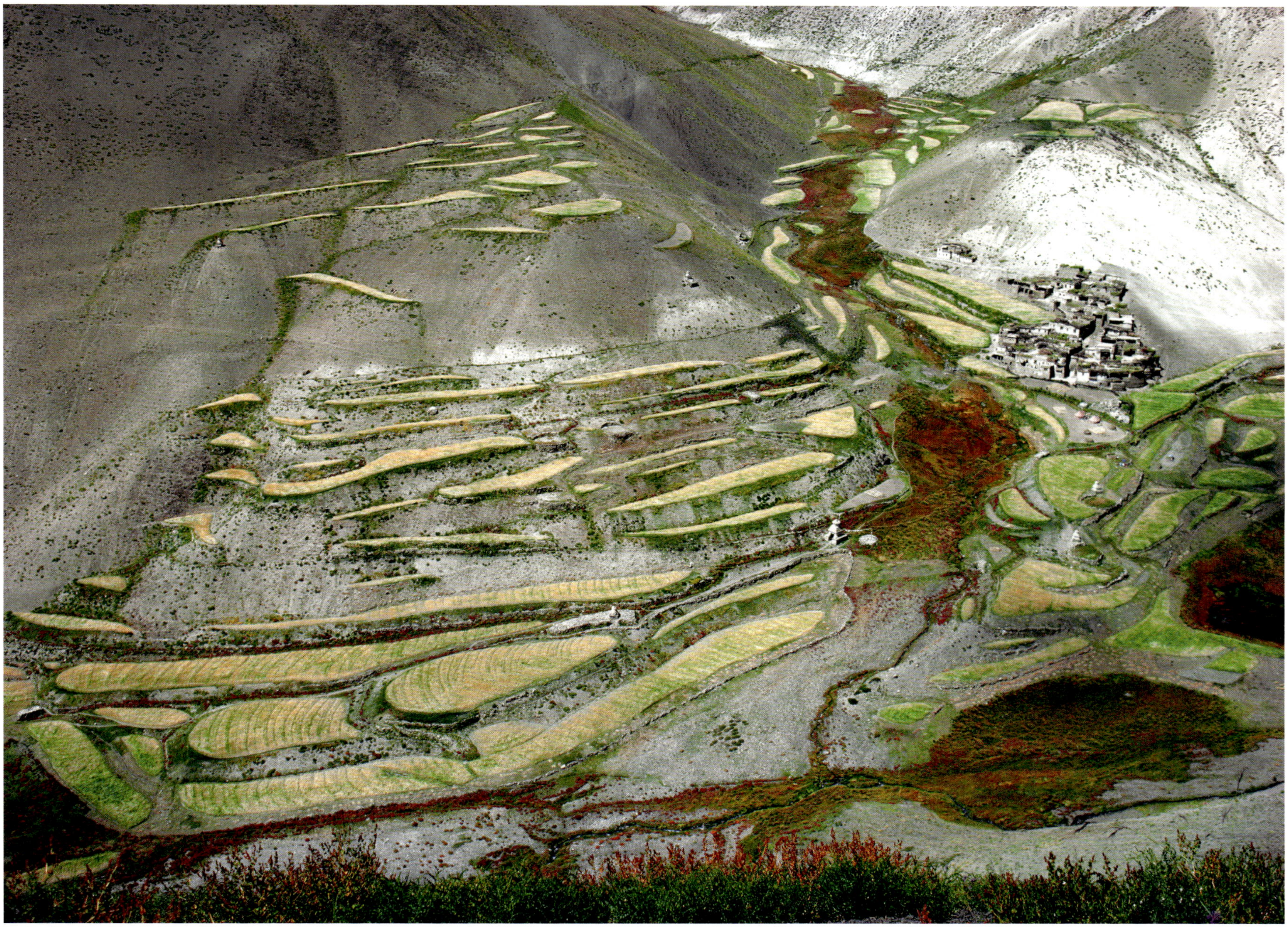

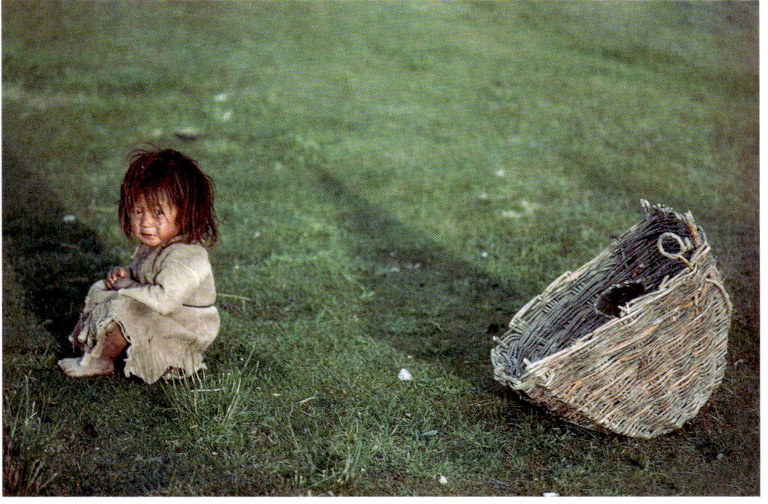

In the remote valleys of Zanskar, people were self-sufficient and no one had ever seen strangers. In the village of Shade, I photographed little Paldmo and, the year after, went back to see her and to give her a print of her photo. But I was disappointed as she looked at it with indifference. Her friend then exclaimed: "Oh! It's you!" Amazed, Paldmo examined the photo: for the first time she saw what her face looked like.

In den entlegenen Tälern von Zanskar lebte man autark. Niemand hatte je Fremde gesehen. Im Dorf Shade fotografierte ich die kleine Paldmo. Ein Jahr später kehrte ich zurück, um ihr einen Abzug des Fotos zu geben. Aber sie warf nur einen gleichgültigen Blick darauf, und ich war enttäuscht. Da rief ihre Freundin: „Oh! Das bist ja du!" Verblüfft sah sich Paldmo das Foto genauer an: Zum ersten Mal entdeckte sie die Züge ihres eigenen Gesichts.

Dans les vallées isolées du Zanskar, on vivait en autarcie et personne n'avait jamais vu d'étrangers. Au village de Shadé, j'ai photographié la petite Paldmo et, l'année suivante, je suis retourné la voir pour lui offrir le tirage de sa photo. Mais elle l'a regardé avec indifférence et j'étais déçu. Son amie s'est alors écriée : « Oh ! C'est toi ! » Stupéfaite, Paldmo a scruté la photo : pour la première fois, elle découvrait les traits de son visage.

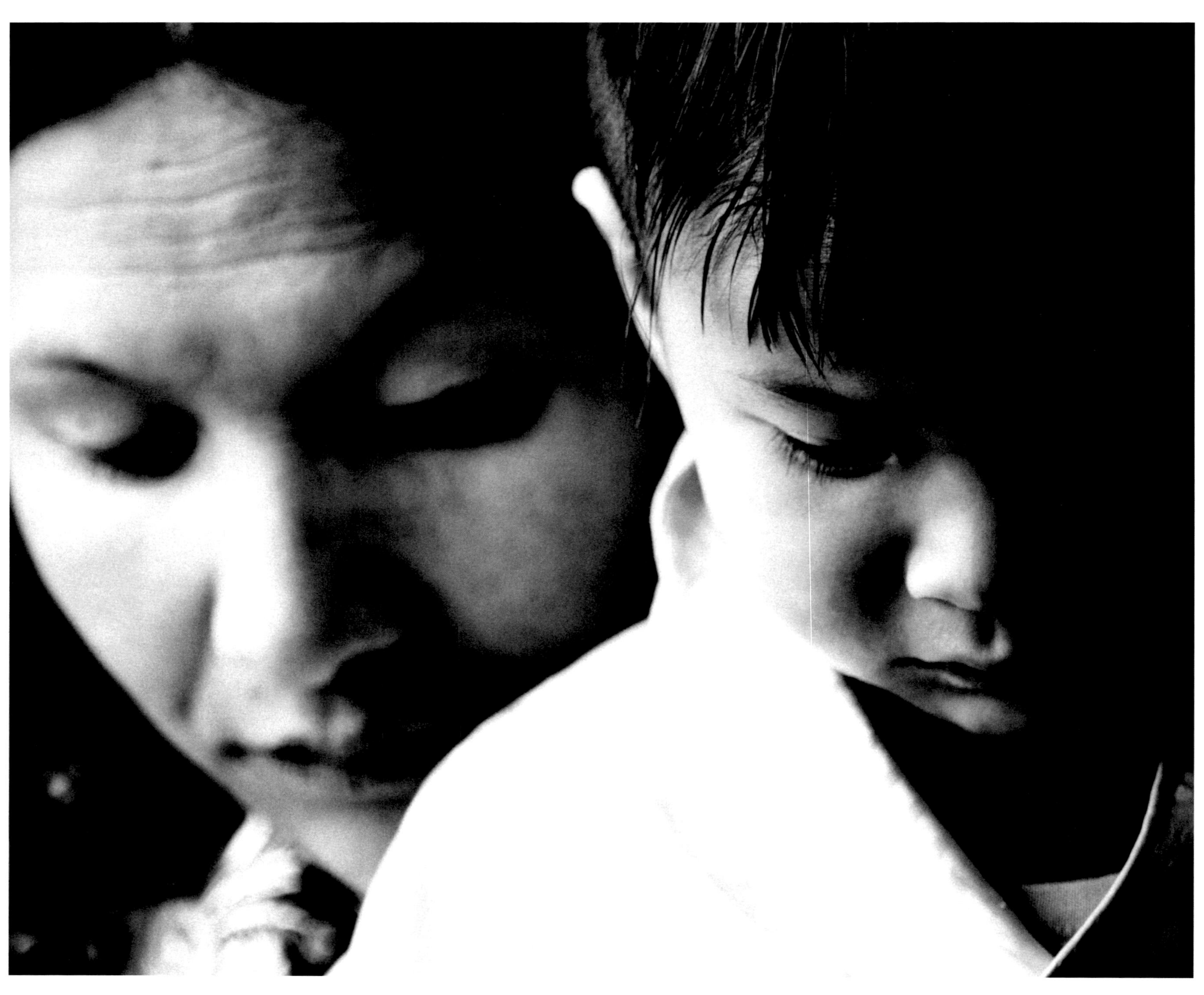

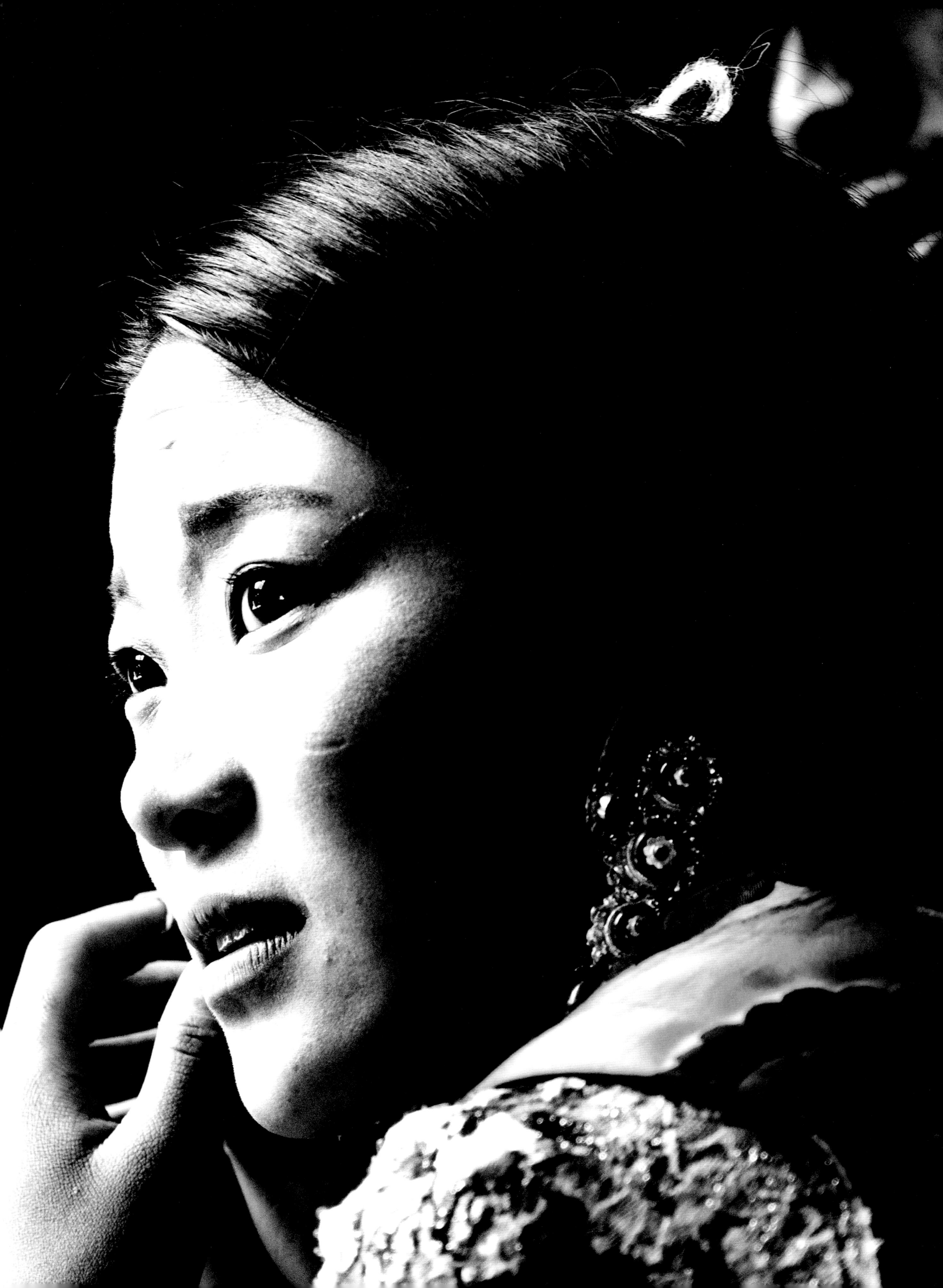

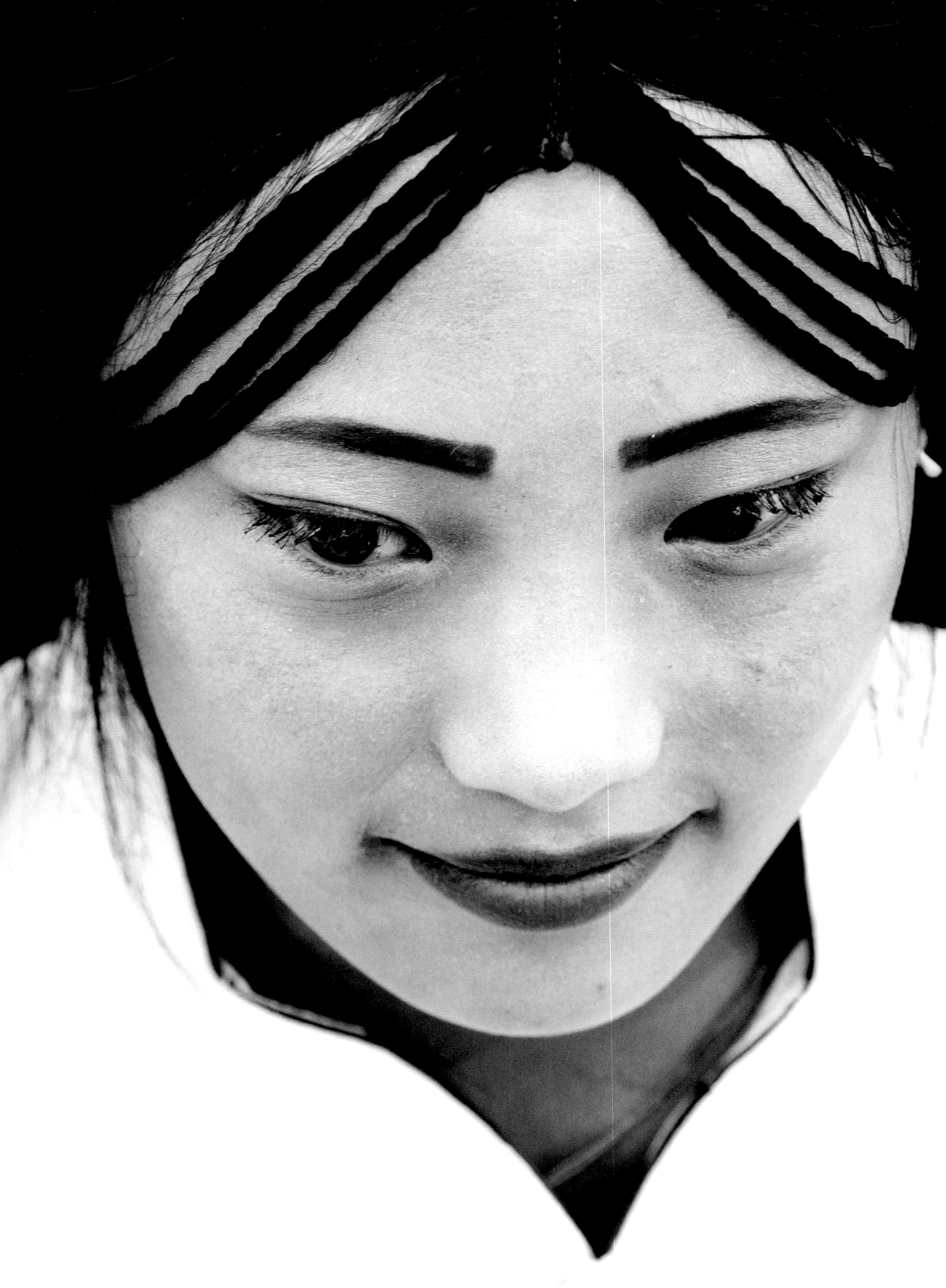

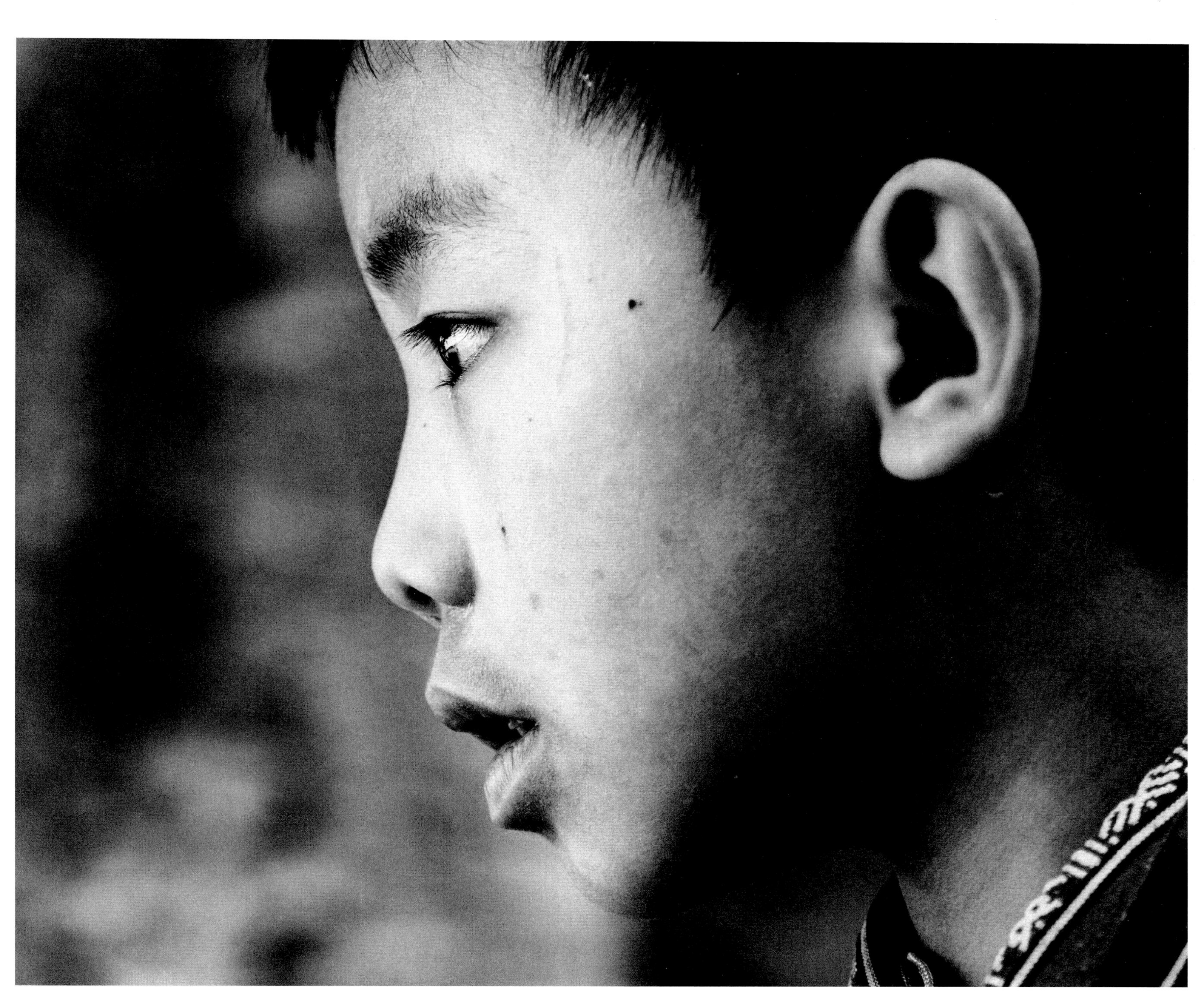

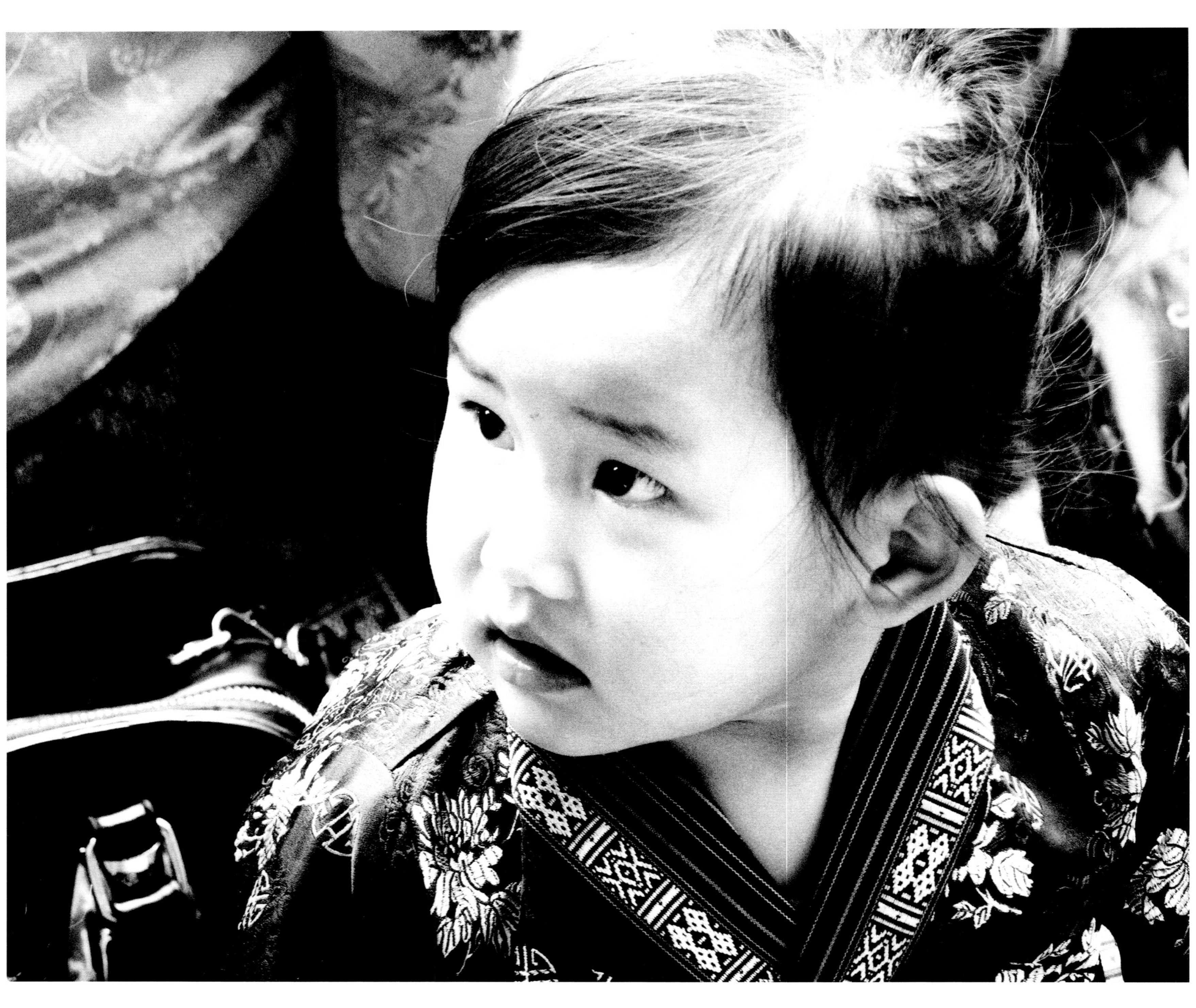

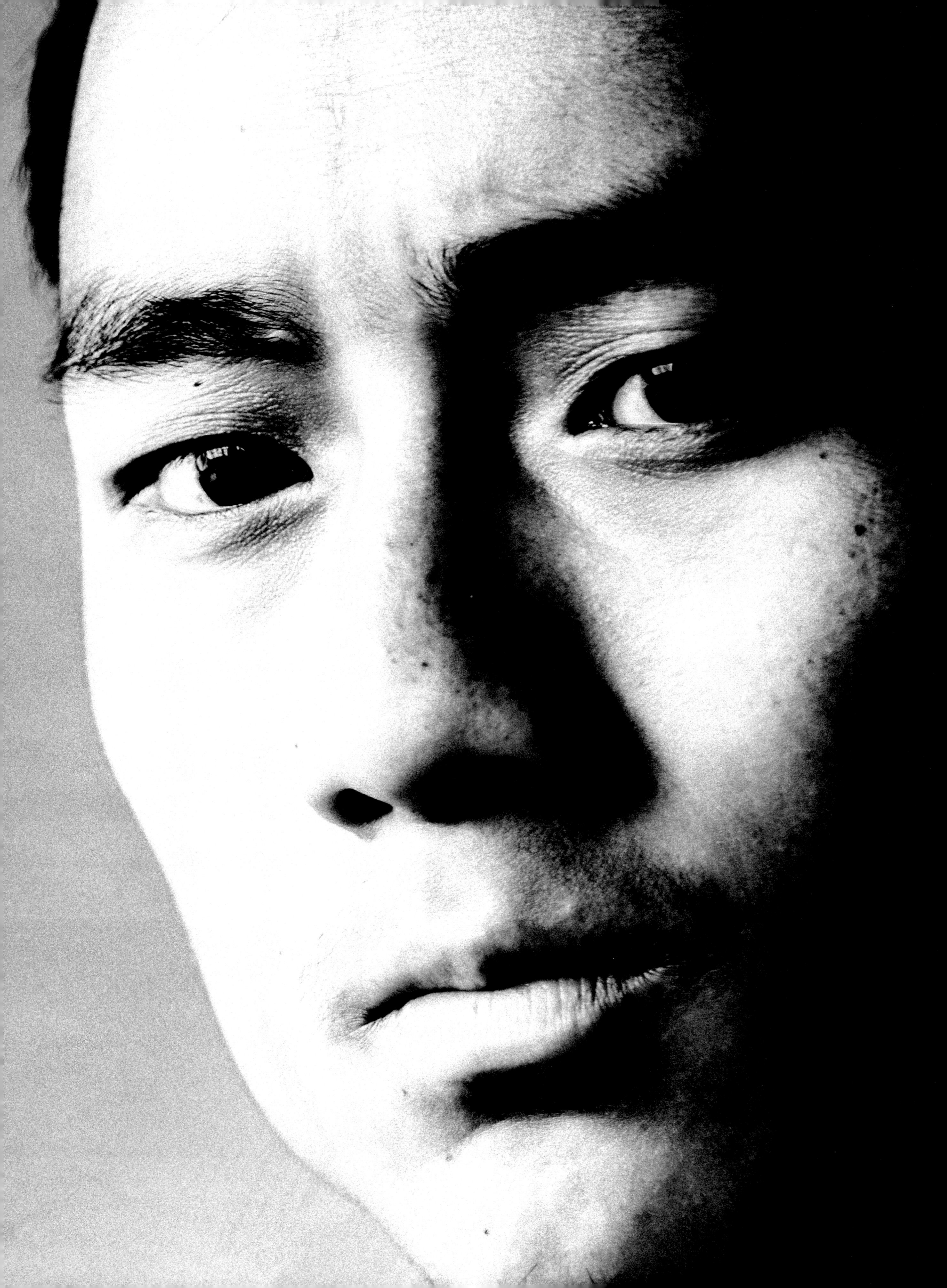

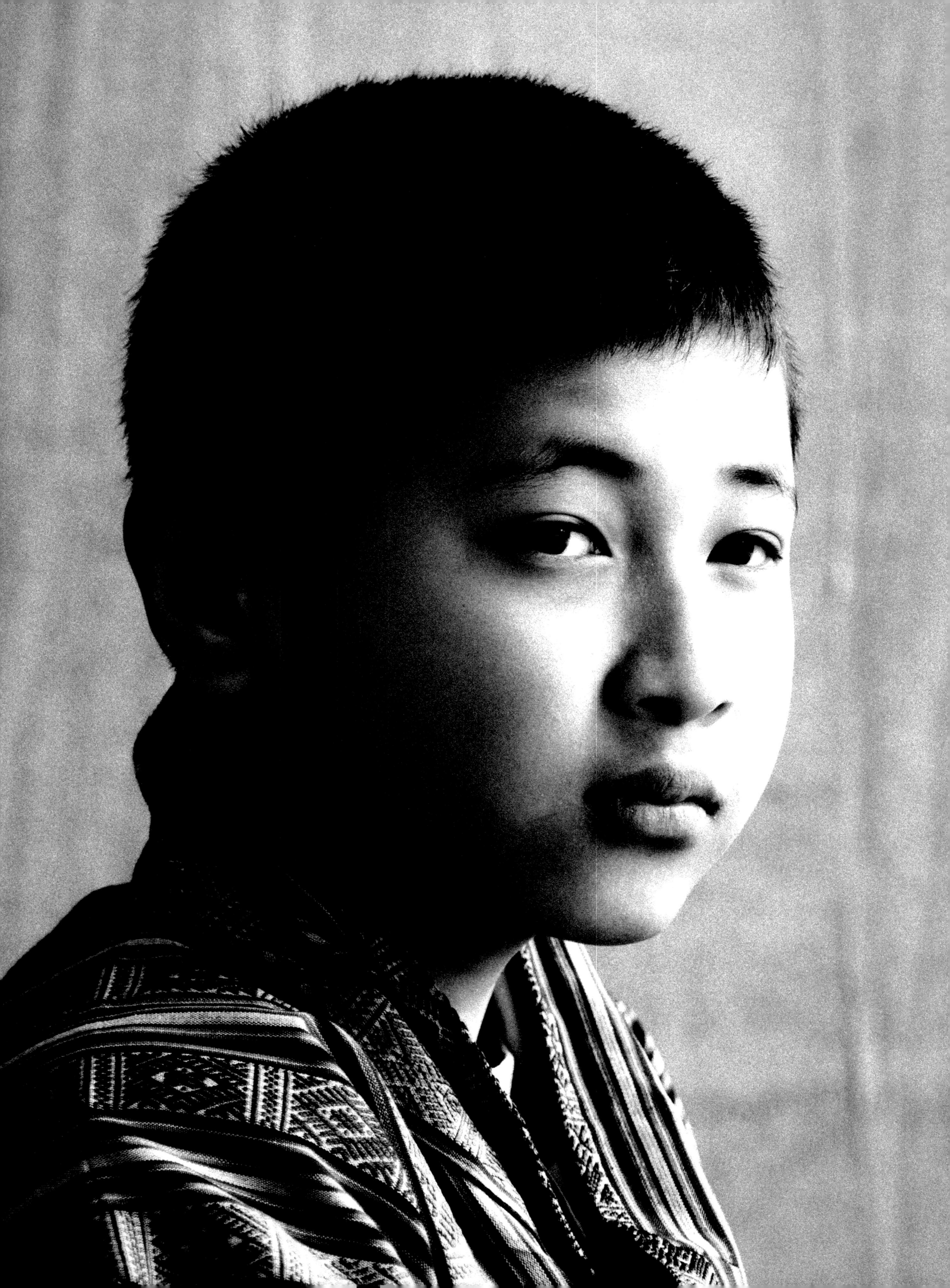

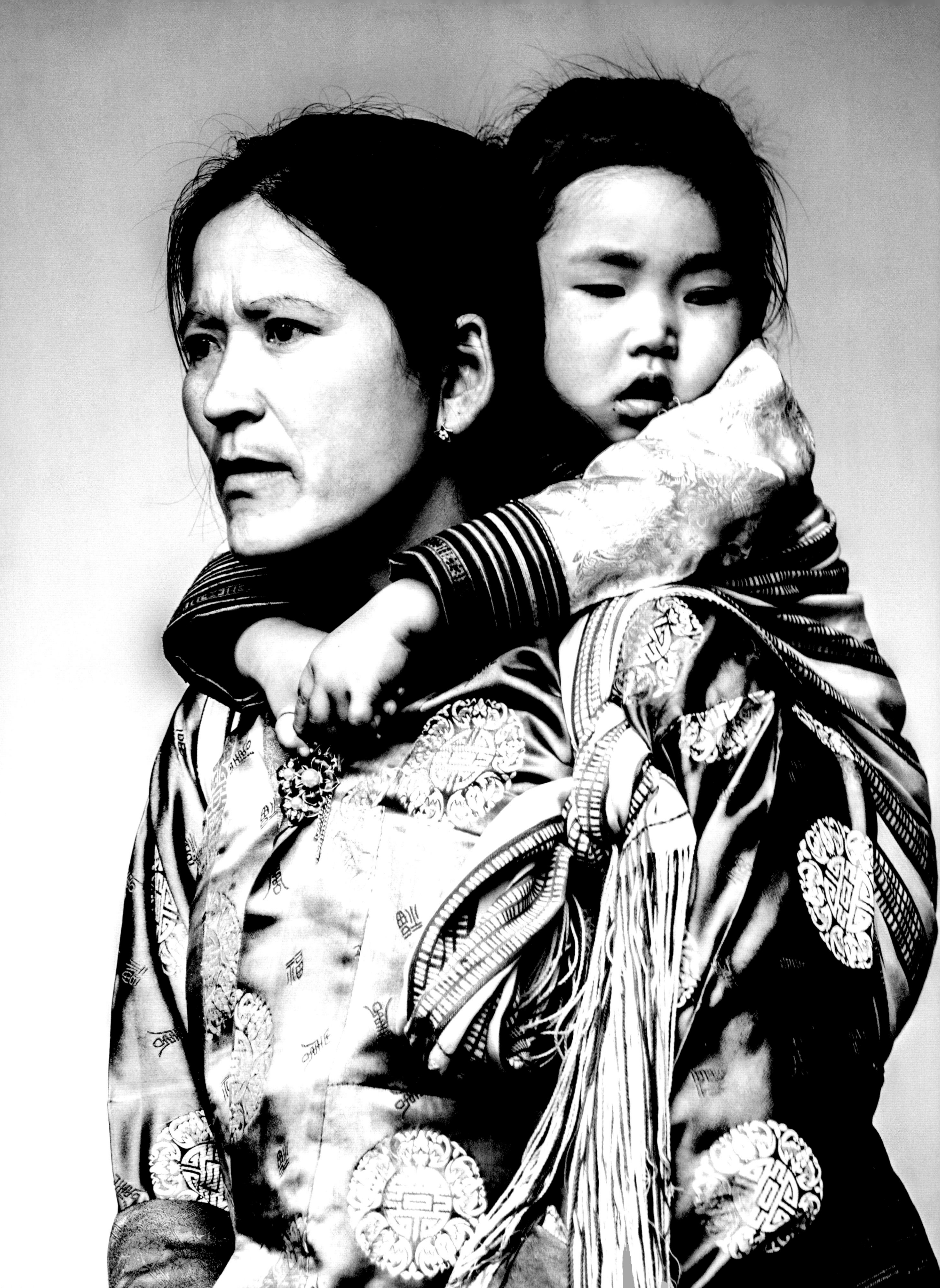

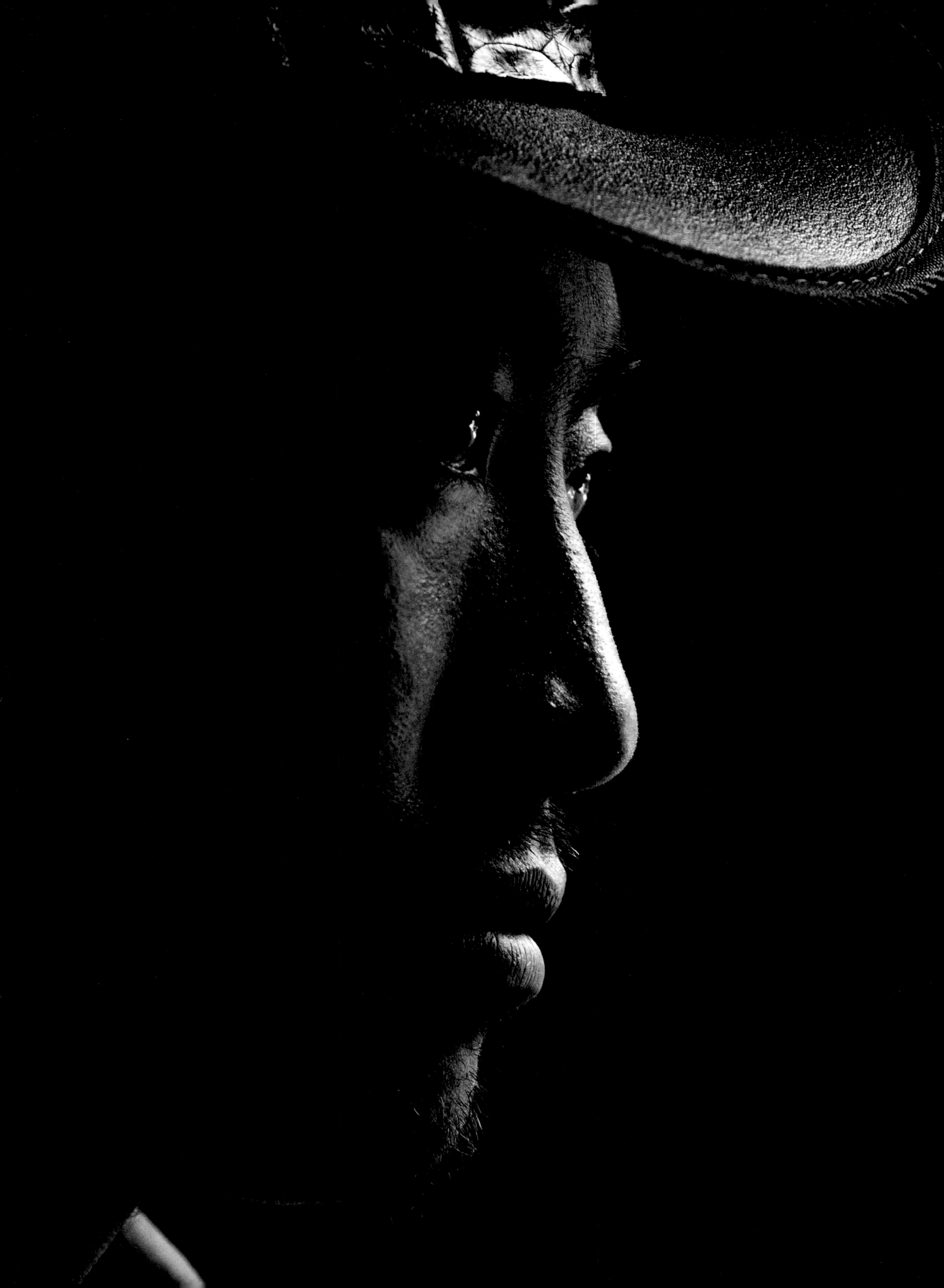

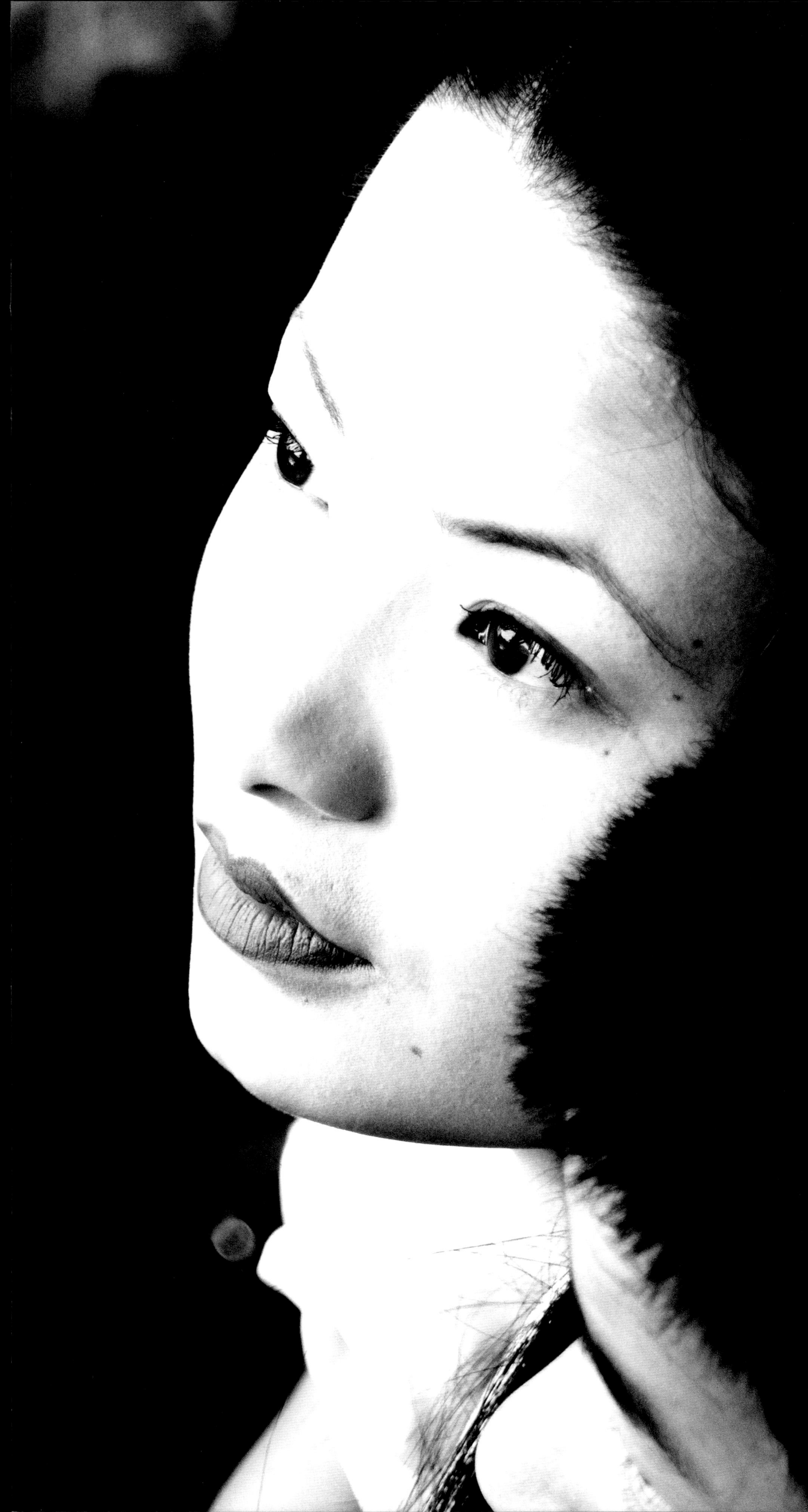

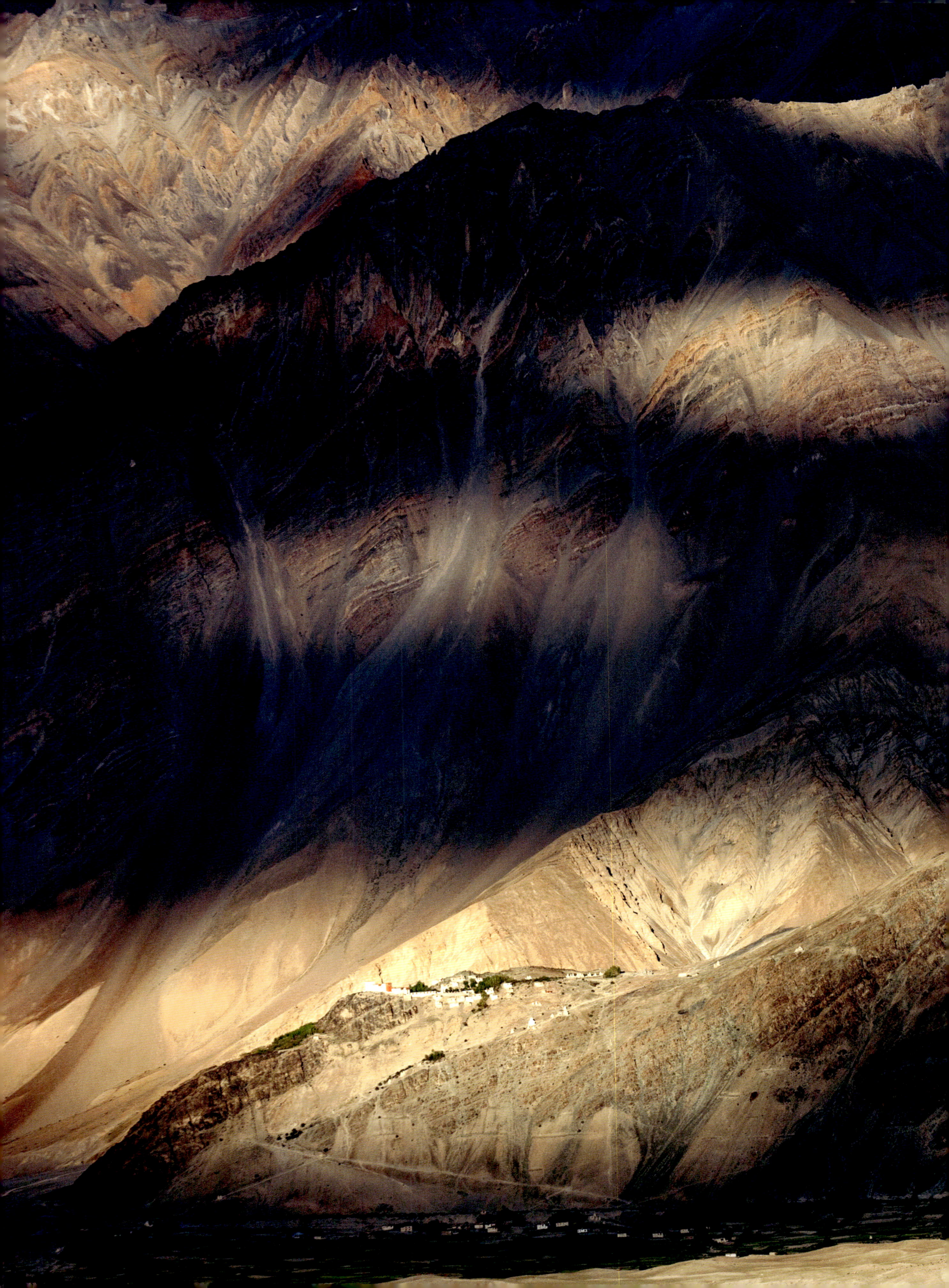

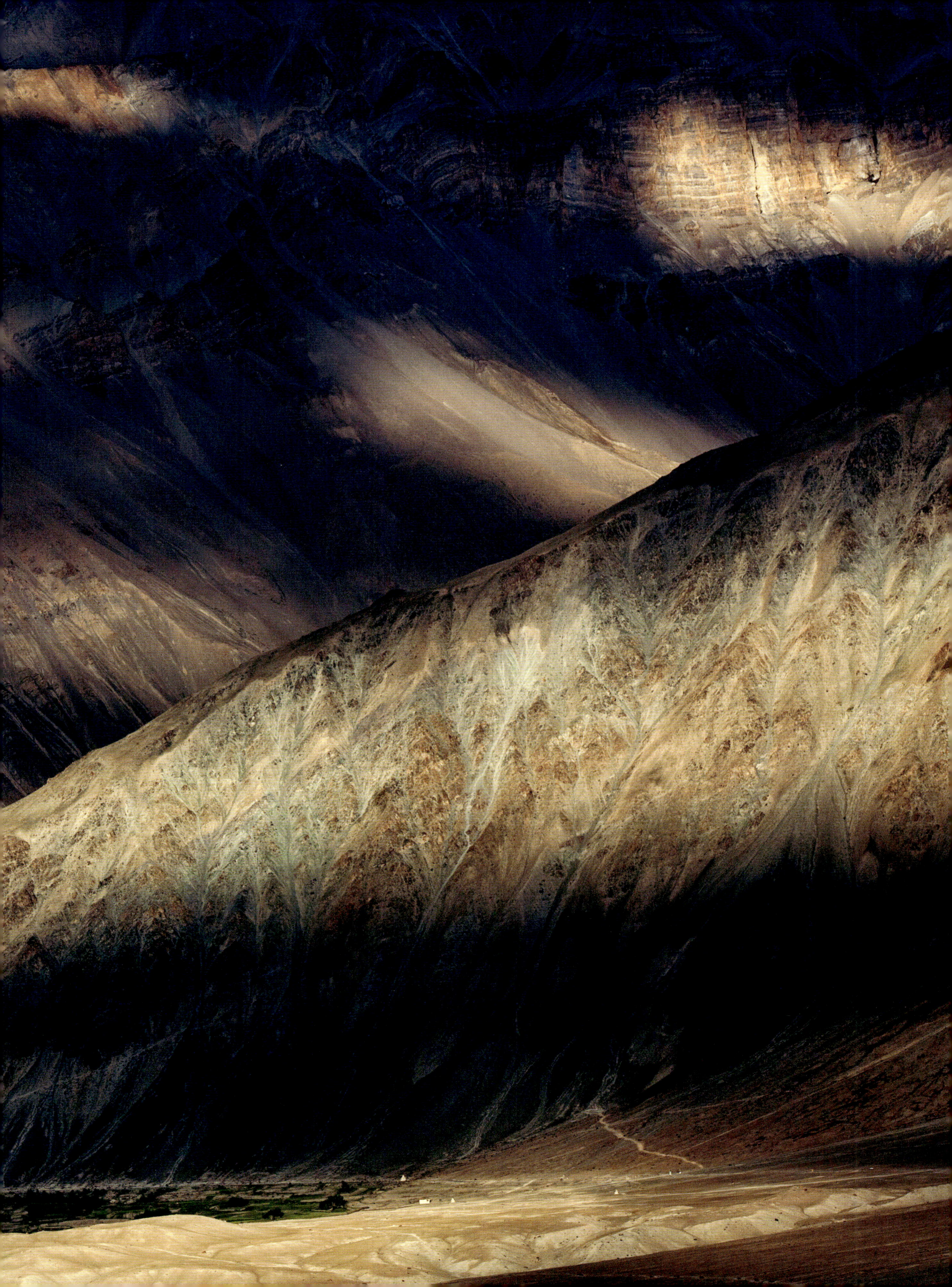

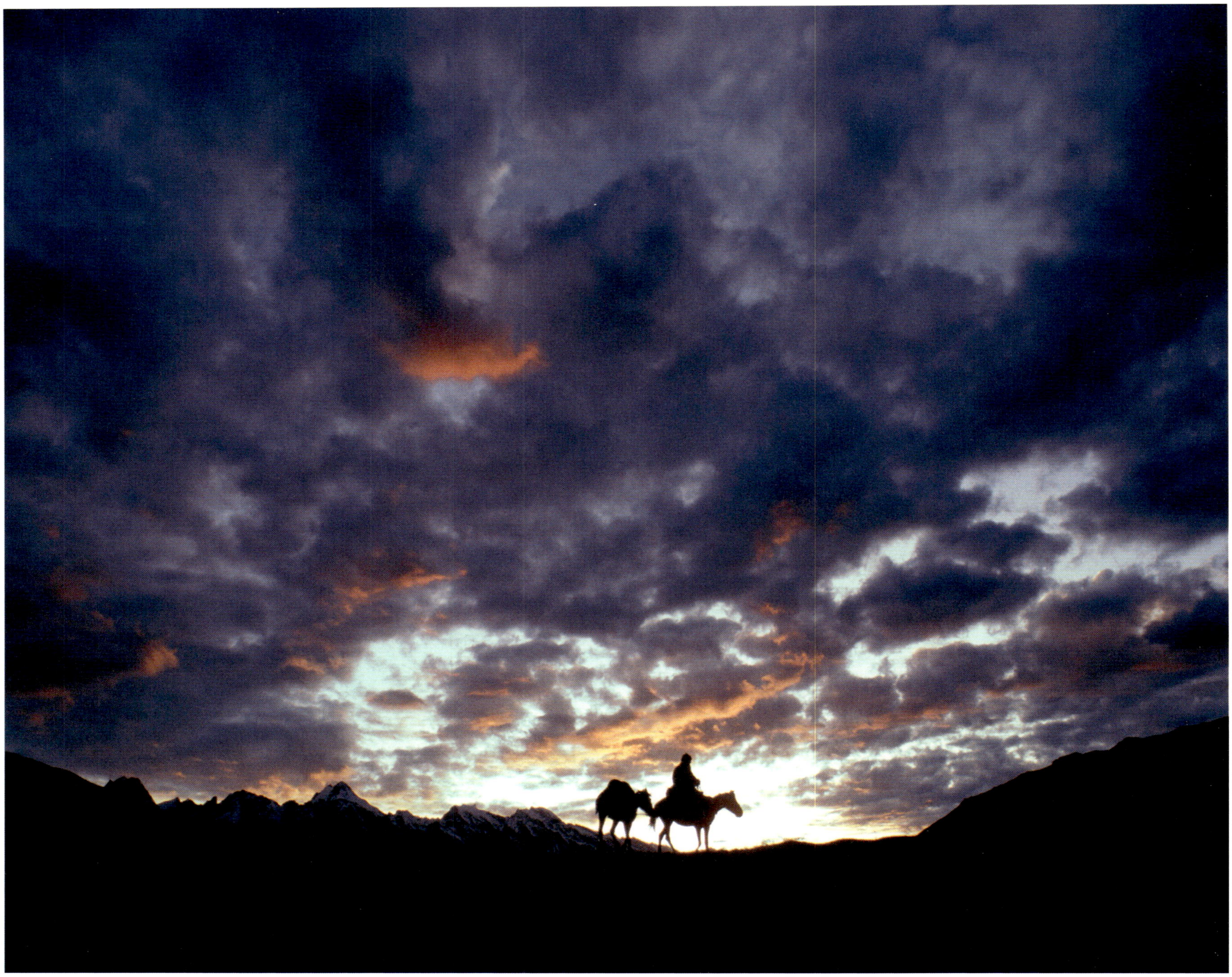

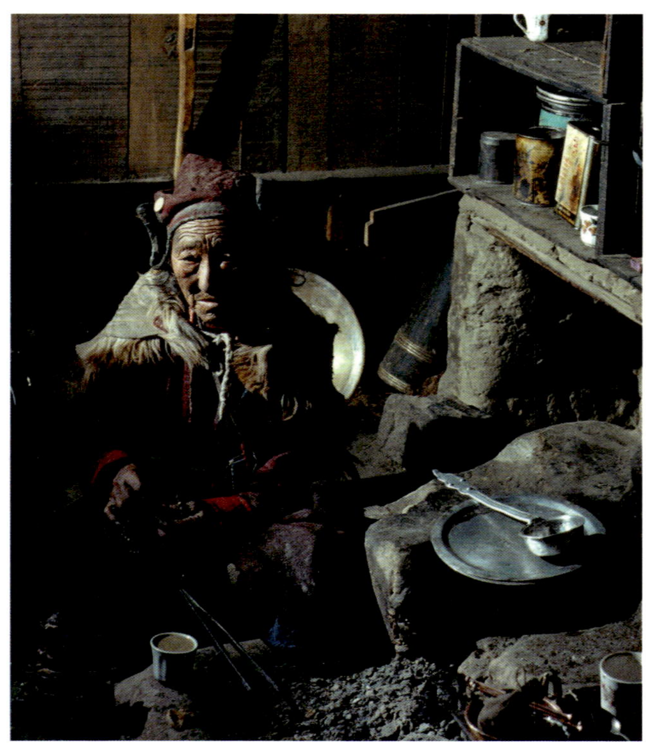

One winter's day in Zanskar, I offered a lump of butter to Abile, a grandmother living with next to nothing by herself in her mud house, and discreetly left her a note of twenty rupees. I went back to see her three days later: "Olivier, you wouldn't happen to have more papers like those you left me, they come in handy for lighting the fire!"

Eines Wintertags in Zanskar gab ich Abile, einer Großmutter, die allein in ihrer Lehmhütte lebte, einen Klumpen Butter. Unauffällig ließ ich außerdem einen 20-Rupien-Schein bei ihr zurück. Drei Tage später suchte ich sie erneut auf. „Olivier, hast du noch andere Papierfetzen wie den, den du mir dagelassen hast?", rief sie. „Sie sind sehr nützlich, um Feuer zu machen!"

Un jour d'hiver au Zanskar, j'ai offert une motte de beurre à Abilé, une grand-mère qui survit seule dans sa maison de terre, et lui ai laissé discrètement un billet de vingt roupies. Je l'ai retrouvée chez elle trois jours plus tard : « Olivier, tu n'aurais pas d'autres bouts de papier comme tu m'as laissé, c'est très pratique pour allumer le feu ! »

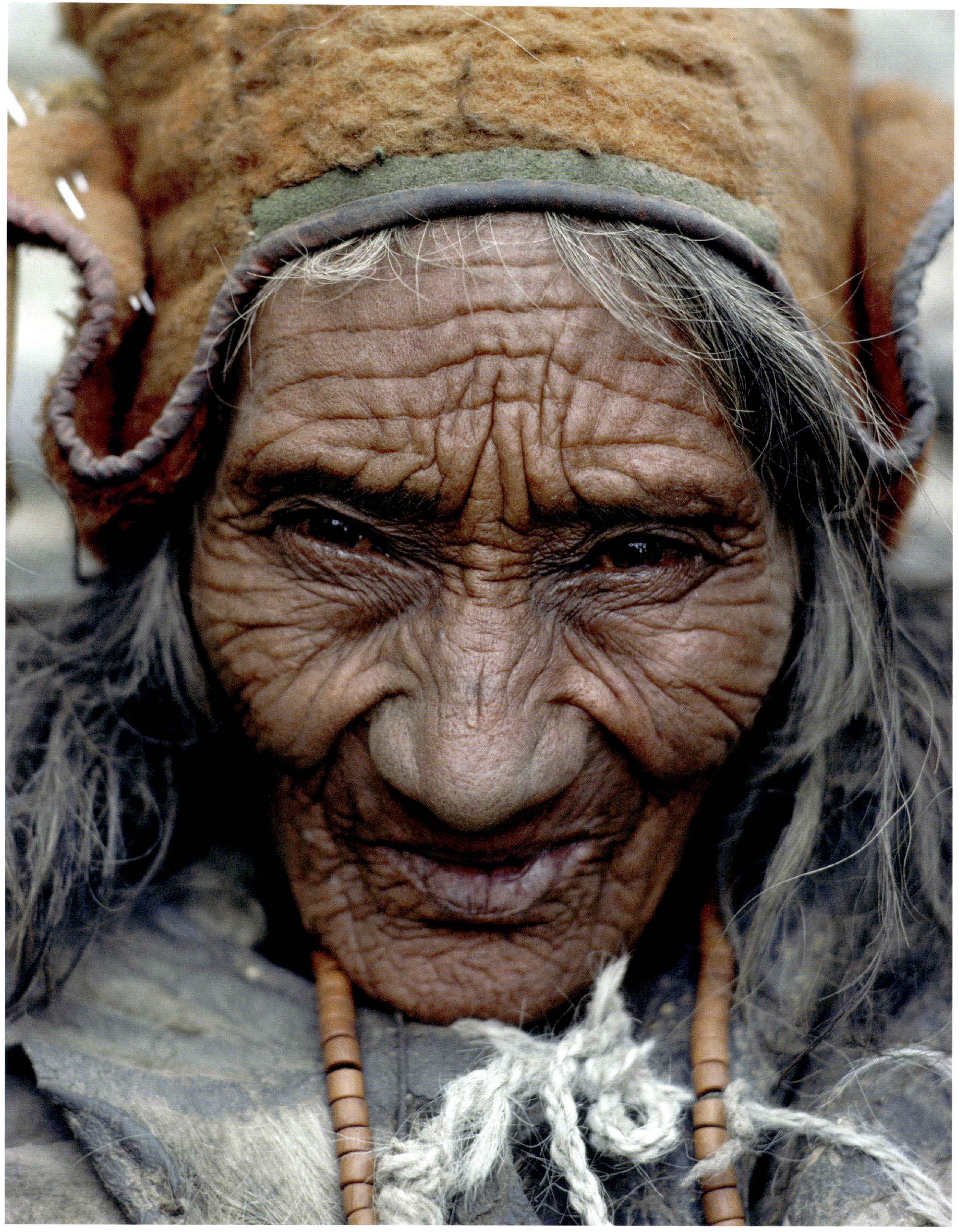

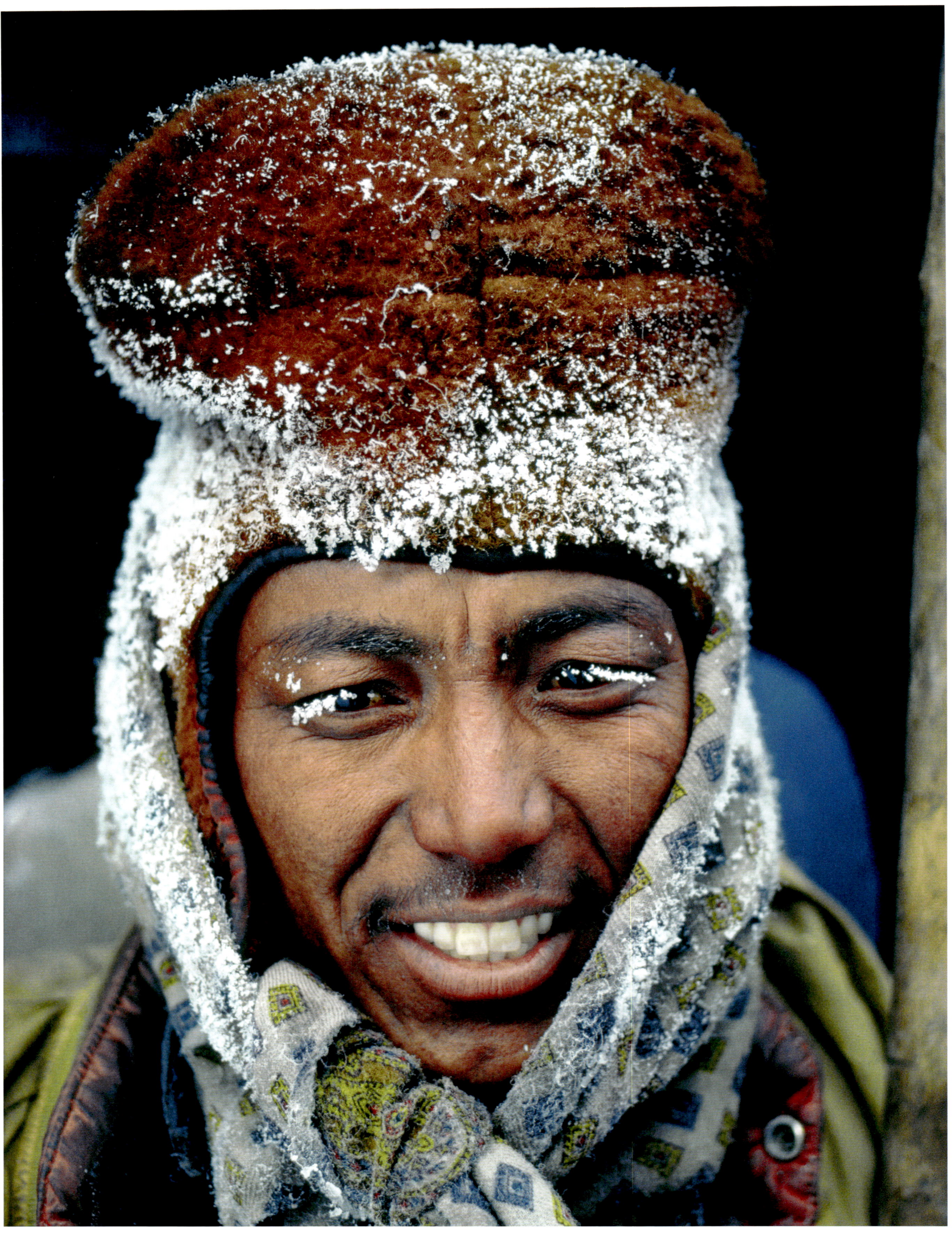

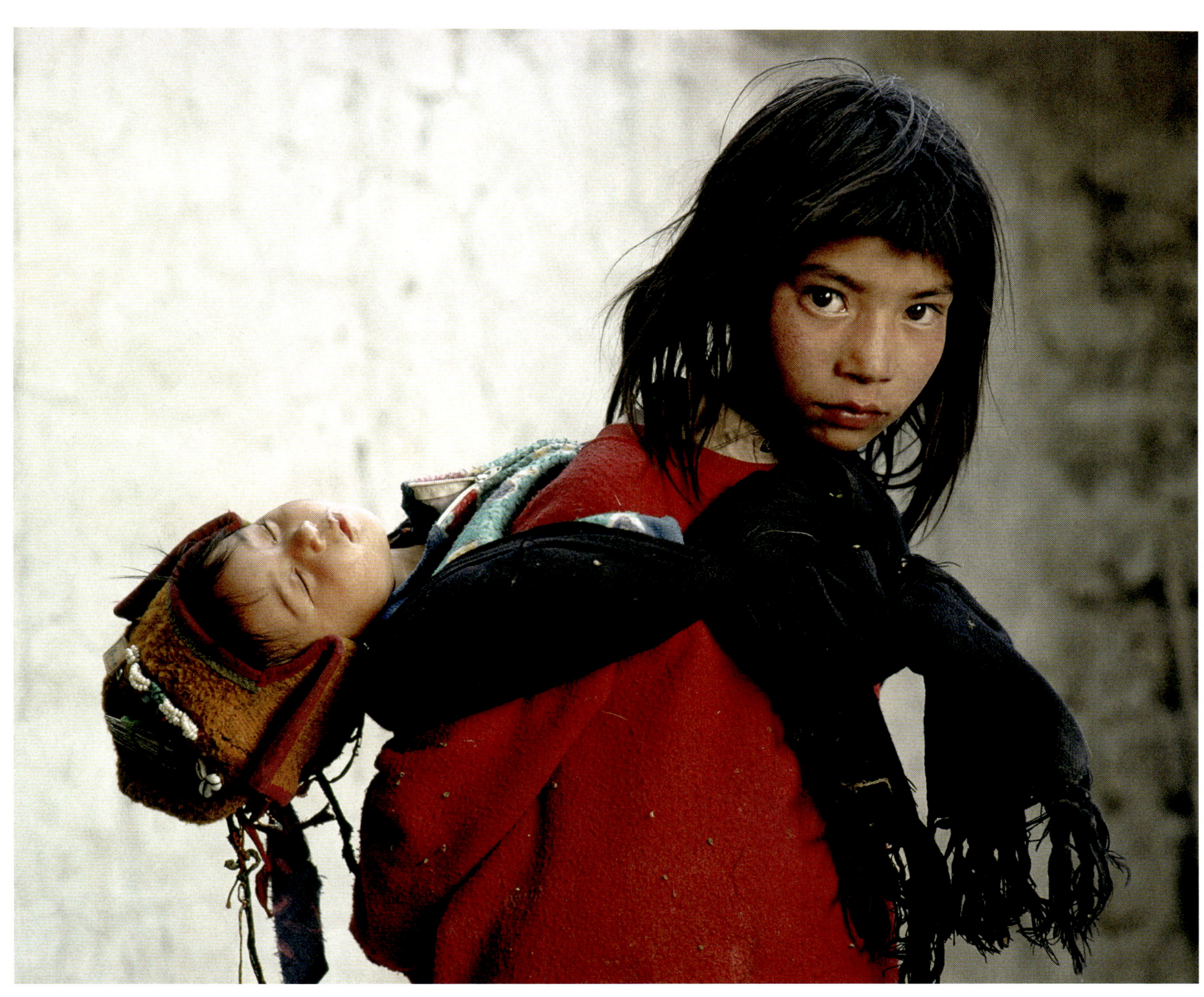

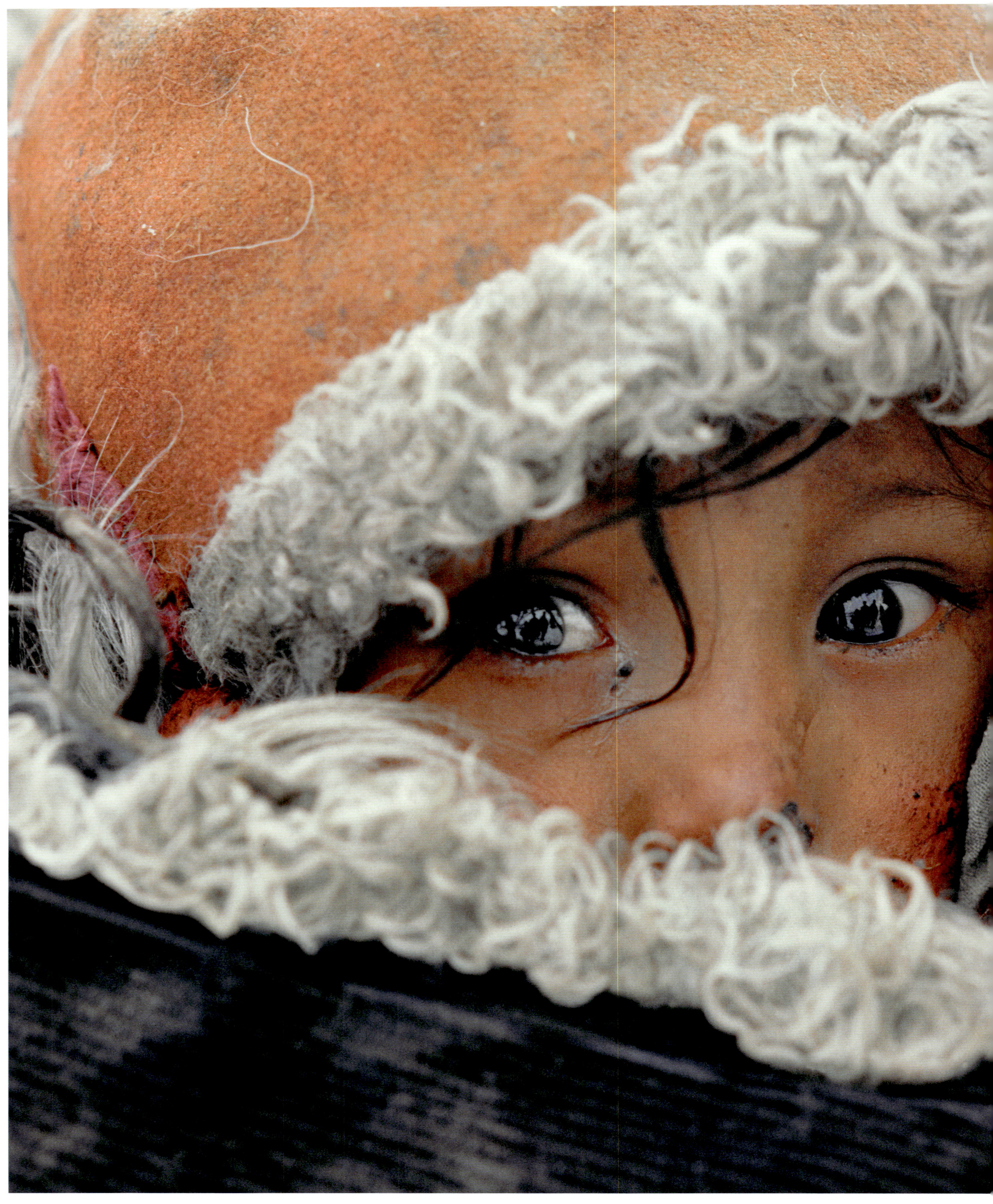

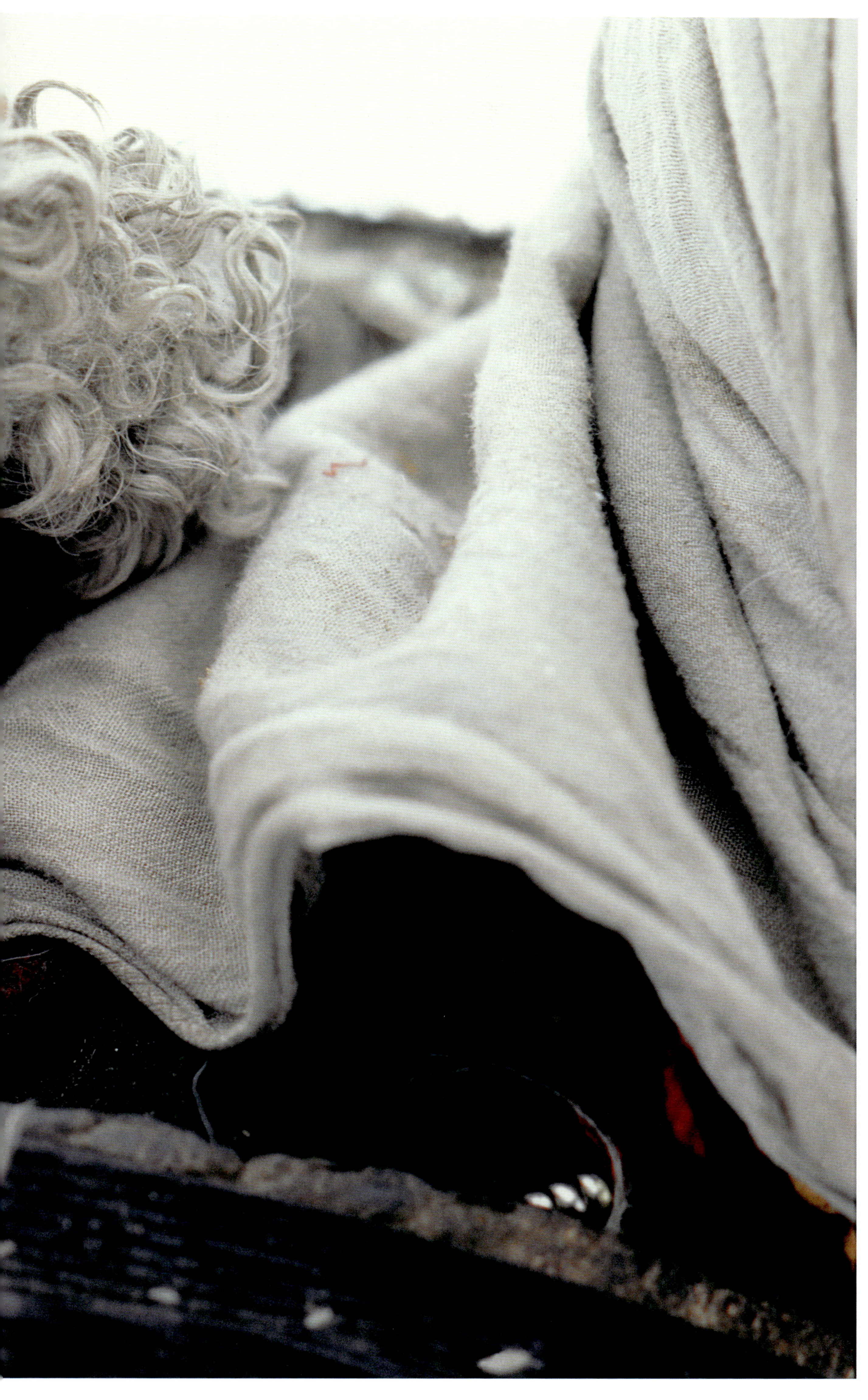

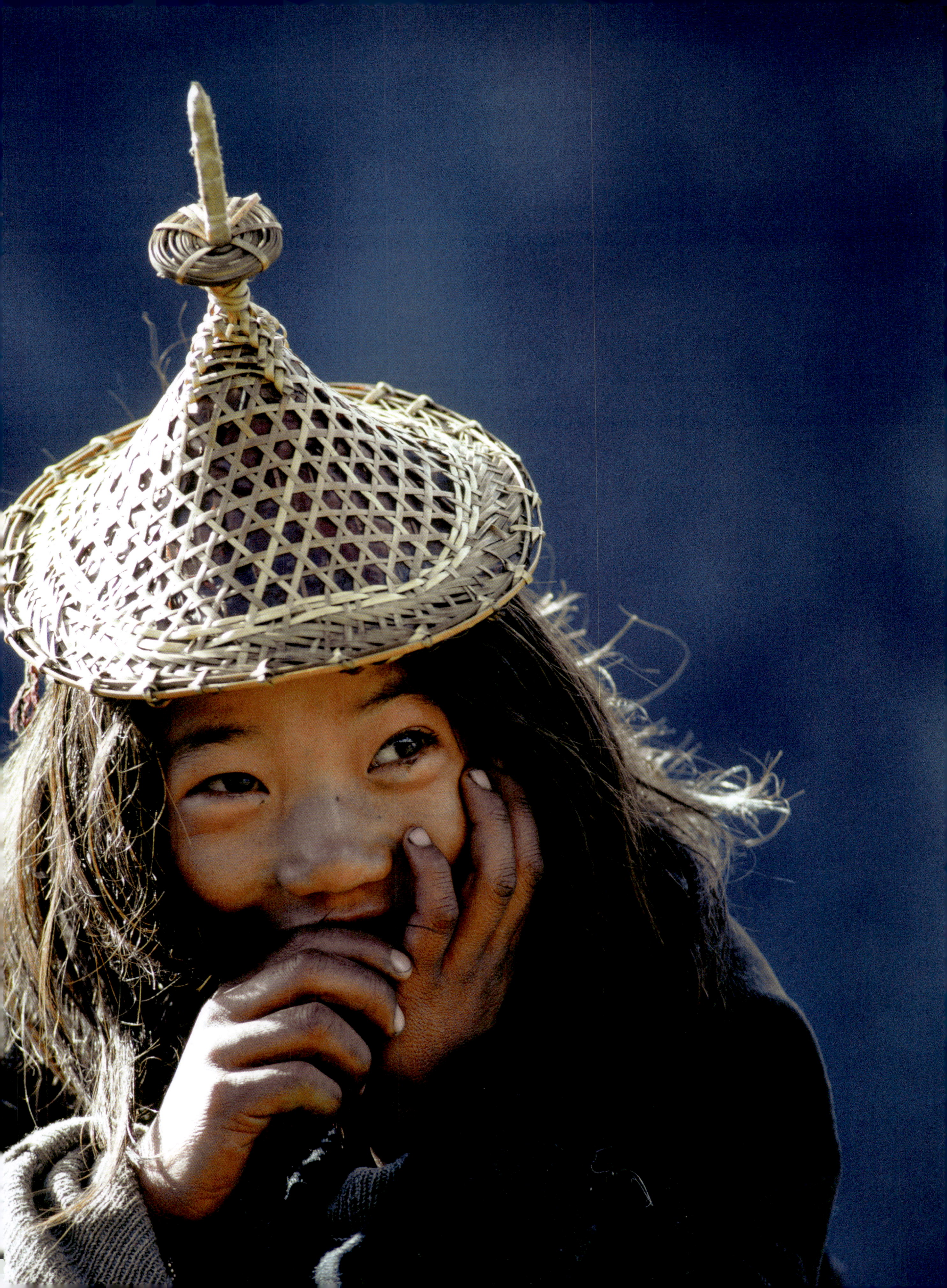

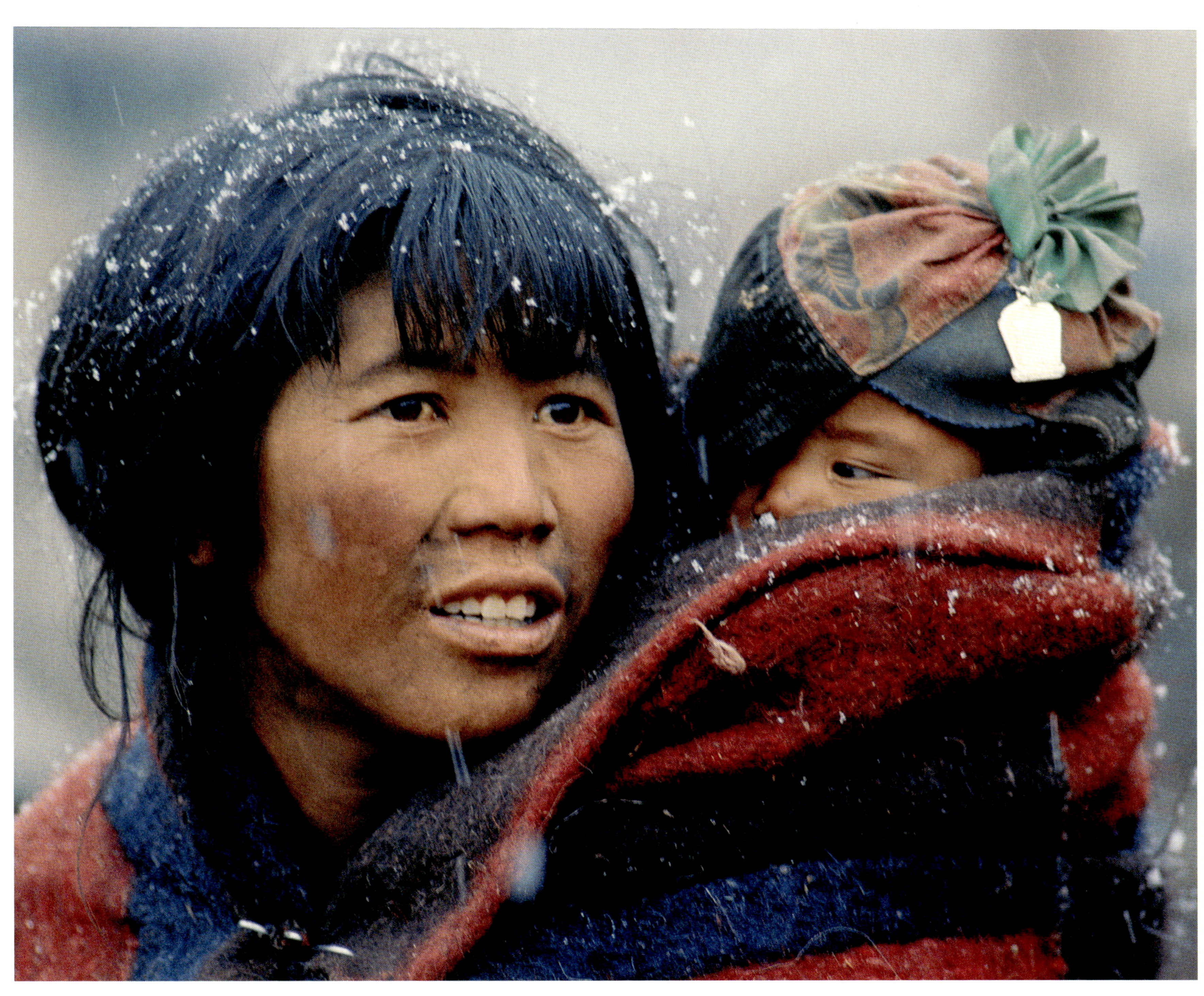

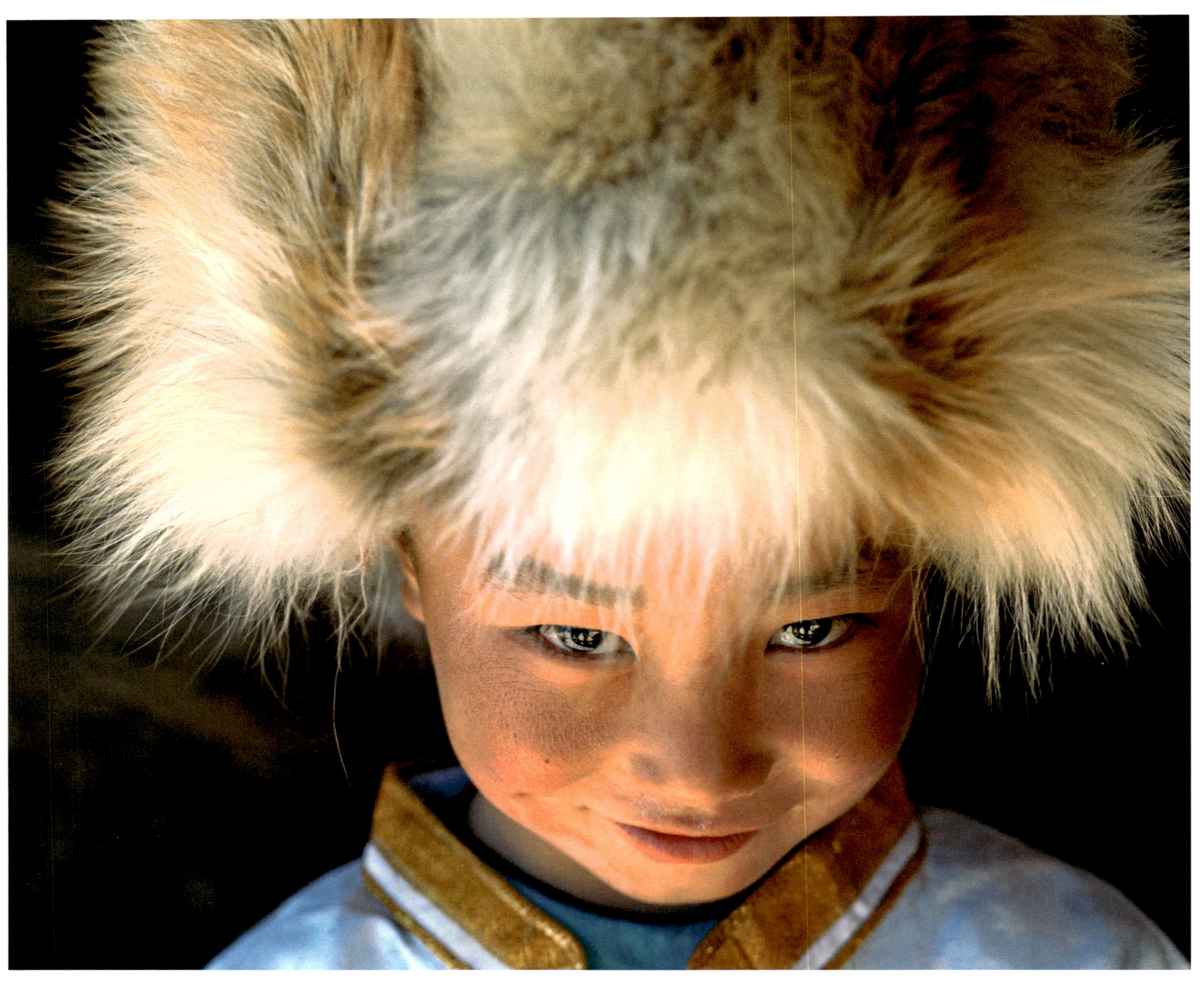

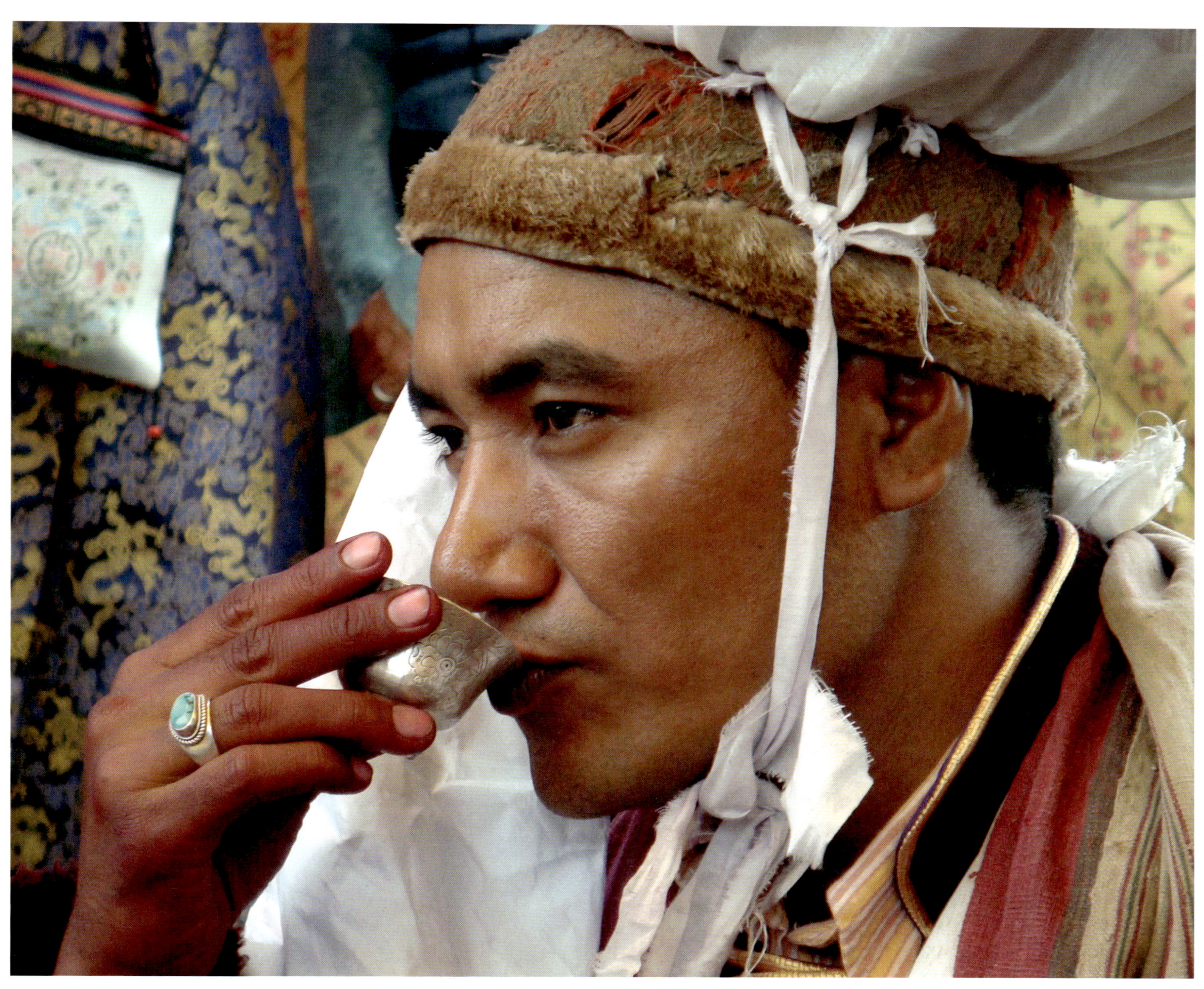

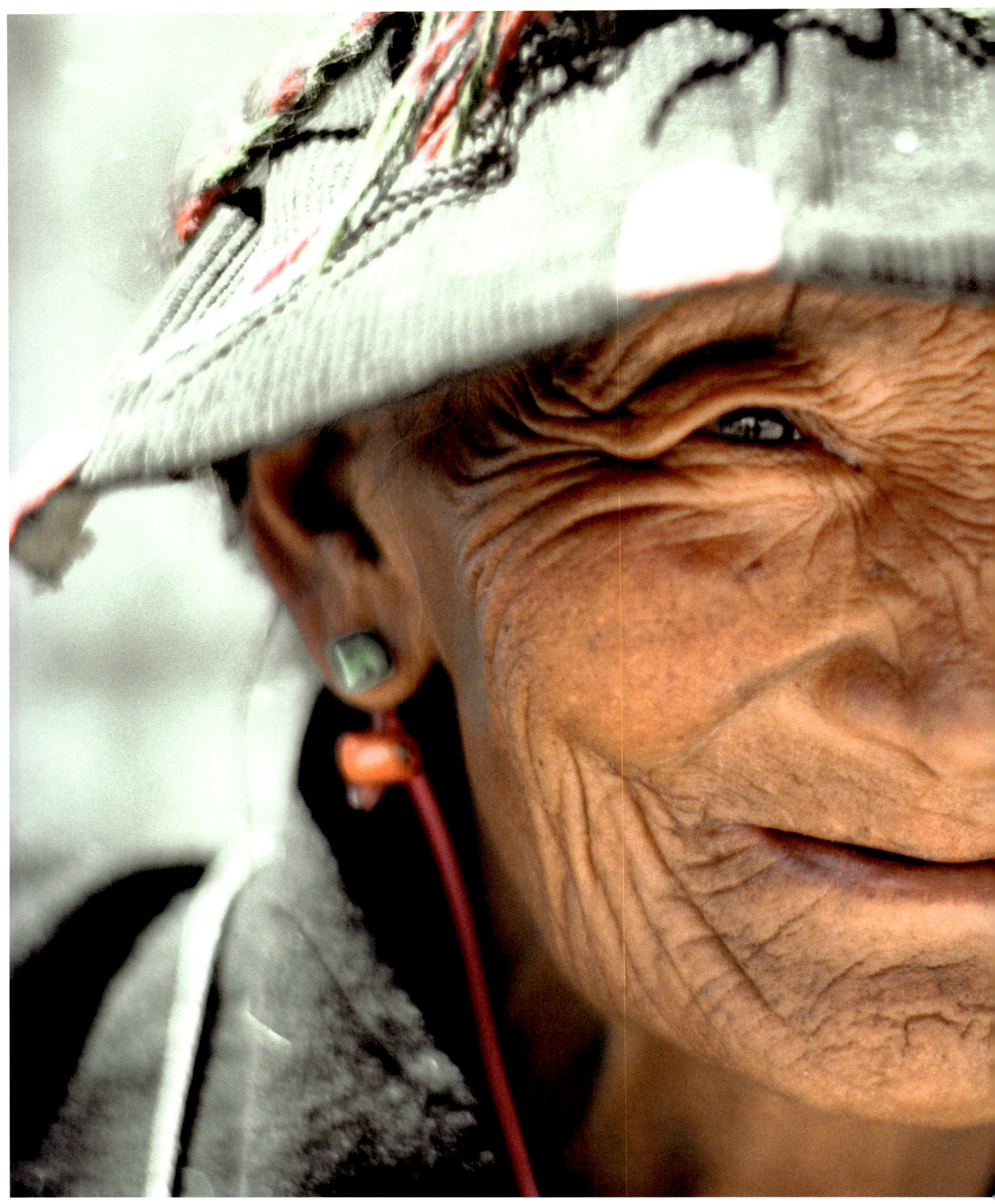

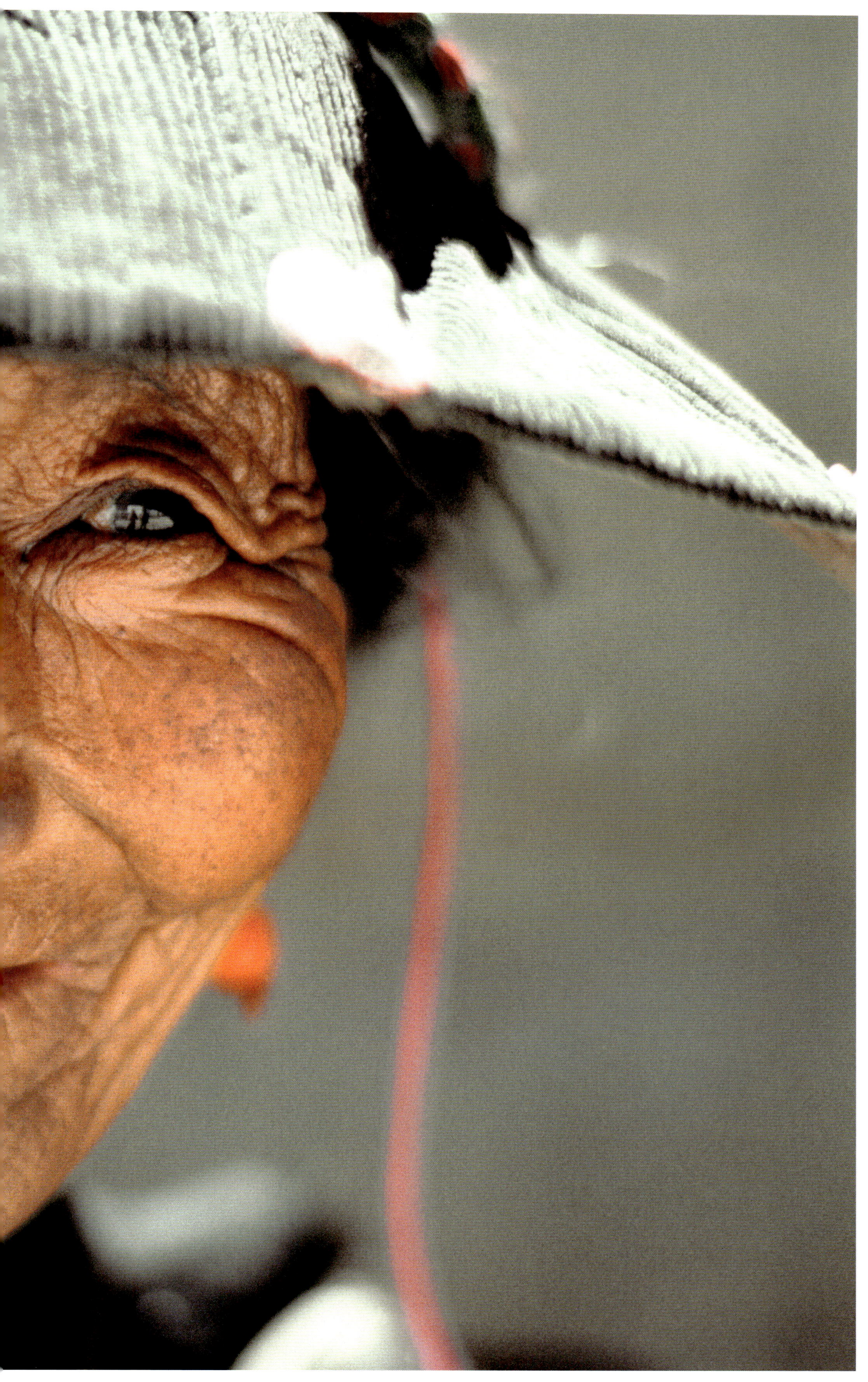

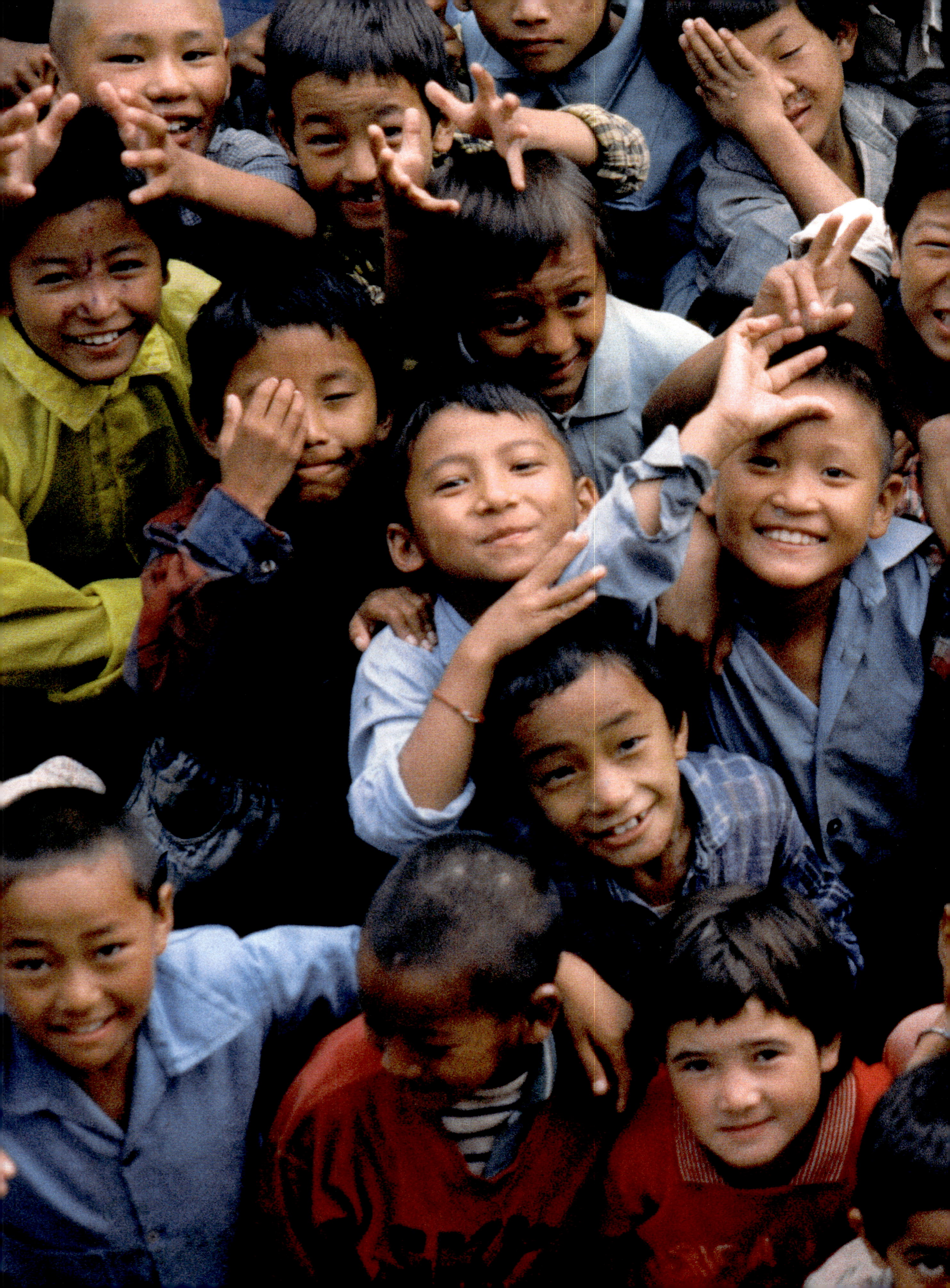

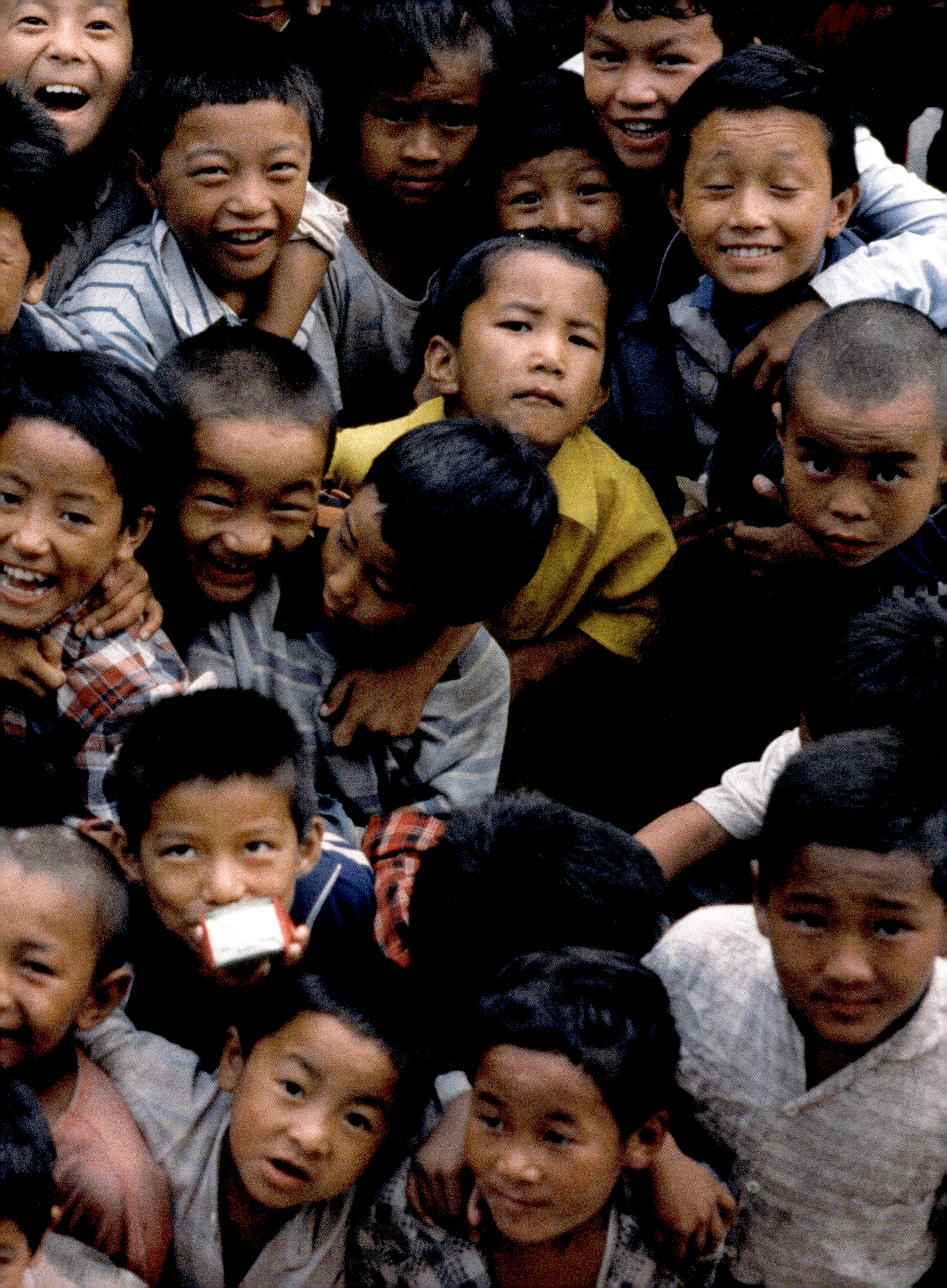

*We are all interdependent
for our daily needs
and it is thus that we have
a debt to all beings.*

Kalu Rinpoche

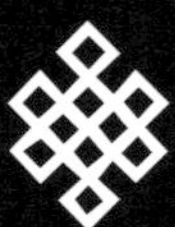

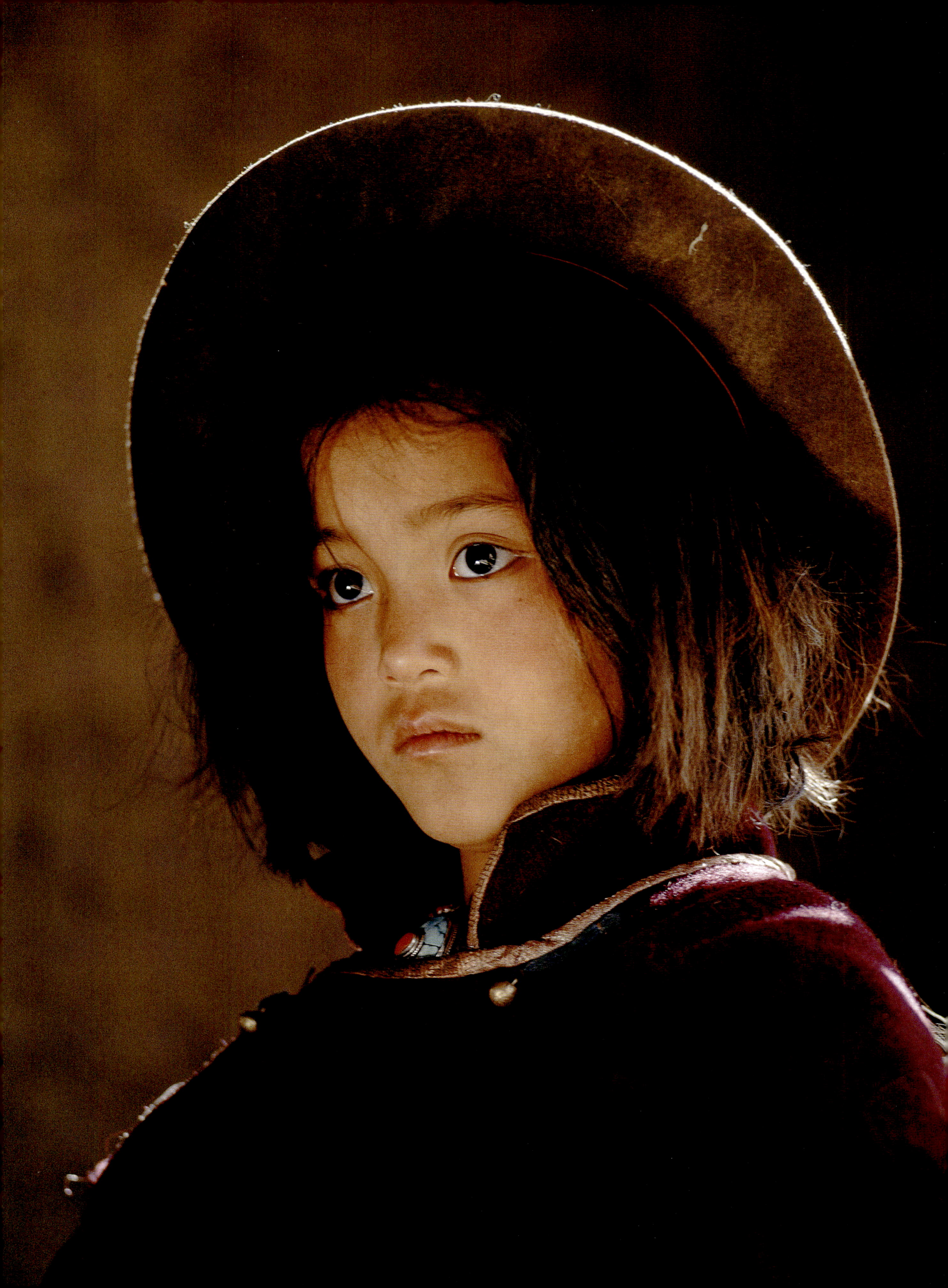

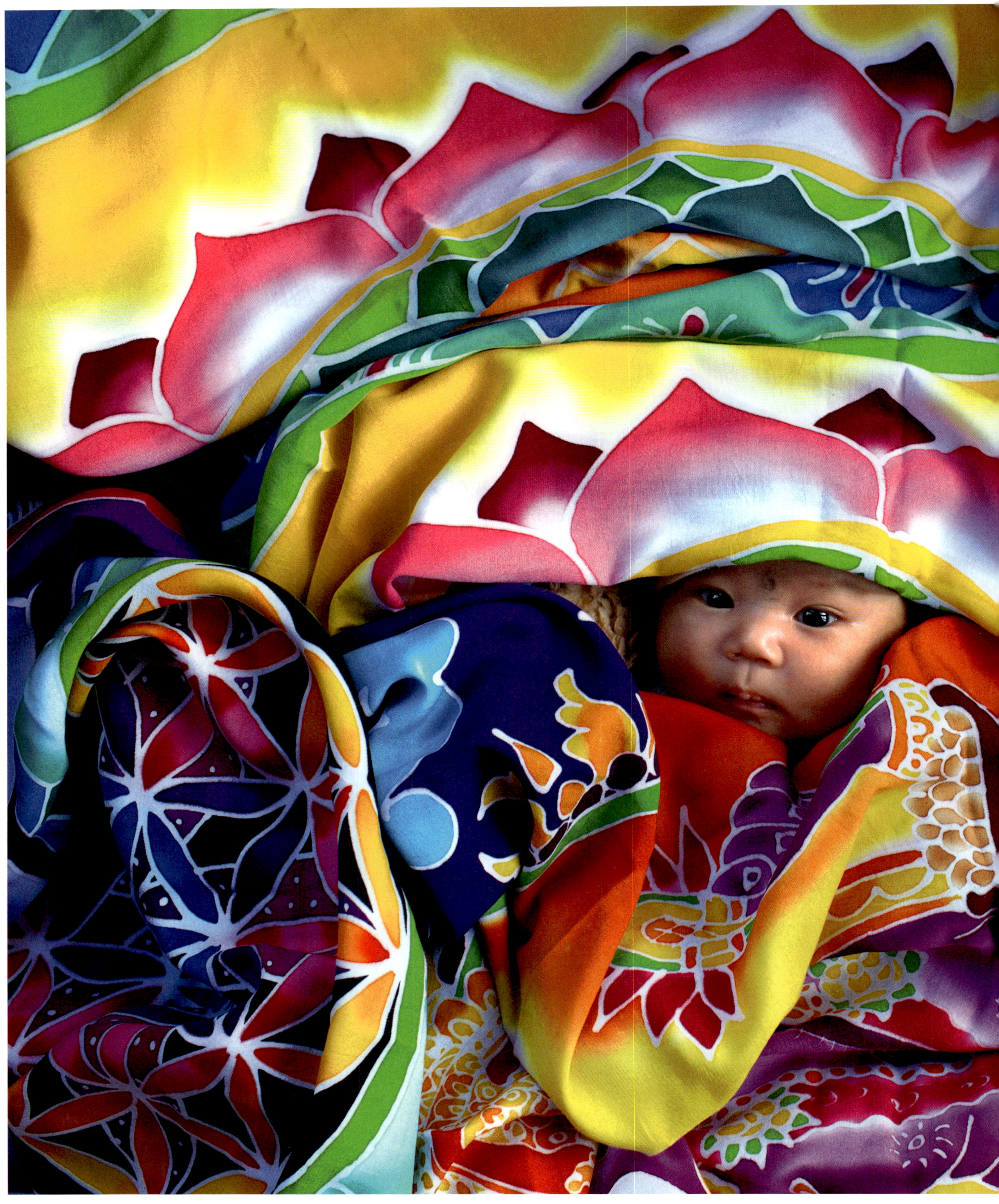

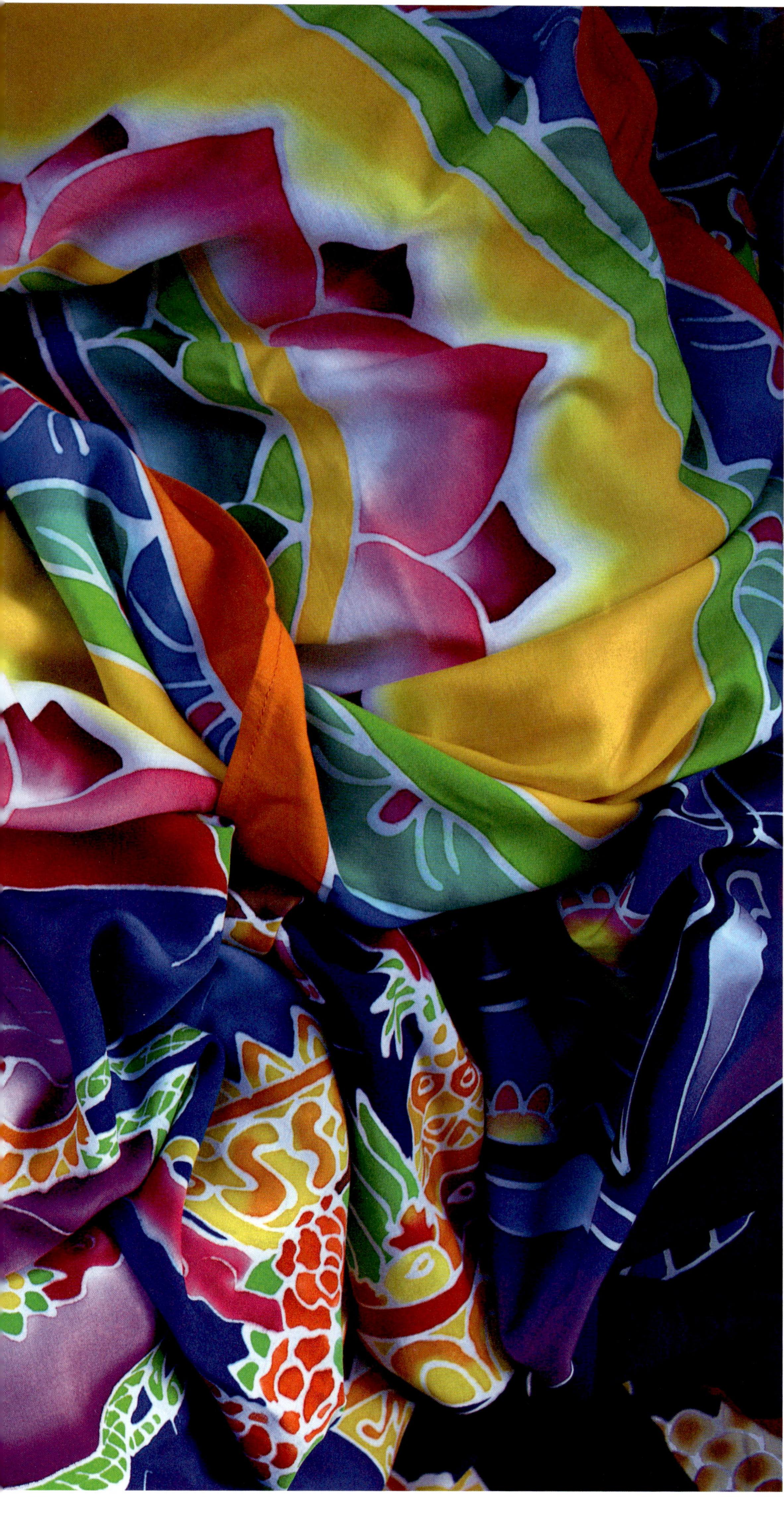

My granddaughter, Sonam Lhazes, was born in the Himalayan valley of Ladakh. Sonam Lhazes means gracious, lucky, and deserving goddess. I contemplated her, impressed: Where do you come from, little seed of Buddha, and what is your destiny in our world? Are you by any chance Maitreya, the future Buddha whom we are all waiting for?

Meine Enkelin Sonam Lhazes ist in einem Himalaya-Tal von Ladakh geboren. Ihr Name bedeutet anmutige, glückliche und verdienstvolle Göttin. Ich betrachtete sie beeindruckt: Von woher kommst du, kleines Samenkorn von Buddha, was ist dein Schicksal in unserer Welt? Wirst du Maitreya sein, der Buddha der Zukunft, auf den wir alle warten?

Ma petite-fille, Sonam Lhazès, est née dans la vallée himalayenne du Ladakh. Sonam Lhazès signifie déesse gracieuse, chanceuse et méritoire. Je la contemplais, impressionné : d'où arrives-tu petite graine de bouddha, quelle est ta destinée dans notre monde ? Serais-tu Maitreya, le bouddha du futur que nous attendons tous ?

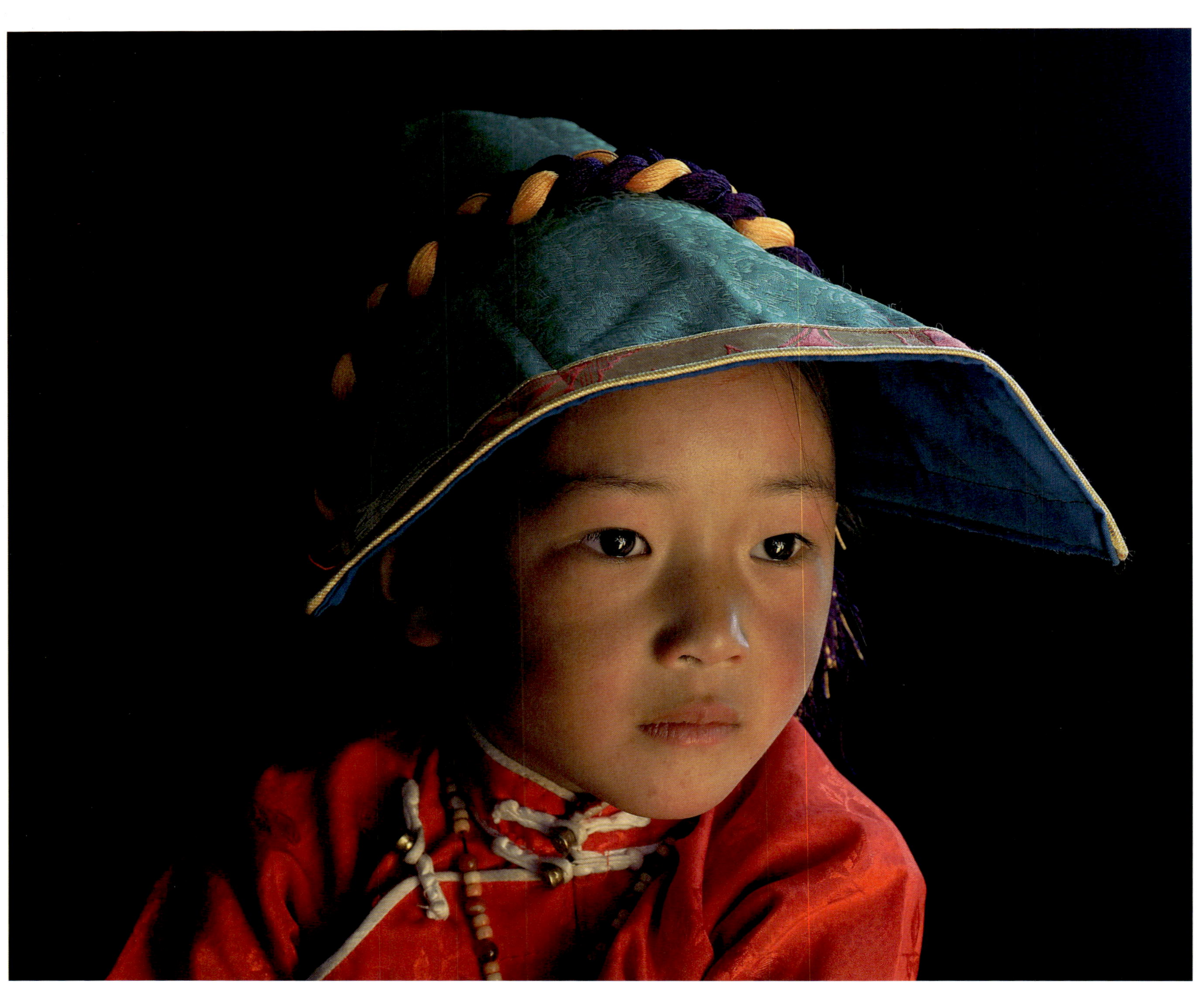

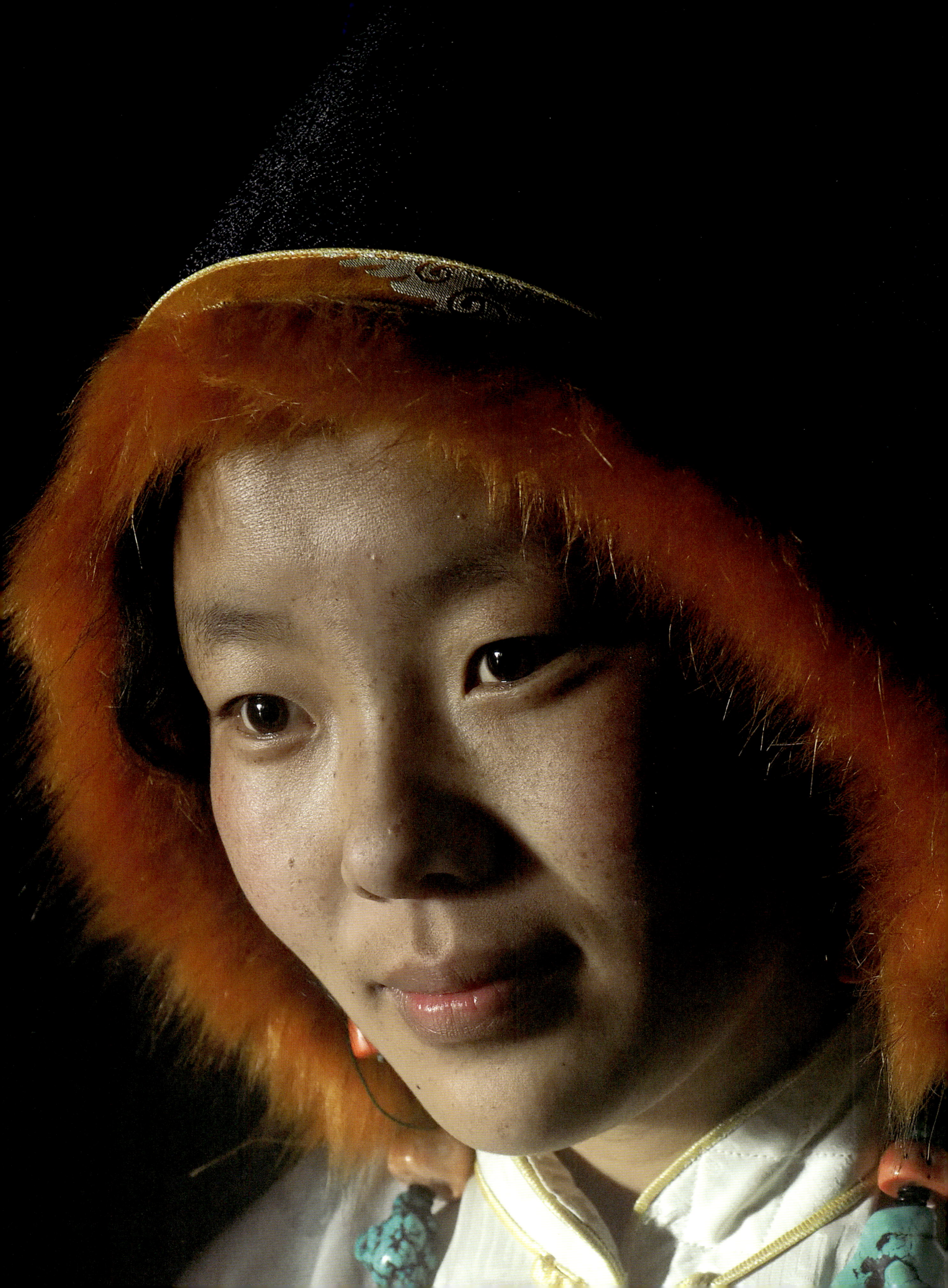

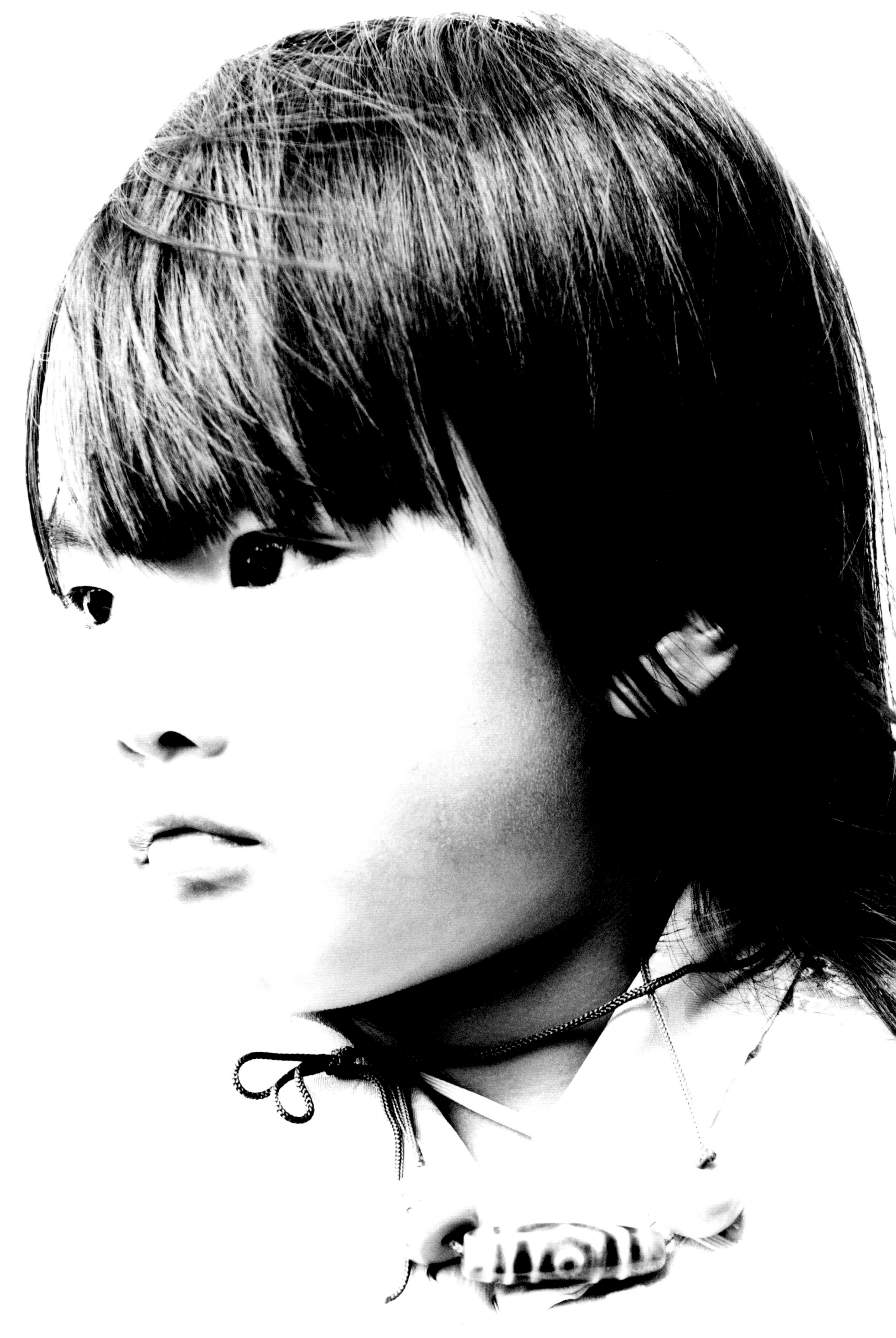

Compassion
Mitgefühl · Compassion

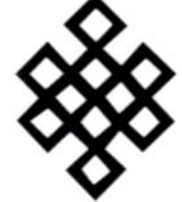

Doing no harm, practicing good, and achieving good for others:
these are the three pure precepts taught by Buddha.

Kein Leid verursachen, Gutes tun und zum Wohle der anderen handeln – das sind
die drei reinen Gebote, wie sie von Buddha gelehrt wurden.

Ne pas causer le mal, pratiquer le bien et réaliser le bien pour les autres
constituent les trois préceptes purs enseignés par Bouddha.

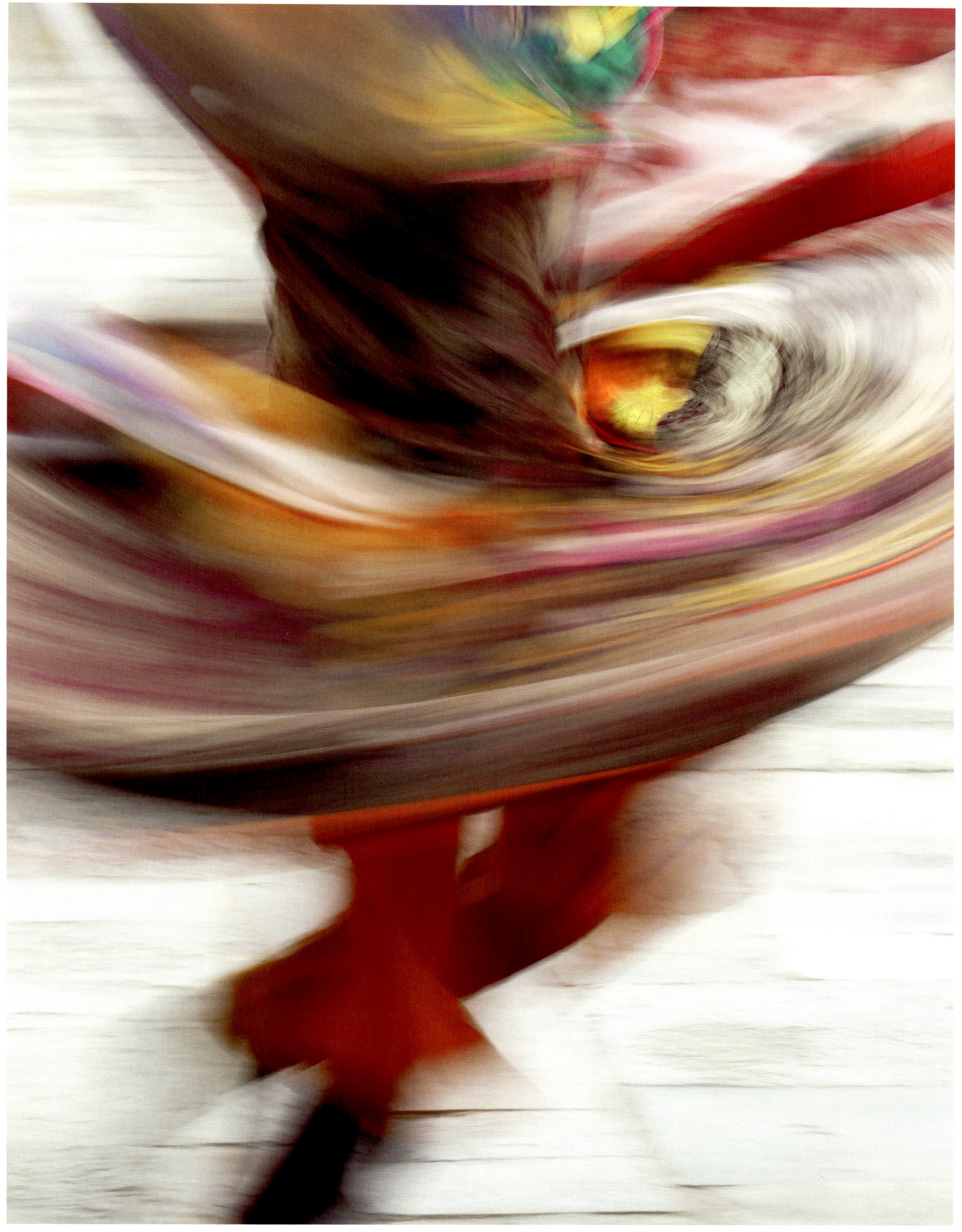

For years I have traveled through the remote valleys of the Himalayas, in Ladakh, Zanskar, Spiti, Dolpo, Mustang, Khumbu, Sikkim, and Bhutan, where the villagers have taught me with spontaneity and innocence the Buddhism of their heart. I then had the privilege of being welcomed by the highly literate and educated Tibetan community exiled in India, in Dharamsala, at the foot of the Himalayas. In their company I discovered the finer details of Tibetan culture adapted to modernity and of Buddhism to which globalization has been applied.

We cannot talk of Peace in the world
if we do not first make Peace with ourselves.
Negative and destructive forces can be fought
by Compassion, Love and Selflessness.
The 14th Dalai Lama

Having already agreed to send our first two children, Motup and Diskit, to the best Tibetan schools that she directed in the Tibetan Children's Village (TCV), Mrs. Jetsun Pema, the Dalai Lama's sister, entrusted to Danielle and me two children for adoption: Tharpa Tsering and Pema Yangdon, who grew up in Europe and are now adults. I cannot therefore mention Mrs. Jetsun Pema without first expressing my immense gratitude to her as well as to all those in the Tibetan community and the leaders of the government in exile, the TCV, and the Tibetan Institute of Performing Arts, whom I have been so fortunate to meet.

OUR CULTURE IS A VEHICLE OF HUMAN, SPIRITUAL, AND MORAL VALUES THAT ARE PART OF THE WORLD'S HERITAGE AND ABLE TO CONTRIBUTE GREATLY TO HUMANITY AS A WHOLE.

Anxious for our children, Tharpa Tsering and Pema Yangdon, to remember their roots, we returned to Dharamsala regularly to visit the Tibetan community. One day, Jetsun Pema invited us to dine with her and her family in her home in the forest beneath the school. We dressed smartly, and the children put on their festive clothes, wearing elegant chubas and shiny polished shoes. Jetsun Pema welcomed us with white silk khatas, and in turn we honored her with our khatas adorned with the eight auspicious signs of Tibetan Buddhism. She had laid out the dinner on a very pretty low table that was decorated

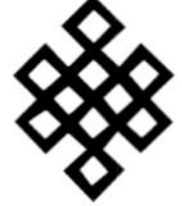

with doilies embroidered with the knot of long life, around which we sat cross-legged on comfortable carpets with snow lion patterns. We talked about the past year and of our joy in returning to the Tibetan Children's Village, speaking in hushed tones out of politeness. Speaking loudly is considered a lack of discernment and self-control.

As Jetsun Pema explained to us, 99 percent of young Tibetans living in refugee camps go to school, and the progress made thanks to the concerted efforts of the Tibetan community is impressive: "The education system in exile first saw the light of day in the 1960s. To begin with we had only four schools. Today we have more than eighty in India, Nepal, and Bhutan. Roughly 30,000 pupils study in them and 44,000 have graduated from them. Education remains our top priority."

The young girl of the house carried in thukpa soup in a large, fine golden tureen, as well as platters of vegetables cooked in curry and mok moks. One object on the table intrigued me: between the tureen and the platters was an ordinary transparent plastic bag. I thought someone must have forgotten to remove it, but the dinner continued without anyone taking it away. A fly buzzed around the table and landed on one of the platters. Jetsun Pema took the bag and placed it delicately on the vegetables. The fly then flew away, trapped in the bag. Jetsun Pema lifted up the mosquito net on the window, freed the fly, and continued her explanation as though nothing had happened. In Tibetan society I have never seen anyone squash or kill an insect.

"Our ideal is not only to educate our children but also to help them become good human beings. They receive an education that, while modern, is firmly rooted in the human values of Buddhism. In our educational efforts, we place great importance on each person's responsibility for the harmonious development of their own life."

Most pupils in the Tibetan Children's Villages have been sent there clandestinely by their parents to avoid the repression they would suffer on the high Tibetan plateaus and to give them every opportunity to grow up with Tibetan values. In Dharamsala, two thousand children live in the TCV year round, and most of them will never see their parents again. How could they, given the geographical isolation and strict political surveillance of their families still living in Tibet? The TVC could well have become centers of violence and places of delinquency for these uprooted children, were their directors not so anxious to pass on the legacy of their Tibetan culture to the new generation. As Jetsun Pema explains: "We try to recreate a family atmosphere by developing the feeling of community, the sense of duty, and the desire to be an example for others. We also instill in our young people compassion, which is the essence of the Buddha's teaching. We teach them very early on to care about the welfare of all beings. Our culture is a vehicle of human, spiritual, and moral values that are part of the world's heritage and able to contribute greatly to humanity as a whole. As citizens of the world, aware of the interdependence of all peoples, we particularly hope to promote peace in the world by instilling in our children the essential values of love and tolerance."

My children, you are human beings. You are not like flowers that wither
under the heat of the sun and are destroyed or scattered by hail and storms.
Unlike plants, you can control your own destiny.
Whatever physical suffering you may encounter, always keep an honest heart
and a sound and stable mind. Acquire knowledge and fight with the weapons
of justice and righteousness. You who are on the threshold of life,
grow stronger each day and do not waste your precious time!
The 14th Dalai Lama, addressing the pupils of the Tibetan Children's Village

In Ladakh, Zanskar, Spiti, Dolpo, Mustang, Khumbu, Sikkim und Bhutan habe ich jahrelang die abgeschiedenen Täler des Himalaya erkundet. Dort lehrten mich die Dorfbewohner mit ihrer Spontaneität und Unschuld den Buddhismus ihres Herzens. Ich genoss später das Privileg, von der hoch gebildeten Gemeinschaft der Exiltibeter im indischen Dharamsala am Fuße des Himalaya aufgenommen und gelehrt zu werden. Dort konnte ich die Feinheiten der an die Moderne angepassten tibetischen Kultur und des von der Globalisierung beeinflussten Buddhismus entdecken.

Wir können nicht vom Frieden in der Welt sprechen,
wenn wir nicht zuerst Frieden mit uns selbst schließen.
Die negativen, zerstörerischen Kräfte lassen sich mit
Mitgefühl, Liebe und Uneigennützigkeit bekämpfen.
Der 14. Dalai Lama

Nachdem sie zugestimmt hatte, unsere ersten beiden Kinder Motup und Diskit in die beste tibetische Schule, die sie im Tibetischen Kinderdorf (TCV) leitete, aufzunehmen, vertraute Jetsun Pema, die Schwester des Dalai Lama, Danielle und mir als Paar zwei weitere Kinder an, damit wir sie adoptierten: Tharpa Tsering und Pema Yangdon, die später in Europa aufwuchsen und nun erwachsen sind. Ich kann Jetsun Pema nicht erwähnen, ohne ihr und allen Verantwortlichen der tibetischen Gemeinschaft, den Protagonisten der Exilregierung, dem TCV und dem Tibetischen Institut der darstellenden Künste (TIPA) meine große Dankbarkeit zum Ausdruck zu bringen.

Damit Tharpa Tsering und Pema Yangdon ihre Wurzeln nicht vergaßen, kehrten wir immer wieder nach Dharamsala zurück, um der tibetischen Gemeinschaft einen Besuch abzustatten. Eines Tages empfing Jetsun Pema uns als Familie in ihrem Haus im Wald unterhalb der Schule. Wir hatten uns in Schale geworfen, die Kinder trugen ihr Festtagsgewand mit eleganter Chuba und polierten Schuhen. Jetsun Pema empfing uns mit Kathas, tibetischen Begrüßungsschals, aus weißer Seide, und auch wir ehrten sie mit unseren Kathas, die mit den acht glücksbringenden tibetischen Symbolen verziert waren. Sie hatte einen sehr schönen niedrigen Tisch für uns gedeckt. Er war mit Deckchen geschmückt, die mit dem Ewigen Knoten bestickt waren. Wir setzten uns im Schneidersitz auf bequeme kleine Teppiche mit Schneelöwenmotiven. So redeten wir über das vergangene Jahr und unsere Freude, wieder im Tibetischen Kinderdorf zu sein. Aus Höflichkeit sprachen wir nur leise. Laut zu reden zeugt von einem Mangel an Umsicht und Selbstkontrolle.

Wie uns Jetsun Pema erklärte, gehen 99 Prozent der tibetischen Jugendlichen im Flüchtlingslager in die Schule. Dank der gemeinsamen Anstrengungen der tibetischen Gemeinschaft durchlaufen sie eine beachtliche Ausbildung: „Das Schulsystem der Exilregierung nahm in den 1960er-Jahren Formen an. Anfangs betrieben wir nur vier Schulen. Heute sind es mehr als 80 in Indien, Nepal und Bhutan. Rund 30 000 Schülerinnen und Schüler gehen dort in die Schule; 44 000 haben bisher ihr Diplom gemacht. Die Bildung hat bei uns weiter hohe Priorität."

Ihre Tochter brachte uns Thukpa, eine tibetische Suppe, in einer großen, schönen vergoldeten Schüssel, außerdem Teller mit gekochtem Curry-Gemüse und Mok Mok. Ein Gegenstand auf dem Tisch überraschte mich: Zwischen der Schüssel und den Tellern lag ein gewöhnlicher Beutel aus transparentem Plastik. Ich dachte, dass er vergessen worden sei, aber wir aßen, ohne dass man ihn anrührte. Da flog eine Fliege um den Tisch und setzte sich auf einen der Teller. Jetsun Pema nahm den Beutel und stülpte ihn vorsichtig über das Gemüse. Die Fliege wollte wegfliegen und verfing sich im Beutel. Jetsun Pema hob das Fliegennetz am Fenster hoch, ließ die Fliege draußen frei und setzte ihre Erläuterungen fort, als sei nichts geschehen. Ich habe in Tibet noch nie jemanden ein Insekt töten sehen.

„Unser Ideal ist es nicht nur, unsere Kinder zu unterrichten, sondern auch, sie zu guten Menschen zu erziehen. Sie bekommen eine moderne Erziehung, die jedoch auf den Idealen des Buddhismus fußt. Wir legen dabei viel Wert auf eine eigenverantwortliche, harmonische Gestaltung des eigenen Lebens."

Die meisten Kinder im Tibetischen Kinderdorf wurden von ihren Eltern heimlich dorthin geschickt, damit sie nicht unter der Unterdrückung auf dem tibetischen Hochplateau leiden müssen und uneingeschränkt mit tibetischen Werten aufwachsen. In Dharamsala leben 2000 Kinder jährlich im Dorf; die meisten sehen ihre Eltern nicht mehr wieder, denn sie sind geografisch zu isoliert oder werden politisch zu stark überwacht. Die Tibetischen Kinderdörfer könnten durchaus zu Heimstätten der Gewalt und Kriminalität für die entwurzelten Jugendlichen werden, würden sich die Verantwortlichen dort nicht sehr darum bemühen, ihnen ihre tibetische Kultur zu vermitteln. Jetsun Pema erklärte es so: „Wir versuchen eine familiäre Atmosphäre zu schaffen, indem wir ein Gefühl der Solidarität, des Pflichtbewusstseins und des Wunsches, für andere ein Vorbild zu sein, fördern. Zudem vermitteln wir der Jugend Mitgefühl, die Quintessenz von Buddhas Lehren. Wir bringen ihnen sehr früh bei, für das Wohlergehen aller Wesen zu sorgen. Unsere Kultur ist Trägerin menschlicher, spiritueller und moralischer Werte, die Teil des universellen Erbes sind und viel Positives für die gesamte Menschheit bewirken können. Als Weltbürger, die sich der gegenseitigen Abhängigkeit aller Menschen bewusst sind, hoffen wir insbesondere, etwas zum Weltfrieden beitragen zu können, indem wir unseren Kindern die unverzichtbaren Werte Liebe und Toleranz beibringen."

> *UNSERE KULTUR IST TRÄGERIN MENSCHLICHER, SPIRITUELLER UND MORALISCHER WERTE, DIE TEIL DES UNIVERSELLEN ERBES SIND UND VIEL POSITIVES FÜR DIE GESAMTE MENSCHHEIT BEWIRKEN KÖNNEN.*

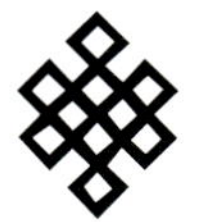

Meine Kinder, ihr seid menschliche Wesen. ihr seid nicht wie die Blumen, die in der Hitze der Sonne verwelken und von Hagel und Sturm zerstört oder zerstreut werden. Im Gegensatz zu den Pflanzen könnt ihr euer Schicksal selbst in die Hand nehmen. Welches körperliche Leid ihr auch immer auf eurem Weg erdulden müsst, bewahrt immer ein ehrliches Herz und einen festen, unbeugsamen Geist. Mehrt euer Wissen und kämpft mit den Waffen der Gerechtigkeit und des Rechts. Ihr steht an der Schwelle zum Leben, werdet jeden Tag stärker und vergeudet nicht eure wertvolle Zeit!
Der 14. Dalai Lama in einer Rede vor den Kindern des Tibetischen Kinderdorfes

Au Ladakh, au Zanskar, au Spiti, au Dolpo, au Mustang, au Khumbu, au Sikkim, au Bhoutan, j'ai parcouru pendant des années les vallées reculées de l'Himalaya, où les villageois m'ont appris avec spontanéité et innocence le bouddhisme de leur cœur. J'ai eu ensuite le privilège d'être accueilli par la communauté tibétaine exilée en Inde, hautement instruite et éduquée, à Dharamsala, au pied de l'Himalaya. Auprès d'elle, j'ai pu découvrir les finesses de la culture tibétaine adaptée à la modernité et du bouddhisme concerné par la mondialisation.

> *Nous ne pouvons pas parler de paix dans le monde*
> *si nous ne faisons pas d'abord la Paix avec nous-mêmes.*
> *Les forces négatives et destructrices peuvent être combattues*
> *par la Compassion, l'Amour et l'Altruisme.*
> Le xiv⁰ dalaï-lama

Après avoir accepté de scolariser nos deux premiers enfants, Motup et Diskit, dans les meilleures écoles tibétaines qu'elle dirigeait au Village des Enfants Tibétains (TCV), Madame Jetsun Pema, sœur du dalaï-lama, a confié au couple que nous formions, Danielle et moi, deux enfants en adoption : Tharpa Tsering et Pema Yangdon, qui ont grandi en Europe et sont adultes maintenant. Je ne peux donc évoquer Madame Jetsun Pema sans commencer par lui exprimer mon immense gratitude, ainsi qu'à tous les acteurs de la Communauté tibétaine, dirigeants du gouvernement en exil, du TCV et du TIPA que j'ai eu tant de chance de connaître.

NOTRE CULTURE EST PORTEUSE DE VALEURS HUMAINES, SPIRITUELLES ET MORALES QUI FONT PARTIE DU PATRIMOINE UNIVERSEL ET PEUVENT BEAUCOUP APPORTER À L'HUMANITÉ TOUT ENTIÈRE.

Soucieux que nos enfants, Tharpa Tsering et Pema Yangdon, n'oublient pas leurs racines, nous retournions régulièrement à Dharamsala rendre visite à la Communauté tibétaine. Un jour, Jetsun Pema nous reçoit en famille dans sa maison, dans la forêt en dessous de l'école. Nous sommes sur notre trente et un, les enfants sont en habit de fête, en chuba élégante, les chaussures sont cirées. Jetsun Pema nous accueille avec des kathas de soie blanche et nous l'honorons aussi de nos kathas ornées des huit signes auspicieux tibétains. Elle a préparé une très jolie table basse, décorée de napperons brodés

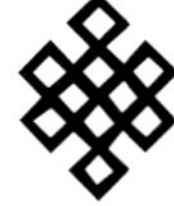

du nœud de longue vie, autour de laquelle nous nous installons en tailleur sur de confortables tapis aux motifs de lions des neiges. Nous évoquons l'année écoulée et notre joie à retrouver le Village des Enfants Tibétains, et parlons à voix basse par politesse. S'exprimer d'une voix forte est un manque de discernement, un manque de contrôle de soi.

Comme nous l'explique Jetsun Pema, 99 % de la jeunesse tibétaine vivant dans les camps de réfugiés est scolarisée, et le chemin parcouru grâce aux efforts conjugués de la Communauté tibétaine est impressionnant : « Le système d'éducation en exil a vu le jour dans les années 1960. Au début, nous n'avions que quatre écoles. Aujourd'hui, nous en avons plus de quatre-vingts en Inde, au Népal et au Bhoutan. Environ 30 000 élèves y étudient et 44 000 y ont été diplômés. L'éducation demeure notre priorité majeure. »

La jeune fille de la maison apporte une soupe de thukpa dans une grande et belle soupière dorée, des plats de légumes cuits au curry et des mok mok. Un objet me surprend sur la table : entre la soupière et les plats trône un vulgaire sac en plastique transparent. Je pense qu'il s'agit d'un oubli, mais le dîner se déroule sans qu'on ne touche au sac. Une mouche tourne autour de la table et se pose sur l'un des plats. Jetsun Pema s'empare du sac et le pose délicatement sur les légumes ; la mouche s'envole, prisonnière du sac. Jetsun Pema soulève la moustiquaire de la fenêtre, libère la mouche et continue son explication, comme si de rien n'était. Chez les Tibétains, je n'ai jamais vu quelqu'un écraser ou tuer un insecte.

« Notre idéal n'est pas seulement d'instruire nos enfants ; il vise aussi à les aider à devenir de bons êtres humains. Ils reçoivent une éducation moderne mais enracinée dans les valeurs humaines du bouddhisme. Dans notre effort d'éducation, nous attachons beaucoup d'importance à la responsabilité de chacun dans le développement harmonieux de sa propre vie. »

La plupart des élèves des Villages des Enfants Tibétains y ont été envoyés clandestinement par leurs parents pour leur éviter la répression sur les hauts plateaux du Tibet et leur offrir toutes les chances de bien grandir avec des valeurs tibétaines. À Dharamsala, 2 000 enfants vivent à l'année au TCV et la plupart d'entre eux ne reverront plus leurs parents, trop isolés géographiquement ou trop surveillés politiquement. Les Villages des Enfants Tibétains pourraient avoir tous les ingrédients pour devenir des foyers de violence et des lieux de délinquance pour ces jeunes déracinés, si ceux et celles qui les dirigent n'étaient pas aussi soucieux de leur transmettre l'héritage de la culture tibétaine. Jetsun Pema l'exprime ainsi : « Nous essayons de recréer une atmosphère familiale en développant le sentiment de solidarité, le sens du devoir et le désir d'être un exemple pour les autres. Nous inculquons aussi aux jeunes la compassion, qui est l'essence de l'enseignement de Bouddha. Nous leur apprenons très tôt à se soucier du bien-être de tous les êtres. Notre culture est porteuse de valeurs humaines, spirituelles et morales qui font partie du patrimoine universel et peuvent beaucoup apporter à l'humanité tout entière. En tant que citoyens du monde, conscients de l'interdépendance de tous les peuples, nous espérons en particulier contribuer à la paix dans le monde en inculquant à nos enfants les indispensables valeurs d'amour et de tolérance. »

Mes enfants, vous êtes des êtres humains. Vous n'êtes pas comme les fleurs qui se fanent
sous la chaleur du soleil et sont détruites ou éparpillées par la grêle et la tempête.
Contrairement aux plantes, vous pouvez prendre en main votre destinée.
Quelles que soient les souffrances physiques que vous rencontriez, gardez toujours
un cœur honnête, un esprit stable et solide. Acquérez des connaissances et battez-vous avec
les armes de la justice et du droit. Vous qui êtes au seuil de la vie, devenez chaque jour plus forts,
et ne gâchez pas votre précieux temps !
Le XIVe dalaï-lama s'adressant aux élèves du Village des Enfants Tibétains

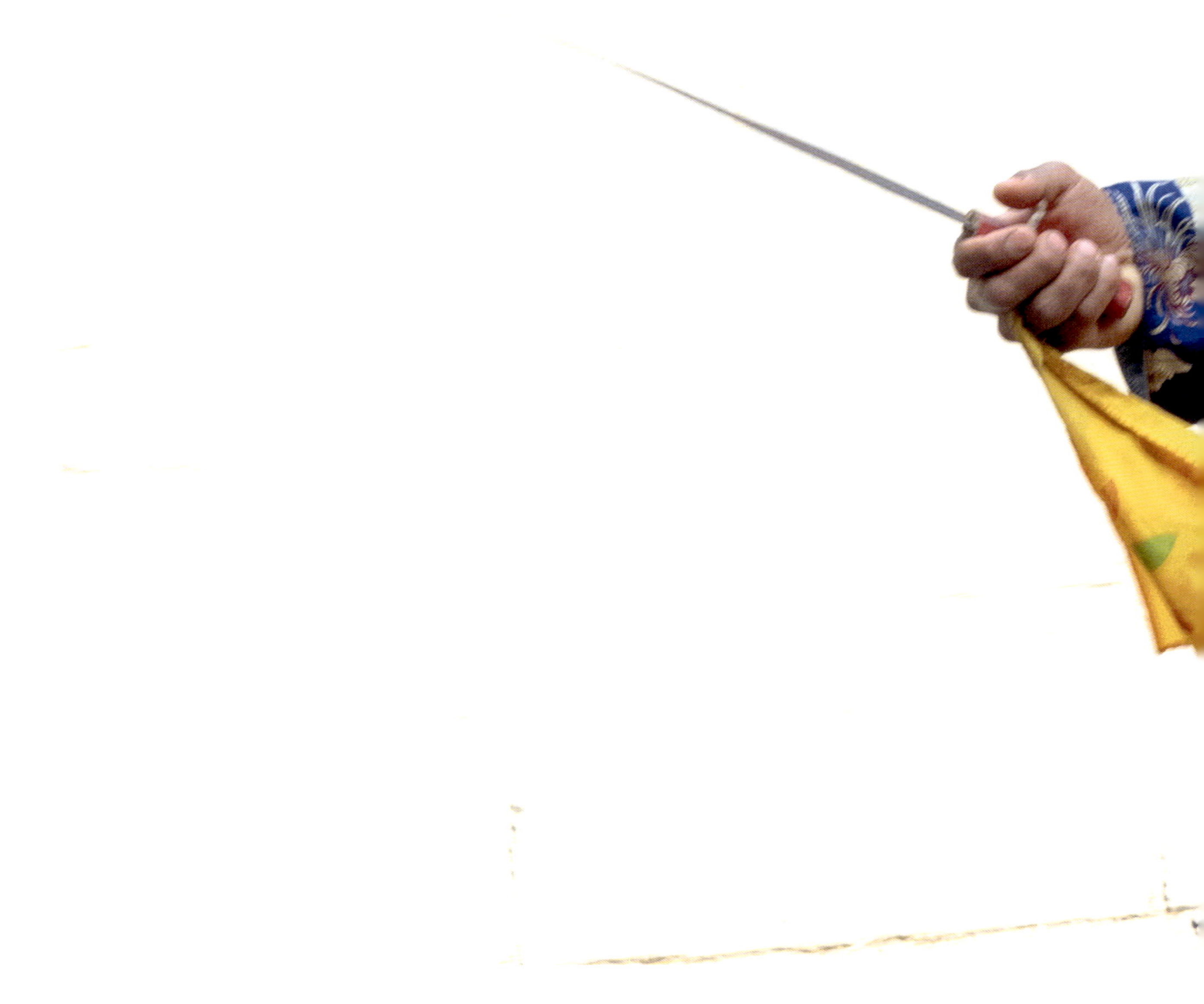

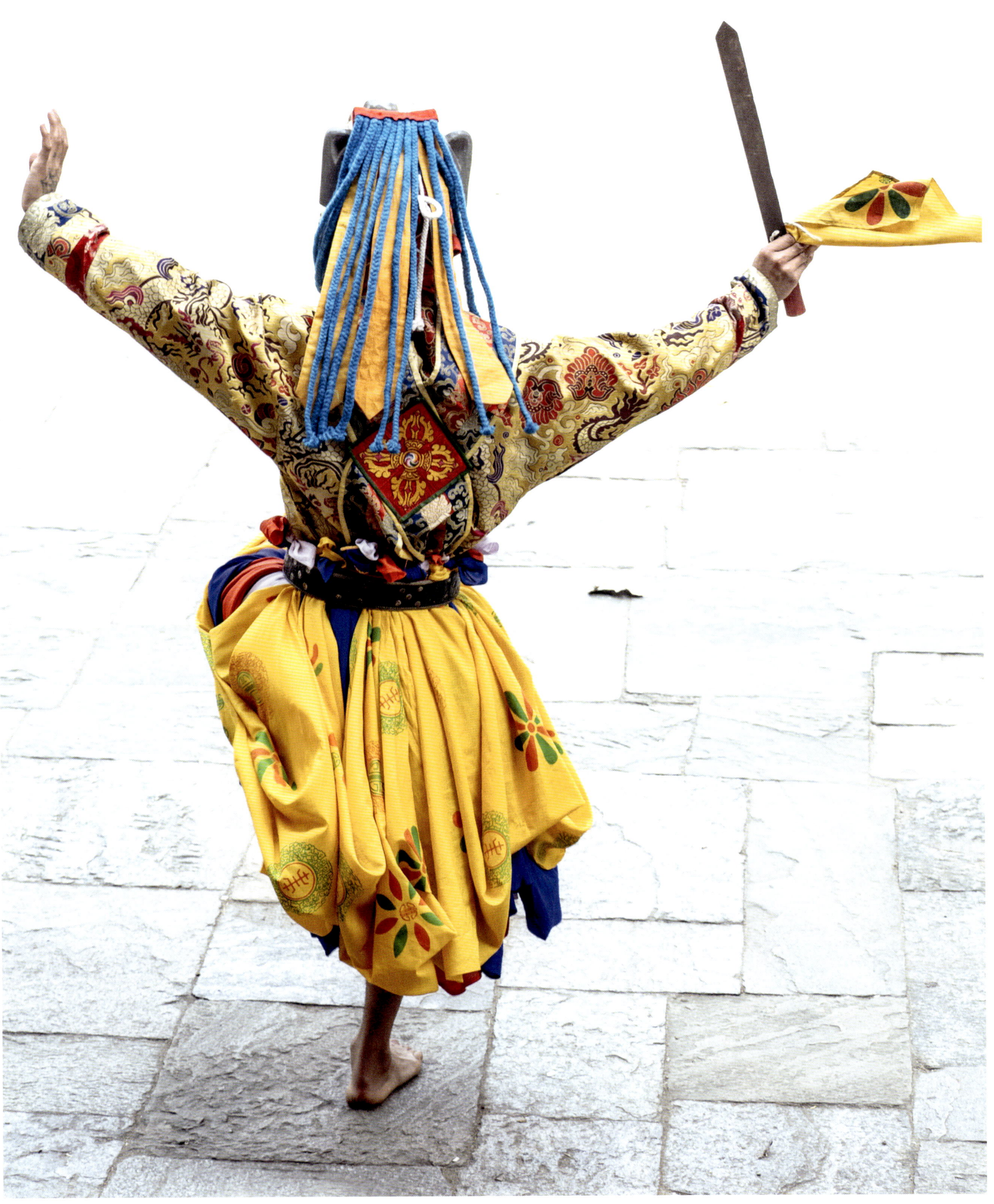

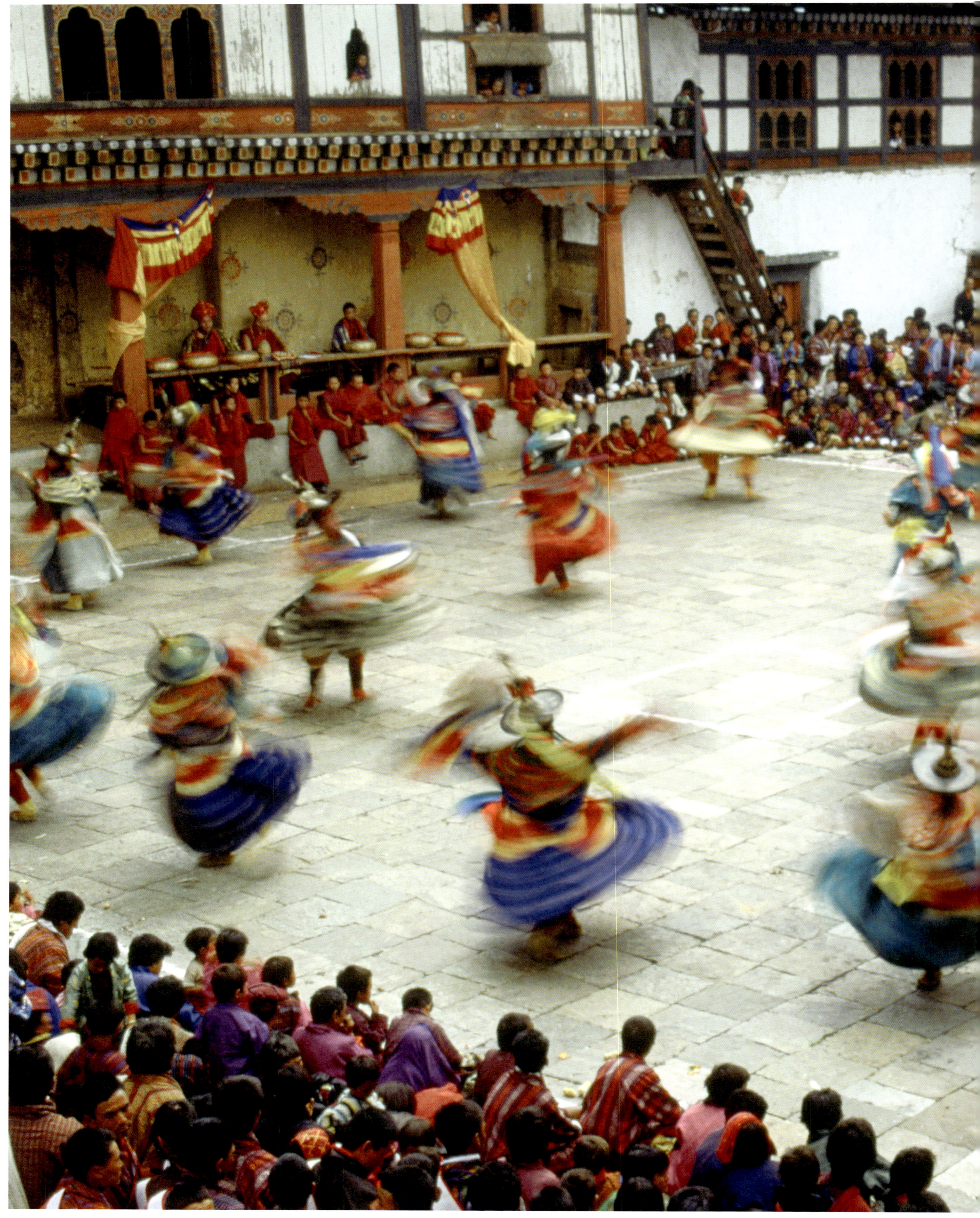

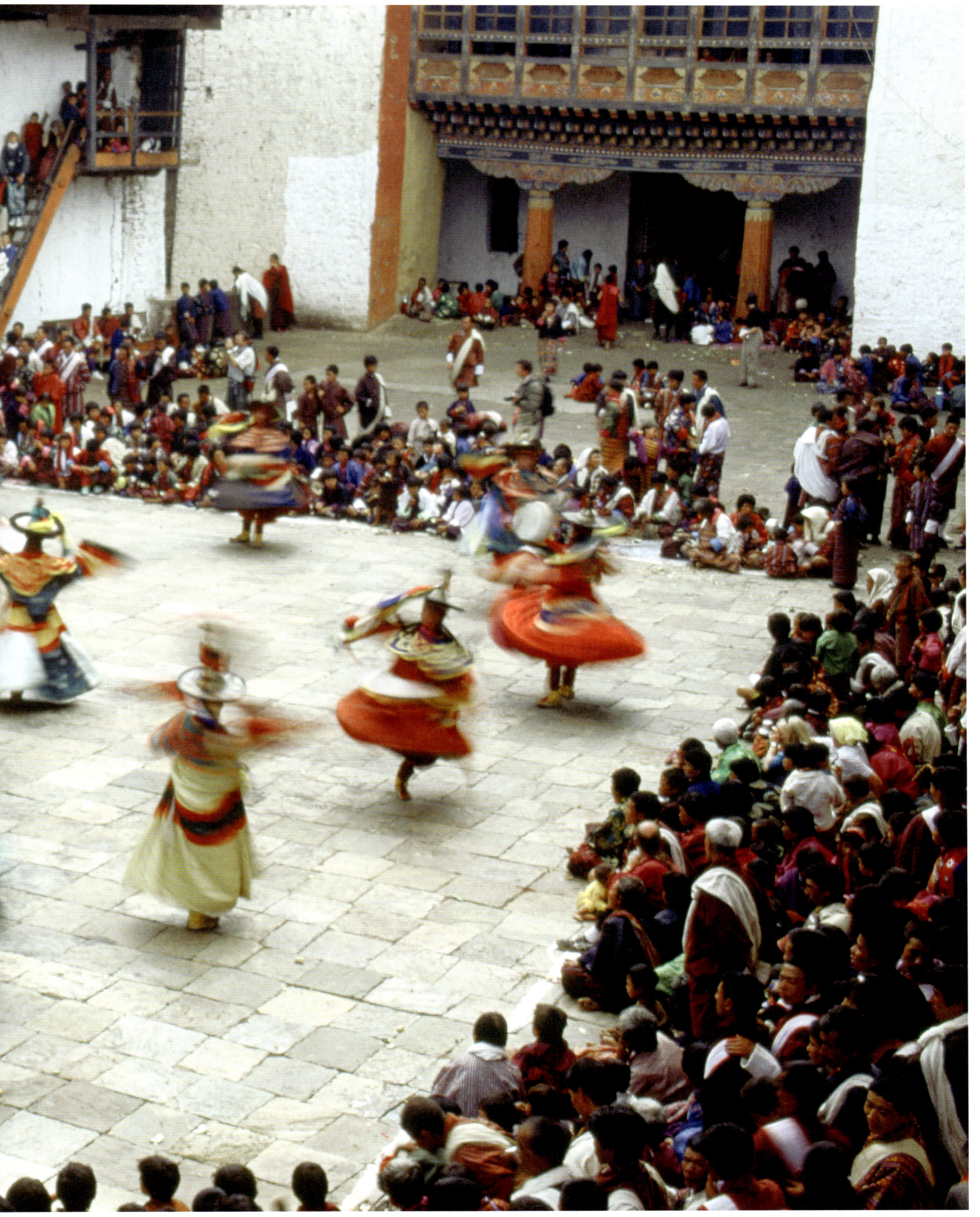

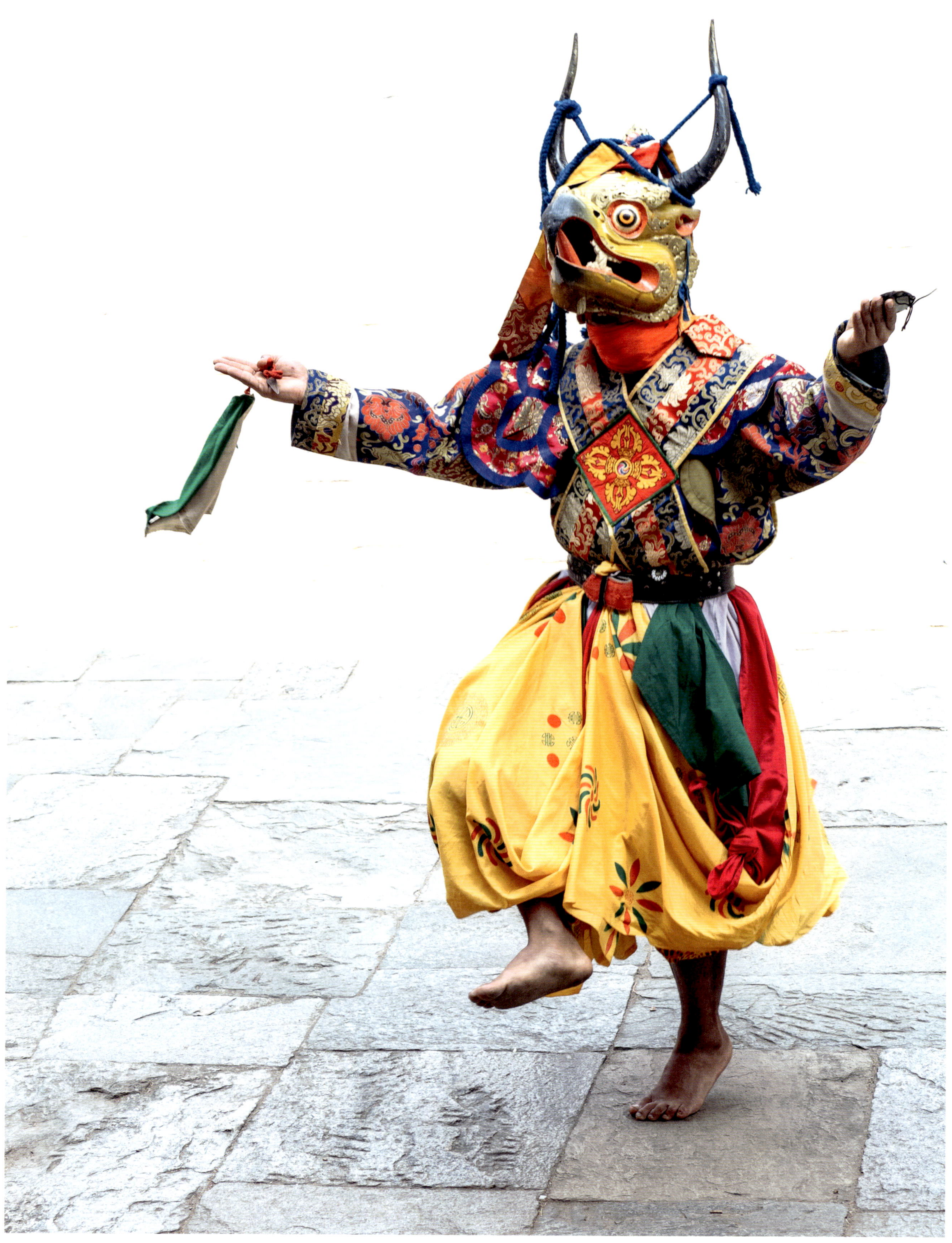

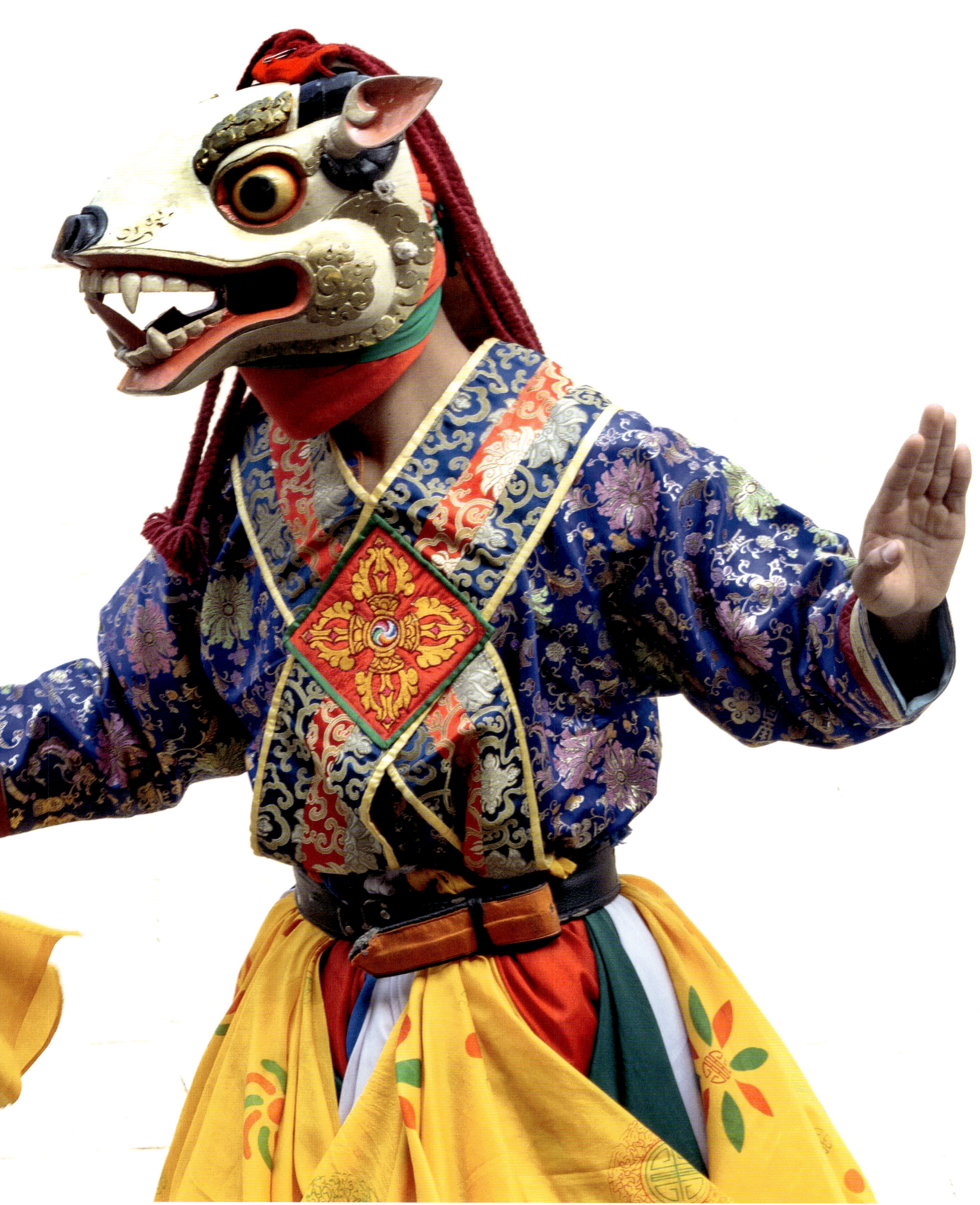

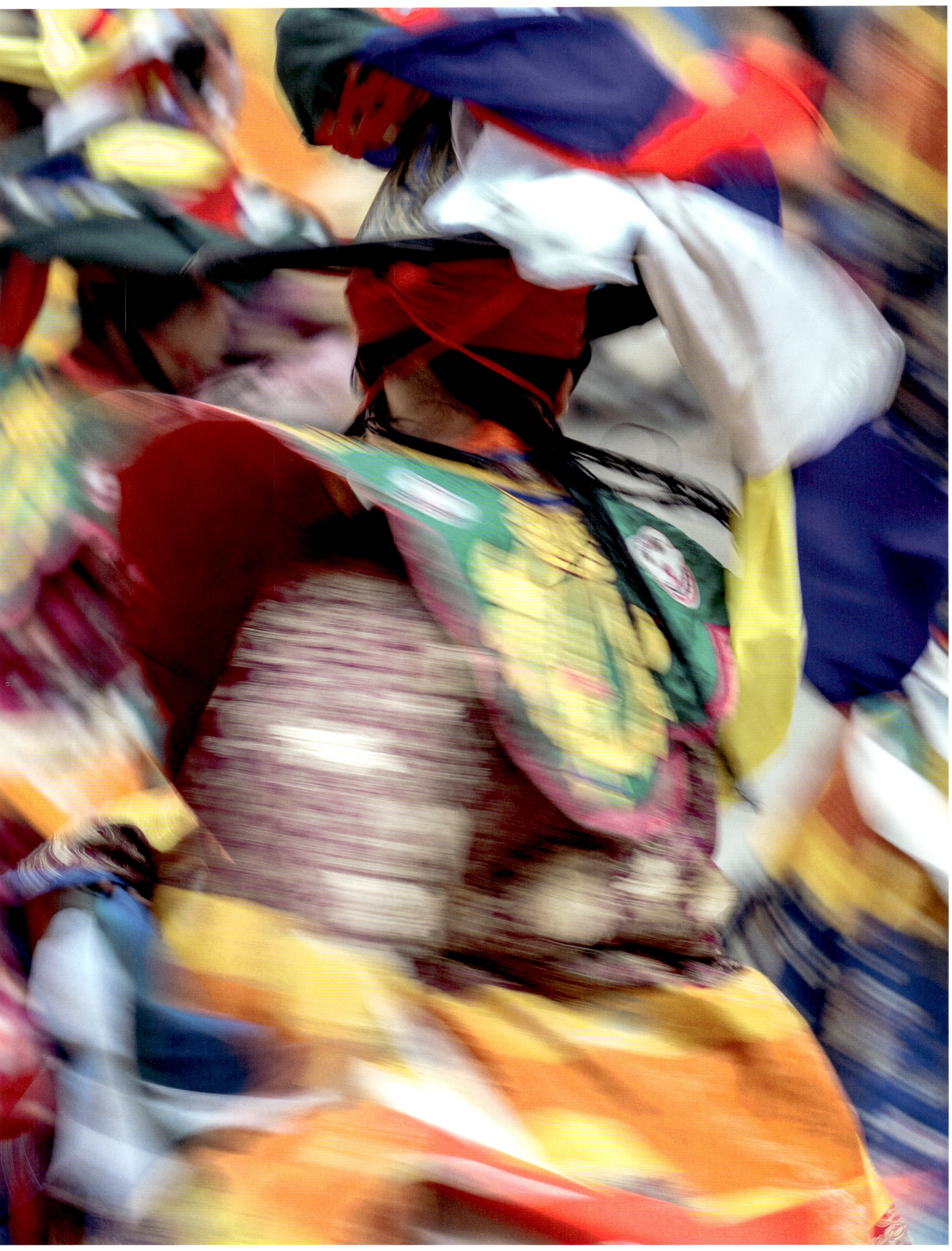

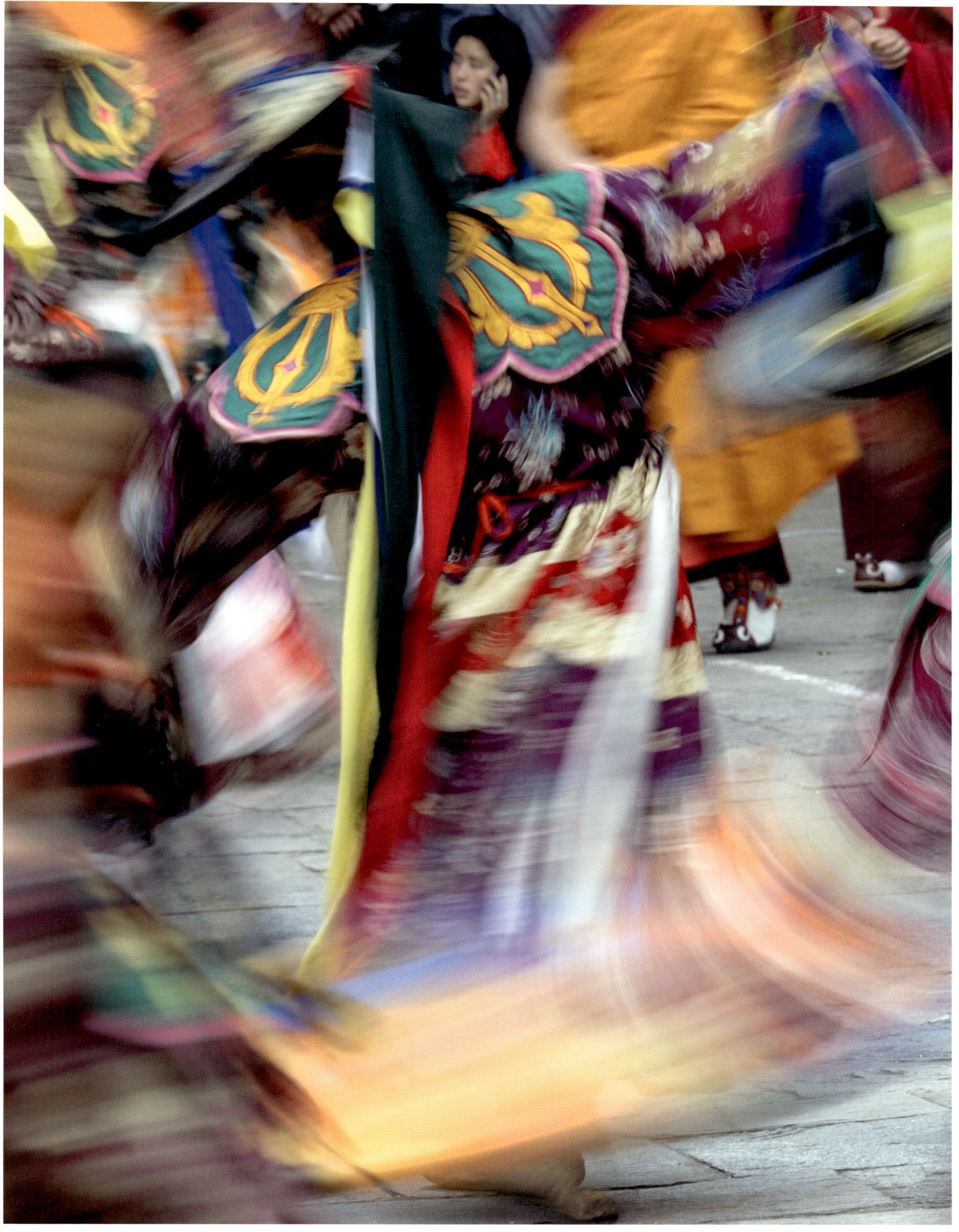

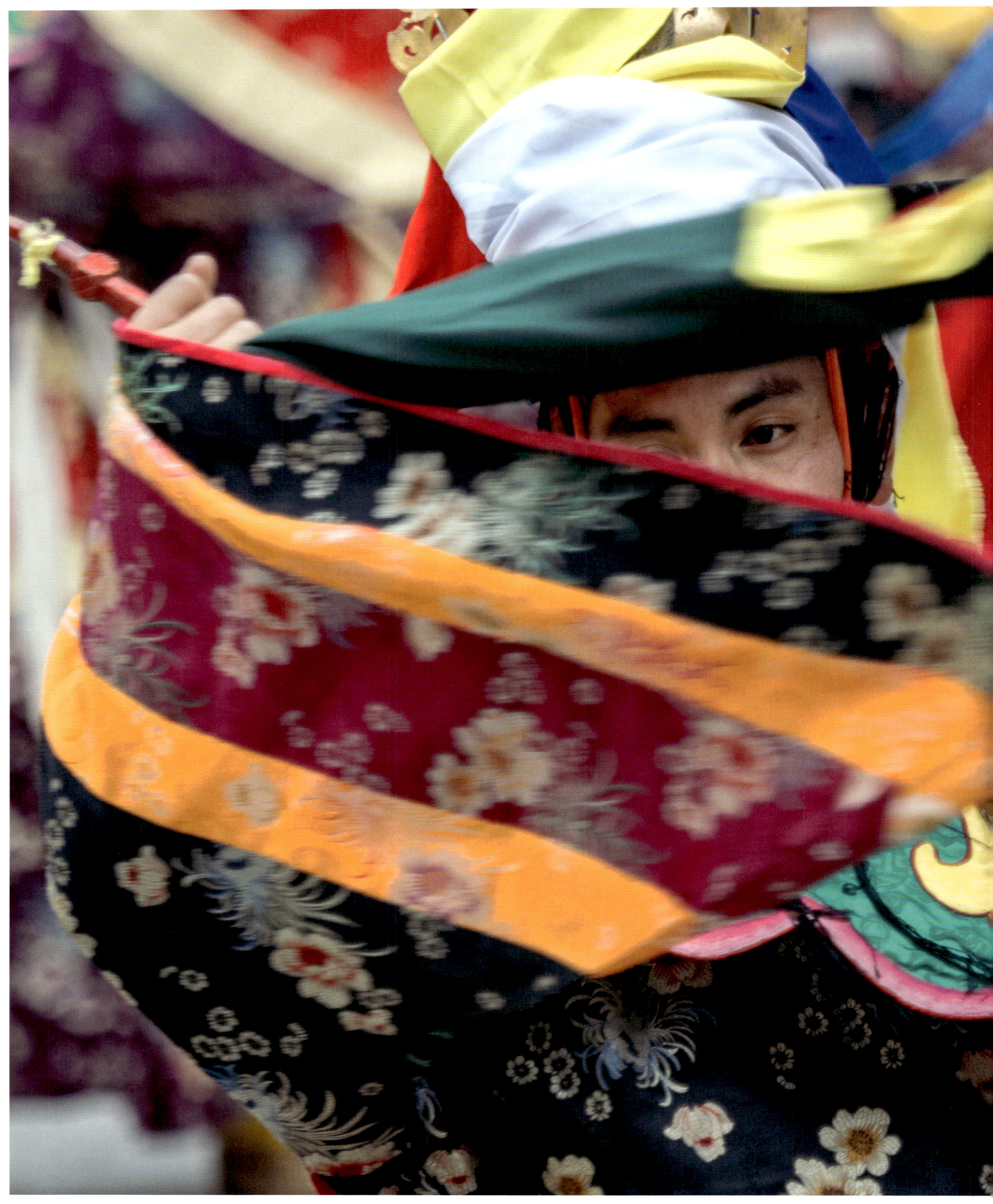

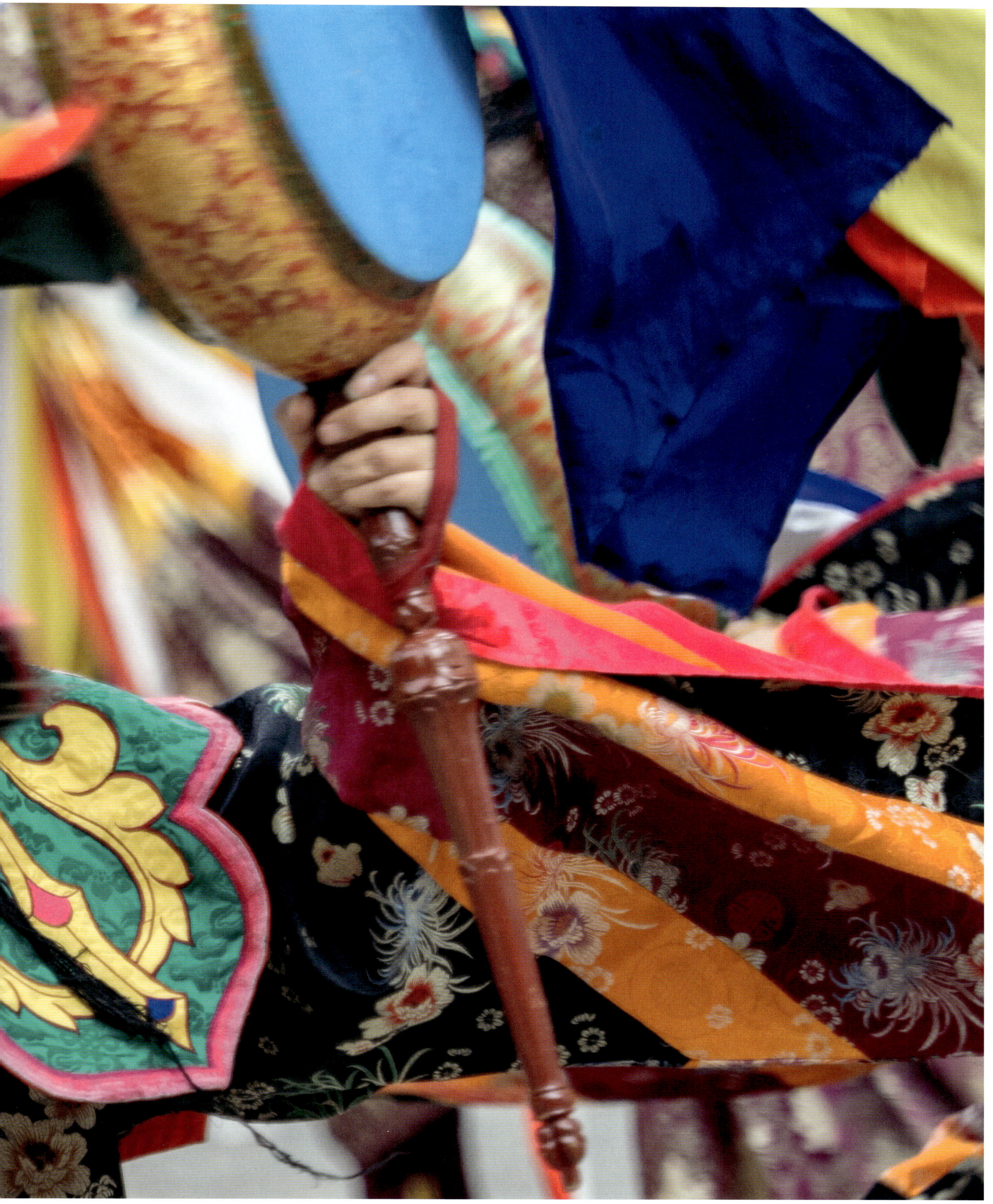

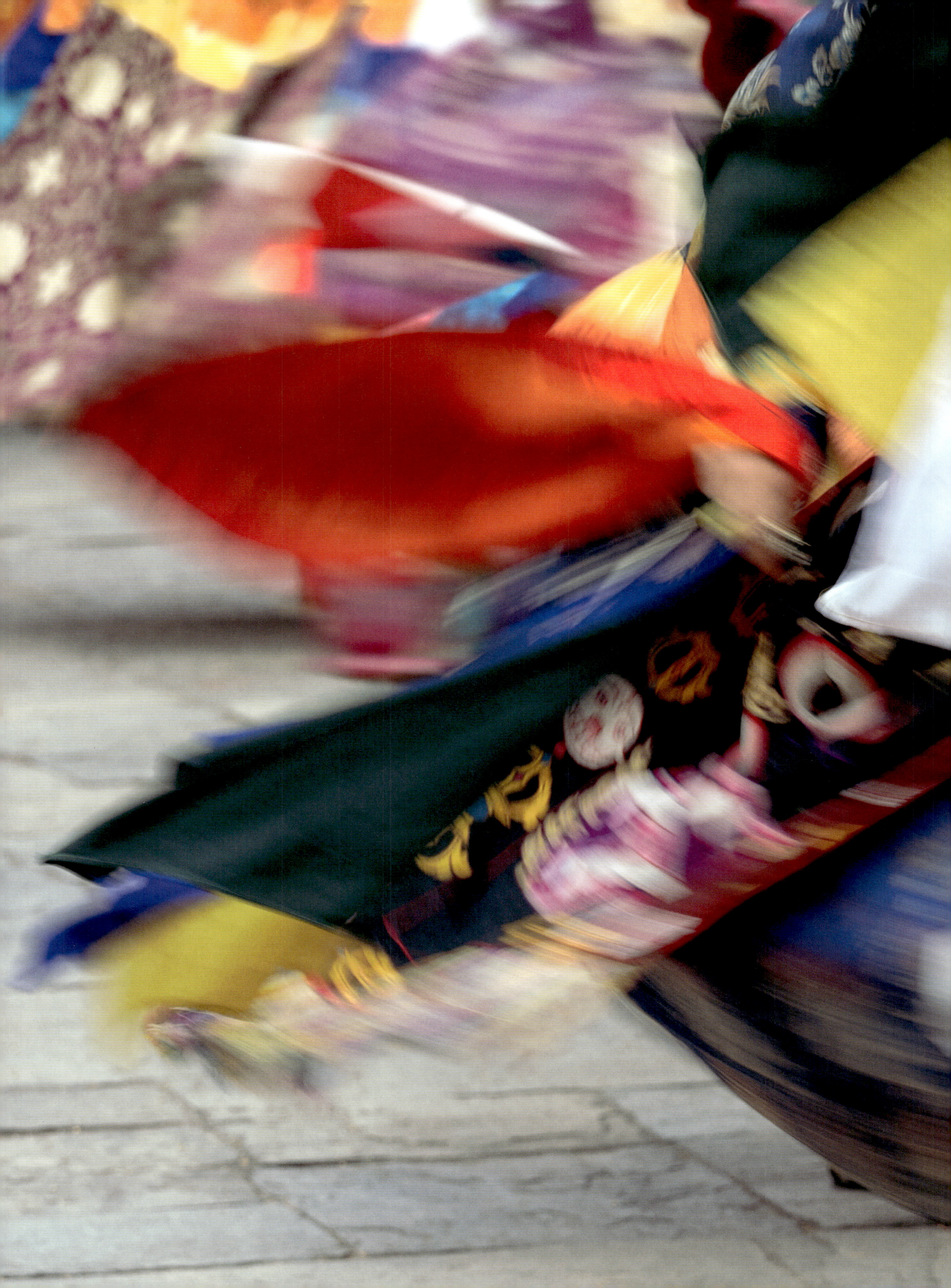

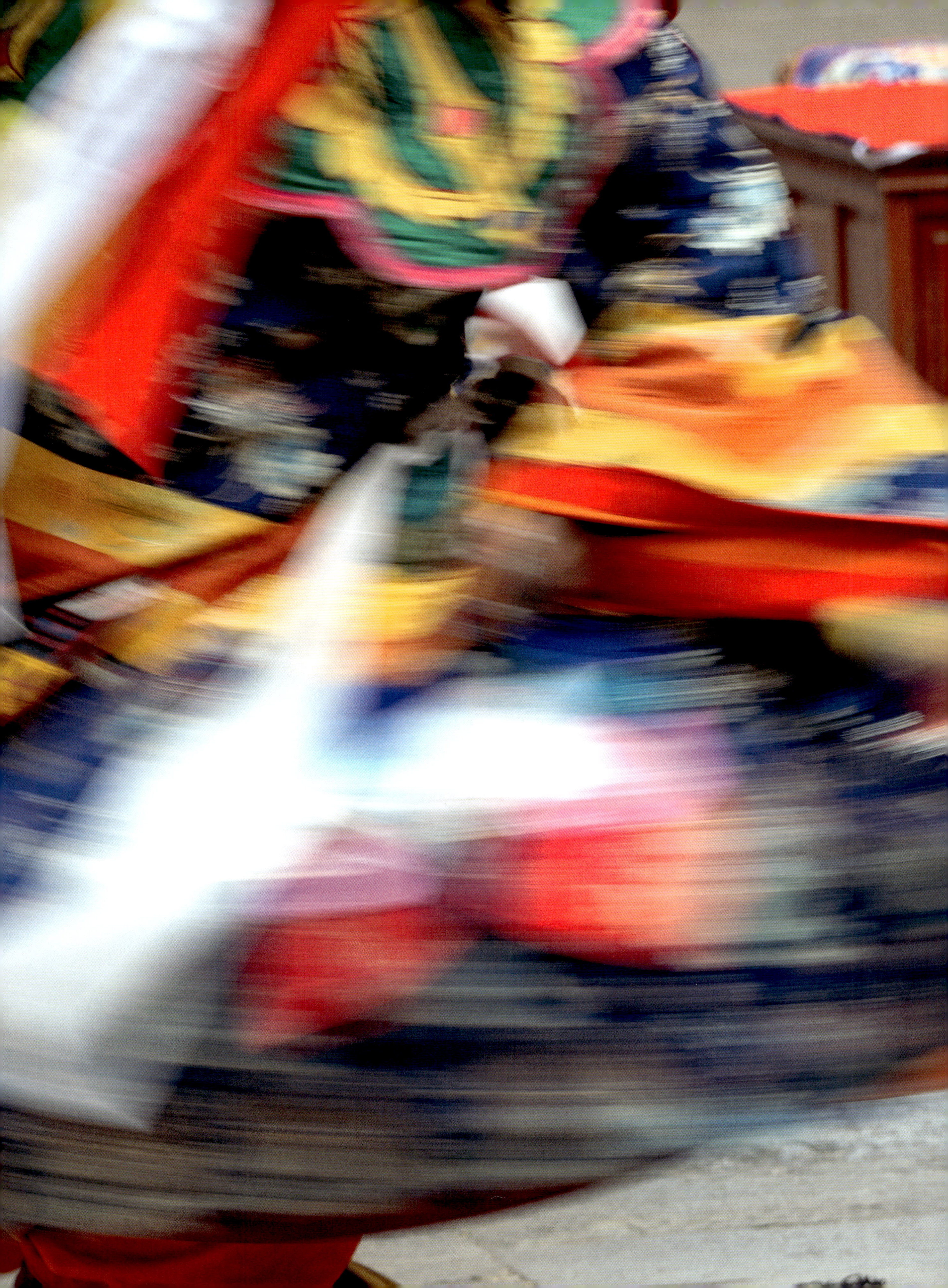

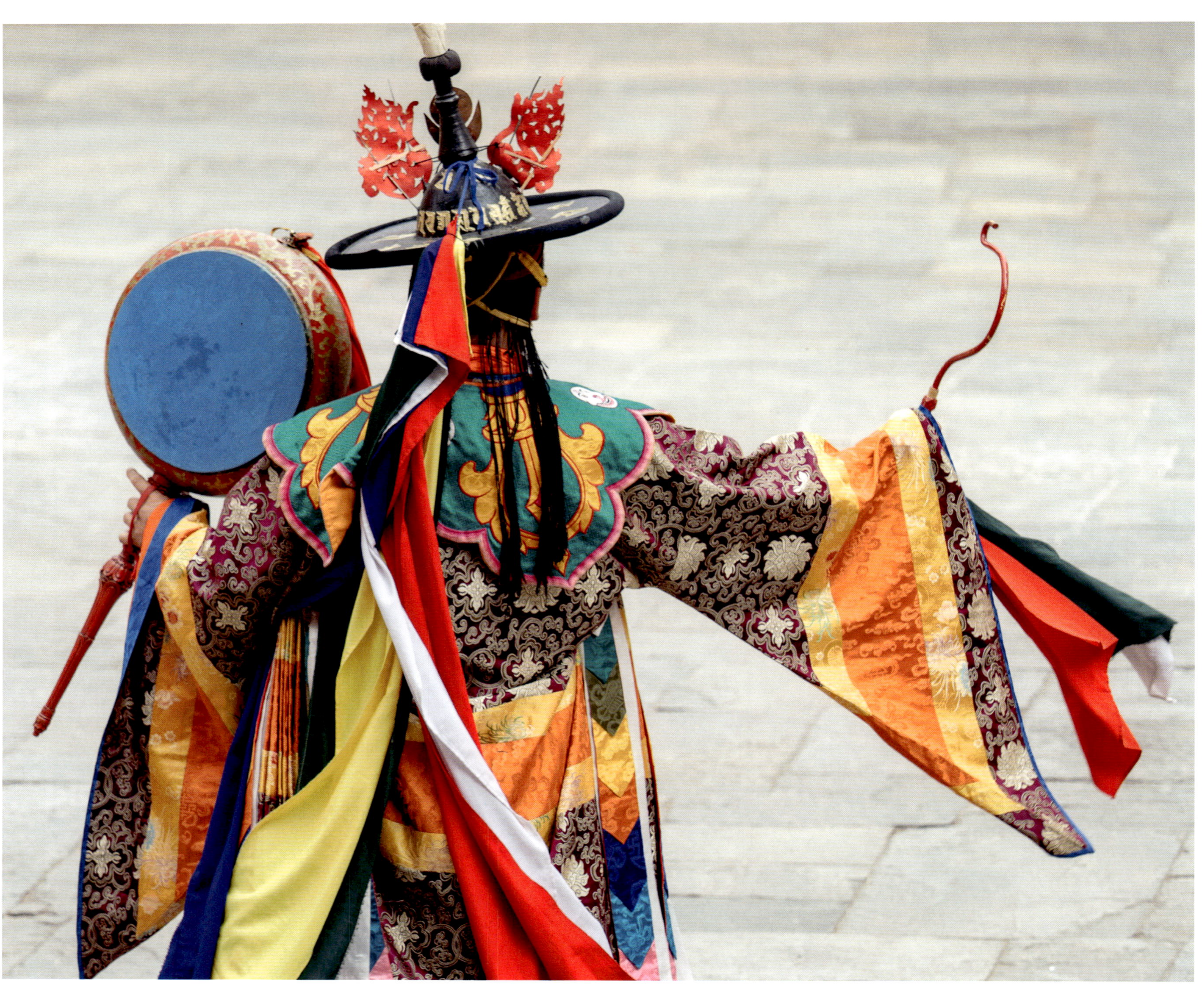

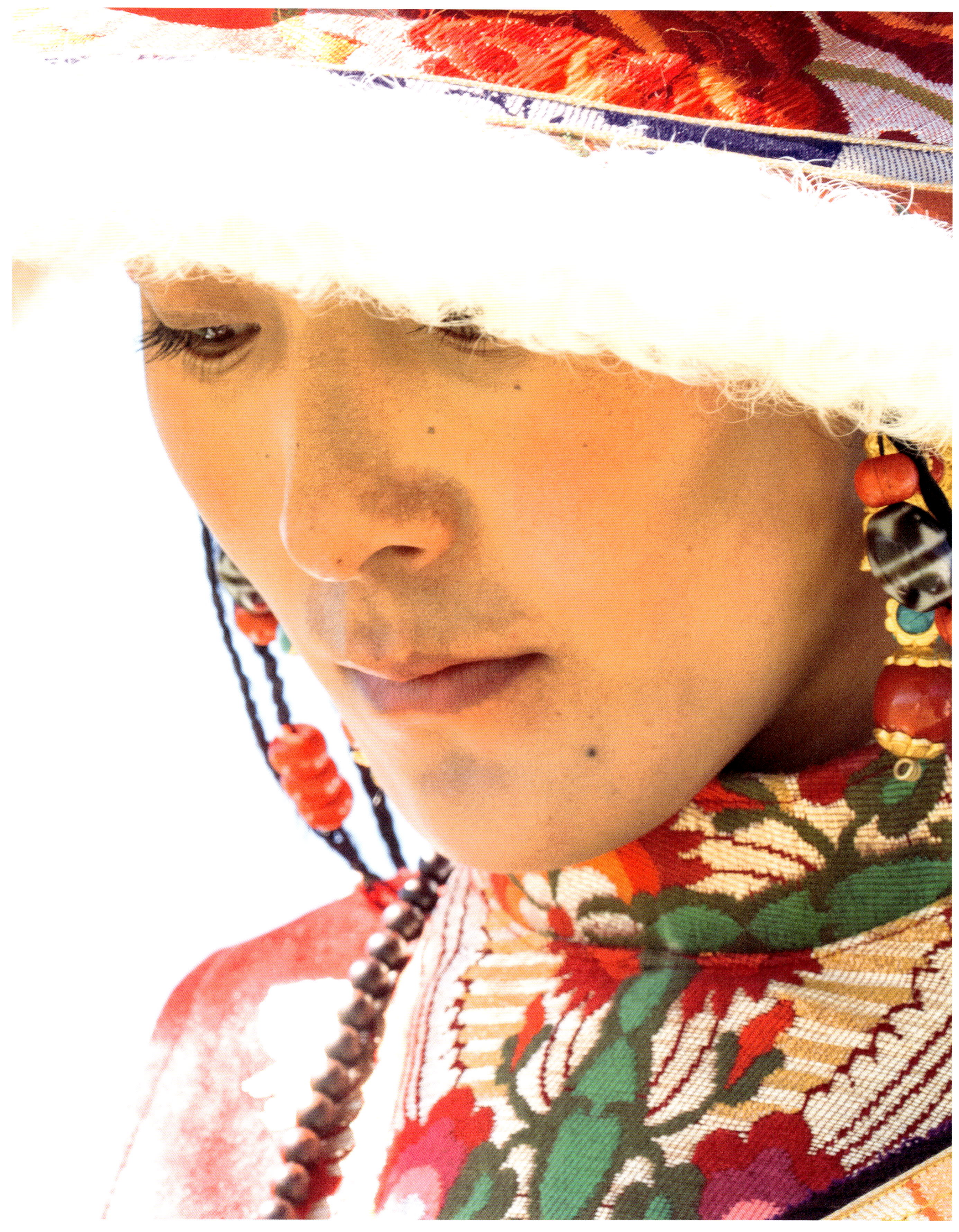

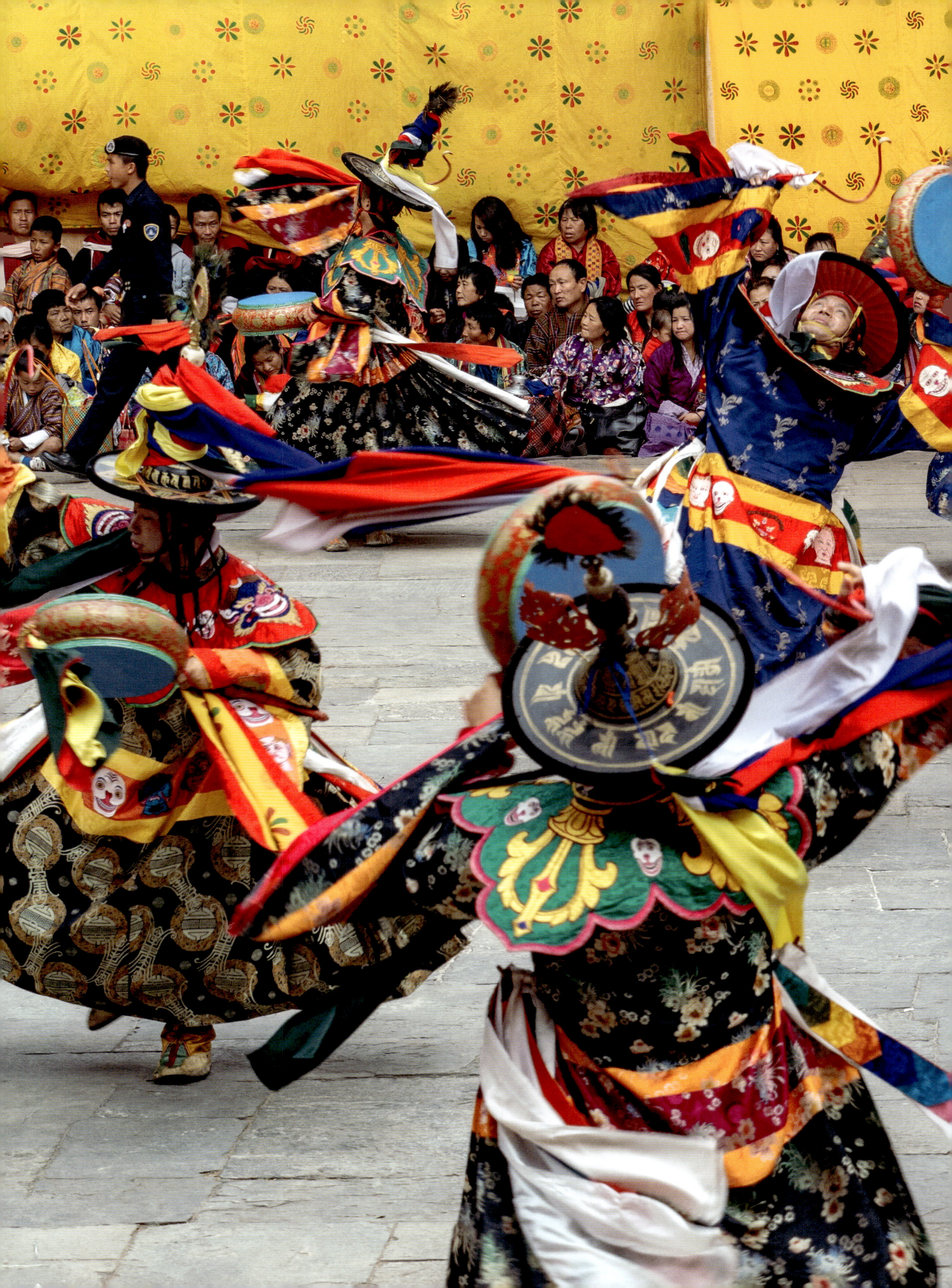

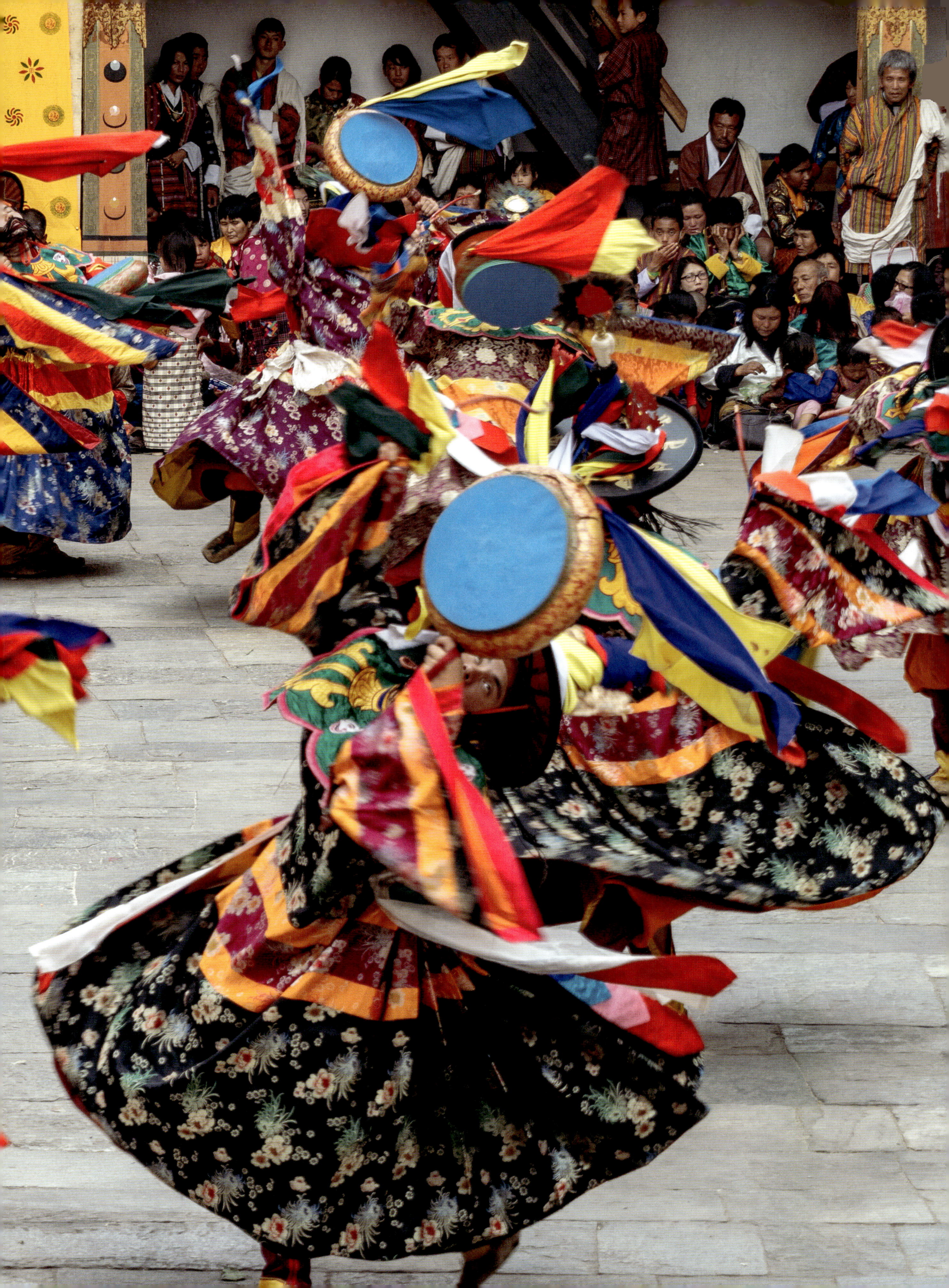

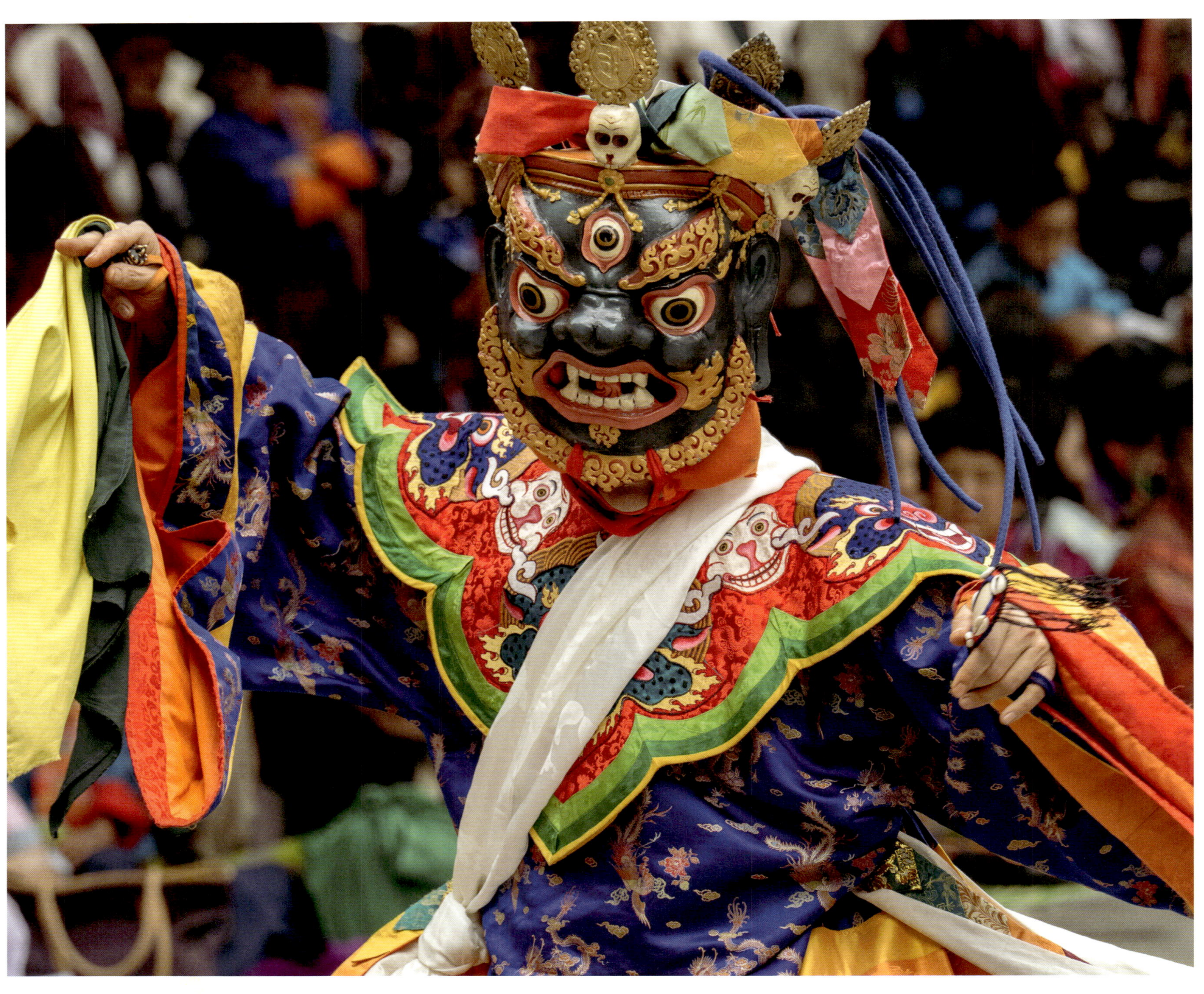

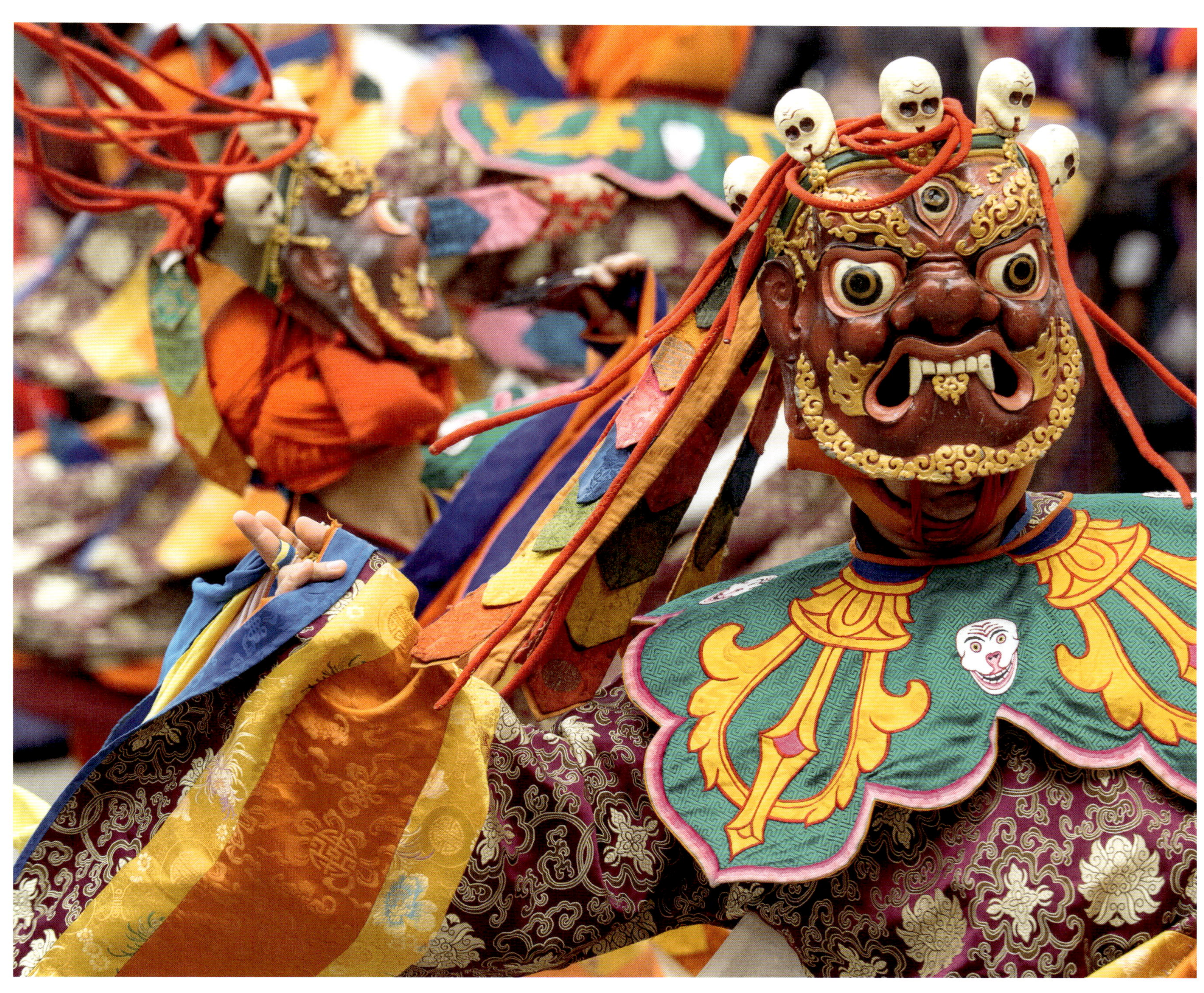

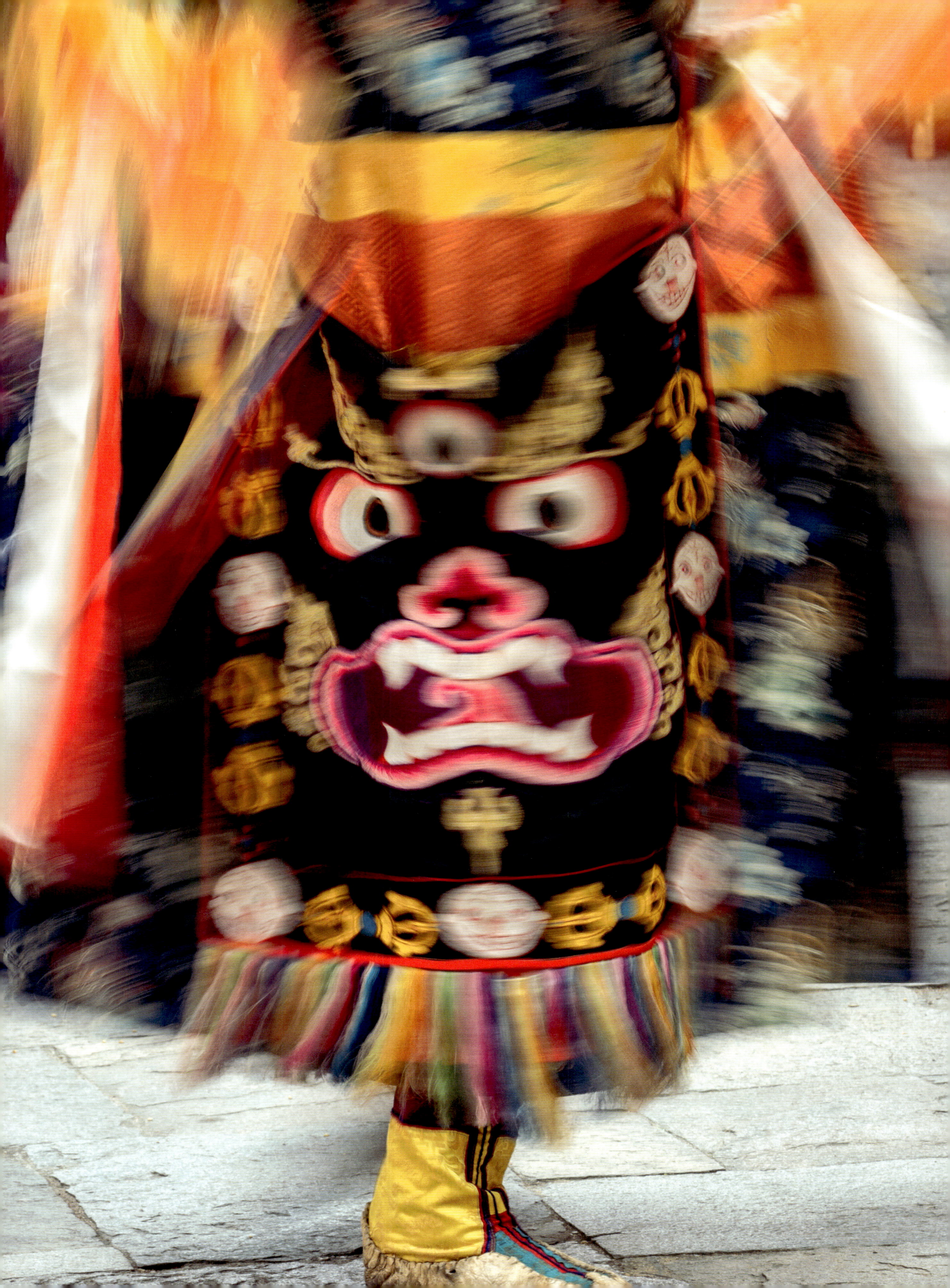

*All those who are unhappy
are so because they sought
their own happiness;
all those who are happy
are so because they sought
the happiness of others.*

Shantideva

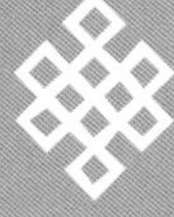

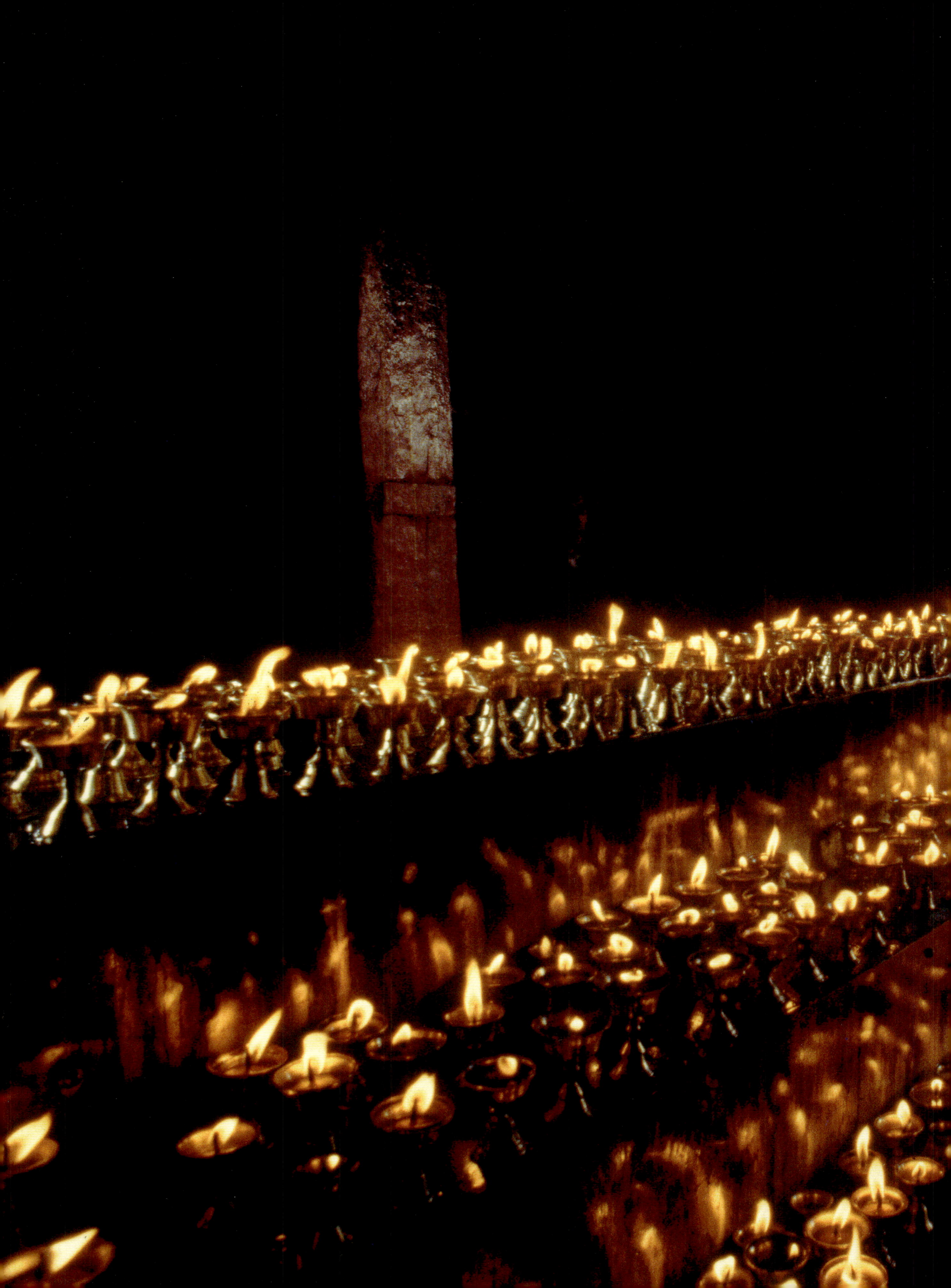

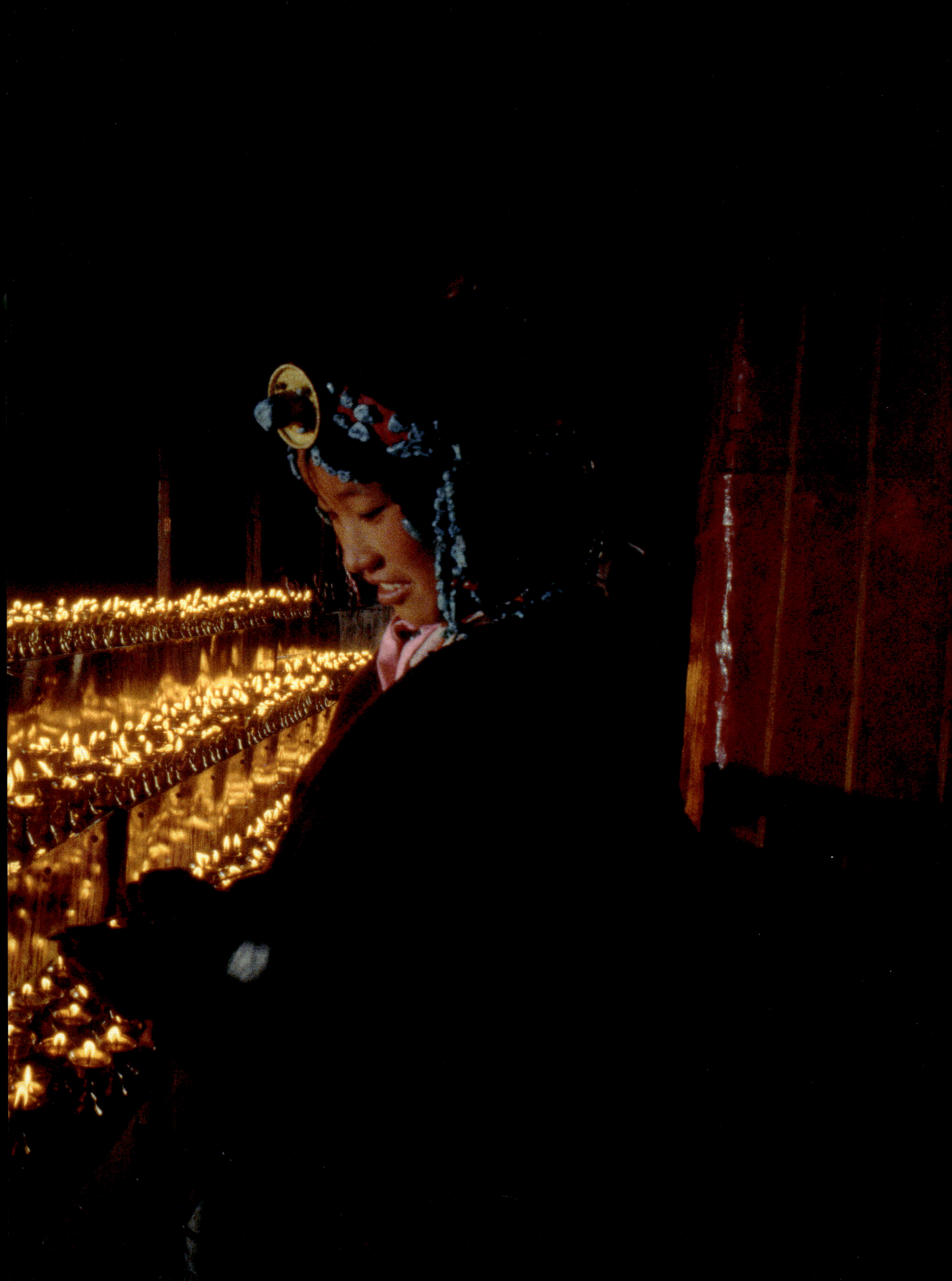

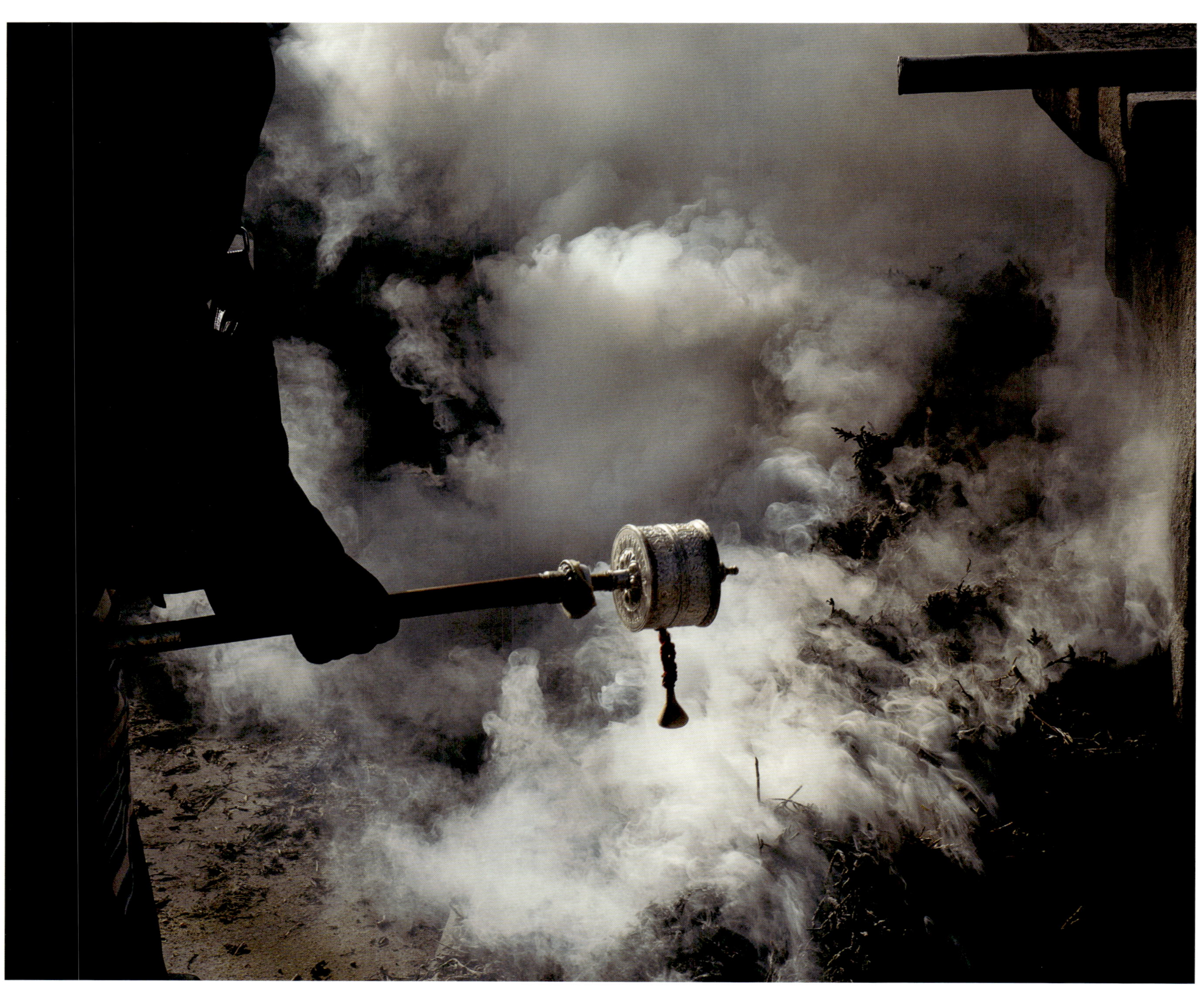

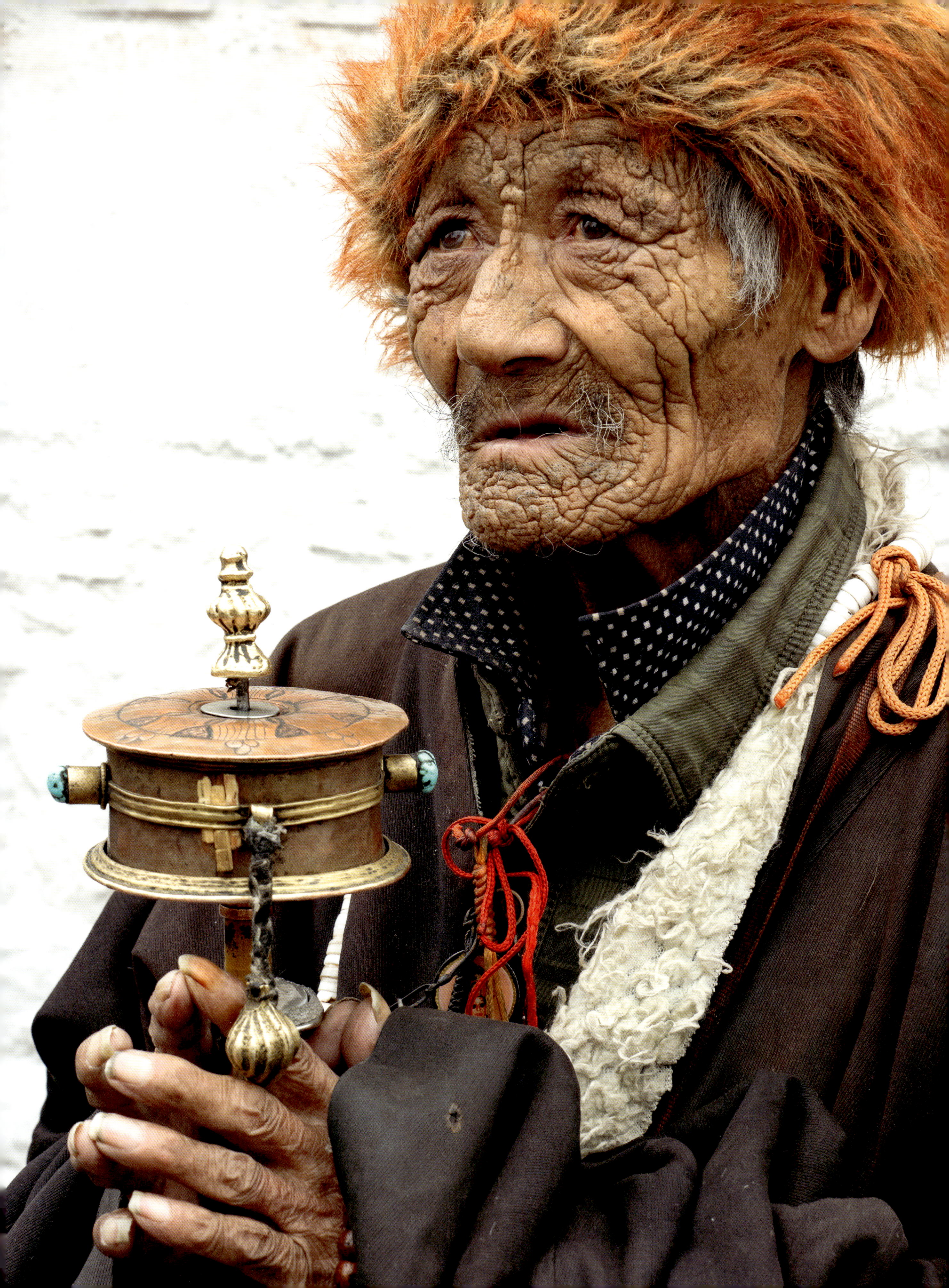

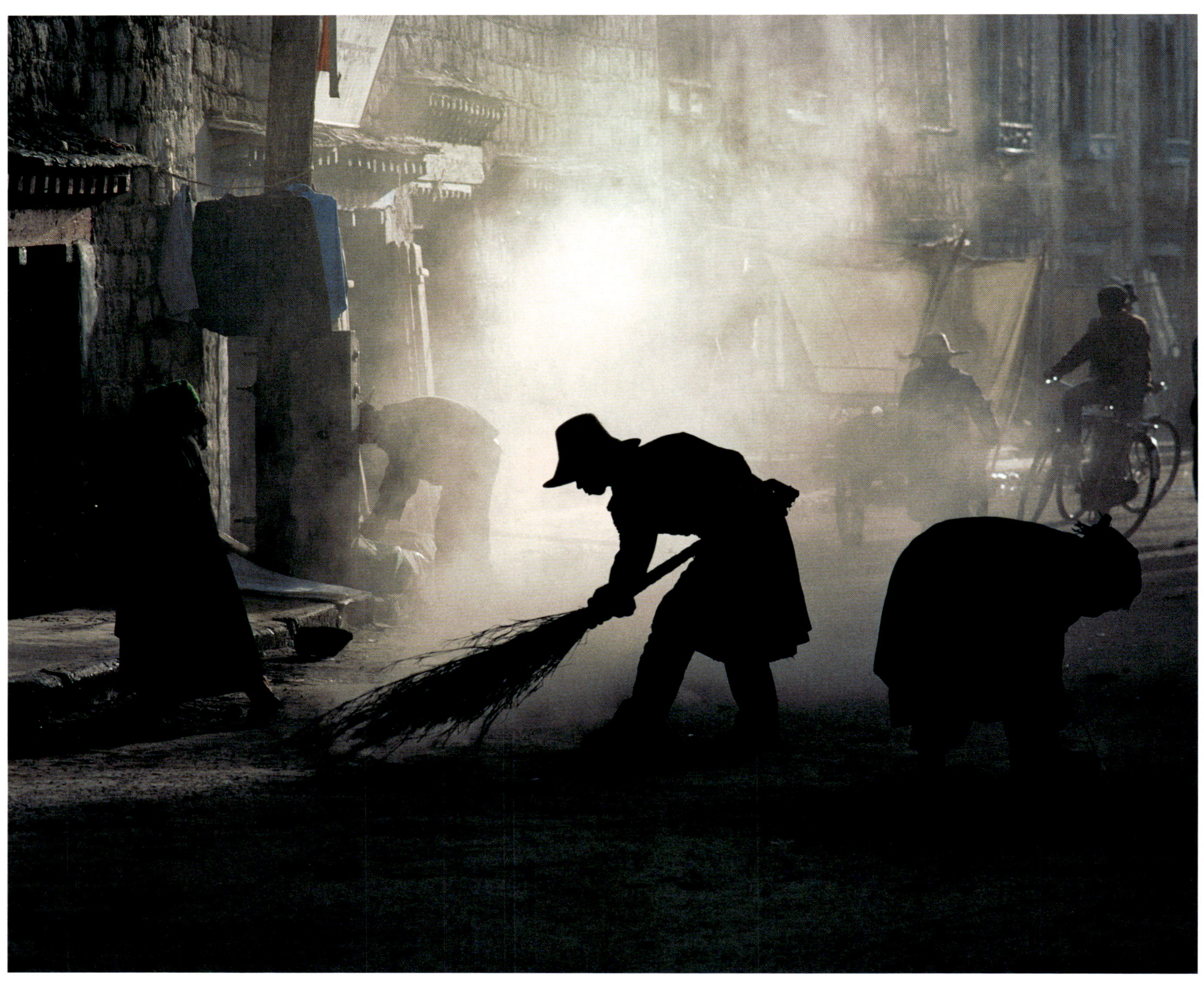

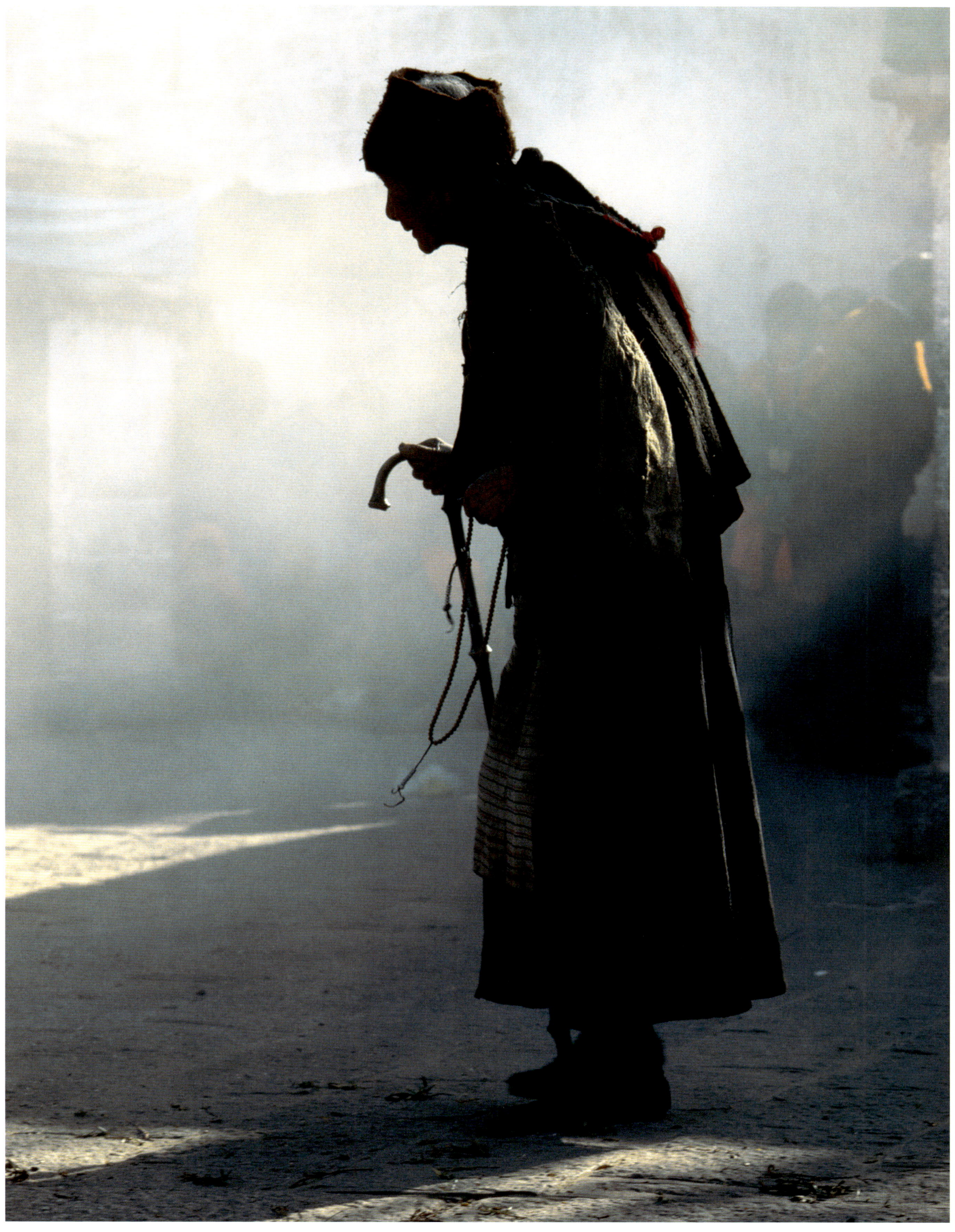

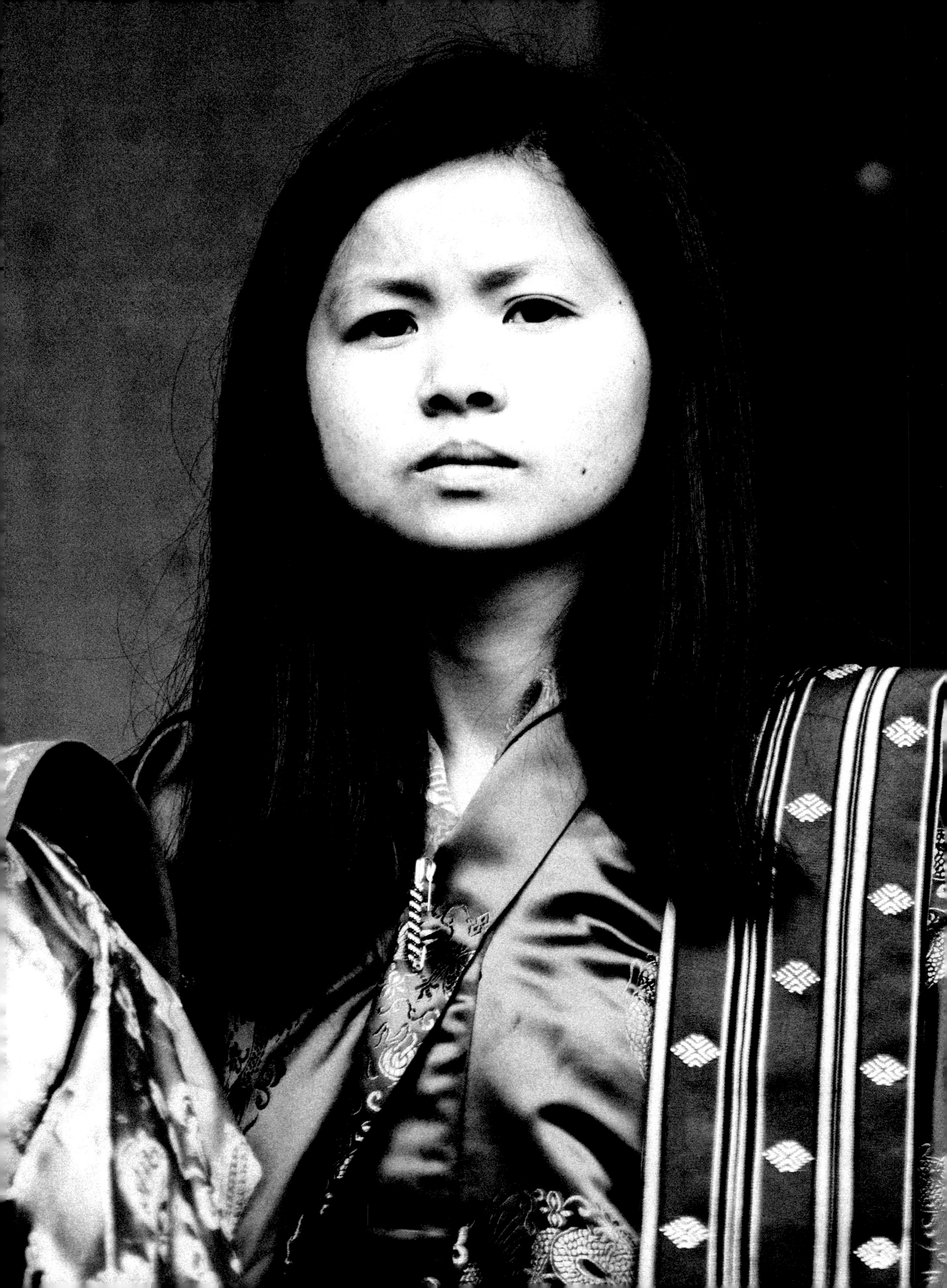

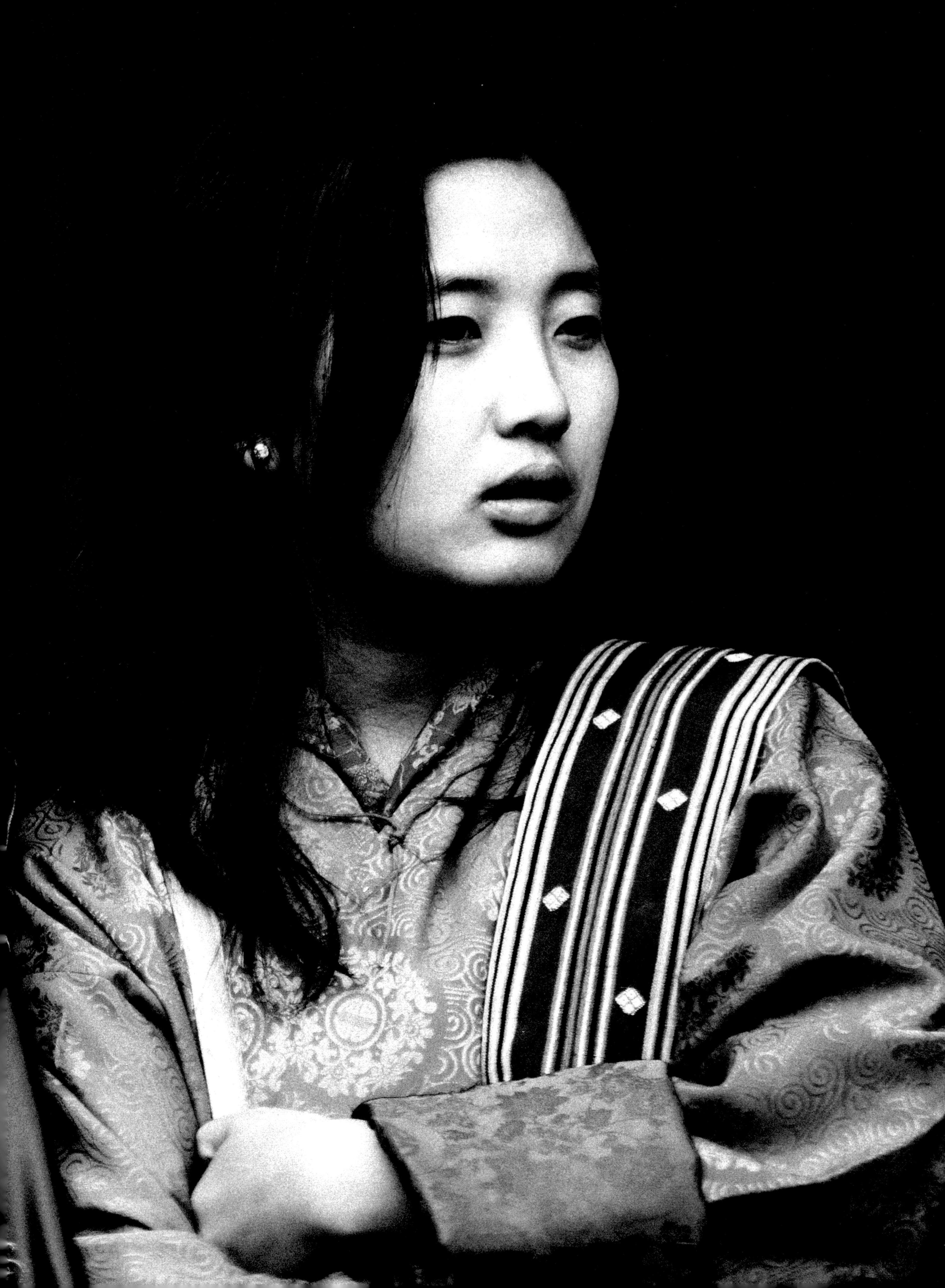

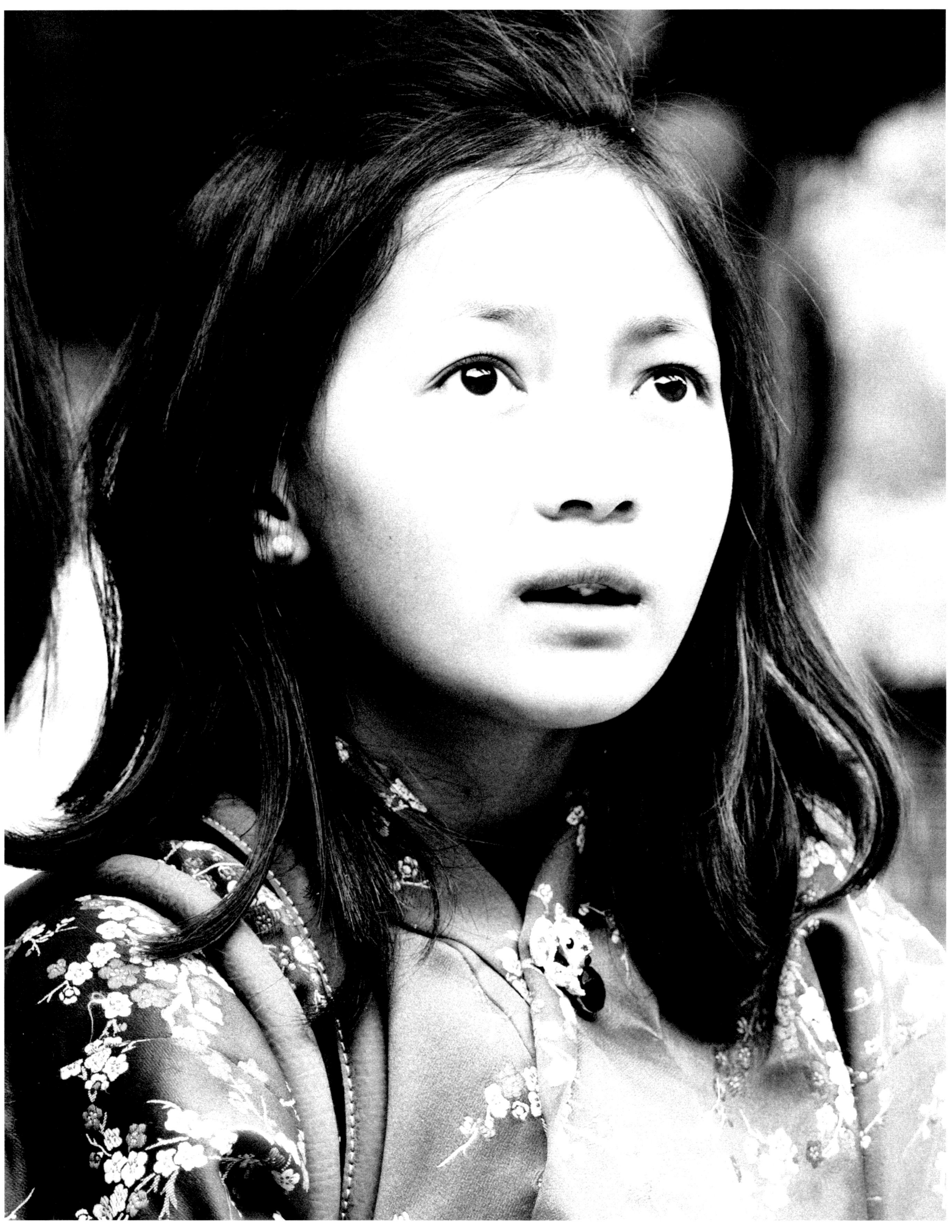

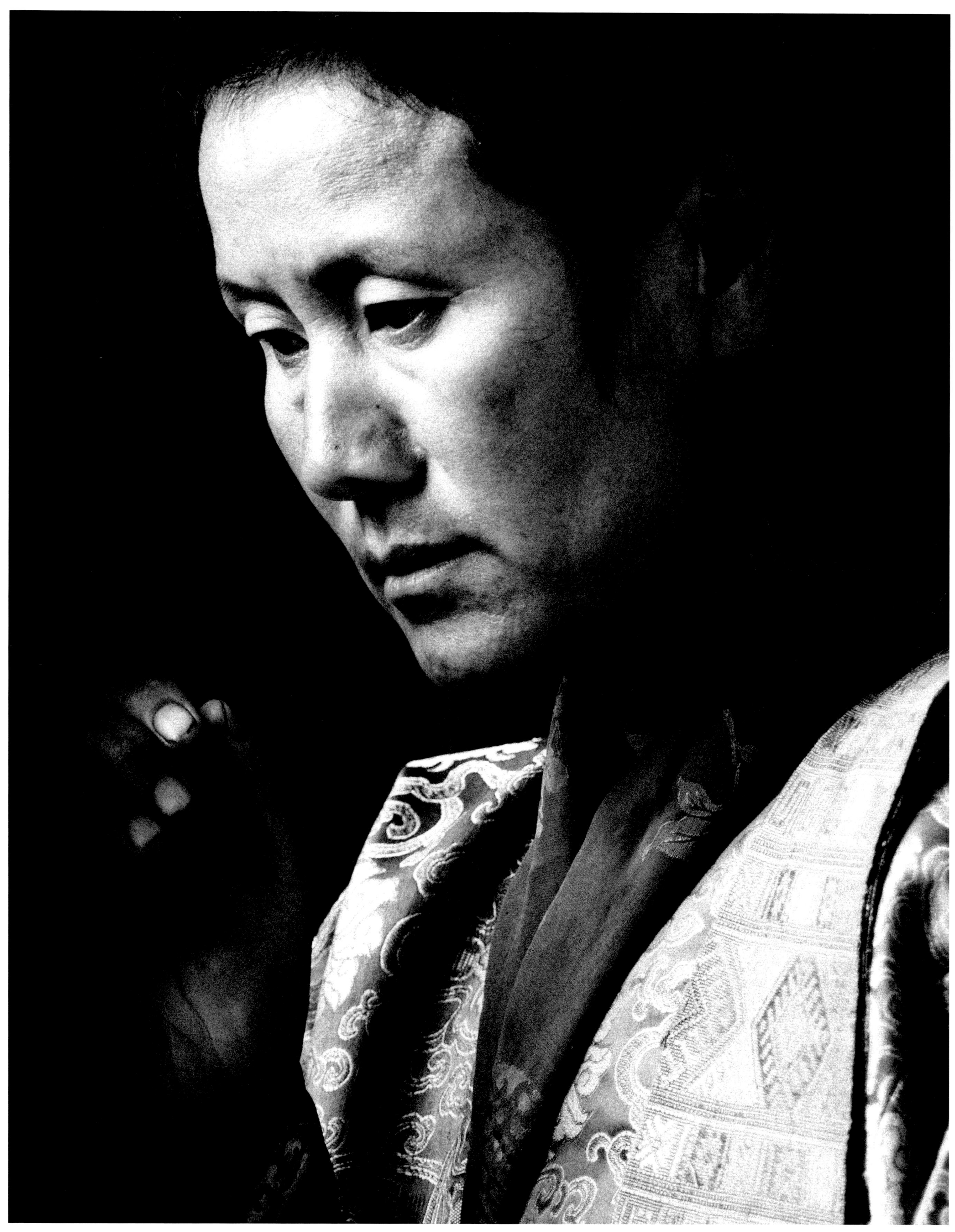

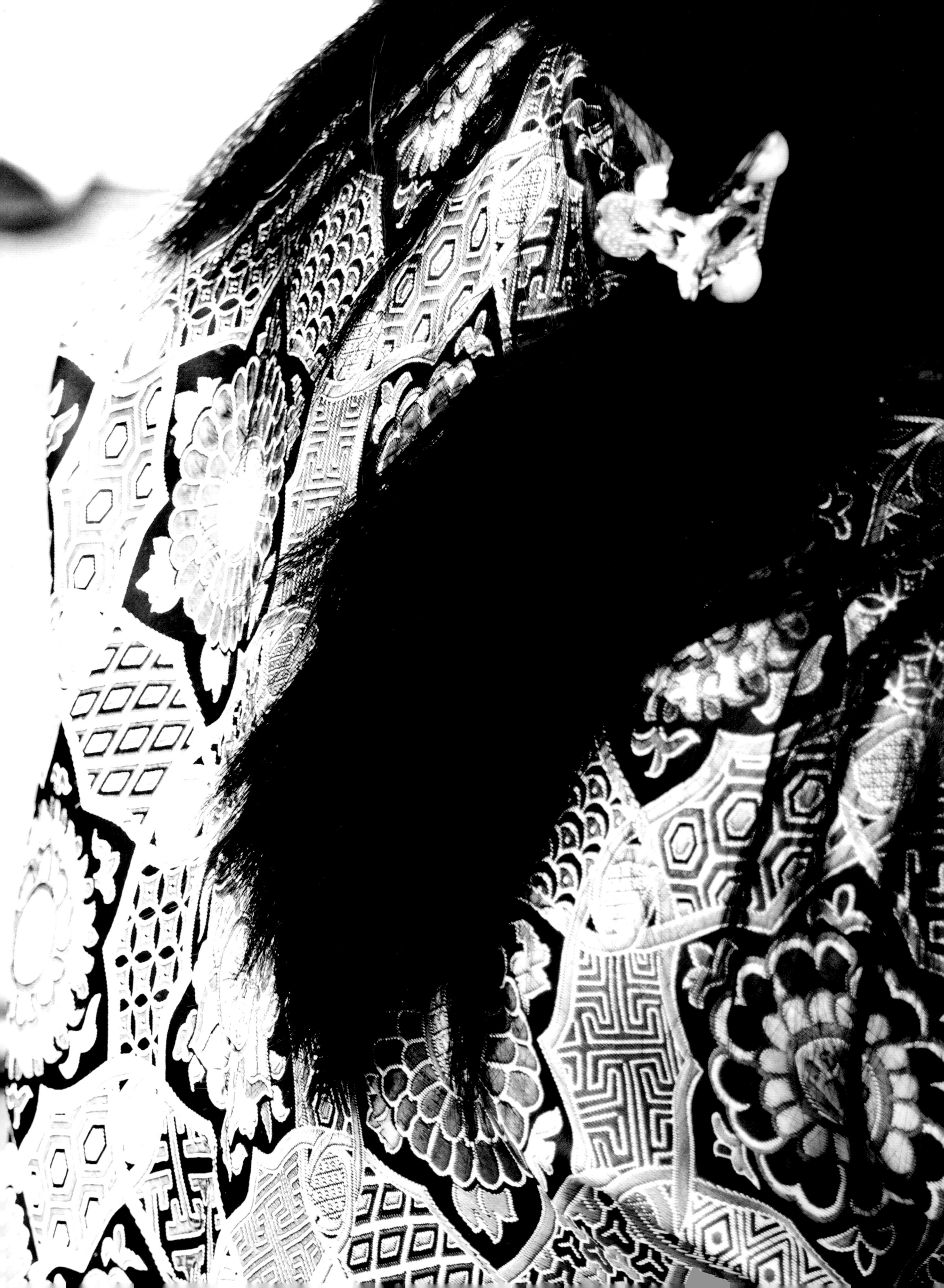

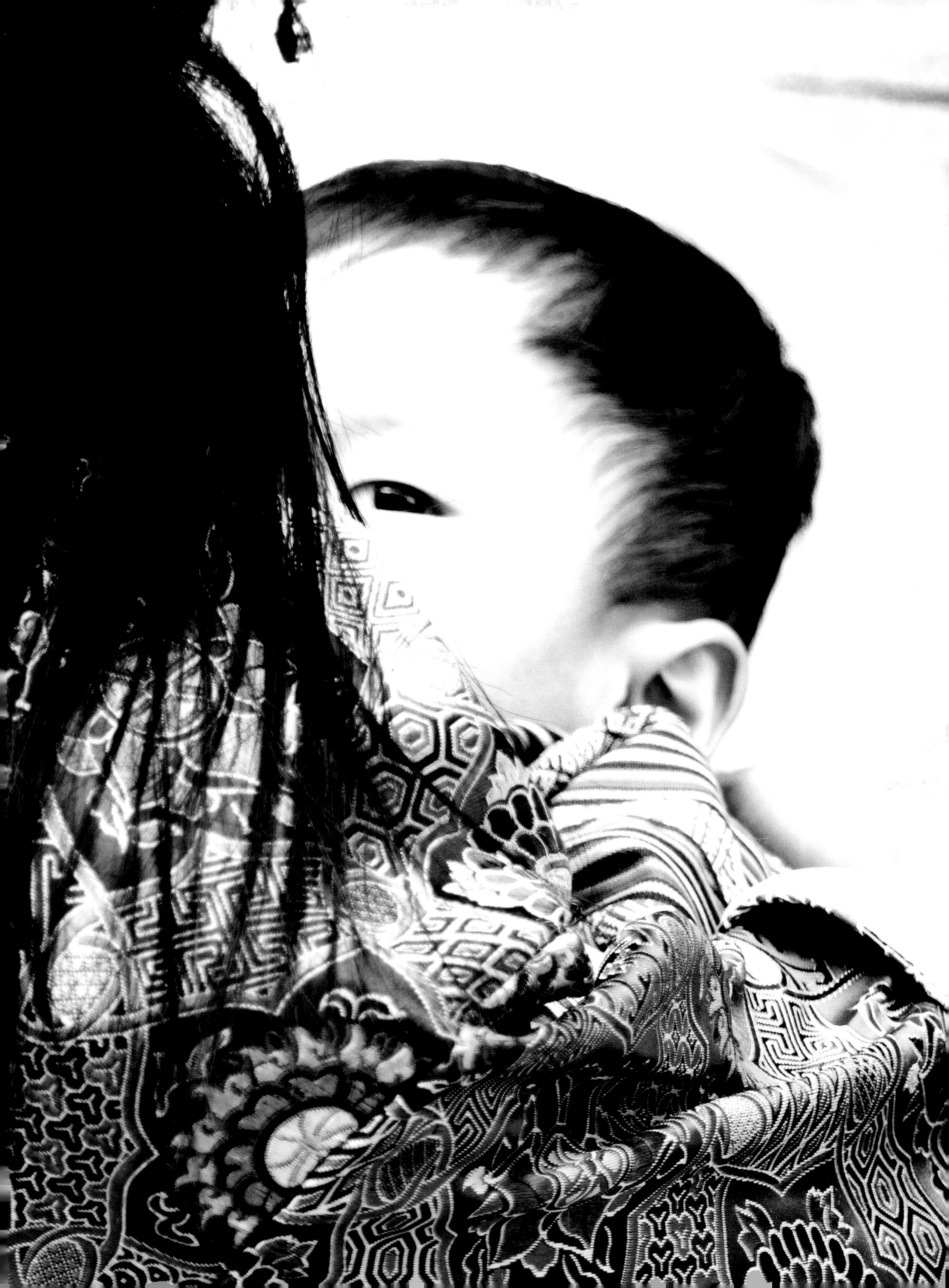

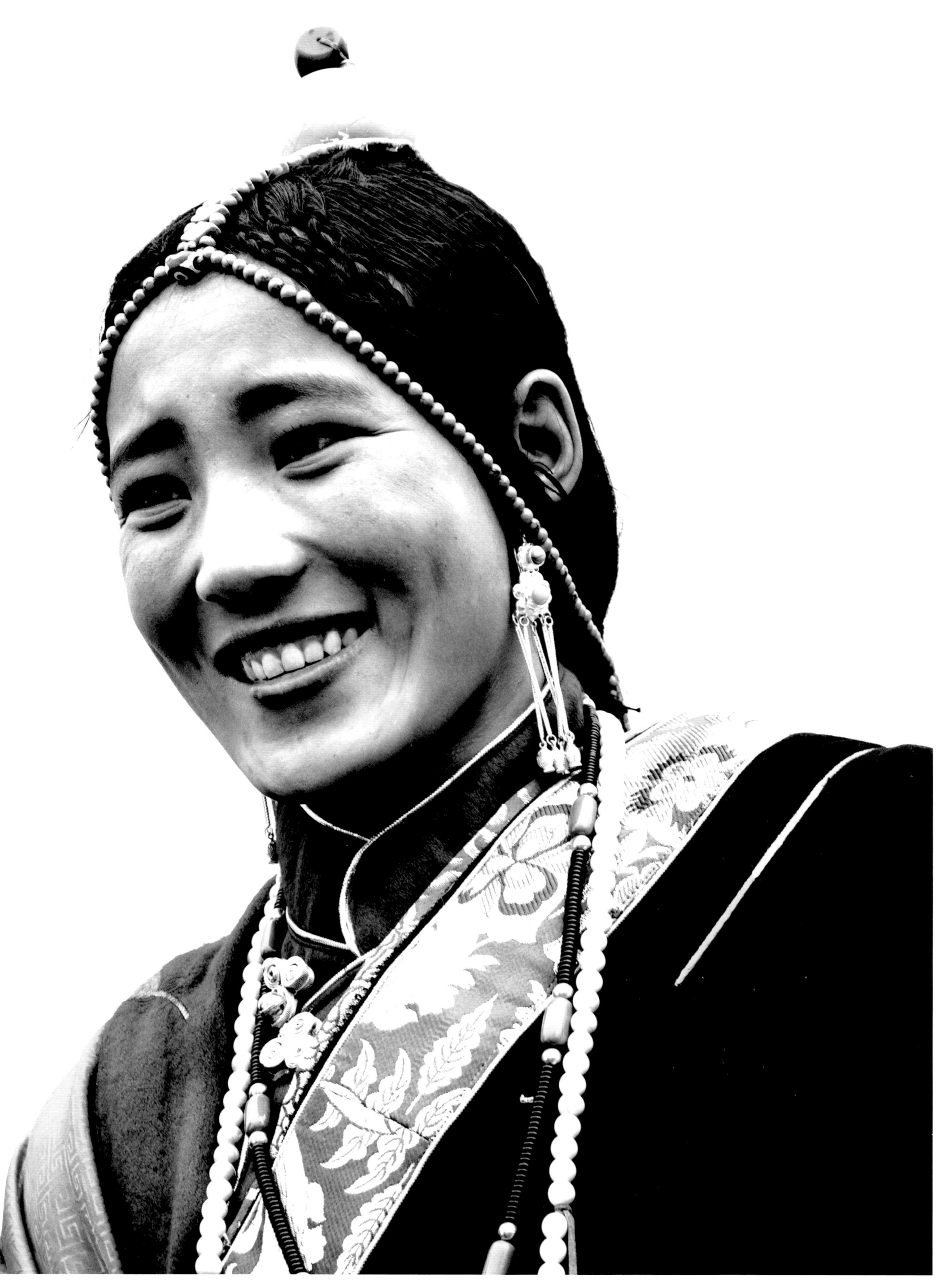

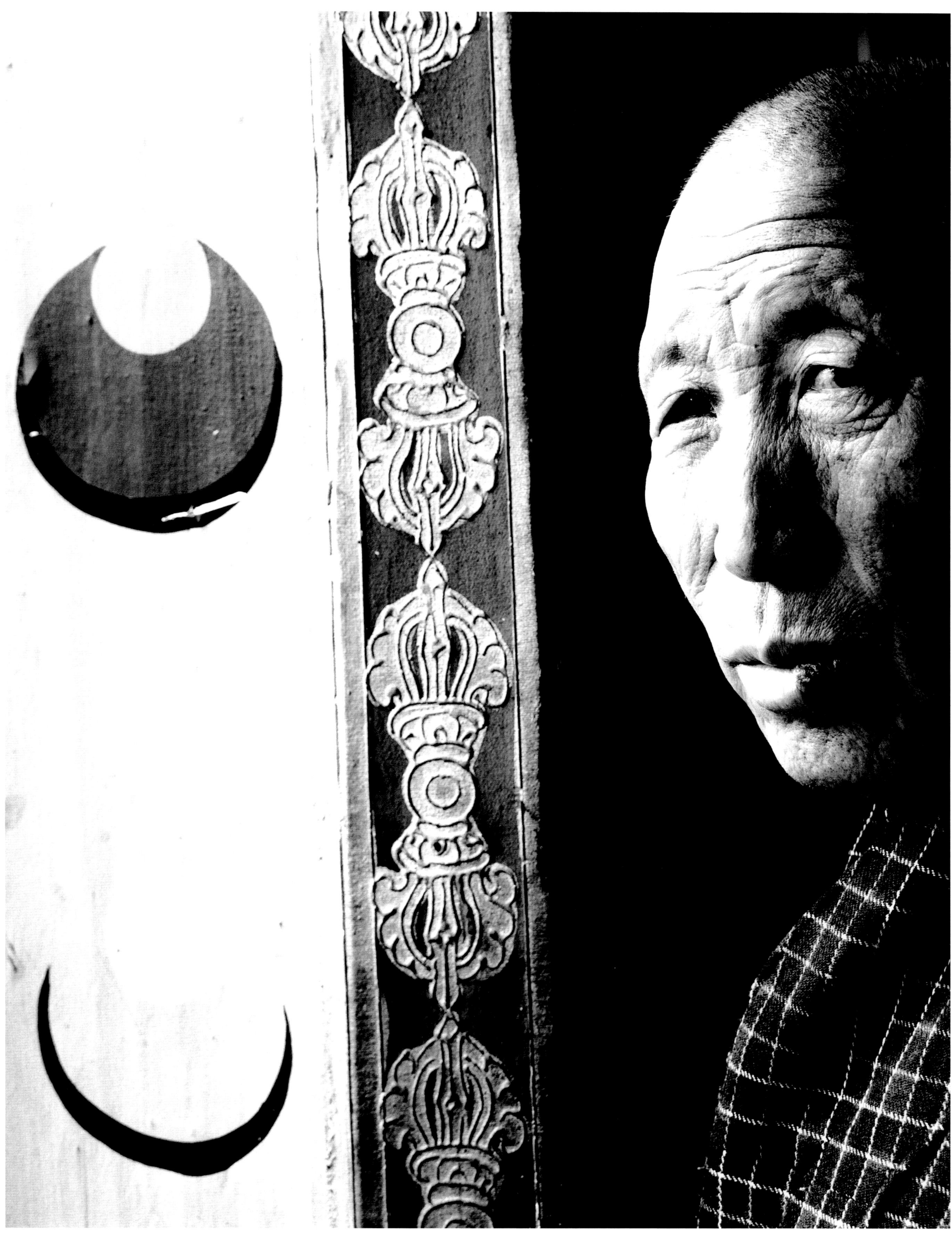

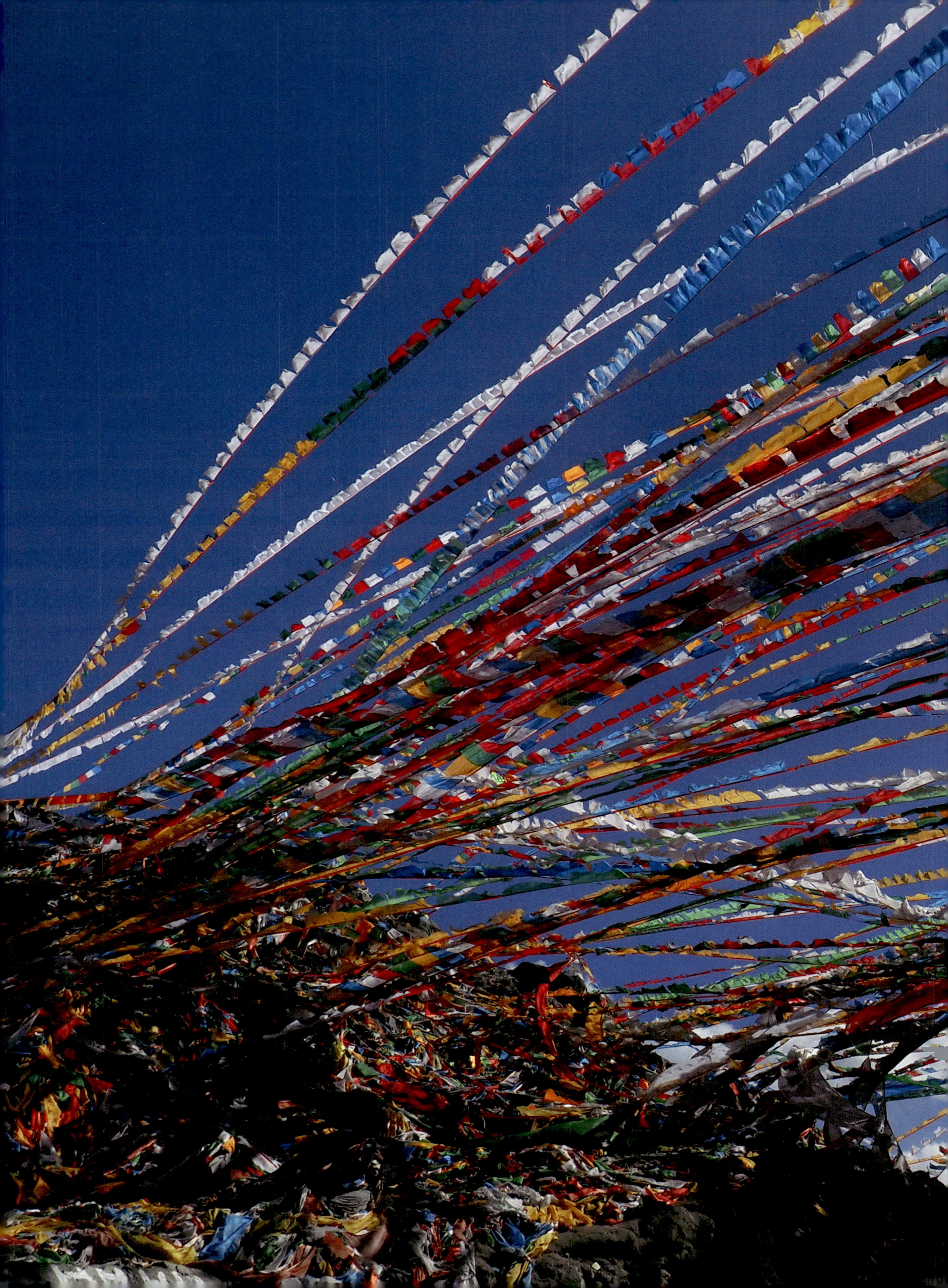

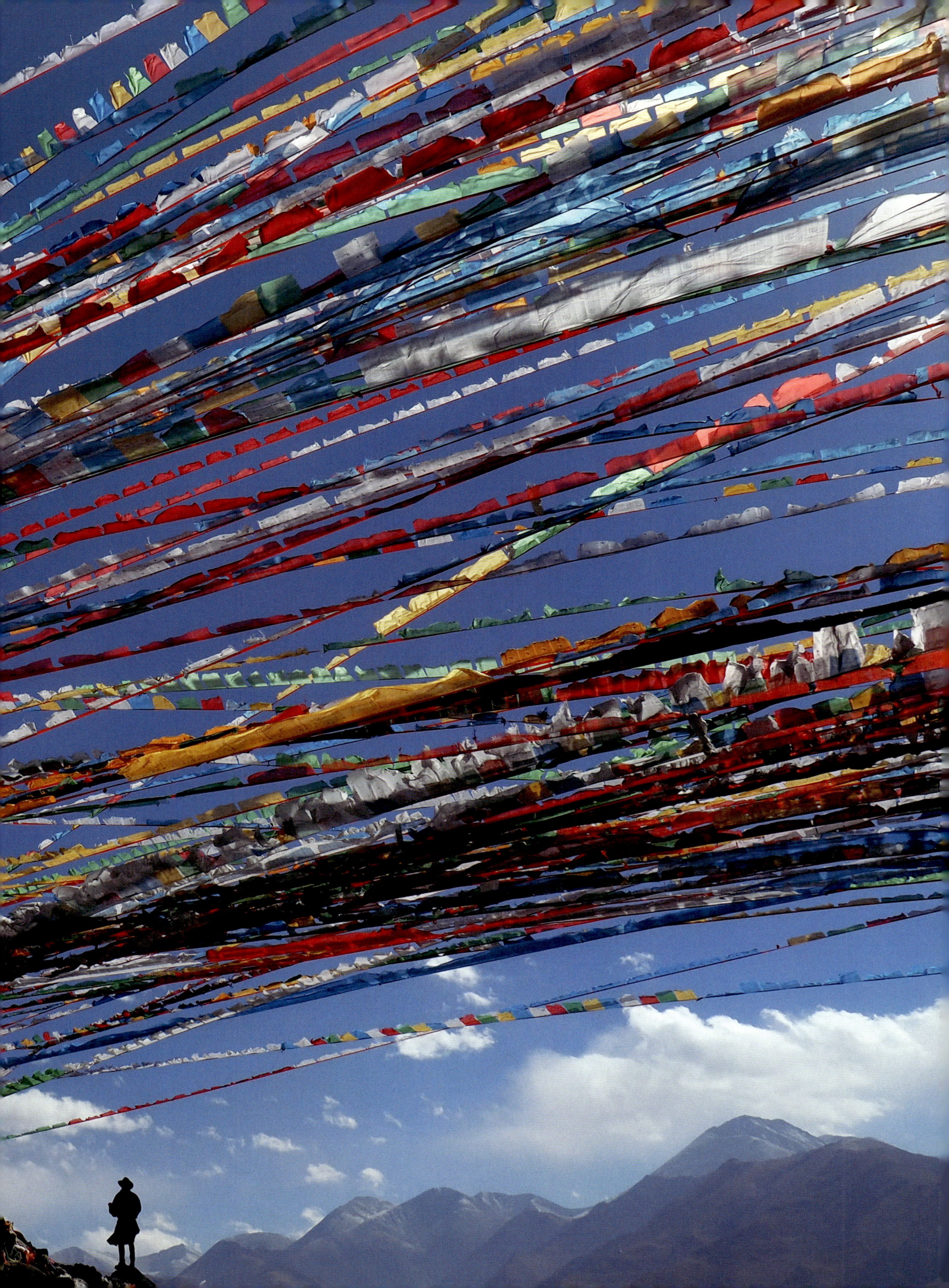

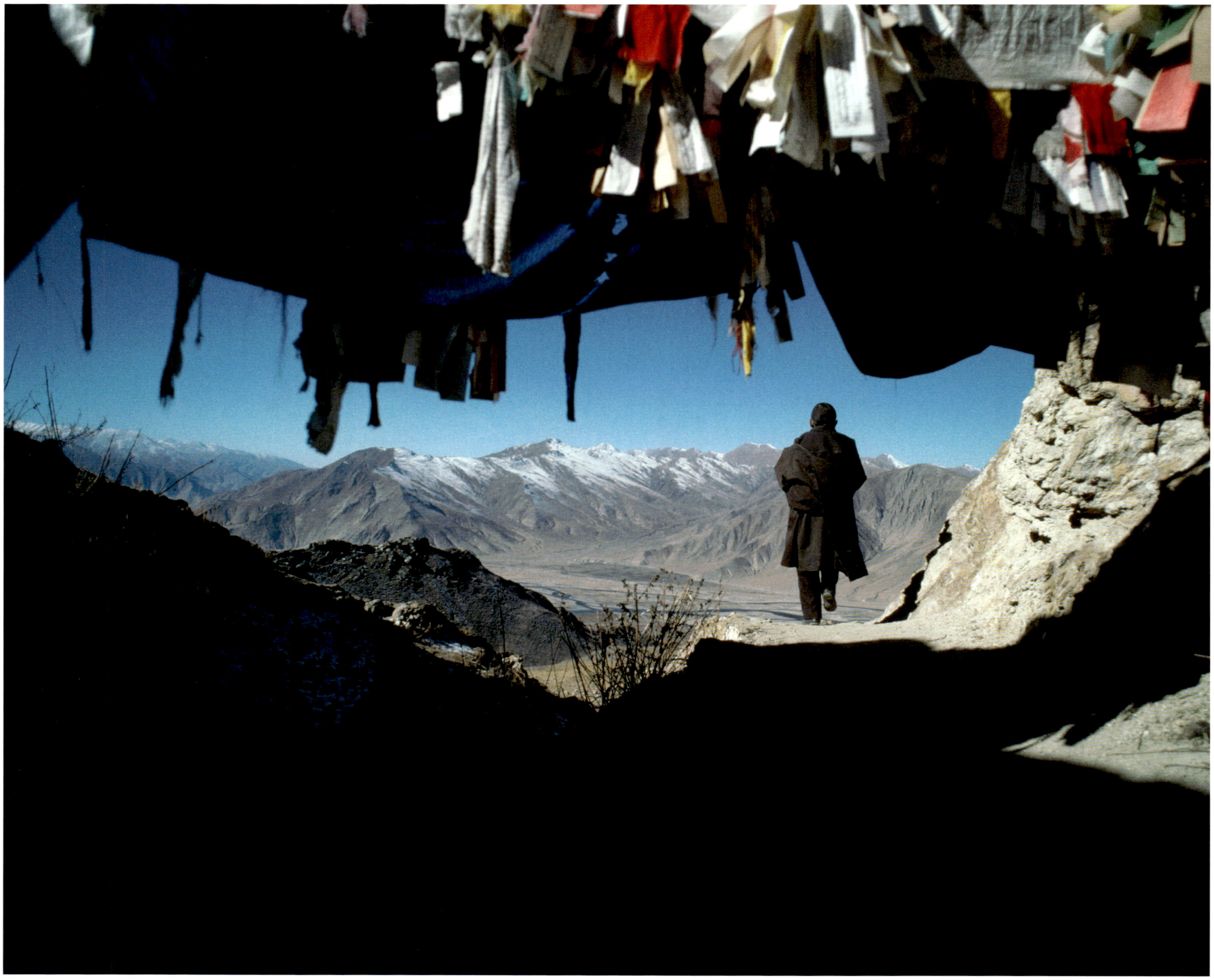

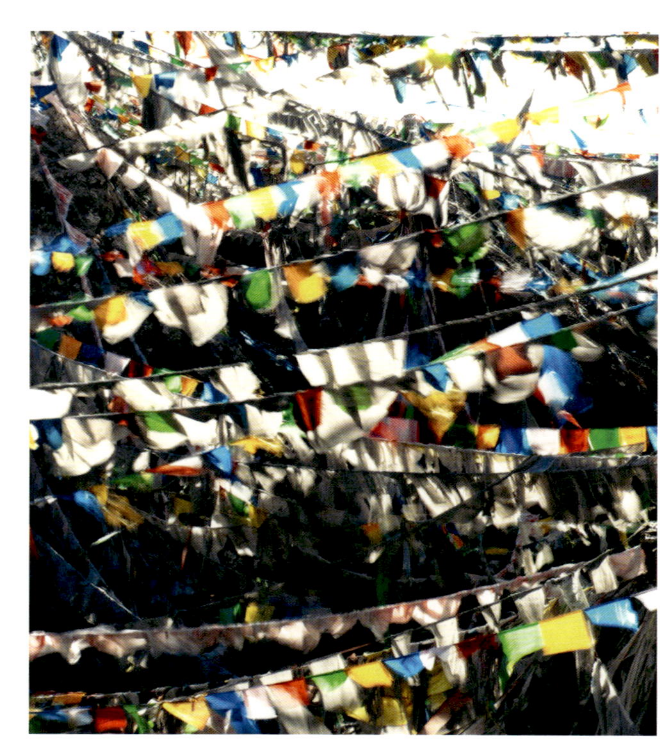

The wind blowing over the high passes of the Himalayas caresses the sacred texts of compassion that are printed on the small colored prayer flags and scatters them in the air, sending them to all those it touches in its mad race. "May all beings be happy and relieved of their sufferings."

Der Wind, der über die Höhen des Himalaya weht, nimmt im Vorbeistreichen die heiligen Formeln des Mitgefühls mit, die auf die kleinen, farbigen Gebetsfahnen aufgedruckt sind, und verteilt sie an jene, die er auf seinem wilden Weg streift. „Mögen alle Wesen glücklich und frei von Leid sein."

Le vent qui souffle sur les hauts cols de l'Himalaya caresse au passage les formules sacrées de compassion imprimées sur les petits drapeaux de prière colorés et les disperse dans l'espace pour les transmettre à tous ceux qu'il touche dans sa course effrenée. « Que tous les êtres soient heureux et soulagés de leurs souffrances. »

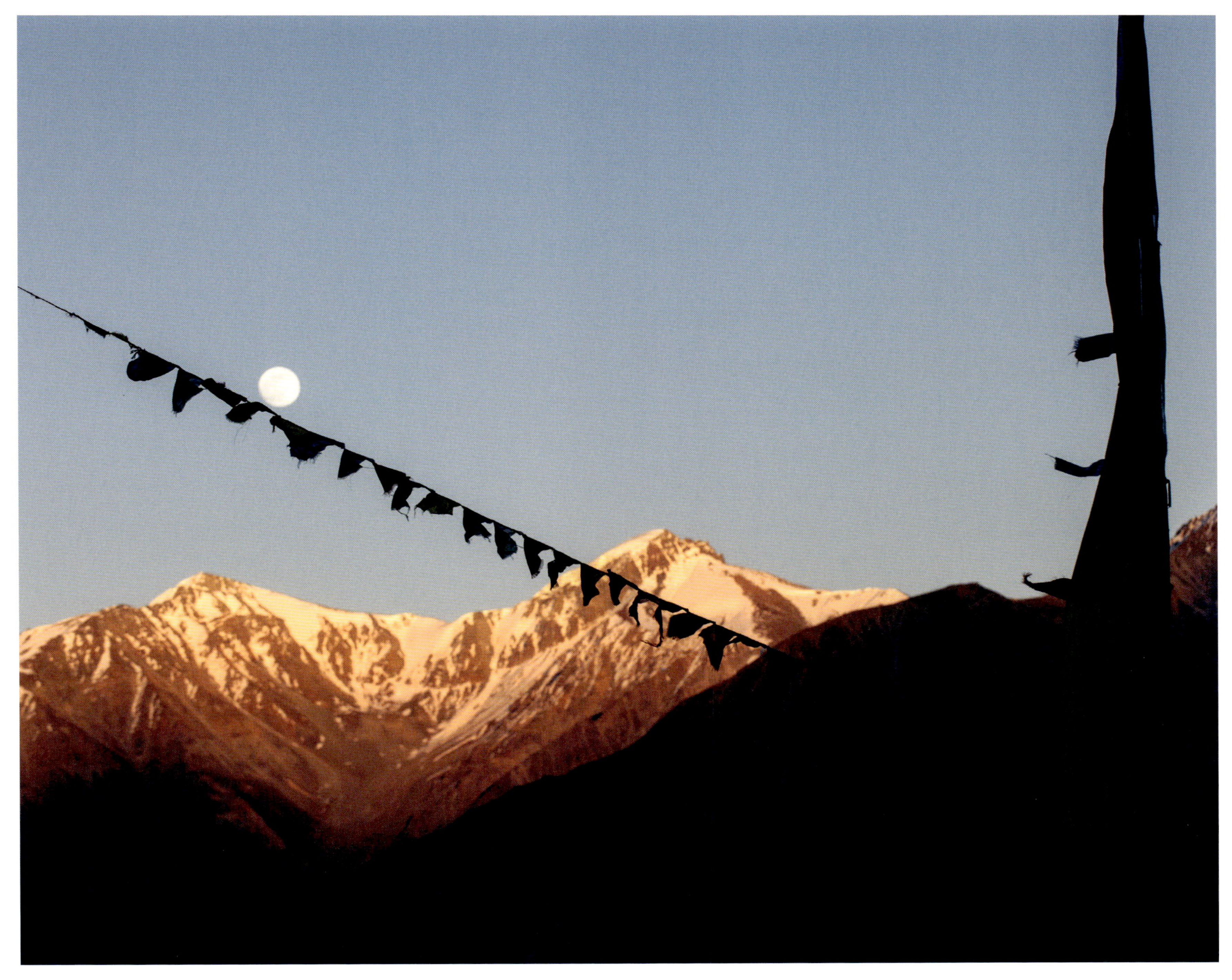

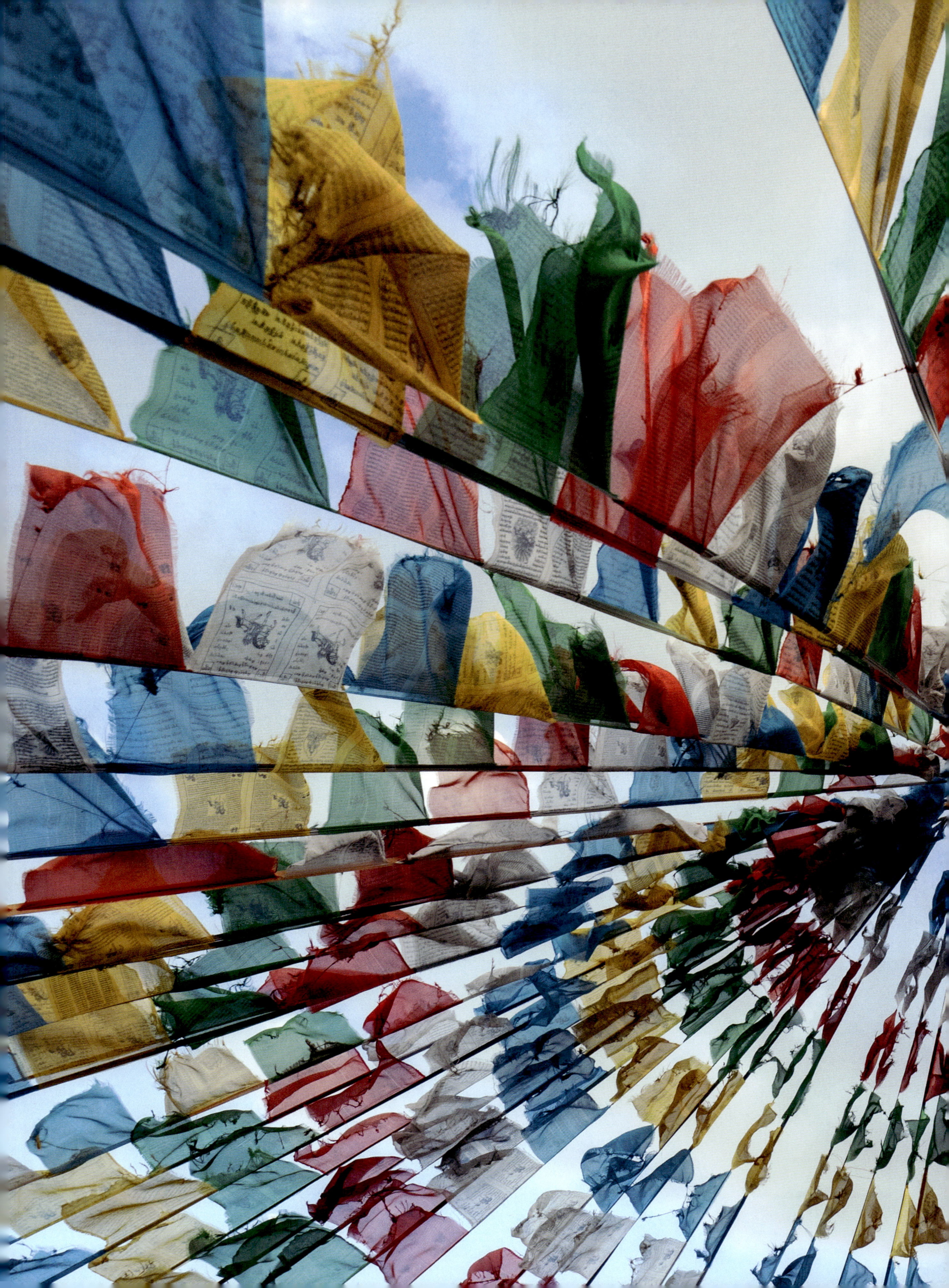

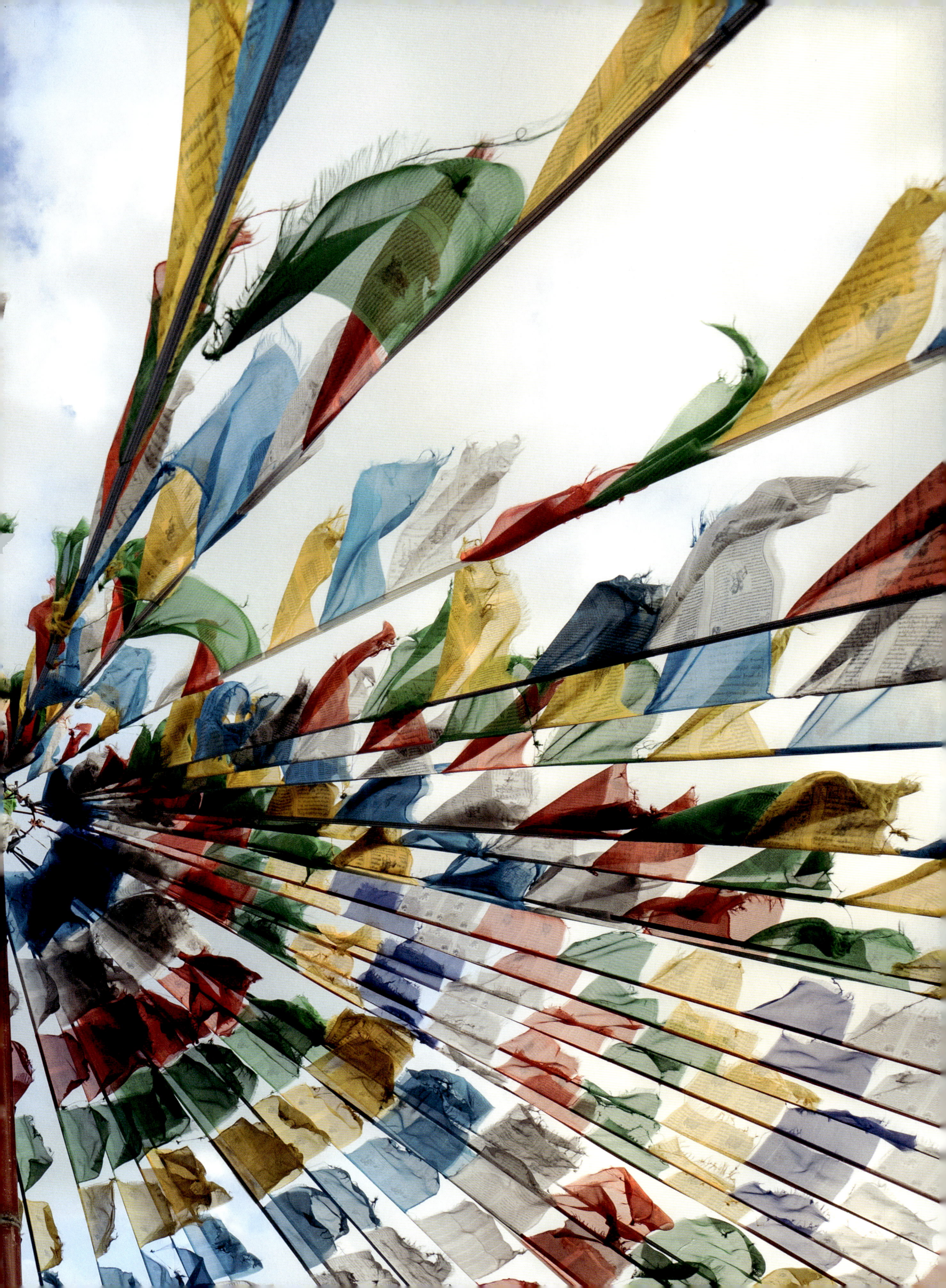

In memory of my very dear and loyal friend and assistant,
Ang Norbu Sherpa, and my very dear Gil Dumas.

To Danielle Föllmi, thanks to whom I built a happy life with in the Himalayas.
To my very dear children, Tenzin Motup, Tenzin Diskit, Yvan Tharpa Tsering Föllmi,
and Pema Yangdon Föllmi, as well as Nyima Lhamo.
To my very dear stepchildren, Tsering Angchuk and Padma Shozin.
To my very dear grandchildren, Karma Otzer, Stanzin Takpa, Karma Paljor Tundup,
Sonam Lazès, and Stanzin Palden.
To my very dear Lobsang Tundup and Dolma Lobzang, Stenzin Rabiang,
Stenzin Sonam Dorjee, Lobsang Khunkyap, and Stenzin Choekyi, as well as Rigzin Dhontup
and Mona, Lia and Marlon Thinley, Kunsang Tsering, and the Venerable Tashi Tundup.

And to my very dear Himalayan friends: Jetsun Pema, Tempa Tsering, Tenzin Geyche Tethong,
Tashi Wangdi, Rigzin and Dolkar Jora, Rajiv and Indra Kaul, Kalsang and Kim Yeshi,
Sawa Thondup, Gyaltsen Gyaltag, Tsewang Yeshi, Tsering Yeshi,
Thupten Dorje, Phuntsok Namgyal, the Venerable Tashi, the Venerable Salden,
Chhime Chhokyapa, Tenzin Takhla, Chhime Rigzing, Tashi Lhamo, Samchoe, Kesang Lhamo,
Sonam Yangzom, Lhamo Youden, Pemba Kyipa and her family, Dickyi Samgmo,
Ngodup Tsering, Tenzin Choeden, Tsering Tashi, Jho Tsering, Sonam Tashi, Mrs. Varma,
Eyshe Tundup, Ang Phurba Sherpa and his family, Ming Ma Lhamo Sherpa, Tsering Zangmo Sherpa,
Sonam Dorjee Sherpa, Phurba Gyaljen Sherpa and his family, Nawang Tashi, Lobsang Palmo,
Ngawang Tsering, Mr. Ashraf, Katcho Esfandhyar Khan, Mr. G. M. Kakpory, Nasir Shoda,
Lhamo, Dr Stanzin Namgyal, Phuntsok Dawa, Sonam Wantchuk, Tondup Namgyal,
Nyima Norboo, Tsering Raften, Sonam Dolma, Tsering Stobden, Tenzin Lhakpa and
their families, Kathup, Yangsom, Dorje, Lhakpa Tsering Sharley,
Tuga Duchunstang, and Dago Beda.

As well as to her Majesty the Queen Grandmother of Bhutan, Ashi Kesang Choden Wangchuck,
to Yetta and John Goelet, and to my very dear André Deom, Philippe Chassot, Noëlle Gojon,
Odile Morard, Corinne Morvan, and my very dear Jef and René Collet.

To all those men and women in Tibet that I cannot name through
fear of placing them in a difficult situation.

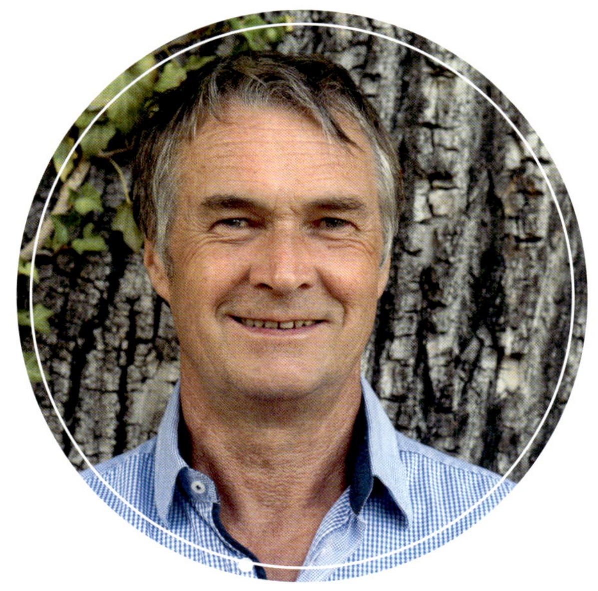

With his roots in France, Switzerland, and Italy, photographer Olivier Föllmi
spent more than 20 years traveling and photographing the most remote areas
of the Himalayas, before he then spent the next 20 years traveling
every continent on Earth. He has published 36 books, which have been translated
into nine languages, sold 1.5 million copies, and have inspired numerous films.
Föllmi is the recipient of numerous awards and prizes, including the World Press
Photo Award, and has exhibited his work in galleries around the world.

Olivier Föllmi, dessen Wurzeln in Frankreich, der Schweiz und Italien liegen, reiste
über 20 Jahre als Fotograf und Menschenfreund zu Fuß durch die abgelegensten
Himalaya-Regionen, bevor er die nächsten 20 Jahre damit verbrachte,
jeden Kontinent der Erde für sich zu entdecken. Er hat 36 Bücher veröffentlicht,
die in neun Sprachen übersetzt und insgesamt mehr als eineinhalb Millionen Mal
verkauft wurden und als Grundlage mehrerer Filme dienten. Seine Arbeit wurde
vielfach ausgezeichnet, unter anderem mit dem World Press Photo Award.
Olivier Föllmi stellt seine Fotografien in Galerien auf der ganzen Welt aus.

Photographe humaniste mêlant des origines française, suisse et italienne,
Olivier Föllmi a commencé par sillonner à pied pendant 20 ans les régions
les plus reculées de l'Himalaya avant de consacrer les 20 années suivantes à explorer
chaque continent de la planète. Traduits dans 9 langues et vendus à plus
d'1,5 million d'exemplaires, ses 36 ouvrages publiés à ce jour
ont inspiré plusieurs films. Ses travaux ont été primés à maintes reprises,
notamment au World Press Photo. Les photographies d'Olivier Föllmi
sont exposées dans des galeries du monde entier.

www.olivier-follmi.net

Olivier Föllmi is honored to be an OLYMPUS Ambassador

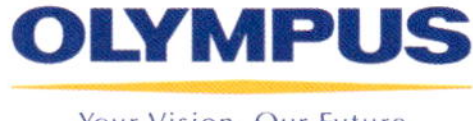

IMPRINT

© 2018 teNeues Media GmbH & Co. KG, Kempen
Photographs © 2018 Olivier Föllmi. All rights reserved.
Portrait © Véronique Girod-Föllmi

Text by Olivier Föllmi
Translations by:
Julia Summerton (English),
Reinhard Ferstl (German)
Copyediting by Megan Conway (English),
Sabine Boccador (French)
Proofreading by Nadine Weinhold
Creative Direction by Martin Graf
Prepress by Christin Steirat
Editorial coordination by Nadine Weinhold
Image delivery and coordination by Corinne Morvan,
Studio Olivier Föllmi
Production by Alwine Krebber
Color separation by Jens Grundei

English Edition: ISBN 978-3-96171-140-6
French Edition: ISBN 978-3-96171-165-9
Library of Congress Number: 2018904684

Printed in Italy

Picture and text rights reserved for all countries.
No part of this publication may be reproduced in
any manner whatsoever.

While we strive for utmost precision in every detail,
we cannot be held responsible for any inaccuracies,
neither for any subsequent loss or damage arising.

Every effort has been made by the publisher to contact
holders of copyright to obtain permission to reproduce
copyrighted material. However, if any permissions
have been inadvertently overlooked, teNeues Publishing
Group will be pleased to make the necessary
and reasonable arrangements at the first opportunity.

Bibliographic information published by the Deutsche
Nationalbibliothek. The Deutsche Nationalbibliothek
lists this publication in the Deutsche Nationalbibliografie;
detailed bibliographic data are available on the Internet
at http://dnb.dnb.de.

Published by teNeues Publishing Group
teNeues Media GmbH & Co. KG
Am Selder 37,
47906 Kempen, Germany
Phone: +49-(0)2152-916-0
Fax: +49-(0)2152-916-111
e-mail: books@teneues.com

Press department: Andrea Rehn
Phone: +49-(0)2152-916-202
e-mail: arehn@teneues.com

teNeues Media GmbH & Co. KG
Munich Office
Pilotystraße 4,
80538 Munich, Germany
Phone: +49-(0)89-443-8889-62
e-mail: bkellner@teneues.com

teNeues Media GmbH & Co. KG
Berlin Office
Kohlfurter Straße 41–43,
10999 Berlin, Germany
Phone: +49-(0)30-4195-3526-23
e-mail: ajasper@teneues.com

teNeues Publishing Company
350 7th Avenue, Suite 301,
New York, NY 10001, USA
Phone: +1-212-627-9090
Fax: +1-212-627-9511

teNeues Publishing UK Ltd.
12 Ferndene Road,
London SE24 0AQ, UK
Phone: +44-(0)20-3542-8997

teNeues France S.A.R.L.
39, rue des Billets,
18250 Henrichemont, France
Phone: +33-(0)2-4826-9348
Fax: +33-(0)1-7072-3482

www.teneues.com

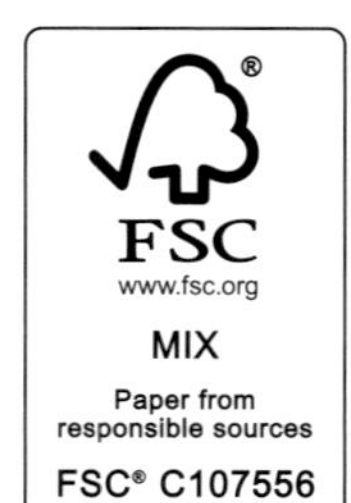